The Case Approach to Financial Planning

Bridging the Gap between
Theory and Practice, Fourth Edition (Revised)

John E. Grable, Ph.D., CFP®

Ronald A. Sages, Ph.D., AEP®, CFP®, CTFA, EA

Michelle E. Kruger, Ph.D.

D1522985

National Underwriter Academic Series

ISBN 978-1-949506-35-8

THE NATIONAL UNDERWRITER COMPANY

Copyright © 2008, 2013, 2016, 2018, 2020
The National Underwriter Company
a division of ALM Media, LLC
4157 Olympic Blvd., Suite 225
Erlanger, KY 41018

Fourth Edition (Revised)

Printed in the United States of America

ABOUT THE AUTHORS

JOHN E. GRABLE, PH.D., CFP®

Professor and Athletic Association Endowed Professor of Financial Planning at The University of Georgia

Professor John Grable teaches and conducts research in the Certified Financial Planner™ Board of Standards Inc. undergraduate and graduate programs at the University of Georgia where he holds an Athletic Association Endowed Professorship. Prior to entering the academic profession, he worked as a pension/benefits administrator and later as a Registered Investment Adviser in an asset management firm. Dr. Grable has served the financial planning profession as the founding editor of the *Journal of Personal Finance* and co-founding editor of the *Journal of Financial Therapy* and *Financial Planning Review*. He is best known for his work in the areas of financial literacy and education, financial risk-tolerance assessment, behavioral financial planning, and evidence-based financial planning. He has been the recipient of numerous research and publication awards and grants and is active in promoting the link between research and financial planning practice where he has published over 150 refereed papers, co-authored several textbooks, co-authored a financial planning communication book, and co-edited a financial planning and counseling scales book. Since earning his Ph.D., Dr. Grable has served on the Board of Directors of the International Association of Registered Financial Consultants (IARFC), as Treasurer and President for the American Council on Consumer Interests (ACCI), and as Treasurer and board member for the Financial Therapy Association. He has received numerous awards, including the prestigious Cato Award for Distinguished Journalism in the Field of Financial Services, the IARFC Founders Award, the Dawley-Scholer Award for Faculty Excellence in Student Development, and the ACCI Mid-Career Award. He currently writes an economics and investing column for the *Journal of Financial Service Professionals* and provides research and consulting services through the Financial Planning Performance Lab.

RONALD A. SAGES, PH.D., AEP®, CFP®, CTFA, EA

Adjunct Professor at The University of Georgia

Lecturer in Wealth Management at Columbia University, New York City

Ron Sages is an Adjunct Professor of Personal Financial Planning at the University of Georgia, Athens, Georgia, where he teaches in the CFP® Board Registered Master's Program. Courses he currently teaches for UGA include Advanced Estate Planning and Practice Management. Dr. Sages also serves as a Lecturer in Wealth Management at Columbia University in New York City. Prior to joining both academic institutions, he was an Assistant Professor of Personal Financial Planning at Kansas State University from 2011 – 2019 where he was a 2016 recipient of the GPIDEA Faculty Excellence Award for his instruction in the Case Studies/Program Development Course. In addition to his responsibilities in academia, Dr. Sages is a Senior Investment Officer and Director of Personal Financial Planning for Eagle Ridge Investment Management,

LLC, a wealth management firm, based in Stamford, Connecticut. A former wealth management entrepreneur for twenty-five years, including an additional twenty years of Money Center Bank experience, Ron earned his doctorate in Personal Financial Planning from Kansas State University in 2012 and his MBA in Finance and Taxation from the University of Connecticut in 1979. His research interests are in behavioral finance, risk management and financial literacy. As a financial planning practitioner and researcher, Ron aspires to bring applied research to financial planning practitioners in an effort to provide practical solutions to client-focused challenges. Ron is a member of the Stamford (CT) CFA Society, Estate Planning Council of Lower Fairfield County (CT), the National Association of Estate Planning Councils, Financial Planning Association, and the Financial Therapy Association.

MICHELLE E. KRUGER

The University of Georgia

Michelle Kruger is a Ph.D. candidate with a concentration in Financial Planning at The University of Georgia (UGA). She graduated magna cum laude with a B.B.A. in Finance from the Terry College of Business at UGA in 2015. Michelle teaches classes in computer application in financial planning, as well as advanced financial planning seminar courses. Her research interests include financial planning interventions, risk tolerance assessment, and behaviors associated with building wealth. In addition to her graduate studies, Michelle works as a research assistant at the Financial Planning Performance Lab, the nation's only applied clinical facility designed to obtain evidence about the effectiveness of the financial planning process. She has worked as a financial planning analyst at Elwood & Goetz Wealth Advisory Group, a fee-only, comprehensive financial planning firm located in Athens, Georgia. She also has served as a financial counselor at the Aspire Clinic, an interdisciplinary teaching and research institution, applying marriage and family therapy theories and techniques to her work with financial clients.

ACKNOWLEDGMENTS

Creating a book of this magnitude is not without challenges. Several individuals have been instrumental in keeping the project on task. First and foremost, we wish to thank our spouses and partners for being patient and supportive during the writing and editing process. As we have all learned, writing a book is a continuous process, and without the support of our families, the process would have stopped long ago. We are also indebted to our editor at The National Underwriter Company—Jason Gilbert. Jason has shown unwavering confidence in this book. Without his editorial leadership this new revised edition of the book would never have come to fruition. Jason's encouragement, patience, and editing skills made this revision come together. Thanks also go to Jay Caslow for fully supporting this book from revision to publication. The anonymous reviewers who spent countless hours evaluating chapters prior to publication and those who have helped improve the book's content also deserve sincere thanks, particularly Sherman Hanna, Luke Dean, David Nanigian, Carolynn Tomin, and Joanne Snider. We are also grateful for the early work Dr. Ruth Lytton and Derek Klock provided on this project.

As a team, we are also thankful for the opportunity to have worked with undergraduate, graduate, and certificate financial planning students over the past decade. The idea of this case book was formulated through this daily work with students. We are immensely thankful for what each student has taught us about what works in and outside the classroom. The writing of this book has reminded us that "to teach is to learn again." Each student we have had in class has challenged us to strive to find better ways to explain and teach financial planning concepts. Additionally, we are very grateful to our colleagues around the country (and world) who have adopted this book and helped make this revision possible. We are honored to be a part of your professional development and learning experience. We certainly hope that you find the material in this book a benefit to your career.

John Grable

Ron Sages

Michelle Kruger

DEDICATION

To Emily, with love, John

To Betsy, Laurie, Patti & Lindsay, with all my love and devotion, Ron

To Joey, with love for you and gratitude for the coffee, Michelle

PREFACE

HOW TO USE THIS BOOK

Since the first edition of this book was published, the demand for more comprehensive and realistic cases has increased dramatically. *A Case Approach to Financial Planning: Bridging the Gap between Theory and Practice, Fourth Edition* has been written to meet this demand. Because of its unique focus, it is very important that readers fully understand the core assumptions imbedded in the book before reading chapters or completing case assignments. The following points comprise the book's underlying assumptions:

- This book is a companion to *Writing a Financial Planning: A Seven Step Process* written by John Grable, Michelle Kruger, and Megan Ford. In fact, some of the material—particularly descriptions of analytical processes—matches what is presented in *Writing a Financial Planning: A Seven Step Process*.

- This book assumes that readers already have a foundation in understanding and applying the process of financial planning or are currently reading *Writing a Financial Planning: A Seven Step Process*; thus, the chapters in this book focus primarily on the analysis of a client's current situation and the development of strategies to help a client reach his or her goals.

- This book is intended for use in mid-level or capstone courses in financial planning programs at colleges, universities, and certificate programs. It is appropriate for use at the undergraduate, graduate, and certificate levels. When used at the undergraduate level, it is assumed that the book will be used in the final course of a student's last year of study, in conjunction with *Writing a Financial Planning: A Seven Step Process* or a similar textbook. Although a review of key financial planning assumptions is provided in each core content chapter, this book is not—nor should it be considered—a replacement for a content specific (e.g., investments, retirement, etc.) financial planning textbook.

- To successfully complete case assignments and questions, students are assumed to have already completed or be enrolled in classes in the six core areas of financial planning: Financial Situation Analysis, Tax Planning, Insurance (Risk Management) Planning, Investment Planning, Retirement Planning, and Estate Planning. This book offers a review of important concepts and strategies, but in no way are the core content chapters intended to provide a comprehensive overview of each financial planning topic.

- This book is not intended for use solely as a CFP® examination study guide. The comprehensive cases, the end-of-chapter materials, and the mini-cases were designed to help faculty and students assess minimum financial planning competencies. The cases can certainly help those who wish to sit for a national financial planning certification examination; however, the material is not intended for that purpose exclusively.

- *A Case Approach to Financial Planning: Bridging the Gap between Theory and Practice, Fourth Edition* is intended to present timely and accurate information; however, the strategies, tools, and techniques presented are designed for educational purposes only. Although the authors and outside reviewers have reviewed the information, data analysis methods, recommendations, strategies, and other material, some material presented in the text could be affected by changes in tax law, court findings, or future interpretations of rules and regulations. Therefore, the accuracy and completeness of the information, data, and opinions in the book are in no way guaranteed. The authors specifically disclaim any personal, joint, or corporate (profit and nonprofit) liability for loss or risk incurred as a consequence of the content of the book.

FEATURES OF THE BOOK

Underlying the development of this text and the various student learning experiences presented throughout the book is Bloom's taxonomy of cognitive skills.[1] For example, *knowledge* and *comprehension* are covered through the traditional presentation and testing of financial planning concepts. *Application* and *analysis* are fostered through discussions of planning strategies, where students are challenged to evaluate the advantages and disadvantages of each, relative to the needs of the individual client situation. The book is designed to help readers build *synthesis* and *evaluation* skills. Designing an integrated, actionable plan matched to a client's needs, capacities, and desires requires competency across Bloom's taxonomy of cognitive skills.

OVERVIEW OF CHAPTERS

One of the purposes of a financial planning case course is to provide a forum for students to develop and critique financial planning strategies matched to a client's needs. For many students, the capstone course is the only place in a college or university curriculum where all core content planning areas are reviewed and integrated in the context of a specific client situation. This book provides a variety of commonly used financial planning strategies matched to each core content planning area for in-class and out-of-class review and discussion. In addition, an assortment of computational examples and end-of-chapter problems are presented in each chapter.

Each chapter lists a set of learning objectives relevant to the chapter. This is followed by a listing of CFP® Board principal knowledge topics. These topics correspond to financial planning learning outcomes that underlie the CFP® national certification examination. Keep in mind that the content within the chapters may not match the order in which the topics are listed. Important equations, relevant to conducting a financial planning analysis, are then listed. Financial planning strategies make up the core of each chapter. Each chapter concludes with an opportunity to apply calculation and strategic planning skills through quantitative/analytical mini-case problems. The elements of the book include:

Part I: Review of the Financial Planning Process and Computational Skills for Developing a Financial Plan

1. *The Financial Planning Process.* This chapter describes the general financial planning process and outline of the book.

2. *Computations for Financial Planning.* This chapter provides a comprehensive review of key concepts related to time value of money and general personal finance calculations.

Part II: Analyzing and Evaluating a Client's Financial Status to Plan for Client Earnings

3. *Cash Flow and Net Worth Planning.* This chapter examines the process of analyzing and evaluating a client's current financial situation. The chapter offers conventional strategies that financial planners regularly use to improve a client's cash flow and net worth position.

4. *Income Tax Planning.* The purpose of this chapter is to review the basic steps involved in analyzing and evaluating a client's current tax planning situation. In addition, the chapter provides a review of several widely used tax planning strategies.

Part III—Analyzing and Evaluating a Client's Financial Status to Plan for Client Risk Protection

5. *Life Insurance Planning.* This chapter reviews the basic steps involved in a financial planner's analysis and evaluation of a client's current life insurance situation. The chapter also presents popular life insurance planning strategies.

6. *Health Insurance Planning.* This chapter reviews the fundamental steps associated with a financial planner's analysis of a client's current health insurance situation. Common health insurance strategies are presented.

7. *Disability Insurance Planning.* This chapter reviews the steps involved in conducting a disability insurance planning analysis. The chapter includes several disability insurance planning strategies that can be adapted to meet client needs.

8. *Long-Term Care Insurance Planning.* This chapter examines the process underlying a financial planner's analysis and evaluation of a client's long-term care insurance situation. The chapter also presents common product and procedural strategies.

9. *Property and Liability Insurance Planning.* This chapter considers issues related to maximizing a client's plan for protecting property and minimizing liability exposures. The chapter reviews the fundamental steps in the analysis and evaluation of a client's current property and liability situation and presents examples of popular strategies used to protect client assets.

Part IV—Analyzing and Evaluating a Client's Financial Status to Plan for the Growth and Distribution of Assets

10. *Investment Planning.* In this chapter, important issues surrounding the analysis of a client's investment situation are explored. The investment planning process is reviewed and examples of how to develop strategies to meet client needs are provided. How investment strategies can influence a client's financial goals is explained.

11. *Education Planning.* The steps typically followed when analyzing and evaluating a client's current educational funding situation are reviewed. A selection of education funding strategies demonstrating how some financial planners strategize when planning for a client's education situation is presented.

12. *Retirement Planning.* This chapter describes the analysis and evaluation of a client's current situation and reviews common retirement planning strategies that can be used to meet retirement objectives. Strategies to develop recommendations for retirement planning across the life cycle are also provided.

13. *Estate Planning.* Essential steps for conducting an estate planning analysis are reviewed. A brief outline of how financial planners estimate a client's gross and taxable estate is provided. Other important issues are presented, such as transferring assets, providing for survivors or other legacy needs, and planning for incapacitation and other end-of-life decisions. The chapter ends with a review of how certain estate planning strategies can be used in the financial planning process.

Part V—Financial Planning Case Studies

14. *Financial Planning Cases.* A variety of multiple-choice cases appear in this chapter. The cases in this section of the book have been designed to help students develop assessment, evaluation, and decision choice competencies. Student success is derived by utilizing correct data inputs to optimize question choices. Many of the case questions require a mathematical analysis and other calculations, most of which can be made using a time value of money calculator. A financial planning ethics case is also presented in the unique format of a dialogue. The ethic's case is designed to test students' knowledge of securities rules and financial planning practice standards.

Case Studies and Quantitative/Analytical Mini-Case Problems

Although successfully developing a financial plan for a client situation is rewarding, the downside to conducting a case analysis is that the process can sometimes seem far removed from reality. This book attempts to bridge the gap between theory and practice by providing short cases and computational problems at the end of chapters 3 through 13. These chapter case studies illustrate how financial planning strategies can be developed and shaped into tools and matched to a client's situation.

End-of-chapter quantitative and analytical mini-cases were written to challenge students to practice calculations and critical thinking. These skills are essential to the application, synthesis, and evaluation competencies needed to artfully analyze a client's situation, identify and match workable strategies to a client's situation, and to integrate these strategies into actionable recommendations for implementation.

This icon represents a unique feature of the book. When this icon accompanies a quantitative and analytical mini-case, the question can be answered using the Financial Planning Analysis Excel™ package included with this book.

All of the cases were designed to remind students that despite the focus on analytical skills and detailed factual knowledge, clients—real people—and their financial goals and dreams are truly the reason for financial planning. As noted earlier, financial planners help clients, people with whom financial planners may develop relationships that span decades and often even generations, *plan* for a better financial future. In this sense, *A Case Approach to Financial Planning: Bridging the Gap between Theory and Practice, Fourth Edition* is focused on helping the next generation of financial planners truly practice financial planning as a humanistic science.

Words of Advice

The case study methodology presented in this book was developed and tested by the instructors at several universities over the past two decades. The outcomes associated with these methods have been successful. During an eighteen-year period, teams of undergraduate students that have used this book, and the tools and techniques presented here, have competed in and won numerous national collegiate financial planning championships. Many students who have applied the concepts presented in this book have gone on to pursue successful careers in the field of financial planning.

Four aspects of student success are tied directly to how well students do when working on the development of financial planning strategies when solving cases:

- First, successful students tend to have a strong proficiency in the use of personal finance calculators.

- Second, the best students have an interest in working with computer spreadsheets and confirming calculations obtained on their calculator with spreadsheets.

- Third, successful students do extremely well at applying critical thinking skills. Exploring issues, looking for the integration of concepts, and willingness to research and use reference materials are all indicators of success for those engaged in the case study method.

- Finally, the most successful students understand that developing a plan in response to a case situation—especially a comprehensive case—takes time. A commitment to taking the time to analyze a situation, develop strategies, craft workable client-centered recommendations, and work on ways to implement and monitor recommendations is critical to plan writing success.

Our sincere hope is that you find the materials, quantitative/analytical mini-case problems, and mini cases helpful as you improve your financial planning skills. We are always interested in feedback about the book. Please feel free to reach out with comments and suggestions.

John Grable

Ron Sages

Michelle Kruger

Endnote

1. Bloom, B.S. *Taxonomy of Educational Objectives, Handbook I: The Cognitive Domain* (New York: David McKay, 1956).

ABBREVIATIONS COMMONLY USED IN FINANCIAL PLANNING

Alternative Minimum Tax—AMT

Assets Under Management—AUM

Accredited Investment Fiduciary®— AIF®

Certificate of Deposit—CD

Certified Financial Planner Board of Standards, Inc.—CFP Board

Certified Financial Planner® Certification Examination—CFP® exam

Certified Investment Management Analyst—CIMA

Certified Investment Management Consultant— CIMC (No longer awarded)

Certified Life Underwriter—CLU

Charitable Remainder Annuity Trust—CRAT

Charitable Remainder Unitrust—CRUT

Chartered Financial Analyst—CFA

Chartered Financial Consultant—ChFC

Chartered Investment Counselor—CIC

Chartered Life Underwriter—CLU

Consolidated Omnibus Budget Reconciliation Act of 1986—COBRA

Coverdell Education Savings Account—Coverdell ESA or CESA

Discretionary Cash Flow—DCF

Employee Retirement Income Security Act of 1974—ERISA

Enrolled Agent—EA

Errors and Omissions— E&O

Exchange Traded Fund—ETF

Financial Industry Regulatory Authority—FINRA

Financial Planning Association—FPA

Flexible Spending Account—FSA

Grantor Retained Annuity Trust—GRAT

Grantor Retained Unitrust—GRUT

Guaranteed Auto Protection Insurance—GAP Insurance

Health Insurance Portability and Accountability Act of 1996—HIPAA

Health Savings Account—HSA

High Deductible Health Plan—HDHP

Homeowners Policy—HO Policy

Incentive Stock Option—ISO

Individual Retirement Arrangement—IRA

Investment Advisor Representative—IAR

Investment Advisor Registration Depository —IARD

Investment Policy Statement—IPS

Internal Revenue Code—IRC

Internal Revenue Code Section 529—529 Plan

Internal Revenue Service—IRS

Irrevocable Life Insurance Trust—ILIT

Joint Tenancy with the Right of Survivorship—JTWROS

Long Term Care—LTC

Million Dollar Round Table—MDRT

National Association of Insurance Commissioners— NAIC

National Association of Personal Financial Advisors—NAPFA

North American Securities Administrators Association—NASAA

Payable on Death—POD

Personal Automobile Policy—PAP

Personal Financial Specialist—PFS

Qualified Personal Residence Trust— QPRT

Qualified Terminable Interest Property Trust—QTIP Trust

Real Estate Investment Trust—REIT

Registered Investment Advisor—RIA

Securities Investor Protection Corporation—SIPC

Self-Regulatory Organization—SRO

Transferable on Death—TOD

Uniform Gift to Minors Act Account—UGMA Account

Uniform Prudent Investor Act—UPIA

Uniform Transfers to Minors Act Account—UTMA Account

U.S. Securities and Exchange Commission—SEC

Variable Universal Life—VUL

SUMMARY TABLE OF CONTENTS

Part I: Review of the Process and Computational Skills for
Developing a Financial Plan

Part II: Analyzing and Evaluating a Client's Financial Status
to Plan for Client Earnings

Part III: Analyzing and Evaluating a Client's Financial Status
to Plan for Client Risk Protection

Part IV: Analyzing and Evaluating a Client's Financial Status
to Plan for the Growth and Distribution of Assets

Part V: Financial Planning Case Studies

DETAILED TABLE OF CONTENTS

Part IV: Analyzing and Evaluating a Client's Financial Status
to Plan for the Growth and Distribution of Assets

Part V: Financial Planning Case Studies

Chapter 1

The Financial Planning Process

Learning Objectives

- Learning Objective 1: Summarize and explain the steps of the financial planning process.

- Learning Objective 2: Describe how the financial planning process, as established by the Certified Financial Planner Board of Standards, Inc. (CFP Board), serves as a framework for guiding financial planners when working with clients.

- Learning Objective 3: Understand the role of case studies when preparing for financial planning certification.

CFP® Principal Knowledge Topics

- CFP Topic: A.1. CFP Board's Code of Ethics and Professional Responsibility and Rules of Conduct.
- CFP Topic: A.2. CFP Board's Financial Planning Practice Standards.
- CFP Topic: A.3. CFP Board's Disciplinary Rules and Procedures.
- CFP Topic: A.7. Fiduciary.
- CFP Topic: B.8. Financial Planning Process.
- CFP Topic: B.14. Client and Planner Attitudes, Values, Biases, and Behavioral Finance.

Chapter Equations

There are no equations in this chapter.

THE CASE STUDY APPROACH

The profession of financial planning has expanded quickly since its inception in 1969. During the 1960s and 1970s, financial planning consisted of little more than a small consortium of financial service professionals interested in offering clients a value-added service, in addition to insurance and mutual fund products. Since its inception, financial planning has grown into a dynamic, growing, and respected profession.

The growth of financial planning, both as a recognized profession and as an important behavioral change force in the lives of individuals and families, has been remarkable. Starting with fewer than fifty Certified Financial Planner (CFP®) professionals in the early 1970s, the number of CFP® certificants has grown to more than eighty thousand today. Worldwide growth in financial planning, particularly among CFP® professionals, is even more stunning. As the profession has expanded in recent years, the number of students studying financial planning has also grown, which has prompted the need for tools students and aspiring financial planners can use to enhance their knowledge, skill set, and confidence. Thus, the purpose of this textbook.

This book has been designed to help students synthesize knowledge obtained in multiple classes into practical techniques that can be used to solve theoretical and practical financial planning case studies. The tools, techniques, and strategies presented here are intended to serve as a manual to help students and aspiring financial planners piece together divergent concepts into strategic recommendations. Before describing each element of the book, it is worthwhile to take a step back and review two important concepts. First, what exactly is meant by the phrase 'financial planning'? And second, what is the relationship between financial planning and the process of financial planning?

FINANCIAL PLANNING DEFINED

Professional organizations and leading members of the financial planning community have defined financial planning in a variety of ways. The most recognized definition, offered by the **Certified Financial Planner Board of Standards, Inc. (CFP Board),** defines financial planning as a process. According to CFP Board,[1] **financial planning** denotes:

"The collaborative process that helps maximize a client's potential for meeting life goals through financial advice that integrates relevant elements of the client's personal and financial circumstances."[2]

Financial planning can be thought of as a humanistic science focused on helping individuals and families manage and improve their financial situation. The term humanistic, as used here, means that a financial planner focuses on individuals and families and the values, capabilities, and capacities clients bring with them when dealing with complex financial questions and issues. Financial planning is a science because financial planning professionals rely on critical thinking, data, and evidence-based practices, rather than generalized rules or dogmas, when formulating client-centered strategies.[3]

THE FINANCIAL PLANNING PROCESS

Traditionally, the practice of financial planning has followed what is generally referred to as the financial planning process. In its Standards of Professional Conduct, CFP Board describes the **financial planning process** as the following seven steps:

1. Understanding the client's personal and financial circumstances

2. Identifying and selecting goals

3. Analyzing the client's current course of action and potential alternative course(s) of action

4. Developing the financial planning recommendation(s)

5. Presenting the financial planning recommendation(s)

6. Implementing the financial planning recommendation(s)

7. Monitoring progress and updating

The financial planning process has been revised over the years. The current seven-step financial planning process represents the latest revision as of 2018. Prior to the revision, the process consisted of six steps. Figure 1.1 compares the current financial planning process with the way nearly all financial planners have traditionally conceptualized the process of financial planning.

Figure 1.1. The Current Financial Planning Process Compared to the Traditional Process

Current Process	Traditional Process
1. Understand the Client's Personal and Financial Circumstances • Obtain qualitative and quantitative information • Analyze information • Address incomplete information	1. Gather Data and Determine the Client's Personal and Financial Goals, Needs, and Priorities
2. Identify and Select Goals • Identify potential goals • Select and prioritize goals	2. Analyze and Evaluate the Client's Financial Status • Identify and evaluate financial planning alternative(s)
3. Analyze the Client's Current Course of Action and Potential Alternative Course(s) of Action a. Analyze current course of action b. Analyze potential alternative courses of action	3. Develop the Financial Planning Recommendation(s)
4. Develop the Financial Planning Recommendation(s)	4. Present the Financial Planning Recommendation(s)
5. Present the Financial Planning Recommendation(s)	5. Agree on Implementation Responsibilities • Select products and services for implementation
6. Implement the Financial Planning Recommendation(s) • Address implementation responsibilities • Identify, analyze, and select actions, product, and services • Recommend actions, products, and services for recommendation • Select and implement actions, products, or services	6. Define Monitoring Responsibilities
7. Monitor Progress and Update • Monitor and update responsibilities • Monitor the client's progress • Obtain current qualitative and quantitative information • Update goals, recommendations, or implementation decisions	

Figure 1.2 illustrates how the financial planning is circular in nature, with ongoing monitoring continually informing the type of information a financial planner must obtain to continually ensure that a client is moving toward goal achievement.

THE ROLE OF FINANCIAL PLANNERS

Figure 1.2. The Circular Nature of the Financial Planning Process

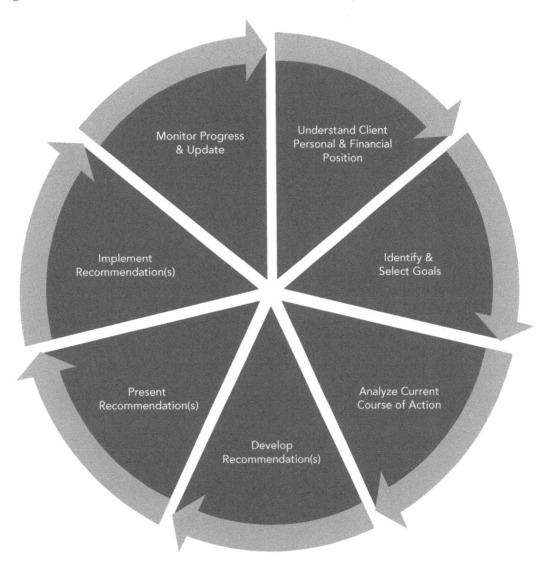

According to the Bureau of Labor Statistics,[4] a **financial planner** is a professional who provides advice on investments, insurance, mortgages, college savings, estate planning, taxes, and retirement to help individuals manage their finances. Financial planners tend to look at a client's financial situation holistically. Unlike a financial advisor who may provide advice and council on investment or insurance topics, or an accountant who may only prepare a client's tax or perform auditing services, a financial planner, by definition, is generally tasked with evaluating a client's overall financial situation and then using professional judgment to make integrated recommendations with the intent of improving a client's financial situation. Subject areas typically reviewed by a financial planner include, but are not limited to, the following:

- Financial statement preparation and analysis (including cash flow and net worth management and budgeting)

- Insurance planning and risk management

- Employee benefits planning

- Investment planning

- Income tax planning

- Education planning

- Retirement planning

- Estate Planning

Essentially, a financial planner is expected to use the financial planning process to guide their client generally and specifically within—and across—each subject area.

Financial Planning Practice Standards and Ethics

Financial planning professionals who are CFP® certificants must also follow practice standards developed and promulgated by CFP Board. These standards are described CFP Board's Standards of Professional Conduct—all of which have evolved within the profession to guide professional actions and benefit consumers. The CFP Board Practice Standards and Code of Ethics are intended to:

- assure that the practice of financial planning by CFP® professionals is based on established norms of practice;

- advance professionalism in financial planning; and

- enhance the value of the financial planning process.[5]

All CFP® professionals must adhere to the following Code of Ethics:

1. Act with honesty, integrity, competence, and diligence.

2. Act in the client's best interests.

3. Exercise due care.

4. Avoid or disclose and manage conflicts of interest.

5. Maintain the confidentiality and protect the privacy of client information.

6. Act in a manner that reflects positively on the financial planning profession and CFP® certification.

CFP Board's Standards of Conduct provide specific guidance to CFP® professionals when working with clients within the scope of the Code of Ethics. There are fifteen actions that comprise a financial planner's duties when conducting financial planning:[6]

1. Fiduciary duty

2. Competence

3. Diligence

4. Sound and objective professional judgment

5. Integrity

6. Professionalism

7. Comply with the law

8. Confidentiality and privacy

9. Disclose and manage conflicts of interest

10. Provide information to a client

11. Duties when communicating with a client

12. Duties when representing compensation method

13. Duties when recommending, engaging, and working with additional persons

14. Duties when selecting, recommending, and using technology

15. Refrain from borrowing or lending money and commingling financial assets

CFP Board also provides guidance on ways a CFP professional must act when applying the financial planning process and when dealing directly with CFP Board. Of particular importance is a rule titled "Rebuttable Presumption that the Practice Standards Apply," which states:

There is a rebuttable presumption that a CFP® professional providing financial advice is required to integrate relevant elements of the client's personal and/or financial circumstances in order to act in the client's best interest, and thus is required to comply with the Practice Standards. Among the factors that CFP Board will weigh are:

a. the number of relevant elements of the client's personal and financial circumstances that the financial advice affects;

b. the portion and amount of the client's financial assets that the financial advice may affect;

c. the length of time the client's personal and financial circumstances may be affected by the financial advice;

d. the effect of the client's overall exposure to risk if the client implements the financial advice; and

e. the barriers to modifying the actions taken to implement the financial advice.

A key takeaway is that a financial planner must act in the best interest of their client at all times while attempting to be holistic in the delivery of financial advice. For the purposes of the Practice Standards, a client is defined as:[7]

"Any person, including a natural person, business organization, or legal entity, to whom the CFP® professional renders professional services pursuant to an engagement."

Within this definition, an **engagement** is defined as:[8]

"A written or oral agreement, arrangement, or understanding."

The Practice Standards apply to the delivery of **financial advice**, which is defined as:[9]

"A communication that, based on its content, context, and presentation, would reasonably be viewed as a suggestion that the client take or refrain from taking a particularly course of action with respect to:

1. the development or implementation of a financial plan addressing goals, budgeting, risk, health considerations, educational needs, financial security, wealth, taxes, retirement, philanthropy, estate, legacy, or other relevant elements of a client's personal or financial circumstances;

2. the value of or the advisability of investing in, purchasing, holding, or selling financial assets;

3. investment policies or strategies, portfolio composition, the management of financial assets, or other financial matters;

4. the selection and retention of other persons to provide financial or professional services to the client; or

5. the exercise of discretionary authority over the financial assets of a client.

When determining whether financial advice has been provided to someone, CFP Board looks at the level of communication specifically provided to a client. For example, if advice is customized and communicated to an individual client, the advice will likely be considered to be financial advice. On the other hand, general education communications will not be viewed as financial advice.

The Role of Fiduciaries

While CFP Board practice standards and guidelines can serve as a performance benchmark for anyone who provides financial planning services, it is important to note that only CFP® professionals and certificants are required to adhere to the standards. CFP Board has no governmental or legal standing beyond the power to reprimand a CFP® professional. At a broader level, the practice of financial planning generally falls under the watchful eye of either the **Securities and Exchange Commission (SEC)** or the **Financial Industry Regulatory Authority (FINRA)**. Although overly simplified, the following guidelines can be used to identify when a financial planner will be subject to SEC or FINRA rules:[10]

- If a financial planner provides advice or counsel on investments and/or securities for a fee, the financial planner must register as an investment adviser with the SEC or appropriate state regulator.[11]

- If a financial planner recommends the purchase or sale of investments and/or securities, and earns a commission based on a transaction, the financial planner must be licensed by FINRA. The most common securities license is the Series 7 license.[12]

A SEC registered financial planner is required, under federal law, to follow a fiduciary standard of care when working with clients. According to the SEC:[13]

"The Investment Advisers Act prohibits misstatements or misleading omissions of material facts and other fraudulent acts and practices in connection with the conduct of an investment advisory business. As a fiduciary, an investment adviser owes its clients undivided loyalty, and may not engage in activity that conflicts with a client's interest without the client's consent."

A FINRA licensed financial planner needs only to follow what is generally referred to as a best interest standard of care when working with clients. Under this rule, a broker-dealer must recommend products that are in a client's best interest while also disclosing any potential conflicts of interest related to such products.[14]

The fiduciary standard of care is growing in importance worldwide. In some European countries, for example, the fiduciary standard has been adopted as the only means of providing financial planning services. There is little consensus in the United States and Canada, however, regarding the adoption of the fiduciary standard, although CFP Board's financial planning standards require any CFP® professional who is providing financial planning services must follow a fiduciary standard of care. Given global trends and CFP Board's standards of practice, the tools, techniques, and strategies presented in this book are designed to adhere to fiduciary standard of care.

FINANCIAL PLANNING AS A CAREER

As someone reading this book, it is likely that you are:

- a student who is nearing completion of a degree in financial planning;

- a financial service professional who is studying to enhance your professional competence; or

- a career changer looking for an exciting occupation that provides daily challenges, rewards, and high compensation.

It is also likely that you would like to sit for and pass the national Certified Financial Planner examination. Becoming a financial planner, and eventually obtaining the CFP® marks (or any of the other valuable credentials available in the marketplace[15]) is a worthwhile career goal. Consider the following statistics as published by the Bureau of Labor Statistics:[16]

- Almost 272,000 individuals work as financial planners and financial advisors.

- Financial planners and other financial advisors have median earnings of $90,640 annually.

- The top 10 percent of financial planners and financial advisors earn more than $208,000 annually.

- The lowest 10 percent of financial planners and financial advisors earn nearly $41,000 annually, which is still above the national median for all occupations.

- The job outlook for financial planners is high and expected to grow much faster than average.

- As many as 40,000 new financial planners and financial advisors are expected to be hired by 2026.

WHY CASE STUDIES?

Financial planning is perennially ranked as one of the top five fastest growing and most prestigious careers. One outcome associated with the growth of the financial planning profession is that the study of financial planning has taken root as an academic discipline on college campuses. It is possible today to obtain an undergraduate and graduate degree in financial planning. The need for a case study textbook to help prepare future financial planners has been ongoing since the first financial planning courses were developed. The 2012 requirement that a financial plan development course be included in all CFP® registered financial planning curriculums has cemented this need. With the growing demand for well-educated financial planners, the need for challenging, yet realistic, cases today is more crucial than ever. *A Case Approach to Financial Planning: Bridging the Gap between Theory and Practice, Fourth Edition* was written to meet this need.

This textbook was not designed to be just another book of cases, nor was it conceptualized as an advanced financial planning book or a CFP® certification exam preparation book—although some have noted that, to some extent, it is a combination of all three. As a financial planning casebook, this text includes numerous analytical problems and questions, various computational examples, and enough ten- and twenty-question cases to keep a dedicated student engaged for an entire semester. If that were not enough, the book also offers students an opportunity to solve comprehensive cases using an advanced spreadsheet tool.

As an advanced financial planning book, this text provides a review of basic—and in some chapters, more advanced—content, particularly as applied to strategy development. What is presented should be familiar—almost a reminder—to those who are enrolled in a financial planning program. For those who studying in a certificate program or on their own, the material and cases can be used to identify areas where further study may be needed, especially in relation to passing one or more national certification examinations. Finally, as a CFP® certification exam preparation book, the text attempts to provide a review of relevant content matched to many of the CFP Board topical areas.

At its core, this book was written to illustrate how the financial planning process can be used to help clients achieve multiple financial goals and objectives through integrative financial planning. A second purpose of the book was to provide quality case studies help students, career changers, and those looking to learn more about financial planning gain confidence in identifying, applying, and integrating synergistic personal financial planning strategies into meaningful recommendations. Several objectives have guided the continual development of this book:

- Provide readers with a review of the steps necessary to complete a current situation analysis in the core content areas of financial planning.

- Present commonly used financial planning product and procedural strategies.

- Review the unique challenges associated with the evaluation of each core financial planning content area.

- Provide students with opportunities to work on challenging cases.

- Present computational questions and client-centered case studies that illustrate the use of specific strategies to meet client needs.

Quantitative/Analytical Mini-Case Problems

Brendan Frazier

1. Brendan Frazier is considering a career change. He recently read an online blog that stated the need for financial planning professionals will continue to grow in the future. Brendan is intrigued by the idea of becoming a financial planner. Based on the readings in this chapter, help Brendan answer the following questions:

    a. In what year did financial advisors meet and formalize what is now known as the profession of financial planning?

    b. How does CFP Board define financial planning?

    c. How do the authors of this book define financial planning?

    d. What are the seven steps in the financial planning process?

Frylyn Babcock

2. Frylyn Babcock is studying for a national financial planning examination. She has several questions about who may be called a financial planner, the types of activities a financial planner

typically engages in, and what standards a financial planner must adhere to. Help Frylyn answer the following questions:

a. If Frylyn's professional practice involves solely doing tax preparation work during the tax season is she a financial planner?

b. When must Frylyn follow CFP Board's financial planning practice standards?

c. If Frylyn becomes certified as a CFP® professional, she must follow CFP Board's Code of Ethics. What elements comprise the Board's Code of Ethics?

d. How does CFP Board define a client?

e. What is a financial planning engagement?

William Gustafson

3. William "Bill" Gustafson started his professional career as a stockbroker. While he has built a successful practice, Bill would like to expand his practice by offering investment management advice for a fee, rather than a commission. He believes that he can immediately begin managing $125 million in client assets on a fee basis. Help Bill understand the regulatory environment as it relates to providing investment advice for a fee by answering the following questions:

a. What agency's rules and regulations must Bill follow when working as a stockbroker?

b. If Bill were to become a Registered Investment Adviser, what federal agency must he register with?

c. As a stockbroker, Bill is allowed to provide investment advice based on a best interest standard of care. If he becomes a Registered Investment Adviser, what standard of care must he follow?

d. Which standard of care is more stringent?

Chapter Resources

Anthony, M. Your Clients for Life: The Definitive Guide to Becoming a Successful Financial Planner. Chicago, IL: Dearborn Financial Publishing, 2002.

Assessing a Client's Financial Risk Tolerance: http://pfp.missouri.edu/research_IRTA.html

Certified Financial Planner Board of Standards, Inc. (www.cfp.net).

Diliberto, R. T. Financial Planning—The Next Step: A Practical Approach to Merging Your Clients' Money with Their Lives. Denver, CO: FPA Press, 2006.

Financial Industry Regulatory Authority (FINRA) (www.finra.org).

FinaMetrica® (www.finametrica.com).

Financial Therapy Association (financialtherapyassociation.org/).

Investment Adviser Registration Depository (www.iard.com/).

Investment Financial Planner Public Disclosure Website: www.adviserinfo.sec.gov/ (S(l2wrhvakmfteghqc1qtt0v5m))/IAPD/Content/IapdMain/iapd_SiteMap.aspx

Kinder, G. Seven Stages of Money Maturity: Understanding the Spirit and Value of Money in your Life. New York: Dell Publishing, 2000.

Kinder, G., and S. Galvan. Lighting the Torch: The Kinder Method™ of Life Planning. Denver, CO: FPA Press, 2006.

Klontz, B., R. Kahler, and T. Klontz. Facilitating Financial Health: Tools for Financial Planners, Coaches, and Therapists; Second Edition). Cincinnati, OH: National Underwriter Company, 2015.

Klontz, B., and T. Klontz. Mind over Money: Overcoming the Money Disorders That Threaten Our Financial Health. New York: Crown Business, 2009.

Lytton, R., J. Grable, and Klock, D. The Process of Financial Planning: Developing a Financial Plan, 2nd Ed. Erlanger, KY: National Underwriter, 2012.

Money Quotient® Putting Money in the Context of Life™ (moneyquotient.org/).

The Kinder Institute of Life Planning (www.kinderinstitute.com/index.html).

The Financial Life Planning Institute (www.flpinc.com/).

U.S. Securities and Exchange Commission (www.sec.gov).

Endnotes

1. While all financial planners generally agree with CFP Board's definition, only CFP® practitioners and students enrolled in a CFP Board registered academic program are required to use this definition. Additionally, only CFP® professionals and candidates must abide by the CFP Board Code of Ethics and follow all CFP Board rules and regulations.

2. Certified Financial Planner Board of Standards, Inc., *CFP Board's Standards of Professional Conduct*. Available at: https://www.cfp.net/for-cfp-professionals/professional-standards-enforcement/standards-of-professional-conduct.

3. Dr. Dave Yeske, a financial planning thought leader, has addressed this issue in numerous articles, including "Evidence-Based Financial Planning: To Learn Like a CFP," and "Finding the Planning in Financial Planning."

4. Bureau of Labor Statistics: https://www.bls.gov/ooh/business-and-financial/personal-financial-advisors.htm.

5. CFP Board: https://www.cfp.net/for-cfp-professionals/professional-standards-enforcement/code-and-standards.

6. Details about each standard of conduct can be found at: https://www.cfp.net/for-cfp-professionals/professional-standards-enforcement/standards-of-professional-conduct.

7. CFP Board: https://www.cfp.net/for-cfp-professionals/professional-standards-enforcement/standards-of-professional-conduct.

8. *Ibid.*

9. *Ibid.*

10. It is possible for a financial planner to be subject to both SEC and FINRA rules. When dual registration occurs, a financial planner must disclose to their client what type of service is being provided, how the financial planner is being paid, and any conflicts of interest.

11. Financial planners who manage more than $100 million must register with the SEC. Others generally must register with the state securities regulator in the state(s) in which the financial planner provides services.

12. Financial planners who sell insurance products must hold a state issued license. An insurance professional who also provides investment advice about variable insurance products may also be required to hold an FINRA license.

13. Securities and Exchange Commission: https://www.sec.gov/divisions/investment/iaregulation/memoia.htm.

14. See: https://www.finra.org/rules-guidance/key-topics/regulation-best-interest.

15. Other highly sought-after financial planning credentials include the Chartered Financial Consultant (ChFC®), Chartered Life Underwriter (CLU®), and Personal Financial Specialist (PFS®) designations.

16. Data obtained from: https://www.bls.gov/ooh/business-and-financial/personal-financial-advisors.htm.

Chapter 2

Computations for Financial Planning

Learning Objectives

- Learning Objective 1: Describe the role of financial calculations in the financial planning process.

- Learning Objective 2: Estimate holding period returns.

- Learning Objective 3: Differentiate between arithmetic and geometric returns.

- Learning Objective 4: Describe the way interest rates can be calculated.

- Learning Objective 5: Evaluate different measures of risk.

- Learning Objective 6: Estimate loan payments based on amortization calculations.

- Learning Objective 7: Master time value of money (TVM) computational skills.

- Learning Objective 8: Apply Modern Portfolio Theory computations methods when evaluating a client's investment holdings.

CFP® Principal Knowledge Topics

- CFP Topic: B.13. Time Value of Money Concepts and Calculations.
- CFP Topic: E.36. Measures of Investment Returns.

FINANCIAL PLANNING COMPUTATIONAL STRATEGIES

Almost all aspects of personal financial planning involve mathematical calculations. The good news is that the math is not extremely complex. Furthermore, sophisticated calculators and software programs are available to do most of the work. The most important caveat when attempting to complete financial planning computations is that outputs depend entirely upon the quality of inputs.

The formulas needed for the majority of the calculations are relatively easy to memorize. Applying the correct formula and related inputs within a calculation usually causes the most difficulty. More important than the formulas themselves is a fundamental understanding of the logic, or reasoning, required to identify the correct mathematical formula for a particular purpose.

Once the logic has been established, there may be multiple ways to derive the correct solution to a financial planning question. For example, one financial planner may choose to adjust a future value calculation for taxes at the end of period, while another may wish to adjust a savings need at the beginning to account for taxes. Both financial planners should arrive at the same answer. This can sometimes be confusing to those who are new to the logic of time value of money computations.

What is important, then, is for financial planners to choose a method that they are comfortable with and practice that method until the process becomes second nature. Then, it is equally important to ensure accuracy—in both the input of the data and the supporting assumptions on which a calculation is based.

The purpose of this chapter is to briefly review some of the most important calculations typically made during the financial planning process. After reading this chapter and practicing material in the chapter, readers should understand rates of return and time value of money formulas and how to set up equations for later use in a spreadsheet application or financial calculator. Keep in mind, however, that each of the strategies, techniques, and approaches presented in this chapter represent minimal competencies for a financial planning professional. Other calculation techniques will be presented throughout this book. It is, then, important to combine the material from this chapter with techniques from other chapters to develop a comprehensive understanding of the computational skills that an adept financial planner needs to exhibit on a day-to-day basis.

Planning Strategy 1: Understand How Investors Earn a Rate of Return

One of the most elementary of all personal finance calculations is determining the **total return** earned on an investment. Financial planners use this calculation to determine how much profit has been earned on an investment during a certain period of time. **Rate of return** describes the relationship between profit or loss relative to the amount saved or invested. For example, assume an investor deposits $1,000 into an account, the account has a stated rate of return of 6 percent, and the investor leaves the deposit in the account for one year. What will be the account balance at the end of the investment period? How much of the account balance is principal and how much is interest? How much will the account be worth in real terms if **inflation**—the general increase in the price of goods and services over time—averages 4 percent over the same time period? How much money will be available after paying taxes on the earnings? All of these questions are answered by using various rate of return calculations.

To calculate that rate of return on an investment, all sources of income must be identified. The two most common sources of return are **income** and **capital gains**. In general, income is derived from periodic payments received by an investor, either in cash or as deposits to an account during the investment period. Examples include stock dividends, bond interest payments, mutual fund dividends, or savings account interest payments. Capital gains (or losses), on the other hand, are generally received or realized when an investment period ends and the investment is sold, liquidated, or matures. If the security is sold for more (or less) than the purchase price, the investor will realize a capital gain (or loss).

These two sources of cash inflow serve as the basis for the nominal return on investment. A **nominal value**, in its simplest form, means an unadjusted value. A nominal value can be thought of as the **gross return**. The most common adjustment made to a nominal value is an inflation adjustment; however, nominal values can be adjusted for many other reasons. Later in the chapter, nominal values will be the basis of adjustments for inflation (real returns), taxes (after-tax returns), compounding frequencies (effective returns), and others. When calculating total returns or future values, it is as important to understand the interrelationship between the nominal and adjusted rate as it is to be able to accurately calculate the nominal rate of return.

Planning Strategy 2: Calculate Holding-Period Returns

Holding-Period Return

A simple method of calculating **nominal returns** involves determining an investor's **holding-period return** (HPR). The formula considers a beginning and ending value for the investment, income earned during the holding period, and transaction costs. The income received could be dividends from an equity (or stock) investment, or the income could be coupon "interest" payments from a debt (or bond) investment. The formula is as follows:

$$HPR = \frac{Income + \left(Ending\,Value - Beginning\,Value\right) - Transaction\,Costs}{Beginning\,Value}$$

Example: Bob purchased one share of stock for $45 per share, received two dividend payments of $1 each that were not reinvested, and paid a transaction fee of $5. Bob then sold the stock for $55. What was Bob's holding-period return?

$$HPR = \frac{\sum Div + (End - Beg) - Costs}{Beg}$$

$$HPR = \frac{(1+1) + (55 - 45) - 5}{45} = \frac{2 + 10 - 5}{45} = 15.6\%$$

A common modification to nominal rates of return is an adjustment for taxes paid at the state and federal levels. However, calculating **tax-adjusted returns** can be complex. First, a financial planner needs to know what type of income was generated as a result of the return. Second, the financial planner must know what tax rate applies to each type of return. For example, interest income, dividends (qualified or nonqualified), and capital gains may be taxed at different rates. The rates may also vary depending on the holding period for the investment (e.g., short-term or long-term capital gains).

To accurately calculate the tax-adjusted rate of return, the HPR must be offset by any tax liability generated as a result of owning the investment. The following adjustment can be used for historical return calculations:

$$Tax\ Adjusted\ HPR = \frac{(Income - Income\ Tax) + (Capital\ Gains - Cap\ Gains\ Tax) - (Costs\ adjusted\ for\ Taxes)}{Beginning\ Value}$$

Obviously, this equation can be used only for historical calculations because the actual amount of tax liability must be determined prior to calculating the return. However, to estimate the after-tax rate of return for projection purposes, where taxation occurs annually, a financial planner can also use the following equation:

$$r_t = R \times (1 - t)$$

Where:

r_t = tax-adjusted return

R = nominal return

t = investor's marginal tax bracket

Example: Expanding on the previous example, assume Bob owned the stock in a non-tax-qualified account and dividends and capital gains are taxed at a short-term tax rate of 15 percent. His after-tax rate of return would be 13.26 percent, as shown below:

$$r_t = 15.6\% \times (1 - 0.15) = 13.26\%$$

Dollar-Weighted Return

The problem with using a holding-period return is that the formula does not account for the timing of subsequent cash flows into or out of an account. A very basic formula that corrects for the timing of subsequent cash flows is the **dollar-weighted return** formula, shown below:

$$\text{Dollar Weighted Rate of Return} = \frac{Inc + [End - (Beg + D - W)] - Costs}{Beg + D_t - W_t}$$

Where:

Inc	=	income
End	=	ending value
Beg	=	beginning value
D	=	deposit amount
W	=	withdrawal amount
Costs	=	transaction costs
D_t	=	D × (1 – timing of deposit)
W_t	=	W × (1 – timing of withdrawal)

Example: Altering the preceding example, assume that one year after Bob made his initial one share purchase he bought an additional two shares of stock at $48 ($48 × 2 = $96). Further, assume that he sold one share at $45 at the end of the second year and liquidated the account after three years at $50 per share ($50 × 2 = $100). He will still receive semiannual dividends of $1 per share ($12 total); the total transaction cost is still $5. What is Bob's dollar-weighted rate of return?

$$\text{Dollar-Weighted HPR} = \frac{\$12 + [\$100 - (\$45 + \$96 - \$45)] - \$5}{\$45 + \left[\$96\left(1 - \frac{12}{36}\right)\right] - \left[\$45\left(1 - \frac{24}{36}\right)\right]}$$

$$= \frac{\$12 + \$4 - \$5}{\$45 + \$64 - \$15} = 11.7\%$$

Time-Weighted Return

An alternative to dollar-weighted returns is a **time-weighted return**. This method of calculation ignores the actual value of the investment during each time period.

Example: Using Bob's situation, it is known that the stock was initially purchased for $45 per share and was valued as follows:

End-of-year 1: $48

End-of-year 2: $45

End-of-year 3: $50

Using the holding-period return formula results in the following annual rates of return:

Year 1: $\dfrac{\$2 + (\$48 - \$45)}{\$45} = 11.1\%$

Year 2: $\dfrac{\$2 + (\$45 - \$48)}{\$48} = -2.1\%$

Year 3: $\dfrac{\$2 + (\$50 - \$45)}{\$45} = 15.6\%$

Average: $\dfrac{11.1\% - 2.1\% + 15.6\%}{3} = 8.2\%$

Thus, the average of the three annual returns results in a time-weighted return of 8.2 percent. Note that the dividend was the same for all three periods because the time-weighted return ignores the number of shares (dollar amount) owned in each period.

Which measure is superior? It depends on **asset control**. Investors who control their own investments (both the timing and amount of purchases) will want to use the dollar-weighted average. In this case, the more money invested when a stock is performing well, the more money the investor will have in the end. However, a person who does not control the timing and amount of the investment, such as a portfolio manager, would want to measure performance using the time-weighted measure. It would be inappropriate to examine a manager's success or failure based on a measure over which the manager does not have complete control.

Planning Strategy 3: Calculate an Average Annual Return

Average annual returns are some of the most quoted statistics in finance. These returns are easy to calculate, relatively simple to interpret, and —for the most part—intuitive. However, the most common usage for these statistics is to incorporate them into models to predict future investment results. It is important to keep in mind that most calculations of historic returns tend to have a **bias** or partial perspective when used to project future or terminal values. A **downward bias** means that the average used to project the future value tends to underestimate the actual outcome. An **upward bias** results in overestimation. Such bias occurs because cumulative return is a nonlinear function of average return.

The following discussion of arithmetic averages and geometric averages not only presents the calculation of the two statistics but also addresses two issues inherent in using either average as a means to project future results: standard deviation and time horizon. Both of these factors play a role in the bias created when projecting terminal values.

Arithmetic and Geometric Means—Calculation and Deterministic Forecasting

Although holding-period based returns are very simple to use and calculate, most returns are quoted on an average annual basis because annual returns are more intuitive for investors to understand and are often required by regulators. A financial planner can use a number of different methods to measure average rates of return. The simplest method is to calculate the **arithmetic mean**, which is a linear interpretation of past performance.

$$\text{Average Return (AR)} = \frac{r_1 + r_2 + r_3 + ... + r_n}{n}$$

Where:

r = return for period

n = number of periods

Example: Consider a client who makes 8 percent, 2 percent, and –5 percent in each of three years, respectively. The average of these returns is 1.67 percent.

$$AR = \frac{8\% + 2\% - 5\%}{3} = 1.67\%$$

The arithmetic mean, although quick to calculate and easy to explain, is often a poor representation of actual performance due to the variability (measured by *standard deviation*) of returns. Therefore, it can be said that the higher the standard deviation of returns, even over a short time period, the greater the potential upward bias of the projection. The resultant overestimation of future values is even more problematic when short-term arithmetic averages are used for long-term forecasting.

For longer forecasting periods, or for forecasting using a more highly varied return, a **geometric average** is more appropriate because this mean estimate is computed using a geometric series. A geometric mean takes on more of the characteristics found in long-term averages and corrects for any upward bias. In other words, future values, by their very nature, are the result of a geometric series of returns rather than linear series. The rule is that, unless the variation of returns is zero, the geometric average will always be lower than the arithmetic return. How much less depends on the variation (standard deviation) of returns. **Standard deviation** is the average difference between an individual outcome (in this case the investment return) and the average, or expected, outcome for the applicable group. Standard deviation will be discussed in more depth later in the chapter.

Consider a $100 stock that rises 50 percent in one year and falls 50 percent the next. The arithmetic mean return is zero. However, when the return is tracked, it is apparent that in the first year the final price was $150. Then the 50 percent drop results in a final value of $75. The total return is obviously less than zero—it is a negative 25 percent total return. It is also a negative 13.4 percent geometric return. For this reason, the geometric mean is recommended for forecasting future values. The geometric mean is often referred to as **geomean**, the annualized return or the **compound annualized growth rate (CAGR)**. The formula for calculating a geometric average is as follows:

$$Geometric\ Mean\ Return = \left[(1+r_1)\times(1+r_2)\times(1+r_3)\times...\times(1+r_n)\right]^{1/n} - 1$$

Where:

r = return for period

n = number of periods

Example: Tonya purchased an investment seven years ago. According to the annual report, the investment earned the rates of return shown in the table below. She wants to know what return she could project for the next seven years by calculating the annualized return.

Year	Rate of Return
1	9 percent
2	–8 percent
3	2 percent
4	12 percent
5	18 percent
6	–7 percent
7	4 percent

$$Geomean = \left[(1+0.09)\times(1-0.08)\times(1+0.02)\times(1+0.12)\times(1+0.18)\times(1-0.07)\times(1+0.04)\right]^{1/7} - 1$$

$Geomean = 3.90\%$

Now compare this result to the simple linear average.

$$Arithmetic\ Mean = \frac{9\% - 8\% + 2\% + 12\% + 18\% - 7\% + 4\%}{7}$$

$Arithmetic\ Mean = 4.29\%$

Clearly, the arithmetic average overstates expected return with an upward bias. For example, seven years ago a client might have asked for the future value of $500,000 in seven years. Using the arithmetic average of 4.29 percent would have resulted in a projected value of $670,916.82; however, the account actually only grew to $653,550.03. Using the arithmetic average to project the future value would have resulted in an overstatement of the actual account value by $17,366.79. This may seem like an insignificant amount given the very fluid nature of financial markets and the subjective nature of projections. But what if the client had $2,000,000 and asked for a twenty five-year projection? In this case, the difference between the arithmetic projection and the geometric projection would have been more than half a million dollars, which would have most likely undermined the client-planner relationship.

Using a geometric average will result in a more precise measure of the client's true return when projecting account values into the future. The arithmetic mean can be useful in certain circumstances or for a quick estimate, but for actual reporting and forecasting, the geometric mean is generally preferred. However, this method, too, is not without flaws. A future value calculated using a geometric average is likely to have a slight downward bias. This means that the actual future value achieved is likely to be slightly greater than the future value projected using the geometric average. The amount of underestimation will depend on the ratio of the sampled estimation period compared to the forecasted period. The closer the ratio is to one, the less likely the downward bias.[1]

The following rules generally hold true: (1) when forecasting periods that are much shorter than the sample period from which the averages were calculated, the true average tends to be closer to the arithmetic mean; and (2) for forecasting periods that are much closer in length to the sample period, the true average will be closer to the geometric mean.

Arithmetic and Geometric Returns Compared

When comparing the arithmetic mean and the geometric mean, it is interesting to note that as the standard deviation of the returns approaches zero, the difference between the arithmetic mean and the geometric mean also approaches zero. This is because the arithmetic mean and the geometric mean are equal if the return is fixed, meaning that the exact same outcome (return) occurs in each period, which results in a standard deviation of zero. However, the inverse is also true. As the standard deviation of outcomes increases, the difference between the arithmetic mean and the geometric mean also increases.

Consider the S&P 500 total returns in Figure 2.1. The difference between the two means is quite large, 1.90 percent (10.10 percent – 8.20 percent), because the standard deviation is nearly 20 percent. As this example illustrates, the relationship between the two statistics becomes quite apparent and very important.

Figure 2.1. Investment Market Returns

Year	Annual Return	Year	Annual Return
Year 1	–3.10%	Year 11	–9.10%
Year 2	30.46%	Year 12	–11.89%
Year 3	7.62%	Year 13	–22.10%
Year 4	10.08%	Year 14	28.68%
Year 5	1.32%	Year 15	10.88%
Year 6	37.58%	Year 16	4.91%
Year 7	22.96%	Year 17	15.80%
Year 8	33.36%	Year 18	5.49%
Year 9	28.58%	Year 19	–37.00%
Year 10	21.04%	Year 20	26.46%
Arithmetic Average	10.10%	Geometric Average	8.21%
Variance	3.89%	Standard Deviation	19.73%

Example: A client has an account balance of $50,000. The client assumes that since the average annual return of the stock market has been 10 percent over the last twenty years, the next twenty years should result in the same return. Even if history were to repeat itself, the client still should not use the 10 percent average annual return but should instead use the 8.2 percent geometric average return. By using the incorrect average return for projecting the value of the account in twenty years, the client will likely overstate the account balance by nearly $95,000. Using the incorrect 10 percent return results in an account balance of $336,375.00; using the more accurate 8.2 percent return results in an account balance of $241,832.81.

One of the most significant issues associated with calculating geometric averages is that individual periodic returns are needed to construct the geometric series; however, the literature and internet sites typically provide only multi-period average returns (e.g., three-, five-, or ten-year). However, if the standard deviation is also available for a corresponding period, then the *geomean* can be estimated. The following formula can be used to back into the geomean if a return series is unavailable:

$$Geometric\ Mean = Arithmetic\ Mean - \frac{1}{2}Variance$$

Example: Using the preceding example where the arithmetic average was 10.10 percent and the variance was 3.89 percent, the geomean can quickly be estimated as:

$$Geometric\ Mean = 10.10\% - \frac{1}{2}*3.89\% = 8.155\%$$

Planning Strategy 4: Calculate a Weighted Average Return

Multi-Asset Portfolio Returns

Sometimes it is necessary to calculate a weighted average return for different assets or values. A **weighted average** is calculated by multiplying an investment return by the proportion of the investment, stated as a percentage of the total portfolio, and then summing the total for all of the investments. For example, Figure 2.2 provides rate of return data from seven mutual funds. The amount invested in each fund is also provided. These data were used to determine that this portfolio has a weighted average rate of return of 5.64 percent.

Figure 2.2. Hypothetical Portfolio Values and Returns

Fund	Objective	Value (A)	Percent of Portfolio (B)	RoR (C)	Weighted Return (D)
	Calculation		(A /E)		(B × C)
Fund A	Moderately Aggressive	$75,000	15.79%	8.00%	1.26%
Fund B	Moderately Conservative	$100,000	21.05%	9.00%	1.89%
Fund C	CD	$94,000	19.79%	3.00%	0.59%
Fund D	Aggressive	$14,000	2.95%	10.00%	0.29%
Fund E	Conservative	$35,000	7.37%	3.00%	0.22%
Fund F	CD	$45,000	9.47%	2.00%	0.19%
Fund G	Conservative	$112,000	23.58%	5.00%	1.18%
Total		$475,000 (E)	100.00%		5.64%*

* Total may differ due to rounding

Scenario-Based Returns

Nearly all financial planning forecasts are based on the notion that the future will closely resemble the past. This is, obviously, a tenuous assumption. **Deterministic modeling** based on historical averages can sometimes be highly misrepresentative of the near-term future. It is sometimes better to account for multiple potential outcomes, where each outcome is assigned a probability of occurrence. Using the same methodology to determine a weighted average return, where the weights each represent a percentage of the entire portfolio, a financial planner can reassign the weights to the probability of occurrence, as shown in Figure 2.3. Then each outcome can be assigned a corresponding potential return.

Figure 2.3. Scenario-Based Potential Returns

Potential Economic Outcome	Probability of Occurrence (A)	Corresponding Return (B)	Weighted Return (A × B)
Super-normal growth	15.0%	20.00%	3.00%
Normal growth	55.0%	12.00%	6.60%
Stagnation	5.0%	3.00%	0.15%
Recession	20.0%	–8.00%	–1.60%
Depression	5.0%	–25.00%	–1.25%
	100.00%		6.90%

Planning Strategy 5: Describe and Calculate Different Types and Forms of Interest Rates

Real and Nominal Rates

Nearly all interest rates quoted online, in magazines, and in annual reports are **nominal rates**, meaning that the rate has not been adjusted to account for inflation. Nominal rates are used when the actual dollar amount of an investment is important. By contrast, the **real rate of return** is the return "left over" after adjusting for inflation. This return provides a more accurate representation of **purchasing power**, which is an important consideration for long-term investments. A client may be interested in having a portfolio value of $1 million when she turns sixty five, but she needs to recognize that the purchasing power of such a portfolio will be far less than what $1 million provides today. This is why adjusting returns to account for inflation is of paramount importance.

Two equations are used to account for the effects of inflation: one if the nominal rate of return is continuously compounded and another if the nominal rate is discretely or not continuously compounded. If the nominal rate of return is **continuously compounded**, it is appropriate to subtract the inflation rate from the nominal rate to determine an approximation of the real rate.

$r = R - i$

Where:

r = real rate

R = nominal rate

i = inflation rate

Example: The nominal annual rate of return on Mary's portfolio is 9 percent and the annual inflation rate is 4 percent. In this case, the nominal rate of return is continuously compounded. What is her real rate of return?

$R = 9\% - 4\% = 5\%$

However, if the nominal rate is not continuously compounded, a different equation, often referred to as the **Fisher Equation**, should be used to take into account the effects of this compounding difference. The result of this calculation is sometimes referred to as a **serial interest rate**.

$$r = \frac{(1+R)}{(1+i)} - 1$$

Where:

> r = real rate
>
> R = nominal rate
>
> i = inflation rate

Example: The nominal annual rate of return on Mary's portfolio is 9 percent and the annual inflation rate is 4 percent. In this case, the nominal rate of return is not continuously compounded. The real rate of return is no longer 5 percent, but slightly less than 5 percent.

$$r = \frac{(1.09)}{(1.04)} - 1 = 4.81\%$$

This calculation should be used whenever a client faces **inflation risk** when making an investment. These are particularly important formulas when determining the present value of an inflation-adjusted dollar amount—as is the case anytime a financial planner or investor is calculating future values but stating the results in today's dollars.

Tax-exempt and Taxable Rates

In addition to the difference between nominal and real rates of return, financial planners need to account for differences between taxable and tax-exempt rates of return. In the earlier discussion of holding-period returns, the concept of **tax impact** was briefly introduced. For the most part, exact **after-tax returns** cannot be determined until the end of an investing period. However, applying a client's **marginal tax bracket** to a return calculation can at least offer a reasonable estimate of future tax impact on a projected return.

Example: A client is in the 25 percent marginal tax bracket and the expected return on an investment is 7 percent. By applying the following formula, a financial planner can determine how much of the return will actually benefit the client. In other words, how much of each dollar earned will be retained after taxes?

$$r' = R \times (1-t)$$

Where:

> r' = after-tax rate
>
> R = nominal rate
>
> t = federal marginal tax rate
>
> r' = $0.07 \times (1 - 0.25) = 5.25$ percent

In this case, the investor's after-tax return will be 5.25 percent. If a client invested $1,000 in a taxable account and the account returned 7 percent per year, or $70, then the client would keep $52.50 of those dollars. The investor would pay $17.50 in taxes. This formula can also be expanded to include impact of state taxes on nominal returns.

In many states, **state income taxes** are levied against gains that remain after the federal tax liability has been applied; in such states, the **state tax rate** cannot simply be added to the federal tax rate in the preceding formula. The state tax rate is, in essence, reduced by the client's federal tax bracket. This is accomplished by using the same formula as above, except that the nominal rate in the formula is replaced by the state tax rate.

$$s' = s \times (1 - t)$$

Where:

s' = applicable state tax rate

s = state tax rate

t = Federal tax rate

Now the combined after-tax rate can be determined by combining both of the preceding equations.

$$r' = R \times [1 - (t + (s \times (1 - t)))] \quad \text{or} \quad r' = R \times [1 - (t + s')]$$

This may seem like a lot of manipulation for a fairly simple projection; however, this approach can be useful when determining the **taxable equivalent yield (TEY)**. A TEY is an investor's implied **required rate of return** on a taxable investment with identical risk/reward characteristics. In other words, if an investor could earn 6 percent on a tax-free investment, the TEY would need to be higher to compensate the investor equally on an after-tax basis. The formula to determine exactly how much higher is a variation of the preceding formulas.

The following formula can be used to determine the TEY on a taxable investment that can then be compared with a federal **tax-free investment** (e.g., an out-of-state municipal bond) using the **federal marginal tax bracket (FMTB)**.

$$TEY = \frac{Bond\ Yield}{(1 - FMTB)}$$

Keep in mind that this formula accounts only for federal taxes and it applies only to certain situations, including: (1) the purchase of out-of-state municipal bonds, (2) the comparison of in-state municipal bonds to Treasury bonds when neither bond is subject to state taxes, or (3) when a client's state of residence does not levy a state income tax. Outside of these situations, the impact of both federal and state taxes should be considered. To include the impact of state taxes, the formula needs to be slightly altered to include the **state marginal tax bracket (SMTB)**.

$$TEY = \frac{Bond\ Yield}{1 - [FMTB + (SMTB \times (1 - FMTB))]}$$

Example: A client desires a fixed-income investment and has narrowed the list of choices to two bonds: (1) an in-state municipal bond with an annual coupon rate of 6 percent and (2) a corporate bond with an annual coupon rate of 8 percent. The investor is in the 25 percent federal tax bracket and the 5 percent state tax bracket. Which would be the better bond to purchase?

At first glance, it would seem that the corporate bond that pays $80 per $1,000 invested would be the better choice. However, the client would have to pay taxes on the $80, leaving the client with less than $80 after taxes. The other choice is the municipal bond that pays only $60, but the client would, under most circumstances, not owe any federal or state taxes on that amount.

By using the TEY formula, the client can determine the required yield on the taxable investment that would provide equal compensation. In other words, this is the yield that is required to net the client the same amount of spendable dollars after paying the tax liability on the earnings.

$$TEY = \frac{0.06}{1-[0.25+(0.05\times(1-0.25))]} = \frac{0.06}{0.7125} = 0.08421 \, or \, 8.421\%$$

Using the formula above, a financial planner can determine that the taxable return would have to be 8.421 percent for the client to maintain the same net return. Therefore, the client would be better off purchasing the in-state municipal bond.

Planning Strategy 6: Describe Common Risk and Return Factors

Inflation risk, default risk, interest rate risk, reinvestment risk, political risk, exchange rate risk, and other factors must be analyzed and either removed, mitigated, or compensated for when making investment planning and rate of return assumptions. To be compensated for these risks (discussed in more detail in Chapter 10), an investor must receive a rate of return high enough to adjust for the risk. The outcome of this adjustment is an investor's **required rate of return**. This rate will nearly always be greater than the **risk-free rate** that simply compensates an investor for delaying consumption. An investor's required rate of return is universally used as the basis for time value of money calculations.

Planning Strategy 7: Make Time Value of Money Calculations

Among financial planners, the notion that a financial plan serves as the foundation of a client's financial future is widely held. If true, then time value of money concepts are the cornerstone of that foundation. The use of **time value of money** (**TVM**) formulas has two primary purposes: (1) to estimate how money can be moved around in time while accurately reflecting its true value or purchasing power; and (2) to solve for complex spending and savings scenarios, such as college or retirement funding. TVM formulas can be used to answer questions such as: What will be the value of a client's savings in ten years? How much does a client need to save today to fund something in the future? What will be the impact of inflation on a client's standard of living?

The underlying assumption behind all TVM calculations is that it is generally more beneficial to receive a dollar today than in the future. Someone who waits to receive a dollar, rather than taking it today, must be compensated for waiting. That person would be willing to spend less than a dollar today in order to receive a dollar in the future. The following discussion provides an overview of some of the cornerstone concepts underlying TVM calculations.

Effective and Nominal Rates of Return

Compound interest is premised on the idea that interest earned in a prior period is reinvested and therefore earns additional interest in subsequent periods. Referred to by Albert Einstein as the "eighth wonder of the world," this mechanism adds a level of complexity when calculating present or future values, which substantiates the less well-known component of his quote: "He who understands it, earns it…he who doesn't, pays it."

The simplest example is that if a $100 investment earns a simple 10 percent per year, then the account will pay the owner $10 the first year, the tenth year, and every year thereafter. If the same investor reinvests or compounds the interest, the account will earn more interest in each subsequent year. While the first year still returns $10, the tenth year will return $23.58 based on a prior year value of $235.79.

For TVM calculations, it is generally assumed that all accounts will compound interest earned; therefore, the **interest rate**, or the investor's required rate of return, is the variable that compounds or discounts the cash flows. **Compound interest** takes into account both principal and the interest earned on the principal. This is the variable that keeps values equal across time. When using TVM formulas, it is critical that the interest rate used be an **effective rate**—one that considers the effects of **compounding** when compounding occurs more than once a year. In other words, this is the actual **accrued annual interest rate**.

If the rate is not an effective rate, then it is a nominal rate, often referred to as an **annual percentage rate** (**APR**). The nominal rate may be used in a financial calculator because the calculator can automatically adjust for the compounding period (**payment frequency**). It generally may not be used in mathematical formulas unless adjustments are made to the formulas. The following formula is used to adjust a nominal rate to an effective rate:

$$\textit{Effective Annual Rate} = \left(1 + \frac{APR}{m}\right)^{m} - 1$$

Where:

APR = annual percentage rate or the nominal rate

m = number of compounding periods per year

The **effective annual rate** (**EAR**) is the rate of return that, under annual compounding, will produce the same future value at the end of one year as produced by more frequent compounding. If compounding occurs on an annual basis, the effective annual rate and the nominal rate are the same. If compounding occurs more frequently, the effective annual rate will be greater than the nominal rate.

In addition to the effective annual rate, there is also an **effective periodic rate** (**EPR**). The EPR, or **iPER**, is the rate charged by a lender or paid by a borrower each period. The EPR can be a semiannual, quarterly, monthly, or daily rate; in fact, it can be any time interval, for example, every ten years.

Example. What is the EAR in a bank account that has an APR of 6 percent, but the interest is compounded quarterly?

$$EAR = \left(1 + \frac{APR}{m}\right)^{m} - 1$$

$$= \left(1 + \frac{0.06}{4}\right)^{4} - 1$$

$$= 1.015^{4} - 1$$

$$= 1.0614 - 1 = 0.0614 \text{ or } 6.14 \text{ percent}$$

Example: What is the effective monthly interest rate on a mortgage with a stated APR of 8 percent? This would be the rate necessary to determine the monthly interest charges on a simple-interest mortgage with a monthly payment.

$$EPR = \frac{APR}{m}$$

$$EPR = \frac{0.08}{12} = 0.0667 \text{ or } 0.667 \text{ percent}$$

Figure 2.4 illustrates common variations of the equations used to adjust between nominal and effective interest rates.

Figure 2.4. Adjusting Between Nominal and Effective Interest Rates

Type of Interest Rate Known	Type of Interest Rate Desired	Formula Needed
EAR	EPR	$(1 + EAR)^{1/m} - 1 = EPR$
EAR	APR	$\left[(1 + EAR)^{1/m} - 1\right] \times m = APR$
EPR	EAR	$(1 + EPR)^{m} - 1 = EAR$
EPR	APR	$EPR \times m = APR$
APR	EPR	$\dfrac{APR}{m} = EPR$
APR	EAR	$\left[1 + \left(\dfrac{APR}{m}\right)\right]^{m} - 1 = EAR$

Note: In all cases, m is the number of compounding periods per year.

One of the most important concepts to understand when manipulating rates of return in TVM equations is that the compounding frequency of the effective rate must match the payment frequency. In other words, the rate used must match the compounding frequency of how often cash flows, or payments, occur. For example, if a payment is occurring monthly, then the effective rate needs to be adjusted so that it is also compounded monthly. This adjustment does not influence the actual interest earned; it simply adjusts how the rate is interpreted within the equation.

Payments are the periodic inflows or outflows that occur during a valuation period. Payments are used only with **annuity equations**. For a cash flow to be considered a *payment*, it must occur more than once and happen on a fixed periodic basis (e.g., monthly, semiannually, annually, etc.). Because the frequency of a payment and the interest rate must match, and the payment frequency is independent, the interest rate must be adjusted to match the payment frequency.

Example: A client is planning to save for retirement by contributing to an employer-sponsored 401(k) plan on a **semimonthly** (twice per month) basis. However, the account reports and compounds at a monthly rate of 0.721 percent. For a TVM equation to be accurate, the rate must reflect the semimonthly compounding period. To make this conversion, two of effective rate equations must be used. Here is the process. First convert the monthly effective rate into an EAR.

$$EAR = (1 + EPR)^m - 1$$

$$EAR = (1 + 0.00721)^{12} - 1 \text{ (m = 12 because the account compounds monthly)}$$

$$EAR = 9.00\%$$

Second, the EAR must be converted back into a semimonthly effective rate.

$$EPR = (1 + EAR)^{\frac{1}{m}} - 1$$

$$EPR = (1 + 0.09)^{\frac{1}{24}} - 1 \quad \text{(m = 24 due to semimonthly payment frequency)}$$

$$EPR = 0.360\%$$

This new EPR can be used in the formula to determine what the required savings amount needs to be, the future value of the account, or whatever else the financial planner may be calculating.

Basic Time Value of Money Calculations

Every TVM calculation involves at least three of six possible variables, including:[2]

1. FV—A single cash flow or series of cash flows (FVA) that occur at any point(s) in time after the present.

2. PMT—A series of equal* and uninterrupted cash flows that occur for multiple consecutive periods (*payments may not be equal, but related, in the case of growing annuities).

3. PV—The value today of a single cash flow or of a series of cash flows (PVA) that will occur in the future. It is important to note, however, that present values can exist at any point in time so long as the cash flows are being discounted.

4. I/Y—The rate of return required by an investor to forgo consumption in the current time period. This is often referred to as the discount rate and can be used interchangeably with internal rate of return (IRR) because this rate equates future benefits with current costs.

5. N—The number of periods (and payments, if an annuity) across which cash flows are being discounted or compounded. Typically, N is used to denote years and M is used to denote periods or payments per year, but often the variable N is used to represent the total number of periods regardless of the duration of the period.

6. G—The growth rate or inflation rate at which a payment increases or decreases over the annuity period. Growth rates apply only to annuities, which are often then referred to as geometrically varying, graduated, or growing annuities.

Understanding not only the definitions of each variable but the impact of changing each variable is paramount to truly understanding TVM computations. Figure 2.5 provides an overview of the assumptions imbedded in TVM formulas.

Figure 2.5. Relationships between Inputs and Outcomes in Time Value of Money Computations

Variable Change (All Others Constant)	Impact On			
	Present Value	Future Value	Present Value of Annuity	Future Value of Annuity
Increase I/Y	Decrease	Increase	Decrease	Increase
Decrease I/Y	Increase	Decrease	Increase	Decrease
Increase N	Decrease	Increase	Increase*	Increase
Decrease N	Increase	Decrease	Increase	Decrease
Increase PMT	N/A	N/A	Increase	Increase
Decrease PMT	N/A	N/A	Decrease	Decrease
Increase G	N/A	N/A	Increase	Increase
Decrease G	N/A	N/A	Decrease	Decrease
* This may counter intuition, but as the number of payments increase, total value decreases.				

Future Value of a Single Sum

One of the most common questions in all of finance is, "How much will a sum invested today be worth in the future?" To answer this question, a financial planner should use a basic **future value** formula. The **future value of a single sum** formula is as follows:

$$FV_n = PV(1 + i)^n$$

Example: Assume that Jack made a $10,000 deposit into a three-year certificate of deposit that paid an annual interest rate of 5 percent. How much will Jack accumulate when the certificate of deposit matures? To answer this question, insert the facts into the formula as follows.

$$FV_3 = \$10,000(1 + 0.05)^3 = \$11,576.25$$

A **financial calculator**, such as a *Texas Instruments BAII Plus*, can also be used to quickly derive the solution to this type of problem. The following inputs correspond to calculator key strokes that can be used to determine the future value of a lump sum.

Input	Keystroke	Result
0	[PMT]	PMT = 0.00
10000 [+/−]	[PV]	PV = −10,000.00
5	[I/Y]	I/Y = 5.00
3	[N]	N = 3.00
[CPT]	[FV]	FV = 11,576.25
Note: The PV is input as a negative because an investment is an assumed outflow.		

Figure 2.6 shows the solution to the same client question assuming various compounding frequencies. It is interesting to note that a continued increase in compounding frequency decreases the marginal effect.

Figure 2.6. Effects of Compounding Frequency on Future Values

Compounding Frequency	Effective Periodic Rate	Effective Annual Rate	Formula	Future Value
Annual	0.05/1 = 0.0500	0.05000	10,000*(1.0500^{3*1})	$11,576.25
Semiannual	0.05/2 = 0.0250	0.05063	10,000*(1.0250^{3*2})	$11,596.93
Bimonthly	0.05/6 = 0.0083	0.05105	10,000*(1.0083^{3*6})	$11,611.12
Monthly	0.05/12 = 0.0042	0.05116	10,000*(1.0042^{3*12})	$11,614.72
Weekly	0.05/52 = 0.0010	0.05125	10,000*(1.0010^{3*52})	$11,617.51
Note: EPRs and EARs are rounded for display but are not rounded for calculation.				

Present Value of a Single Sum

A **present value** formula is used to determine the value of a future asset in today's dollars. The **present value of a single sum** formula follows:

$$PV_n = \frac{FV}{(1+i)^n}$$

Planning Tip

The Rule of 72: A quick estimate for calculating the future value of a single sum is the rule of 72, which can be used whenever a client wishes to know approximately how long it will take to double an investment. To answer such a question, 72 is divided by the interest or discount rate earned. For example, it will take approximately eight years to double an investment that earns 9% annually (72/9 = 8).

A financial planner can also use this shorthand tool to determine the rate of return needed to double a client's initial investment. For example, if a client has six years to meet a goal that requires the doubling of an asset's value, what rate of return must be achieved? In this case, the client must earn 12% on average over the six-year period (72/6 = 12).

Example. Assume that Melissa needs to accumulate $50,000 in 10 years. She is confident that she can earn an annual effective rate of 8 percent per year in her portfolio. How much does Melissa need to deposit into the account today to achieve her goal? The present value of a single sum formula can be used to solve this question. The answer to Melissa's question is easily found by entering the known variables into the formula, as shown below:

$$PV_n = \frac{\$50,000}{(1+0.08)^{10}} = \$23,159.67$$

Here are the keystrokes needed to solve this problem using a financial calculator:

Input	Keystroke	Result
0	[PMT]	PMT = 0.00
50000 [+/−]	[FV]	FV = 50,000.00
8	[I/Y]	I/Y = 8.00
10	[N]	N = 10.00
[CPT]	[PV]	PV = −23,159.67

Note: In this case, the present value answer is given as a negative because this is the amount Melissa would have to part with today.

Both future value of a lump sum and present value of a lump sum calculations assume that a client is dealing with a single **lump sum** of money being invested or received. However, sometimes a client needs to know the future or present value of a series of equal payments rather than a lump sum. A series of equal payments or receipts is known as an **annuity**. For a series of payments to be considered an annuity, the series must adhere to three rules: (1) the payments must be equal in amount; (2) the payments must continue on a fixed frequency (e.g., monthly, annually, weekly, etc.); and (3) the required rate of return must remain constant over the entire period of the annuity payments. If the series of payments adheres to these three rules, then the payments may be treated as an annuity.

The annuity equation is set up to perform two calculations simultaneously. First, it discounts (or compounds) each cash flow payment to a common point in time—most often the current time. Second, it summates the now discounted (or compounded) payments. The annuity equation is represented as either:

$$FVA_n = \sum_{n=1}^{t} CF_n (1+i)^n \quad \text{or} \quad PVA_n = \sum_{n=1}^{t} \frac{CF_n}{(1+i)^n}$$

Planning Tip

Using a Financial Calculator to Solve Annuity Problems with Non-Annual Payments. Using the formulas to solve annuities with non-annual payments is as simple as it is for lump sums. Simply change your interest rate into the corresponding EPR form and solve for the answer. However, using the financial calculator is a bit more involved in that you have to manually change some of the basic calculator settings.

To adjust your calculator for non-annual payments, you must press the [2nd] key, then press the [I/Y] key. This allows access to the payments-per-year setting. Once "P/Y = M" (where M is the number of payments per year) is displayed, you must type the number of payments desired (e.g., 12 for monthly payments) and then press [Enter.] You may now exit the settings by pressing the [2nd] key and then the [CPT] key.

To enable this functionality when solving, you must now get in the habit of entering N as the number of years the payment is occurring rather than as the total number of payments that occur. So instead of entering the total number of payments and then pressing the [N] key, you must first get the calculator to multiply the N you entered with the M you previously set. To do this, press the [2nd] key and then the [N] key. Now that the calculator has multiplied N by M, press the [N] key a second time. What is now displayed is the total number of payments.

Another result of changing this setting is that when you changed the payments per year the calculator also adjusted the compounding period per year to correspond. The benefit is that the calculator will now calculate the appropriate EPR behind the scenes; therefore, you can input the APR as usual.

These equations show how each payment will be discounted (or compounded). Once this is established, the sum of the number of payments to occur is totaled. A discussion of future and present value annuities follows.

Future Value of an Annuity

The **future value of an annuity** values a series of uninterrupted payments as of when the last payment occurs. That is, if an annuity pays twenty annual installments starting at time one and ending at time twenty, then the future value formula will provide a value for the series of payments at time twenty. The formula for the future value of an ordinary annuity follows:

$$FVA_n = \frac{PMT}{i}\left[(1+i)^n - 1\right]$$

Example: Thomas would like to know how much he will accumulate if he invests $5,000 per year in a Roth IRA for twenty years earning an annual 9 percent rate of return. As shown below, answering Thomas's question is easy using the future value of an ordinary annuity formula or a financial calculator.

$$FVA_{20} = \frac{\$5,000}{0.09}\left[(1.09)^{20} - 1\right] = \$255,800.60$$

Input	Keystroke	Result
5000	[PMT]	PMT = −5,000.00
0	[PV]	PV = 0.00
9	[I/Y]	I/Y = 9.00
20	[N]	N = 20.00
[CPT]	[FV]	FV = 255,800.60
Note: In this case, the payment is given as a negative because this is the amount that Thomas would have to pay each year.		

Present Value of an Annuity

The **present value of an annuity** is used to determine the value of a series of equal, uninterrupted payments as of the beginning of a period in which the first payment occurs. If an annuity pays annual payments beginning at time one and lasting for four years, the present value equation will return a value at the beginning of period one or time zero. The present value of an ordinary annuity formula is as follows:

$$PVA_n = \frac{PMT}{i}\left[1 - \frac{1}{(1+i)^n}\right]$$

Example. Consider Erik and Erin, who want to make an immediate lump sum deposit into an account earning an annual rate of 5 percent to fund four years of college expenses beginning at the end of this year. Current college costs are assumed to be $15,000 per year and are not expected to change. How much do they need in the account today? To gauge the true amount needed, the present value of an annuity formula should be used as follows:

$$PVA_0 = \frac{\$15,000}{0.05}\left[1 - \frac{1}{(1.05)^4}\right] = \$53,189.26$$

The calculator keystrokes necessary to solve the problem are:

Input	Keystroke	Result
15000	[PMT]	PMT = 15,000.00
0	[FV]	FV = 0.00
5	[I/Y]	I/Y = 5.00
4	[N]	N = 4.00
[CPT]	[PV]	PVA = −53,189.26
Note: In this case, the present value is given as a negative because this is the amount Erik and Erin would have to pay today.		

In other words, Erik and Erin need to deposit $53,189.26 into an account today, earning 5 percent per year, to fund college costs of $15,000 per year for four years with the first payment occurring one year from today.

Example. Reconsider Erik and Erin, who still want to make an immediate lump sum deposit into an account earning an annual rate of 5 percent to fund four years of college expenses beginning at the end of this year. However, now it is assumed that college costs are paid $7,500 per semester (six months apart) and are not expected to change. How much do they need in the account today?

First, it is necessary to calculate the appropriate EPR for semiannual payments.

$$EPR = \frac{APR}{m} = \frac{0.05}{2} = 0.025$$

Now, using the EPR, it is possible to solve for the present value normally, as follows:

$$PVA_0 = \frac{\$7,500}{0.025}\left[1 - \frac{1}{(1.025)^8}\right] = \$53,776.03$$

The calculator keystrokes for this problem are as follows:

Input	Keystroke	Result
7500	[PMT]	PMT = 7,500.00
0	[FV]	FV = 0.00
5 (as APR)	[I/Y]	I/Y = 5.00*
4	[2nd] [N] [N]	N = 8.00
[CPT]	[PV]	PVA = –53,776.03
* After adjusting the m to two periods per year, the APR will still display on the calculator screen although the EPR is actually being used for the calculation.		

Present Value of a Delayed Annuity

What happens when a financial planner needs to know the present value of an event in the future rather than today? For example, assume a financial planner needs to estimate the cost of college on a child's fifth birthday, rather than simply at the beginning of college? Again, consider Erik and Erin, who are planning for future education expenses, perhaps for a younger child. In the previous example, it was assumed that the first tuition payment occurred at the end of the first year. What would happen if that tuition payment was not due for ten years?

The clients would need to know how much they need to save by the beginning of college, but they now have ten years for an account to accumulate the required amount before the first tuition payment. The formula to solve for this type of equation is a combination of two of the previous formulas: the present value of an annuity and the present value of a single sum. The two equations are:

$$PVA_n = \frac{PMT}{i}\left[1-\frac{1}{(1+i)^n}\right] \quad \text{and} \quad PV_n = \frac{FV}{(1+i)^n}$$

The solution to this situation begins in the same way as the previous example, by solving for the present value of the annuity for the four years of college. However, in the first example this answer was as of today (T_0); now, it is as of ten years from today (T_{10}).[3] Therefore, the value would have to be discounted a second time—back to today. This is referred to as **double discounting** because the first equation discounts the four payments to the beginning of the payment period and the second equation discounts the result back to today. Functionally, the first answer, which was solved for as a present value, becomes a future value when solving for the second answer. These equations may be combined into one equation that handles both steps. The equation on the left is then substituted into the numerator of the equation on the right, as shown below:

$$PVA_n = \frac{PMT}{i}\left[1-\frac{1}{(1+i)^n}\right] \quad \rightarrow \quad PV_0 = \frac{PVA_n}{(1+i)^d}$$

Where:

n = number of payments

d = number of periods delayed

Combining the two equations results in the following:

$$PV_0 = \frac{\dfrac{PMT}{i}\left[1-\dfrac{1}{(1+i)^n}\right]}{(1+i)^d}$$

Example: To return once again to Erik and Erin, the financial planner would solve for the present value of the annuity at year ten, which is $53,189.26, and then discount that result back to today. The final need can then be determined as $32,653.59. The calculation is shown in the following equation.

$$PV_d = \frac{\dfrac{\$15,000}{0.05}\left[1-\dfrac{1}{(1.05)^4}\right]}{(1.05)^{10}}$$

$$PV_d = \frac{\$53,189.26}{1.62889} = \$32,653.59$$

In essence, in the second discounting period (during periods 1–10), the equation backs out the interest earned between today (T_0) and the beginning of the year in which the first payment occurs (T_{10}).

This is also the first instance where it may be simpler to use the equations than to use TVM keys on a financial calculator. This is because the calculator cannot handle both steps of the equation simultaneously. Instead, it is a two-step solution, as shown below:

Step 1:

Input	Keystroke	Result
15000	[PMT]	PMT = 15,000.00
0	[FV]	FV = 0.00
5	[I/Y]	I/Y = 5.00
4	[N]	N = 4.00
[CPT]	[PV]	PVA10 = –53,189.26

Step 2:

Input	Keystroke	Result
0	[PMT]	PMT = 7,500.00
53,189.26	[FV]	FV = 53,189.26
5	[I/Y]	I/Y = 5.00*
10	[N]	N = 10.00
[CPT]	[PV]	PV_0 = –32,653.59
* The present value of the annuity at time 10 in Step 1 becomes the future value of the lump sum in Step 2.		

This type of combined equation can be used anytime a stream of payments begins after the first period. In such a case, it is appropriate to discount the cash flow twice: once to bring the stream back to the beginning of the year in which the first payment occurs, T_n; and once again to bring that result back to the present time, T_0.

Future Value of a Geometrically Varying Annuity (Growing Annuity)

Up to this point, the assumption has been that the dollar amount of each payment received or paid during an annuity is fixed. To differentiate, this assumption is sometimes referred to as a **fixed, constant-dollar**, or **level-payment annuity**. However, there is an alternative. Sometimes a client's payment will increase from year to year by a constant percentage. (Note: The rate of change must always be at a constant percentage amount and *not* a constant dollar amount.) This can occur based on a number of factors (e.g., changes in salary, changes in disposable income, etc.), but the most common reason for an increasing payment is inflation.

A **growing annuity** is actually very common. In fact, most payments (e.g., college, retirement, and Social Security) typically change over time by some rate of inflation. The issue is that rates of inflation are not constant, so to be able to treat a series of payments as an annuity one must make an assumption about what the average rate of change will be. For example, actual annual inflation is almost never constant, but this simplifying assumption is needed to make the formula work.

If a client wants a payment, either in or out of an annuity, to keep pace with inflation, then a growth rate must be applied. The growth rate may be positive or—though it apparently contradicts its name—negative, but it cannot be equal to the rate of return. If the growth rate is zero, then the fixed annuity equation should be used. Growing annuities apply to either present value or future value situations. The equation for the **future value of a growing annuity** follows:

$$FVGA_n = \frac{PMT_1}{(i-g)}\left[(1+i)^n - (1+g)^n\right]$$

Where:

    i = interest rate (i ≠ 0)

    g = growth rate of payment (i ≠ g)

The growing annuity equation performs three calculations simultaneously. First, it changes the payment at a constant rate. Second, it compounds each payment to a common point in time. Third, it summates the now compounded payments. Breaking the annuity equation into its component parts looks like this:

$$FVGA_n = PMT_1(1+g)^{n-n}(1+r)^{n-1} + PMT_1(1+g)^{n-(n-1)}(1+r)^{n-2} + \ldots + PMT_1(1+g)^{n-1}(1+r)^{n-n}$$

Consider a client who participates in a 401(k) or 403(b) plan. Usually, defined contribution plan salary reductions are based on a percentage of an employee's annual income. So, if the client's income increases by 3 percent annually it follows that the retirement plan contribution will also increase by the same percentage. A basic future value of annuity formula cannot account for this assumption. A **geometrically varying annuity** formula must be used to determine a future value whenever a payment is expected to increase at a fixed geometric rate.

Example: Assume that Jorge will make annual payments[4] into a 401(k) for twenty years, earning an effective annual rate of 9 percent. He will begin with a $3,000 contribution, which is 5 percent of his income. Every year thereafter, he will increase his deposit by 3 percent to reflect the expected increase in his salary. Using this assumption, how much will Jorge accumulate at the end of twenty years?

$$FVGA_n = \frac{\$3,000}{(0.09-0.03)}\left[(1.09)^{20} - (1.03)^{20}\right]$$

$$FVGA_n = \$50,000 * 3.7983 = \$189,914.98$$

In this case, the fact that Jorge's subsequent deposits into the 401(k) grow by 3 percent annually means that he will have approximately $189,915 in the account at the end of twenty years. When using growing annuities, it is often beneficial—or at least interesting—to compare the results of a growing annuity and a fixed annuity, keeping all of the variables besides the growth rate fixed.

Solving the example, but without growing the payment by 3 percent per year, can be done using the same formula and entering a zero for the growth rate, or it can be solved using the fixed annuity equation as shown below:

$$FVGA_n = \frac{\$3,000}{(0.09 - 0.00)}\left[(1.09)^{20} - (1.00)^{20}\right]$$

$$FVGA_n = \frac{\$3,000}{0.09}\left[(1.09)^{20} - 1\right]$$

$$FVGA_n = \frac{\$13,813.23}{0.09} = \$153,480.36$$

By removing the growth rate, the value in Jorge's account at the end of twenty years is $36,435 ($189,915 − $153,480) less if he chooses not to increase his annual payment. As shown here, increasing payments over a long-term planning horizon can have a significant impact on meeting a client's financial goals.

It is also important to note that when using a growing annuity equation, the payment used in the calculation will be the first payment. Similarly, when using the equation to solve for the payment amount, the equation solves for the first payment (PMT_1). It is important to understand that this distinction is relevant because the value increases or decreases across the series of payments in a growing annuity, whereas in a fixed annuity all of the payments are the same, so no differentiation is needed. All other payments must be derived by using PMT_1 and then increasing payments by the growth rate. Therefore, PMT_2 equals $PMT_1 * (1 + g)$, and so on.

Present Value of a Geometrically Varying Annuity

An equation that is very similar in form and function to the present value of a fixed annuity equation is the one used to estimate a present value of a growing annuity. As was the case with the future value of a growing annuity, a growth rate must be assumed. For instance, a client may desire to know the amount that must be saved, or available, at the beginning of a withdrawal period if the desired withdrawal amount changes over time. This is a likely scenario because of the effects of inflation on purchasing power. In this situation, the client wants to know the **present value of a growing annuity**. The following formula can be used for this purpose:

$$PVGA_n = \frac{PMT_1}{(i - g)}\left[1 - \frac{(1 + g)^n}{(1 + i)^n}\right]$$

The growing annuity equation does three calculations simultaneously. In this case, it (1) changes the payment at a constant rate, (2) discounts each payment to a common point in time, and (3) summates the now discounted payments. Breaking the present value of a growing annuity equation into its component parts looks like this:

$$PVGA_n = \frac{PMT_1(1+g)^{n-(n-0)}}{(1+r)^{n-(n-1)}} + \frac{PMT_1(1+g)^{n-(n-1)}}{(1+r)^{n-(n-2)}} + \ldots + \frac{PMT_1(1+g)^{n-1}}{(1+r)^{n-(n-n)}}$$

Example: Middle-aged clients, Joshua and Rebecca Rosenbaum, want to know how much they need to have saved by retirement to withdraw $80,000 in the first year and to have that amount increase by 4 percent per year. They assume that they can earn an EAR of 8.5 percent throughout their twenty five years of retirement.

$$PVGA_n = \frac{\$80,000}{(0.085-0.04)}\left[1 - \frac{(1.04)^{25}}{(1.085)^{25}}\right]$$

$$PVGA_n = \$1,777,777.78[0.65319] = \$1,161,228.92$$

In this case, the Rosenbaums must save $1,161,228.92 by the time they retire to meet their withdrawal goal. However, similar to the previous comparison conducted with the future value of a growing annuity, they need to save only $818,735.26 if they choose not to increase their annual withdrawal by 4 percent. Note again that assuming the growth rate is zero allows the fixed payment annuity equation to be used.

$$PVGA_n = \frac{\$80,000}{(0.085-0.00)}\left[1 - \frac{(1.00)^{25}}{(1.085)^{25}}\right]$$

$$PVGA_n = \frac{\$80,000}{0.085}\left[1 - \frac{1}{(1.085)^{25}}\right]$$

$$PVGA_n = \frac{\$69,592.50}{0.085} = \$818,735.26$$

The Serial Interest Rate

Another method for solving growing annuity equations is to calculate the **serial interest rate**. In fact, if a financial calculator is to be used, the serial rate will be required. The serial rate is calculated using the same equation used to determine the real rate.

$$Serial\ Rate = \left[\frac{(1+i)}{(1+g)}\right] - 1$$

Where:

i = interest rate

g = growth rate of payment (could be the inflation rate)

Example: Consider the first step to the previous retirement savings example, where Joshua and Rebecca needed to determine how much to save by retirement to fund a growing stream of retirement payments. Using assumptions identical to those above, the problem may also be solved using the fixed annuity equation by substituting the serial rate for i. First, solve for the serial rate:

$$Serial\ Rate = \left[\frac{(1.085)}{(1.04)}\right] - 1 = 4.327\%$$

Second, the serial rate should then be inserted into the adjusted present value of a fixed annuity formula as follows:

$$PVA_n = \frac{PMT/(1+g)}{i}\left[1 - \frac{1}{(1+i)^n}\right]$$

$$PVA_n = \frac{\$80,000/1.04}{0.04327}\left[1 - \frac{1}{(1.04327)^{25}}\right]$$

$$PVA_n = \$1,777,746.17[0.65320] = \$1,161,219.63$$

The difference from the earlier calculation is caused by rounding. If the serial rate 4.327 percent were not rounded, the PVA_n would equal $1,161,228.91.

It is worth noting the small adjustment that was made to the present value formula. Notice how the payment was adjusted down by the factor of $(1 + g)$. Why was this necessary? It was necessary because the serial rate cannot distinguish when the payment needs to grow (e.g., from time one to time two) or when it does not grow (e.g., from time zero to time one). Refer again to the present value of a growing annuity formula, this time simplified with N = 5:

$$PVGA_n = \frac{PMT_1(1+g)^{5-(5-0)}}{(1+i)^{5-(5-1)}} + \frac{PMT_1(1+g)^{5-(5-1)}}{(1+i)^{5-(5-2)}} + ... + \frac{PMT_1(1+g)^{5-1}}{(1+i)^{5-(5-5)}}$$

$$PVGA_n = \frac{PMT_1(1+g)^0}{(1+i)^1} + \frac{PMT_1(1+g)^1}{(1+i)^2} + ... + \frac{PMT_1(1+g)^4}{(1+i)^5}$$

The calculation shows that the relationship between the number of periods of growth and the number of periods of discounting is off by one period. This is because payment one is given in terms of time one and not time zero. Said another way, the first payment does not grow, but it is still discounted. The serial rate is constant for all time periods, so an adjustment must be made to allow the serial rate to both grow and discount the first payment; this adjustment is made by forcibly reducing the value of the first payment to its time zero equivalent.

The use of the serial rate is also required when using a financial calculator to solve growing annuity calculations. Keep in mind that a financial calculator does not provide a separate input for "g." The following keystrokes can be used to determine the amount the Rosenbaums' need to save for retirement:

Input	Keystroke	Result
80000/1.04	[PMT]	PMT = 76,923.08
0	[FV]	FV = 0.00
4.327	[I/Y]	I/Y = 4.327
25	[N]	N = 25.00
[CPT]	[PV]	PVA = –1,161,219.64
Note: The initial payment is adjusted by the factor of (1 + g) to resolve the serial rate issue previously discussed.		

Revisiting the prior problem, what if the Rosenbaums needed to determine the future value of their retirement annuity? (Not that this is a realistic issue, because knowing the future value of a prior payment stream at death is not very useful, but it serves for demonstration purposes). This now becomes a two-step solution, as shown below:

Step 1:

Input	Keystroke	Result
80000/1.04	[PMT]	PMT = 76,923.08
0	[FV]	FV = 0.00
4.327	[I/Y]	I/Y = 4.327
25	[N]	N = 25.00
[CPT]	[PV]	PVA = –1,161,219.64

Step 2:

Input	Keystroke	Result
0	[PMT]	PMT = 0.00
–1,161,219.64	[PV]	PV = –1,161,219.64
8.5	[I/Y]	I/Y = 8.50*
25	[N]	N = 25.00
[CPT]	[FV]	FV = 8,926,019.42
* The nominal rate is used to determine the compound future rate.		

Annuity Due Payments (Payments Occurring at the Beginning of Each Period)

So far, all of the examples presented in this chapter have assumed that each payment has occurred at the end of each time period or "in arrears." This is not always the case.

For example, tuition is normally paid at the beginning of each semester, "in advance." The term **annuity due** is used whenever the present value of an "in advance" payment is needed. This obviously influences the value or cost of college in that each payment is now taken out six months earlier, meaning six months of interest will not be earned.

Planning Tip

Using a Financial Calculator to Estimate Future-Value of Growing Annuities Problems: This situation presents an interesting challenge.

Refer to Table 2.5. Did you notice in the present value of an annuity, a change in G has the opposite effect as a change in I/Y? As a result, a lower rate to account for a higher payment is reasonable.

When calculating the serial rate, increases in G functionally serve to decrease I/Y.

Keep in mind that the serial rate cannot be used to directly solve for future values of growing annuities. Instead, the serial rate is used to determine the present value of the growing annuity, and the second step is to calculate the future value of that lump sum using the original interest rate.

The only way to make up for this is to save more money. So, it stands to reason that the present value of an annuity due will need to be greater than that of an ordinary annuity. How much greater? The answer will need to be approximately one period of interest greater for each payment because not only will the first payment be removed six months early, *every* payment will be removed six months early. Therefore, the present value of every payment will have to increase. The **present value of an annuity due** formula is presented below:

$$PV\ Ordinary\ Annuity = \frac{PMT_1}{(1+i)^1} + \frac{PMT_2}{(1+i)^2} + ... + \frac{PMT_n}{(1+i)^n}\ or\ \frac{PMT}{i}\left[1 - \frac{1}{(1+i)^n}\right]$$

$$PV\ Annuity\ Due = \frac{PMT_1(1+i)^1}{(1+i)^1} + \frac{PMT_2(1+i)^1}{(1+i)^2} + ... + \frac{PMT_n(1+i)^1}{(1+i)^n}$$

Simplifying the numerator by removing the (1 + r) adjustment from each leaves:

$$PV\ Annuity\ Due = \left[\frac{PMT_1}{(1+i)^1} + \frac{PMT_2}{(1+i)^2} + ... + \frac{PMT_n}{(1+i)^n}\right](1+i)\ or\ \frac{PMT}{i}\left[1 - \frac{1}{(1+i)^n}\right](1+i)$$

The difference in value between an ordinary annuity and an annuity due is simply a factor of (1 + i). Reworking the problem of Erik and Erin, who want to fund four years of college expenses starting at the *beginning* of this year, is as simple as this:

$$PVA_0 = \frac{\$15,000}{0.05}\left[1 - \frac{1}{(1.05)^4}\right](1.05) = \$53,189.26(1.05) = \$55,848.72$$

This adjustment also works when calculating the future value of an annuity. Even if it is a growing annuity, the adjustment remains the same. The factor (1 + i) always works!

Present Value of a Growing Perpetuity

Although not very common, there are certain instances when a payment will either be made or received indefinitely. For example, this might occur in retirement planning scenarios when a client wants to be very conservative. The **present value of growing perpetuity (PVP)** assumes that the principal of an investment is never liquidated and continues in "perpetuity."

Planning Tip

Annuity Due Rule: The following rule applies when making present value calculations: income is considered to be received at the beginning of a period (annuity due), whereas savings is assumed to occur at the end of a period (regular annuity).

Example: A client wants to make sure that he leaves a legacy for his wife and children, but he also wants to ensure a comfortable retirement while alive. He requires an annual rate of return of 7.0 percent. He wants an initial annual payment of $100,000 that will keep pace with expected inflation of 3.5 percent. How much does the client need to save by the beginning of the withdrawal period? The following formula can be used to answer the question:

$$PVP = \frac{PMT}{(i-g)}$$

$$PVP = \frac{\$100,000}{(0.070-0.035)} = \frac{\$100,000}{0.035}$$

$$PVP = 2,857,142.86$$

In order for the client to ensure that he will not outlive his money, nor lose purchasing power to inflation, he needs to have nearly $2.9 million saved on the first day of retirement.

An interesting thing about perpetuities is that the present values are not significantly larger than traditionally estimated annuities. See Figure 2.7 for a summary of present values for different terms.

Figure 2.7. Comparison of Present Values by Term Length

Periodic Payment	Discount Rate	Periods	Present Value
$1,000	7%	20	$10,594
$1,000	7%	35	$12,948
$1,000	7%	50	$13,801
$1,000	7%	65	$14,110
$1,000	7%	Infinite	$14,286

Planning Strategy 8: Estimate a Solution to a Fluctuating Payment Problem

A **net present value** (**NPV**) method of calculation can be used when a series of payments, either made by the client or received by the client, fluctuates on a per-period basis. The traditional present value of annuity calculation assumes that payments remain fixed, or if they do change, that the rate of growth is fixed. NPV is defined as the present value of a stream of earnings less the present value of contributions. The formula for NPV is:

NPV = PV of Cash Inflows – PV of Cash Outflows

Where:

NPV = net present value

PV   = present value

NPV compares benefits and costs. The rule for NPV is that if the present value of benefits *exceeds* the present value of costs (NPV > 0), then the investment should be accepted; if the present value of benefits *does not exceed* the present value of costs (NPV < 0), then the investment should be rejected. The following formula illustrates how a present value cost is subtracted from the discounted future value benefits of a particular investment opportunity:

$$NPV = \frac{PMT_1}{(1+r)^1} + \frac{PMT_2}{(1+r)^2} + ... + \frac{PMT_n}{(1+r)^n} + \frac{FV_n}{(1+r)^n} - PV$$

Planning Tip

Similar to NPV rules, as discussed previously, if the IRR of an investment exceeds the required rate of return, then accept the investment; if IRR does not exceed the required rate of return, reject the investment.

A simple example can be used to illustrate the NPV method.

Example: Assume that a client is considering an investment of $5,000. Currently, the client is making 11 percent on the $5,000 in an alternative investment. The client anticipates that the investment will make payments back as shown below:

Year 1:	$1,500
Year 2:	$1,000
Year 3:	$500
Year 4:	$500
Year 5:	$4,000

Should the client make the investment? A quick way to answer this question might be to compute NPV using the cash flow functions in a financial calculator (shown in the next section). However, the formula may also be used to find a solution.

$$NPV = \frac{\$1,500}{(1.11)^1} + \frac{\$1,000}{(1.11)^2} + \frac{\$500}{(1.11)^3} + \frac{\$500}{(1.11)^4} + \frac{\$4,000}{(1.11)^5} - \$5,000$$

$$NPV = \$1,351.35 + \$811.62 + \$365.60 + \$329.37 + \$2,373.81 - \$5,000$$

$$NPV = \$5,231.75 - \$5,000 = \$231.75$$

When using the NPV method, it is critical to understand what the answer is saying. When the NPV is positive, it means that the internal rate of return (IRR) is greater than the required rate, and therefore, the investment should be accepted. If the NPV is negative, it means that the IRR is less than the required rate, and therefore, the investment should be rejected. If the IRR equals the required rate, then the investment should be accepted because the required rate is expected to be achieved. The NPV as a planning tool is generally constrained to investment scenarios where a known initial investment has or will be made. Additionally, NPV estimates assume that and investment generates an investment return.

Planning Strategy 9: Calculate an Internal Rate of Return

What if a financial planner knows both how much a client is willing to spend today (PV) and the values of the future cash flows (FV)? This raises an interesting and different question: what is the **internal rate of return (IRR)** on the investment? The IRR, and its close cousin NPV, are more sophisticated methods that determine whether or not an investment is expected to meet a client's required rate of return.

The IRR measures the discount rate at which the present value of cash inflows (returns or benefits) equals the present value of cash outflows (investments or costs). IRR takes into account the time value of money by considering the amount and timing of cash inflows and outflows over the life of an **investment**. Calculating the IRR can be done through a trial-and-error process. IRR can be calculated manually by completing multiple iterations of NPV estimates with different interest rates until the NPV is equal to zero. The trial-and-error calculation can also be automated by using the IRR function in a computer spreadsheet program or using the cash flow functions in a financial calculator.

As a reminder, an IRR measures the present value of a series of cash flows in relation to an initial (and possibly subsequent) investment amount. The formula for calculating IRR is used when both the value of each subsequent cash flow and the present value are known:

$$PV = \frac{PMT_1}{(1+r)^1} + \frac{PMT_2}{(1+r)^2} + \ldots + \frac{PMT_n}{(1+r)^n} + \frac{FV_n}{(1+r)^n}$$

Where:

   PV   = present value

   FV   = future value

   PMT = periodic payment

   R   = internal rate of return

As noted earlier, it would take multiple iterations to determine the rate that would result in the NPV being equal to zero. Using the formula for calculating IRR can be tiresome. Fortunately, IRRs can be determined relatively easily using a financial calculator. There are two main methods for determining the IRR: (1) using the TVM keys if future cash flows can be considered as an annuity or (2) using cash flow functions if the future cash flows are uneven; this is often called a **mixed sum**.

Using TVM Keystrokes to Solve for IRR

Using TVM keystrokes to solve for IRR is as simple as using a calculator to solve any other TVM problem. As long as at least three inputs are known, it is as simple as entering the known variables and solving for those remaining.

Example: Assume that Jesus invests $1,000 today in an investment that will pay him $100 per year for ten years. At the end of the investment period, Jesus receives $2,000. What rate of return did he earn? Entering these data into a financial calculator, as shown below, results in an IRR equal to 14.94 percent.

Input	Keystroke	Result
100	[PMT]	PMT = 100.00
–1000	[PV]	PV = –1,000
10	[N]	N = 10.00
2000	[FV]	FV = 2000
[CPT]	[I/Y]	I/Y = 14.94%

Although the method for calculating IRR looks innocuous enough, its application can become quite tedious, especially when the periodic payments fluctuate every period. However, a financial calculator can also be used if the periodic cash flows are not fixed.

Using Cash Flow Functions to Solve for IRR

By using the built-in **cash flow functions** or registers, individual cash flows may be entered separately in a financial calculator. To enter the cash flow functions in the BA II Plus calculator, press the [CF] key. Always begin by clearing the register of any previous work by pressing the [2nd] key and then the [CLR WORK] key in succession. It is important to remember a major difference between using the TVM keys and the CF functions: in order to enter the value into the tables, the [enter] key must always be pressed after entering the desired value.

Example: Assume that Shameka is considering an investment that requires a $5,000 payment today. The required rate of return, based on her next best investment choice, is 11 percent in a mutual fund. If she anticipates receiving the following payments, should she make the investment?

Year 1:	$1,500
Year 2:	$1,000
Year 3:	$500
Year 4:	$500
Year 5:	$4,000

Calculating the IRR of these individual cash flows is possible using the following formula; however, it would require a great deal of time and some more difficult algebra.

$$\$5,000 = \frac{\$1,500}{(1+r)^1} + \frac{\$1,000}{(1+r)^2} + \frac{\$500}{(1+r)^3} + \frac{\$500}{(1+r)^4} + \frac{\$4,000}{(1+r)^5}$$

Instead, it is much easier to let a financial calculator handle the algebra and use the cash flow functions as demonstrated below. There are always two sets of entries when using cash flow functions: the amount of each cash flow and the number of consecutive times the cash flow happens, which is known as the **frequency of the cash flow**. Once all of the cash flows have been entered into the cash flow table, IRR can be computed by pressing the [IRR] key and then pressing the [CPT] key, as shown below:

Input	Keystroke	Result
	[CF]	Turn-on functions
[2nd]	[CLR WORK]	Clear register
–5000	[ENTER]	CF0 = –5,000,00
[↓] 1500	[ENTER]	CF1 = 1,500.00
[↓] 1*	[ENTER]	F01 = 1.00
[↓] 1000	[ENTER]	CF2 = 1,000.00
[↓] 1	[ENTER]	F02 = 1.00
[↓] 500	[ENTER]	CF3 = 500.00
[↓] 2	[ENTER]	F03 = 2.00
[↓] 4000	[ENTER]	CF4 = 4,000.00
[↓] 1	[ENTER]	F04 = 1.00
[IRR]	[CPT]	IRR = 12.55%
* One is the default entry for the frequency of the cash flow.		

In this case, the IRR is 12.55 percent, which is greater than her next best alternative of 11 percent. Therefore, applying the decision rule previously discussed, she would accept this investment alternative.

To solve for NPV, however, an estimated rate of return must be entered. After the [NPV] key is pressed, the calculator will ask for the required rate of return—in this case, 11 percent. Once the return is entered, pressing the down arrow key again will display the NPV, which will be computed when the [CPT] key is pressed. For this example, the NPV is $231.74. The keystrokes required to arrive at this conclusion are:

Input	Keystroke	Result
[NPV] 7	[ENTER]	I/Y = 11.00%
[↓]	[CPT]	NPV = $231.74
Note: One is the default entry for the frequency of the cash flow.		

Basically, this means that if Shameka's required return is 11 percent, she should be willing to pay up to $231.74 more ($5,231.74) for the agreed upon cash flows. Both the IRR and NPV methods of computing the value of cash flows produce the same decision conclusion—accept the investment.

Planning Strategy 10: Develop and Use a Loan Amortization Schedule

An amortized loan is a liability where the payment is normally fixed and set to repay the obligation over a fixed period of time. Every payment for a loan is composed of principal and interest and, as the loan is paid back, the percentage of each payment attributable to interest declines. This happens because a simple interest loan (which represents the majority of loan structures to individuals) recalculates the interest expense each period based on the remaining outstanding balance. Therefore, as the outstanding balance declines, so does the periodic interest expense. This also means that lenders receive more interest at the beginning of a loan repayment period than at the end of the period.

A widely used method of presenting this information to a client is with an amortization table. An **amortization schedule** can be created for any loan that has a fixed rate of interest and a known number of payment periods. Although an outstanding loan balance can be calculated using a financial calculator or present value of an annuity formula, it is sometimes more helpful to create an amortization schedule using a computer spreadsheet. A spreadsheet can more easily display different loan payoff amounts at different times. It can also be used to illustrate how a change in interest rates or duration can change a client's cash flow situation. Figure 2.8 provides an example of how an amortization schedule can be created in a computer spreadsheet.

Figure 2.8. Partial Amortization Spreadsheet with Formulas

Inputs	Interest Rate Present Value Term		7% annual [AFR] (0.583% monthly EPR) $100,000 30 years (360 months)		
A Month	B Beginning Balance	C Total Monthly Payment	D Monthly Interest Payment	E Monthly Principal Payment	F Ending Balance
			(B * EPR)	(C – D)	(B – E)
1	$100,000.00	$665.30	$583.33	$81.97	$99,918.03
2	$99,918.03	$665.30	$582.85	$82.45	$99,835.58
...					
359	$1,319.05	$665.30	$7.69	$657.61	$661.44
360	$661.44	$665.30	$3.86	$661.44	$0.00

Another method can also be useful and much quicker when trying to determine the outstanding balance of a loan. This method uses the previously discussed present value of an annuity (PVA) formula. It stands to reason, because the original payment for the loan could be determined with the PVA formula, that the same formula can be applied to that payment to determine the outstanding balance. The key is to change the n (number) in the equation to reflect the number of payments remaining.

Example: Recall the sample loan from Figure 2.8. The Figure illustrates how the loan is amortized, but in this example, it does not show the outstanding balance at all points in time. If a client wanted to pay off this loan after the 120th payment (in conjunction with the 121st payment), the client would need to know the outstanding balance at that time. To provide the client with the necessary information, the financial planner would solve for the PVA with the PMT equaling $665.30, the periodic interest rate equaling 0.583 percent, and the number of payments remaining equal to 240 (360 total payments – 120 payments previously paid). The formula is shown below:

$$PVA_n = \frac{PMT}{i}\left[1 - \frac{1}{(1+i)^n}\right]$$

$$PVA_{120} = \frac{\$665.30}{0.00583}\left[1 - \frac{1}{1.00583^{240}}\right]$$

$$PVA_{120} = \$114,116.64[0.75220] = \$85,838.54$$

Although it hardly seems to make sense that more than 85 percent of the loan remains outstanding, this is a common occurrence because the progression of a geometric function is not linear over time. In other words, the loan balance does not decline in a straight line.

Another useful application based on the TVM formulas is to determine how much money has already been paid on a loan. This is necessary information when determining the total amount of interest paid because the difference between the total amount of payments and the change in the outstanding balance is the total interest paid to date. The following formula is used to determine the total amount paid to date on a loan:

Total Payments = PMT Amount × Number of PMTs

Example: Revising the previous example, it had already been determined that the client had reduced the outstanding balance of the loan by $14,161.46 ($100,000 – $85,838.54); however, this does not indicate how much the client has paid in total. Nor does it tell how much interest the client has paid over the first 10 years of the loan. To determine the total amount paid, the monthly payment should be multiplied by the number of payments made, as shown below:

Total Payments = $665.30 × 120 = $79,836.00

To determine the total amount of interest paid, the change in outstanding balance should be subtracted from the total amount of payments. In this example, the total interest paid to date is $65,674.54.

Total Interest = Total of PMT – Change in Balance

Total Interest = $79,836.00 – $14,161.46 = $65,674.54

Quantitative/Analytical Mini-Case Problems

1. Holding-Period Returns

    a. Last year Marla purchased 100 shares of stock for $8 per share. She paid a flat $75 to purchase the shares. Since making her purchase, she has received $200 in dividends. Marla is concerned that the stock price will fall below its current FMV of $7. Calculate her holding-period return if she sells today and pays a $75 commission.

    b. Swarn bought 200 shares of a stock for $36 per share. He paid $245 in trading commissions. He has received dividends in the amounts of $98, $156, and $300 over the last three years, respectively. Assuming that Swarn is in the 15 percent marginal tax bracket for capital gains and dividends, what is his holding-period return if he sells all of the shares at $40 each with a $245 trading commission? What is Swarn's tax-adjusted holding period rate of return?

2. Dollar-Weighted Returns

    a. Brad purchased ten shares of stock for $10 per share. He paid a $5 commission. One year later, he purchased another ten shares at $9 per share. Again, he paid a $5 commission. In the second year, his disappoint got the best of him and he sold ten shares at $7 per share, paying another $5 commission. At the end of third year, Brad liquidated his holdings, paying $5 in commissions at $8 per share. What was his dollar-weighted rate of return?

    b. Buckley purchased a collectible stamp for $600. He was thrilled to learn that the stamp price had moved up, so one year later he purchased another stamp for $700. At the end of the second year, he sold one of the stamps for $800. He held his original stamp for the third year. Buckley then sold his stamp at the end of the fourth year for $1,000. What was Buckley's dollar-weighted rate of return?

3. Time-Weighted Returns

    a. Camerin purchased one ounce of gold for $1,400. The following year, the price of gold shot up to $1,800, but in the third year, prices fell back to $1,500. What was Camerin's time-weighted return?

    b. Marybeth purchased one share of stock for $92. At the end of year one, the stock was worth $95. At the end of year two, the stock was worth $100; and at the end of year three, the stock was worth $92. What was Marybeth's time-weighted return? How does this compare to her holding period rate of return?

4. Mean Returns

    a. Maurice purchased a coin collection several years ago. Each year he has had the collection appraised by a reputable coin dealer. Maurice has calculated the yearly percentage gain or loss based on the appraisal, as shown below:

Year	Return
Year 1:	10%
Year 2:	5%
Year 3:	9%
Year 4:	–5%
Year 5:	2%
Year 6:	–3%
Year 7:	12%

    b.   What is the average (mean) return of the coin collection over the seven-year period?

    c.   Use the rate of return data provided by Maurice to calculate the geometric mean return. How does this compare to the mean return?

5.   Weighted Average Returns

    a.   Sherman is a novice investor. The following table shows his portfolio holdings and market values for each holding. Calculate Sherman's weighted average return for his portfolio.

	Market Value	Rate of Return
Junk Bond Fund	$ 13,000.00	7.50%
Gold Fund	$ 19,500.00	12.00%
Small Cap Fund	$ 36,000.00	3.40%
Index Fund	$ 9,800.00	6.20%
CD	$ 41,000.00	1.00%

    b.   Sheri and Jarius own several pieces of expensive jewelry. The following table summarizes their most important gem assets:

	Market Value	Purchase Price
Diamond Ring	$ 12,000.00	$ 7,250.00
Sapphire Necklace	$ 23,000.00	$ 18,875.00
Emerald Pendant	$ 19,500.00	$ 19,000.00
Ruby Brooch	$ 21,200.00	$ 23,000.00
TOTAL	$ 75,700.00	$ 68,125.00

         Use this information to calculate the holding-period return.

6.   Serial Interest Rates

    a.   Consumer prices have been averaging 3.50 percent in South Korea. If So-Hyun can earn a nominal rate of return on her investment portfolio of 10.25 percent, what is her real rate of return, assuming continuous compounding?

b.   Farrell wants to retire in six years. To have sufficient assets to fund retirement, Farrell needs to accumulate an additional $400,000 between today and retirement. As his planner, you assume that inflation will average 5 percent. You are also confident that you can build a portfolio that will generate an 8 percent compounded annual after-tax return. What serial payment should Farrell invest at the end of the first year to fund this goal?

7.   Tax-Exempt and Taxable Rates

a.   Thomas Jones is in the 25 percent marginal federal tax bracket, the 4 percent marginal state tax bracket, and the 2 percent marginal city tax bracket. If he earns 9.25 percent on his portfolio, what is his after-tax rate of return?

b.   Stephanie is considering purchasing a fixed-income investment. She has narrowed her list of bond choice to two AAA-rated investments. The first is a corporate bond that matures in seven years. The bond yields 6.35 percent. The second bond also matures in seven years; however, this bond is a municipal bond issued by the state in which Stephanie resides. The bond has a current coupon rate at 4.79 percent. Stephanie is in the 25 percent marginal federal tax bracket and the 3.50 percent marginal state tax bracket. Which bond should she invest in to maximize her after-tax rate of return?

8.   Effective Rate Conversion Problems

a.   A client was earning an EAR of 7 percent. The client was contributing to the account on a monthly basis. What would be the appropriate EPR?

b.   A client wants to compute the estimated future value of a bank account. The account pays a semiannual rate of 4 percent (EPR). The client is investing in the account on a biweekly basis. What is the appropriate EPR to be able to solve for an estimated future value for the client?

9.   Future Value Problems

a.   Ted has $1,000. He can earn an annual effective rate of 5 percent. How much will he have in 10 years?

b.   Lanisha currently earns $45,000 per year. She expects her salary to increase by 3.5 percent per year. She plans to work for another 20 years. How much will she earn in her final year of work?

10. Present Value Problems

a.   Tammy has determined that she will need $3 million when she retires in 45 years. The current interest rate is 7 percent (EAR). How much does she need today to fully fund this goal at that rate?

b.   David and Iantha expect their ten-year-old daughter to get married someday. They estimate that her wedding would cost $30,000 today. Wedding costs will increase by 3 percent per year, and she will marry in fifteen years. David and Iantha earn a pre-tax annual rate of 5 percent. They are in the 20 percent marginal tax bracket. What amount do they need to set aside today for their daughter's wedding?

11. Future Value of Annuity Problems

    a. Sue wants to save $1,000,000 in twenty years. She estimates she can earn 8.5 percent on savings. She intends to make deposits at the beginning of every year in a series of equal payments starting today. How much does she need to save each year to reach her goal?

    b. Merita has been offered a choice of either receiving $100,000 in ten years or receiving $7,000 per year (at the end of each year) for the next ten years. Which is the better option if her required annual rate of return is 7 percent?

12. Present Value of Annuity Problems

    a. Mike needs to receive $40,000 per year (at the beginning of each year) from his investments for the next thirty years. His opportunity cost of money is 5 percent. How much does he need in an account today to generate this level of income if he fully depletes the account?

    b. Roshanna has just won the lottery. Her required rate of return is 6 percent. Should she take the annual annuity payment of $125,000 for the next twenty years (assume she will receive her first payment at the end of the year) or an immediate lump-sum payout of $1.5 million?

13. Future Value of Growing Annuity Problems

    a. Martha wants to start saving for college. She estimates that she will need $50,000 when she starts college four years from now. She plans to save $9,500 this year and increase deposits by 5 percent annually (payments at the end of each year). She can earn 7 percent on her savings. Will she meet her savings goal of $50,000 for college four years from now?

    b. Todd is saving $3,000 annually into an account (payments at the end of each year). He plans to increase the annual level of savings by 5 percent each year. He can earn 9 percent annually. How much will he have in the account at the end of twenty years?

14. Present Value of Growing Annuity Problems

    a. Mike wants to receive $40,000 per year pretax from his investments for the next thirty years. He is concerned about inflation, which he expects to average 3 percent. He can earn a pretax rate of 6 percent on his money. How much does he need in an account to generate $40,000 in annual inflation-adjusted income (payments at the end of each year)?

    b. A client is doing some investment/retirement planning. She is attempting to determine how much of her estate she needs to set aside today to fully fund her retirement. She desires annual beginning-of-period withdrawals for the next twenty five years. She would like inflation-adjusted withdrawals that start at $50,000 per year. Assume an annual post-tax rate of return of 7.5 percent and that inflation will increase at an annual effective rate of 3.5 percent. What amount does she need to dedicate to this goal?

15. Present Value of Delayed Annuity Problems

    a. Jonas desires fixed annual income of $85,000 beginning twenty years from now and lasting for 20 years. He plans to deplete the account. His annual required return is 9.5 percent. How much does he need to invest today to achieve his goal?

b.   An investor has two options: (1) $50,000 received at the end of this year, or (2) $10,000 received each year for ten years but beginning 10 years from now. Assume the rate of return is 7 percent. Which option has the higher present value?

16. Present Value of Perpetuity Problems

a.   An investment would provide end-of-year annual income of $2,000. The client's required rate of return is 12.5 percent. What price should the client be willing to pay for the investment?

b.   Jose Marie and his wife, Ayna, want to ensure that they do not outlive their money. They want to make end-of-year withdrawals that start at $80,000 after tax and increase by 4 percent per year. They can earn an annual effective rate of 7.2 percent after tax. How much do they need to have invested to make withdrawals that last forever?

17. Internal Rate of Return

a.   Demi invested $16,000 in an exchange-traded fund six years ago. Dividends and earnings were automatically reinvested in new shares. Although Demi considers herself to be a buy-and-hold investor, she nonetheless made a few trades during the time period, as follows:

$3,025 redemption at the end of the second year

$1,825 redemption at the end of the third year

$4,200 additional investment into the fund at the end of the fifth year

$19,885 received at the end of the sixth year, when Demi redeemed the shares.

What was Demi's internal rate of return on the investment?

b.   Lawrence Block is considering investing in a gold coin. The coin costs $47,500. He anticipates spending $1,000 to have the coin's value reevaluated by experts at the end of the first year. Lawrence believes that he can receive $3,500 in exhibitor fees by allowing a major museum to showcase his coin during the second year of ownership. He would like to sell the coin, but he will need to market and promote it first. He anticipates spending $2,000 by the end of the third year on the process. If he can receive $50,000 at the end of the fourth year, should Lawrence make this investment if he needs to earn 4.50 percent on it?

18. Net Present Value

a.   Bruce invested $12,000 in a mutual fund five years ago. He received a dividend check for $1,000 after the first year. He received $750 after the second year. At the end of the third year, he received a check for $1,500. After the fourth year, he collected $750. His final dividend check of $1,000 was received at the end of the fifth year. Assume that Bruce sold the mutual fund at the end of the fifth year for $18,000. What was Bruce's internal rate of return on this investment?

b.   Kristy purchased shares of a mutual fund five years ago. She has since made the following additional transactions:

End of year 2, invested additional $2,500 in the fund

End of year 3, invested additional $9,000 in the fund

End of year 5, redeemed all of her shares in the fund, receiving $16,000

Kristy just told you she achieved an annual return of 9 percent in this investment. If Kristy is correct, what was her initial investment in the fund?

19. Loan Amortization Problems

   a.   Willy and Ursha have just purchased a new car for $38,000. They financed $35,000 for five years at 6.75 percent (APR). What is the monthly payment and total interest expense?

   b.   Assume an initial loan amount of $150,000, an APR of 6.5 percent, fixed monthly payments, and an amortization period of twenty years. What is the outstanding balance on the loan after sixty payments have been paid?

20. Kristin and Dan Peterson

   Kristin and Dan Peterson wonder how much they will need to save to fully fund four years of college for their daughter, Samantha, who is twelve years old today. She plans to attend college at age eighteen. They know that their first choice of college currently costs $13,000 per year. College costs are increasing 5 percent annually. They feel that it is possible to earn an effective annual rate of 8.3 percent (8 percent compounded monthly), both before and during college.

   a.   How much will Samantha's first year of college cost?

   b.   How much do the Peterson's need to fully fund college costs when Samantha begins college?

   c.   How much do Kristin and Dan need to deposit in an account today to fully fund four years of expenses?

   d.   How much will they need to save on a monthly basis starting at the end of this month to fully fund four years of expenses?

21. Tony Mitchell

   Tony Mitchell has been eyeing a new car. Last weekend, he went to the dealership and noted that his dream car would cost $23,000 if purchased today. Tony currently has $9,000 saved. He does not want to go into debt to buy the car, so he has decided to save toward the purchase for three years. Tony estimates that inflation will average 4.5 percent per year. He earns 7 percent (EAR) on his savings.

   a.   How much will the car cost in exactly three years?

   b.   How much must he save per year (at end of each year) to purchase the car in three years?

22. John Johnson

   John Johnson is an avid stamp collector. He has been noting the rapid rise in prices for stamps printed in the 19th century. Some of the best stamps from that time period have been increasing in value by 12 percent per year. John has the rare opportunity to purchase several impressive stamps from a reputable dealer.

The dealer has offered to sell the stamps to John for $65,000 today. As an alternative, John can put down $10,000 toward the purchase today and buy the stamps outright for an additional $89,500 in four years. Assume an annual discount rate of 12 percent. Assuming John has the cash for either deal, which should he take?

Endnotes

1. E. Jacquire, A. Kane, and A. Marcus, "Geometric or Arithmetic Mean: A Reconsideration," *Financial Analyst Journal* 59, no. 6 (2003): 46–53.

2. Additional information about the use of a Texas Instrument BAII Plus can be found at: Texas Instruments BAII Plus Reference Manual (http://education.ti.com/guidebooks/financial/baiiplus/BAIIPLUSGuidebook_EN.pdf).

3. T_0 is always the present time, "today." Future points in time are then counted, with the first period (T_1) being one period in the future. For example, 10 periods in the future would be designated as T_{10}. The period could be years, months, or any other definable period.

4. Annual payments are assumed because the growth rate is annual. Semimonthly or biweekly payments would be expected. However, the growing annuity equation assumes that the payment change frequency caused by applying the growth rate is the same as the payment frequency.

Chapter 3

Cash Flow and Net Worth Planning

Learning Objectives

- Learning Objective 1: Develop cash flow and net worth statements.

- Learning Objective 2: Estimate a client's cash flow and net worth position.

- Learning Objective 3: Describe appropriate funding techniques for an emergency fund.

- Learning Objective 4: Analyze a client's mortgage and refinancing situation.

- Learning Objective 5: Evaluate a client's financial capacity using financial ratios.

CFP® Principal Knowledge Topics

- CFP Topic: B.9. Financial Statements.
- CFP Topic: B.10. Cash Flow Management.
- CFP Topic: B.11. Financing Strategies.
- CFP Topic: B.12. Economic Concepts.
- CFP Topic: B.16. Debt Management.

Chapter Equations

Discretionary Cash Flow:

Total Income – Dedicated Expenses – Discretionary Expenses

Net Worth:

Total Assets – Total Liabilities

Section 79 Taxable Income:

$$Taxable\ Income = \frac{Insurance\ in\ Excess\ of\ \$50,000}{\$1,000} \times Table\ Factor \times 12$$

After-Tax Rate of Return:

Nominal Rate × (1 – Marginal Tax Bracket)

Months to Breakeven on Mortgage Refinance:

$$Breakeven\ months = \frac{Total\ Cost\ of\ refinance}{Original\ PMT - New\ Payment}$$

Cost to Refinance:

$$Costs\ of\ refinance = \frac{PMT_S}{i_S}\left(1 - \frac{1}{(1+i_S)^{\Delta}}\right) + \frac{\left[\frac{PMT_O}{i_O}\left(1 - \frac{1}{(1+i_O)^{t-\Delta}}\right) - \frac{PMT_A}{i_A}\left(1 - \frac{1}{(1+i_A)^{T-\Delta}}\right)\right]}{(1+i_s)^{\Delta}}$$

Cost to Refinance (reduced form):

$$Costs\ of\ refinance = \sum_{t=1}^{\Delta}\left(PV\ IPMT_O - PV\ IPMT_A\right)$$

CASH FLOW AND NET WORTH PLANNING STRATEGIES

Nearly all financial plans begin with an analysis of a client's current cash flow and net worth position. The goal of the analysis is to identify earning, spending, and saving strengths and weaknesses exhibited by a client. In this regard, financial planners should develop and analyze a cash flow statement, a net worth statement, and a spending plan (budget). A related skill is the ability to evaluate a client's current position using financial ratios, and then using these data to develop client-specific recommendations.

Any number of financial planning techniques can be used to increase discretionary cash flow, increase assets, or reduce and possibly eliminate non-tax-efficient liabilities. The choice of strategies will depend entirely on the situation being addressed. Although this is true of all financial planning decisions, the fundamental connection between cash flow and net worth management and the achievement of client goals tends to be particularly important. It is at this stage of the analysis of a client's situation that sources of cash flow and assets are identified to be used throughout the financial planning process. The following financial planning strategies represent just a few approaches that can be used when working with clients.

Planning Strategy 1: Develop a Cash Flow Statement

A **cash flow statement** (sometimes called an income and expense statement) is designed to summarize yearly (sometimes monthly) income flows and fixed and variable expenses. Subtracting expenses from income results in an estimate of **discretionary cash flow**. It is worth noting that discretionary cash flow is not necessarily the same as savings. Often, savings is shown as a **dedicated expense** (fixed expense) within a cash flow statement.

Examples of fixed savings include retirement plan contributions, educational funding savings, and earmarked allocations for other specific goals.

Discretionary cash flow is what remains for future allocation after all known expenses have been paid. Figure 3.1 shows examples of income typically found in a cash flow statement. Figure 3.2 illustrates the way in which expenses are often organized in a cash flow statement. Figure 3.2 also shows the way discretionary cash flow can be presented to a client. Both spreadsheets are available in the Financial Planning Analysis Excel package included with this book.

Figure 3.1. Income Sources within a Cash Flow Statement

DISCRETIONARY CASH FLOW WORKSHEET

Yearly Income	Current	Recommended
Salary Client One	$ -	
Salary Client Two	$ -	
Qualified Cash Dividends		
Taxable Interest Received		
Tax-Free Interest Received		
Short-Term Capital Gains		
Long-Term Capital Gains		
Client One Business/Self-Employment Income		
Client Two Business/Self-Employment Income		
LLC Rental Business		
Client One Bonus Income	$ -	
Client Two Bonus Income	$ -	
Pension Income		
Social Security Income		
Group Benefit Income (Sec 79)		
Other Income		
Total Income	**$ -**	**$ -**

Figure 3.2. Expenses within a Cash Flow Statement

Dedicated Yearly Expenses	Current	Recommended
Mortgage Payment		
Automobile Payment(s)		
Home Equity Loan		
Student Loan(s)		
Credit Cards		
Loan Payment Total	**$ -**	**$ -**
Life Insurance		
Disability Insurance*		
Medical Insurance*		
Long-Term Care Insurance		
Homeowner's Insurance		
Automobile Insurance		
Group Benefit Insurance		
Condo Fees		
Umbrella Liability Insurance		
Insurance Total	**$ -**	**$ -**
Federal Income Taxes Paid		
State Income Taxes Paid		
FICA Paid		
Real Estate Taxes Paid		
Personal Property Taxes Paid		
Other Taxes Paid		
Tax Total	**$ -**	**$ -**
Regular/Allocated Savings		
Unallocated Savings		
Reinvested Div/CG/Interest		
Retirement Plan Contributions*		
After-Tax Retirement Savings		
Savings Total	**$ -**	**$ -**

*Pre-Tax Expenses

Discretionary Yearly Expenses	Current		Recommended	
Electricity/Utilities				
Other Household Utilities				
Telephone				
Cable/Satellite TV				
Other				
Other				
Utility Total	$	-	$	-
Home Maintenance & Repair				
Home Improvements				
Other Home Expenses				
Home Expense Total	$	-	$	-
Food at Home				
Clothing				
Laundry				
Child Care				
Personal Care				
Automobile Gas & Oil				
Automobile Repairs				
Daily Living Expense Total	$	-	$	-
Non-Auto Transportation				
Bank Charges				
Entertainment & Dining				
Recreation & Travel				
Club Fees & Dues				
Hobbies				
Gifts & Donations				
Other Expense Total	$	-	$	-
Unreimbursed Medical Expenses				
Miscellaneous Expenses				
Miscellaneous Expense Total	$	-	$	-

Discretionary Cash Flow	Current		Recommended	
Total Income	$ -		$	-
Total Dedicated Expenses	$ -		$	-
Total Discretionary Expenses	$ -		$	-
Discretionary Cash Flow (DCF)	$	-	$	-
DCF + Unallocated Savings	$ -		$ -	

Planning Strategy 2: Develop a Balance Sheet

A **balance sheet** summarizes a client's current asset and liability situation. **Assets** include all property owned by a client. **Liabilities** include debts and obligations owed to others by the client. Subtracting liabilities from assets results in an estimate of a client's **net worth position**. Figure 3.3 shows the types of assets typically found within a balance sheet. Figure 3.4 illustrates the types of liabilities generally recorded on a balance sheet. Figure 3.4 also shows how an estimate of net worth can be presented to a client.

Figure 3.3. Assets in a Balance Sheet

BALANCE SHEET WORKSHEET

Assets	Current	Recommended
Cash		
Checking Accounts		
Savings Accounts		
Certificates of Deposit		
Money Market Funds		
Other Monetary Assets		
Monetary Asset Total	$ -	$ -
EE/I Bonds		
Stocks		
Bonds		
Mutual Funds		
Brokerage Account Investments		
Investment Real Estate		
Other Investments		
Life Insurance Cash Value		
Investment Asset Total	$ -	$ -
Primary Residence		
Second Home		
Third Home		
Other Housing		
Housing Asset Total	$ -	$ -
Vehicle One		
Vehicle Two		
Vehicle Three		
Other Automobiles		
Vehicle Asset Total	$ -	$ -
Artwork		
Collectibles		
Books		
Furniture and Household Goods		
Sporting Equipment		
Boat		
Other Personal Property		

	Current		Recommended	
Personal Property Asset Total	$	-	$	-
Client 401(k)				
Spouse 401(k)				
Client IRA				
Spouse IRA				
Other Retirement Assets				
Retirement Asset Total	$	-	$	-
Loans and Money Owed				
Market Value of Business				
Business Assets				
Other Asset Total	$	-	$	-

Figure 3.4. Liabilities in a Net Worth Statement

Liabilities and Debts	Current		Recommended	
Current Bills				
Other Short-Term Amounts Due				
Current Liability Total	$	-	$	-
Visa Credit Card(s)				
MasterCard Credit Card(s)				
Discover Credit Card(s)				
Other Credit Card(s)				
Credit Card Liability Total	$	-	$	-
First Mortgage				
Home Equity Loan				
LLC Rental Mortgages				
Housing Liability Total	$	-	$	-
Vehicle Loan One				
Vehicle Loan Two				
Vehicle Loan Three				
Other Automobile Loans				
Lease Liability				
Vehicle Liability Total	$	-	$	-
College Loans				
Life Insurance Policy Loans				
Retirement Plan Loans				
Bank Loans				
Installment Loans				
Other Loans				
Other Debt Liability Total	$	-	$	-

Net Worth Calculation				
	Current		**Recommended**	
Total Assets	$	-	$	-
Total Debt and Liabilities	$	-	$	-
Net Worth	$	-	$	-

Planning Strategy 3: Use Financial Ratios to Assess a Client's Financial Situation

Once a client's cash flow and net worth statements have been completed, the next step in the planning process involves interpreting the findings. **Financial ratios** can be used to help a financial planner better understand a client's current financial position by providing a quantitative measure of financial health that can be compared to a **financial benchmark**. Several financial ratios are commonly used when establishing baseline information about a client's financial situation. These ratios are summarized in Figure 3.5.

Figure 3.5. Commonly Used Financial Ratios

Ratio	Formula	Benchmark
Current ratio	$\dfrac{\text{Monetary assets}}{\text{Current liabilities}}$	> 1
Emergency fund ratio	$\dfrac{\text{Monetary assets}}{\text{Monthly living expenses}}$	3–6+ months
Savings ratio	$\dfrac{\text{Personal savings and employer contributions}}{\text{Annual gross income}}$	> 10%
Debt ratio	$\dfrac{\text{Total liabilities}}{\text{Total assets}}$	< 40%
Long-term debt coverage ratio	$\dfrac{\text{Annual gross income}}{\text{Total annual long-term debt payments}}$	> 2.5
Debt-to-income ratio	$\dfrac{\text{Annual consumer credit payment}}{\text{Annual after-tax income}}$	< 15%
Credit usage ratio	$\dfrac{\text{Total credit used}}{\text{Total credit available}}$	< 30%
"Front-end" mortgage qualification ratio	$\dfrac{\text{Annual mortgage (PITI) payment}}{\text{Annual gross income}}$	< 28% to 30%
"Back-end" mortgage qualification ratio	$\dfrac{\text{Annual mortgage (PITI) and credit payment}}{\text{Annual gross income}}$	< 36% to 43%
Rental expense ratio	$\dfrac{\text{Annual rent and renter's insurance premium}}{\text{Annual gross income}}$	< 25%

The **current ratio** is a measure of client liquidity. This ratio indicates whether sufficient current monetary assets are available to pay off all outstanding short-term debts. The recommended benchmark for the current ratio is a number greater than one, which means that if all current liabilities were paid the client would still retain some monetary assets.

The **emergency fund ratio**, sometimes called the **month's living expenses covered ratio**, is very important because it indicates how long a client could live in a crisis situation without liquidating non-monetary assets or being forced into an unfavorable employment situation. A benchmark of three to six months of expenses is recommended. The rationale for having a range rather than a single value is based on several factors. In addition to general economic conditions, including job and income stability, the number of household earners and the relative economic contribution of each, types and amount of available credit, the current credit usage ratio, and the current savings ratio all play a role in shaping the appropriate dollar amount.

An alternative approach for calculating the emergency fund ratio uses monetary assets divided by monthly **emergency fund expenses**, rather than **monthly living expenses**. For example, this number can be computed by taking gross living expenses and subtracting federal, state, and FICA taxes paid, dedicated savings, and other expenses that are not essential to the maintenance of a household, assuming that the emergency is caused by loss of employment, disability, or a similar event.

Another approach focuses on **fundamental living expenses** that clients must continue to pay regardless of employment status, such as auto and home loans, insurance premiums, utilities, and other variable expenses (e.g., grocery costs, utilities, home repairs). Regardless of what is or is not included, emergency fund expenses represent the bare minimum level of expense a household must pay in case of a financial crisis.

One of the most important questions clients ask financial planners is, "Am I saving as much as I should?" The **savings ratio** can be used to answer this question. This ratio sums a client's personal savings and employer contributions to retirement plans and divides this amount by the client's annual gross income. A benchmark of 10 percent or more is generally recommended. In other words, at least 10 percent of *gross* earnings should be saved annually. (Note: This ratio is very subjective and should not be blindly applied; rather, great care should be taken to match a client's total savings need to their total goal-funding need.)

Clients often wonder whether they have too much debt. The **debt ratio** provides a guideline to help answer this question. This ratio shows the percentage of total assets financed by borrowing. A benchmark of 40 percent is typically used for this ratio. That is, the typical client should strive to have no more than four dollars in liabilities for every ten dollars in assets.

As is the case with most financial ratios, the interpretation of this benchmark needs to be flexible, depending on a client's unique circumstances and stage in the life cycle. For example, clients in the early stage of their careers may not have much choice except to exceed the optimal percentage because of car loans, education loans, revolving credit accounts (for furniture and appliance purchases), and other household formation costs. Older clients, and those with few debts, may easily meet the ratio benchmark.

The **long-term debt coverage ratio** tells how many times a client can make debt payments, based on current income. This formula can be calculated in several ways. A common method involves dividing annual gross income by total annual **long-term debt payments**. Another method uses after-tax income as the numerator.

Examples of long-term debt payments include *mortgage payments, automobile loan payments, student loan payments,* and other debts that take more than one year to repay. If a client's monthly *credit card payment* is large enough that servicing the debt could take more than one year, this amount can also be included in the denominator of the formula.

A long-term debt coverage ratio of at least 2.5 is recommended. The inverse of this formula tells an interesting story. The inverse of a long-term debt coverage ratio of 2.5 is 0.40. This means that a client should allocate no more than 40 percent of income to cover long-term debt payments.

Related to the long-term debt coverage ratio is the **debt-to-income ratio,** which measures the percentage of take home pay committed to consumer credit payments, defined as all revolving and installment non-mortgage debts. A ratio of less than 10 percent of take home, or disposable, income is optimal, although up to 15 percent is considered safe. Between 15 and 20 percent is considered a questionable practice, while consumer debt repayments more than 20 percent of take home pay are usually considered a severe problem. Because automatic payments, optional salary deferral retirement plans, and other employee benefits can further reduce after-tax income, it is important that financial planners use care when calculating this ratio. However, the interpretation is rather clear: when clients commit fifteen to 20 percent (or more) of disposable, or take home, pay to consumer debt repayments, usually little is left for meeting all other financial obligations.

The **credit usage ratio** is not only a factor used to determine the adequacy of the emergency fund ratio, but it is also one of the key factors in determining a **credit score.** High credit usage, such as balances above 50 percent of a credit limit, is usually considered negative. This is because creditors may think more credit is being used than can be repaid. (Note: For clients with very high credit scores, as little as 20 percent credit usage can have a minor negative impact on a credit score.)

Lenders also use mortgage qualification ratios to measure repayment ability for mortgage qualification. Variations of debt-to-income ratios, in this case referred to as **mortgage qualification ratios,** are used to determine how much of a client's annual income can be used to pay for proposed monthly mortgage and existing non-mortgage, or consumer, debt payments. Two **debt limit ratios** are widely used.

The first is called the **28 Percent Rule**, or what some refer to as the **front-end mortgage qualification ratio** or the **mortgage debt service ratio**. This ratio results from a comparison of the projected total mortgage payment for **principal, interest, taxes, and insurance** (PITI) to gross household income. To pass this ratio, PITI generally cannot exceed 28 percent of gross annual income.

The second qualification ratio is called the **36 Percent Rule**, the **back-end mortgage qualification ratio**, or the **debt repayment ratio**. This rule states that a client should pay no more than 36 percent of gross income on the projected mortgage PITI plus other regular monthly consumer debt payments (e.g., credit card, student loan, auto).

These qualification ratios are currently applied throughout the mortgage industry for conventional loans, although the range may vary slightly by lender. Special loan programs or government-subsidized loan programs allow for more relaxed qualification ratios. Clients whose ratios exceed these benchmarks may not qualify for a mortgage or refinance option. If allowed, a lender may require a higher rate of interest or suggest using other available assets to reduce debt. One final but important note: for a client to qualify for a maximum mortgage, these two ratios implicitly limit other consumer debt payments to 8 percent of gross income. This corresponds closely to the original debt-to-income ratio that recommends a consumer credit payment limit of 10 percent of take home income.

The **rental expense ratio** compares the cost of rent and renter's insurance to annual income. Renter's expenses are not too different from homeowner's expenses in that the rental income likely subsidizes principal, interest, taxes, and property insurance for the landlord, who also benefits from equity appreciation in the property. Given this analogy to PITI, it is prudent to apply a slightly stricter benchmark to the rental expense ratio (< 25 percent to < 28 percent of gross income) similar to the front-end mortgage ratio. Although the cost of rent in major urban areas could make this benchmark unachievable, offsetting reductions in other expenses that are not part of the urban lifestyle can balance the increased housing costs.

Planning Strategy 4: Refinance Mortgage with a Fixed Rate, Fixed-Term Loan

The analysis of a client's current financial situation often results in the conclusion that a client will need additional cash flow to meet their long-term financial goals. Many financial planners begin the process of building additional cash flow by paying down debt and refinancing currently held debt. Related to this is the notion of refinancing a client's mortgage. This strategy offers clients one of the best ways to decrease expenditures for housing while increasing annual discretionary cash flow, assuming the term of the new loan is equal to or greater than the loan being replaced. A break-even analysis comparing monthly savings to total refinancing costs will indicate how long it will take to break even on a refinance decision. Things to consider before recommending a refinance solution include:

- Refinancing a mortgage can be expensive, often requiring a client to pay closing costs equal to or greater than 3 percent of the amount borrowed.

- Choosing a short loan term can increase annual expenses.

- Interest for itemized deductions can decrease after implementing a refinance recommendation, resulting in a marginal increase in a client's tax liability. Because of this, a complete break-even analysis should be completed to determine the payback period and cost effectiveness of any refinance strategy.

Planning Strategy 5: Obtain or Refinance with an Adjustable Rate Mortgage (ARM)

This strategy is effective when a client must significantly reduce housing expenses to increase annual discretionary cash flow. The strategy works best in a declining interest rate environment, unless the adjustable rate mortgage offers a conversion to a fixed rate option. This strategy can also work well if the sale of a client's house is planned during the initial fixed rate period of the ARM. Keep in mind, however, that using an adjustable rate mortgage can subject a client to fluctuations in interest rates in the future. If rates increase, a client's annual housing expenses will likely increase as the mortgage payment rises. This strategy also presents clients with **refinancing risks**—if rates do increase, a client could be forced to lock in a new mortgage with a higher interest rate.

Planning Strategy 6: Use an Interest-Only Mortgage

Interest-only mortgages, as the name implies, allow a client to make monthly mortgage payments consisting entirely of interest for a predetermined number of years, after which the payments include both principal and interest. This strategy can reduce a monthly mortgage payment by as much as 50 percent when compared to a conventional mortgage. This is an effective strategy for clients who need to decrease housing expenditures as a method to increase discretionary cash flow. The use of an interest-only mortgage is also a potentially effective strategy for a disciplined client who believes earnings on the money invested elsewhere will exceed the mortgage rate. Interest-only mortgages are also attractive for those who know that they will live in the house for only a brief period of time. In some high-priced housing markets, an interest-only mortgage can be an effective way to finance a house that would be unaffordable with a traditional mortgage.

The recommendation of this strategy is based on the notion that future housing prices will steadily appreciate, which is not always the case. Clients who use this approach must be willing to assume that their future home value will be substantially greater than the mortgage amount. Meeting this assumption is crucial so that future equity will be sufficient to reduce the outstanding mortgage. If housing prices do not increase as predicted, an interest-only mortgage can leave a client with a large outstanding balance, even after paying mortgage payments for many years.

Planning Strategy 7: Consolidate Debts with a Home Equity Loan

Although beginning in 2018, home equity loan interest for non-property improvement expenditures is no longer tax deductible, this strategy can still be effective for those who need to lower the overall interest paid on debts. Using this strategy, it may be possible for total loan payments to be lower than payments made individually on unconsolidated debt. This is true because, generally, home equity loans carry a longer duration and a lower interest rate than open ended and collateralized loans typically used to purchase consumer assets. It is worth noting that although this strategy can result in increased levels of discretionary cash flow, using a home equity loan to consolidate debt places the client's home at risk in case of default.

Planning Tip

Some qualified defined contribution plans (e.g., 401(k) and 403(b) plans) allow participants to borrow up to $50,000 or 50 percent of the employee's account balance, whichever is larger. This loan provision can be used as an emergency source of funds or as a source to pay down high cost credit debt. Remember, however, that there is an opportunity cost involved, in that the borrowed money will no longer be earning market rates of return.

Planning Strategy 8: Establish a Home Equity Line of Credit as a Source of Emergency Funds

This strategy is useful whenever assets designated for emergency savings are depleted for another purpose, or when a client's monetary assets are insufficient to meet the minimum of three to six months of emergency expenses. Essentially, the line of credit substitutes for actual assets. A home equity line of credit can typically be obtained with little or no closing costs, and there is no requirement that the line of credit be used. It is important to note that anything purchased using a line of credit subjects the client's home equity to risk. However, this option offers several benefits over other types of consumer credit or lending sources. Spending of equity should be restricted to true emergency situations. Failure to meet qualification standards can restrict the use of this strategy or increase associated costs.

Planning Strategy 9: Pay off Unsecured Debt with Assets Earning Lower Rates of Return

This strategy is most appropriate for clients who currently have a revolving balance on their credit cards or other unsecured debt. Implementing this strategy decreases annual interest expenses, thereby increasing annual discretionary cash flow for funding other financial goals. In the event of an emergency where assets are needed immediately, a client could re-incur debt, if necessary, to cover expenses. This strategy applies to a wide range of client situations. Two potential disadvantages are associated with this strategy:

- First, some clients find it psychologically difficult to reduce the level of cash or cash equivalents in their portfolio. Suggesting this strategy can cause stress for a client struggling with the thought of being "cash poor" until the liquidated assets can be restored.

- Second, for clients who fail to control spending, paying off debt can lead to the accumulation of more debt and a further reduction in net worth.

Planning Strategy 10: Identify Client Expenses That Can Be Reduced

This strategy can be used to uncover hidden or excessive lifestyle expenses that a client does not consciously consider on a daily basis. Reframing the importance of other goals can be used to override the short-term benefits of these expenses and encourage the client to curtail or eliminate these costs. Keep in mind that discussions that involve cutting expenses tend to be very sensitive. A financial planner must know the needs and wants of each client, using a sincere appreciation of a client's values and spending motives, before making spending cut recommendations. Keep in mind that typically clients are committed to their lifestyle and the associated expenses. Asking a client to reduce or eliminate select expenses can cause a negative reaction. Nevertheless, a financial planner must clearly communicate the benefits (short- or long-term) of this strategy and give the client responsibility for the identification of acceptable spending changes. In the end, this strategy can effectively increase discretionary cash flow without the cost of incurring liabilities or selling assets.

Planning Strategy 11: Use the Cash Value of Life Insurance as an Emergency Source of Income.

The cash value portion of a life insurance policy can be designated and, if necessary, used as a source of emergency income. The cost of a life insurance policy loan is relatively inexpensive, and no qualification standards need to be met. Taking a **policy loan** generally reduces the death benefit and the cash surrender value while the loan is outstanding. The loan also incurs an interest expense. Depending on the policy, the return on the cash value could be reduced until the loan is fully repaid. Loans against a policy value reduce the amount of assets available for earnings used to offset future premium payments. Further, loans that go un-serviced for too long (i.e., no regular payments being submitted) can cause a policy to lapse, which can create a taxable event that could generate a substantial embedded tax liability.

Planning Strategy 12: Use Financial Assets to Reduce Mortgage Debt

Using financial assets to reduce the outstanding balance of mortgage debt lowers the **loan-to-value (LTV) ratio** of a mortgage, which can increase the options available for refinancing. Lenders are more willing to finance real estate that has an LTV ratio of less than 80 percent. This means a homeowner can gain access to a wide set of mortgage options, including a shorter loan term, a fixed versus variable rate, and a lower interest rate. Using assets that have a lower expected rate of return than the after-tax interest rate on a mortgage can also optimize overall investment returns. It is important to note that using financial assets to pay down mortgage debt can reduce financial flexibility in the event of an emergency. This can also have unintended consequences on the achievement of other financial goals.

Planning Strategy 13: Implement an Income Shifting Strategy When Appropriate

This strategy is designed to leverage the use of client monetary assets in a tax efficient manner. Consider the following case scenario. A client, age fifty five, works for a college and has saved a substantial ($100,000) emergency fund that is earning less than 1 percent annually. Also assume that the client's primary goal is to accumulate enough savings to reach retirement in twelve years. The client's secondary goal is to reduce taxes paid on her $90,000 salary.

Here is how an **income shifting strategy** can work. First, the client would immediately maximize contributions to all available defined contribution plans at work. Because she is employed by a college, she is eligible for both a 403(b) and 457 retirement plan. Each has a contribution limit of $19,500 in 2020, plus a $6,000 catch-up provision because she is older than age fifty. She can effectively defer $51,000 in salary this year, which leaves taxable income equal to $39,000 ($90,000 − $49,000). While the client may like the fact that the contributions move her into a lower tax bracket, she may be concerned about a lack of cash flow to meet daily living expenses. This is where the income shift occurs. She should then supplement her income with savings. Given the balance of her emergency fund account, she can shift income for two years.

The downside to this strategy is that her emergency savings fund will be depleted. However, should she need an emergency source of funds she can rely on other sources of credit, including credit cards and possibly a loan from the 403(b) account. In the case of a severe emergency, she could take distributions from the retirement accounts. Given her age and the purpose of the distribution, this may or may not trigger a penalty. It is worth noting that this type of strategy may also be effective for families who want to minimize their adjusted gross income in order to qualify for college and university grants, aid, and scholarships.

Quantitative/Analytical Mini-Case Problems

Emily and Joel Schumaker

1.   Emily and Joel Schumaker are married clients who have just been approved for a twenty-year, $150,000 mortgage. They have been given a choice of two loans. One loan has an annual percentage rate (APR) of 8 percent and does not carry a fee, and the other has an APR of 7.5 percent but carries a discount fee of 2 percent of the initial loan amount. The fee for the second mortgage is payable in cash at loan inception and cannot be financed with the loan.

From a present value cost perspective, which loan is the better deal, assuming (a) they sell their home immediately after making ten years' worth of payments and (b) they require a 9 percent effective annual rate of return? Stated another way, which option has the lower cost?

When conducting the analysis, assume all required payments are made at the end of each month and that interest is compounded monthly. Remember to consider the difference in loan payment, the difference in remaining balance at the time of sale, and the present value of the discount points on an after-tax basis assuming the points are fully deductible. For the purposes of this question, assume the clients are in a marginal 25 percent tax bracket. (Hint: You can solve this problem at either T_0 or T_{120}.)

Bev Mickelson

2.   Suppose Bev Mickelson is in the market to purchase a new car. Bev can afford to spend $500 per month, but she decides it is best to buy an inexpensive car now and use what is left of the $500 to save for a more expensive car later. These savings will earn an effective annual rate of 9 percent interest. Suppose she decides to borrow $15,000 to buy a car today. The loan is for forty-eight months at a 7.8 percent APR. Also assume that in three years she will sell this car for $4,500.

How much money will Bev have for her new car after paying off the old one assuming that all payments and compounding occur monthly? (Do not consider sales or income taxes in the calculations.)

Nina and Rafael Ruiz

3. Nina and Rafael Ruiz are married clients have just been approved for a thirty-year, $150,000 mortgage, with an APR of 7 percent. However, they know that they want to make more than the regular payment in order to pay off the loan before thirty years. They have come to you to analyze two options. Option One requires a fixed monthly payment of $1,200. Option Two requires they start with the regular payment but then increase that amount by an effective monthly rate of 0.35 percent.

    Provide Nina and Rafael answers to the following questions.

    a. Which payment method will result in a faster payoff?

    b. What is the difference in total interest payments between the two alternative payment methods? Hint: The total of payments for Option Two involves using a formula for the partial sum of a geometric series.

    c. Which repayment method results in higher home equity (the lower loan balance) after fourteen years?

Puneet and Theresa Chatterjee

4. Puneet and Theresa Chatterjee are both twenty-eight years old and have a two-year old child, Edward. They have asked you to construct financial statements based on the information provided below. Use this information to calculate the following financial ratios:

    a. Current Ratio

    b. Emergency Fund Ratio

    c. Savings Ratio

    d. Debt Ratio

    e. Long-term Debt Coverage Ratio

    f. Debt-to-Income Ratio

    g. Front End Mortgage Ratio

    h. Back End Mortgage Ratio

    Summarize the Chaterjees' financial situation based on your analysis of these financial ratios.

Income and expense (cash flow) information:

- Income: Puneet and Theresa earned $95,000 in salary. Puneet earned $50,000 as a data analyst, and Theresa made $45,000 as a nursing supervisor. Puneet and Theresa also received $35 in interest from their money market account, which they reinvested.

- Taxes: Their W-2 tax statements indicate that they paid $7,267 in FICA taxes, $10,500 in federal income tax, and $2,900 in state income taxes. Real estate taxes on their home were $1,800. Personal property taxes on the two vehicles they own equal $360.

- Insurance: Medical insurance is provided by their respective employers; however, they must pay a portion of the premium, which amounted to $1,400. Their personal automobile policy premiums totaled $1,600. Homeowner's insurance premiums for the year were $1,200. Puneet and Theresa own term life insurance policies, and they paid $500 in premiums for both policies.

- Loan payments: Mortgage payments amounted to $20,253. Auto loan repayment for their two vehicles totaled $6,600. Student loan payments for Theresa's student loans when she was working toward her master's degree in nursing equal $4,500 for the year, and the boat payments for the year equal $3,112.

- Savings payments: Puneet and Theresa contributed $4,000 to their retirement accounts, $1,200 to an education fund for their child, and $1,200 to their money market account, and the $35 in interest that they reinvested in the money market account.

- Daily living expenses: Puneet and Theresa estimate, based on checking account records and credit card statements, that they spent approximately $4,000 on food at home. Clothing expenditures were estimated to be $1,800; laundry and dry-cleaning expenses were $300; and personal care expenses were $1,000. Day care for Edward was $6,000. Expenses for gas and maintenance for their vehicles were $2,000. This year there were no auto repair costs.

- Variable expenses: They estimate that they spent $1,600 on entertainment, which includes dining out and admission charges for plays, movies, and sporting events. Puneet and Theresa also spent $1,500 on recreation and travel, which is how they categorize vacation expenses. Charitable contributions for the year totaled $2,000. Hobby expenses were $360 for the year. Gifts for family and friends throughout the year were $2,000.

- Utilities: Utilities for the year cost $4,000, which included $1,840 for gas and electricity, $720 for water, and $1,440 for telephone, Internet access, and cable television.

- Home maintenance and improvements: They spent $1,200 annually in this category.

- Miscellaneous expenses: Unreimbursed medical expenses amounted to $300.

Asset and liability information:

- Assets: They have $2,000 in their checking account, $11,000 in their money market account, $6,000 in a mutual fund investment account, $5,500 in the education savings account for Edward, and $20,000 in their retirement accounts. Their home has a fair market value of $185,000, and the blue book value of their vehicles is $7,000 for Vehicle 1 and $5,500 for Vehicle 2. Their furniture and household goods have an estimated value of $20,000; they have sporting equipment estimated at $2,500, and a boat valued at $12,500.

- Liabilities: Theresa's and Puneet's current unpaid bills equal $500 and they owe $700 on their Visa credit card but will pay the entire balance off before the due date. They routinely charge during the month, but always pay the balance in full each month. The balance on their home mortgage is $182,510; their auto loan balance for Vehicle 1 is $8,500, and $2,000 for Vehicle 2. The balance on the loan for the fishing boat is $11,855, and Theresa's student loan balance is $5,700.

Ledio and Isabel Greene

5. Ledio and Isabel Greene have the following assets, liabilities, income, and expenses. Use this information to answer the questions that follow:

- Yearly income: $99,000

- Value of home: $190,000

- Value of cars: $32,000

- Monetary assets: $30,000

- Mortgage on house: $150,000 with twenty-four years remaining on the loans

- Auto loans: $14,000 with three years remaining on the loans

- Student loans: $92,000 with five years remaining on the loans

- Mortgage payment: $1,200

- Utilities: $500

- Car payments: $550

- Groceries: $900

- Taxes: $3,000

- Discretionary expenses: $1,000

a. What is their current net worth situation?

b. What is their current discretionary cash flow position?

c. What is their current ratio?

d. What is their debt ratio?

e. What is their savings ratio (assume that any discretionary cash flow is used for savings)?

f. Ledio and Isabel are considering purchasing a new car. The car will cost $30,000. They plan to borrow the entire amount of the car purchase. By how much will their net worth increase or decrease?

Butterfield Case

6.   Using the Butterfield case from Chapter Fourteen, calculate and interpret the following financial ratios. All needed information is provided, except for the total credit available, which is $10,000 on the Visa credit card and $11,500 on the MasterCard. Answer the following questions based on your findings.

   a.   How would you rate the Butterfields' overall level of liquidity?

   b.   How would you rate the Butterfields' overall level of solvency?

   c.   Does their periodic savings rate meet the minimum suggested threshold?

   d.   Are they spending too much on housing?

   Be sure to frame your answers as if you are speaking to or presenting them to the client.

Chapter Resources

Bradley, Susan, and Mary Martin. Sudden Money: Managing a Financial Windfall. New York: John Wiley & Sons, 2000.

Home Affordable Refinance Program (HARP) (http://www.makinghomeaffordable.gov).

Leimberg, Stephan R., Michael S. Jackson, and Martin J. Satinsky. Tools & Techniques of Financial Planning, 12th Ed. Cincinnati, OH: National Underwriter Company, 2017.

Chapter 4

Income Tax Planning

Learning Objectives

- Learning Objective 1: Calculate a client's current year tax liability.

- Learning Objective 2: Identify client characteristics that uniquely affect the client's income tax planning goals.

- Learning Objective 3: Explain the nine-step tax planning procedure and demonstrate how income taxes are determined at the federal level.

- Learning Objective 4: Explain the significance, and provide examples, of above-the-line and below-the-line deductions.

- Learning Objective 5: Identify income tax planning strategies that can be used to help clients reach their income tax planning goals.

- Learning Objective 6: Describe how a client's tax return can be used to recognize other financial planning opportunities.

CFP® Principal Knowledge Topics

- CFP Topic: F.42. Fundamental Tax Law.
- CFP Topic: F.43. Income tax Fundamentals and Calculations.
- CFP Topic: F.44. Characteristics and Income Taxation of Business Entities.
- CFP Topic: F.45. Income Taxation of Trusts and Estates.
- CFP Topic: F.46. Alternative Minimum Tax (AMT).
- CFP Topic: F.47. Tax Reduction/Management Techniques.
- CFP Topic: F.48. Tax Consequences of Property Transactions.
- CFP Topic: F.49. Passive Activity and At-Risk Rules.
- CFP Topic: F.50. Tax Implications of Special Circumstances.
- CFP Topic: F.51. Charitable/Philanthropic Contributions and Deductions.

Chapter Equations

$$\text{Exclusion Ratio} = \frac{\text{Total after} - \text{tax contribution}}{\text{Total expected distribution}}$$

$$\text{Taxable Equivalent Yield (Federal Tax-exempt)} = \frac{\text{Tax-exempt bond yield}}{(1 - \text{FMTB})}$$

$$\text{Taxable Equivalent Yield (State Tax-exempt)} = \frac{\text{Tax-exempt bond yield}}{(1 - \text{SMTB})}$$

$$\text{Taxable Equivalent Yield (Fully Tax-exempt)} = \frac{\text{Tax-exempt bond yield}}{[1 - (\text{FMTB} + (\text{SMTB} \times (1 - \text{FMTB})))]}$$

$$\text{After-tax yield} = \text{Taxable rate} \times (1 - (\text{FMTB} + (\text{SMTB} \times (1 - \text{FMTB}))))$$

TAX PLANNING STRATEGIES

Tax planning typically follows a cash flow and net worth analysis. Sequencing tax planning early in the analytical process is useful in identifying strategies that can reduce future tax liabilities and increase discretionary cash flow. Additionally, results from a tax plan can be used as an educational tool. In addition to providing clients with background terms, definitions, and calculations, a tax plan can prompt client dialog about retirement funding, insurance needs, college planning, and other client goals that can be impacted by tax issues.

Tax policy in the United States tends to be either progressive or regressive. With **progressive taxes**, the percent of tax paid someone increases as taxable income increases. The federal income tax and the Alternative Minimum Tax (AMT) are progressive. With **regressive taxes**, the tax rate decreases as a person's taxable income increases. Self-employment and **sales taxes** are examples of regressive taxes. A 5 percent tax rate on food, for example, is proportionately more burdensome on someone earning $20,000 per year than on a person earning $100,000 annually, assuming that both consume the same amount and quality of food.

It makes sense for financial planners who do not consider themselves tax specialists to establish working relationships with tax professionals such as a **certified public accountant (CPA), tax attorney,** or **enrolled agent (EA)**. The Internal Revenue Service (IRS) recognizes these professionals as qualified to represent clients in tax disputes. A financial planner should also take time to understand a client's knowledge of taxes and determine whether any previously undisclosed tax issues are present in the client situation. Referring a client to a CPA, attorney, or EA for complex tax help is often prudent, but such referrals do not remove the basic fact-finding obligations associated with comprehensive financial planning. For instance, a client might not initially disclose an outstanding tax debt with the IRS or state taxing agency. Calculating tax liabilities and making recommendations without such information can cause serious tax and legal problems for the client. In this situation, information about the client issue is an essential data point when making a referral decision.

Keep in mind that relying on the help of a CPA, attorney, or EA may be important, but it does not eliminate the need for a clear understanding of current tax laws. This is true because almost every aspect of financial planning is either influenced by or directly influences a client's tax situation. Consider a recommendation to increase contributions to a 401(k) retirement plan. This recommendation may appear to have only retirement planning implications, but it also influences a client's cash flow and tax situation. Contributions to a qualified retirement plan help reduce the amount of income reportable for income tax purposes. This, in turn, helps reduce a client's annual withholding requirement, which can increase discretionary cash flow during the year. Conversely, by not reducing the withholding requirement, the client can avoid or reduce additional tax payments for investment earnings. The combined tax ramifications of this simple recommendation can be significant.

Planning Tip

Unless a financial planner is also a CPA or an EA, it is prudent to include a tax planning disclaimer when presenting any tax calculations, estimates, or recommendations, such as:

"Before implementing the advice provided, please confirm these suggestions with your tax professional."

The purchase, sale, or refinancing of a personal residence provides an example of how client actions can trigger tax issues that call for advanced financial planning. Under current tax law, a married couple can exclude up to $500,000 ($250,000 for a single taxpayer) in gains on the *sale of a primary residence*. But to receive this exclusion, the client must have owned and used the home as a personal residence for any two of the past five years—typically referred to as the **holding period requirement**. Note that losses on the sale are regarded as personal losses and are not deductible. Any gains exceeding the excluded amount are generally taxed at the capital gains tax rate. The itemized deduction for home mortgage interest is often cited as a tax benefit, but the deduction applies only to interest paid on **primary mortgage initial acquisition debt**. In 2018, the law was changed so that only the interest on loans used to acquire property after December 15, 2017, up to a cumulative value of $750,000, can be deducted. Interest paid on home equity loans and home equity lines of credit are no longer deductible unless the loan is used to acquire property or upgrade property.[1]

While maintaining a perspective on the client's tax planning situation, a financial planner must also consider anticipated changes in the tax code. Tax planning involves taking actions that maximize each client's situation in anticipation of household and/or tax code changes. A client's wishes and concerns, as well as potential changes in the client's tax situation, should be considered when developing planning strategies and recommendations. In this regard, a financial planner must often utilize a variety of recommendations within a tax plan. The following tax planning strategies represent a few of the most important of these strategies.

Planning Strategy 1: Apply the Tax Cuts and Jobs Act of 2017

A notable change in the federal tax code was implemented in December 2017. Known as the Tax Cuts and Jobs Act (TCJA), the law effectively limited the use of several of the most widely used tax planning strategies and recommendations. However, the SECURE Act (2019) and the Taxpayer Certainty and Disaster Relief Act of 2019 further modified several of these more restrictive provisions. The following discussion highlights some of the most essential elements of these recent tax legislative changes.

- The deduction for medical expenses must exceed 7.5 percent of AGI.

- The Kiddie Tax applies if a child's unearned income exceeds $2,200 in 2020. Earnings that exceed this amount are taxed at the custodial parent's highest marginal tax rate.

- Clients may deduct the value of charitable contributions up to 60 percent of adjusted gross income. Non-itemizers (those filers claiming the standard deduction) may deduct charitable contributions up to $300.

- A pass-through deduction for sole proprietorships, LLCs, S-corporations, and partnerships was created. The pass-through deduction allows business owners to deduct 20 percent of pass-through income. The deduction lowers taxable income not AGI. A phaseout income limit exists for those who provide professional services: $326,600 for those who are married and file a joint return.

- The TCJA divides pass-through businesses into two classes:

  - Those that provide personal services, such as law firms, medical practices, consulting firms, and professional athletes; and

  - All other businesses.

- Business owners are then divided into three groups:

  - Singles making less than $163,300 or joint filers making less than $321,400 in total taxable income. These taxpayers may take the full 20 percent deduction on their pass-through income.

  - Singles making more than $213,300 or couples making more than $426,600 are subject to different rules. These taxpayers may not take the pass-through business deduction if they own a personal service firm. If the taxpayer owns another type of business, the deduction is limited based on the type of property owned and wages paid.

  - Taxpayers with incomes between the thresholds are eligible for a limited deduction.

  - To calculate the deduction, a taxpayer first must calculate **Qualified Business Income** (QBI), which is usually a firm's net income. The 20 percent deduction is based on QBI.

    - The QBI deduction cannot exceed the greater of:

      - 50 percent of the business owner's W-2 wages paid by the qualified business during the year or

      - The total of twenty-five percent of W-2 wages paid plus 2.5 percent of the cost of qualified property (depreciable tangible property owned and used by the business). The W-2 limitation only applies to those who have income that exceeds $163,300 for single filers and $326,600 for married filers.

        - Example. John is a financial planner who owns his firm as an LLC. John earned $135,000 from his practice. John's spouse earned $170,000 working as a university faculty member. After taking the standard deduction, their taxable income is $280,200 ($305,000 - $24,800 [in 2020]). Since their taxable income is less than the income threshold, John and his spouse are eligible for a $27,000 QBI deduction ($135,000 × .20).

- AMT exemption amounts are now indexed for inflation. For example, in 2020, the AMT exemption amount for married couples filing jointly is $113,400.

- The value of transportation benefits (e.g., transit pass and parking) provided by an employer can be received tax free as long as the combined value of commuter highway vehicle transportation and transit passes does not exceed $270 per month.

- Although not directly impacted by TCJA, clarifications about Social Security and FICA tax withholding was an element of the law. As a reminder, FICA includes taxes paid for Social Security and Medicare. In 2020, earnings up to $137,700 (the wage base) are taxed at 6.20 percent. The tax rate for Medicare is 1.45 percent of all earnings (in other words, there is no wage base limit). Keep in mind that these rates apply to all income earned by a client (although some fringe benefits are exempt from taxation).

  - FICA taxes are paid jointly by the employee and the employer. If, for example, someone earns $150,000 in, she will pay $8,537.40 Social Security taxes ($137,700 × 6.20 percent). She will also pay $2,175 in Medicare taxes ($150,000 × 1.45 percent). Her employer must pay the same amount.

  - A self-employed client must pay both the employee and employer element, of which one half of the tax is deductible for AGI.

  - An additional 0.9 percent Medicare tax on earnings over $250,000 (for those filing married jointly and $204,100 for those filing single) threshold amount (based on filing status) must also be paid by the employee (not employer).

The TCJA also introduced new marginal income tax brackets and rates. Figure 4.1 shows the seven tax brackets and rates for 2020:

Figure 4.1. 2020 Income Tax Brackets and Rates

Filing Status				
Marginal Tax Rate	Single	Married, Filing Jointly	Head of Household	Married, Filing Separately
10%	$0 to $9,875	$0 to $19,750	$0 to $14,100	$0 to $9,875
12%	$9,875 to $40,125	$19,750 to $80,250	$14,100 to $53,700	$9,875 to $40,125
22%	$40,125 to $85,525	$80,250 to $171,050	$53,700 to $85,500	$40,125 to $85,525
24%	$85,525 to $163,300	$171,050 to $326,600	$85,500 to $163,300	$85,525 to $163,300
32%	$163,300 to 207,350	$326,600 to $414,700	$163,300 to $207,350	$163,300 to $207,350
35%	$207,350 to $518,400	$414,700 to $622,050	$207,350 to $518,400	$207,350 to $311,025
37%	Over $518,400	Over $622,050	Over $518,400	Over $311,025

One of the most controversial aspects of the TCJA was the elimination of the personal exemption. Instead of allowing a taxpayer to deduct an amount for each dependent, the TCJA increased the standard deduction, as shown in Figure 4.2.

Figure 4.2. Standard Deduction Amounts in 2020

Filing Status	Deduction Amount
Single	$12,400
Married, Filing Jointly	$24,800
Married, Filing Separately	$12,400
Head of Household	$18,650
Married, Older/ Retired	Married, Over age 65: Additional $2,600 ($1,300 each) Single, Over Age 65: Additional $1,650

The loss of personal exemptions was partially offset by an increase in the **child tax credit**. A $2,000 tax credit is available for qualifying children under age 17. The amount of the credit that may refunded is $1,400. Although the tax credit can be phased out based on income. Some clients with dependent children older than age 17, and those who provide support for elderly parents, may be eligible for a $500 tax credit per dependent.

Capital gain tax rates were also adjusted in the TCJA. Figure 4.3 shows the 2020 tax rates for long-term capital gains. The dollar amounts shown in Figure 4.3 are related to a client's maximum taxable income.

Figure 4.3. Capital Gain Tax Rates in 2020

	Filing Status			
Capital Gain Tax Rate	Single	Married, Filing Jointly	Head of Household	Married, Filing Separately
0%	Up to $40,000	Up to $80,000	Up to $53,600	Up to $40,000
15%	$40,000 to $441,450	$80,000 to $496,600	$53,600 to $469,050	$40,000 to $248,300
20%	Over $441,450	Over $496,600	Over $469,050	Over $248,300

Note: A 3.8 percent net investment income tax applies to high income earners.

Financial Planners engaging in longer-term client projections should note that many of these provisions are scheduled to sunset after December 31, 2025.

Planning Strategy 2: Estimate a Client's Tax Liability

The estimation of a client's tax liability is based on identifying all sources of income. Two approaches can be used to determine a client's tax liability. The first approach uses actual IRS tax forms, such as **IRS Form 1040** and IRS Schedules A, B, C, and D. The second approach, which may be slightly less accurate but more efficient, involves using some form of tax calculator or estimator. Either approach should lead to the same conclusion: the client will receive a refund, owe nothing, or owe additional tax.

The following is a basic nine-step income tax calculation process that can be used when estimating a client's tax liability:

Step 1: Record potential gross income.

Step 2: Exclude nontaxable income and pretax items.

Step 3: Calculate gross income.

Step 4: Subtract expenses for adjusted gross income (AGI) "above-the-line" deductions.

Step 5: Reduce taxable income by either the standard deduction or by the itemized deduction amount "below-the-line" deductions.

Step 6: Calculate tax liability.

Step 7: Reduce tax liability using credits.

Step 8: Add in other tax liabilities.

Step 9: Determine the additional tax liability or the amount of the tax refund.

Following this nine-step tax calculation approach ensures that all income is appropriately accounted for, expenses are recorded, and appropriate tax-reduction tools and techniques are utilized. Of the nine steps, Steps Two, Four, Five, and Seven are areas where a financial planner can add the most value. At Step Two, a financial planner can help a client identify areas within the household budget that can be converted to a pre-tax expense. At Steps Four and Five, a financial planner can help a client maximize "above-the-line" and "below-the-line" deductions, or adjustments to income that occur before the determination of adjusted gross income (AGI) or itemized deductions that occur after the determination of AGI. At Step Seven, a financial planner can assist clients maximize available tax credits. A more detailed explanation of the steps where a financial planner can add value to the tax planning process are discussed in greater detail below.

Step One involves identifying client income. This step in the calculation process requires a financial planner to know the delivery schedule of tax reporting forms, including Form 1099s, as well as obtaining aggregate tax reports from the client.

At Step Two, a financial planner can help her or his clients maximize income from sources that are not subject to taxation. **Municipal bonds** and tax-free money market accounts can be used to reduce a client's reported income.

Step Three involves adding together sources of income to determine gross income that may be subject to taxation.

At Step Four, tax planning strategies can be used to help clients manage tax liabilities. It is important to remember, however, that many of the benefits available in the tax code are subject to income limits. The limit most often imposed is based on **adjusted gross income (AGI)** or **modified adjusted gross income (MAGI)**. The actual definition or calculation of MAGI can vary with the tax issue in question. There are two methods used to reduce AGI. One is to minimize the amount of income reported. The other is to increase negative adjustments to income.

A financial planner can suggest ways a client can maximize her or his **above-the-line deductions**, which are also referred to as **adjustments to gross income**. Although these deductions change from year to year, current examples of expenses that can be used to reduce gross income include *educator expenses, student loan interest, tuition fees,* and *IRA early withdrawal penalties*. Other examples include making deductible contributions to a traditional IRA (phase-out thresholds based on income for qualified plan participation typically apply) and contributing to a *healthcare savings account* (HSA). For those who are self-employed, paying one-half of *self-employment taxes*, contributing to a self-employed retirement plan (e.g., a *Keogh* or *SIMPLE plan*), or purchasing health care insurance are additional options that can be used to reduce gross income. Adjustments to AGI provide a marginal benefit for clients. For instance, if a client is in the 24 percent marginal tax bracket, a $1,000 deduction for AGI will result in approximately $240 in tax savings.

At Step Five, a financial planner can assist her or his clients maximize below-the-line deductions. If above-the-line adjustments are either unavailable or exhausted, attention should turn to below-the-line taxable income reductions by identifying available **itemized deductions which, in the aggregate, exceed the allowable standard deduction**. Three areas where many clients can increase deductions, and thereby reduce taxable income (assuming the client is not subject to the AMT), include:

1. converting non-tax-advantaged interest paid to *deductible mortgage interest,*

2. increasing or accelerating taxes paid in a year subject to the $10,000 limitation imposed by the TCJA, and

3. increasing gifts to charitable organizations.

Whether a financial planner is directly involved in the preparation of a client's income tax return or indirectly involved in the analysis of a client's tax situation, as part of a comprehensive planning engagement, the financial planner may be responsible for implementing the changes necessary to increase a client's tax efficiency. For example, investment planning strategies that minimize tax liabilities should always be considered and accounted for when calculating a client's tax liability. Tax planning strategies should not, however, be considered in isolation. Strategies should be considered in conjunction with each client's other financial planning needs. As an example, increasing a client's municipal bond allocation can be a viable strategy to reduce taxable income. However, if the tax-free rate of return offered by the bonds does not exceed the after-tax return on another fixed-income investment, the client may be better off paying taxes. To make matters even more complicated, high levels of tax-exempt interest can trigger the AMT, thus effectively reducing the availability of several deductions, including home equity interest.

Step Six involves estimating a client's tax liability. This is done using effective marginal tax rates at the time the estimate is made.

At Step Seven, a financial planner should take steps to identify and maximize available **tax credits**—a dollar for dollar reduction in tax liabilities. A few of the most commonly used tax credits include the *child and dependent care credit*, the *Lifetime Learning education credit*, and the *saver's tax credit*. Maximizing available tax credits is an effective tax planning strategy because rather than reducing a client's taxable income, a tax credit reduces a client's tax liability directly. Keep in mind, however, that the availability of tax credits may depend on a client's AGI or MAGI, meeting various qualification thresholds, and potential changes in the tax code.

The last step in the process, Step Nine, involves determining a client's additional tax liability or the amount of the tax refund. While it is possible to use IRS Form 1040 and related schedules to derive an analysis a client's tax situation, nearly all financial planners use software or an Excel sheet to make estimates. Figure 4.4 shows the tax estimator available in Financial Planning Analysis Excel™ package that accompanies this book. This sheet is fully integrated, which means that data are automatically pulled from other worksheets to facilitate an accurate estimate of a client's tax situation.

Figure 4.4. Federal Tax Planning Estimator

Federal Tax Planning Estimator	Assumption:
Gross Income	$0.00
Long-Term Capital Gains & Qualified Dividends	$0.00
Pre-Tax Retirement Contributions	$0.00
Other Pre-Tax Payroll Deductions	$0.00
Adjustments	$0.00
Less Exclusions	$0.00
Reportable Gross Income	
Less Deductions for Adjusted Gross Income	
Educator Expenses	$0.00
One-Half Self-Employment Tax	$0.00
Student Loan Interest	$0.00
Archer MSA Deduction	$0.00
Tuition Deduction	$0.00
IRA Contribution	$0.00
Keogh Contribution	$0.00
Other Deductions	$0.00
Early Withdrawal Penalty	$0.00

Adjusted Gross Income	
Number of Children Dependents Under Age 17	0
Number of Children Dependents Over Age 17	0
Itemized Deductions	
Medical and Dental Expenses	
AGI Medical Deduction Requirement	$0.00
Amount of Deduction	$0.00
Taxes Paid	$0.00
Home Mortgage Interest	$0.00
Investment Interest	$0.00
Home Purchase Points	$0.00
Gifts to Charity	$0.00
Other Deductions	$0.00
Total Itemized	$0.00
Standard Deduction	
Taxable Income	
Tax on Income	
Long-Term Capital Gain and Qualified Dividend Tax	
Social Security & Medicare Taxes	
FICA Taxes Withheld	$0.00
Tax Withheld or Paid	$0.00
Less Tax Credits	
Earned income tax credit (refundable)	$0.00
Credit for child and dependent care expenses	$0.00
Foreign tax credit	$0.00
Adoption credit	$0.00
Retirement savings credit	$0.00
Education credits	$0.00
Credit for elderly	$0.00
Child tax credit/Credit for other dependents	$0.00

Planning Strategy 3: Convert Taxable Interest to Tax-Exempt Interest

Helping a client reduce taxable income is one way to increase her or his discretionary cash flow. One way to do this is to reduce the amount of interest income subject to tax. Using a tax-exempt interest strategy is most appropriate for clients in a high marginal tax bracket. This strategy can also be beneficial for clients in lower brackets whenever the return on a tax-exempt investment exceeds the after-tax return on taxable investments. Three potential drawbacks are associated with this strategy.

- First, obtaining tax exempt interest can be challenging. Municipal securities tend to trade less frequently and in smaller markets. Investors who use this strategy with individual securities may subject themselves to more illiquidity and less marketability than investors who purchase individual taxable securities.

- Second, the difference between a taxable and tax-free rate is not stable. In some instances, tax-free rates exceed after-tax rates of return. In other cases, a fully taxable security will provide a better return, even for high-marginal-tax-bracket clients.

- Third, certain types of tax-free interest can trigger the AMT. Clients with significant amounts of tax-free interest should be aware that they may end up paying a higher tax rate if receipt of interest triggers the AMT.

Planning Strategy 4: Consider Investing in a Roth rather than a Traditional IRA

A **traditional IRA**, with deductible contributions and tax deferral, provides a way to reduce taxable income while saving for retirement. An alternative strategy involves making nondeductible contributions to a **Roth IRA**. Roth IRAs provide a great deal of flexibility. For example, all contributions made to a Roth may be distributed tax and penalty free at any time. This makes a Roth IRA a suitable holding for an emergency savings fund (distributions of earnings may be subject to tax and penalty). Additionally, qualified distributions from a Roth IRA can be received tax free. Tax-free distributions of income from a Roth IRA in the future can, under certain circumstances, provide greater after-tax benefits than an immediate tax deduction and tax deferral offered by a traditional IRA. Keep in mind that this strategy subjects a client to two risks. First, Congress may someday repeal the tax-free status of Roth IRAs, which could subject Roth distributions to taxation. Second, if marginal tax rates are lower when a client retires, the traditional IRA may be preferable. Keep in mind that income restrictions apply that may prohibit Roth IRA contributions for some clients.

Planning Strategy 5: Compare 529 Plans, UGMAs, and UTMAs to Save Taxes and Pay for College

Section 529 plans have gained popularity among financial planners and clients for two reasons. First, contributions are often given special state tax incentives. Second, withdrawals from such plans, if used in accordance with the rules, are tax free. Furthermore, in 2020, the annual gift exclusion of $15,000 applies to contributions per child; however, a special five-year provision can be elected that allows up to $75,000 to be contributed in one year to a Section 529 plan per beneficiary without triggering a gift tax liability. The maximum account balance per beneficiary is $475,000, making these accounts very attractive for families who anticipate large college expenses. Additionally, any unused account balance may be transferred to other beneficiaries as noted below or up to $10,000 may be used to pay down student loan debt on a tax free basis:

- Spouse

- Son, daughter, stepchild, foster child, adopted child, or a descendant of any of them

- Brother, sister, stepbrother, or stepsister

- Father or mother or ancestor of either

- Stepfather or stepmother

- Son or daughter of a brother or sister

- Brother or sister of father or mother

- Son-in-law, daughter-in-law, father-in-law, mother-in-law, brother-in-law, or sister-in-law

- The spouse of any individual listed above

- First cousin

UGMA (Uniform Gifts to Minors Act) or **UTMA** (Uniform Transfer to Minors Act) accounts can also be used to save for college. Effective tax planning is needed at the outset and throughout the planning process to make this recommendation work effectively. The only way to entirely avoid long-term capital gain taxes on custodial accounts is to make sure that asset sales do not trigger the Kiddie Tax. To obtain a low capital gains rate, asset sales in an account must generally occur after the child beneficiary turns age nineteen (age twenty-four if a full-time student). Asset sales prior to age nineteen (age twenty-four if a full-time student) can result in distributions being taxed at the marginal tax rate, in effect in the year in which any capital asset sales takes place, of the parent, guardian, or another adult custodian.

A significant disadvantage financial planners and clients must understand about the use of a UGMA or UTMA account is that funding educational expenses with these accounts does not guarantee that assets will be used for this purpose. With custodial accounts, parents lose control of the assets. Legally, assets are the property of the child, and at the age of majority, age eighteen or twenty-one in most states, the child is entitled to control the use of the assets.

Planning Strategy 6: Match Withholdings to a Client's Tax Liability

Without proper financial planning, a client may find that she or he is under- or over-withholding taxes. In situations where a client is over-withholding taxes, it is a best practice for a financial planner to show how matching liabilities to withholdings can enhance a client's financial situation. If a client can reduce withholdings, the client can invest the increased cash flow immediately instead of waiting for a tax refund. In cases where a client owes more than was withheld, it is important to show both how the tax liability can be paid and how tax liabilities and withholding can be matched in future years. Failure to withhold enough or to make estimated payments, if required, can result in the client needing to pay interest and penalties. Adjustments to withholdings can be made using a **W-4** IRS form. Keep in mind that matching tax withholdings to tax liabilities does not work well for clients who need a measure of forced savings. By reducing monthly withholdings, discretionary cash flow will increase. Clients who tend to spend rather than save may find that this strategy reduces their net worth while decreasing their annual level of discretionary cash flow.

Planning Strategy 7: Maximize Deductions for Adjusted Gross Income

This strategy provides clients one of the best ways to decrease taxable income. Examples of deductions for AGI include educator expenses, contributions to traditional IRAs, student loan interest, tuition fees, one-half of self-employment taxes, self-employed qualified plan contributions, and IRA early withdrawal penalties. It may be possible to prepay some of these expenses in high-income years, thus reducing income for tax purposes. The primary disadvantage associated with this strategy is that many of the deductions for AGI are applicable to particular taxpayers (e.g., some deductions apply only to those who are self-employed). Also, some deductions from AGI are subject to a phase-out based on adjusted gross income.

Planning Strategy 8: Increase Tax Credit Items

A tax credit decreases tax liability dollar for dollar. Compared to a tax deduction, a tax credit is extremely valuable. As such, financial planners should focus on strategies to uncover and use tax credits when possible. Some of the most common tax credits include:

- The foreign tax credit

- The credit for child and dependent care expenses

- The credit for the elderly or the disabled

- Education credits

- The retirement savings contributions credit

- The child tax credit

- The adoption credit

Paying for the educational expenses of a client (typically a client's children/ grandchildren or other dependents) is a way to take advantage of education tax credits. For example, the use of the American Opportunity Tax Credit can reduce a client's tax liability by up to $2,500 in any given year, assuming a client meets AGI income limits. One disadvantage of this strategy is that the approach may not work for higher-income clients. Some of the most common tax credits are subject to income phase-out restrictions, taking many credits out of reach for high-income clients. Another potential disadvantage is that some of the credits listed above are intended to help younger taxpayers and families, and as such, may not be available or of use to others.

Planning Strategy 9: Maximize Pre-tax Retirement Plan and Benefit Contributions

An optimal way to minimize taxes is to legally reduce the amount of income reported for tax purposes. Maximizing pre-tax retirement plan and benefit contributions is one method that can be used to reduce reportable taxable income. Contributing more to a qualified retirement plan, such as a 401(k) or 403(b) plan, is one strategy that can reduce current taxes while increasing savings for retirement.

Other contribution alternatives that can reduce taxable income include taking full advantage of employer provided health benefits, including medical, dental, eye, and disability insurance. Deductions for employer sponsored insurance typically reduce taxable income because the employee premium payments are not subject to income or FICA taxes. This tax-reduction strategy, in effect, reduces the overall cost of policy premiums, making group benefits more affordable in many cases.

Section 125 plans, also known as cafeteria plans or flexible benefit plans, allow employers to offer employees a choice between cash and a variety of nontaxable benefits. The benefits are typically paid for with pre-tax dollars from employee salary reductions or employer credits. Pre-tax salary reduction plans are also available to fund a high deductible health plan and health savings account, as well flexible spending accounts for health care and dependent care expenses. Although restrictions apply, all these benefit options offer the potential for significant tax savings.

Planning Tip

The wide range of credits available (i.e., child and dependent care; elderly and disabled; education; retirement savings; adoption) offer a tax reduction for almost every taxpayer.

Like many of the strategies presented in this chapter, tactics associated with reducing taxable income are not available to all clients at all times. Furthermore, the types of group benefits provided by an employer may be limited. Additionally, it is possible that the purchase or use of certain employer provided benefits may reduce or prompt extra taxes. This is particularly true when a client purchases group term life insurance. Where the face amount of insurance is greater than $50,000, the client will likely trigger a **Section 79 imputed income** tax liability.

Planning Strategy 10: Maximize Qualified Dividends while Reducing Interest Received

Qualified dividends generally, are taxed as follows:

Tax Rate	Single	Married, Filing Jointly
0%	$0 to $40,000	$0 to $80,000
15%	$40,000 to $441,450	$80,000 to $496,600
20%	Over $441,450	Over $496,600

This means that income received in the form of qualified dividends will typically be taxed at a lower rate than ordinary interest income. Although dividends are currently taxed at a low rate compared to regular interest, implementing this strategy for any reason other than to increase the rate of return on long-term savings or to supplement a fixed-income portfolio can be risky. For example, using dividend paying stocks as the basis of an emergency fund can create a liquidity risk for a client. Further, tax laws are constantly in flux. It is possible that the federal tax-advantaged nature of dividends will be repealed in the future. State income taxes may also apply.

Planning Strategy 11: Consider Long-term versus Short-term Capital Gains

Investment property sold for a **long-term capital gain** (which requires than an asset be held for longer than one year) is taxed at the same rates as qualified dividends (as described above). State income taxes may also apply. Investment property that is held for one year or less generates a **short-term capital gain**, which is taxed at the same rate as ordinary income. Because the tax rates for a long-term capital gain are lower than the ordinary income rates for all taxpayers, holding capital assets for more than one year can reduce a client's tax liability. However, employing this strategy imposes an opportunity cost on clients by creating an incentive to hold an asset longer than might otherwise be prudent. For instance, a gain can quickly turn to a loss over a relatively brief period of time. It is sometimes better to capture a short-term gain than to risk a loss to ensure a lower capital gain rate. As with all tax laws, it is possible that the tax advantage associated with long-term capital gains will be repealed in the future.

Planning Strategy 12: Donate Appreciated Investments to Charity

Donating appreciated property to a charity can be one of the best strategies to reduce current taxable income and eliminate assets from a client's gross estate. If an appreciated asset, such as a stock or mutual fund, is sold first with the proceeds donated to charity, a client will need to pay a capital gains tax on the sale. Even though the long-term capital gains tax rate is relatively low, selling first reduces the amount of the total donation to the charity by up to 20 percent, in addition to any applicable state tax. Instead, clients should generally donate property and securities rather than selling assets first. The charity can then sell the property on a tax-free basis. In this way, the total amount of capital gains can be excluded from income. This strategy also maximizes the total amount of the charitable donation. This strategy is beneficial only if the property donated provides a long-term gain. Short-term gain property donated to a qualified charity is deductible only up to the client's basis in the property. In such cases, the client loses the capital appreciation amount as a potential donation.

Planning Strategy 13: Shift Medical Expenses to a Lower Income Year

It can be difficult for clients to treat unreimbursed medical expenses as an itemized deduction because the IRS imposes a **10 percent medical deduction AGI rule**. Only those medical expenses that exceed 10 percent (2019 and beyond) of a client's AGI may be itemized on Schedule A. One strategy that can work for clients who do have large medical bills is to shift these expenses into years when household income is lower. For example, if a client knows that they will terminate employment or retire, it may be helpful to postpone major medical expenses until that year, if possible. The primary disadvantage associated with this strategy is that it may be difficult, if not impossible, to postpone certain medical expenses. In many cases, medical bills and related expenses are the result of an emergency or unplanned event, and as such, a client may have little control over the timing of care and payment of expenses.

Planning Strategy 14: Recommend that a Client Establish a Business

All the strategies discussed so far have been general in nature and applicable to almost any client situation. This strategy, on the other hand, should be considered whenever a client's income exceeds phase-out limits for certain deductions and credits. Several forms of business ownership are available. Figure 4.5 shows each business ownership option and the resulting tax implication for a business owner.

Establishing a business can be an effective way to convert non-tax-deductible expenses into income tax reducing deductions. For example, someone who opens a consulting practice can begin to deduct some expenses related to travel, entertainment, and marketing. Other potential deductions include home office expenses, cell phone charges, and computer equipment. A business owner may also deduct contributions to certain types of retirement plans. Additionally, a **pass-through deduction** for sole proprietorships, LLCs, S-corporations, and partnerships is available for some business owners. The pass-through deduction allows business owners to deduct 20 percent of pass-through income. Keep in mind that a phase-out income limit exists for those who provide professional services.

Figure 4.5. Forms of Business Ownership

Type of Business	Does Business Entity Provide Liability Protection	Tax Implications
Sole Proprietorship	No	• All income passes directly to the business owner; income reported on Schedule C.
Partnership	No	• The proportional share of business income flows through to the owner; income reported on Form 1065 and shown on Form 1040.
Limited Liability Company	Yes	• The proportion share of business income flows through to the owner; income reported on Form 1065, 1120S or Schedule C depending on entity.
Corporation	Yes	• Income taxed at corporate marginal rate; dividends from corporation taxed at owner's marginal tax rate; taxes filed on Form 1120.
S Corporation	Yes	• Income flows through to owner; taxes filed on Form 1120S

It is worth noting that tax laws require a business to show an operating profit in at least three out of five years, or at least show an honest attempt to generate a profit. Some clients who attempt to implement this recommendation run afoul of **hobby loss rules**, which severely limit the type of expense that are deductible. The IRS looks very critically at a commercial enterprise that may really be a hobby rather than a legitimate business.

Planning Strategy 15: Use Like-Kind Exchange Strategies Appropriately

While the Internal Revenue Code (IRC) addresses a dozen or more non-taxable exchanges, the two most common deal with investment property (Section 1031) and insurance policies (Section 1035).

U.S. Internal Revenue Code Section 1031 features a provision for owners of appreciated real estate to exchange a property for a similar piece of real estate without incurring immediate taxation. For this to be an effective tax-postponing strategy, a client must exchange the property for a similar kind or class of asset. Beginning in 2018, 1031 exchanges can only be made using real estate. Taxes on personal property can no longer be postponed using this technique.

Boot, defined as the receipt of non-like-kind property, can trigger taxation. Sometimes clients attempt to exchange investment securities for personal use property. The IRS will not allow such transfers on a tax-free basis. Furthermore, real estate can be exchanged only for real estate (foreign real estate is excluded), which is defined as improved or unimproved land, buildings, warehouses, etc.

For example, exchanging a mortgage for a piece of land would not be permitted under Section 1031.

Keep in mind that the amount *realized* for tax purposes is often different from the amount *recognized* for tax purposes. In general, investors need only recognize for tax purposes the value of the boot received even though they may have realized an amount greater than reported for tax purposes.

U.S. Internal Revenue Code Section 1035 provides for a tax-free insurance product exchange for owners of a life insurance policy, an endowment, or an annuity. Restrictions apply, but eligible product exchanges allow a client to avoid taxes due on the sale or redemption of an insurance product. Otherwise, the two-step process of the sale or redemption, minus the taxes owed, can result in a smaller amount for a subsequent insurance product purchase.

Planning Strategy 16: Describe the Difference between Realized and Unrealized Gains

A **realized gain** (or **realized loss**) is calculated by subtracting the adjusted basis in a property from the sale price of the property. Realized gains (or losses) are reported on a client's Form 1040. Sometimes a gain (or loss) is realized but not immediately recognized (i.e., reported on Form 1040). In these situations, the gain (or loss) is *unrecognized*.

Examples of situations that might result in an unrecognized gain (or loss) include completing a Section 1031 like-kind exchange, the sale of personal use assets, and some gains on the sale of a personal residence (e.g., a $250,000 gain for a single taxpayer).

Understanding when a gain or loss must be reported can be an effective tool to help clients maximize discretionary cash flow by managing and minimizing tax liabilities. Misinterpretation of gains rules can result in tax penalties.

Example. Selling personal property for a loss is not an eligible tax deduction strategy; however, selling personal property (e.g., sales at a garage sale) that results in a gain is technically taxable. As such, care must be taken whenever a like-kind exchange strategy is employed.

Planning Strategy 17: Calculate the Exclusion Ratio to Reduce the Tax on Annuity Distributions

Careful attention should be paid to situations where a client is taking distributions from an annuity, IRA, or qualified plan. If any contribution is made using after-tax dollars, or if any of a contribution has been taxed previously, a portion of the total distribution will be considered a tax-free distribution. Calculating the exclusion ratio can reduce the possibility that a client will pay unnecessary taxes. The exclusion ratio formula is as follows:

$$\text{Exclusion Ratio} = \frac{\text{Total after} - \text{tax contribution}}{\text{Total expected distributions}}$$

Where the "total expected distributions" is calculated by multiplying the monthly distribution amount by the number of expected distributions (i.e., twelve per year).

Example. Assume a client expects to receive $2,000 per month over a twenty-year period. If the client originally invested $300,000 on an after-tax basis, the exclusion ratio will indicate that 62.5 percent of each distribution will be received tax free. That is, 37.5 percent of each distribution will be taxable.

It is possible that distributions will last longer than the expected duration used in the formula. In these situations, all the after-tax contributions will have been accounted for. This will result in all future distributions being fully taxable. Clients who fail to track cumulative distributions can incur tax penalties at some point in the future.

Planning Strategy 18: Compare Taxable and Tax-free Interest on a Taxable Equivalent Yield Basis

Financial planners should be adept at calculating **taxable equivalent yields** as a means of comparing taxable and tax-free sources of income. An analysis may be required to determine whether municipal securities, for example, are appropriate for a client. Some bonds are exempt from federal income tax, some are exempt from state income tax, and some are fully exempt, meaning the bond incurs neither federal nor state income tax liability. The following formulas should be used as a means of determining the yield needed for a taxable fixed-income investment to match that of a state and/or federally tax-free fixed income investment:

Taxable Equivalent Yield (Federal Tax-Exempt)

$$\text{TEY (Federal Tax-Exempt)} = \frac{\text{Tax-exempt bond yeild}}{(1 - \text{FMTB})}$$

Taxable Equivalent Yield (State Tax-Exempt)

$$\text{TEY (State Tax-Exempt)} = \frac{\text{Tax-exempt bond yeild}}{(1 - \text{SMTB})}$$

Taxable Equivalent Yield (Fully Tax-Exempt)

$$\text{TEY (Fully Tax-Exempt)} = \frac{\text{Tax-exempt bond yeild}}{[1 - (\text{FMTB} + (\text{SMTB} \times (1 - \text{FMTB})))]}$$

Where:

TEY   = Taxable Equivalent Yield

FMTB = Federal Marginal Tax Bracket

SMTB = State Marginal Tax Bracket

Example. If a client lives in a state with a 5 percent marginal tax rate and is in the 24 percent federal marginal tax bracket, it is possible to compare two bonds—a fully taxable 8.25 percent corporate bond and a 6.0 percent municipal bond. The TEY on the municipal bond is 8.45 percent if the bond is issued from a municipality in the same state as the client's state of residence. In other words, a fully taxable bond would need to have an annual yield of 8.45 percent or greater to be the better investment. However, if the client purchased a municipal bond from another state, the interest would not be state tax exempt, so the TEY would be only 7.89 percent. In this case, the client should purchase the corporate bond and pay the tax.

A similar formula is used to determine **after-tax yield** (or equivalent tax-free rate of return), which can be calculated using the following formula:

$$\text{After Tax Yield} = \text{Taxable Rate} \times (1 - (\text{FMTB} + (\text{SMTB} \times (1 - \text{FMTB}))))$$

Several assumptions are associated with the use of the preceding formulas. It is possible (and likely) that over time marginal tax rates in a particular state will change. When this happens, it is important to rerun previously conducted analyses. Also, bond rates change on a regular basis. What may be an attractive tax-free rate today may be a less appealing rate tomorrow. Again, the use of a formula is not a one-time calculation. Financial planners are encouraged to conduct yield analyses on an ongoing basis. Finally, it is important to remember that the tax-exempt status of municipal bonds does not extend to all instances, especially in the context of AMT calculations.

Planning Strategy 19: Understand When a Client Should Itemize Deductions

According to the IRS, financial planning clients should itemize deductions if their allowable itemized deductions are more than the **standard deduction**. Schedule A is used to itemize deductions. There are many rules and limitations applicable to itemizing deductions, but whenever clients have eligible expenses that exceed the standard deduction, they should claim the higher itemized amount. However, this in turn can create additional income reporting confusion for the subsequent year.

Example. Clients who claim *state income tax* as an itemized deduction are required to report any refund of state tax overpayment as income on their federal income tax form the following year. Forgetting to claim the state tax refund as income can result in fines and penalties.

Planning Strategy 20: Review Cost Basis Rules when Advising Clients about Gifts

Sometimes clients get confused when calculating the tax gain or loss on an investment asset received as a **gift**. The rules relating to **non-cash investment gifts** can be found in IRS Publication 550. A summary of these rules follows:

- The holding period of the asset in the hands of the donor, generally, is transferred to the donee.

- If an asset is gifted at a value on date of gift that is below the donor's original basis the asset will have a dual basis in the hands of the done: gain will be based on the difference between the sale price of the asset and the donor's original basis and will be deemed to be a long-term holding; loss will be based on a sale at a price below the gift tax value of the asset and the holding period resets from the date of the gift. A sale of the asset at a price between gift tax value and the donor's original basis results in no taxable gain or loss.

- If the asset is sold for more than the original basis of the asset (i.e., the amount paid by the donor when the asset was originally purchased), the original basis is used.

Example: Assume a client's father purchases bonds for $20,000. The father gifts the bonds to your client. At the time of the gift, the bonds are worth $10,000. If the bonds are sold for $9,000, the client will record a $1,000 loss. If the bonds are sold for $25,000, the client will record a $5,000 gain. If the bonds are sold for $15,000, no gain or loss will be recorded.

Planning Tip

When a donor pays a gift tax on a gift, the donee's basis is equivalent to the donor's basis plus the amount of the gift tax attributable to the appreciation of the gift above the donor's adjusted basis. The following formula can be used to determine the new basis:

New Basis = Donor's Basis + ((Unrealized Appreciation of Gift/Taxable gift) × Gift Tax Paid).

For example, assume your client receives a stock worth $1,014,000 with the donor's adjusted basis being $764,000. Also assume the donor was subject to a 40 percent federal and state gift tax rate and that the gift tax exclusion is $15,000. Given this information, your client's new cost basis is: $862,521, after accounting for the excluded portion of the gift.

Solution:

$764,000 + (($1,014,000 − $764,000)/$1,014,000) × (($1,014,000 − $15,000) × 0.40) = $862,521

It is worth noting that whenever a client gives or receives a gift that can be deemed an investment, she or he should record and retain information related to the date of the gift, its original basis, and the fair market value of the asset on the gift date. Without this information, the IRS can limit claims of loss or maximize a sale gain if the client is audited. It is also worth noting that in cases where the current value of an asset is less than the original basis but more than the date-of-gift fair market value, the donee should be advised to sell the asset, capture the tax loss, and then transfer the assets to the giftee.

Planning Strategy 21: Consider Roth IRA Conversion Options

Clients who own a traditional IRA may convert their IRA into a Roth IRA at any time, regardless of household income. The primary advantages of conversion include the ability to take contributions out without tax or penalty, no-required minimum distributions, and the potential tax-free receipt of distributions in retirement. Two downsides are associated with this strategy: (1) the conversion will increase taxable income in the year of the conversion, and (2) once completed, the action is irrevocable.

In general, conversion to a Roth IRA is advantageous for a client who anticipates being in a higher marginal tax bracket in retirement, compared to the year of conversion. Four approaches are typically used in relation to conversion:

1. Convert an amount from a traditional IRA that moves a client up to the maximum income in a given marginal bracket. For example, assume a married client is in the 32 percent marginal income tax bracket, making $350,000 in taxable income. Using this approach, $50,000 would be converted this year into a Roth IRA. The $50,000 would keep the client in the 32 percent marginal tax bracket. A higher distribution would shift the client into either the 35 or 37 percent bracket.

2. Convert a traditional IRA into a Roth prior to required minimum distributions. For instance, assume a client is age sixty nine and is in the 24 percent marginal tax bracket. Also assume that once required minimum distributions begin, the client will shift into the 32 percent bracket. By converting now, and paying taxes at the 24 percent rate, the client can effectively avoid paying higher taxes in the future.

3. Convert a traditional IRA into a Roth once required minimum distributions begin. For planning purposes, assume that distributions will force a retired client to pay taxes on 85 percent of Social Security benefits. If the client makes a series of conversions prior to age sixty-two, the distributions will not negatively influence Social Security or Medicare benefits, but will reduce future required minimum distributions and taxes. This strategy can also be used with qualified retirement plans.

4. Convert traditional IRAs and qualified retirement plan assets of older married clients. The logic is that the marginal tax rate, and standard deduction, will be larger for a married couple compared to the rate and deduction for a single person. Consider the following example. Assume a married couple earns $90,000 annually, with a large percent of earnings from required minimum distributions. As a couple, the marginal tax rate is 12 percent. Without conversion, and at the death of one of the spousal partners, the surviving spouse will be subject to a 22 percent marginal rate. Converting prior to the death of a partner can ensure that taxes remain manageable in the future.

Planning Strategy 22: Understand Passive Activity Rules

Owners of rental real estate sometimes fall under **passive activity loss** rules. A passive activity is one in which someone makes an investment but does not materially participate in the business. A business owner who has passive losses may deduct losses only to the extent that the owner has passive income from other sources. Beginning in 2018, a business owner's ability to deduct excess business losses in the current year is limited. Although the rules are complicated, the general rule is:

- A current year business loss cannot be used to offset more than $250,000 (for a single tax filer) or $500,000 (for a married tax filer) of income from other sources.

Any losses carried forward can be used to shelter 80 percent of future taxable income. For example, assume a single business owner generates $600,000 in real estate losses from a property, while earning $300,000 from other real estate operations. In this case, the excess business loss is $50,000. This $50,000 can be carried forward. Keep in mind that had the owner of these businesses lost $250,000 or less, there would be no excess business loss.

Planning Tip

The passive activity loss rules apply to rental real estate owners who do not activity participate in the business. The IRS deems active participation as being a real estate professional.

Besides holding a real estate sales license, the IRS defines active participation in rental real estate as making management decisions in a significant and bona fide manner. Decisions that indicate active participation include approving new tenants, deciding on rental terms, approving expenditures, and making other impactful property decisions. A real estate investor must document working at least 10 hours per week in the business to avoid passive activity loss rules.

Planning Strategy 23: Apply a Systematic Approach when Developing Tax Planning Recommendations

Tax planning is integrative to the extent that tax recommendations are incorporated into other parts of a client's financial plan. Effective tax planning can provide insights into ways to increase monthly discretionary cash flow. Tax planning can also be used to prompt deeper client-financial planner discussions regarding retirement, investment, insurance, and education planning. Figure 4.6 illustrates a process that can be used to narrow strategies down into one or more client recommendations. Note that this process is premised on the notion that, regardless of the approach chosen, the recommendation(s) match a client's tax planning goals and objectives.

A best practice involves reviewing common tax planning pitfalls before making tax planning recommendations or recommendations in other core content planning areas. These issues include:

- possible AMT triggers;

- contribution levels to employer provided tax-advantaged benefit plans;

- allocations among pre-tax, taxable, and tax-free investment assets;

- present and future business ownership interests;

- non-tax-advantaged debt compared to home equity debt; and

- where applicable, the ability to meet tax adjustment, deduction, and credit income limits.

Figure 4.6. Decision Tree for Developing Tax Planning Recommendations

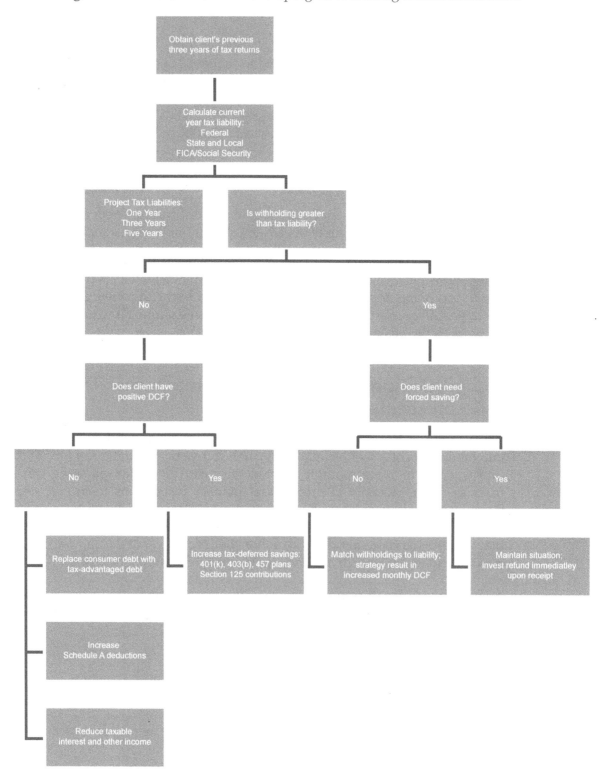

Planning Strategy 24: Incorporate Elements of the CARES Act into Work with Clients

On March 27, 2020, the U.S. House of Representatives joined the United States Senate in passing a financial stimulus bill known as the CARES Act. President Trump signed the Act into law on the same day. A significant number of provisions affecting and benefiting individual taxpayers, college students, unemployment compensation and health care coverages, as well as both large and small businesses were put into place to help combat the Covid-19 pandemic. Many of the measures were temporary; however, a few elements of the law were made permanent. The following are of particular importance to financial planners:

- Withdrawals from IRAs and qualified plans prior to age 59½ up to $100K will avoid the 10 percent early withdrawal penalty if made for Coronavirus-related purposes, which is defined as a positive diagnosis for the account owner, spouse of account owner, or dependent, or due to adverse financial consequences resulting from being quarantined, furloughed from work, lack of child care prohibiting ability to work, or from having work hours reduced. Amounts withdrawn are taxable but allowed to be allocated to gross income in 2020, 2021, and 2022. Optionally, amounts withdrawn for these purposes can be recontributed without being subject to income taxation if recontributed within three years of withdrawal.

- Beginning January 1, 2020, individuals who otherwise claim the standard deduction and wish to make *cash* charitable contributions will receive an "above the line" (itemization not required) deduction against Adjusted Gross Income (AGI) of up to $300.

- Under the Tax Cuts and Jobs Act of 2017, the limitation on the deductibility of charitable contributions in any calendar year was raised from 50 percent of AGI to 60 percent of AGI, for those taxpayers who itemize deductions. Any excess over the limit is eligible to be carried forward for up to five years. Under the CARES Act, the 60 percent of AGI limitation was increased to 100 percent of AGI for charitable contributions made *in cash* during calendar year 2020 to qualifying charities. Taxpayers opting to make cash charitable contributions of this magnitude must elect 100 percent of AGI treatment on their tax return reporting the deduction. The 100 percent of AGI limitation dollar amount must be reduced by any other charitable contributions made during the calendar year (for example, gifts of appreciated securities). Further, the term "qualifying charity" does not include cash contributions to private foundations, supporting organizations or donor-advised funds.

Quantitative/Analytical Mini-Case Problems

Liama MacDonald

1. Liama MacDonald just turned thirty years old. She is currently single. Liama has gross wages of $95,000 (before deferrals) and has had $14,000 withheld for federal income tax. Given the information presented below, and in the chapter, will she likely have too much or too little withheld for the current tax year (do not consider AMT in your calculations)? Based on your analysis, what should Liama do?

   • She estimates total itemized deductions of $11,450.

   • She will not have any interest or dividend income or capital gains.

   • She will not contribute to an IRA.

   • She will defer 5 percent of her gross salary into the qualified retirement plan.

Randy Cross

2. Randy Cross, a new financial planning client, makes a tax-deductible contribution of $4,000 to a traditional IRA. The client is in the 24 percent marginal tax bracket. How much are the approximate tax savings?

Frank and Louisa Beamer

3. Frank Beamer and his wife Louisa have owned and lived in their personal residence for ten years. They purchased the home for $300,000. They sell the home for $900,000. How much of the gain is taxable? If a portion of the sale is taxable, calculate the tax liability.

Luke Heckman

4. Luke Heckman has asked you to analyze the following investment alternatives to determine the highest after-tax rate of return under the assumption that he is subject to a 32 percent marginal federal income tax and a 5 percent state income tax (disregard the AMT for this problem). Which bond should he purchase?

   • A corporate bond with a 7 percent pre-tax return.

   • An out-of-state municipal bond with a 5.75 percent pre-tax return.

   • An in-state municipal bond with a 5.5 percent pre-tax return.

Anabell Snyder

5. A financial planner has just completed an analysis of Anabell Snyder's fixed-income holdings. The financial planner has determined each of Anabell's after-tax yields, but is cautioning Anabell

that the tax implications of her holdings might change if Congress alters marginal tax rates. Based on the following after-tax yields, which of these bonds would offer the greatest after-tax return if Anabell's federal marginal tax bracket increased from 24 percent to 32 percent, while her state marginal bracket remained at 4.5 percent?

- A corporate bond with a 5.1 percent after-tax return.

- An out-of-state municipal bond with a 5.0 percent after-tax return.

- An in-state municipal bond with a 4.8 percent after-tax return.

Jacque Smith

6. Jacque Smith, an interior designer, is one-year shy of her thirtieth birthday. She has come to you for help in preparing her taxes. Use the information in the chapter, as well as the assumptions below, to answer the following questions:

   - She is single;

   - She has one child;

   - She made $39,500 in wages last year;

   - She earned $300 in taxable interest last year;

   - Last year she received a $100 tax refund from the State of Georgia, where she is resident;

   - She paid $250 in student loan interest;

   - She incurred $2,450 in medical expenses, $2,800 in state and property taxes, and made a $3,000 charitable donation to her church;

   - She is thinking about going to graduate school next year, which will cost $5,000; she has not yet started saving for this potential expense; and

   - She had $4,000 withheld from her pay for federal taxes.

     a. How many personal exemptions may she claim?

     b. What is Jacque's filing status?

     c. How much must she report on Line 7 of Form 1040 (wages, salaries, etc.)?

     d. What is Jacque's total income for the year?

     e. What is Jacque's AGI?

     f. What deduction amount should Jacque claim?

     g. How much taxable income must she report this year?

     h. What marginal tax bracket does Jacque fall?

    i.   What is her tax liability for the year?

    j.   How much may Jacque claim in tax credits for the year?

    k.   Is Jacque due a refund this year? Why or why not?

Chapter Resources

Internal Revenue Service (www.irs.gov).

Leimberg, S. R.; J. Katz; R. Keebler; J. Scroggins; M. Jackson. *The Tools & Techniques of Income Tax Planning*, 5th Ed. Cincinnati, OH: National Underwriter Company, 2016.

Tax Facts on Insurance & Employee Benefits. Erlanger, KY: National Underwriter Company (published annually).

Tax Facts on Investments. Erlanger, KY: National Underwriter Company (published annually).

Endnote

1.   According to the IRS, interest on a home equity loan used to build an addition to an existing home is typically deductible, while interest on the same loan used to pay personal living expenses, such as credit card debts, is not. Similar to the prior law, the loan must be secured by a client's main home or second home (known as a qualified residence), not exceed the cost of the home, and meet other requirements.

Chapter 5

Life Insurance Planning

Learning Objectives

- Learning Objective 1: Describe the personal characteristics that influence the underwriting process.

- Learning Objective 2: Compare different types of life insurance policies.

- Learning Objective 3: Evaluate a client's life insurance need.

- Learning Objective 4: Explain how life insurance can be used as a business management tool.

- Learning Objective 5: Describe the role of annuities in a client's financial plan.

CFP® Principal Knowledge Topics

- CFP Topic: D.23. Analysis and Evaluation of Risk Exposures.
- CFP Topic: D.27. Annuities.
- CFP Topic: D.28. Life Insurance (Individual).
- CFP Topic: D.29. Business Uses of Insurance.
- CFP Topic: D.30. Insurance Needs Analysis.
- CFP Topic: D.31. Insurance Policy and Company Selection.

Chapter Equations

$$\text{Present Value of an Annuity (PVA)} = \frac{\text{PMT}}{i}\left[1 - \frac{1}{(1+i)^n}\right]$$

$$\text{Present Value of a Growing Annuity Due (PVGA)} = \frac{\text{PMT}_1}{(i-g)}\left[1 - \frac{(1+g)^n}{(1+i)^n}\right](1+i)$$

$$\text{Present Value of Perpetuity (PVP)} = \frac{\text{PMT}}{i}$$

$$\text{Yearly Price per Thousand of Coverage (YPT)} = \left[\frac{(\text{PMT} + \text{CV}_o) \times (1+i) - (\text{CV}_1 + \text{Div})}{(\text{DB} - \text{CV}_1) \times (0.001)}\right]$$

LIFE INSURANCE PLANNING STRATEGIES

Financial planners use numerous life insurance planning strategies to meet client objectives. It is a financial planner's professional duty to continually improve product knowledge and keep abreast of new strategies and products that can appropriately be used to help their client's needs. The following strategies represent a sampling of some of the most widely used life insurance planning techniques used by financial planners.

Planning Strategy 1: Estimate a Client's Life Insurance Need Using a Consistent Methodology

Financial planners generally use one of five approaches to estimate a client's life insurance need:

1. Income Multiplier Approach

2. Human Life Value Approach

3. Capital Retention Approach

4. Income Retention Approach

5. Needs Analysis Approach

Planning Tip

In some cases, financial planners substitute a household's current living expenses less the survivor's earnings for current income. The decision to make this choice will depend on a client's unique situation. The use of current living expenses will likely increase the amount of insurance needed. An alternative consideration involves whether current living expenses will be defined to include or exclude savings. Including current savings for the cost of education, for example, would increase, and potentially over-estimate, the insurance need.

Income Multiplier Approach

The **income multiplier approach** is a very simple model for determining a life insurance need. The following formula can be used to determine a life insurance need:

Current Need = Insured's Current Gross Income × Chosen Multiplier

The process begins by multiplying a client's gross income by a factor between five and fifteen. A high factor should be used when a client has more financial needs to be met in the case of death and/or the availability and continuity of a survivor's income is problematic. The choice of multiplier is subjective and generally based on a financial planner's past experience in similar situations. Typical factors include:

*   A multiplier of seven for a client with no financial dependents and few debts and/or final expenses.

*   A multiplier of twelve when a client has more than one dependent children and other ongoing financial demands.

*   A multiplier of fifteen for a client who has high debts and/or a client who wishes to leave a sizable legacy to beneficiaries, who are living well beyond their financial means or have a desire to leave a large legacy to children or charity.

Human Life Value Approach

The **human life value (HLV) approach** is based on estimating the amount needed to replace current income in case a client were to die. Two inputs are needed:

1. The current income of the insured, and

2. The years remaining until the expected retirement of the insured.

The calculation involves solving for the present value of a client's lost income stream using a present value of annuity calculation, where:

$$PVA = \frac{PMT}{i}\left[1 - \frac{1}{(1+i)^n}\right]$$

PVA = present value of an annuity

PMT = insured's current income

i   = projected after-tax rate of return on investment assets

n   = insured's remaining work-life = (projected retirement age – current age)

The basic HLV approach can be adjusted to account for the impact of inflation. A growing annuity formula can be used as shown below:

$$PVGA = \frac{PMT_1}{(i-g)}\left[1 - \frac{(1+g)^n}{(1+i)^n}\right]$$

Planning Tip

The human life value approach has two weaknesses. First, the formula does not consider other sources of income. Second, the formula does not consider to what extent a decedent's income supports the client's family. Using a replacement ratio (also known as family member support ratio) to determine the annual income need for a client's survivor(s) is one method that can be used to adjust for any possible overstatement in required income.

Capital Retention Approach

The **capital retention approach** also bases the insurance need on the current income of a client. However, the capital retention approach uses a perpetuity to determine the need, as follows:

$$PVP = \frac{PMT}{i} + \text{First Year's Payment to Make Equation an Annuity Due}$$

PMT = insured's current gross income

i   = projected rate of return on investment assets

This estimation method assumes the survivor will not liquidate investment assets to generate current income (i.e., the capital is retained). Keep in mind that this approach can overestimate the required amount of insurance coverage needed.

Planning Tip

Keep in mind that the human life value, capital retention, income retention approaches usually estimate a client's insurance need using the normal retirement age to calculate the number of periods in the estimates. It is assumed that the surviving partner will continue to save for retirement from insurance proceeds.

Income Retention Approach

The **income retention approach** estimates a client's life insurance need based on the expected income needs of a client's survivor(s). The process begins by reducing a client's gross income by:

1. Any continuous income earned by the survivor;

2. The income taxes associated with the decedent's income;

3. Any preretirement benefits received from Social Security or pensions; and

4. Other reasonable adjustments (e.g., annuity payments, interest, or dividend income).

This approach often yields the lowest approximation of required insurance coverage. The following formula can be used to estimate the income retention need:

$$PVA = \frac{PMT}{i}\left[1 - \frac{1}{(1+i)^n}\right]$$

PVA = present value of an annuity

PMT = survivor's net income need after considering all sources of continuing income)

i = projected after-tax rate of return on investment assets

n = survivor's remaining work-life = (projected retirement age – current age)

This formula is the same as the one used to estimate a need using the HLV approach. The primary difference is the way in which the payment is calculated.

Needs Analysis Approach

While each of the valuation approaches described above can be used to quickly estimate a client's life insurance need, nearly all financial planners prefer to use a needs analysis approach to obtain a more accurate estimate of the additional insurance a client should purchase. Figure 5.1 illustrates the type of information typically included in a needs analysis model. This spreadsheet is available in the Financial Planning Analysis Excel package included with this book.

Planning Tip

Each of the formulas can be adjusted by applying a growth rate to the formula (a growing annuity). The growth rate "g" should be a reasonable estimate of the average annual increase in income. This adjustment will always result in a higher present value need. The following growth-adjusted formula can be used in this regard:

Present Value of a Growing Annuity

$$(PVGA) = \frac{PMT_1}{(i-g)}\left[1 - \frac{(1+g)^n}{(1+i)^n}\right](1+i)$$

By assuming a salary growth rate equivalent to the inflation rate, a client's life insurance need will increase. As such, it is more likely that the assets provided from a life insurance settlement will be sufficient to provide the surviving household or partner an increasing stream of income over the survivor's life.

Figure 5.1. Life Insurance Needs Analysis Spreadsheet

LIFE INSURANCE NEEDS ANALYSIS ESTIMATOR		
Assumptions		
Insured's Name	0	0
Insured's Earned Income	$ -	$ -
Insured's Age	0	0
Survivor's Earned Income	$ -	$ -
Survivor's Age	0	0
Final Expenses		
Estate Administration		
Federal Estate Taxes		
State Estate Taxes		
Other Final Needs		
Credit Card Debt		
Installment Debt		
Automobile Debt		
Mortgage Debt		
Other Debt		
Transitional Child Care Expenses		
Other Transitional Needs		
Household Expenses Needed in the Event of Death		
Capital Retention Replacement Ratio		
Investment Rate of Return		
Marginal Tax Bracket (State & Fed.) Before Retirement		
Marginal Tax Bracket (State & Fed.) After Retirement		
Inflation Rate		
Tax-Adjusted Rate of Return Before Retirement	0.00%	0.00%
Real Rate of Return Before Retirement	0.00%	0.00%
Real Rate of Return During Retirement	0.00%	0.00%

While Children Are at Home		
Number of Survivors		
Expense Reduction Ratio	100.00%	100.00%
Household Expense Need	$ -	$ -
Social Security Survivor Benefits		
Other Income		
Income Need	$ -	$ -
Years Until Youngest Child Turns 18		
Value of Need	**$0.00**	**$0.00**
Educational Needs		
Educational Expenses for Children/Grandchildren		
From Time Children Leave to Age 60 for Survivor		
Number of Survivors	1.00	1.00
Expense Reduction Ratio	100.00%	100.00%
Household Expense Need	$ -	$ -
Social Security Survivor Benefits		
Other Income		
Income Need	$ -	$ -
Years From Last Child 18 to Age 60	60	60
Value of Need	**$0.00**	**$0.00**
From Age 60 to Full Retirement		
Survivor's Full Retirement Age	0	0
Survivor's Age at Death	0	0
Income Need While Retired		
Survivor's Age 60 Social Security Benefit		
Other Income		
Survivor's Earnings		
Income Need	$ -	$ -
Value of Need	**$ -**	**$ -**
From Full Retirement to Death		
Income Need While Retired		
Survivor's Social Security Benefit		
Other Income		
Survivor's Earnings		
Income Need	$ -	$ -
Value of Need	**$ -**	**$ -**
Needs Summary		
Immediate Needs	$0.00	$0.00
While Children Are at Home	$0.00	$0.00
Educational Needs	$0.00	$0.00
From Time Children Leave to Retirement for Survivor	$0.00	$0.00
From Age 60 to Full Retirement	$0.00	$0.00
From Full Retirement to Death	$0.00	$0.00
TOTAL GROSS NEED	**$0.00**	**$0.00**

NET NEED	**$0.00**	**$0.00**
ALTERNATIVE LIFE INSURANCE NEEDS APPROACHES		
HUMAN LIFE VALUE APPROACH		
Gross Need	$0.00	$0.00
Net Need (Subtracting Current Insurance & Assets)	*$0.00*	*$0.00*
INFLATION ADJUSTED HUMAN LIFE VALUE APPROACH		
Gross Need	$0.00	$0.00
Net Need (Subtracting Current Insurance & Assets)	*$0.00*	*$0.00*
CAPITAL RETENTION APPROACH		
Gross Need		
Net Need (Subtracting Current Insurance & Assets)		
CAPITAL RETENTION APPROACH ALTERNATIVE		
Gross Need		
Net Need (Subtracting Current Insurance & Assets)		
INCOME RETENTION APPROACH		
Ratio Reduced Current Living Expenses Until Retirement	$0.00	$0.00
Investment Income Until Retirement	$0.00	$0.00
Spouse Income Until Retirement	$0.00	$0.00
Pre-Retirement Social Security and Other Survivor Benefits	$0.00	$0.00
Yearly Income Need	$0.00	$0.00
Gross Need	$0.00	$0.00
Net Need (Subtracting Current Insurance & Assets)	*$0.00*	*$0.00*
10x GROSS INCOME APPROACH		
Gross Need	$0.00	$0.00
Net Need (Subtracting Current Insurance & Assets)	*$0.00*	*$0.00*
Weighted Average Need		
Needs Approach, HLV, CR, & IR Average		

Planning Strategy 2: Recommend a Whole Life Policy

Once a client's life insurance need has been estimated, a financial planner's attention usually changes to identifying appropriate life insurance products to meet the need. For a client who demands greater product certainty, purchasing a whole life policy provides a fixed annual premium, guaranteed cash value, known rate of return, and guaranteed death benefit. Clients who are considered a substandard risk often find that whole life is the only type of cash value policy available. It is important to note, however, that whole life insurance does not allow clients to control the rate of return earned on cash values in the policy. Typically, the rate of return is quite modest—generally not more than five percent annualized. Furthermore, both face value and premium are fixed, which reduces policy flexibility.

Planning Strategy 3: Recommend a Universal Life Policy

Universal life provides clients with the opportunity to earn a conservative rate of return greater than that offered in a whole life policy. This strategy should be considered for clients who desire a guaranteed fixed rate of return with the opportunity to earn more as the investment performance of the insurance company improves. Universal life also provides clients with some flexibility in terms of changing the annual premium.

Keep in mind that universal life insurance does not allow a client to fully manage assets held in the policy—and consequently the rates of return—in the cash account. Also, it is unlikely that a client will earn more than a one to two percent real return over an extended period of time. The greatest shortcoming associated with universal life policies, however, is that unless a policy is properly funded and possibly prefunded, it is possible for the coverage to **lapse** (i.e., that coverage be terminated) because of nonpayment of premium and/or a reduction in cash value due to low rates of return earned on the cash account. Although lapsing is possible with any form of universal life policy, the flexibility associated with the frequency and amount of premium payments could make this a greater risk for some clients.

Planning Strategy 4: Recommend a Variable Life Policy

This strategy offers clients the opportunity to manage their investments in the policy's cash account, which makes it possible to earn a higher tax-advantaged rate of return. More diversification is possible than that provided by a whole life or universal life policy. Variable life insurance is appropriate for clients who demand some guarantee in terms of annual premium but are willing to assume greater investment risk over time. It is worth noting that variable life insurance is relatively inflexible. Premiums are fixed on a yearly basis, regardless of how well the cash value is invested, and the death benefit is typically fixed.

Planning Strategy 5: Recommend a Variable Universal Life (VUL) Policy

Variable universal life (VUL) insurance is the most flexible type of cash value policy. Premiums can be changed annually. A client can also direct the investments held within the policy's cash account, and the death benefit can grow to exceed the face value. It is also possible to skip premium payments if the policy account earns a sufficiently high rate of return. The use of a VUL also provides high-income clients with an opportunity to maximize diversified tax-advantaged savings. For example, high earning clients can quickly maximize contributions to qualified retirement plans. Although clients will not receive an immediate reduction in taxable income, contributions to a VUL can be (1) quite large in comparison to qualified plans and (2) provide maximum tax deferral across time. A client with an above-average financial risk tolerance may find this strategy appealing because a VUL will allow the client to invest the cash held in the policy more aggressively.

Keep in mind, however, that whenever a VUL policy is sold, the insurance company must provide a cash value growth illustration to the client; some illustrations can be overly optimistic. The premium, based partially on the assumed rate of return, can, in reality, be too low to fully fund the policy. A policy that assumes high returns in policy subaccounts can end up being underfunded as a result of lower realized market returns achieved over a given period. If a VUL policy becomes underfunded, the insurance company will require the client to increase the premium. Additionally, a VUL strategy can also subject a client to relatively high administrative, insurance, and subaccount fees. Consequently, a client will need to obtain above-average returns on investments just to cover administrative, premium, and interest costs.

Planning Strategy 6: Recommend a Single-Premium Variable Universal Life Policy

This strategy allows a client to pay a one-time premium that will result in a higher guaranteed face value in the future. Some financial planners recommend this strategy as part of an estate reduction plan that allows a client to reposition assets to reduce estate taxes or to leverage assets for gifts to beneficiaries or charities. For example, an average fifty-year-old client can use a $10,000 one-time premium to purchase between $25,000 and $30,000 of life insurance. As with any variable life insurance strategy, this approach can fail if the realized rate of return earned in the cash account falls below projections. Also, a single-premium policy is generally classified as a modified endowment contract (subject to less favorable tax treatment), which can make implementation of the strategy problematic.

Planning Strategy 7: Recommend a One-Year Term Policy

The average client who does not require a forced savings or large tax deferral benefit may not need a cash value policy (i.e., whole, universal, variable, or VUL policy). Purchasing a term policy may be a more appropriate strategy. Buying a one-year term policy provides the maximum amount of pure coverage at the lowest annual cost. This purchasing approach is appropriate for a client who needs to minimize the impact of income loss due to death over short periods of time. For example, this strategy satisfies a temporary need caused by a change in employment or other life-cycle event that dramatically increases the need for insurance protection. Without a **guaranteed renewable provision** (i.e., the right to renew the policy on the policy's anniversary date at a higher premium without fear of denial), this strategy can expose a client to the possibility of becoming uninsurable when the policy terminates. This strategy also eliminates multiple-year cost savings and guarantees that the client will pay a higher premium when the new policy is issued.

Planning Strategy 8: Recommend a Multiyear Term Policy

Rather than recommend that a client purchase a one-year term policy, nearly all financial planners who utilize term solutions recommend multiyear term policies. This strategy allows a client with a limited insurance budget to purchase the maximum amount of pure life insurance over an extended period of time. The annual premium is fixed for the term of the policy. Policies can be purchased with terms ranging from two to forty years. Usually, this strategy is presented as a **buy term and invest the difference** tactic based on the term policy premium and premium for a comparable cash value policy. Essentially, a client who buys term and invests the difference takes what would have been paid for a cash value policy and invests the difference between that premium and the cost of the term policy in a basket of stocks and bonds. Over time, the value of the investments held outside of the insurance should grow large enough to replace the face value of the term policy when the insurance coverage expires. This strategy can fail when a client fails to actually save the difference in premiums or when the investment rate of return achieved on the savings is below expectations. Regardless, however, because of the term nature of the insurance, coverage ceases at the end of the term, and the annual premium will increase upon policy renewal.

Planning Strategy 9: Recommend a Return-of-Premium Term Policy

A return-of-premium term insurance policy is a hybrid between pure term and whole life insurance. These polices guarantee to repay all premiums to the policy owner if the insured outlives the term of the policy. If the insured dies during the term of the policy, the full-face value is paid to the named beneficiary. This type of policy appeals to young, healthy clients who want some kind of return on their premium investment but do not want to spend the extra premium to purchase a cash value life insurance policy. Return-of-premium polices offer two significant advantages. First, the cost can be as much as 60 to 70 percent less than the premium for a cash value policy. Second, the returned premium can be received on a tax-free basis.

The primary disadvantage associated with this strategy deals with a client's self-discipline. If a client allows a policy to lapse, the return-of-premium option is of little value. Returned premiums seldom exceed 35 percent of actual premiums paid if a policy lapses. Another disadvantage is that the premiums repaid do not earn interest during the term of the policy. Therefore, the inflation-adjusted "time value of money" of the returned premiums can be greatly reduced depending on the term of the policy. Obviously, the longer the term, the greater the loss of purchasing power. However, some money received can be better than no money returned.

Planning Strategy 10: Utilize Insurance through a Group Term Policy

This strategy is designed for clients who are able to purchase life insurance on a pretax, group-rate basis, which makes the insurance very affordable. Coverage is typically available to any employee (or in some cases, members of fraternal, professional, or other groups), regardless of insurability factors. This provides at least a minimum level of insurance to pay for final debts and expenses. Aside from the benefits of guaranteed insurability and relatively low cost, lack of coverage diversification can be a major disadvantage of this strategy. If most or all of a client's life insurance is purchased through an employer, conversion to individual coverage is typically unavailable should the client cease working. Even a change in position with a reduction in salary can affect insurance coverage and cost. Payment of income taxes on employer-provided premiums (generally for coverage in excess of $50,000), also known as **Section 79 imputed income**, is another potential disadvantage.[1]

Planning Strategy 11: Combine a Group Term Policy with a Low-Cost Private or Individual Policy

This combination insurance strategy is most appropriate for clients who have access to low priced group term life insurance, but also want the assurance of supplemental, continuous coverage of a private policy. This strategy is also appropriate for clients who anticipate leaving employment before retirement, or those who fear a **substandard risk classification** in the future due to health habits, medical history, or work history. As a precaution, insurance diversification and lifetime coverage can be assured by purchasing a cash value policy or guaranteed renewable term rather than depending solely on employer-provided coverage. The primary disadvantage associated with this strategy is that the additional insurance will probably be more expensive than group coverage and will not offer the ability to purchase coverage with pretax dollars.

Furthermore, to be most cost effective, the purchase should be made at a relatively young age.

Planning Strategy 12: Combine a "Base" Cash Value Policy with Group or Private Term Policies

This combination strategy offers the guarantee of permanent insurance protection coupled with the lower cost options provided by group and/or private term insurance. Combining types of coverage offers clients increased flexibility to add lower cost term coverage during periods of high insurance coverage need (e.g., when children are young or in college), while maintaining a smaller "base" amount of permanent protection. Keep in mind that during the early years of strategy implementation, when client earnings may be lower, the higher cost, cash value policy can limit the amount of coverage a client can afford relative to the amount of term insurance that could have been purchased.

Planning Strategy 13: Include Conversion and Renewability Features in Term Policies

An attractive feature offered in most term polices is a **conversion provision**, which allows the policy owner to exchange a term policy for a cash value policy without proof of insurability. This rider is valuable for those who think that they might become uninsurable in the future or face a significantly higher risk classification. When purchasing a term policy, it is also possible to obtain a **guaranteed renewable provision**, which guarantees that the policy owner can renew the policy for an extended period of time without proof of insurability. A conversion provision usually has time limits. The guaranteed renewable provision does not guarantee a fixed premium rate, only the ability to lengthen the term of the policy regardless of underwriting considerations. An alternative for clients interested in locking in a steady annual premium involves purchasing a cash value policy.

Planning Strategy 14: Include a Disability Waiver Provision when Purchasing a Policy

Almost all life insurance policies provide a **disability waiver provision**. This optional provision enables an insurance policy to remain in effect during a period of a disability without the additional cost of continuing premium payments. Essentially, this provision supplies a waiver of premiums if the policy owner becomes disabled. This strategy is worth consideration because the probability of becoming disabled far exceeds the probability of premature death during most of a client's working years. Consequently, from a cost/benefit analysis perspective, this provision is generally worth the expense. A variation of the idea of continuing coverage for the client is a **waiver of premium for unemployment** if an individual is unemployed and eligible for unemployment benefits. Restrictions apply regarding how long premiums will be paid or how often the waiver can be used.

As with other policy provisions, the inclusion of a disability waiver or the unemployment waiver will increase the annual cost of the policy, sometimes substantially. The unemployment waiver provision may be offered as a no-cost rider or added for a fee. When recommending any rider, a client's unique situation and risk tolerance must be considered in the cost-benefit analysis in consultation with an insurance professional.

Planning Strategy 15: Beware of Modified Endowment Contracts

Modified endowment contract (MEC) status applies to any contract purchased after June 1988 that fails the **seven-pay test**. As defined by Internal Revenue Code section 7702A, the seven-pay test refers to any contract "if the accumulated amount paid under the contract at any time during the first seven contract years exceeds the sum of the net level premiums which would have been paid on or before such time if the contract provided for paid-up future benefits after the payment of seven level annual premiums." This basically means that if a contract could have been self-supporting after seven years based on the premiums of the first seven years and additional amounts were deposited, some of the tax benefits of the life insurance contract will be lost. The purpose of the test is to discourage policyholders from making very large premium payments during the first seven years of the contract to create a **paid-up policy** that leverages the tax advantaged status of the deposits. If a policy is an MEC, any death benefit provided under the contract will qualify for income tax-free treatment. However, any distribution—whether a loan, withdrawal, surrender, or settlement from an MEC—will be taxed on an income-first basis. Furthermore, if the insured is less than age 59½, a 10 percent penalty will also apply to the taxable portion of most distributions.

Planning Strategy 16: Determine the Cost per Thousand Paid for a Cash Value Policy

Financial planners are commonly asked to review cash value policies in terms of premium cost. When a policy is deemed too expensive, a 1035 exchange may be an appropriate recommendation. A number of approaches can be used to evaluate the cost-effectiveness of cash value life insurance policies. Commonly used methods include the **traditional net cost method**,[2] the **interest-adjusted net cost method**,[3] the **internal rate of return yield method**,[4] and the **yearly price per thousand method** (also known as the **yearly rate of return method**).[5] The yearly-price-per-thousand formula can be used to answer the "maintain or replace" question.

The information needed to calculate the yearly-price-per-thousand formula is generally available from the insurance company underwriting the policy. The yearly-price-per-thousand method formula is:

$$\text{YPT} = \left[\frac{[(\text{PMT} + \text{CV}_0) * (1 + i)] - (\text{CV}_1 + \text{Div})}{(\text{DB} - \text{CV}_1) * (0.001)} \right]$$

YPT = yearly cost per thousand in coverage

PMT = annual premium payment

CV_0 = cash value at beginning of the year

CV_1 = cash value at end of the year

i = projected after-tax rate of return

Div   = current policy dividend

DB   = death benefit (most often face value)

The interest rate used in the formula should be the rate of interest that can be earned in another investment with similar safety and liquidity characteristics as those offered in a life insurance policy. The rate of return should be equivalent to a net after-tax yield. Once the cost per thousand of coverage is calculated, this amount should be compared to benchmark prices as illustrated in Figure 5.2 as an example.

Figure 5.2. Sample Benchmark Premium Prices Based on the Yearly-price-per-thousand Formula

Age of Client	Yearly Price per $1,000 (Benchmark)
Less than 30	$1.50
30–34	$2.00
35–39	$3.00
40–44	$4.00
45–49	$6.50
50–54	$10.00
55–59	$19.00
60–64	$29.00
65–69	$39.00
70–74	$50.00
75–79	$80.00
80–84	$129.00
Source: Adapted from Belth, J. M. *Life Insurance: A Consumer's Handbook*, 2nd Ed. (Bloomington, IN: Indiana University Press, 1985).	

The yearly-price-per-thousand formula results in three outcomes:

- If the cost is less than the benchmark price, the client should maintain the policy.

- If the cost is greater than the benchmark price but less than two times the benchmark price, the client should still retain the policy.

- Only when the cost per thousand is greater than two times the benchmark price should a client consider replacing or exchanging a policy; the new policy should be priced favorably according to the yearly-price-per-thousand formula guidelines.

Consider the following example. Tucker is 36 years old. Tucker is currently paying $13.11 per $1,000 of life insurance coverage, whereas the recommended benchmark for a male his age is $3.00 per $1,000 of life insurance coverage. Given that the premium cost per $1,000 of coverage is more than four times greater than the recommended yearly-price-per-thousand benchmark, and holding other factors constant, a recommendation to replace the policy (assuming the coverage is needed) should be made.

$$YPT = \left[\frac{[(PMT + CV_0) * (1 + i)] - (CV_1 + Div)}{(DB - CV_1) * (0.001)} \right]$$

$$YPT = \left[\frac{[(600 + 475) * (1.069)] - (500 + 0)}{(500,000 - 500) * (0.001)} \right] = \$13.11$$

Planning Strategy 17: Use Nonforfeiture Options in Cash Value Policies Effectively

When a cash value life insurance policy is terminated, the policy holder may be entitled to additional benefits, which are called nonforfeiture options. State laws specify standard nonforfeiture options that insurance companies must offer policyholders. A policy owner may use the cash in the account to purchase a paid-up cash value policy. The new face value of the policy will almost always be lower than the original policy. Alternatively, the policy owner may use the cash value to purchase extended-term insurance. The term of the new policy will be based on the amount of insurance that can be purchased with the cash value. An example of a nonforfeiture table is shown in Figure 5.3.

Figure 5.3. Sample Whole Life Insurance Nonforfeiture Table

End of Policy Year	Cash/Loan Value	Paid-up Insurance	Extended-term Insurance	
			Years	Days
1	$14	$30	0	152
2	$174	$450	4	182
3	$338	$860	8	65
4	$506	$1,250	10	344
5	$676	$1,640	12	360
6	$879	$2,070	14	335
7	$1,084	$2,500	16	147
8	$1,293	$2,910	17	207
9	$1,504	$3,300	18	177
10	$1,719	$3,690	19	78
11	$1,908	$4,000	19	209
12	$2,099	$4,300	19	306
13	$2,294	$4,590	20	8
14	$2,490	$4,870	20	47
15	$2,690	$5,140	20	65

16	$2,891	$5,410	20	66
17	$3,095	$5,660	20	52
18	$3,301	$5,910	20	27
19	$3,508	$6,150	19	358
20	$3,718	$6,390	19	317
Age 60	$4,620	$7,200	18	111
Age 65	$5,504	$7,860	16	147

Source: Sample Life Insurance Policy. Education and Community Services, American Council of Life Insurance, Washington, DC.

In this example, the policy has a $10,000 face value. The nonforfeiture options include:

1. Requesting the insurance company return the **cash surrender value** of the policy, as shown in the second column. After ten years the amount returned will be $1,719. The value of the cash received in excess of the net paid premiums is subject to federal and state income taxation.

2. Requesting the cash value of the policy be used to purchase a fully **paid-up cash value policy**. This will result in a significantly reduced face value policy, as shown in the third column. If this choice is made after ten years, the new policy face value will be $3,690. The benefit, however, is that no additional premiums will have to be paid.

3. Requesting the cash value can be used to purchase a **fully paid term policy**. The face value of the original cash value policy is retained in this case. The length of the term policy is then determined by the amount of the cash value available in the policy. If this election is made after ten years, a $10,000 face value policy will be in effect for nineteen years and seventy-eight days.

Planning Skill 18: Use a Section 1035 Exchange Option as a Way to Obtain Different Coverage

A **Section 1035 exchange** is an alternative to using a nonforfeiture option within a life insurance policy. Internal Revenue Code Section 1035 allows for a policy owner to exchange a life insurance policy (contract) for another life insurance contract on a tax-free basis. Five types of Section 1035 exchanges are allowed:

1. A currently owned life policy for a newly issued policy;

2. An endowment contract policy for another endowment contract, with certain restrictions, or for an annuity contract;

3. A currently owned life policy for an annuity contract;

4. An annuity contract for another annuity contract; or

5. An annuity or life insurance contract for a long-term care contract.

The process of transferring policies on a tax-free basis is similar to conducting a custodian-to-custodian rollover of qualified retirement plan assets. A Section 1035 tax-free exchange strategy should be considered whenever a currently owned cash value policy is disadvantaged in terms of performance or premium cost.

Planning Strategy 19: Know the Different Options to Access Policy Benefits and Avoid Income Taxes

State and federal laws offer consumers options for terminating life insurance policies and accessing benefits within life insurance policies prior to the death of the insured. The decision to terminate or take distributions from a life insurance policy can be prompted by a variety of reasons, including the need to pay unexpected medical bills, to reduce cash flow expenses, or to meet other short- and long-term client needs. Distributions can be taken as a loan or as a 1035 exchange or as a distribution of cash held in a policy. Sometimes a distribution can entail receiving some of a policy's face value prior to the death of the insured. Regardless of the manner in which a distribution is made, a client's need for life insurance protection, available cash flow to pay premiums, and the tax implications of alternatives must be considered. The complexity of these decisions can often prompt collaboration with a client's insurance professional or tax consultant. A review of these options is shown in Figure 5.4.

Figure 5.4. Options for Accessing Life Insurance Policy Proceeds

Action	Immediate Benefit	Effect on Face Value	Effect on Premium	Tax Consequences
Nonforfeiture – surrender	Cash value accumulated in the policy	Policy contract ends	Ceases	Taxes due if the proceeds exceed the expenses of the policy
Nonforfeiture – paid up term		Face value remains constant, but only for the specified term	Ceases	None
Nonforfeiture – paid up whole life		Face value reduced based on policy cash	Ceases	None
Accelerated Death Benefits • Terminal • Critical • Chronic	Percentage of face value available to the insured	Reduced to percentage remaining, paid at death of the insured to the beneficiary	Continues	Generally, none, except in the case of critical care if the amount exceeds the tax free daily rate set by the IRS

Viatical Settlement (fees may apply)	Percentage of face value available to the terminally ill insured	At death of insured, full face value paid to the viatical settlement company	Ceases, paid by settlement company	Generally, none
Life Settlement (fees may apply)	Percentage of face value available to the elderly insured	At death of insured, full face value paid to the life settlement company	Ceases, paid by settlement company	Taxes due if the proceeds exceed the expenses of the policy

Planning Strategy 20: Structure a Life Insurance Contract to Avoid Future Problems

Determining the face amount of coverage and the specific policy or policies to purchase—in other words, the strategy—is not enough information to provide a client. A recommendation should include more details. Specifically, a recommendation should go beyond the strategy to clearly state how a life insurance policy contract should be structured. Considerations unique to life insurance recommendations include:

- Who owns the policy;

- Who receives the benefit from the policy; and

- How policy proceeds will be disbursed.

This attention to the structure of a policy contract promotes smooth and timely asset transfer by maximizing tax benefits and minimizing legal issues upon the death of the insured. When purchasing a policy, care must be taken to consider the income, gifting, and estate tax implications of potential scenarios. Periodically, during client-financial planner review meetings, it is important to reconsider policy beneficiaries to ensure that previous choices still match a client's wishes. A review may also be necessary after significant life or family events. The following reminders can be used to guide ongoing insurance reviews:

- Avoid having the insured (client) as owner of the policy if the client's estate is likely to be greater than the federal estate tax exclusion amount.

- Avoid naming the policy owner or the owner's estate as beneficiary because of (1) possible estate tax or state inheritance tax implications, (2) lack of protection of the funds from creditors, and (3) delays with the probate court that will make the funds inaccessible.

- Avoid establishing a trust to manage life insurance proceeds and naming an individual as the beneficiary of the policy. The proceeds will go to the beneficiary instead of the trust.

- Avoid delays in updating the policy beneficiary after major life events. In some states, divorce automatically revokes a beneficiary designation naming the ex-spouse. Otherwise, an ex-spouse can receive policy proceeds years after the divorce.

- Avoid naming only a single, primary beneficiary and opt instead for naming a primary beneficiary with one or two contingent beneficiaries. Should a sole beneficiary predecease the insured, the insurance proceeds would then be payable to the estate unless a second in-line contingent beneficiary (or two) is named.

- Avoid naming minor children as beneficiaries unless the will names a guardian or trust to manage the funds on behalf of the children. If the court has to appoint someone, there will be an additional expense—paid from the insurance proceeds.

- Avoid stating a specific amount of policy proceeds to be paid to multiple beneficiaries, opting instead for a stated percentage of the policy proceeds. Because of dividends, outstanding loans, or other variations, the face value of the policy might not, at the time of death, be exactly the face amount initially stated in the distribution.

- Avoid a deliberate or inadvertent policy structure known as "The Unholy Trinity" a/k/a "Goodman Triangle" a/k/a "Triangle Policy" where the owner of the policy, policy beneficiary and insured are all different parties. Adverse gift tax implications can result upon the death of the insured.

Quantitative/Analytical Mini-Case Problems

Theresa Cortez

1. Theresa Cortez is the primary breadwinner for a family of four. Her husband has been unable to work since the onset of severe vertigo over two years ago. Their two children are both in high school and, presumably, college bound. After attending your seminar about life insurance planning, Theresa has come to you to determine whether she has enough life insurance currently in place. Besides a small disability check that her husband receives, she is the only source of income—albeit a good income of $84,000 per year. At your request, she has brought her most recent annual income and expense statement that shows the family's annual expenses of $55,000, annual taxes of $17,000, and savings of $12,000.

   Calculate Theresa's current insurance need using the Human Life Value approach for each of the following four scenarios, assuming her remaining working life is twenty six years and the projected discount rate is 8.0 percent before taxes, compounded daily.

   a. Using her gross income.

   b. Using her gross income and a growth rate of 3.5 percent.

c.   Using her net income.

d.   Using her net income and a growth rate of 3.5 percent.

e.   Which of these four methods will result in the most reasonable estimation of the insurance need?

John Wilson

2.   John Wilson is a forty-year old computer programmer, husband, and father of four. He wants to use the capital retention approach to determine how much life insurance he should purchase. Because of his $105,000 salary and the need to care for the family's four children, his wife does not work outside the home. The family's current annual living expenses are approximately $75,000, including $8,000 in annual IRA contributions. John prefers to use the capital retention approach (CRA) so that he can be reasonably assured that his family will not exhaust the proceeds of a life insurance policy. However, he also wants to consider the possible reduction in expenses and apply a 70 percent replacement ratio to the calculation.

a.   Calculate John's insurance need using the capital retention approach and an after-tax discount rate of 5.5 percent (assume end-of period payment of benefits).

b.   Calculate John's insurance need using the human life value approach (HLV), an after-tax discount rate of 5.5 percent, and a remaining working life of twenty five years (assume end-of period payment of benefits).

c.   After your presentation, John was bewildered about why the HLV and CRA calculations resulted in significantly different insurance needs. Using the two formulas as a guide, explain to John why this result occurred.

Morgan Hanna

3.   Morgan Hanna is a thirty two-year old nurse. She is in good health and has applied for a new cash value life insurance policy. She is interested in knowing whether she should surrender her current policy and purchase the new policy offered through an AAA-rated firm. If all of the contract and company characteristics are similar, and the current face value of her policy is sufficient, should she maintain or replace her current policy? Assume the following factors:

- Yearly premium: $1,900

- Cash value at the beginning of the period: $13,456

- Cash value at the end of the period: $13,927

- Projected after-tax rate of return: 3.50 percent

- Current policy dividend: $350

- Death benefit: $200,000

Stephen Watkins

4. Stephen plans to retire in twenty years at age sixty seven, at which time he will be in the 24 percent marginal income tax bracket. He is considering the purchase of a $200,000 face value whole life policy. The annual premium is $4,000. Alternatively, he is thinking that he could buy a twenty-year $200,000 face value term policy for $500 per year.

    a. If he implements a buy term and uses 'the invest the difference' strategy, and can earn 8 percent annually in a Roth IRA (assume he saves annually for twenty years), how much will be in his account when the term policy expires?

    b. If Stephen were to die at age sixty eight (one year after the term policy expires and he has stopped saving), which strategy (buy the cash value policy or buy the term policy and invest the difference) is the better choice if he continues to save in a Roth IRA?

    c. If instead Stephen were to purchase a twenty five-year term policy for $500 per year in premiums, and he were to die at age seventy three (one year after the term policy expires and he has stopped saving), which strategy (buy the cash value policy or buy the term policy and invest the difference) is the better choice if he continues to save in a Roth IRA?

    d. Would your answers change if Stephen used a traditional IRA?

    e. Stephen was recently diagnosed with cancer. He underwent treatment and was found to be healthy and cancer free. However, Stephen worries that in the future he might have a reoccurrence, which could affect his chances of obtaining life insurance. If his budget is constrained and he can only afford a twenty-year term policy, what feature(s) or policy rider(s) should he purchase to enable him to continue coverage in the future even if the cancer returns?

Jamal and Chyna Gwynn

5. Your clients, Jamal and Chyna Gwynn, would like you to estimate their life insurance needs based on a comprehensive needs analysis. Their son, Jarius, is currently thirteen years of age. Jamal and Chyna have high hopes for Jarius's future education. They would like to accumulate a $240,000 (in today's dollars) educational savings fund to pay for four years of college. In event of Jamal's or Chyna's passing, they will need $10,000 in transitional child care expenses. When making your estimate, the Gwynns would like to pay off all debt and liabilities at the death of the first spouse. Use the following information to determine the life insurance need for Jamal and Chyna separately:

    • Jamal: Age forty eight; Life Expectancy: Age ninety seven

    • Chyna: Age fifty; Life Expectancy: Age ninety-five

    • Desired Retirement Age: Age sixty two

    • Full Retirement Age: Age sixty seven

    • Earned Income: Jamal $145,000

- Earned Income: Chyna $210,000

- Bonus: Jamal $25,000

- Investment Rate of Return: 7.90 Percent

- Inflation Rate Assumption: 3.00 Percent

- Marginal Federal and State Marginal Tax Rate Before Retirement: 29 Percent

- Marginal Federal and State Marginal Tax Rate After Retirement: 29 Percent

- Final Expenses: Jamal and Chyna $40,000 Each

- Estate Administration: Jamal and Chyna $12,000 Each

- Other Final Needs/Expenses: Jamal and Chyna $20,000 Each

- Jointly Held Credit Card Debt: $45,000

- Jointly Held Installment Debt: $82,000

- Jointly Held Automobile Debt: $19,000

- Jointly Held Mortgage Debt: $345,000

- Jointly Held Other Debt: $190,000

- Transitional Child Care Expenses: $10,000 Each

- Household Expenses Needed in Event of Death: $296,000 Each

- Capital Retention Replacement Ratio: 80 Percent

- Expense Reduction Ratio While Jarius is at Home: 100 Percent

- Social Security Benefits While Jarius is at Home: $0

- Expense Reduction Ratio After Jarius Leaves Home but Survivor Turns Age sixty: 80 Percent

- Social Security Benefits After Jarius Leaves Home but Survivor Turns Age sixty: 80 Percent

- Income Needed from Age sixty to Full Retirement: $190,000 Each

- Income Need While Retired: $190,000 Each

- Social Security Benefit of Survivor: Jamal $42,000

- Social Security Benefit of Survivor: Chyna $39,000

- Other Income in Retirement: $80,000 Each

- In-force Cash Value Life Insurance: Jamal $300,000

- In-force Term and Cash Value Life Insurance: Chyna $500,000

- Combined Retirement Assets: $1,500,000

- Combined Other Savings: $200,000

- Other Assets: $0

    a. Approximately how much additional life insurance does Jamal need?

    b. Approximately how much additional life insurance does Chyna need?

    c. How do these estimates compare to the need from the human life value approach? What helps explain the difference?

Chapter Resources

Baldwin, B., *The New Life Insurance Investment Advisor* (New York: McGraw Hill, 2002).

Belth, J. M., *Life Insurance: A Consumer's Handbook*, 2nd ed. (Bloomington, IN: Indiana University Press, 1985).

General life insurance and tax source: *Tax Facts on Life Insurance & Employee Benefits* (Cincinnati, OH: National Underwriter Company, published annually).

Leimberg, S. R.; Buck, K.; and Doyle, R.J. *The Tools & Techniques of Life Insurance Planning*, 6th ed. (Cincinnati, OH: National Underwriter Company, 2015).

Life and Health Insurance Foundation for Education, general life insurance information (www. naifa.org/consumer/life.cfm).

Endnotes

1. Issues related to Section 79 imputed income are addressed in Chapter 3.

2. The traditional net cost method subtracts total premiums paid from a policy's projected dividends plus cash surrender value. What remains is divided by the projected holding period. This equates to an annual cost of ownership. One criticism of this methodology is that the calculation does not account for the time value of money associated with premium payments. This evaluation procedure is not widely used because the calculation often results in a negative cost of ownership.

3. This method of evaluation adjusts the traditional net cost estimate for the time value of money associated with premium payments.

4. Sometimes called the net payment cost index, this approach assumes that premiums and policy dividends are accrued over a set period of time, typically 20 years, with a fixed rate of return (e.g., 4 percent) paid on the policy cash value. Total dividends are then subtracted from the total of all premium payments. This figure is then averaged, using a time value of money adjustment, to estimate an average annual net premium cost.

5. Joseph Belth originally developed the yearly price per thousand method. A complete description of the method can be found in Belth, J. M., *Life Insurance: A Consumer's Handbook*, 2nd Ed. (Bloomington, IN: Indiana University Press, 1985).

Chapter 6

Health Insurance Planning

Learning Objectives

- Learning Objective 1: Evaluate a client's health insurance need.

- Learning Objective 2: Integrate health insurance into a client's risk management strategy.

- Learning Objective 3: Conduct a health insurance needs analysis.

CFP® Principal Knowledge Topics

- CFP Topic: D.23. Analysis and Evaluation of Risk Exposures.
- CFP Topic: D.24. Health Insurance and Health Care Cost Management (Individual).
- CFP Topic: D.30. Insurance Needs Analysis.

Chapter Equations

There are no equations in this chapter.

HEALTH INSURANCE PLANNING STRATEGIES

Health insurance is a topic included in nearly all comprehensive financial plans. It is important to keep in mind that, unlike life insurance, financial planners typically have limited control over the products and procedures used in the context of health insurance planning. Typically, clients gain access to health insurance through an employer or a governmental exchange. This means that financial planners are most often called on to help choose between health insurance plans based on expected costs and benefits, associated health savings options, and private market solutions.

Even so, it is important for a financial planner to integrate appropriate health insurance planning strategies into overall risk management recommendations. As with all areas of financial planning practice, there are numerous strategies that can be used to help a client accomplish his or her goals. It is a financial planner's ability to synthesize and evaluate client data that leads to optimized recommendations. Within the health insurance domain, it is important to exhibit a thorough understanding of insurance contracts, especially the way benefits are often coordinated among contracts. Additionally, a competent financial planner must be able to differentiate between and among tax-advantaged accounts to meet a client's needs. Increasing a client's confidence to handle the monetary loss associated with a serious or chronic illness, and to minimize the lingering financial and emotional effects of that loss, solidifies a strong client-financial planner working relationship.

The following array of strategies represents a cross-section of approaches often used by financial planners to meet a client's health insurance needs over a client's life cycle. Understanding a client's needs, as well as preferences, related to health care coverage can further inform the review of specific strategies. When completing case work, a financial planner should anticipate questions related to appropriate strategy selection, recommendation implementation, and ongoing monitoring of recommendations.

Planning Strategy 1: Define the Terminology of Health Insurance

A competent financial planner should be familiar with common terms and phrases used in the health insurance planning process. The following include some of the most widely used health insurance terms and definitions:

- current **deductible**—amount the insured pays before the insurance company contributes;

- current **copayment**—fixed fee the insured pays for services in addition to what the insurance company will pay;

- current **coinsurance**—percentage of service expense paid by the insured above the deductible amount (e.g., if a plan has a 20 percent coinsurance clause, the insured is responsible for paying the deductible and 20 percent of each bill up to the maximum annual stop-loss limit);

- current **stop-loss limit**—the maximum amount of out-of-pocket expenses paid by an insured, which includes deductibles, copayments, and coinsurance (i.e., cost sharing);

- excluded coverage—what a plan will not pay for (e.g., elective cosmetic surgery);

- out-of-network restrictions, freedom of choice, network of providers, and cost differentials if a HMO, PPO, POS, or EPO;

- current annual **premium**—the cost of insurance; and

- access to COBRA and HIPAA benefits (discussed later in the chapter).

Planning Strategy 2: Determine the Impact of the Patient Protection and Affordable Care Act (PPACA) of 2010 on a Client's Health Plan

The **Patient Protection and Affordable Care** Act of 2010 (often called Obama Care) changed the way health insurance planning is conducted. The Act established Health Insurance Exchanges, expanded Medicaid coverage, and provided incentives for employers to offer health insurance. Additionally, the Act strengthened consumer protections, limited premium increases, encouraged preventive care, and required all Americans to purchase health insurance. The following is a summary of the principal elements imbedded in the Act (more information can be found at www.healthcare.gov):

- The Act effectively eliminated insurance restrictions based on pre-existing conditions; waiting periods are now prohibited.

- Programs are now in place to help those who are fifty-five or older obtain insurance prior to enrolling in Medicare at age sixty-five.

- Tax credits up to 50 percent of employer contributions to health insurance plan premiums help small businesses offer plans.

- Children up to age twenty-six may stay on their parents' insurance regardless of financial dependence, student status, marital status, employment, or residency (some states, like New York, have even more generous laws).

- Lifetime limits on coverage are now prohibited.

- The Act banned rescissions in which insurance companies could drop someone from coverage due to a paperwork mistake after they got sick.

- Health insurance plans must provide preventative services without copayments, coinsurance, or deductibles.

- The Act formalized an appeals process for individuals and groups who feel that their insurance company has denied a claim in error.

- The choice of a primary care provider is now guaranteed, assuming the provider is available to accept new patients.

- Direct access to OB/GYN services is guaranteed; further, insurance companies can no longer force an insured to use a network OB/GYN service provider.

- The Act prohibits employer sponsored plans from excluding employee participation based on salary or income.

- Lower income households may receive subsidies to make health insurance premiums more affordable.

- The Act guarantees everyone access to health insurance without regard to age, sex, occupation, or health status.

Planning Strategy 3: Describe the Key Differences Between and Among Common Health Insurance Plans

Figure 6.1 provides a comparison of the five primary health insurance plans available in the marketplace. As illustrated, **preferred provider organization (PPO)** plans, **point-of-service (POS)** plans, and **health maintenance organization (HMO)** plans are three common **managed care** designs. A PPO offers the most flexibility for those seeking health care, whereas a HMO is typically the most restrictive. The hybrid POS plan shares features of a PPO and HMO. An **exclusive provider organization (EPO)** plan is another type of plan that is more restrictive in its provider network than a HMO.

Figure 6.1. Comparison of Health Insurance Plans

Plan Type	Traditional Indemnity Plan	Preferred Provider Organization (PPO)	Point-of-Service (POS) Plan	Health Maintenance Organization (HMO)	High-Deductible Health Plan (HDHP)
Cost	Highest	Middle-high	Middle-low	Lowest of managed cost plans	Lowest of all plans available
Physician Choice	Least restrictive, but restrictions are increasing to control costs	Restricted to network; may go outside network with higher deductible and copayment	Restricted, but insured may see out-of-network provider for additional cost	Restricted	Depends on whether the HDHP is an indemnity, PPO, POS, or HMO plan, but certain requirements must be met to qualify as a HDHP. Offers copays for office visits only after the deductible has been met. For 2020, the minimum deductible for one insured is $1,350; $2,700 for families. Out-of-network providers can cost more than in-network providers.

Hospital Choice	Least restrictive, but restrictions are increasing to control costs	Restricted to network; may go outside network with higher deductible and copayment	Restricted to network	Restricted	Similar to a physician choice plan, the choice depends on whether the HDHP is an indemnity, PPO, POS, or HMO plan, but certain requirements must be met to qualify as a HDHP. Offers copays for office visits only after deductible has been met. For 2020, the minimum deductible for one insured is $1,350; $2,700 for families. Out-of-network providers can cost more than in-network providers.
Appropriate for Whom?	Households that demand maximum choice	Households that would like some choice but with lower expenses than a traditional plan	Households that use medical services frequently, but occasionally visit out-of-network providers	Households that use medical services frequently	Households that are • Generally healthy and medical expenses are limited to preventive care *OR* not healthy and typically hit the lower limits on catastrophic coverage in other plans and incur out-of-pocket expenses for exclusions (e.g., drug or other costs); • Financially disciplined savers who can fund the annual maximum of the HSA ($3,550 for individuals; $7,100 for families in 2020) to cover expenses; and • Comfortable with in-network providers to maximize savings.

Among Firms Offering Health Benefits, Availability of this Plan, 2016-2017[1]	3 percent	50 percent	24 percent	16 percent	23 percent
Estimated Annual Group Plan Cost for a Family, 2016-2017	$20,000+	$19,500	$18,297	$17,978	$16,737

[1] Source: Kaiser Family Foundation. 2016 Employer Health Benefits Survey. Available at: https://www.kff.org/health-costs/report/2016-employer-health-benefits-survey/: Because some firms offer more than one type of plan columns do not sum to 100 percent

Sources:

- Lyke, B., & Peterson, C. L. (2009). *Tax-Advantaged Accounts for Health Care Expenses: Side-by-Side Comparison.* Washington, DC: Congressional Research Service.
- IRS Publication 969, *Health Savings Accounts and Other Tax-Favored Health Plans.*
- U.S. Department of the Treasury. Resource Center-Health Savings Accounts (HSAs). Available at: https://www.treasury.gov/resource-center/faqs/Taxes/Pages/Health-Savings-Accounts.aspx

Planning Strategy 4: Establish an HSA in Conjunction with a Qualified HDHP (For clients aged sixty-four or younger and not a dependent of another individual)

This strategy works well for self-employed clients, for those without access to cost efficient group plans, and those with access to qualifying **high deductible health plans** (HDHPs). The combination of an **HSA** and an **HDHP** offers several benefits to those who (1) have minimal health care needs and (2) want greater control over the cost of medical care and insurance. Because of the high-deductible associated with the plan, premiums are significantly lower than typical health care plans.

To qualify as a HDHP in 2020, an individual insurance plan must have at least a $1,400 deductible and an annual stop-loss limit of no more than $6,750. For a family plan to qualify, the deductible must be at least $2,800, with a maximum stop-loss limit of $13,800. Advantages associated with the use of an HSA include:

- An HSA is similar to an individual retirement account (IRA) for health care-related expenses. The plan provides access to catastrophic health coverage, while allowing an above-the-line tax deduction for post-tax contributions or a tax-exemption for pretax contributions to the account.

- An HSA can be funded up to the 2020 contribution limit of $3,550 for an individual and $7,100 for a family, with pretax salary reductions or with employer contributions that may be available through a Section 125 Plan.

- Contributions are not subject to state or federal income tax or FICA withholding. A catch-up contribution of $1,000 is also available for persons aged fifty-five to sixty-four.

- Assets in the account grow tax deferred as they accumulate.

- Distributions for qualifying medical expenses are excluded from income.

- Any funds remaining in the account not used for medical expenses can be used after age sixty-five for any purpose without penalty.

- Other allowable coverage includes dental and vision insurance as well as coverage for a specific disease or illness if it pays a specific dollar amount when the policy is triggered.

- Beginning in 2020, clients with HSA assets (as well as those with FSAs and HRAs, may purchase over-the-counter medications and receive reimbursement without the needing a prescription. This provision includes expenses for menstrual care products (the employer plan document must be written to allow for these reimbursements under IRC 105(b)). When these medical expenses are covered in a health plan, such expenses may not be reimbursed.

There are drawbacks associated with HSAs:

- Only clients covered by a qualifying HDHP are eligible for an HSA.

- Annual contribution limits, as well as the allowable above-the-line tax deduction, are limited, but contribution limits do increase annually.

- Distributions made for any reason other than to pay for qualified medical expenses are subject to income taxes. In addition, such distributions are subject to a 20 percent penalty unless made after death, disability, or age sixty-five.

- Premiums paid for a high-deductible health plan may not be used as an itemized tax deduction.

- Also, a participant must be younger than age sixty-five, the age of eligibility for Medicare.

- In addition, an account cannot be established if the participant is a dependent of another person.

HSA accounts provide financial planners an opportunity to add value to the client-financial planner relationship. HSAs are portable and require contributions to be managed, typically through mutual funds or bank accounts. As is the case whenever an investment is made, the custodian of the account should be evaluated in terms of investment alternatives, costs, and fee structure. Many smaller banks—and even some specialty banks—act as HSA trustees. They offer fixed-interest funds and other account types for qualified deposits.

Planning Strategy 5: Maximize the Benefits of a Section 125 Plan (for Employed Clients)

Internal Revenue Code Section 125 provides employed clients with several advantages for choosing, using, and paying for health insurance premiums, health care expenses, and other benefits. **Section 125 plans**, commonly known as **cafeteria plans** or **flexible benefit plans**, make it possible for employers to offer employees a choice between cash and a variety of nontaxable benefits. These plans must allow employees to choose between two or more qualified benefits (i.e., life insurance, health insurance, accidental death and dismemberment, long-term disability insurance, child and dependent care costs or adoption assistance, group legal services, or medical expense reimbursement) and cash, or another taxable benefit that is treated as cash. Nontaxable benefits, such as disability insurance purchased with after-tax dollars, can also be included in a cafeteria plan.

The benefits selected are typically paid for with pretax dollars through employee salary reduction agreements or credits provided by the employer. Employee contributions are made by contributing a portion of salary, on a pretax basis, to pay for qualified benefits. Salary reduction contributions are not considered to be actually or constructively received by the participant. Therefore, contributions are generally not considered wages for federal or state income tax purposes (some exclusions apply). Also, plan contributions generally are not subject to FICA withholdings. In addition, employer-provided credits, often stated in dollar amounts, are used to purchase qualified, or nontaxable, benefits. Although the credits may vary with employee age, service, or salary, a plan cannot offer an undue advantage to highly compensated employees.

Because of their complexity, cafeteria plans are generally available to those working in midsize to large firms and organizations. Self-employed clients are not eligible to establish these plans, although other tax advantages for health and retirement plan contributions are available to self-employed clients.

Once an employee has elected benefits for a plan year, the choice can be changed only in limited circumstances. Under **change-in-status rules**, a plan may permit participants to revoke an election or make a new election with respect to accident and health coverage, dependent care expenses, group-term life insurance, or adoption assistance if a qualifying event occurs and the participant makes the change in a plan within thirty-one days of the qualifying event. **Qualifying change-in-status events** include:

- a change in legal marital status;

- a change in number of dependents or eligible family members;

- a change in employment status of the employee or changes affecting the employment of a covered family member;

- cases where the dependent satisfies or ceases to satisfy the requirements for eligibility;

- a change in residence for the employee, spouse, or dependent; and

- the commencement or termination of an adoption proceeding, for purposes of adoption assistance.

Many cafeteria plans offer a **salary reduction agreement**, or **premium-conversion plan**, or **premium-only plan** for the purchase of health or life insurance coverage. Pretax salary reduction agreements can also be used to fund an HSA and HDHP.

A flexible spending arrangement, also referred to a **flexible spending account (FSA)**, is another tax-advantaged tool that allows employees to accumulate pretax dollars (exempt from state, federal, and Social Security taxes) through salary reductions to be used for the reimbursement of select expenses. Both health care FSAs and dependent care FSAs are established and maintained in a similar manner. For both, allowable reimbursements are limited to those eligible for a medical deduction or the dependent care tax credit, respectively.

A **health care FSA** can be used to pay for cost sharing (e.g., copayments, coinsurance, and deductibles), as well as other medical, dental, or eye care costs not covered by health insurance Beginning in 2020, clients with FSA assets may purchase over-the-counter medications and receive reimbursement without the necessity of a prescription–assuming their employer's plan documents allow for these expenses. In addition, expenses for menstrual care products may be paid for from FSA funds. Vitamins, dietary supplements, and cosmetic procedures continue to be prohibited, but expenses for herbal remedies or a weight loss program, if prescribed by a physician as medically necessary, can be covered. Keep in mind that if a client uses an HSA, the client may not also use a health care FSA. A **dependent care FSA** can be used to pay for qualified dependent care expenses, such as child care and elder care costs incurred, when both spouses are employed, unless one is disabled or a full-time student. In 2020, the maximum tax-free reimbursement for a dependent care FSA is $5,000 ($2,500 for married employees filing separate tax returns), although income restrictions apply to determine the maximum allowable contribution.

It is important to recognize that a health care FSA and dependent care FSA differ on the uniform coverage, or risk-of-loss, rule. **Uniform coverage** means that the maximum amount of reimbursement (i.e., the annual election) must be available to the health FSA participant at all times. For example, if an employee elects a monthly salary reduction of $100 for an FSA, then the annual election of $1,200 (less any prior year reimbursements) must be made available for employee reimbursement at any time during the plan year without regard to the employee's actual accumulated balance. The plan may not accelerate the payment schedule based on the employee's prior claims. Conversely, a dependent care FSA account can reimburse only with funds deposited into the account, based on the monthly salary deductions available in the participant's account to date.

For both health and dependent care FSAs, reimbursements can be made only for claims incurred during a plan year and cannot be paid in advance. FSA expenses are treated as having been incurred when the participant is provided with the medical care or dependent care resulting in an expense, not when the participant is billed or pays for the care. Reimbursement requests can be submitted, with restrictions, after the plan year ends for expenses incurred during the plan year. An employer may offer those with remaining FSA assets a 2½-month grace period for the use of assets or a $500 maximum allowable carryover option, but not both.

Section 125 plan options usually must be selected before the beginning of a plan year during the open enrollment period. Once established, adjustments to the amount of salary reduction during the year are not allowed, unless there is a qualifying change of family or work status.

Careful estimates of out-of-pocket medical and dependent care expenses are necessary to avoid the loss of contributions if flexible spending accounts are used. Because of the 'use it or lose it' rule, any balance remaining in an account at year-end will most likely be forfeited. Preplanning medical expenses to occur within one year is a way to coordinate the use of medical services to avert the loss of account funds. In addition to non-qualifying health expenses, premiums for other health care coverage or for long-term care insurance are also excluded. Keep in mind that dependent care reimbursements from an FSA reduce the total dependent care expenses eligible for calculation of the dependent care credit.

Planning Strategy 6: Recommend a Medigap Policy to Supplement Medicare Coverage (for Clients Age Sixty-five or Older)

Traditional **Medigap insurance** is available to residents of most states. Medigap policies are sold by private insurance providers to help clients pay for health care costs not provided by Medicare Parts A and B, such as out-of-pocket expenses for copays, co-insurance, or deductibles. Some Medigap plans also fill in for 'gaps' in coverage not provided by Medicare Parts A and B. A few states—Massachusetts, Minnesota, and Wisconsin—have their own specific Medicare supplemental policies and are not considered here. Acceptance by an insurance company into a Medigap plan is guaranteed once a client reaches age sixty-five and enrolls in Medicare. Clients have six months to apply for a Medigap policy. Clients cannot be turned down, regardless of health status, if they apply within the six-month window. However, anyone covered by Medicaid or by a Medicare Advantage Plan is typically not eligible to purchase Medigap insurance.

Planning Tip

Keep the following in mind regarding Medigap coverage: It is illegal for an insurance company to sell clients a Medigap policy that substantially duplicates any existing coverage, including Medicare coverage.

A client may postpone purchasing a Medigap policy if the client works past age sixty-five and is covered by employer-sponsored health insurance, or if not working but still covered by a spouse's employer-sponsored plan. Clients may enroll in Medicare, with the employer-sponsored insurance being the primary payer.

Medicare will pay any costs that are not covered by the employer's plan. If clients find themselves in this situation, they may want to enroll in Medicare Part A, because it is free. Remember, however, that if clients enroll in Medicare Part B, the open enrollment period for Medigap begins at that time.

Nearly all Medigap insurance is sold as a standardized plan that must meet federal and state laws. As shown in Figure 6.2, ten standard plans are available, ranging from the most basic coverage in Plan A to other plans, with unique features, having different alphabetical titles up to Plan N. Every insurance company offering Medigap insurance is required to provide the same standard coverage for each plan, although premiums may differ significantly. Each company offering Medigap insurance must offer Plan A, but companies may have some, all, or none of the other plans available in a state or geographic region within a state. Basic benefits include:

- In-patient hospital care, which covers the cost of Part A coinsurance and the cost of 365 extra days of hospital care during the client's lifetime after Medicare coverage ends;

- Medical costs, which covers the Part B coinsurance (generally 20 percent of Medicare-approved payment amount) or copayment amount, which may vary according to service; and

- Blood, which covers the first three pints of blood each year.

Figure 6.2. Standard Medicare Supplement, or Medigap Plans, and the Percentage of Costs Covered for Benefits

Benefits	A	B	C	D	F*	G	K**	L**	M	N
Part A coinsurance and hospital costs up to an additional 365 days after Medicare benefits are used	100%	100%	100%	100%	100%	100%	100%	100%	100%	100%
Part B coinsurance or copayment	100%	100%	100%	100%	100%	100%	50%	75%	100%	100%***
Blood (first 3 pints)	100%	100%	100%	100%	100%	100%	50%	75%	100%	100%
Part A hospice care coinsurance or copayment	100%	100%	100%	100%	100%	100%	50%	75%	100%	100%
Skilled nursing facility care coinsurance			100%	100%	100%	100%	50%	75%	100%	100%
Part A deductible		100%	100%	100%	100%	100%	50%	75%	50%	100%
Part B deductible			100%		100%					
Part B excess charges					100%	100%				
Foreign travel emergency care (up to plan limits)			100%	100%	100%	100%			100%	100%

Note: The Medicare supplement policy covers coinsurance only after the insured has paid the deductible (unless the supplement policy also covers the deductible).

*Plan F also offers a high-deductible plan. If this option is chosen, the insured must pay for Medicare covered costs up to the deductible amount before the Medicare supplement plan pays anything.

**Plans K and L do not include the entire benefit package. These plans offer catastrophic coverage at a lower premium. After meeting the annual out-of-pocket limit and the annual Part B deductible, the Medicare supplement plan pays 100 percent of covered services for the rest of the calendar year.

***Plan N pays 100 percent of the Part B coinsurance, except for a copayment of up to $20 for some office visits and up to a $50 copayment for emergency room visits that do not result in an inpatient admission.

Source: Centers for Medicare and Medicaid Services. *Choosing a Medigap Policy: A Guide to Health Insurance for People with Medicare*, p 11. Available at: www.medicare.gov/Publications/Pubs/pdf/02110.pdf.

An alternative to a Medigap plan is a **Medicare SELECT plan**. These plans are like traditional Medigap plans, with a key difference being that SELECT coverage utilizes a managed care approach, similar to an HMO or PPO, where clients must use either an in-network or preferred provider, which can make the premiums less expensive than comparable plans.

Medigap insurance offers the advantage of a standardized insurance policy, with a range of supplemental coverage, for those on Medicare. With careful selection and attention to company ratings and consumer satisfaction rankings, a Medigap policy can be a cost-effective solution to dealing with the limitations of Medicare coverage. To make a cost-effective selection, financial planners and their clients should compare the projected Medigap premium with potential out-of-pocket costs for deductibles, coinsurance, and other health care needs not covered by Medicare. Medigap policies are particularly useful for clients who are not offered or cannot afford to continue any company-provided health benefits after retirement.

Planning Strategy 7: Establish an HSA in Conjunction with a Qualified HDHP (for Young Adult Clients)

This strategy works well for young, healthy adults because the use of an HSA provides another avenue to save for retirement. An ideal time to maximize contributions to an HSA is when a client is healthy, single, and without dependents. Because an HSA can be invested in a wide variety of risk- and age-appropriate investment assets, it is possible to accumulate a sizable account balance that can be used later in life for health and/or retirement needs.

Some health insurance experts and financial planners advocate contributing to an HSA before maximizing Roth or Traditional IRA contributions. While all original contributions to a Roth IRA can be withdrawn at any time, earnings withdrawn within five years of opening an account may be fully taxable and subject to a 10 percent early withdrawal penalty (if the owner is under age 59½). To withdraw earnings, in addition to the five-year rule, one of several qualifying events or exceptions must be met. One exception deals with unreimbursed health care expenses; however, to meet the exception rule, the unreimbursed health care expenses must exceed 7.5 percent of the account owner's adjusted gross income. No such limitation exists for HSA withdrawals, plus any money remaining in the account when the account owner reaches age sixty-five may be withdrawn for any reason without a tax penalty, although ordinary income tax will be owed.

Additionally, although the income-based phase-out limits on a Roth IRA are quite high, the phase-out on a deductible, Traditional IRA, if the account owner is eligible for a qualified retirement plan, is relatively low. Single clients with income exceeding the phase-out threshold could instead make a deductible contribution to an HSA even if they had maximized their Roth IRA contribution because HSA deposits are not included in the combined maximum funding levels.

As with all strategies, several caveats are worth noting. Overfunding an HSA in preference to a Roth IRA can create additional tax consequences at retirement given that qualified Roth IRA distributions are tax free, whereas distributions from an HSA at age sixty-five or after will be taxed at ordinary income tax rates. Also, an HSA acts more like a Traditional IRA than a Roth IRA in that contributions to an HSA are made on a pretax basis, but again are taxed upon withdrawal. An additional issue is that if the account owner must take a withdrawal from an HSA prior to age sixty-five, or for a reason other than a qualified medical expense, the penalty on the withdrawal is 20 percent—twice the penalty rate on IRA accounts.

Planning Strategy 8: Use Supplemental Health Policies Cautiously

Supplemental health policies are a form of **limited insurance coverage** that pay benefits for the actual diagnosis and/or treatment of a specific illness or complications arising from the treatment of a specific illness. **Cancer insurance** is the most common limited insurance policy. When clients ask about these forms of insurance it is best to proceed with caution. Supplemental insurance should never be used as a substitute for comprehensive health insurance or for supplemental Medicare coverage. A **critical illness policy** (also called a **specified disease policy**) provides hospital and medical benefits for other diseases in addition to cancer, such as heart disease, stroke and Alzheimer's disease.

Financial planners should focus on recommending the purchase of insurance that provides the best coverage available for the cost that covers expenses regardless of the type of illness or injury involved. *Supplemental policies and critical illness policies should only be recommended when a client can afford the coverage without threatening the accomplishment of other financial planning goals.*

There are two traditional types of supplemental insurance policies. The first (sometimes known as an **expense incurred policy**) pays a percentage of all expenses up to the policy's maximum dollar limit. The second type (sometimes called an **indemnity policy**) also provides payments, but the payments are limited to a fixed dollar amount not the actual expenses incurred.

It is not uncommon for certain cancers (e.g., skin) to be excluded for coverage. Limited insurance and critical illness policies have provisions related to waiting periods, pre-existing conditions, and limits on duplicate coverage payments. The marketplace for these products is dynamic. For example, it is possible to purchase a **First Occurrence Cancer Policy** that pays a lump sum upon the first diagnosis of cancer. The benefit can range from $2,000 to over $100,000. A First Diagnosis Critical Illness Policy can include coverage for other specified illnesses, such as heart attack, stroke, or Alzheimer's disease, paying a lump sum amount as defined in the policy.

In most states, consumers have a 'free look' right that provides a minimum number of days to review and return a policy for any reason. One reason to cancel a purchase is a poor review from one of the following **insurance rating companies**:

- A.M. Best

- Demotech, Inc.

- Fitch

- Moody's

- Standard & Poor's

Planning Strategy 9: Monitor Health Insurance Coverage and Encourage Clients to Do the Same

Financial planners should routinely conduct ongoing reviews of clients' health insurance plan coverage as part of the comprehensive financial planning process. This may seem redundant and unnecessary; however, including this strategy as a specific recommendation, or in a structured client-financial planner to-do list, reminds clients that they too have a responsibility for staying abreast of plan changes and insurance triggers. Both financial planners and clients need to monitor the ongoing changes to Obama Care to ensure that previously implemented strategies remain appropriate across time.

Planning Tip

Coordination of Plan Changes: Nearly all clients will be eligible to make changes to their health plan only during the annual open-enrollment period or in response to a qualifying midyear event. Of course, these limitations do not apply if the client purchases an individual policy, but this is the exception and not the rule. As with any sound recommendation, health care recommendations must be developed in anticipation of events that could create coverage gaps or restrictions.

It is important to remember that in many cases, the flexibility to change a health plan within a given year will be severely constrained and likely limited to the plan's open enrollment period. Nevertheless, it is prudent to recommend that clients continue to monitor potential employer-provided and Obama Care-mandated alternatives or modifications available to them or their spouse/partner, as well as any other household changes that could affect health care planning options.

Planning Strategy 10: Use COBRA to Bridge Employment Termination or Continue Group Health Coverage for Dependents

The Consolidated Omnibus Budget Reconciliation Act (COBRA) of 1985 law requires employers with twenty or more employees offering group health plans to provide employees and certain family members the opportunity to continue group health coverage in a number of instances when coverage would otherwise have lapsed. The lapse must occur as the result of an employee qualifying event, defined as:

- voluntary or involuntary termination of employment, except in the case of gross misconduct;
- coverage termination due to a reduction in hours worked;
- eligibility for Medicare;
- divorce or legal separation; or
- death.

Two other nonemployee qualifying events also are included in COBRA:

a. dependents who cease to meet the dependency definition; and

b. the filing of Chapter 11 bankruptcy by the employer.

The employee must pay for the entire cost of continuing coverage through COBRA. The employee or qualified beneficiary may be charged 102 percent of the applicable premium for this benefit. Although expensive, coverage remains available, whereas a privately provided individual policy might not be available, might offer more limited coverage, or be equally expensive.

Employers must send COBRA notifications to employees and their spouses when the employee is first covered under a group health plan. The employer must also send notices to both the employee and qualified beneficiaries whenever a qualifying event occurs. The latter notice must be sent within fourteen days of learning of the qualifying event.

Qualified beneficiaries have sixty days to elect continuation of coverage. The maximum period that this continued coverage must be provided is generally eighteen months, but in some cases, it is thirty-six months. Depending on the state, there may be a **small group COBRA benefit** available. Given time constraints, a timely response is required. Election of coverage continuation must occur within sixty days of employer-provided COBRA notification. The cost of insurance continuance can be 102 percent of total premiums, calculated as the employer and employee contributions and a 2 percent surcharge. Thus, it is possible that a policy that costs a client $2,500 annually as an employee may actually cost, for example, as much as $6,500 when COBRA benefits are used. The effect on cash flow must be weighed relative to the potential monetary loss of an uninsured accident or illness for one or more household members.

Planning Strategy 11: Maximize the Benefits of HIPAA to Extend COBRA Coverage

The original COBRA law was amended by the **Health Insurance Portability and Accountability Act (HIPAA)** of 1996. The first change dealt with the extension of COBRA coverage to disabled beneficiaries. COBRA required that the eighteen-month maximum coverage continuation period be extended to twenty-nine months if the qualified beneficiary was determined under the Social Security Act to have been disabled at the time of the qualifying event. HIPAA provided that if the disability existed at any time during the first sixty days of COBRA coverage, then a twenty-nine-month period applies. The twenty-nine-month period also applies to a nondisabled qualified beneficiary of the covered employee.

HIPAA also provides that a newborn infant or child placed for adoption with a covered employee during the period of COBRA coverage is entitled to receive COBRA continuation coverage as a qualified beneficiary. COBRA coverage can be terminated early for individuals who are covered under another group health plan. HIPAA provides that COBRA coverage can be cut short even if the new plan has a pre-existing condition exclusion unless the exclusion applies to a condition for which the insured is receiving treatment.

To take advantage of HIPAA, a person must prove that they were insured during the previous twelve months and has not been uninsured for more than sixty-three days. Workers who might be unemployed for more than sixty-three days should consider purchasing a (1) **COBRA bridge** or (2) an individual short-term policy to maintain continuous coverage, and thus avoid loss of coverage for pre-existing conditions.

Life events that should trigger either a COBRA or HIPPA discussion and necessitate a health care policy review include:

- childbirth;

- marriage/divorce/widowhood;

- employment change (especially retirement);

- a child reaching the age of twenty-six, if ineligible for an employer-provided plan; or

- a change in the overall health of the client or other household member.

In addition to coordinating the timing of plan changes, a client may also need to coordinate the timing of health care expenditures to maximize benefits. For example, combining medical expenses in one year may allow a client to periodically satisfy the 7.5 percent floor for claiming an itemized tax deduction. Conversely, the same strategy can allow for more effective management of a health FSA or the coordination of periodic elective expenses (e.g., new eyeglass frames) with health FSA funding.

Quantitative/Analytical Mini-Case Problems

Xuan Chen

1. Xuan Chen, a forty-year-old, unmarried client has been contributing to an HSA for the last three years using a salary reduction agreement through his employer. The stated effective annual rate on the account is 3 percent, and the interest is compounded monthly. The client is in the 24 percent marginal federal tax bracket and the 6 percent marginal state tax bracket. Use this information to answer the following questions.

    a. How much money does Xuan currently have in the HSA if he has deposited $200 per month and has not made any withdrawals?

    b. Because Xuan is in exceptionally good health, he is also using this account as an additional retirement savings vehicle. How much money will Xuan have in the account at age 65 if he maintains his current level of contribution?

    c. How much will Xuan have at age sixty five if he contributes $2,850 every year?

    d. How much will Xuan have at age sixty five if he contributes $2,850 every year if it is also assumed that the contribution and catch-up provision limits increases by 2.5 percent each year? (Ignore any minimum or maximum dollar change limitations.)

So-hyun Joo

2. So-hyun Joo, a fifty two-year-old client, has come to you for assistance with funding her HSA. Her doctor has told her that she will be facing knee replacement surgery within the next five years. She was also told that her out-of-pocket expenses (deductibles, copays, and various other uncovered expenses including rehabilitation) for the operation would total $4,000 if the operation happened today. Her health insurance enrollment period is currently open. She plans to wait exactly five years for the surgery.

    How much money should she contribute monthly if the account pays a stated rate (APR) of 4 percent compounded quarterly? To determine her out-of-pocket expenses at the time of her surgery, inflate the current cost by an effective annual rate of 7 percent.

Ludwig Lindamood

3. Ludwig Lindamood has just accepted a position at a midsize firm that provides three health insurance plan choices for employees. Basic information about each plan is provided below (note: Plan C is a high-deductible health plan with a savings option). Ludwig must make a plan choice immediately. He can afford the annual premium for any of the plans and/or the HSA contribution. Although no one can predict a future health emergency, Ludwig estimates that he will likely incur $500 in medical expenses during the next year. Given this forecast, what policy should he purchase to minimize his net health insurance cost for the year?

Plan provisions	Plan A	Plan B	Plan C
Annual deductible	$300	$150	$1,500
Coinsurance	20%	35%	20%
Annual stop-loss limit	$1,400	$2,000	$3,000
HSA eligible	No	No	Yes
HSA yearly employer contribution	NA	NA	$400
HSA minimum employee contribution	NA	NA	$100
Yearly premium	$190	$175	$94

David Cohen

4. David Cohen, a twenty four-year-old, single, healthy male has just opened an HSA in conjunction with a qualified HDHP. He wants to determine how much the account might be worth if he funds the HSA primarily for retirement purposes.

    a. How much will the account be worth at age sixty five if David makes a deposit of $3,100 per year for the next seven years before changing to his employer's standard health plan because of family health concerns and discontinuing contributions to the HSA? Assume that David earns 3 percent per year for the next seven years while he might need the money, but after he changes plans (and increases his risk tolerance), the return will be 6 percent annualized.

b. How much will the account be worth at age seventy if David makes the maximum deposit of $3,100 per year for the next eight years, but also takes a $5,500 qualified distribution at age twenty eight? Assume David earns 2 percent per year for the next seven years while he might need the money, but after he changes plans the return will be 7 percent annualized.

c. If David takes a $10,000 nonqualified distribution from his HSA prior to age sixty five, how much in federal income tax and penalties will he owe? Assume that he is in the 24 percent marginal tax bracket.

Amy Hunter

5. Amy, who is thirty seven years old, is a single mother with two children. Amy is employed as a laboratory chemist with a national company. She is in good health. Her son Jimmy, age five, is an active and healthy boy. Lane, her daughter, is an inquisitive and healthy eight-year-old girl. Amy has come to you for advice about choosing the most appropriate health insurance plan for her family, as well as preparing for future health insurance issues.

a. If Amy decides to join an HDHP at her work, what must she also contribute to at that time?

b. What factors should Amy consider when deciding to use an HDHP with an HSA?

c. Amy is wondering which of the following events will allow her to change her employer-sponsored FSA election: (a) She gets married, (b) she adopts a baby, (c) her son is admitted to a hospital for surgery, or (d) if she is married and her spouse is fired from his job.

d. If Amy uses an HDHP plan, with an HSA, may she contribute to a health care FSA? May she contribute to a dependent care FSA?

e. Although Amy is too young to purchase a Medigap or Medicare SELECT plan, she would like to learn more about these policies for when she retires. If she were to purchase a Medigap policy, she would want the policy to cover very large, unexpected, and catastrophic expenses. She is also interested in a lower price plan. What plan would be appropriate for Amy (select from one of the standard plans)?

f. When would it make sense for Amy to purchase a specified disease policy?

g. What health factors should be monitored as an element of the comprehensive financial planning process?

h. At which age will Amy trigger a qualifying event under COBRA?

i. Health care coverage is a primary concern for many single mothers. The idea of being without adequate insurance to cover health expenses for children is a worry for many. What options are available to Amy should she accept a position at another firm and be without coverage for a short period of time?

Chapter Resources

Health insurance cost information: www.nchc.org

Health savings account information: www.treasury.gov/resource-center/faqs/Taxes/Pages/Health-Savings-Accounts.aspx

IRS Publication 969, *Health Savings Accounts and Other Tax-Favored Health Plans.*

Medicare information: www.medicare.gov

Patient Protection and Affordable Care Act (PPACA) of 2010: www.dol.gov/ebsa/healthreform/

Chapter 7

Disability Insurance Planning

Learning Objectives

- Learning Objective 1: Explain the role of disability insurance in a client's comprehensive financial plan.

- Learning Objective 2: Calculate a client's short- and long-term disability insurance need.

- Learning Objective 3: Describe the tax implications associated with different disability policies.

- Learning Objective 4: Identify appropriate disability planning recommendations based on a client's goals, resources, and household characteristics.

CFP® Principal Knowledge Topics

- CFP Topic: D.23. Analysis and Evaluation of Risk Exposures.
- CFP Topic: D.25. Disability Income Insurance (Individual).
- CFP Topic: D.30. Insurance Needs Analysis.

Chapter Equations

There are no equations in this chapter.

DISABILITY INSURANCE PLANNING STRATEGIES

The following disability insurance planning strategies represent a concise sample of approaches and planning alternatives used by financial planners in practice. When planning for a client's disability income needs, it is important to include details about structuring insurance contracts, coordinating benefits between group and individual contracts, and coordinating benefits with social insurance when developing strategies.

Planning Strategy 1: Estimate a Client's Disability Insurance Need Using a Consistent Methodology

The Americans with Disabilities Act defines a **disability** as a physical or mental impairment that substantially limits a person's major life activities.[1] Many people are surprised to learn that the typical working adult is more likely to become disabled than to die in any given year. Numerous factors shape a client's probability of becoming disabled, including:

- Gender

- Age

- Lifestyle

- Occupation

Factors that can be used to determine a client's need for disability income replacement coverage include:

- The number of wage earners in the household

- Whether the client provides support for minor children or disabled adults

- The availability of assets or credit

- Whether the client qualifies for Social Security Disability Insurance

- The hazard level of the client's job and whether they are self-employed

- The client's lifestyle choices

- The client's risk tolerance

Calculating the appropriate amount of disability insurance requires consideration of income and expenses, assets available to support a client's lifestyle (i.e., bank accounts, undrawn lines of credit, cash value life insurance, etc.), and employee benefits (i.e., vacation and sick leave, Family Medical Leave Act (FMLA) availability, group disability policies). Five questions should be answered when evaluating an existing or new disability policy:

1. How restrictive is the definition of disability within the policy?

2. How long must the insured wait before benefits are paid?

3. How much of a client's expenses will be replaced during the benefit period?

4. Will the benefits remain fixed or is it possible for benefits to increase with the rate of inflation?

5. How long will the benefits continue?

Although the estimation of a disability insurance need can be quite complex, a simple approach can be used to determine a client's basic need. Consider the example in Figure 7.1. In this example, the analysis is based on a key assumption: to provide long-term coverage with a ninety-day elimination period (the **elimination period** is the time between the diagnosis of the disability and the contractual point at which time benefits are paid). As shown in Figure 7.1, the estimate can be calculated using either annual or monthly data. Since disability insurance is usually issued on a monthly dollar replacement basis, the monthly estimates may be more appropriate for most client situations.

Figure 7.1. Basic Approach to Estimate Disability Insurance Need

Inputs	Yearly Example	Monthly Example	Monthly Calculation
Determine Household Income Need in the Event of a Disability	$90,000	$7,500	
Determine an Appropriate Income Replacement Ratio	80%	80%	
Estimate Net Household Income Needed	$72,000	$6,000	$7,500 × 80%
Determine Spouse/Partner Income While Insured is Disabled	$50,000	$4,167	
Calculate Disability Need	$22,000	$1,833	$6,000 – $4,167
Long-Term Disability Benefits	$0	$0	
Social Security Disability Benefits	$0	$0	
Estimate Earnings from Assets while Insured is Disabled	$12,000	$1,000	
Sum of Disability Benefits + Earnings	$12,000	$1,000	$0 + $0 + $1,000
Calculate Long-Term Disability Insurance Need	$10,000	$833	$1,833 – $1,000
Estimate Short-Term (90 Day) Elimination Period Need	$5,500	$5,500	$1,833 × 3
Current Emergency Fund Value	$10,000		
Short-Term Disability Insurance Need	$0		$5,500 – $10,000

In this example, the client has a monthly long-term disability need of $833. This estimate assumes that the policy will begin paying benefits ninety days after the diagnosis of a covered disability. This implies that the client should have an emergency fund of at least $5,500 to cover the first ninety days of disability. Because the client has $10,000 currently saved, no short-term disability coverage is needed at this time.[2]

The disability need calculation can be easily automated. Figure 7.2 shows the information typically included in a needs analysis model. The spreadsheet approach includes more assumptions (e.g., including estimates of after-tax investment earnings) that make an estimate more precise. The spreadsheet shown in Figure 7.2 is available in the Financial Planning Analysis Excel package included with this book.

Figure 7.2. Disability Needs Analysis Spreadsheet

DISABILITY NEEDS ANALYSIS		
ASSUMPTIONS		
Client's Name	0	0
Client's Income		
Length of Short-Term Disability (Months)		
Length of Long-Term Disability (Months)		
Does Client Have Short-Term Disability Policy? 1 = yes; 0 = no		
Does Client Have Long-Term Disability Policy? 1 = yes; 0 = no		
Short-Term Elimination Period (Months)		
Long-Term Elimination Period (Months)		
Short-Term Benefit Period (Months)		
Long-Term Benefit Period (Months)		
Value of Assets to be Used for an Elimination Period		
Value of Other Assets to be Used for Disability Needs		
Household Income Replacement Ratio		
Yearly Expense Needs In Disability	$0.00	$0.00
Continuing Earned Household Income While In Disability	$0.00	$0.00
Before-Tax Investment Return		
Federal Marginal Income Tax Bracket	0.00%	0.00%
State Marginal Income Tax Bracket	0.00%	0.00%
Monthly After-Tax Investment Income	$0.00	$0.00
After-Tax Continuing Income While In Disability	$0.00	$0.00
Yearly Shortfall While In Disability	$0.00	$0.00
Monthly Income Shortfall	**$0.00**	**$0.00**
SHORT-TERM DISABILITY		
Monthly Tax-Free Short-Term Disability Benefits	$0.00	$0.00
Monthly Tax-Free Short-Term Social Security Disability Benefits	$0.00	$0.00
Monthly Taxable Short-Term Disability Benefits	$0.00	$0.00
Monthly Other Taxable Benefits or Income for Short-Term Disability Use	$0.00	$0.00
Monthly Investment Earnings	$0.00	$0.00
Total Monthly Short-Term Income Available While In Disability	*$0.00*	*$0.00*
Monthly Short-Term Disability Need	$0.00	$0.00
Assets Needed to Fund Short-Term Disability Need	$0.00	$0.00
Does Client Have Sufficient Elimination Period Assets to Meet Short-Term Disability?	No	No
LONG-TERM DISABILITY		
Monthly Tax-Free Long-Term Disability Benefits	$0.00	$0.00
Monthly Tax-Free Long-Term Social Security Disability Benefits	$0.00	$0.00
Monthly Taxable Long-Term Disability Benefits	$0.00	$0.00
Monthly Other Taxable Benefits or Income for Long-Term Disability Use	$0.00	$0.00
Monthly Investment Earnings	$0.00	$0.00
Total Monthly Long-Term Income Available While In Disability	*$0.00*	*$0.00*
Monthly Long-Term Disability Need	-	-
Assets Needed to Fund Long-Term Disability Need	$0.00	$0.00
Does Client Have Sufficient Monetary and Investment Assets to Meet Long-Term Disability Needs?		
SUMMARY		
Monthly Short-Term Disability: How Much is Needed?		
Monthly Long-Term Disability: How Much is Needed?		

Planning Strategy 2: Recommend an Own-occupation Policy

Disability insurance policies are designed to provide a monthly income after a client is medically diagnosed as disabled. It is important to note that several definitions of disability exist. The most advantageous disability insurance definition is known as **own-occupation disability coverage**. Under this definition, an insured client will receive benefits if, as the result of sickness or injury, the client is unable to perform the specific duties of their own occupation. A less favorable definition is any-occupation disability coverage. The difference between an "own" and "any" occupation definition is significant. It is quite possible that a client will become disabled and unable to work in their chosen occupation but may be able to perform the duties of another, unrelated occupation. If this happens, and the client's coverage is any-occupation, no benefit will be received. Nearly all clients prefer an own-occupation policy.

Planning Tip

The insurance industry is moving away from offering more narrowly defined own-occupation policies. As a result, own-occupation coverage can be more difficult to find. Policies that are available can be quite expensive: a premium equivalent to 5 percent of a client's gross income is not unrealistic.

Planning Strategy 3: Recommend a Modified Own-occupation Policy

Trends within the privately provided or non-group disability insurance market indicate that the number of policy options available in the future may be somewhat limited. Although own-occupation policies are appropriate for many clients, finding such a policy is becoming increasingly difficult. Several insurance companies have either stopped offering own-occupation policies or significantly reduced the number of policies issued on a yearly basis. When and if an own-occupation policy can be obtained, the annual premium can be quite expensive.

The primary reason insurance companies are backing away from own-occupation policies is the probability of being deemed disabled has increased over the years. Increasing costs are due, in part, to the types of disabilities that precipitate these claims. For instance, in the past nearly all disabilities were physical in nature. More recently, the number of mental and emotional disability claims has skyrocketed. This has had the most significant negative impact on coverage availability and premiums.

To meet the needs of the market while protecting the underwriting profitability of insurance companies, some firms have started to offer modified own-occupation and split-definition disability policies (see below). A **modified own-occupation** policy is one that pays only if an insured is unable to engage in their chosen occupation and is also unable to work in a reasonable alternative occupation—or one for which the client is qualified by education, training, or experience. This product is appropriate in cases where a client does not qualify for an own-occupation policy or is unable to afford the premium for an own-occupation policy. The premium for a modified own-occupation policy can be significantly less than the premium charged for an own-occupation policy.

Keep in mind, however, that although the premium is less for modified-occupation coverage, some clients may find that the premium still exceeds their modified insurance budget. A projection of 1 percent to 3 percent of gross client income can be used to estimate the premium cost for a disability policy. The elimination period, benefit period, age, optional riders, premium structure, occupational class, gender, state, health, amount and type of coverage, and benefit amount can also influence the cost of a policy.[3]

Planning Strategy 4: Recommend a Split-definition Policy

A **split-definition policy** incorporates the aspects of the modified own-occupation definition with a short- and long-term disability definition. Specifically, to obtain benefits, an insured must be unable to engage in his or her own occupation for a certain period of time, usually two years. After the specified period, benefits are continued only if the insured is unable to engage in a suitable and reasonable occupation.

It should be apparent from these definitions that insurance companies want to encourage clients to re-enter the workforce as soon as possible. To this end, a **loss-of-income test** is frequently used to determine benefit eligibility. This test considers earnings before a disability, earnings in a new position, and the maximum benefit coverage originally provided by the policy. If eligible, the insured will receive a percentage of the maximum monthly benefit relative to the percentage of earned income lost between the two jobs.

Planning Strategy 5: Recommend an Employer- or Group-provided Policy

This strategy is based on having a client purchase **group disability plan coverage**, which typically costs less than a private policy. When implementing this strategy, a client may use pre-tax dollars or, in some cases, after-tax dollars to fund premiums. Medical examinations are usually not required. An initial waiting period might apply to new employees, while existing employees may be eligible to enroll only during an annual open-enrollment period.

Planning Tip

It is important to remind clients that if they use pre-tax dollars to pay premiums, any benefits received will be taxed at the client's current federal marginal tax bracket.

Before making this recommendation, it is important to note that group coverage is typically standardized across employees. In a fluctuating job environment, primary coverage through an employer can be problematic. Disability coverage ends at termination of employment, leaving clients vulnerable to disability losses at the most inopportune time.

Planning Strategy 6: Consider a Mortgage Disability Insurance Policy

This strategy offers a client another insurance alternative if the earned **income replacement ratio** is lower than needed to meet household expenses, or if the client provides the sole source of household income. Disability insurance offered through a mortgage provider may have several drawbacks. For example, the insurance policy itself may be a **fully restrictive policy**, meaning that a client must be completely unable to engage in gainful employment to collect benefits. Additionally, there may be a waiting period before the policy starts to pay, even though premiums still must be paid. This is not always the case, so research is necessary. Finally, the cost of such insurance is often based on the amount of the loan. Private disability insurance is based on an income needed and is usually a percentage of a client's latest salary; thus, a traditional disability policy will provide more flexibility and a higher payout.

Planning Strategy 7: Recommend a Policy with a Social Security Rider

Monthly benefits for private or group coverage can be influenced by policy provisions that coordinate the benefit amount with Social Security or workers' compensation benefits. Known as a **Social Security disability rider**, this provision decreases the amount of policy benefits paid if the insured meets both the policy definition of disability and qualifies for Social Security benefits. The inclusion of this rider should substantially reduce the policy premium (group policies specifically offset Social Security in policy contracts).

There are several types of Social Security offset riders available in the individual market. In some instances, individual policy Social Security offset riders assure a client a certain level of benefits if Social Security does not pay benefits. This is often the case because of the broadly defined any-occupation definition. To encourage rehabilitation, the total combined benefit is often less than the income received before the disability. For example, group benefits, which are typically limited to 60 to 70 percent of salary, will likely be reduced if the client is also eligible for Social Security or workers' compensation benefits.

Planning Strategy 8: Ensure Continuation of Coverage by Including Appropriate Provisions

The availability of policy provisions that help ensure continuity or continuation of coverage should be a key decision point when recommending a disability insurance policy. The following provisions are typically reviewed during the recommendation development phase of the disability insurance planning process:

- A **group disability replacement rider** guarantees a client the ability to convert a certain percentage of a group disability benefit into an individual plan, thus making the group long-term disability policy portable.

- A **waiver-of-premium clause,** which pays all future premiums in the event of disability, is also an important provision to consider. Obviously, it would not be beneficial for a disabled client to lose coverage because of nonpayment just when coverage is needed most.

- A **guaranteed-renewable disability provision** protects a client from policy cancellation by allowing the client to renew a policy without proof of insurability.

- A **noncancelable disability provision** allows for the guaranteed renewal of a policy at a predetermined premium—an essential provision for controlling costs. The policy cannot be cancelled (except for nonpayment of premiums), and if desired, the insured can renew for a specific number of years or until age sixty-five or sixty-seven, depending on the policy.

A common recommendation is to purchase a noncancelable and guaranteed-renewable policy, if available and affordable. Otherwise, purchase a guaranteed-renewable policy. Including both riders is ideal, but both may not be available to all clients. These provisions are typically offered only to low-risk occupational groups at a high premium. A guaranteed-renewable policy provision provides continual coverage subject to premium increases (any premium increase applies to all policyholders in the same insurance classification and cannot be modified for individuals). Any premium increase must be approved by the state insurance department contingent on a company's adverse claims history.

Planning Strategy 9: Recommend a Policy with a Recurrent Disability Provision

A common client question is: "What happens if I become disabled a second time as the result of a previous injury or illness?" Having an answer to this question is important because it is not uncommon for an insured to become disabled, recover from the disability, return to the workforce, and then become disabled a second time. This is referred to as a recurrent disability.

It is important for those employed in high-risk professions to obtain a **recurrent disability provision** as part of the original disability contract. Recurrent disability provisions state that if a policyholder becomes disabled again within six months or up to one year, the disability will be considered a continuation of the previous claim. Without a recurrent disability provision, an insurance company can impose another elimination period before beginning benefits a second time. As with all other policy provisions, adding a recurrent disability provision will increase the cost of coverage, which can negatively impact other short- and long-term financial objectives by diverting cash flow that could be used for other objectives.

Planning Strategy 10: Recommend a Policy with Partial or Residual Benefit Provisions

Although often overlooked, a **residual disability provision** may be the most important policy rider or provision to include in a disability policy. A significant percentage of all disability insurance claims either start or end in a residual disability claim. The basis of a **residual claim** is that those who are insured will typically return to the workforce, but because of the original disability, sickness, or injury, they will either lose time on the job or suffer from lost productivity, resulting in reduced income.

Preferred residual provisions provide coverage based on lost income rather than on the loss of job responsibilities caused by a disability. The amount of the benefit will be prorated according to the disability. For example, someone who is 50 percent disabled will receive a 50 percent benefit. Someone who is determined to be 30 percent disabled will receive a 30 percent benefit. It is assumed that the person will then work part time to increase monthly income. The primary disadvantage associated with this strategy is that the policy provision adds to the cost of the policy. Keep in mind that nearly all residual benefit provisions have a benefit floor of $250 to $500 to minimize the administrative cost of very small benefit payments.

Planning Strategy 11: Reduce Premium Costs by Relying on Social Security Benefits

The Social Security Administration applies a very stringent definition of disability. Qualification for coverage is based strictly on an any-occupation definition. To collect benefits, an insured must be currently eligible to receive Social Security benefits and be permanently and totally disabled. According to the Social Security Administration, **permanently disabled** means that the disability is expected to last at least twelve months, while **totally disabled** means that the insured is unable to work in or at any occupation. Furthermore, there is a five-month elimination period, and benefits do not include reimbursement for related medical expenses. Finally, the recipient of benefits is limited in the total amount of earned income per month they can receive (usually less than $1,800 is allowed).

Planning Tip

Depending on cost, availability, and willingness to pay, the following policy recommendations should be made and ranked as follows: own-occupation, modified own-occupation, and split-definition. Only after these policies have been explored should an any-occupation policy be considered.

The one advantage to Social Security coverage is that the cause of a disability does not have to be work related to qualify. If the disability meets the other permanent and total criteria, benefits can be received after the elimination period. Given the restrictions on the definitions of permanent and total disability, the mandatory elimination period, and the lack of reimbursement for related medical expenses, the general recommendation for clients is not to rely solely on Social Security disability benefits. It is best to consider these benefits only as a supplement to an existing long-term policy. In other words, this is not an optimal financial planning strategy, but it is one that reduces cash flow dedicated to insurance needs.

Planning Strategy 12: Coordinate Noninsurance Strategies with Short-term Disability Coverage

For the average worker, the likelihood of short-term disability far exceeds that of long-term disability. One way to deal with short-term needs is by managing employer-provided sick leave and/or vacation time. Taking paid time off from work can help fill in income gaps during a short-term need. Emergency funds or other financial assets can be liquidated, if necessary, to extend the elimination period on a short-term policy and reduce premium costs. If group or individual short-term coverage is unavailable or judged to be too expensive, noninsurance strategies can be a cost-effective alternative; but management of client resources will be necessary.

It is worth remembering that contingent on individual client and employer-provided benefits, noninsurance strategies might not be available, or there may be employer restrictions on sick leave or vacation reserves. Additionally, extending a policy elimination period by increasing an emergency savings fund can subject a client to potentially significant opportunity costs.

Planning Strategy 13: Pursue Other Sources of Disability Benefits, When Available

An important source of disability income for some clients comes from workers' compensation benefits. **Workers' compensation** is administered through state compensation boards and funded by participating employers. These programs grant benefits to employees who are injured at work or suffer a work-related illness. Although specific program provisions vary from state-to-state, benefits include medical treatment, partial wage replacement, and survivor benefits. In some states, clients might also be eligible for compulsory temporary benefits. These are basically state-sponsored disability insurance pools.

Generally, a workers' compensation program can be thought of as a combination health and disability policy. But unlike Social Security benefits, workers' compensation covers only disabilities that occur during the normal course of employment. The other basic difference from Social Security is that employees are eligible for workers' compensation benefits for short-term, long-term, partial, and total disabilities.

Because of the broad coverage, some disabled workers can file claims with both Social Security and their state office of workers' compensation, but the combined benefit amount cannot exceed 80 percent of the worker's average current earnings. Clients who find themselves unemployed after a disability may also be eligible for state-sponsored unemployment insurance, although some restrictions may apply, and benefits generally end after thirty-nine weeks. Private unemployment insurance can also be available on a limited basis. However, the costs associated with this type of insurance can be prohibitively high. Benefits from private policies are based on previous earnings and typically equal no more than 50 percent of a person's earnings. This is further limited by a total dollar maximum monthly benefit. It is important to note that neither state-sponsored nor private unemployment benefits are designed for long-term disability situations.

Finally, settlements from a liability or negligence claim resulting from a disabling accident can sometimes provide assets or income for a disabled client. But this is a worst-case scenario. The receipt of any financial benefits can potentially be delayed for years. Restrictions on applicability, availability, benefit amounts, and benefit periods limit the usefulness of these sources of disability benefits in the financial planning process. Even so, for eligible clients, these benefits can be a useful income supplement that should not be overlooked.

Planning Strategy 14: Increase the Waiting Period and Increase Emergency Savings Fund

Financial planners often recommend disability policies that have the longest **elimination period** that is financially feasible. At a minimum, a ninety-day elimination period is common. The reason is that policy premiums are inversely related to the elimination period. Elimination period expenses can be covered from employer-compensated sick leave or vacation time, emergency savings and other emergency income sources, or if necessary, supplemented with available lines of credit.

Extending the elimination period in a policy significantly reduces the cost of coverage for a short- or long-term disability policy. If a large enough emergency fund or other assets earmarked for liquidation are available, it may be possible to eliminate the need for short-term coverage. Compared to a ninety-day wait period policy, a one-hundred-and-eighty-day elimination period can reduce the cost of long-term coverage by approximately 1 percent of a client's gross income. It is important to note that increasing the elimination period and increasing an emergency savings fund can subject a client to potentially significant opportunity costs. A client may need to sacrifice higher rates of return on assets held as emergency savings to implement this strategy. The untimely forced sale of assets earmarked for this purpose can result in significant losses.

Planning Strategy 15: Reduce the Wage Replacement Ratio

Some clients find the cost of disability coverage to be prohibitively high. This strategy reduces the premium cost relative to a policy with a higher wage replacement ratio. Reducing the amount of cash flow needed to fund a disability policy can provide a more cost-effective solution that ensures some income protection. Essentially, this strategy allows a client to accumulate other assets to meet a potential disability need.

Keep in mind that recommending a policy with, say, a 60 percent wage replacement ratio can leave a client underinsured. This can negatively impact other short- and long-term financial objectives, unless the client has the financial wherewithal to cover any possible difference between the benefit amount and actual living expenses. It is important to note that in most situations, this strategy should be reserved for two-income households, although reducing the replacement ratio can be a better alternative than not having any income protection.

Quantitative/Analytical Mini-Case Problems

Tarek Framborgia

1. Tarek Framborgia is considering the purchase of a disability policy. He is currently thirty five years old and earns $50,000 per year as a quality control engineer for a major industrial company. He worries that with his moderately strenuous job responsibilities, and his potential for increasing earnings, he may not be adequately covered should an off-the-job accident keep him from continuing his career. He has come to you with the following list of problems and questions.

    a. If I purchase a policy that pays a fixed benefit of 90 percent of my current salary, how long will it be before this amount covers only 70 percent of my future salary if I assume salary increases of 4 percent per year?

b. Assuming the same policy as above, if I purchase a policy with a provision for future increases of $1,000 per year, how long will this new policy cover at least 70 percent of my income?

c. If I assume that both my salary and the inflation rate increase at 4 percent per year, and that there is no floor or ceiling to my potential benefit increases because I purchase both a COLA and future increase option provisions on the above policy, how much should my annual benefit be in twenty five years?

Samantha O'Reilly

2. Samantha O'Reilly has come to your office for a second opinion about purchasing an individual long-term disability policy. She was told that her best option for reducing the cost of a policy is to choose a long elimination period. But she has become worried that she will not be able to pay her monthly expenses during an extended (year-long) elimination period. She has some savings, but she is afraid what she has is not enough.

a. If Samantha's current annual salary is $43,000, her taxes are $8,000, and she just barely manages to fund her Roth IRA each year with $5,000, how much of an emergency fund will she need to meet only her living expenses?

b. How long will it take Samantha to achieve the emergency fund goal from above if she currently has $18,500 saved, invests $300 per month, and earns an annual percentage yield (APY) of 4.25 percent after taxes in her money market mutual fund?

c. If she could reduce the policy elimination period to nine months for an additional premium of $10 per month, how much will she need to save monthly in the same money market account to reach her emergency fund goal within twelve months? Can she afford this savings payment if she suspends her IRA contribution for one year?

Deshawn Carter

3. Deshawn Carter has just received his open-enrollment benefits notification from his employer and has asked you to assess his disability insurance coverage. He currently has a long-term, any-occupation disability policy available through his employer that pays a benefit of 80 percent of his $85,000 gross annual income. Deshawn previously elected to have his premiums deducted from his salary on a before-tax basis. The premium dollars are not being added back into his taxable income. He has asked you to determine the net after-tax benefit he will receive should he become disabled under each of the following situations:

a. No changes are made to his policy.

b. He elects to have the pre-tax dollars used to pay his policy premiums added back into his taxable income. (Remember to remind Deshawn that this is an irrevocable election.)

c. His employer has offered to pay 50 percent of the premium on his behalf, with Deshawn electing to pay the other half of the premium with after-tax dollars. (Remember to address with Deshawn how the income tax impact of this election will change his net benefit over the next several years, assuming his salary remains static.)

Social Security Benefits Integration

4. One of your clients just realized that her own-occupation disability policy has a Social Security benefits integration clause, meaning that the policy will have a dollar-for-dollar reduction in benefits paid if she qualifies for Social Security disability payments. According to her most recent Social Security benefits statement, she is eligible for $1,325 per month for a permanent and total disability. How much will her disability policy pay as a monthly benefit under the following circumstances if her current annual salary is $62,000, her policy pays 70 percent of gross income, and she pays for the policy with after-tax dollars?

    a. Her disability meets the definition for her policy, but it does not meet the Social Security definition.

    b. Her disability meets the definition for her policy and meets the Social Security definition.

    c. How much will her total combined monthly disability benefits equal if she meets both definitions of disability and her policy does not have a benefits integration clause? Why can this be problematic? In other words, why might this create a moral hazard?

Jamal and Chyna Gwynn

5. Your clients, Jamal and Chyna Gwynn, would like you to estimate their disability insurance needs. Use the following information to determine the disability insurance need for Jamal and Chyna separately:

    *   Jamal: Age forty eight; Life Expectancy: Age ninety seven

    *   Chyna: Age fifty; Life Expectancy: Age ninety five

    *   They would like to plan for disability until they turn age sixty seven

    *   Jamal Short-term Disability Benefits: None

    *   Chyna Short-term Disability Benefits: None

    *   Long-term Elimination Period: Six Months

    *   Long-term Benefit Period: Until Age sixty seven

    *   Earned Income: Jamal $145,000

    *   Earned Income: Chyna $210,000

    *   Unallocated Monetary Assets: $95,000

    *   Unallocated Investment Assets: $400,000

    *   Bonus: Jamal $25,000

    *   Household Income Replacement Ratio in the Event of Disability: 80 Percent

- Federal Marginal Tax Rate: 24 Percent

- State Marginal Tax Rate: 5 Percent

- Emergency Fund Value: $50,000

- Value of Other Assets to be Used for Disability Needs: $200,000

- Before-Tax Investment Return: 4.50 Percent

- Jamal Group Monthly Long-term Benefits: $5,000 (premium paid with after-tax dollars)

- Chyna Group Monthly Long-term Benefits: $7,000 (premium paid with pre-tax dollars)

- Does Jamal Wish to Consider Social Security Disability Benefits? No

- Does Chyna Wish to Consider Social Security Disability Benefits? No

    a. Approximately how much short-term disability insurance does Jamal need?

    b. Approximately how much long-term disability insurance does Jamal need?

    c. Approximately how much short-term disability insurance does Chyna need?

    d. Approximately how much long-term disability insurance does Chyna need?

Chapter Resources

Council for Disability Awareness (http://www.disabilitycanhappen.org/).

Disability Insurance Education—Glossary of Disability Insurance Terms. Available at: https://www.tdi.texas.gov/consumer/glossary.html.

Elias, Stephen, and Kevin Urbatsch. *Special Needs Trusts: Protect Your Child's Financial Future*. Berkeley, CA: Nolo Press, 2011.

Gay Lesbian Alliance Against Defamation organization (http://www.glaad.org/)

General disability insurance information: https://www.healthcare.gov/glossary/.

Information about Medicare: www.medicare.gov.

Nadworny, John W., and Cynthia R. Haddad. *The Special Needs Planning Guide: How to Prepare for Every Stage of Your Child's Life*. Baltimore: Brookes Publishing, 2011.

Rajput, Minoti. "Planning for Families of Children with Disabilities." *Journal of Financial Planning,* August, 2001: 74–84.

Russell, L. Mark, and Arnold E. Grant. Planning for the Future: Providing a Meaningful Life for a Child with a Disability after Your Death. Planning for the Future, Inc., 2005.

Social Security Benefit Calculator (disability, retirement, survivor): http://www.socialsecurity.gov/planners/benefitcalculators.htm.

2018 Social Security & Medicare Facts. Erlanger, KY: National Underwriter Company, (revised annually).

Endnotes

1. U.S. Equal Employment Opportunity Commission, *Facts About the Americans With Disabilities Act.* Available at http://www.eeoc.gov/eeoc/publications/fs-ada.cfm.

2. This approach takes into account investment earnings for the long-term disability need. Investment earnings are not used to offset the elimination period or the overall short-term disability need. This make the estimate very conservative.

3. Guardian Disability Insurance Brokerage, *Common Questions: How Much Does Disability Insurance Cost?* Available at http://www.disabilityquotes.com/disability-insurance/disability-insurance-cost.cfm.

Chapter 8

Long-Term Care Insurance Planning

Learning Objectives

- Learning Objective 1: Evaluate a client's long-term care insurance situation.

- Learning Objective 2: Describe activities of daily living that are commonly used to document the need for long-term care.

- Learning Objective 3: Perform a long-term care insurance needs analysis.

- Learning Objective 4: Develop a long-term care plan that incorporates insurance, savings, and the use of household assets.

CFP® Principal Knowledge Topics

- CFP Topic: D.23. Analysis and Evaluation of Risk Exposures.
- CFP Topic: D.26. Long-Term Care Insurance (Individual).
- CFP Topic: D.30. Insurance Needs Analysis.

Chapter Equations

There are no equations in this chapter.

LONG-TERM CARE PLANNING STRATEGIES

The long-term care planning landscape continues to change rapidly. Several important trends continue to shape the marketplace for long-term care products, including increasing premium costs, the exit of prominent insurance companies from the market, and the application of more stringent underwriting requirements.

When recommending the purchase of long-term care insurance, it is a best practice to discuss with clients methods that optimize the cost/benefit ratio of a recommended policy. One of the easiest ways to accomplish this, aside from adjusting the amount of benefits, is to weigh the benefit period and the elimination period against the premium. A long benefit period and a short waiting period will result in a relatively expensive policy. Conversely, a policy with a short benefit period and a long elimination period may leave the client uninsured when insurance is most needed.

A client's sex must also be considered. Because women tend to live longer than men, the benefit period for a female client may need to be longer. This will, by definition, increase the premium. But if a client can afford the premium, a lifetime benefit, regardless of sex, may be appropriate.

When conducting a cost/benefit analysis, it is important to keep in mind that the average stay in a long-term care facility is thirty months, but the median length of stay, according to the American Association for Long-Term Care Insurance (AALTCI), is between twelve and thirty-six months. Keep in mind that clients have a 50 percent chance of incurring a stay of longer than three years.[1] To err on the side of caution, all the following strategies assume that a client will spend at least three years in a long-term care facility and insure the projected total cost. The following strategies provide an insight into some of the most widely used tools and techniques used by financial planners when helping clients navigate the long-term care insurance marketplace.

Planning Strategy 1: Estimate a Client's Long-Term Care Insurance Need Using a Consistent Methodology

The need for long-term care (LTC) insurance is based on (a) client preferences, (b) net worth, and (c) the projected need for care based on age, personal health, family health history, lifestyle choices, and occupational choice. The first two factors can usually be easily identified, while the last factor can sometimes be more time consuming to identify. All three factors significantly influence the projected cost of care and the amount of insurance to be purchased. Specifically, five factors should be considered when quantifying the amount of insurance coverage to purchase:

1. Range of services covered and benefit amount;

2. Coverage period;

3. Method by which benefits are paid (i.e., pool-of-money or indemnity);

4. Elimination period; and

5. Inflation rider to increase coverage limits.

Financial planners who are asked to evaluate an existing ltc policy should first determine whether the client really needs coverage or if self-insurance is a better option. Once a determination has been made, factors that determine the amount of insurance needed, as well as riders that affect coverage, should be reviewed. If the decision to discontinue a policy is made, a client usually has the option to (1) let the policy lapse; (2) exercise the nonforfeiture clause, if available; (3) exercise a contingent benefits nonforfeiture provision, if available; or (4) exercise a section 1035 exchange for another, more suitable ltc insurance contract. With the last option, care must be taken because the new policy premium will reflect the client's current age.

The actual steps required to determine a LTC insurance need are relatively straightforward. The process is shown in Figure 8.1. The following inputs are needed:

• current age of client

• assumed age at need

• annual cost of care today

• the LTC inflation rate

• the value of any funds set aside for LTC expenses

• the before tax-rate of return

• the client's marginal tax bracket

• the expected increase in future savings for long-term expenses

As illustrated in Figure 8.1, the analysis shows the client will need to fund LTC needs in the amount of $101,728. This is the total amount that will pay for three years of LTC needs. If the client's net worth is high enough, it may be possible to self-insure the need. For risk averse clients, and those with limited assets, purchasing a LTC insurance policy may be appropriate. Keep in mind, however, that nearly every input used in a LTC calculation is an assumption. As such, the derived estimates should be used only as a starting point in further discussions with clients.

Figure 8.1. Estimating a Client's LTC Insurance Need

Client Data Input	Data Input Example	Calculation
Current Age	60	
Age LTC Benefits Begin	65	
Annual LTC Inflation Rate	3%	
Number of Years Benefits are Needed	3	
Before-Tax Rate of Return	8%	
Marginal Tax Bracket	24%	
Annual Increase in Savings	0%	
Current Dollars Set Aside for LTC Needs	$50,000	
Estimate Annual Cost of LTC	$50,000	Calculate FV of Cost N = 5 I/Y = 3 PV = $50,000 CPT FV = $57,964
Estimate Total LTC Need (based on three years stay in nursing home)		Calculate Need on First Day of Care 1. Determine After-Tax Return 8% × (1 – .24) = 6.08% 2. Calculate Serial Rate (1.0608/1.03) – 1 = 2.99% 3. Calculate PV (Annuity Due) N = 3 I/Y = 2.99 PMT = $57,964 PV = $168,892
Calculate Current Value of Assets Set Aside for LTC Needs	$50,000	Calculate FV of Assets N = 5 I/Y = 6.08 PV = $50,000 FV = 67,164
NET LTC NEED		Determine Difference Between Need and Resources $168,892 – $67,164 = $101,728

Note: This calculation approach assumes the client uses assets from an emergency savings fund to pay for services during the policy's elimination period.

The LTC need calculation can be easily automated. Figure 8.2 shows the information typically included in a needs analysis model. The spreadsheet approach includes more assumptions (e.g., including estimates of after-tax investment earnings) that make an estimate more precise. The spreadsheet shown in Figure 8.2 is available in the Financial Planning Analysis Excel package included with this book.

Figure 8.2. LTC Needs Analysis Spreadsheet

LONG-TERM CARE ANALYSIS	
ASSUMPTIONS	
Cost of Care Today	
Age Today	0
Age of LTC Need	
Years Until Need	0
Years of Stay	
LTC Inflation Rate	
Before-Tax Rate of Return	
Marginal Tax Bracket	0.00%
After-Tax Rate of Return	0.00%
Salary Inflation Rate	0.00%
Value of Assets Set Aside	
CALCULATIONS	
Cost of LTC at Age of Need	$0.00
Cost of Total Stay for One Person	$0.00
Cost for Couple (Joint Stay)	$0.00
FV of Assets	$0.00
Net LTC Need Per Person	$0.00
Net LTC for Couple	$0.00

Planning Strategy 2: Match the Appropriate LTC Product to Each Client's Needs

Insurance companies continue to refine LTC offerings to the meet the needs of financial planning clients. The latest trend involves packaging life insurance and LTC products together. Some insurance companies are also packaging annuity and LTC products jointly. These innovations occurred as a result of the Pension Protection Act of 2006. The Act made clear that investments in life insurance and annuity contracts may fund a LTC insurance rider. If used, the benefit payments are not treated as taxable distributions of policy gains. However, any LTC benefits used will reduce the investment value in a contract, which may have implications if the contract is surrendered or upon the death of the owner. The combining of products, often referred to as **linked-benefit products** or **asset-based products**, makes LTC insurance planning both flexible and complicated. Planning strategies four and five provide more details about linked-benefit products.

Another innovation is a **partnership plan**. These plans help families meet LTC insurance needs by providing tax and asset protection benefits. Partnership plans encourage LTC planning by linking insurance coverage and Medicaid eligibility with the goal of reducing Medicaid spending for a rapidly increasing elderly population (more information on partnership plans is presented in planning strategy six). Consider the following example from the State of New York:[2]

> The New York State Partnership for Long-Term Care combines private LTC insurance and Medicaid Extended Coverage (MEC). The program works by allowing an individual or couple who purchases a partnership insurance policy (and keeps the plan in effect) to hold onto all or part of their assets under the Medicaid program if their long-term care needs extend beyond the period covered by the policy. If a client were to purchase a partnership plan and use the benefits according to the conditions of the program, the client can apply for MEC, which will assist in paying for on-going care. Unlike regular Medicaid, MEC allows a client to protect some or all of their assets, depending on whether the client selects a dollar-for-dollar plan or total asset protection plan (MEC does require someone claiming benefits to contribute income to cover the cost of care). Essentially, this and other partnership plans help clients pay for LTC without having to 'spend down' assets, as is typically required under Medicaid rules.

Planning Strategy 3: Understand the Role of IRC Section 1035 in Relation to LTC Insurance

The Pension Protection Act of 2006 also modified provisions of **IRC Section 1035** to allow for the tax-free exchange of a life insurance or annuity product to purchase a qualified LTC policy, or the exchange of one LTC policy for another. This change protects from taxation a client's gains from existing life insurance or annuity contracts by allowing an exchange on a tax-free basis. The 1035 exchange rule makes it possible for clients to protect future assets by means of a deferred annuity with a LTC benefit, to exchange an annuity or life insurance product to purchase a LTC insurance policy, or to exchange an annuity or life insurance contract for a similar product with a qualified LTC rider.

Planning Tip

It is important to note that neither an annuity contract nor a traditional LTC contract can be exchanged, tax-free, for a life insurance policy with or without a qualified LTC rider. A nonqualified single-premium immediate annuity may be eligible for a tax-free exchange to purchase LTC insurance. Care must be taken to handle the exchange appropriately through the insurance companies, with the advice of a tax professional, and to be certain that any death benefit surrendered (in the case of life insurance) is no longer needed.

Planning Strategy 4: Consider Hybrid Life Insurance/LTC Products

The question 'what if I never need long-term care?' coupled with the expense of insurance are primary reasons people fail to purchase LTC coverage. Realizing that clients often feel constrained when faced with what they consider to be a lose-lose scenario, a few insurance companies have created a product that combines the advantages of cash value life insurance with LTC coverage. Financial planners and consumers have enthusiastically embraced these combination or hybrid products because of the perceived dual value: obtaining LTC coverage while building cash value that can be used if the LTC benefit is never needed.

Although products vary by company, most hybrid products add a LTC rider to a cash value (whole or universal) life insurance policy. Policies are available as a single premium or, in some cases, with a recurring premium. Regardless of the product, an accelerated benefits rider makes the policy death benefit available to pay for LTC expenses. An **extension of benefits option** adds a multiple to the face value of a policy for additional LTC expenses. For example, with this option, a $100,000 face value policy might provide an additional $200,000 in LTC coverage. This means that both the death benefit of the policy and the extension of benefits will be available to pay LTC costs. Keep in mind, however, that unlike traditional LTC policies that offer greater choice in the length of time qualifying care must be provided before policy benefits begin, a ninety- or 100-day elimination period is common with a hybrid product.

According to the AALTCI, insurance companies use different formulas when qualifying claims. **Reimbursement plans** repay actual expenses up to the policy maximum monthly benefit amount. Another approach is known as an **indemnity plan**, which pays a monthly maximum if the policyholder provides evidence of an ongoing need within covered expenditures. An indemnity plan tends to be more expensive.

Policyholders determine the total LTC amount and maximum monthly payment when purchasing a policy. Typical payment periods range from twenty-four to sixty months, although a few lifetime plans are also available. Policies may pay for a range of care options (in-home, assisted living, or adult day care) or be limited to nursing home care. Regardless of policy type, the benefit amount must fall within IRS defined guidelines and conform to federal regulations for both life insurance and LTC insurance coverage to maintain qualified tax status.

It is worth noting that clients must meet underwriting standards for a hybrid policy. Underwriting requirements vary by product. Applying for a hybrid policy before it is needed is an important element of proper financial planning. Some insurance companies offer joint policies for couples, which may ease underwriting concerns if one spouse is reasonably healthy.

The following example, described by the AALTCI, illustrates how a linked-benefit life and LTC plan works:[3]

> A client with $400,000 in retirement assets is sixty years old and in good health. He plans to leave his nest egg to his adult children. The client could purchase a $200,000 face value hybrid policy, naming his children as beneficiaries. By adding an extension of benefits rider, he could have up to $400,000 in LTC coverage, or $6,000 per month for five years. Using a return of premium option, the client can cancel at any time and receive his premium payments back, but if necessary, the policy can be used to protect retirement assets intended for the heirs. Typically, the LTC benefit rider is paid with a one-time premium of available assets. For planning purposes, a minimum premium of $65,000 should be used. A Section 1035 exchange of an existing life insurance policy can be used to help fund the policy.

Planning Strategy 5: Consider Hybrid Annuity/LTC Products

Hybrid products combining annuity and LTC features appeal to clients who want protection for LTC costs but fear that they will not ultimately need the coverage. Although features vary by company and individual product, several general product characteristics add to the appeal—and the complexity—of hybrid annuity products. It is important to note that product availability also varies by state. Thus, working with a knowledgeable insurance professional is important. Many financial planners, in the best interests of their clients and to remain within their competence limits, collaborate with someone who specializes in LTC products once a client's LTC insurance need has been established.

Both fixed and variable annuities may offer a **LTC rider**, although fixed products are more common. Some linked-benefit annuity and LTC products require health underwriting, whereas others do not. The latter feature is particularly attractive to those who may be uninsurable. However, the available term of LTC benefits varies for these products. Annuities that do not require underwriting typically limit coverage to no more than thirty-six months. Longer benefit periods are available for products that require health underwriting.

Funding options vary by product. Lump-sum, or single, payments are generally required, but if funds are not available, a traditional annuity or a life insurance contract can be exchanged, through IRC Section 1035, for an annuity with a LTC rider. For annuities that require health underwriting, up to 60 percent of the value in a qualified account, such as a 401(k) or IRA, can be used through a Section 1035 exchange to purchase a product. This option can benefit couples, in that qualified funds of one spouse may be used to purchase a shared-benefit product that can offer protection for both. **Linked-benefit annuity** and LTC products have certain disadvantages, including high surrender charges, low fixed returns on premiums, and the opportunity costs associated with funding LTC insurance with a lump-sum payment rather than over time.

An example reported in bankrate.com illustrates how this type of product can be used:[4]

> Consider a sixty-year-old female who purchases a twenty-year long-term-care fixed annuity with a 5 percent inflation-adjustment rider for LTC coverage and a lump-sum premium of $50,000. This coverage provides the client with an initial $100,000 (two times the premium) in LTC coverage for a maximum of the six-year benefit period. If no distributions are taken from the policy, the account will increase to $265,330 of LTC coverage, or a maximum of $3,685 per month at the end of twenty years, assuming a 3.5 percent compound interest rate less administrative fees. If the LTC coverage is not needed, the client may continue to defer the account value or begin taking distributions when the annuity matures. Upon her death, her heirs will receive the premium of $50,000 less any LTC benefits paid *or* the accumulated annuity value, whichever is larger.

Despite the complexity of hybrid annuity products, the LTC protection available, if needed, is typically based on four factors:

1. the amount of the single premium paid;

2. the term of benefits selected (generally four or six years);

3. the addition of an inflation factor and its amount (e.g., 3 percent or 5 percent); and

4. the multiplier (sometimes called the **leverage factor**) applied to the initial premium paid to determine the maximum LTC benefit, typically one-and-a-half or two times if inflation protection is chosen *or* two or three times if inflation protection is not chosen.

Clients should be cautioned to fully understand and compare products prior to purchase. Recall that, as a result of the Pension Protection Act of 2006, distributions for long term-care coverage are made on a tax-free basis. This tax savings can benefit a client who previously purchased a traditional annuity, but who can now purchase a hybrid product with a Section 1035 exchange and avoid the taxes that would have been paid on the gains in the original product.

Planning Strategy 6: Understand the Role of Medicaid in LTC Insurance Planning

Medicaid is a federally funded program that provides health and LTC services to those with few resources and very limited income. States administer the Medicaid program individually to provide nursing home care and, to a limited extent, in-home and community care services to those who meet financial and functional eligibility requirements. Medicaid will not pay for long-term custodial care for individuals until most of the person's assets have been spent and income is limited.

Financial planners are not allowed, under current law, to recommend that clients forgo the purchase of a LTC policy with the intent of spending down assets to become Medicaid eligible. When someone applies for Medicaid, the Medicaid agency reviews all transfers of assets that the applicant or their spouse have made in the prior sixty months. This is called the **look-back period**. Nonexempt transfers or transfers disallowed by Medicaid during this period can cause the loss of Medicaid eligibility (what is called a **penalty period**) that begins when the individual is eligible for Medicaid benefits. The length of the penalty period is determined by dividing the value of the transferred asset by the average monthly private-pay rate for nursing facility care in the state. This penalty means that more of an individual's assets must be liquidated or, if unavailable, that the person's extended family may have to offer assistance.

Planning Tip

Medicaid planning involves efforts to distribute or "spend down" assets to meet the means tests (i.e., a maximum of $2,000 in "countable" assets are owned in the individual's name, although this amount may vary by state) and other eligibility requirements for Medicaid LTC benefits. Financial planners are prohibited from providing spend down recommendations.

According to the Omnibus Budget Reconciliation Act of 1993, each state has the right to reclaim the amount paid for the care of a Medicaid applicant. Because of means testing to qualify for Medicaid, a client's home is usually the only property of substantial value that a Medicaid recipient is likely to own. Fortunately, federal law allows a married Medicaid recipient to transfer equity in a home to their spouse without penalty. Should the spouse choose to protect the home, some states allow the spousal owner to gift the home to others. This creates several issues, beyond the obvious question of whether the donor will be able to remain in the home. A second issue focuses on the donor's potential need for LTC. If Medicaid is needed, all transfers within the prior sixty months will be reviewed, and any **nonexempt transfer** or a disallowed transfer of assets, during that prior five-year period will trigger a penalty period and ineligibility for aid. A third issue is the potential gift tax that could result.

The role of partnership plans. When analyzing a client's capacity to fund a long-term stay in a care facility, financial planners must consider a client's desires regarding the location, the type of care anticipated, and family or charitable legacies relative to the assets available. Public/private partnership plans encourage LTC planning by linking insurance coverage and Medicaid eligibility. Partnership programs, which are now available in more than thirty-five states, split the cost of custodial care between personal assets and state payments while allowing the recipient to maintain assets based on a predetermined formula established by the state.

It is important to note that although these plans help protect assets from liquidation, partnership plans do not waive the income limit or functional eligibility required for Medicaid—functional eligibility requirements that may exceed the eligibility requirements for the private policy that had been providing care services. Another downside associated with partnership plans is that benefits may or may not be portable from state to state, depending on individual state agreements that allow for reciprocity among states. Finally, Medicaid plans typically restrict coverage to services provided in a nursing home. Out-of-pocket expenses to supplement the cost of care provided by the private policy also must be considered.

Planning Tip

Partnership plans encourage consumers to partner with a state-based program as they purchase qualified private LTC insurance policies. Partnership qualified policies are available from licensed insurance professionals and financial planners. To qualify, policies must meet state and federal partnership requirements. People who purchase a qualifying LTC policy may still qualify for Medicaid after depleting their insurance benefits, provided they meet all other Medicaid eligibility criteria. In effect, a LTC partnership program provides dollar-for-dollar asset protection. Each dollar paid by a partnership policy entitles a consumer to keep a dollar of assets sheltered from Medicaid recovery.

Planning Strategy 7: Utilize a Policy with a Lifetime Benefit Period and a 180-day Elimination Period

This strategy is appropriate in cases where the probability of needing skilled care for an extended period is high, based on defined risk triggers. Assuming a three-year or longer care period and having a 180-day elimination period results in a client self-funding for six months up front, but it ensures that the client will never exhaust coverage. This strategy is most suitable for clients who are predisposed to chronic diseases that may result in incapacitation for years, such as Alzheimer's disease, severe osteoarthritis, Type 2 diabetes, or Parkinson's disease.

Two disadvantages are associated with this strategy. First, the cost of insurance for this level of coverage can be very high. Second, this strategy requires a client to maintain assets equivalent to the cost of care during the elimination period, which in light of current average monthly costs could equal $20,000 to $50,000, not including projected LTC expense increases. An alternative to reduce the cost of coverage includes extending the elimination period to a full year, if this option is available from the insurer and the client has enough assets to cover the cost. Another option is to limit the lifetime benefit period, a feature that significantly increases the premium.

Planning Strategy 8: Utilize a LTC Policy with a Four-year Benefit Period and a Ninety-day Elimination Period

This strategy is appropriate in cases where the probability of needing skilled care for an extended period is moderate to average, based on defined risk triggers. This strategy is most suitable for a client who is predisposed to terminal coronary artery disease or stroke, where the length of stay is not as long and has a higher probability of meeting the requirements for Medicare and/or Medicaid coverage. Should the length of stay exceed the benefit period, a client and the client's family has some time to consider alternatives for meeting the cost of care. According to the AALTCI, only 12 percent of patients stay for an average of five years or more in a nursing home. The largest distinct group of patients, 30 percent, stay an average of one to three years.[5]

Three possible disadvantages are associated with this strategy. First, insurance for this level of coverage can be expensive. Second, this strategy requires a client to maintain assets equivalent to the elimination period, in this case, $10,000 to $25,000, not including projected increases in annual costs. Third, the client could exhaust coverage should the LTC extend beyond the four-year coverage period. A longer elimination period will reduce the cost of insurance but doing so will increase the client's savings requirement.

Planning Strategy 9: Utilize a Fixed-premium, Restricted-coverage LTC Policy with a Four-year Combined Benefit Period and a Ninety-day Elimination Period

This strategy is appropriate in cases where the probability of needing custodial care is below average to low. The fixed premium results in a higher initial premium. Restricting the types of coverage reduces the overall cost of the insurance. One method of restricting the coverage involves having two years of coverage for assisted living care and two years for nursing care. Assuming a three-year combined care period, and having a ninety-day elimination period, results in a most up front self-funding. As long as one type of care does not exceed two years, a client's coverage should not be exhausted.

The primary disadvantage associated with this strategy is that the total four-year benefit period will not be available for either assisted living or nursing care. Insurance experts typically advise against limiting policy coverage to the point that the policy offers a false sense of security for the premiums paid but actually offers little protection. Eliminating benefits or key provisions from a comprehensive policy to make the premium affordable may be less effective than having no coverage at all.

Planning Strategy 10: Utilize a Fixed-premium LTC Policy with a Two-year Benefit Period and a 180-day Elimination Period

This strategy is appropriate in cases where the probability of needing custodial care is below-average to low. Although locking in the premium results in a higher initial cost, this can make sense when a client needs more certainty within a budget. Assuming a three-year care period, and having a 180-day elimination period, results in a client self-funding expenses for six months initially and again at the end payment period. If funding allows, and the option is available, a one-year elimination period may be preferable because this option substantially reduces the cost of insurance while requiring the client to self-fund only one year of coverage.

The three primary disadvantages associated with this strategy are: (1) the cost of insurance may still be significant for some clients; (2) this strategy requires a client to maintain an emergency level of savings equivalent to the elimination period; and (3) the shorter coverage period can leave a client unprotected in the event of an abnormally long care period.

Planning Strategy 11: Self-Insure the LTC Need

This strategy is appropriate in cases where the probability of needing custodial care is modest and a client has the financial resources to meet ongoing expenses. If a client's asset base is sufficient to support up to four years of expenses in today's dollars, LTC insurance may not be needed. This strategy is particularly appropriate for clients with a net worth in excess of $1.5 million and whose insurance coverage and other assets are adequate to care for surviving family members.

If a client is strongly committed to leaving a legacy gift or inheritance to individuals or assets to charity, this strategy can significantly diminish the assets available. With nursing home care costs ranging from approximately $40,000 to $200,000 annually, contingent on location and care provided, the cost of even four years of nursing care can be a significant sum. Assisted living facility care is almost as expensive and often precedes a move to a nursing facility. Clients who wish to leave a legacy should consider the benefits of a LTC insurance policy.

Planning Strategy 12: Self-Insure with a Life Insurance Backup

This strategy is best suited for a client whose asset base is sufficient to support at least partial funding of a LTC stay. If a life insurance policy is available that allows for a living benefit to be paid for the costs associated with LTC, even if the client is not terminally ill, then LTC insurance may not be needed. This can be a good strategy for a client who has a life insurance need but wants added protection should nursing care, such as skilled care or hospice, be needed. Before implementing this strategy, clients should be counseled that using the living benefit will reduce the amount of the legacy and/or leave survivors underinsured at the time of death. Because policies vary regarding the qualifications that must be met to receive a living benefit, a complete understanding of the requirements, as well as an evaluation of the cost of the rider, should always be considered.

Planning Strategy 13: Self-Insure with a Medicaid Backup

This strategy is appropriate for clients with less than $250,000 in net worth, exclusive of the home. Clients with this asset profile may find that the premiums associated with LTC insurance outweigh the benefits provided. It is possible that a client's asset base could be depleted if nursing home care is required, which would result in the client becoming dependent on Medicaid to pay for care.

Planning Strategy 14: Take Advantage of Available Policy Discounts

In some states, a 10 to 30 percent discount is available for married couples who insure jointly with the same insurer. Another way to decrease the cost of coverage for a married couple is by sharing a common benefit pool. Some individual plans allow couples to transfer benefits to each other from the same policy or sometimes between policies. A **spousal survivorship option**, available on some plans, requires both spouses to buy separate coverage. If one spouse dies after coverage has been in effect for a predetermined number of years, usually ten years, the surviving spouse's policy becomes paid up. As with health insurance, LTC insurance offers "good-health" discounts for people who do not take unnecessary health risks or have a history of debilitating diseases.

Planning Strategy 15: Use Caution When Recommending a LTC Policy to Young Clients

Clients younger than age fifty generally should not be encouraged to purchase LTC insurance unless they know that they have a high likelihood of needing care at an early age and for an extended time. One possible scenario making early age purchase viable may be if a client knows of a genetic predisposition for early-onset Alzheimer's disease or Parkinson's disease, which might make insurability problematic in the future. Clients who wait until at least age fifty to purchase LTC coverage implicitly self-insure the risk of needing LTC coverage earlier than age fifty. As with most LTC recommendations, it is good policy to have a client sign an acknowledgment that their LTC situation was evaluated and discussed, and that the client opted to postpone a LTC purchase.

Planning Strategy 16: Recommend a Joint LTC Policy

It can be significantly less expensive for a married couple (or an unmarried couple that meets the policy definitional requirements) to purchase a joint policy rather than purchasing two individual policies with the same benefit amount and period. With a joint policy, a couple shares the pool of benefits, either individually or simultaneously. This can be a very useful strategy when both partners want/need LTC coverage but only one has a high propensity for using the policy. Generally, this strategy should be recommended in situations where both spouses are close in age. Wide dispersions in age between spouses can trigger excessive policy premiums. However, a joint policy allows a couple to maximize eligible tax deductibility for the premium when there is a difference in ages between the spouses.

Although the annual premium for this type of coverage will be lower than purchasing two policies, the total benefit available for each spouse will also be lower should both become benefit eligible. To compensate, a large inflation factor is recommended to increase the daily or monthly benefit should both members of the couple require benefits simultaneously. This strategy may be unsuitable for spouses who are of significantly different ages because of the higher premiums.

Planning Strategy 17: Recommend Linked, or Shared-Care, Policy Riders

For a married couple (or an unmarried couple that meets policy definitional requirements), benefits can be increased by linking individual policies with a shared-care rider, which essentially provides sequential access to the benefits available to each individual, thus doubling the benefit, if necessary. Benefits can be drawn on simultaneously by each spouse, but combining the benefits is only available after one spouse has exhausted individual coverage. Thus, assets will be needed to supplement the cost of care if benefit coverage is insufficient for all costs. Discounts can be available when spouses apply for coverage at the same time.

The **shared-care rider** adds to the cost of the policies, but it is less expensive than buying additional benefits. Linking policies with reduced individual benefits can be a viable strategy unless the cost of care for one partner exceeds the benefit available, which will then require other assets to supplement the cost. The second spouse to need benefits will have access only to the remainder of his/her unused benefits, which can be insufficient.

Planning Strategy 18: Increase the Coverage Period but Decrease the Daily Benefit

If a client has adequate funds to self-insure but does not want to risk the chance of depleting savings, then sharing the cost of care might be an excellent alternative strategy. By choosing a lower daily benefit, such as $75 or $100, and increasing the benefit period to five years or more, a client should have adequate protection in the event of an abnormally long care period. Without incorporating an **inflation guard rider** in the policy, choosing a low initial benefit amount can put undue strain on a client's finances, regardless of the coverage period. To offset this possibility, a financial planner could recommend a **pool-of-money policy**, rather than a stated period, or indemnity, policy so that a client can draw a higher amount, up to actual costs incurred, until the policy is exhausted.

Planning Tip

Rather than adding an inflation guard rider, it may be less expensive to buy a greater fixed daily dollar benefit amount. If the premium, for example, for a $100 daily benefit with a 3 percent inflation guard rider is $250 per month, a $200 daily benefit without an inflation guard rider might only cost $140 per month. The difference in premium can be invested and used to self-insure future expenses.

Planning Strategy 19: Inform Clients that LTC Costs Are Generally Not Covered by Medicare

Clients are often misinformed about Medicare coverage and may need guidance to prepare for unexpected LTC costs. **Medicare** coverage for home care is limited to skilled-nursing care when homebound under a doctor's care. Skilled nursing home care, limited to one hundred days, is covered only within thirty days of a three-day or longer hospital stay. Hospice care in a Medicare-approved hospice is available only if a doctor certifies that the individual has six or fewer months to live. Furthermore, restrictions on the services covered, benefit periods, benefit payments, and client copayments apply in each situation. Without LTC insurance, and with only limited Medicare benefits, clients are effectively self-insuring against the costs associated with skilled nursing care. Unfortunately, clients who wish to rely on Medicare are often unaware of the actual costs involved, or how dramatically different costs can be in one area or one type of facility versus another. Implications for adult children who may provide care or share in the cost of insurance premiums or the cost of care services must also be considered.

Planning Strategy 20: Recommend Appropriate LTC Policy Provisions

LTC policy provisions customize a policy to better meet the needs of a client. Guaranteed renewability or better yet, noncancelability, is a recommended provision that adds to the cost of a policy. **Guaranteed renewable** means that as long as premiums are paid on time, the insurance company cannot cancel the policy, unless it does so for an entire risk category. Keep in mind that premiums can continue to increase. **Noncancelable** also means that a policy is in force as long as premiums are paid, but unlike the guaranteed renewable policy, premiums are fixed for the duration of the policy. Not all companies offer noncancelable policies. Guaranteed renewable policies are more commonly available.

Some policies offer ways for clients to shorten the length of time that premiums are due. **Accelerated payment options** include ten-pay, twenty-pay, or pay-until-age-sixty-five options. Each of these payment options allows for a fixed payment period beyond which no further premiums are due. This can be a very beneficial feature for clients who can afford to pre-pay a higher premium, thus avoiding payment later when income may be reduced, or medical expenses may have accelerated.

Another feature available on some LTC policies is a **restoration of benefits provision**. This feature is conditional and restores benefits that have been used under a policy, as long as the benefit pool has not been exhausted. For example, if a client has a six-year benefit policy and uses five years of benefits, all the policy benefits can be restored if a claim is not made for a certain length of time, typically twelve months. To trigger the restoration, a physician must certify that the insured no longer needs LTC, and the insured must resume paying premiums if a waiver of premium had been granted.

A **return of premium provision** adds approximately 70 to 80 percent to the base premium, but the provision will repay the difference between premiums paid and benefits collected upon the insured's death. To collect on this feature, most insurers require a policy to have been in force for a certain period of time, such as ten years. Although this feature is moderately expensive, it may be a useful planning tool if a client is uncertain about the probability of using the policy but wants the assurance of coverage for care, if needed.

A **bed hold provision** or **reservation feature** preserves a bed or room in a LTC facility should a client need to leave for a period of time, typically two weeks to two months, or for a certain cause, such as a stay in a hospital. In other words, the facility cannot "rent out" the client's room because it is temporarily unoccupied. This can be a very valuable feature if care facility vacancies in a geographic area are at a premium.

A **residual death benefit** makes a life insurance benefit available if the LTC coverage feature is not used. Some policies provide a minimal residual death benefit to cover final expenses if all policy benefits are exhausted. Inflation protection can also be purchased. This additional feature provides some protection against increasing long term-care costs.

One of the most beneficial options that can be purchased with a LTC policy is a **nonforfeiture clause provision**, especially if a client is young or still in exceptional health. In some policies this is known as a **benefit bank**. This clause allows the insured to receive some residual benefit in the event of policy lapse or death before making a claim. Many states require nonforfeiture on policies, or an insurance company may voluntarily offer the benefit as an option. A nonforfeiture option adds to the cost of a basic policy premium—in some cases, as much as 40 percent, and by some estimates as much as 100 percent.[6] Different types of nonforfeiture options are available, and costs vary by company.

Nonforfeiture options are similar to those for cash value life insurance. These options include a reduced lifetime (or paid-up) benefit, a reduced benefit period, or a return of premium. The **reduced paid-up coverage option** provides that a specified amount of coverage is available until the death of the client, but the daily benefit is permanently reduced, and with some companies the coverage is limited to nursing home care. The **shortened benefit period option** provides the insured the benefit originally offered, but the duration of coverage is limited based on the dollar amount of the premiums paid. With the **return of premium option**, a percentage of the premiums paid is returned after a policy lapses or death occurs.

For insureds who do not purchase a nonforfeiture option, some policies offer **contingent benefits nonforfeiture benefits** (CBL) upon lapse. Based on a standardized table recommended by the National Association of Insurance Commissioners (NAIC) 2000 Model Act and Regulation, this benefit is available when a policy lapses because of increased premium costs. Availability of the option is based on a comparison of an insured's age and the percentage increase in premium cost, either for a single increase or for cumulative increases, compared to the initial premium amount. Like other nonforfeiture options, CBL is available only when required by state law or when voluntarily offered by an insurance company. The options are reduced paid-up benefits (available indefinitely, but with a reduced daily benefit) or a shortened period of benefits (with the original coverage benefit available, but for a limited time).

For clients who are considering a LTC policy lapse or replacement provision, financial planners must carefully study the nonforfeiture and CBL options available. In some cases, continuing a policy for even a brief period of time can affect the nonforfeiture benefits available. As is true with other types of insurance, clients should be cautioned not to cancel a policy until another is in force. Furthermore, a pre-existing condition clause in a new policy can limit coverage initially. Also, premium costs will reflect the increased age of the client at the date of purchase. These are two distinct disadvantages that should not be overlooked.

Planning Strategy 21: Use Tax-advantaged Methods to Purchase LTC Coverage

A portion of the LTC premiums paid for a tax-qualified policy may be eligible for a medical expense deduction for clients who own their own businesses (including S-corporation owners, LLC members, and partnership owners) and individual taxpayers who file Schedule A as part of IRS Form 1040. For individuals, tax-qualified LTC insurance premiums paid for themselves, their spouses, or any tax dependents (e.g., parents) can be claimed as a personal medical expense.

Additionally, clients who purchase health insurance through a high-deductible health plan and a health savings account (HSA) can use distributions from the HSA to pay LTC insurance premiums up to a maximum eligible premium amount. This results in a pretax purchase method for LTC insurance. Some states also offer tax incentives (i.e., deductions or credits) for LTC premiums. If an HSA is used to purchase LTC coverage, clients will lose the IRS Schedule A deduction. Bear in mind that distributions from Section 125 plans and flexible spending accounts may not be used to pay LTC insurance premiums.

Planning Strategy 22: Consider Group LTC Coverage

For those who need LTC insurance, group coverage may be an acceptable option, especially for clients who might not meet the underwriting standards to qualify for an individual policy. However, for those who can qualify individually, adverse selection may force healthy clients to pay increasing premiums to subsidize the costs of others in the group. Nearly all group policies are guaranteed or modified-guaranteed (i.e., little or no medical history or health underwriting required). This means that clients should expect regular premium increases. Additionally, most group policies do not offer automatic inflation protection.

Quantitative/Analytical Mini-Case Problems

Ambra Turco

1. Ambra Turco is age fifty and single. She is concerned about funding long-term care insurance costs in the future. Based on family history, she has determined the following:

   • She will likely need long-term care coverage beginning at age seventy eight;

   • She will need coverage for six years;

- Long-term care costs in her area are currently $72,000 per year;

- Long-term care costs are increasing by 5 percent annually;

- She can earn 7 percent on her savings and assets;

- She currently earns $98,000 per year; and

- She has saved $75,000 that she is willing to earmark for long-term care costs.

Use this information to answer the following questions:

a. What is the future value cost of long-term care coverage when Ambra enters a nursing facility?

b. What is the total cost of coverage for six years when Ambra enters a nursing facility (present value of cost determined at age seventy eight)?

c. How long will Ambra's long-term care savings last when she enters a nursing facility?

d. Assume that Ambra has other property valued at $250,000. If she is willing to use this asset to help pay for long-term care costs, does she need long-term care insurance at this time?

Dan and Terry Ogelsmith

2. Recently, a married couple—Dan and Terry Ogelsmith—requested that you assist them by writing a modular, or targeted, long-term care financial plan. The clients both turned fifty four this month and are fairly wealthy but not rich. Specifically, they wanted to consider self-insuring for any long-term care costs. However, they do not know whether they have adequate assets to self-insure. Use the following client assumptions to answer their questions.

- The current cost of an assisted living facility is $95 per day and a nursing care facility is $135 per day.

- Cost of care will increase at an annual effective rate of 6 percent throughout the time period. Assume cost increases occur annually.

- Both clients will simultaneously enter care facilities at age seventy seven, spend three years in assisted living, and one year in nursing care, and die at age eighty one.

- For simplicity, assume that all expenses, whether premium payments or direct costs, are to be paid at the end of each year.

- The policy includes a *waiver of premium provision*. In other words, once the clients begin to receive benefits for a long-term care stay, premium payments cease.

- Premiums are not paid during the elimination period.

- The clients currently have $40,000 that could be set aside for long-term care expenses. But if long-term care insurance is purchased, this same account will be used to pay for insurance premiums.

- The effective annual required rate of return on invested funds is 6.5 percent.

- For simplicity, assume that all months have thirty days.

Use this information to answer the following questions:

a. How much will assisted living care cost per year when the clients reach age seventy seven?

b. How much will nursing care cost per year when the clients reach age eighty?

c. What is the total present value need for one person at age seventy seven?

d. Given the future value of assets saved for long-term care needs compared to future costs, should the couple plan to self-insure the need?

Lakned Jones

3. Lakned Jones is fifty years old. He is working with you, his financial planner, to calculate his long-term care insurance need. Please use the following assumptions to calculate Lakned's net LTC need:

- Current Annual Cost of LTC: $73,000

- Age at which Lakned will need LTC Services: seventy

- LTC Inflation Rate: 4.50 percent

- Number of Years Benefits will be Needed: sixBefore-Tax Rate of Return: 7 percent

- Marginal Tax Bracket: 24 percent

- Annual Increase in Savings: 0 percent

- Current Value of Assets Set Aside for LTC Need: $100,000

Afra Jenner

4. Afra Jenner's financial planner determined that Afra needs to purchase a long-term care policy.

a. If Afra expects her expenses to fluctuate month-to-month in the event she was to need long-term care assistance, which policy type should her financial planner recommend?

b. To prepare for the possibility of needing long-term care assistance, Afra has been gifting assets to family, friends, and charitable organizations. Which of the following asset transfers will most likely trigger Medicaid to consider the transfer non-exempt?

  - A gift of $50,000 in home equity to her husband.

  - A $35,000 gift of stock to her church six years ago.

  - A $100,000 transfer of bank assets to her daughter four years ago.

  - A $25,000 gift of clothing and household items to Goodwill two years ago.

   c.   After reviewing the cost of long-term care coverage, Afra is reluctant to buy a LTC policy. She may be willing to buy a policy if the premium can be reduced. When choosing between extending the elimination period or increasing the benefit period, which will reduce her annual premium?

   d.   Afra's husband, Rex, believes that insurance of any type is a rip-off. He worries that if he does not need LTC care, all the premiums paid will have been for nothing. However, he does not want to pay 100 percent of LTC costs if he needs care. What policy provision can Rex add to a policy that will provide some piece of mind?

Jamal and Chyna Gwynn

5.   Your clients, Jamal and Chyna Gwynn, would like you to estimate their LTC insurance needs. Use the following information to determine the disability insurance need for Jamal and Chyna separately:

- Jamal: Age forty eight; Life Expectancy: Age ninety seven

- Chyna: Age fifty; Life Expectancy: Age ninety five

- Cost of Care Today: $78,000

- Age of LTC Need: seventy three for Jamal and seventy five for Chyna

- Length of LTC Need: four years

- Federal Marginal Tax Bracket: 24 percent

- State Marginal Tax Bracket: 5 percent

- Rate of Salary Increase: 0 percent

- Assets to Be Used in Case of LTC Need: $150,000

   a.   What is the LTC need for one person?

   b.   What is the LTC need combined?

   c.   How much, if any, LTC insurance should Jamal and Chyna purchase?

Chapter Resources

AARP (www.aarp.org/).

Administration on Aging (www.aoa.gov).

American Association for Long-Term Care Insurance (www.aaltci.org/).

Commission on Accreditation of Rehabilitation Facilities/Continuing Care Accreditation Commission (CARF/CCAC) (www.carf.org/Providers.aspx?content=content/Accreditation/Opportunities/AS/CCAC.htm).

Comparison of Nursing Homes (www.medicare.gov/NHcompare).

Comprehensive long-term care insurance information (www.longtermcarelink.net).

LeadingAge (www.leadingage.org/).

Long-term Care Partnership Only (ltcpartnershiponly.com/index.html).

Medicare (www.medicare.gov).

National Clearinghouse for Long-term Care Information (www.longtermcare.gov).

Weiss Ratings (www.weissratings.com).

Patient Protection and Affordable Care Act (PPACA) of 2010: www.dol.gov/ebsa/healthreform/

Endnotes

1. American Association for Long-Term Care Insurance. 2008 LTCi Sourcebook. Available at: www.aaltci.org/long-term-care-insurance/learning-center/fast-facts.php.

2. New York Partnership for Long-Term Care: https://nyspltc.health.ny.gov/

3. American Association for Long-Term Care Insurance. Available at: https://www.aaltci.org/about/linked-benefit-compared-to-traditional-long-term-care-insurance.php

4. J. L. Phipps *New: A Hybrid Annuity with LTC Coverage.* Available at: www.bankrate.com/finance/insurance/new-a-hybrid-annuity-with-ltc-coverage-1.aspx.

5. American Association for Long-term Care Insurance, *What Is the Probability You'll Need Long-term Care? Is Long-Term Care Insurance A Smart Financial Move?* Based on the 2008 LTCi Sourcebook. Available at: www.aaltci.org/long-term-care-insurance/learning-center/probability-long-term-care.php. (updated 2019)

6. What if You Cannot Afford to Continue Paying the Long-Term Care Premium? Nonforfeiture Benefits in Long Term Care Insurance Policies. Available at: law.freeadvice.com/insurance_law/long_term_care/can-not-afford-to-continue-paying-long-term-care.htm.

Chapter 9

Property and Casualty Insurance Planning

Learning Objectives

- Learning Objective 1: Evaluate a client's property and casualty insurance need.

- Learning Objective 2: Identify liability exposures associated with the ownership of property.

- Learning Objective 3: Assess a client's need for property replacement and liability insurance coverage.

- Learning Objective 4: Compare different homeowner's and personal automobile insurance policies.

- Learning Objective 5: Identify the appropriate standard and supplemental coverages a client can use to reduce liability exposures and the possibility of property losses.

- Learning Objective 6: Describe the role of excess liability insurance in a client's risk management strategy.

- Learning Objective 7: Recommend appropriate property and casualty insurance policies.

CFP® Principal Knowledge Topics

- CFP Topic: D.22. Principles of Risk and Insurance.
- CFP Topic: D.23. Analysis and Evaluation of Risk Exposures.
- CFP Topic: D.31. Insurance Policy and Company Selection.
- CFP Topic: D.32. Property and Casualty Insurance.

Chapter Equations

Coinsurance Penalty:

$$\frac{\text{Amount of HO Insurance Coverage}}{80\% \text{ Replacement Cost}} \times \text{Value of Loss} = \text{Value of the Claim} - \text{Deductible} = \text{Reimbursement Amount}$$

PROPERTY AND LIABILITY INSURANCE PLANNING STRATEGIES

Reviewing a client's current property coverage and liability limits can help a financial planner and the financial planner's clients discover gaps in property and casualty exposures. This can lead to recommendations to enhance in-force policies and add new coverage to fill any insurance gaps. The way an insurance contract is structured will affect the cost and amount of insurance obtained. The following discussion describes commonly used property and liability insurance strategies financial planners use in the financial planning process. When reviewing these strategies, it is important to consider that, in practice, financial planners often go beyond these basic approaches to help their clients navigate the complex property and casualty insurance environment.

Planning Strategy 1: Describe the Types of HO Policies Available

HO policies are generally packaged as **standard policy forms**. Figure 9.1 compares the seven most widely used HO policy forms. An important feature that differentiates HO policies is protection from **perils**. A **named perils policy** protects against economic loss resulting from perils that are specifically named within a policy. **Open peril** is a term used to describe an **all-risk policy** that covers losses from all causes unless specifically excluded in the insurance contract. These exclusions typically include flood, earthquake, war, nuclear accident, and mold. Corresponding to these types of policies is the related issue of **burden of proof**. With a named perils policy, the homeowner (or renter) must provide evidence that the loss was caused by a named peril listed in the policy. In contrast, with the open peril policy, a loss is covered unless the insurance company can provide evidence that the loss was excluded from the policy.

Once the type of policy is selected, both homeowner and renter have choices on the level of protection offered (known as a policy's loss settlement clause). Some policies use **actual cash value (ACV)** as the basis for replacing property. Although typically applied to replacement of possessions, ACV may also apply to claims on a structure. Actual cash value provides reimbursement based on the replacement value of the property less depreciation. Older property, whose age exceeds the specified useful life of "x" years, has little or no reimbursement value. Consequently, reimbursement could be pennies on the dollar relative to the value of the loss or the amount needed for even minimal replacement. Keep in mind that the term market value refers to reimbursement based on the value of similar items in the secondary market, whereas replacement cost coverage pays for a similar new product.

A **replacement cost coverage endorsement** provides for lost, stolen, or destroyed property to be replaced with equivalent property with no reductions for depreciation. Although slightly more expensive, replacement cost coverage is recommended in most situations.

Although not available in every state or from every insurance company, homeowners also may have the choice of **guaranteed replacement cost** or **extended replacement cost** for claims on the structure. With both, the amount paid on a claim to replace or repair the structure may exceed the amount of coverage on which the premium is based. Guaranteed replacement coverage pays the full amount, while extended replacement coverage pays a specified amount, typically 20 to 25 percent above the policy coverage limit. These endorsements protect the insured in the case of a total loss or when a natural disaster may cause widespread market increases in construction costs. It is important to note that costs of upgrading a home to comply with current building codes are not typically included.

Condominium or cooperative owners must also consider the level of coverage on unit property for which they are responsible, such as built-in cabinetry, appliances, or other surface treatments (e.g., carpet, tile, wall paper, etc.) relative to the actual cash value or replacement cost decision. Upgrading to replacement cost and inflation guard protection offers broader protection, but it will increase premium costs as well.

Figure 9.1. Common HO Policy Forms and Coverage

Seven Forms of Homeowners Policies*						
Form	Part A Dwelling	Part B Other Structures	Part C Personal Property	Part D Loss of Use	Part E Typical Personal Liability Limit	Part F Typical Medical Payments to Others Limit
Broad Form (HO-2) Named 16 perils policy**	Replacement value	10% of dwelling coverage	50% of dwelling coverage; actual cash value	30% of dwelling coverage	$100,000	$1,000 per person per incident
Special Form (HO-3) Named 16 perils policy for personal property	Replacement value	10% of dwelling coverage	50% of dwelling coverage; actual cash value	30% of dwelling coverage	$100,000	$1,000 per person per incident

Contents Form (HO-4) Named 16 perils policy for personal property***	Does not apply	Does not apply	Usually stated in dollar amount; actual cash value	30% of personal property coverage	$100,000	$1,000 per person per incident
Comprehensive Form (HO-5) All perils, except specific exclusions	Replacement value	10% of dwelling coverage	50% of dwelling coverage; actual cash value	30% of dwelling coverage	$100,000	$1,000 per person per incident
Unit Owner's Form (HO-6) Named 16 perils policy**	$1,000 - $5,000 minimum limited to semi-permanent features in the unit	Does not apply or included in Part A	Usually stated in dollar amount; actual cash value	50% of personal property coverage	$100,000	$1,000 per person per incident
Modified Coverage Form (HO-8) Named 11 perils policy††	Market value of structure or cost to repair replace with functional equivalent	10% of dwelling coverage	50% of dwelling coverage; actual cash value	10% of dwelling coverage	$100,000	$1,000 per person per incident

* This summary is based on the standard Insurance Service Office (ISO) policy forms used throughout the United States. Policy variations may apply as some insurers use American Association of Insurance Services (AAIS) forms, while some insurers design their own forms, and in some instances, state mandated modifications may apply. For more information see www.iso.com. HO-1 policies are generally no longer available.

†† The named 11 perils typically include: (1) Fire or lightning; (2) windstorm or hail; (3) explosion; (4) riot or civil commotion; (5) damage caused by aircraft; (6) damage caused by vehicles; (7) smoke; (8) vandalism or malicious mischief; (9) theft; (10) volcanic eruption; and (11) falling objects.

** The additional five perils (leading to a total of 16) include: (12) weight of ice, snow or sleet; (13) accidental discharge or overflow of water or steam from within plumbing, heating, air conditioning, automatic fire-protective sprinkler system, or from a household appliance; (14) sudden and accidental tearing apart, cracking, burning, or bulging of a steam or hot water heating system, an air conditioning or automatic fire-protective system; (15) freezing of a plumbing, heating, air conditioning, automatic, fire-protective sprinkler system, or of a household appliance; and (16) sudden and accidental damage from artificially generated electrical current (does not include loss to a tube, transistor or similar electronic component). See the Insurance Information Institute at http://www.iii.org/policymakers/home/ for more information.

Planning Strategy 2: Recommend an HO-3 Policy with Appropriate Liability Coverage

An **HO-3 policy** provides the broadest open perils coverage available for a given structure. According to the Insurance Information Institute, an HO-3 policy provides coverage for the structure of the home and personal belongings as well as personal liability coverage.[1] An HO-3 policy also provides the broadest coverage, protecting against the following 16 events:

- Fire or lightning

- Windstorm or hail

- Explosion

- Riot or civil commotion

- Damage caused by aircraft

- Damage caused by vehicles

- Smoke

- Vandalism or malicious mischief

- Theft

- Volcanic eruption

- Falling object

- Weight of ice, snow or sleet

- Accidental discharge or overflow of water or steam from within a plumbing, heating, air conditioning, or automatic fire-protective sprinkler system, or from a household appliance

- Sudden and accidental tearing apart, cracking, burning, or bulging of a steam or hot water heating system, an air conditioning or automatic fire-protective system

- Freezing of a plumbing, heating, air conditioning or automatic, fire-protective sprinkler system, or of a household appliance

- Sudden and accidental damage from artificially generated electrical current (does not include loss to a tube, transistor or similar electronic component)

Planning Tip

Play it safe by recommending an in-home safe to store valuables and the verifications for property values. Buying a safe retains the risk and reduces the probability of loss. Purchasing insurance coverage (i.e., endorsement or floater) is a form of loss sharing.

Keep in mind that an HO-3 policy covers personal property losses for named perils *only*. An endorsement to provide open perils coverage on the contents is available for those who prefer the most comprehensive coverage, assuming an HO-5 is unavailable. If the HO-3 provides only $100,000 in liability coverage, it should be increased to a minimum of $300,000, which is what many financial planners consider a minimum level of protection and in some cases required by the insurance company as a minimum for adding an umbrella policy. Increasingly, a minimum of $500,000 of liability protection is recommended. An umbrella policy can be added for additional liability protection. Choosing the open perils coverage on contents, or the higher liability limit, will add to the cost of the policy but this expense can be partially offset by a higher deductible.

Planning Strategy 3: Use the 80 Percent Rule to Determine Adequacy of Insurance Coverage

Two out of every three homes in the United States are underinsured.[2] Some homeowner's policies include an **80 percent rule** (or "coinsurance" rule) to determine the level of reimbursement when a loss is incurred. Every financial plan should include an 80 percent rule analysis when a client owns a home.[3] The 80 percent rule provides a way to verify whether an HO policy limit is sufficient to provide full replacement for a major loss. Based on the replacement value of the residence at the time of loss, if the amount of coverage is equal to or greater than 80 percent of the replacement cost, full replacement of the damaged portion will be paid, up to the limits of the policy less the deductible, with no reduction for depreciation. If the insured does not carry insurance equal to at least 80 percent of the replacement cost, the insured is penalized through a coinsurance clause when the loss is paid.

Planning Tip

Although 80 percent coverage is the minimally acceptable level of coverage on a structure, 100 percent coverage with an inflation endorsement is a standard planning strategy.

If the amount of insurance on a structure, divided by 80 percent of the applicable replacement cost, is equal to or greater than 1.0, then the homeowner will be reimbursed for the lesser of the replacement cost or the amount of the policy. However, if the amount of insurance on the structure, divided by 80 percent of the applicable replacement cost, is less than 1.0, then the insured will not qualify for full repair or replacement. The reduction in reimbursement is sometimes referred to as a **coinsurance penalty**. If an insured is penalized, the insured will be paid the actual cash value of the part of the structure damaged or destroyed less the deductible *or* the reimbursement amount calculated using the following formula:

$$\frac{\text{Amount of HO Insurance Coverage}}{80\% \text{ Replacement Cost}} \times \text{Value of Loss} = \text{Value of the Claim} - \text{Deductible} = \text{Reimbursement Amount}$$

Planning Tip

The deductible amount will be subtracted from all settlements, regardless of whether the insured has met the 80 percent rule. Actual cash value settlements typically depreciate a property to account for its age. Replacement cost settlements typically do not include depreciation.

Assume, for example, that a client owns a home with a replacement value of $190,000. Unfortunately, over the years the policy has not kept pace with the rising values of construction, with the home being currently insured for $130,000 with a $500 deductible. If the insured incurs a loss of $20,000, the insurance company will value the claim at only $16,605, as shown below:

$$\left(\frac{\$130,000}{80\% \times \$190,000} \times \$20,000 \right) - \$500 = \$17,105 - \$500 = \$16,605$$

The $2,895 not reimbursed on the $20,000 claim is considered to be the client's coinsurance penalty. However, this is the reimbursement before applying the $500 deductible. Therefore, the actual amount received by the client will be $16,605. To maintain full reimbursement to the limit of the policy, the house should have been insured for a minimum of $152,000 ($190,000 multiplied by 80 percent).

Planning Tip

For clients who rent or own a condominium or cooperative, the 80 percent rule is not an effective measure of coverage. Other factors must be considered because the client is only responsible for the interior of their property. Foremost is the named perils coverage on contents, which some clients may wish to extend to protect against all risks except specific exclusions. Clients protected by an HO-4 or HO-6 policy should include replacement cost and inflation guard (discussed later in the chapter) endorsements for maximum protection.

In general, it is important to remember three rules when evaluating the current coverage limits on a client's home:

- The 80 percent rule applies primarily to partial losses;

- If the actual cash value exceeds the 80 percent rule limit, the insured receives the larger amount; and

- The total reimbursement will never exceed the face amount of the policy less the deductible.

Planning Strategy 4: Maximize HO Coverage with Endorsements

To personalize and maximize coverage, a wide variety of endorsements, such as a personal articles endorsement, personal injury endorsement, an identity theft endorsement, an inflation endorsement, or home office coverage, can be written as an addendum to a HO contract. These choices must be considered in light of a client's property, risk tolerance, and emergency funds available for unreimbursed losses, as well as the projected probability for loss relative to the additional premium cost of the endorsement.

Three endorsements are generally recommended:

- A **replacement cost endorsement** for the structure, the contents, or both.

- An **inflation endorsement**.

- A **building code upgrade endorsement.**

The need for these endorsements will vary with the individual insurer and the HO policy. Whenever major repairs or reconstruction must occur, building codes mandate that the work must be updated to the standards of the current building code requirements. Bringing a home up to date in an affected area can significantly add to replacement costs. Some HO policies provide coverage that helps offset expenses associated with bringing a dwelling up to residential code standards after a loss; however, the amount of coverage is typically limited to 10 percent of the amount of insurance on the dwelling. Other policies provide no coverage for this necessary expense.

Planning Tip

Four parameters can be used whenever an HO policy is recommended to a client.

- First, clients should purchase maximum liability protection, but generally never less than a $300,000 limit. This should be coordinated with an umbrella policy of at least $1 million.

- Second, the coverage should be as comprehensive as possible.

- Third, first-party losses should be paid on a replacement cost basis, with an annual inflation adjustment.

- Fourth, any and all discounts should be explored, including the use of higher deductibles.

Premium discounts also may be earned by implementing property protection devices and by buying all policies from the same insurance company.

Planning Strategy 5: Recommend Excess Liability Coverage through an Umbrella Liability Policy

Rapidly increasing jury awards for liability claims have escalated the need for additional liability insurance to protect current assets and future income. High net worth clients are especially at risk for liability exposure.

The annual cost for an **excess liability coverage** (an **umbrella policy**) is quite reasonable. A $1 million policy can be purchased for $300 or less annually in most cases.

HO and personal automobile policy (PAP) liability limits generally must be increased to obtain an umbrella policy. A minimum of $300,000 in liability coverage for a HO policy typically is most often required. Higher split-limit PAP coverage, such as 250/500/100, or a $500,000 single limit, is normally required. If needed, a client's HO policy or PAP provides the first level of coverage in case of litigation. Once these policy limits are reached, the umbrella policy provides additional protection up to the limits of the policy.

If an umbrella policy is used for a claim that is excluded from HO or PAP coverage, a deductible ranging from a low of perhaps $250 to as much as several thousand dollars may be imposed. For example, payment of a deductible would be required for a lawsuit that is excluded from HO coverage. This must be considered when establishing emergency fund needs.

Planning Strategy 6: Review the Possibility of Dropping Collision Coverage on Autos Six to Eight Years of Age or Older

The costs associated with repairing significant damage on a late model automobile almost always exceeds the book value of the automobile. In such cases, an insurance company may elect not to repair the car. Rather, the insurance provider may pay the insured the book value (minus the deductible) and declare the car a total loss. Paying premiums for collision coverage on a car in this situation may not be cost effective.

Dropping collision coverage will reduce the premium paid and increase annual discretionary cash flow. However, the insured must recognize that, without physical damage protection, any loss other than an at-fault accident caused by another driver with insurance will mean that the insured must pay for all repair costs or replace the vehicle with another automobile. This strategy is least effective when a client owns a high value or collectible car.

Planning Tip

Four personal automobile policy rules should be followed.

- First, clients should obtain the maximum affordable level of liability coverage, which should be coordinated with coverage for uninsured and underinsured motorists and an umbrella policy.

- Second, medical expense coverage should be evaluated. Policy payments to others within the policy should be maximized if the insured frequently has passengers who are not family members.

- Third, clients need to take advantage of premium reductions for discounts and higher deductibles.

- Fourth, collision insurance, which covers damage to a policy holder's auto resulting from physical contact with another object, should be monitored yearly and eliminated if the automobile's value drops substantially.

It is also important to monitor comprehensive insurance coverage as well. In situations where a client owns an older car, comprehensive coverage can be reduced or eliminated as a way to decrease the annual premium.

Planning Strategy 7: Choose the Highest Deductible a Client Can Afford

Generally, a higher deductible is preferred across policies unless a client has limited emergency savings. Raising an HO policy deductible from $500 to $1,000, for example, can save a client up to 25 percent in annual premium costs.[4] Similarly, raising a PAP deductible from $200 to $500 can reduce collision and comprehensive coverage costs by 15 to 30 percent. Increasing a deductible to $1,000 can save 40 percent or more in annual premium costs.[5] Because client out-of-pocket expenses will increase in case of a loss, this strategy requires a client to increase their emergency fund holdings, which may temporarily divert savings and assets from funding other goals. Financial planners should conduct a cost-benefit analysis to determine how long it will take to recoup costs if a claim occurs earlier or later in the savings process.

Planning Strategy 8: Increase Liability Limits

In general, liability limits in an HO policy should be increased to a minimum of $300,000. Insurance experts often recommend that clients have a minimum of $100,000/$300,000/$100,000 in split-limit coverage in a PAP. A minimum of $500,000 **combined single-limit coverage** is recommended, with the insurance company paying covered liabilities up to this amount regardless of the distribution between bodily injury and property damage liability.

Increasing liability coverage decreases the likelihood of being **underinsured for losses** caused to others. Furthermore, these amounts are generally the minimum required to purchase excess liability insurance.

Increasing liability limits will result in an annual premium increase. But the premium cost must be considered relative to the protection of assets and future income, in the event of a large award from an at-fault accident. The increased premium cost can be partially offset by (1) comparing costs from different insurers; (2) taking advantage of all discounts; and (3) increasing the deductible on collision and comprehensive coverages, as generally no deductible applies to the liability coverage for auto on homeowner policies.

Planning Strategy 9: Reduce Premiums with Discounts

Clients may be eligible for insurance premium discounts. For example, an older client who drives infrequently may be eligible for a low-mileage discount, whereas clients with teenagers or college-age children should inquire about good student discounts. In many states, it is also possible to receive a discount for taking a driver's education course. Clients who insure a home and automobile with a single insurer may receive a **multi-policy discount**. HO policy discounts may be available for smoke detectors or security systems, including dead-bolt locks. The only real disadvantage associated with this strategy is the amount of time involved in researching, requesting, or validating eligibility for certain discounts. Clients should instruct their insurance agent to recommend applicable discounts.

Planning Strategy 10: Review Insurance Rates before Purchasing a New Car

Insurance rates are, in part, based on the type and value of the car being insured. Cars with lower repair rates will be less expensive to insure than those with higher repair histories. Likewise, a lower-priced car will be less expensive to insure than a more valuable one. Cars with outstanding safety records, passive restraint systems, and antitheft devices may also be subject to lower premiums. Unfortunately, implementing this strategy can significantly limit a client's choice in vehicles. Additionally, adding features that will reduce premium costs may increase the overall cost of a vehicle. The best advice is to check the cost of coverage on all models being considered by a client.

Planning Strategy 11: Bundle HO and PAP Coverages to Reduce Annual Premiums

Financial planners should help their clients should shop aggressively for HO and PAP bundled coverage. The marketplace is competitive and discounts are widely available for those with a strong history of premium payments and a low incident level of filing claims. An easy way to reduce annual premiums involves bundling a PAP and HO policy together, using a replacement value endorsement. When determining the level of HO insurance to purchase, insurance agents and brokers often recommend using the **cost per square foot** associated with building in a local area as a guide. Average insurance rates, for bundled and unbundled policies, can be obtained at www.homeownersinsurance.com.

A clear disadvantage associated with bundling coverage relates to sometimes being held captive by one insurance company. Although a single provider may offer competitive rates on, for example, HO policies, there is no guarantee that the company will also be competitive with PAP coverage rates. It is important for financial planners to work with their clients to shop competitively for bundled policies that provide the lowest net premium cost.

Planning Strategy 12: Use an Appropriate Business Structure to Help a Client Limit Liability

Although not entirely a property and casualty insurance issue, clients who own a business as a sole proprietorship, who also use personal property as a function of their business, need to understand that they are exposed to potential unlimited **personal liability** for claims against either the business or the individual. Normally, this liability cannot be controlled with an HO policy or an excess liability insurance contract. Although a **sole proprietorship** can be easy to manage, there are better alternatives to protect clients from liability. Five alternatives should be considered when working with small business owners. These alternatives, with a brief description, are listed below:

- **C-corporation:** Limited liability for owners; relatively complex to manage. The corporate structure can provide an effective way to provide tax-advantaged fringe benefits for employees and owner-shareholders.

- **S-corporation:** Limited liability for owners; income flows through from corporation to owners; may not have more than one hundred shareholders.

- **LLC:** Liability limited to member's contribution to firm; members rather than shareholders; less cumbersome than a corporation.

- **LLP:** Liable for actions of all partners, but not liable for errors and omissions of partners.

- **Partnership:** Liable for action of all partners; this form of business ownership provides little liability protection.

The costs, both financially and administratively, are higher for these arrangements than for sole proprietorships. Also, changing from a corporate structure back to a sole proprietorship can be expensive. Sometimes clients feel these costs outweigh the potential liability associated with owning a business; nonetheless, financial planners should always address liability exposure and recommend alternative forms of business ownership, when appropriate, within a comprehensive financial plan.

Planning Strategy 13: Account for Special Client Situations when Completing a Property Insurance Analysis

Planning for property and liability risk management issues can be a challenge because of the property owned or lifestyle activities of clients. A financial planner must be cognizant of special situations and client needs when developing property insurance recommendations. Consider the following situations:

Jewelry Owners. Very few people typically walk around with thousands of dollars in their pocket. Yet, a diamond ring, wedding band, watch, or other jewelry can easily amount to $10,000 or more. Jewelry owners often make three common mistakes.

- First, they sometimes assume that jewelry is covered by their HO policy, not realizing that relatively low limits apply (typically $2,500).

- Second, they do not understand that policies rarely cover loss, damage, or the loss of a diamond from the setting.

- Third, they forget that a deductible will also apply, further reducing the stated, limited protection.

Personal Article Policies, which are relatively inexpensive, provide comprehensive jewelry coverage, typically without a required deductible. The annual premium for a personal article floater can be estimated using the following formula:

- Value of Property × 2 percent.

For example, a ring valued at $5,000 can be insured for approximately $100 per year.

Another common mistake is the failure to periodically update jewelry appraisals based on fluctuations in the price of gold, silver, diamonds, or other precious stones and metals. Recommendations on how often new appraisals should be performed vary, but waiting more than, say, ten years is inadvisable. Without a current assessment, a gap in coverage can result in a loss of not only the item of jewelry, but also in the amount of insurance proceeds to replace it.

A personal articles policy is an all-perils policy and protects from loss, theft, or damage to the item, as well as loss of gemstones and diamonds. A **pair and set clause** offers additional protection for items sold as a pair or a set, as in a matching diamond ring and wedding band or a pair of earrings. A broad form pays for full replacement of both items, but a standard form pays only to replace, or duplicate, the missing component. Personal articles policies typically include inflation protection, based on the purchase price or appraised value when insurance is initially purchased, and require no deductible.

Another common mistake is failure to maintain an up-to-date inventory of items owned. Appraisals required to purchase personal article policies (or to add a personal article endorsement) provide needed documentation, but it is still important to maintain a complete inventory of all jewelry. Care should be taken to continually update the inventory and buy coverage for new purchases. In fact, specialized insurance is available to protect items purchased during a specific time period, such as while traveling, so that insurance is immediately available until a personal articles policy or endorsement can be obtained.

Planning Tip

Completing periodic reviews of a client's insurance coverage is an important task. At a minimum, insurance policy documents should be reviewed annually for accuracy to ensure the following are accurate:

- Names and addresses

- Social Security numbers

- Dwelling construction type

- Dwelling or outbuilding additions

- Auto, motorcycle, or watercraft coverage

- Deductibles

- Schedules and endorsements

- Any new purchases that may require coverage

- Coordination of coverage if not purchased through the same company

If any item on a policy document is incorrect or inaccurate, immediate steps should be taken to correct it. Accurate documentation will lead to more efficient claims settlement should a loss occur.

Those Serving on Corporate or Nonprofit Organization Boards. Individuals are often honored, and quite motivated, to serve on the board of directors of a nonprofit organization. Most corporations and nonprofit organizations purchase **directors' and officers' (D&O)** liability insurance to protect those serving in this capacity. If the coverage is inadequate or is not purchased, then a liability suit that names the officers and directors can expose a client's personal assets to claims or jury awards. An excess, or umbrella, liability policy provides limited protection in this situation, specifically for bodily injury or property damage. An umbrella policy may help pay for the costs of defending the client.

A better option is for the client to purchase a directors and officers liability policy to protect against non-bodily injury claims (e.g., discrimination or termination of employment) arising from misstatements, misleading statements, breach of duty, or errors and omissions. The policy may or may not provide for legal and court fees, and deductibles often apply.

Pet Lovers. The financial planning data collection and discovery process can reveal a family's love for animals. Consider the potential liability a client may face if they serve on a local animal shelter board. Someone who visits the shelter and is bitten by a dog can sue both the shelter and board members. A qualified insurance specialist is best equipped to address this possibility and to recommend the necessary insurance protection.

A financial planner can play a pivotal rule in asking the questions to uncover the issue and to recommend the necessary actions to be taken. In this case, obtaining Directors & Officers insurance is a necessity. If the same person were to own a dangerous pet, such as a dog or exotic animal, they should check with their insurance agent to ensure that their HO and umbrella coverages are still valid. The client may be required to obtain additional coverage or to remove the animal from the home.

Protecting Against Identity Theft. Clients may not have considered insurance coverage in the event of a stolen identity. In fact, according to the Federal Trade Commission (FTC), one of their top consumer complaints is related to identity theft.[6] Placing fraud alerts with credit reporting bureaus, shredding documents with personal or financial information, and using strong passwords are all recommended methods of prevention. There are times, however, when these measures fail. According to the FTC's *2016 Identity Fraud Study*, $112 billion was stolen from individuals from 2010 through 2016.[7] Identity theft can continue undetected until the victim checks their credit report, notices an incorrect charge on a credit card statement, or is contacted by a debt collector.

One method to mitigate such loss at the household level is to insure for the loss. Some HO policies provide at least a modest form of coverage. This may be limited to a particular type of transaction (e.g., forgery, electronic fund transfer, or credit card fraud) or a nominal amount of coverage (e.g., $500 to $1,000) depending on the insurance company. The first layer of additional protection is available with an endorsement to an HO policy to enhance both the scope and coverage amount for a potential loss. Additional coverage may be available with an excess liability policy.

Planning Strategy 14: Understand the Needs of Cohabitating Couples, Housemates, or Partners

Insurance companies can deny claims from an auto accident caused by a driver who routinely has access to a car but is not included on the policy as a driver or for a fire caused by a live-in partner or roommate who is not included on the HO policy.

Often, property owners, of a car or home, may never suspect that they, and the actions of their partners, are not protected in these situations. It is essential that financial planners review the titling—and insurance coverage—of jointly used assets as part of the insurance planning analysis.

In the case of a vehicle, nearly all insurance companies will allow a multicar policy for unrelated individuals who share the same "garage address" for vehicles. If this is unavailable or is not the method preferred by a nontraditional couple or housemates, then the other option is to add the partner or roommate to the auto policy of each of the insured's vehicles. With either method, the premium cost will be based on the driving records of both individuals. This is required for regular access to, and use of, the other partner's car. If access to the other partner's car is limited to a random, occasional occurrence, then it is not necessary to add the partner as a driver. If there is only one car, but both partners routinely drive it, then both must be named as insured drivers on the policy.

Similarly, if a home is owned by one partner, coverage must be extended to the housemate or partner. Typically, HO policies are written to match the deed and protect only the insured and the insured's immediate family. To extend coverage, several options are available. The non-owner's name may be added to the policy as an additional insured, although not all companies will allow this. Some companies add a rider, or **cohabitant form**, for an additional occupant. If this is not available or is not the method preferred by the client(s), then the non-owner should purchase a renter's policy, even if no rent is actually being paid. The renter's policy will provide protection for the personal property in the home, and more importantly, provide liability and other HO-4 coverage, if needed. If the home is rented, a joint renter's policy may be available; otherwise, each partner should purchase an individual policy.

Contingent on the insurance options chosen from these alternatives, a similar strategy may be available to purchase excess liability insurance. State laws and company policies vary, so it is important to consult with an insurance professional. However, individuals who are not married or do not own property jointly typically cannot purchase an excess liability policy together; individual umbrella policies will be necessary. Either way, the protection should be matched, at a minimum, to the net worth of the individuals, and potentially to an even higher amount to protect assets adequately.

Quantitative/Analytical Mini-Case Problems

Ricardo Juarez

1. Ricardo Juarez is purchasing a HO insurance policy. He is very concerned about inflation and wants to make a determination about purchasing an optional inflation protection rider. Ricardo has identified several scenarios and wants to know how often he needs to revisit his coverage to maintain at least 80 percent of replacement cost. Base all calculations on an initial home value of $250,000 and initial coverage of 100 percent on the dwelling and contents.

    a. Ricardo believes that current housing prices will increase at 4 percent per year. How long will his coverage meet the 80 percent rule if he does not buy inflation protection? How long will he be covered if he purchases an inflation protection rider that offers annual compound increases of 3 percent?

b.   Given recent declines in housing values, Ricardo believes a recovery is coming and that housing prices will increase at 7 percent per year for the next five years before slowing to a permanent 4 percent annual appreciation rate. How long will his coverage meet the 80 percent rule? First assume that Ricardo does not purchase an inflation protection rider, and second assume that he purchases an inflation protection rider that offers annually compounded increases of 3 percent.

c.   Ricardo believes that housing prices still have a way to fall before any meaningful recovery. He believes that future housing prices will decrease at an annual rate of 4 percent for the next three years before the long-term trend of 5 percent annual increases resumes. Assuming that he does not purchase an inflation protection rider, how long will his coverage meet the 80 percent rule?

d.   Ricardo believes that future price increases will be very unstable. With this uncertainty, he wants to have the inflation rider protection of 3 percent compounded annually. Assume actual housing price changes for the next five years are 3, -7, -2, 8, and 12 percent. Will his coverage meet the 80 percent rule at the end of this five-year period? What if he does not purchase the optional rider?

e.   Based on the results from the analyses, what can be said about how frequently insurance coverage needs to be reevaluated?

Narang Park

2.   Your client, Narang Park, has coverage of $90,000 on a dwelling. The replacement value of the dwelling is $125,000. The policy coinsurance requirement is 80 percent. Narang has chosen a $500 deductible. Calculate the amount of loss reimbursement she should receive for each of the following losses.

a.   The amount of the loss is $60,000.

b.   The amount of the loss is $90,000.

c.   The amount of the loss is $120,000.

Now assume that Narang increases the amount of coverage to $105,000. To offset some of the premium increase, she chose to increase the deductible to $1,050. The policy coinsurance requirement is 80 percent. The replacement value of the dwelling is $125,000. Calculate the amount of loss reimbursement for each of the following losses.

a.   The amount of the loss is $90,000.

b.   The amount of the loss is $105,000.

c.   The amount of the loss is $120,000.

Michael Kruger

3. Michael has split-limit coverage equal to 50/100/25 on his vehicle. Yesterday, Michael rear ended a new Mercedes as he was driving to work. The damage to the other car totaled $33,000, while the medical bill for the other driver was $15,000.

    a. If Michael incurred $4,500 in damage to his own car, how much will Michael's insurance company pay (without regard to the deductible) from his split-limit policy?

    b. How much will Michael's insurance company pay (without regard to the deductible) for the damage he caused to the other driver?

    c. Michael and his two friends, Amy and Sarah, have been thinking about starting a new business together. Michael is worried about getting sued if a customer gets hurt when working with the new company. Right now, Michael, Amy, and Sarah have narrowed their choice of business entities to a partnership, S-Corporation, and an LLC. Which of these will provide the *least* amount of liability protection?

        * C-Corporation

        * LLC

        * S-Corporation

        * Partnership

Chapter Resources

Insurance Institute for Business and Home Safety (www.disastersafety.org).

Insurance Information Institute (www.iii.org).

National Flood Insurance Program (floodsmart.com or www.fema.gov/nfip/ or 1-800-638-6620).

Policy Forms Used by the Top 10 Homeowners' Insurance Groups in Nevada (doi.nv.gov/scs/Homeowners.aspx). Nevada is the only state offering this service to consumers, but other states are expected to follow this initiative.

Property Casualty Insurers Association of America (www.pciaa.net/web/sitehome.nsf/main).

United Policyholders™ Empowering the Insured (www.uphelp.org).

Endnotes

1. Source: https://www.iii.org/article/homeowners-insurance-basics

2. Source: Nationwide Insurance Company. *Underinsurance: A Common Problem.* Available at http://www.nationwide.com/underinsurance.jsp.

3. The 80 percent rule is rarely used for those who own a condominium or cooperative apartment.

4. Source: Insurance Information Institute. *How to Save Money on Your Homeowners Insurance.* Available at: www.iii.org/article/how-to-save-money-on-your-homeowners-insurance

5. *Ibid.*

6. Federal Trade Commission, *Top 10 Consumer Complaint Categories: Is Your Industry on the List?* Available at: www.ftc.gov/news-events/blogs/business-blog/2016/03/top-10-consumer-complaint-categories-your-industry-list.

7. *Ibid.*

Chapter 10

Investment Planning

Learning Objectives

- Learning Objective 1: Describe how the concepts of risk and return serve as the foundation of investment planning.

- Learning Objective 2: Identify investment asset classes that are most often used within diversified household portfolios.

- Learning Objective 3: Describe the different types of investment/ financial risks and how to measure each risk.

- Learning Objective 4: Calculate measures of modern portfolio theory.

- Learning Objective 5: Explain how portfolio performance can be measured and assessed.

- Learning Objective 6: Develop an investment policy statement that incorporates strategic and tactical investment strategies.

CFP® Principal Knowledge Topics

- CFP Topic: B.12. Economic Concepts
- CFP Topic: E.33. Characteristics, Uses, and Taxation of Investment Vehicles
- CFP Topic: E.34. Types of Investment Risk
- CFP Topic: E.35. Quantitative Investment Concepts
- CFP Topic: E.36. Measures of Investment Returns
- CFP Topic: E.37. Asset Allocation and Portfolio Diversification
- CFP Topic: E.38. Bond and Stock Valuation Concepts
- CFP Topic: E.39. Portfolio Development and Analysis
- CFP Topic: E.40. Investment Strategies
- CFP Topic: E.41. Alternative Investments

Chapter Equations

Variance:

$$\sigma_i^2 = \frac{1}{T-1} \sum_{t=1}^{T} (r_{i,t} - \bar{r}_1)^2$$

Semi-variance:

$$\sigma_i^2 = \frac{0.5}{T-1} \sum_{t=1}^{T} (r_{i,t} - \bar{r}_1)^2$$

Coefficient of Variation:

$$CV = \frac{\sigma}{\bar{r}}$$

Beta:

$$\beta = \frac{\sigma_{i,M}}{\sigma_M^2}$$

Sharpe Ratio:

$$S_i = \frac{R_i - R_f}{\sigma_i}$$

Modigliani Measure:

$$M_i^2 = \left[R_f + \sigma_m \left(\frac{(R_i - R_f)}{\sigma_i} \right) \right] - R_m$$

Treynor Index:

$$T_i = \frac{R_i - R_f}{\beta_i}$$

Jensen's Alpha:

$$\alpha = R_p - [R_f + \beta [(R_m - R_f)]$$

Information Ratio:

$$IR = \frac{(r_p - r_B)}{\sqrt{Var\,(r_p - r_B)}} = \frac{a}{E_T}$$

Duration:

$$\sum_{t=1}^{n} (PV)\,(CF_t) \times t \div \textit{Market Price of Bond}$$

Modified Duration:

Duration/1 + (YTM/Number of Coupon Periods per Year)

Tax-free Rate:

Taxable Rate × (1 − Marginal Tax Bracket)

Discounted Dividend Valuation Model:

$$Value = \frac{D_0\,(1+g)}{(i-g)}$$

Variance Average Return:

$$(AR) = \frac{r_1 + r_2 + r_3 + \cdots + r_n}{n}$$

Asset Variance:

$$\sigma^2 = X_t - \mu$$

Average Variance:

$$\sigma_i^2 = \frac{(x_1 - \mu)^2 + (x_2 - \mu)^2 + (x_3 - \mu)^2 + \cdots + (x_4 - \mu)^2}{n-1}$$

Asset Standard Deviation:

$$\sigma_i = \sqrt{\frac{(x_1 - \mu)^2 + (x_2 - \mu)^2 + (x_3 - \mu)^2 + \cdots + (x_4 - \mu)^2}{n-1}}$$

Asset Coefficient of Variation (CV):

$$CV = \frac{\sigma}{\mu}$$

Required Return of Asset A to Equalize the CV:

$$\frac{\sigma A}{CV\,of\,Asset\,B}$$

Covariance:

$$\sigma_{ij} = \sigma_i \sigma_j \rho_{ij}$$

Correlation:

$$\sigma_{ij} = \frac{1}{n-1} \sum_{t-1}^{n} a(r_{i,t} - \mu_i)(r_{j,t} - \mu_j)$$

Correlation:

$$\rho_{i,j} = \frac{\sigma_{i,j}}{\sigma_i \sigma_j}$$

Standard Deviation of Two-Asset Portfolio:

$$\sigma_p = \sqrt{w_i^2 \sigma_i^2 + w_j^2 \sigma_j^2 + 2w_i w_j \sigma_{ij}}$$

Expected Return:

$$E(r) = r_f + IP + DP + BP + \ldots$$

Expected Return Using Probabilities:

$$E(r) = (p_1 \times r_1) + (p_2 \times r_2) + (p_{n-1} \times r_{n-1}) + \ldots + (p_n \times r_n)$$

Capital Asset Pricing Model (CAPM):

$$R_{Exp} = R_f + \beta(R_m - R_f)$$

Variance:

$$\beta = (\sigma_p / \sigma_m) \times \rho_{p,m}$$

INVESTMENT PLANNING STRATEGIES

Analyzing a client's current investment situation involves a combination of qualitative and quantitative assessments. To this end, investment planning is as much an art as it is a logical system based on fixed rules. A financial planner must understand a client's perspectives on wants and needs and hopes and reality, as well as a broad range of personal characteristics that can influence investment decisions.

Temperament, personality, attitudes, and beliefs are particularly salient factors in the development of efficient and effective investment planning recommendations. Too often, investment planning decisions are based initially on assets available, with insufficient consideration of other client characteristic and factors. Although the assessment of a client's investment planning need is multifaceted, nearly all financial planning professionals agree that an investment plan should be based on five key interrelated factors:

1. a client's risk tolerance,

2. a financial planner's expectations about future market conditions,

3. a client's financial knowledge and experience,

4. time horizon, and

5. a client's financial capacity to incur financial losses.

The first three factors represent client characteristics that are subjective in nature (although each can be measured using a scale). Insights into a client's temperament and personality, as well as attitudes, beliefs, and behaviors, should guide a financial planner when formulating an investment plan. The last two factors, time horizon and financial capacity, can be objectively measured. For example, financial capacity can be assessed using financial ratios and/or measures of insurance coverage.

Planning Tip

Risk tolerance is a widely misunderstood concept. In the context of investment planning, risk tolerance refers to a client's willingness to engage in a financial behavior in which the outcome of the behavior is both unknown and potentially negative.

It is useful to consider both qualitative and quantitative client characteristics before and during the development of investment strategies. An increased focus on the codification of investment policy statements is an example of focusing on the client holistically. For example, an investment plan, client communication, and client education might, of necessity, be quite different for a highly emotional and reactive client who is unduly influenced by short-term market trends than for a client who has a more tolerant, long-term outlook.

Arguably, the most important situational factor in the investment planning process is a client's **risk tolerance**, which can be thought of as the maximum level of uncertainty a client is willing to accept when making an investment decision that entails the possibility of a loss. Interrelated to the concept of risk tolerance is developing an understanding of, and an appreciation for, both the time and psychological dimensions of risk.

It is possible for a client to have both a long-time horizon and a low tolerance for risk. When this situation is present, a client's risk tolerance should generally supersede other factors when making asset allocation recommendations. To help mitigate the effects of risk-averse behavior, a financial planner must be willing to explain to clients that goal achievement may be impossible in a given time horizon if the client is unwilling to accept a higher degree of investment and/or portfolio risk. This is the basic argument underlying the notion of **goals-based investment planning**. A goals-based approach sets a required rate of return needed to achieve one or more goals. The client is then given the option of accepting the target and accompanying level of risk or reducing the investment need to align more closely with the client's tolerance for risk. The second factor influencing investment planning decisions involves managing a client's **expectations**. Expectations include perceptions of a financial planner's abilities and skill set, the general economy, and most importantly, achievable rates of return. It is important to note that successful financial planners rarely compete in the marketplace based on their ability to generate the highest possible rates of return or excess risk-adjusted returns (i.e., alpha). The reason is that it is difficult to consistently beat the broad markets after accounting for fees and expenses. Instead, financial planners with growing practices generally spend more time managing client expectations regarding performance in relation to reasonable benchmarks.

Consider a financial planner who suggests an allocation designed to achieve a 10 percent annualized return but only manages to generate an 8 percent return. The 8 percent return might be low, average, or high in relation to the market environment. In fact, the return may be superior to almost all other strategies available; however, clients working with this financial planner might very well be disappointed because the expectation of 10 percent earnings was established early on in the financial planning-client relationship. This can cause some clients to terminate their relationship with a financial planner.

Planning Tip

Regardless of what financial planning model is used for investment planning, a client's goals and objectives should serve as the foundation of all investment recommendations. If goals have not been determined, it is essential to do so before proceeding with any investment planning. Without a clear understanding of a client's goal(s) (e.g., new home, retirement, university endowment), when the goal(s) needs to be funded, the goal(s) time horizon (e.g., next year, ten years, at age sixty-five), and the amount of funding needed, it is unrealistic to assume that an investment plan can be drafted that will remain valid over time.

Now consider a financial planner who consistently informs clients that a 6 percent return is reasonable, but over the course of three to five years the financial planner generates an 8 percent return for clients. Clients working with this financial planner are likely to feel that they have received a bonus. This demonstrates the importance of managing client expectations when it comes to establishing anticipated investment returns. A financial planner should attempt to achieve the appropriate amount of risk-adjusted return, but in some cases, it is wiser to under-promise and over-deliver.

An investment plan should be tempered by a client's expectations. Managing expectations requires a financial planner not only to measure but also to understand a client's view of market trends, both past and future. It is, therefore, necessary to account for investment and economic expectations when developing investment plans. A client's outlook, be it negative or positive, should be used as a moderating factor when developing an investment plan. The portfolio for a pessimistic client may look different than the portfolio for an optimistic client, even if both share a similar risk profile.

Figure 10.1 provides an example of the type of questions that can be used to measure a client's expectations about the future economy and current financial situation satisfaction. Answers to the first question are particularly important when developing investment planning strategies. If a client believes strongly that the economy will perform worse in the future, and if the financial planner concurs, the level of risk taken to meet a financial goal should be reduced accordingly. Similar adjustments, either positive or negative, can be made based on responses to other questions. For instance, if a client is dissatisfied with their career, this can be an indicator that a career change is possible or that the potential for significant promotions or salary increases may be limited. It would be imprudent to invest a client's assets aggressively—thereby reducing **marketability** (i.e., holding assets in markets that promotes the quick sale of the assets) and **liquidity** (i.e., how quickly assets can be converted to cash)—if there is a possibility that those assets will be needed to fund job search expenses and other costs. Furthermore, the capacity to withstand **financial risk** (i.e., variability of returns), and the availability of assets to invest, must be realistically assessed.

Figure 10.1. Examples of Expectation and Satisfaction Questions

1. Over the next five years, do you expect the U.S. economy, as a whole, to perform better, worse, or about the same as it has over the past five years?
   a. Perform better
   b. Perform worse
   c. Perform about the same

2. How satisfied are you with your current level of income?
   1 2 3 4 5 6 7 8 9 10
   Lowest level   Highest level

3. How satisfied are you with your present overall financial situation?
   1 2 3 4 5 6 7 8 9 10
   Lowest level   Highest level

4. Overall, how satisfied are you with your current job or position within your chosen career?
   1 2 3 4 5 6 7 8 9 10
   Lowest level   Highest level

5. Rate yourself on your level of knowledge about personal finance issues and investing.
   1 2 3 4 5 6 7 8 9 10
   Lowest level   Highest level

Additionally, a financial planner is expected to know the investment environment, as well as a client's level of **investment knowledge and experience**. Beyond the regulatory requirements of understanding a client's financial knowledge, a financial planner will have fewer objections to overcome if they present investment alternatives that the client already understands or has experience with. The fifth sample question from Figure 10.1 can be helpful to determine how much reduction in the variance of returns or overall volatility of a portfolio should be taken based on client knowledge and experience.

Although the qualitative factors of investment planning are critical in shaping the long-term viability of an investment plan, two quantitative factors—time horizon and risk—are just as important in the short term. Suggesting that a client invest aggressively in a retirement account is certainly sound advice if a client is young and risk tolerant. But making the same suggestion to an older less risk tolerant client who does not have an emergency fund may be problematic because the recommendation ignores the time available to realize the goal and the client's financial capacity to take on aggressive risk.

Planning Tip

Expectation and attitude assessments provide only a starting point in financial planning for a client. Questionnaires and scale items are not necessarily prescriptive. It takes a financial planner's insights and experience to decipher the impact that a client's temperament, personality, attitudes, and beliefs can have on the investment planning process.

For the purposes of investment planning, **time horizon** can be defined as the time period between goal formation and goal achievement. For instance, someone who starts planning for retirement at age twenty five will find that time is a great ally. Someone else who waits until age fifty to plan for retirement will most likely discover that time is a limiting factor. A long time period between goal establishment and achievement allows a client to invest more aggressively. Another way of viewing a longer time horizon is that a client can invest less money on a periodic basis, at a higher expected rate of return, because there is less need to worry about short-term risk (i.e., volatility).

For example, assume that two clients have the same goal of saving $1 million by age sixty five. Both have $250 per month available to save. One client is twenty five years old. The other is thirty five years old. In this situation, the older client needs an average rate of return of close to 13 percent to reach the goal. This is possible, but at what level of risk? Comparatively, the younger client needs only to average about 9 percent to achieve the same goal. This is also possible, even probable—and at a much lower level of risk.

As the example illustrates, the more time a client can devote to saving and investing for a goal, the higher the likelihood that the client will accomplish the goal. Because **risk and return** in the securities market are highly positively correlated (i.e. risk and return generally move in the same direction), those with longer time horizons tend to be in a position to reach financial objectives.

Finally, a client's capacity to deal with a financial loss is an important factor to consider when making investment plans. **Risk capacity** measures the amount of financial cushion or the safety net available to a client both before and after an investment decision has been implemented. Some clients are not prepared to take risks with their investments because they just do not have enough assets and/or discretionary cash flow compared to their other financial obligations.

Documenting and assessing a client's risk capacity is especially important when tempering initial portfolio risk profiles based on time horizon and risk attitude. Factors that increase risk capacity include having adequate insurance in place and funded, a well-funded emergency fund, a stable source of household income, low debt, and high savings. Without these factors in place, the maximum amount of risk that a client should be willing to take, given the client's time frame, risk tolerance, expectations, and attitudes, may be higher than what the client can fiscally afford to lose.

Planning Tip

An effective way to assess a client's risk capacity involves using a financial ratio analysis. Determining how many ratios meet prescribed benchmarks and the availability of an emergency fund can provide an insight into the level of a client's risk capacity. A client who has several ratios that meet or exceed benchmark levels can be classified as having a high-risk capacity. Excess capacity gives a client additional flexibility when making long-term investments because the client has the capital to cover an unexpected expense without liquidating long-term assets. Another client who meets or exceeds only one or two ratios might be considered to have a lower capacity to handle risk. The need for additional liquidity and stability may indicate that a financial planner should not recommend long-term volatile investments, even if the client has the willingness to take on such risks.

Once a client's investment profile has been established, the next step when analyzing a client's current situation, and certainly a step that must be completed before a financial planner can recommend additional or alternative investments, entails documenting and evaluating all investment plans currently in place and evaluating whether assets are allocated or unallocated for a specific goal. An initial assessment might focus on a client's stage in the **financial life cycle** (e.g., whether a client is closer to the beginning or end of their working life) and whether current investment plans match life cycle objectives and other client characteristics. It must be noted that changing **family dynamics** (e.g., delayed marriage, remarried or re-partnered families) can limit the usefulness of the life cycle approach, but even broad generalizations can be very important when educating clients. The financial life cycle is typically conceptualized in three stages: (1) protection, (2) accumulation, and (3) distribution.

These categorizations provide direction and meaning within the investment planning environment by helping clients understand and anticipate how each financial decision can influence subsequent decisions. The following is a short discussion of how the investment focus, or overall objective, can change as a client progresses through the life cycle stages.

During the **protection stage of the life cycle**, a client will generally develop a budget and emergency fund to meet unexpected expenses. Regrettably, some young clients can focus on other distant goals too early and be unprepared for the unexpected. As a result, some young clients can find themselves raiding investment assets in the event of an emergency or to fund other short-term needs. Having a financial planner focus on protection investment ensures that a client's future risk capacity matches or exceeds the client's risk tolerance. Also, having the tolerance to invest aggressively, but lacking the capacity to do so, can result in unnecessary frustration for both a client and financial planner.

Next is the **accumulation stage of the life cycle**, during which a client begins to build wealth. This stage can last from ten to forty years or longer. Generally, clients want to save for retirement, purchase a new or second residence, fund a child's education, and/or buy new cars. This is just a sampling of items that may need to be funded at this stage of the life cycle. A financial planner's responsibility is to recommend actions that will enable a client to meet these savings objectives as efficiently as possible. By closely monitoring a client's investment profile for changes and reallocating the portfolio as necessary, a financial planner can safely and effectively guide a client through a challenging stage of a client's financial life that requires both saving for the future and spending for the present.

Although the last stage of the life cycle—**distribution stage**—may seem to be neatly separated from the accumulation stage by retirement, many clients continue to accumulate wealth well into retirement. At this point in the life cycle, the role of a financial planner typically involves suggesting titling and gifting strategies that minimize potential asset transfer and estate planning difficulties. Portfolio allocation and reallocation also become much more intense because investment plan failure in this stage can result in disastrous outcomes for a client.

Once the five initial factors of investment planning have been established (i.e., risk tolerance, expectations about future market conditions, knowledge and experience, time horizon, and capacity to withstand risk) within the context of the life cycle, a financial planner can begin to combine these characteristics into a client's **investment profile**. Initially, this can be estimated by evaluating a client's goal time horizon and risk tolerance for goal achievement. Figure 10.2 illustrates how the combination of time horizon and risk tolerance can be used to estimate a baseline level of investment risk (i.e., volatility) that would be appropriate for a given client goal.

Figure 10.2. Portfolio Risk Guidelines Based on Client Time Horizon and Risk Tolerance

Time Horizon	High Risk Tolerance	Moderate Risk Tolerance	Low Risk Tolerance
10+ years	Aggressive	Moderately Aggressive	Moderate
7 to 10 years	Moderately Aggressive	Moderate	Moderate
3 to 7 years	Moderate	Moderate	Moderately Conservative
1 to 3 years	Moderately Conservative	Moderately Conservative	Conservative
Less than 1 year	Conservative	Conservative	Conservative

The fact that clients typically have more than one goal, each with a different time horizon, implies that multiple investment strategies may need to be designed. To use Figure 10.2 appropriately, it is essential that a financial planner use a reliable and valid risk-assessment instrument.[1] It is also important to remember that the guidelines shown in the table must be tempered by an assessment of a client's attitudes, expectations, and risk capacity. Given this caveat, however, the guidelines provide general guidance on the level of risk that could be appropriate for a client.

> *Example.* Assume a client is saving for retirement in twenty years. After taking a risk-tolerance assessment quiz, it becomes apparent that the client is neither a real risk taker nor a risk avoider. Given the length of time for goal achievement, this should be used as the primary investment planning factor, with an aggressive portfolio being prescribed as a starting point in client discussions.

Knowing only a client's goal time horizon and risk tolerance is not enough to formulate an investment profile or an effective investment plan. These factors alone tell less than half the story. As noted above, to obtain a full picture of a client's investment profile, it is also important to assess a client's **investment attitudes** and **investment expectations**. For instance, some clients might be open to holding any type of investment within their portfolio, while others may prefer to employ screens to eliminate certain types of investments. Screens related to *socially responsible investing, religious beliefs,* or *political affiliations* are examples of how attitudes and preferences can affect the structure of an investment plan. Other types of attitudes need to be evaluated as well. It would be helpful, for example, to know whether a client is content with regard to their current level of investment income, taxes paid on investment earnings, and level of volatility.

Answers to these kinds of questions can help a financial planner identify a client's investment or risk profile. These inputs should also be used to shape investment recommendations. Figure 10.3 presents attitudinal questions a financial planner can ask to more clearly identify a client's investment profile. Specifically, a financial planner can use a client's strong preferences to better understand what might be driving a client to seek help with investments.

Figure 10.3. Client Investment Attitude Questionnaire

Name _____ Investment Attitudes Questionnaire					
Place an X in the box to the right that reflects your first reaction to the statement.	Strongly Disagree	Disagree	Neutral	Agree	Strongly Agree
1. Keeping pace with inflation is important to me.					
2. I am comfortable borrowing money to make a non-home purchase investment.					
3. Diversification is important to investment success.					
4. The current return I am making on my investments is acceptable.					
5. I need to earn more spendable income from my investments.					
6. I am comfortable with the volatility I experience with my current portfolio.					
7. Reducing the amount of taxes paid on my investments is a top priority.					
8. I am willing to risk being audited by the IRS in exchange for higher returns.					
9. I am willing to risk being audited by the IRS in exchange for paying less tax.					
10. My friends would tell you that I am a real risk taker.					

The process of documenting a client's investment preferences and evaluating investment and portfolio alternatives is the basis of constructing an investment policy statement. An **investment policy statement (IPS)** is a document used to acknowledge agreement with and willingness to follow the parameters guiding the investment or management of a client's assets. An IPS, normally drafted by a financial planner and signed by both financial planner and client, integrates a client's risk tolerance, risk capacity, investment philosophy, and overall client investment profile with a financial planner's proposed investment methods to establish parameters for investment strategies.

Some financial planners develop multiple IPS documents individually matched to the investment management plan aligned with different client goals. For example, two investment policy statements might be necessary when managing retirement assets if risk tolerance factors and acceptable investment management strategies are very different for spouses or partners.

Planning Tip

Today's litigious environment suggests that financial planners—even those whose investment advice is secondary to their planning activities—should use an IPS to disclose and document the professional expectations for the management and investment of client assets. Practicing full disclosure with a client signed IPS is a prudent procedure because the process establishes a mutually agreed-upon standard of conduct while reducing the possibility of a future lawsuit brought by a client who claims misrepresentation or poor performance.

Once a client's investment profile has been identified and the outline of an IPS has been developed, a financial planner can turn their attention to developing and recommending specific investment planning recommendations. The following investment planning strategies represent just a few approaches that can be used when working with clients.

Planning Strategy 1: Match a Client's Investment Profile to Portfolio Alternatives

Taken together, a client's investment profile, consisting of risk tolerance, time frame, knowledge, expectations, and risk capacity, can be used as the basis for better understanding a client's current situation. Once an investment profile has been established, it is appropriate to look at portfolio characteristics in more detail. Specifically, it is important to document whether a client's current portfolio matches the client's investment profile and goal(s).

Example. Assume a client has a long-time horizon, a moderate level of risk tolerance and financial knowledge, generally positive attitudes and expectations regarding investing, and an intermediate level of risk capacity, but a portfolio that is invested fairly conservatively. A financial planner may conclude that more portfolio risk could—and probably should—be taken by the client, thus increasing the expected return of the portfolio.

One of the key questions that should be asked before conducting a current situation investment planning analysis is whether a client needs to make a portfolio change to better meet financial goals. There is no definite, quantitative way to answer this question. But distinct approaches can be employed to make the process easier.

One approach to quantifying how a portfolio corresponds to a client's investment profile is to document relevant portfolio characteristics using a standardized form, and then compare these characteristics to market benchmarks. Figure 10.4 is an example of a form that can be used in this process.

Figure 10.4. Investment Profile and Portfolio Summary Form

Investment Profile and Portfolio Summary Form			
Client Investment Profile			
Qualitative	Circle the appropriate response.		
Risk tolerance	High	Moderate	Low
Knowledge/experience	High	Moderate	Low
Market expectations	Positive	Neutral	Negative
Quantitative			
Time horizon	Long	Intermediate	Short
Risk capacity	High	Moderate	Low
Client risk profile*		Client allocation profile**	

Portfolio Measures	Current Statistics	Benchmark Statistics	Comparison to Benchmark
Targeted portfolio allocation profile**			
Observed portfolio allocation profile**			
Portfolio statistics			
Beta			
Alpha			
R^2			
Sharpe ratio			
Treynor ratio			
Fixed income measures			
Bond duration			
Average bond quality			
Asset allocation (%)			
Cash			
U.S. stock			
Foreign stock			
Bond			
Other			
Sensitivity analysis			
3-year average return			
Worst 1-year loss			
Best 1-year gain			
Does portfolio match investment profile?	Yes No	Yes No	

* Scale: 5: High; 4: Above average; 3: Moderate; 2: Below average; 1: Low

** Scale: 6: Aggressive growth; 5: Growth; 4: Moderate growth; 3: Balanced growth; 2: Conservative growth; 1: Income

The **Investment Profile and Portfolio Summary Form** begins by documenting client characteristics and factors that shape a client's investment profile. A client's investment profile, based on these factors, is then determined. This form uses a five-step investment risk profile scale (5 = High; 4 = Above Average; 3 = Moderate; 2 = Below Average; 1 = Low). A financial planner should then match these risk classifications with recommended portfolio allocations.

The client portfolio allocation profile can then be used as the basis for choosing a benchmark portfolio. Benchmark statistics should then be entered into the table. For example, if a financial planner determines that a client's investment profile falls in the moderate range, then statistics for a balanced growth portfolio could be entered in the benchmark column. Next, relevant portfolio statistics should be summarized and actual portfolio statistics compared to the benchmark.

Planning Strategy 2: Use Financial Market Benchmarks to Document an Investment Need

A **market index** can be used by financial planners to track the performance of a select group of equities, bonds, or other classes of investments. The news media typically report index performance as indicators of general market conditions or movements. Economists use the performance of market indexes as **leading economic indicators**. Financial planners, on the other hand, find indexes to be useful as benchmarks or standards of measurement for client portfolio performance. For a meaningful comparison, it is important to select a **benchmark** that most closely matches both the type of security (or portfolio) and the corresponding level of risk in inherent in an investment or portfolio.

The simplest method used to determine the best benchmark(s) is to first find one or more benchmarks that fit well with a client's portfolio. For example, the S&P 500 index is often used as a benchmark for portfolios made up of primarily large-capitalization U.S. stocks, mutual funds, or exchange traded funds. Next, it is best to perform a linear regression of historical returns of the investment or portfolio versus the historical returns of the benchmark. A financial planner can then review the **coefficient of determination** (R^2)—this statistic indicates the amount of explained variance in portfolio performance that is accounted for by the index—for each regression and select the benchmark that results in the largest R^2 coefficient. When evaluating R^2, it is important to remember that values can run a continuum from zero to one. A larger R^2 means that more variability in returns of the investment or portfolio can be explained by variability in returns of the benchmark.[2]

To gauge overall portfolio performance, the returns for several indexes, reported over the same time period, can be matched proportionately to assets held in a portfolio. Information to track the performance of most securities over time should be readily available, either free from the online sources or from a financial planner's custodian, broker dealer, or other third-party source. Although numerous indexes track different market segments (nationally, regionally, and internationally), some of the most commonly used indexes are listed in Figures 10.5 and 10.6. It is worth noting that a decision to purchase or sell a security should not be based solely on performance relative to a benchmark. Instead, security selection and portfolio management issues should consider other aspects of a client's situation as well.

Figure 10.5. Widely Used Equity Market Indexes

	Corresponding Index by Provider			
Market Sector **All U.S. stocks**	**S&P/Barra** **S&P Total Mkt**	**Russell** **3000**	**Morgan Stanley** **Market 2500**	**Wilshire/DJ** **Wilshire 5000**
U.S. Equity (Size segmented)				
Mega-cap	—	—	—	DJIA 30
Large-cap	S&P 500	1000	Large-cap 300	Wilshire 750
Mid-cap	S&P 400	Mid-cap	Mid-cap 450	Wilshire 500
Small-cap	S&P 600	2000	Small-cap 1750	Wilshire 1750
U.S. Equity (Style segmented)				
Large growth	Barra Growth	1000 Growth	—	Target large Growth
Mid-growth	—	Mid-cap Growth	—	Target large value
Large value	Barra Value	1000 Value	—	Target mid-growth
Mid-value	—	Mid-cap Value	—	Target mid-value
U.S. Equity (Sector segmented)				
Consumer	S&P Consumer	—	—	—
Health care	S&P Health Care	—	—	DJ Health Care
Utilities	S&P Utilities	—	—	—
Financials	S&P Financials	—	—	DJ Insurance
Technology	S&P Technology	—	—	DJ Telecom
International Equity (Region segmented)				
Global	S&P Global 1200	—	AC World Index	—
International (non-emerging)	S&P 700	—	AC World Index (Ex. U.S.)	DJ Developed Mkts
Emerging market	IFCI	—	Emerging Markets	DJ Emerging Mkts & DJ Latin America

In some cases, a benchmark analysis can lead to quick and apparent conclusions. For example, a portfolio that carries a higher **risk profile**, as measured by **beta**, a lower annualized rate of return, and hence a negative **alpha** compared to a benchmark often leads to the conclusion that a client is taking too much risk for the return received. When faced with this situation, a financial planner should implement steps to reallocate the client's portfolio.

However, not all analyses are that simple. During the early 2000s, for instance, portfolios that were over-weighted in bonds and cash tended to outperform portfolios that were balanced among bonds, cash, equities, and real estate. Fixed-income weighted portfolios almost always showed betas that were lower, alphas that were higher, and returns that were superior to balanced portfolio indexes. On paper, these portfolios looked better than what might actually be the case going forward. Over the long run, it is worth remembering that risk and return are positively related. In the short term, this relationship might not hold true. To believe that risk and return will continue to be uncorrelated—as many investors did during the Great Recession—can lead to a serious underachievement of client goals if and when the risk-return relationship reverts back to normal.

Figure 10.6. Widely Used Fixed-Income Market Indexes

	Corresponding Index by Provider		
Market Sector	**S&P**	**Wilshire/DJ**	**Barclay's**
All U.S. bonds	—	—	*U.S. Universal*
U.S. Treasury (Term segmented)			
Long-term	BG Cantor U.S. T-bond	—	
Intermediate	—		U.S. Treasury
Short-term	BG Cantor U.S. T-bill		—
TIPS	BG Cantor U.S. TIPS		U.S. Treasury TIPS
Corporate Debt (Quality segmented)			
U.S. Investment Grade	—	—	U.S. Long Credit
U.S. High-Yield	—	—	U.S. Corp High-Yield
International (Region segmented)			
Global	—	—	Multiverse
International	Int'l Corp Bond	—	Global Aggregate
Emerging market	—	—	Global Emerging Markets
Specialty			
Real Estate (REITS)	U.S. REIT	Wilshire RESI*	—
Global Real Estate	—	Global RESI*	—
U.S. municipal	Municipal Bond	—	U.S. Municipal
U.S. mortgage-backed	—	—	U.S. MBS
*Real Estate Securities Index			

Planning Strategy 3: Use a Goals-Based Approach to Determine a Client's Required Rate of Return

There are times when investment decisions must be based on projected investment outcomes rather than current client and financial planner derived attitudes and financial circumstances. In such cases, rather than making allocations that are designed to match a client's risk tolerance and attitudinal preferences, a financial planner and client can allocate a portfolio to achieve a predetermined rate of return that will make goal achievement possible.

A goals-based approach can be seen with a client who is in their mid-thirties and wants to retire at the normal Social Security age with $1 million. If the client has $250 to invest on a monthly basis, the portfolio must be allocated to achieve an annual rate of return of nearly 13 percent (ignoring the impact of income taxes). This rate of return is simply the **required rate of return** that achieves the objective. The return does not consider the client's risk tolerance, risk capacity, or investment profile.

Calculating a required rate is a simple time value of money equation where the future value, in this example, is $1 million, the present value is $0, the periodic payment is $250, and the number of periods is 360 [(65 – 35) × 12]. In practice, having a required rate of return dictate an asset allocation, rather than having the client's risk profile dictate the targeted return, is a problematic proposition and should be recommended only for a knowledgeable client with the capacity to accept the risk. Why? The reason is simple. If a client's investment profile does not match the required portfolio return projection, then the client will have a difficult choice to make. The client must adapt and learn to be comfortable with the additional risk required, increase the amount of money available for savings, reduce the desired goal amount, or delay goal achievement. Any of these compromises can derail an investment plan and undermine the financial planner-client relationship.

Planning Strategy 4: Identify Appropriate Portfolio Components

Asset allocation represents the way a client's investment dollars are spread among different financial asset classes. **Financial assets** can be broken into many categories for asset allocation purposes, based on either a client's preferences or current and projected market conditions. Figure 10.7 outlines the primary asset classes used by financial planners in client portfolios and a suggested use for each asset.

Figure 10.7. Summary of Investments by Asset Classification

Equity (stocks). The primary use of equities is capital appreciation. Stocks have historically had the highest asset returns after adjusting for inflation. A secondary purpose is to generate current income. This is possible if dividend paying stocks are used in a portfolio.

Sub-classifications:

- Large-cap—stocks with a market capitalization over $10 billion. These stocks are typically mature, dividend-paying companies.

- Mid-cap—stocks with a market capitalization between $2 billion and $10 billion. These stocks may not pay dividends, but most have higher growth rate prospects than large-cap companies.

- Small-cap—stocks with a market capitalization under $2 billion. These stocks typically do not pay dividends because these companies are less mature but fast-growing firms that retain earnings to fuel growth.

Debt (bonds). The primary purpose of debt investing is to generate current income. Bonds typically pay interest on a regular and recurring basis without the possibility of interest reinvestment. A secondary purpose is to generate capital appreciation, which is possible if investing in a declining interest rate environment.

Sub-classifications:

- Treasury/government agency—bonds issued by the Treasury Department or a federal government agency.

- Municipal—bonds issued by state and local governments; can be further classified as general obligation bonds or revenue bonds.

- Corporate—bonds issued by public corporations; can be further classified as investment-grade or high-yield issues.

- Zero coupon—bonds sold at a discount to par value that do not pay a periodic payment. Typically, these bonds are issued by the federal government in the form of Treasury Strips; however, other zero-coupon issues are available.

International Investing. The primary purpose of international investing is capital appreciation, especially during times of superior international growth, and diversification. Sub-classifications include the equity and debt of both developed markets and emerging markets.

Commodities. The primary purpose of investing in commodity assets, for the average investor, is capital appreciation, especially in times of rapid hard asset price growth, and diversification. Commodities can serve as an inflation hedge. Sub-classifications include precious metals, natural resources, energy products, livestock, and agricultural products.

Real estate. The primary purpose of real estate investing is the generation of current income. Real estate investment trusts (REITs) typically pay dividends on a regular and recurring basis. Capital appreciation, as a secondary focus, is possible with some forms of direct real estate investment. Sub-classifications include raw land, agriculture, commercial, residential, and mortgage-backed obligations.

Planning Strategy 5: Determine the Riskiness and Potential Returns of Different Financial Assets

When allocating a client's financial assets, financial planners must consider not only the asset classes available, but also client situational and external asset allocation factors. **Client situational asset allocation factors** are client-centric and provide answers to two questions. First, what is a client's goal—**current income, capital appreciation** or **capital preservation**? Second, how aggressively allocated does a portfolio need to be to achieve the goal? **Aggressiveness** can be loosely defined as the amount of additional risk a portfolio will be subject to in order to achieve a corresponding incremental increase in potential returns. In other words, the more aggressive the portfolio, the greater the expected return of the portfolio, but also the higher the anticipated volatility—or risk.

Figure 10.8 summarizes the risk and return characteristics of investments commonly included in client portfolios. The level of aggressiveness required within an asset allocation structure depends heavily on the difference between the current value of invested assets and the desired level of invested assets. From a time value of money perspective, there are only two factors that control the difference between the amount of money initially (or periodically) invested and the desired future value of the portfolio: rate of return and time horizon. Unless a client wants to delay the realization of a goal or is willing and able to invest more money, a financial planner's only choice is to increase the aggressiveness of the portfolio in an attempt to achieve a greater rate of return.

Figure 10.8. Summary of Investment Characteristics by Investment Type

Asset	Liquidity	Marketability	Risk	Current Income	Capital Appreciation
Direct Investment					
Cash	High	High	Low	Low	None
Savings accounts	High	High	Low	Low	None
Certificates of deposit	Moderate	High	Low	None	Low to average
Treasury bills	High	High	Low	None	Low to average
Treasury bonds	High	High	Low	Low to average	Low to average
EE and I savings bonds	High	High	Low	None	Low to average

HH savings bonds	High	High	Low	Low to average	None
Federal agency bonds	High	High	Low	Average	Average
Municipal bonds	Moderate	Moderate	Moderate	Average	Average
Investment-grade corporate bonds	Moderate	High	Moderate	Average	Low
Speculative-grade corporate bonds	Moderate	Moderate	Moderate	High	Low to high
Zero-coupon bonds	Moderate	Moderate	Moderate	None	Average to high
Preferred stock	Moderate	Moderate to High	Moderate	Average to high	None to low
Common stock	Moderate to High	High	Moderate to High	Low to average	Low to high
Collectibles (coins, stamps, art, etc.)	Low	Low to moderate	High	None	Dependent on supply and demand
Precious metals	Low to moderate	Moderate	Moderate to High	None	Dependent on supply and demand
Real estate	Low	Low	High	Low to high	Dependent on supply and demand
Indirect Investment					
Money market funds	High	High	Low	Low to average	None
Bond funds/ ETFs	High	High	Low	Average to high	Low to average
Stock funds/ ETFs	High	High	Moderate	Low to average	Average to high
Commodity funds	Moderate to High	Moderate to High	High	Low to average	Low to high

Real estate investment trusts (REITs)	Moderate to High	Moderate to High	High	Average to high	Low to average
Derivative Investment					
Options and Warrants	Low	Low to Moderate	High	None to average	Dependent on underlying security
Futures	Low	High	High	None	Dependent on underlying contracts

Planning Strategy 6: Understand the Role of External Factors in Shaping Portfolio Decisions

Investments are bought and sold not only because of changing investor goals, risk attitudes, and time horizons, but also because of changing external factors. **External asset allocation factors**, such as the current and prospective economic environment, are not client specific. Financial planners should be engaged in asking, answering, and monitoring answers to the following questions:

- What are the recent and long-term returns of various asset classes?

- Are domestic interest rates (currently and projected) rising or falling?

- What is the difference in stock yields and bond yields?

- Is projected monetary policy and fiscal policy of the United States conducive to strong long-term growth?

- Will the U.S. dollar rise or fall in value relative to foreign currencies?

- What are projected domestic and international growth rates?

- Will inflation or rising commodity prices stunt growth domestically or internationally?

- Will foreign investments offer superior risk-adjusted returns?

Planning Strategy 7: Identify External Factors that Influence Asset Choices

When working with clients, a financial planner should take care to help their clients understand why certain asset allocations are being recommended. A financial planner should be careful not to overwhelm a client with too much financial or economic information, even when large amounts of data have been used to arrive at a recommendation decision. To begin the economic allocation process, it is common for financial planners to mentally segregate assets into a two-by-two investment selection matrix as shown in Figure 10.9.

Figure 10.9. Investment Selection Matrix

		Goal	
		Appreciation	Income
Inflation	High	Commodities	Real estate
	Low	Stocks	Bonds

The matrix shown in Figure 10.9 consists of stocks, bonds, commodities, and real estate (**hard assets**, such as collectibles, are typically not considered investment assets because hard asset value is determined primarily by supply and demand). Each one of the categories offers advantages and disadvantages; however, the use of a strategic allocation approach that includes all types of assets often yields the greatest benefit, especially in terms of diversification. The basic premise behind this type of accounting is that real assets, such as commodities and real estate, often perform better than financial assets, like stocks and bonds, in times of high or increasing inflation; the opposite often holds true in times of low or decreasing inflation.

By considering the impact of economic conditions—particularly inflation—a financial planner can optimize portfolio allocation choices by changing the weight of a particular class of assets. An example of an allocation that might perform equally well in times of high or low inflation is a portfolio split 25 percent among each asset class. However, this might not work if a client needs or wants to maximize current income.

The current income versus capital appreciation question helps a financial planner develop basic guidelines for the allocation that best suits their clientele. Typically, financial planners recommend real estate and bond holdings to maximize the income potential of a portfolio. Stock and commodity holdings are used to maximize appreciation potential. These recommendations generally work well over extended periods of time, but for clients with a short time horizon, a bias in one of more assets might not work well if, for example, high inflation is anticipated.

Once a general allocation decision has been made, the next question is whether the investment focus should be foreign or domestic. The primary outcomes associated with including foreign investments in a portfolio is risk reduction (i.e., a decrease in the **systematic risk** associated with investing in only one country or region). However, superior returns can also be achieved with international investing by capitalizing on changes in **currency exchange rates** or higher international growth rates associated with emerging or recovering markets. In either case, adding international diversification to an **asset allocation framework** can increase the overall risk-adjusted return of a client's portfolio.

The issue of current and projected interest rates is something that has a significant impact on all allocation decisions. The rule for fixed-income securities (bonds) is that as rates rise values fall. Two approaches are often used in relation to fixed-income assets. Some financial planners allocate a portfolio so that returns are not overly sensitive to rising or falling interest rates. Other financial planners attempt to anticipate changes in interest rates and adjust bold durations accordingly. For example, during a time of rising interest rates a financial planner might reduce the bond allocation or reduce average duration within the bond portfolio to mitigate possible negative consequences.

Planning Strategy 8: Relate Risk with Returns When Developing Asset Allocation Strategies

Once classes of appropriate assets have been selected for a client, a financial planner must determine how to combine each asset into a cohesive portfolio. **Portfolio construction** begins with the client and is based on the client's risk tolerance, risk capacity, time horizon, and investment objectives, essentially the client's investment profile. The construction of a portfolio often begins by targeting a specific risk level. It is then up to the financial planner to optimize the return. Risk can be qualified either by **standard deviation** or beta (each is described in more detail later in the chapter), but it is important to remember that a client may not be satisfied with a significant potential or real loss even if the loss is less than that of the overall market.

Financial planners should use caution when attempting to risk-weight a portfolio. **Beta**, which is a risk measure relative to a benchmark, is representative only if the asset allocation model is very similar to the benchmark from which beta was calculated. As such, risk-weighting only works if the R^2 of a portfolio, relative to the benchmark, is very high (i.e., .80 or greater). A second issue arises from the fact that the **capital asset pricing model (CAPM)** derives beta using a linear regression model. Because all asset class betas are linear, the beta of a targeted portfolio becomes the weighted average beta of the underlying asset classes. While more information about specific investment metrics is available in the chapter appendix, the following is an example of the difference that can result from attempting to target a portfolio beta versus a portfolio standard deviation.

Consider the data shown in Figure 10.10. Assume a client has an asset allocation of 50 percent domestic equities, 25 percent international equities, 10 percent commodities, and 5 percent each to real estate, bonds, and cash. Given the data and allocation, it is possible to achieve a portfolio beta of 0.88 as indexed to the S&P 500. This portfolio has a standard deviation of 23.6. The S&P 500 has a standard deviation across the same period of only 21.1. Although the portfolio exhibits only 88 percent of the systematic risk of the market, the portfolio has close to 112 percent of the total variability of return. Using the same data, it is also possible to construct a portfolio with a beta of 0.92 with a standard deviation of only 20.8, which means the portfolio exhibits 92 percent of the systematic risk and 98 percent of the total risk.

Figure 10.10. Sample Risk and Return Statistics

Asset	10-year Arithmetic Average Return	5-year Standard Deviation	Asset Beta vs. Best Index
Equity 1	7.00	20.21	0.757
Equity 2	8.41	19.08	0.887
International equity	9.29	28.51	1.046
Real estate	17.10	35.19	1.131
Commodity	14.59	39.42	0.682
Real estate bond	5.93	3.18	1.058
Treasury bond	6.32	3.77	1.066
Corporate bond 1	10.33	13.09	1.372
Corporate bond 1	3.57	11.33	0.850
Money market	3.50	1.78	0.211

Based on this example, it is easy to see that portfolios with similar betas can have very different total risk profiles. Developing an asset allocation framework based on standard deviation that gives the client a strong understanding of how much the value of the portfolio can change over time in absolute terms rather than one based on beta, which explains the changes only in relative terms, can go a long way toward helping a financial planner manage a client's risk expectations.

Planning Strategy 9: Determine the Appropriate Use of Strategic and Tactical Asset Allocation Models

Strategic asset allocation is the process of setting target (percentage) allocations for each class of asset within a portfolio based on the long-term objective of the portfolio. Once established, the portfolio is then periodically rebalanced back to the original asset allocation percentages. This is necessary because different asset classes appreciate and depreciate at varying rates and times in the market cycle. This is the basis of a **buy-and-hold investing strategy**, where strategic asset allocations change only as a client's goals and needs change. In the long run, strategic allocations are the most important determinant of total return within a broadly diversified portfolio.

Historically, a standard **three-asset-class model** has predominated modeling techniques, where a portfolio is divided among domestic equities, debt, and cash. However, based on continued research and in light of recent economic events, a more diversified approach has become more popular. Currently, a **five-asset-class model** is more common. In addition to the original three asset classes, real estate and commodities are often included when developing a strategic asset allocation. Greater emphasis is also placed on international equity and debt holdings.

For example, if a client wants a portfolio designed for maximum capital appreciation with tax minimization, with a secondary goal of maintaining purchasing power over an extended period of time, a financial planner might recommend a portfolio that is comprised of 50 percent domestic equities, 25 percent international equities, 10 percent commodities, and 5 percent each to real estate, zero-coupon bonds, and cash. This allocation can then be rebalanced annually to maintain these targets until a change in the client's situation dictates a reallocation. For instance, if the client were to lose her job, it might be prudent to alter the composition of the portfolio to reduce volatility.

Tactical asset allocation, on the other hand, allows for a more active management style by setting a range of percentages in each asset class (e.g., a domestic equity range of 45 percent to 60 percent) rather than a fixed target percentage. The use of a range gives a financial planner the ability to be more opportunistic about changing allocations to match current market conditions. Based on economic forecasts, tactical allocations attempt to add value by overweighting asset classes that are expected to outperform on a relative basis and underweighting those expected to underperform. The value added can be measured with alpha. **Alpha** is calculated by subtracting expected returns (usually estimated using the capital asset pricing model) from actual portfolio returns. This should not be confused with attempting to **time the market** (i.e., predicting short-term swings in the market). Tactical asset allocation opens the door for changes to an allocation when longer-term economic conditions might favor one asset class over another. For instance, having 5 percent of a portfolio invested in real estate might make very good sense over the long-term, but not having as much or any exposure to real estate in 2008 would have turned out to have been a very wise move.

To some extent, tactical asset allocation is similar to a **dynamic allocation strategy** that actively adjusts the apportionment of a portfolio based on short- and long-term market forecasts, with the objective of increasing appreciation potential. **Sector rotation** is a basic form of tactical asset allocation in which an investor attempts to outperform a market index, such as the S&P 500, by tracking the **economic cycle**. Sector rotation, as an investment approach, was first introduced as a way to incorporate **National Bureau of Economic Research (NBER)** data on the business cycle into investment decisions. Proponents of sector rotation use their analyses of the current phase of the business cycle, and relative currency valuations, to anticipate industrial and household demand for goods and services. For example, during an economic contraction, demand for commodities typically decreases, which then relaxes the general price pressure on downstream goods. This tendency will influence the types and timing of assets purchased in a portfolio.

Another form of tactical allocation is the construction of **core-and-satellite portfolios**. The core-and-satellite investing style is designed to maximize returns while minimizing **trading expenses** and **tax liabilities**. The approach comprises two types of investments: **core holdings** and **satellite investments** (i.e., speculative or rotational). Financial planners who use this strategy first decide how much to allocate to core portfolio investments, which are those that an investor intends to hold through a number of business and market cycles. This is essentially an investor's strategic allocation. Often, core investments are held as index positions. Core investments are rarely managed tactically, resulting in high tax efficiency. The remainder of portfolio assets can then be dedicated to the satellite portion of the portfolio. Satellite holdings are actively managed. These investments tend to be short-term holdings that allow a financial planner to position assets tactically for maximum capital gain potential.

Core-and-satellite portfolios are used to add alpha by enhancing the return of an asset class upswing by adding exposure to that class of assets. When an investor increases a position in or exposure to a market movement she is adding leverage. For example, if a portfolio has a "normal" strategic allocation that results in a portfolio beta of 0.8, the market increases 12 percent, and the risk-free rate is 2 percent then, according to capital asset pricing model (CAPM), the portfolio should rise 10 percent [2% + (0.8 × (12% − 2%))]. However, if the portfolio is changed to have a beta of 1.1, then the CAPM will suggest that the portfolio should rise by 13 percent [2% + (1.1 × (12% − 2%))]. If the investor mistimes the market and increases the beta just before a market downturn of 12 percent, then the portfolio will be predicted to lose 13.4 percent [2% + (1.1 × (-12% − 2%))]. More information about the CAPM formula can be found in the appendix.

Planning Strategy 10: Measure and Monitor Portfolio Risk

Measures of excess performance can be separated into two categories: absolute measures and ratio measures. As summarized in Figure 10.11, various measures categorize risk differently and provide a more specific description of what risk is: **total risk** versus **downside risk** or **systematic risk** versus **unsystematic risk**. Total risk is a basic measure that quantifies the general likelihood of an unexpected outcome, whereas downside risk limits the quantification of risk to both unexpected and negative outcomes. Systematic risk measures quantify the risk inherent in the entire market, whereas unsystematic risk quantifies the risk associated with a single asset or asset class within a market.

Precision of measurement is important for a financial planner when attempting to make decisions about the effectiveness of portfolio management or asset selection choices. The more active a financial planner is in attempting to mitigate a specific type of risk, or maximize a return based on a particular investment philosophy, the more precise the financial planner must be in isolating those variables to make accurate comparisons.

Figure 10.11. Summary of Commonly Used Portfolio Risk Measures

Name (Symbol)	Definition/Formula
Variance (σ^2) and Std. deviation (σ)	These are absolute measures of the average variability or spread of periodic returns. These measure the *total risk* of unanticipated outcomes. $$\sigma^2_i = \frac{1}{T-1} \sum_{t=1}^{T} (r_{i,t} - \bar{r}_1)^2 \qquad \sigma = \sqrt{\sigma^2}$$
Semi-variance (σ^2) and Semi-deviation (σ)	These are absolute measures of the average variability or spread of periodic returns that do not meet the targeted return (*downside risk*).[3] $$\sigma^2_i = \frac{0.5}{T-1} \sum_{t=1}^{T} (r_{i,t} - \bar{r}_1)^2 \qquad \sigma = \sqrt{\sigma^2}$$
Coefficient of variation (CV)	This is a measure of dispersion of a probability distribution. CV is defined as the ratio of the standard deviation (σ) to the mean (μ). Formula = $CV = \dfrac{\sigma}{\bar{r}}$
Coefficient of determination (R^2)	This is a measure of systematic, or market-related, variability. R^2 ranges from 0 to 100 and reflects the percentage of an asset's movements that are explained by movements in the benchmark. The remainders (residuals) are a rough measure of the *unsystematic* component of risk. Formula = Linear regression-based
Beta (β)	The beta coefficient is a measure of a security's volatility relative to the market. Beta is a "relative" measure of volatility. Because beta reflects only the market-related or *systematic* portion of a security's risk, it is a narrower measure than standard deviation. Formula = $\beta = \dfrac{\sigma_{i,M}}{\sigma^2_M}$

Five other performance statistics are commonly used to make risk-adjusted, return-based portfolio evaluations. The first two statistics are the Sharpe ratio and the Modigliani measure. These are based on a measure of total risk. The next two, the Treynor index and Jensen's alpha, are based on a measure of systematic risk. The final performance measure, the information ratio, is not actually a risk-based adjustment; rather, it tries to capture whether a financial planner or asset manager is enhancing portfolio performance through active management. Each statistical tool is described in greater detail below.

Sharpe Ratio

The **Sharpe ratio** standardizes portfolio performance in excess of the risk-free rate by the standard deviation of the portfolio. Higher Sharpe ratio scores are indicative of better risk-adjusted performance. However, the ratio is not useful unless an investor has a comparable portfolio to judge the score against. Additionally, because the Sharpe ratio uses a measure of **total risk** (i.e., standard deviation) for risk adjustment, a financial planner should use this method primarily for comparing undiversified portfolios or concentrated positions. The Sharpe ratio can be calculated using the following formula:

$$S_i = \frac{R_i - R_f}{\sigma_i}$$

Where:

S_i = Sharpe ratio

R_i = Actual return of the asset (or portfolio)

R_f = Risk-free rate

σ_i = Standard deviation of asset (or portfolio)

Example: Assume that Laini's portfolio achieved an average annual return of 12 percent with an annualized standard deviation of 16 percent, while the market portfolio achieved an annual return of 13 percent with a standard deviation of 18 percent. Also assume that a risk-free opportunity returned 5 percent per year. Applying the formula, Laini's Sharpe ratio would be $(12 - 5)/16 = 0.437$. But what does this mean? Without a point of comparison, it is hard to tell. By calculating the Sharpe ratio of the market for a comparison $(13 - 5)/18 = 0.444$, it can be determined that Laini's portfolio provided an inferior return compared to the market portfolio.

Modigliani Measure

The **Modigliani measure** (**M²**), which calculates the absolute amount of risk-adjusted return within a portfolio, is based on the Sharpe ratio. The Modigliani measure helps put a portfolio's results into perspective by providing an intuitive estimate of what the return should have been given the amount of total risk taken. The calculation starts with the Sharpe ratio and then applies a risk adjustment to convert the Sharpe back into percentage return form, adding the risk-free rate, then subtracting the return of the market. The formula is:

$$M_i^2 = \left[R_f + \sigma_m \left(\frac{(R_i - R_f)}{\sigma_i} \right) \right] - R_m$$

Where:

M^2 = Modigliani measure

R_f = Risk-free rate

R_i = Return of the asset or portfolio

$$\sigma_m \quad = \text{Standard deviation of the market or benchmark}$$

$$\sigma_i \quad = \text{Standard deviation of the asset or portfolio}$$

$$R_m \quad = \text{Return on the market}$$

Example. Returning to the previous example and based on the formula above, Laini's M² measure is -0.125 percent. Although she returned 1 percent less than the market with a standard deviation less than the market, her risk-adjusted return remained negative. In other words, this is her risk-adjusted return. This coincides with the fact that the Sharpe ratio was lower than the market ratio. The Modigliani measure nicely quantifies the exact amount of risk-adjusted performance achieved by an investor.

Treynor Index

The **Treynor index** is also a measure of standardized risk-adjusted performance. Instead of using standard deviation as a measure of absolute volatility, the formula uses *beta* as a measure of **systematic risk**—risk that cannot be reduced through diversification. Just like the Sharpe ratio, the Treynor index outcome is useful only in terms of comparing one portfolio to another. Because the Treynor uses a systemic measure of risk, this index should be used only with well-diversified portfolios. A Treynor index score can be calculated using the following formula:

$$T_i = \frac{R_i - R_f}{\beta_i}$$

Where:

$T_i \quad = \text{Treynor index}$

$R_p \quad = \text{Actual return of the portfolio}$

$R_f \quad = \text{Risk-free rate}$

$\beta_i \quad = \text{Beta}$

Example. Assume Jack's portfolio returned 12 percent, the risk-free rate was 3 percent, and the beta of Jack's portfolio was 0.85. The Treynor index for the portfolio would be 0.106 [(0.12 – 0.03)/0.85].

Jensen's Alpha

Another useful statistic is **Jensen's alpha** or the **Jensen Performance Index. Alpha** measures the relative under- or over-performance of a portfolio compared to a benchmark—typically a representative, diversified market portfolio such as the S&P 500. Alpha measures the difference between the actual returns of a portfolio and the portfolio's expected risk-adjusted performance. The following formula is used to determine the Jensen alpha of a portfolio:

$$\alpha = R_p - \left[R_f + \beta \left(R_m - R_f \right) \right]$$

Where:

α = Alpha (derived from the assumption of investment risk)

R_p = Actual return of the portfolio

R_f = Risk-free rate

β = Beta

R_m = Return on the market

Notice that the calculation is based on the **CAPM** ($R_f + \beta(R_m - R_f)$). A positive alpha indicates that a portfolio exceeded expectations on a risk-adjusted basis. A negative alpha indicates that a portfolio underperformed the market on a risk-adjusted basis. A reallocation of assets might be warranted if a portfolio shows a long history of significant underperformance.

> *Example.* Returning to Jack's portfolio from the previous example, if Jack actually earned a rate of return of 12 percent over the three-year period, he could conclude that on a risk-adjusted basis he did better than expected. His portfolio would have generated a positive alpha of 1.35 percent (12% − 10.65%). If the portfolio were managed by a financial planner, Jack could conclude that the financial planner added value above what would have been expected given the risk taken.

Information Ratio

The **information ratio** can be used to estimate the excess return of a portfolio (alpha) generated by active management compared to the standard deviation (tracking error of alpha) generated by active management. The information ratio is most useful when a financial planner is attempting to outperform a benchmark through superior asset selection or market timing. The information ratio differs from other ratios in that the benchmark is no longer the risk-free asset, as assumed in the Sharpe ratio and Treynor index. The ratio can be calculated using the following formula.

$$IR = \frac{\left(r_p - r_B\right)}{\sqrt{Var\left(r_p - r_B\right)}} = \frac{\alpha}{\varepsilon_T}$$

Where:

IR = Information ratio

α = Alpha (derived from active management, not solely investment risk) where alpha is the difference between the portfolio return and the benchmark return

ε_T = Tracking error of alpha where the error is the standard deviation of the alpha return

Example. If a financial planner achieved an annual alpha of 2.5 percent with an annualized tracking error of 6.25 percent, then the information ratio would be 0.4. What does 0.4 mean? Generally, a positive estimate is good indicator of performance.

Each of the measures discussed above is based on concepts imbedded in **modern portfolio theory**. This theory introduced the process of mean-variance optimization, its related statistics, and various other investment rules that can be used to determine whether a client's portfolio is efficient. While data can and should be used to guide portfolio choices, professional judgment must also play a role in the decision-making process. Experience, knowledge, and skill help a financial planner determine whether a portfolio is appropriate for a client's needs considering the current economic situation, client attitudes and expectations, and an analysis of risk tolerance and capacity. The integrated nature of these, and other client focused factors, makes investment planning challenging. Figure 10.12 provides a summary of the relative portfolio performance measures as illustrated in this discussion.

Figure 10.12. Summary of Relative Portfolio Performance Measures

Name (Symbol)	Definition/Formula
Sharpe ratio	A measure of risk-adjusted performance calculated by dividing the excess return of a portfolio by a measure of *total risk*. Higher values are desirable. This measure is most appropriate when analyzing portfolios where unsystematic risk is still prevalent. $$S_i = \frac{R_i + R_f}{\sigma_i}$$
Modigliani measure (M²)	A measure of risk-adjusted performance that results in a percentage measure for under- (negative values) or over- (positive values) performance, based on *total risk* within the asset or portfolio. $$M^2_i = \left[R_f + \sigma_m \left(\frac{(R_i - R_f)}{\sigma_i} \right) \right] - R_m$$
Treynor index	A measure of risk-adjusted performance calculated by dividing the excess return of a portfolio, return beyond the risk-free rate, by its beta. Higher values are desirable and indicate greater return per unit of *systematic* risk. This measure is most appropriate when analyzing portfolios where only systematic risk remains. $$T_i = \frac{R_i - R_f}{\beta_i}$$
Jensen's alpha (α)	Return in excess of capital asset pricing model (CAPM) return. In other words, alpha is the difference between the security's actual performance and the performance anticipated in light of the security's *systematic risk* (beta) and the market's behavior. $$\alpha = R_p - [R_f + \beta [(R_m - R_f)]$$
Information ratio	A measure of risk-adjusted performance calculated by dividing the excess risk-adjusted return (alpha) of a portfolio by the tracking error (standard deviation of alpha). Higher values are desirable. This measure is most appropriate when analyzing actively managed portfolios where either market timing or asset selection is being used in an attempt to exceed a benchmark. $$IR = \frac{(r_p - r_B)}{\sqrt{Var\,(r_p - r_B)}} = \frac{\alpha}{E_T}$$ or $IR = \frac{\alpha}{E_T}$

Planning Strategy 11: Adjust the Duration of a Bond Portfolio if Changes in Interest Rates are Anticipated

Duration is a term used to describe the level of price volatility a bond will exhibit if interest rates in the economy change. Duration measures the number of years an investor needs to wait to recover the cost of a bond. A bond with a higher duration will show greater price volatility than a bond with a smaller duration. Three calculations are needed to estimate a bond's modified (true) duration. First, a bond's price must be estimated. The following formula can be used (the same calculation can be made on a time value of money calculator):

$$\sum_{t=1}^{N} CPN_t / (1 + YTM_t)^t + P_n / (1 + YTM_n)^n$$

Where:

CPN = Coupon payment

P = Principal payment

YTM = Yield to maturity

n = Number of compounding periods

t = Time period

Three rules emerge with the use of the bond pricing formula:

- The price value of bonds moves inversely with change in market interest rates.

- Lower coupon bonds exhibit greater interest rate sensitivity.

- Longer-term bonds exhibit greater interest rate sensitivity.

The second step in the calculation process involves estimating duration using the following formula:

$$\sum_{t=1}^{N} (PV)(CF_t) \times t \div Market\ Price\ of\ Bond$$

Where:

$(PV)(CF_t)$ = Present value of bond coupon at period t

t = Time to each cash flow in years

n = Number of periods to bond maturity

The third step in the calculation process involves modifying the duration formula as follows:

Modified Duration = Duration /1 + (YTM / Number of Coupon Periods per Year)

Where:

Duration = Estimated bond duration

YTM = Yield to maturity

Example. Assume a client holds a bond with a three-year maturity, an 8 percent coupon (paid annually), and a $1,000 face value. Also assume that current interest rates are 5 percent and that the bond has a yield to maturity of 5 percent. Using the three formulas, it is possible to estimate the bond's modified duration as follows:

- Bond price: $1,081.70

- Value of cash flow year 1: $76.19[4]

- Value of cash flow year 2: $72.56

- Value of cash flow year 3: $932.94

- Duration estimate: (1 × $76.19 / $1,081.70) + (2 × $72.56 / $1,081.70) + (3 × $932.94 / $1,081.70) = 2.79 years

- Modified duration estimate: 2.79 / 1 + (.05/1) = 2.66

Interpreting the modified duration estimate is straightforward: For every 1 percent decrease (increase) in market interest rates, this bond will increase (decrease) in value by 2.66 percent.

In other words, the modified duration of a bond or bond portfolio tells an investor approximately how much a bond or portfolio will change in value in relation to a change in interest rates. A modified duration equal to five means that if interest rates increase by 1 percent over a one-year period, the bond will decline in value by approximately 5 percent. If interest rates decline by 1 percent over a one-year period, the same bond should increase by approximately 5 percent. Knowing this, an investor can adjust a bond portfolio's exposure to interest rate changes by adjusting duration. For instance, if a financial planner believes that interest rates will fall, they could increase the duration of the bond portfolio to capture the increase in principal that should accompany the interest rate change. If, on the other hand, interest rates are expected to increase, the duration of the bond portfolio could be reduced.

In general, this strategy is an effective way to reduce interest rate risk within a bond portfolio. However, duration can be misleading in certain situations. For instance, the duration of a **mortgage-backed security** is often deceptive. If interest rates rise, mortgage-backed bond prices will fall. If interest rates decline, these same bonds might not go up in value as much as their duration indicates because of the negative convexity induced by the fixed interest rates of the mortgages within the bond. The reason for this phenomenon is that as interest rates decline, home owners tend to refinance their mortgages, leading to prepayment of mortgage loan obligations. This effectively reduces the duration and potential capital gain advantage of mortgage-backed securities.

Planning Strategy 12: Use Zero-Coupon Bonds if Interest Rates are Expected to Decline

Zero-coupon bonds are purchased at a discount to the bond's face value. Zero-coupon bonds pay no interest. Instead, bond owners accrue interest over time. Zero-coupon bonds are unique in that maturity and duration of the bonds are basically the same. This means that a bond with a maturity and **modified duration** (i.e., an estimate of the amount the value of a bond will increase or decrease as a result of a change in interest rates) of five years will typically move up or down by approximately 5 percent with a 1 percent change in interest rates over a one-year period. A financial planner who believes that interest rates are going to fall can speculate on rising bond prices by purchasing long-maturity zero-coupon bonds to obtain the maximum price appreciation. On the other hand, a financial planner who believes that interest rates will increase might sell long-term zero-coupon bonds and replace them with short-maturity bonds.

Planning Tip

It is important to keep in mind that clients who use zero-coupon bonds in their taxable portfolios should be aware that, although they receive no income from the bonds, all accrued interest is taxable in the year of accrual. Any capital gains captured from this strategy will also result in a tax liability. The price of zero-coupon bonds is sensitive to changes in interest rates, and as such, zero-coupon bonds should generally be held in tax-efficient portfolios.

Planning Strategy 13: Understand the Role of Bond Convexity

The concept of bond convexity is associated with the notion of bond duration. **Convexity** refers to the relationship between a change in interest rates and the change in the value of a bond. Consider the price curve shown in Figure 10.13.[5]

The figure shows that for a $1,000 face value bond with a ten-year maturity, that pays $50 semi-annually (10 percent yield), rather than being a fixed linear relationship between changes in interest rates and bond values, the relationship is actually convex.

Figure 10.13. Bond Convexity

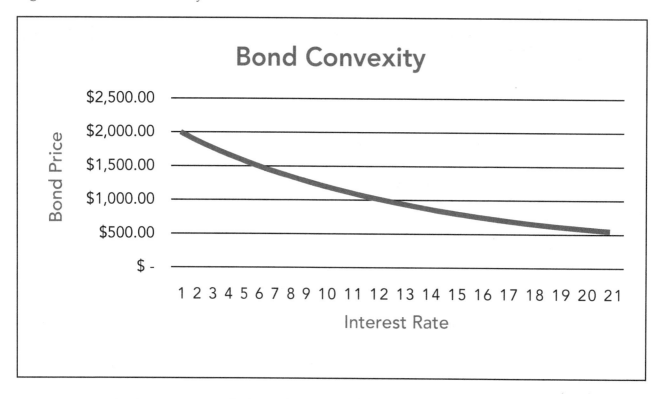

As interest rates decline, this bond's value grows at an increasing rate. On the other hand, when interest rates increase, this bond's value falls at a decreasing rate. Holding this particular bond in a declining interest rate environment will result in a proportionately greater gain compared to the potential loss if interest rates decline. It is worth noting that some bonds (e.g., callable and mortgage-backed bonds) exhibit negative convexity. The convexity of any bond is derived by estimating the present value of interest payments. A financial planner can use this information strategically. Bonds with lower initial yields will almost always have greater convexity. This explains the role of zero-coupon bonds as a capital appreciation asset (in declining interest rate environments).

Planning Strategy 14: Increase Client Income by Investing in Real Estate Investment Trusts (REITs)

REITs are structured in a way that allows investors to pool their investments in a publicly traded company that then purchases a portfolio of real estate. REITs can invest in land, buildings, shopping centers, apartment buildings, offices, and mortgages. REIT investments are attractive for income-oriented investors because REITs are required to distribute 90 percent of income received from rents, dividends, interest, and other gains, such as income from the sale of securities and property. Although REITs tend to be high-income-producing investments, several factors can make these securities problematic for some clients. First, real estate tends to be cyclical, and given that REITs can invest in local markets, rates of return earned on real estate assets are usually tied to local market conditions. There is no guarantee that high yields will persist into the future. Furthermore, lack of liquidity in the commercial real estate markets means that REITs carry more risk than other dividend-paying stocks.

Planning Strategy 15: Increase Portfolio Income by Reducing Bond Quality Mix in a Portfolio

Because of the inverse relationship between bond quality and interest rates—the lower the grade, the higher the interest rate paid—clients who need additional income may want to include lower-grade (Standard and Poor's BB-or lower rated) speculative bonds (**junk bonds**) in their portfolios. One way to do this is through junk bond mutual funds, which provide diversification and professional management as a way to reduce the increased risk associated with this strategy. This strategy has many potential pitfalls. First, clients who purchase lower-grade bonds, especially junk bonds, run the risk that the bonds will not be redeemed because of **default**. Also, lower-grade bonds are more volatile whenever interest rates change. An increase in interest rates will result in a greater loss in value than would a similar higher-rated bond. Finally, junk bonds tend to trade more like stocks than bonds. This means that lower-grade bonds are impacted by both a company's financial situation and interest rates, which subjects a bond holder to greater overall risk.

Planning Strategy 16: Reduce Tax Costs by Investing in Dividend Paying Stocks

Taxes on **qualified stock dividends** are based on the current capital gains rate. This means that clients who need income from their investments should consider shifting assets toward dividend paying stocks. The net after-tax yield, given the lower tax on dividends, means a higher return for clients. It is important to remember that some dividends from stock and bond mutual funds are not considered to be qualified for the lower tax rate. To take advantage of this strategy, a client may need to build a diversified portfolio of individual stocks. This means potentially higher transaction costs, which for smaller portfolios can negate the tax advantage associated with receiving dividends. Furthermore, the costs—particularly in time—to manage a stock portfolio may not be worth the marginal tax benefit.

Planning Strategy 17: Decrease Tax Liability by Investing in Municipal Securities

One of the basic tenets of investing is that an analysis of tax-free yields compared to fully taxable yields should be conducted on a regular basis for those investing in fixed-income securities. Clients in the highest marginal tax brackets often find that municipal securities provide a higher after-tax return than similar fully taxable bonds, even if the initial yield is higher on the taxable bonds. The following **tax-equivalent formula** can be used to determine whether owning a tax-free bond investment is better than owning a taxable security.

Tax-free Rate = Taxable Rate × (1 – Marginal Tax Bracket)

For example, assume a client can earn 4 percent in a fully taxable bond fund and is in the 22 percent marginal federal tax bracket. The equivalent tax-free rate is 3.12 percent (0.04 × [1 – 0.22]). In this case, the client would be just as well served by investing in a municipal bond fund with a yield of at least 3.12 percent.

This strategy is even more effective if a client purchases municipal securities from the state in which the client lives. In such cases, interest earned is usually both federal and state tax free. The primary disadvantage associated with this strategy is that sometimes a client will conduct a tax-equivalency calculation and determine that the relationship between taxable and tax-free rates is fixed. In fact, the relationship between rates can change frequently, meaning that this analysis should occur at least annually. Also, clients should be informed that municipal securities generally have a lower degree of liquidity and marketability than some corporate and nearly all federal government debt. The importance of assessing each credit agency's debt rating cannot be overemphasized.

Planning Strategy 18: Use a Variable Annuity to Reduce Current Taxes

Variable annuities provide clients with multiple advantages. Notably, annuities can be tax efficient. Dividends, interest, and capital gains earned in any given year are deferred until a later date. This can be quite beneficial for clients who will be in a lower marginal tax bracket in retirement than the rate being paid today, and for clients who employ tactical asset allocation strategies, annuities can shelter trading gains from taxes. Keep in mind that variable annuity products should be used only in situations where a client has a long-term investment horizon. This strategy is inappropriate for clients who need assets to fund short-term expenses, such as the purchase of a home, car, or business. Some variable annuity products can be quite expensive. Additionally, income distributions are taxed at the client's full marginal income tax bracket.

Planning Strategy 19: Hedge Inflation in a Fixed-Income Portfolio with Treasury Inflation-Indexed Securities

Treasury inflation-protection securities (**TIPS**) are bonds with a ten-year maturity issued by the federal government. Purchasing TIPS is a strategy designed to reduce inflation risk. The principal value of a TIP security is adjusted on a semiannual basis to account for inflation, as measured by the **consumer price index**. At maturity, the redemption price is equal to the greater of the inflation-adjusted principal amount or par value. The coupon rate for TIPS is fixed, but payments to bond holders can increase over time as the inflation-adjusted principal amount increases.

This strategy is not appropriate for all clients. Two potential disadvantages are associated with TIPS. First, the initial coupon rate for new issues tends to be significantly less than yields on comparable non-inflation-adjusted debt. This means that if inflation stays stable or there is deflation, the bond holder will receive less annual income than other investors. Second, bond holders must pay taxes on the increase in the inflation-adjusted principal amount on a yearly basis, not at maturity. This is why TIPS make the most sense in tax-deferred portfolios.

Planning Strategy 20: Hedge a Portfolio against Inflation with Hard Assets and Precious Metals

During times of high inflation, hard assets and precious metals tend to outperform other assets, especially fixed-income and equity assets. There are many reasons for this phenomenon, but in general, the limited supply of these assets makes them an attractive alternative to other securities during inflationary times. The disadvantages associated with this strategy can offset the advantages associated with holding hard assets. First, hard assets and precious metals entail **holding costs** that can be substantial. A place needs to be devoted to holding the physical assets, and insurance may have to be purchased to cover potential losses due to theft or destruction. These costs work to erode the potential for gains that this strategy offers. Also, the value of hard assets and precious metals is determined primarily by **supply and demand** factors. If a new supply enters the market, the value of existing assets will almost certain to fall. When inflation becomes less of a factor, the value of hard assets tends to stagnate or fall.

Planning Strategy 21: Protect a Client against Interest Rate Risks by Creating a Laddered Fixed-Income Portfolio

Clients occasionally need to limit the maturity and duration of a fixed-income portfolio to reduce interest rate risk. Unfortunately, doing so often reduces the level of income generated from the portfolio. One strategy to increase the average yield from a portfolio of fixed-income securities, while limiting average portfolio maturity, involves creating a bond ladder. For example, a client could purchase equal dollar amounts of three-, six-, nine-, and twelve-month **certificates of deposit** (CDs). Whenever one CD matures, another twelve-month CD would then be purchased. This plan provides a weighted average maturity of less than twelve months but a yield greater than that offered on a three-month CD. Furthermore, this strategy enhances a client's liquidity situation. Obviously, this strategy can be extended beyond twelve months by adding CDs with longer maturities. The same strategy can be used to develop bond portfolios.

Planning Tip

It is important to note that although a laddered fixed-income strategy is relatively simple to implement, it requires constant monitoring to remain effective. New securities must be purchased on a regular basis. This makes analysis of the fixed-income market extremely important. Replacing securities that mature with assets of similar credit quality and yields requires more work than simply buying and holding one or a few securities.

Planning Strategy 22: Utilize Rental Real Estate to Reduce Taxes and Generate Cash Flow

A client's comfort level, knowledge, and experience with certain types of investments often dictates which strategy will dominate an investment plan. Some clients prefer to invest directly in real estate rather than through stocks, bonds, and other investment assets. **Rental real estate** can provide clients with deferred capital gains, an inflation hedge, and cash flow. Lack of liquidity and potentially limited marketability are two significant disadvantages associated with this strategy. Clients who are considering rental real estate must also remember that costs for ongoing operating expenses can sometimes escalate more quickly than rents in certain locations. This is especially true in cases where the client hires a management firm to handle all aspects of rental ownership. Another disadvantage associated with real estate investing is that it requires the temperament and skill of a trained **property manager** to consistently make money. For example, client owners of rental properties must sometimes be plumbers, electricians, painters, sales agents, and evictors. Not everyone is capable of performing these activities. It may be possible to hire a management firm to oversee properties, but the costs associated with management can erode the return on investment generated from a property. It is important to also note that beginning in 2018, passive losses from rental real estate, for those who are not actively engaged in the rental real estate market, can only be used to offset passive gains. This limits the use of rental real estate as a tax planning tool.

Planning Strategy 23: Understand the Purpose of Call and Put Options

During periods of market volatility, financial planners are often called upon to recommend ways to hedge the inherent risks associated with investments in equities. **Options** provide one mechanism to reduce the risk related with owning a basket of securities. A **call option** allows an investor to purchase an asset at a predetermined price in the future. For example, an investor might believe that the price of a stock will increase in the future. Rather than purchase the shares directly, the investor can purchase a call option. If the stock should increase in value, the investor can "call" their broker, pay the predetermined price (which will be lower than the current stock price), and then sell the stock in the market for a higher price. The net result is a profit with very little initial investment.

A **put option** is a way for an investor to sell an asset at a predetermined price in the future. Put options are often used to hedge a portfolio of stocks. Say an investor owns a diversified portfolio. The investor is worried that the markets might fall. The investor can purchase a put option. If prices do indeed decline, the value of the portfolio will fall, but the value of the option will increase, thus hedging the portfolio. Put and call options can be purchased for individual securities or for larger baskets of investments, which are called **index options**.

Two disadvantages are associated with **option trading**: the risk of loss and the added costs of trading. It is important to note that options have a limited duration—usually from a few days to a few months. If an option is not exercised by the owner, the value eventually declines to zero. Additionally, if the option is exercised, the investor must also pay a commission on the shares acquired. Options are usually a good investment only in a volatile marketplace. This is the reason that some investors not only buy options, they sell them as well.

> *Example.* Assume that a client owns 100 shares of stock X. The client believes the stock price will remain about where it is for the next year. That client could sell a call option into the marketplace. Basically, the client is betting against the person who buys the option. The buyer believes the price of the stock will go higher, whereas the seller (client) thinks the price will decline or stay the same.

Some speculators sell **naked call options** and **naked put options**. This is a very risky approach to investing. A naked option writer sells calls and puts without actually owning the underlying security. If the price moves against the seller, they will be forced to enter the market and pay market prices for the security. This strategy exposes the seller to unlimited market risk. In summary, although options trading can be an effective way to hedge a portfolio against market risk, the costs associated with the strategy must be incorporated into the return expectations associated with investing.

Planning Strategy 24: Write (Sell) Covered Calls to Increase Portfolio Income

Suppose a client owns a stock that has appreciated in value. The client would like to sell the stock to capture the profit, but at the same time would not mind holding the stock if income could be generated from the asset. Writing a **covered call option** can be a good strategy to achieve the client's objective. Writing a call option provides immediate premium income for the client, which effectively reduces the cost basis of the original stock. If the price of the stock goes up, the stock may be called away, but this results in generally the same outcome as selling the stock now. If the price of the stock should fall, the call option serves as a hedge, reducing or eliminating the loss on the stock price decline.

It is worth noting that opportunity costs are linked with this strategy. If the price of the stock goes up dramatically, the client will lose both the stock and the price appreciation. If the client purchases back the option, the client will pay much more than the premium earned originally, which will result in a reduced gain. Further, the commission associated with writing covered calls can be quite high, as a percentage of assets, for those selling one or a few options. The strategy is only cost effective if large blocks of options are traded.

Planning Strategy 25: Balance Long- and Short-Term Tax Gain and Loss Selling to Maximum Tax Savings

This strategy is premised on the IRS rule that only $3,000 in **losses** can be used to offset regular income in any given year. If a client has more recognized losses than short- and long-term gains, those losses must be carried forward into future years. By matching investment losses with asset gains, it may be possible to minimize the negative impact of taxes on portfolio performance. Clients should be reminded that it may not always be possible to match losses and gains. It might be better to take a loss than to wait and potentially have the investment liquidated with no value at all.

Planning Strategy 26: Consider Mutual Fund Investments in a Client's Portfolio

Mutual funds represent the most widely used investment company product. Mutual funds are professionally managed, **pooled-asset investment companies** formed to meet a specific investment objective. In effect, mutual funds pool assets from a number of investors and then hire a portfolio manager who uses the assets to purchase stocks, bonds, or other assets. Mutual funds are an attractive investment choice for clients, because mutual funds tend to provide diversification at a relatively low cost. Additionally, mutual funds provide investors of modest means access to professional management at very reasonable entry price point levels. Shares in some funds can be purchased for as little as $100. Figure 10.14 provides a summary reference of key mutual fund terminology.

Figure 10.14. Mutual Fund Terminology

Term	Definition
Mutual Fund	Pooled investment that can issue an unlimited number of shares.
Close-End Fund	Mutual fund with a fixed number of shares sold at one time as an initial public offering and later traded in the secondary market.
Unit Investment Trust	Pooled investment based on a single sale of shares; the trust has a predetermined dissolve date.
Hedge Fund	A private, unregistered investment pool that is limited to accredited investors (i.e., wealthy sophisticated individuals).
Net Asset Value (NAV	The price investors pay to purchase or sell shares in a fund.
Load	Commission (sales fee) paid by investor to purchase shares.
Deferred Sales Charge (Load)	Fee paid when shares are sold; sometimes called a contingent or back-end load.
Management Fee	Fees paid from a fund's net assets to pay for portfolio management services and trading fees.
12b-1 Fees	Fees paid from a fund's net assets to cover costs associated with marketing and selling a fund to new shareholders.
Expense Ratio	The total annual operating expenses of a fund.
No-Load Fund	A mutual fund that does not charge a sales commission to purchase shares.
Break Points	Dollar thresholds where the commission (load) is reduced for new purchases.
Classes of Funds • A Shares • B Shares • C Shares	• Funds that charge a front-end load. • Funds that charge a back-end load. • Funds with a higher 12b-1 fee and a lower front- or back-end fee.

Prospectus	A fund's selling document that outlines all applicable fees, expenses, and investment goals of the fund.

Types of Funds
• Money Market Fund
• Bond Fund
   o Corporate
   o Government
   o Municipal
• Stock Fund
   o Growth Funds
   o Value Funds
   o Income Funds
   o Balanced Funds
   o Index Funds
   o Sector Funds
	• Fund aims to maintain a constant $1 NAV.
	• Fund that invests primarily in fixed-income securities.
	
	• Fund that invests in stocks and other equities.

Source: Securities and Exchange Commission: www.sec.gov/investor/pubs/inwsmf.htm	

One of the most useful predictors of a fund's future performance is a mutual fund's **expense ratio**. Mutual funds with lower expense ratios historically and empirically tend to outperform others. While some mutual funds charge a load to purchase and/ or sell shares, it is the ongoing expense ratio that has the greatest impact of long-term mutual fund performance.

Planning Strategy 27: Consider Adding Exchange-Traded Funds to Client Portfolios

Exchange-traded funds (ETFs) are a popular investment company product. Unlike traditional mutual funds, ETFs can be traded throughout the day, similarly to a stock, bond, or option. This gives ETFs a unique advantage over mutual funds while retaining most of the attributes offered by mutual funds.

ETFs are distinguishable from mutual funds in two respects. First, very few ETFs are actively managed. Until recently, nearly all ETFs mimicked a market index, such as the **S&P 500, Dow Jones Industrial Average**, or other market index. Second, investment companies develop ETFs using creation units, which are then pooled into baskets of securities. These baskets of securities mirror an underlying index, with the securities bought and sold by investors. This allows an investor to purchase one or more units of an ETF, and when an ETF investor wishes to sell, the investor can either sell units to other investors on the secondary market or sell units back to the investment company, though this is rarely done.

An ETF investment strategy provides investors with multiple advantages, as summarized in Figure 10.15. In general, ETFs allow clients to develop well-diversified portfolios with low annual expenses. ETFs also offer liquidity and marketability to a greater extent than index mutual funds. Moreover, ETFs are completely transparent, which means that the exact components and weightings of securities held in portfolios are always known. Mutual funds, on the other hand, are only partially transparent, because fund managers need only make their holdings known on a periodic basis, and even then, managers are allowed to delay the publication of data for a **certain period of time** to **protect portfolio marketability**.

Other ETF advantages include **tax efficiency** and **investment style stability**. ETFs are tax efficient because **portfolio turnover** is low (sometimes zero), which results in few taxable distributions. ETFs also allow financial planners to develop portfolios with fixed **allocations** to certain market benchmarks. Unlike mutual funds that tend to exhibit **style drift**—a phenomenon where a mutual fund's underlying investment approach moves from one predominant market capitalization and/or style (growth or value) target over time—investing via an **ETF** almost always guarantees exposure to a chosen asset class and market.

Figure 10.15. ETF and Mutual Fund Comparison

Investment Attribute	ETF	Index Fund	Managed Fund
Tradability	Can trade during market hours	Can trade once per day	Can trade once per day
Ability to sell short	Yes	No	No
Transparency	High	Moderate to high	Low to moderate
Diversification	Low to high	Moderate to high	Low to high
Tax efficiency	Very high	High	Low to high
Subject to style drift	Low	Low	Low to high

The primary disadvantage associated with ETFs is the lack of **active management**. Once an ETF is created, the underlying assets do not change. This means that the opportunity to outperform the market, on a risk-adjusted basis, is very low. Also, because ETFs are traded like stocks, clients incur trading commissions whenever shares are bought and sold.

Planning Strategy 28: Use the Discounted Dividend Valuation Model to Value Shares of Stock

The **discounted dividend valuation model**, sometimes referred to as the **dividend growth model**, can be used to value a share of stock using the present value of all future dividends. This method of valuation provides a starting point in valuing a stock. The formula is:

$$Value = \frac{D_0(1+g)}{(i-g)}$$

Where:

D_0 = Current dividend

i   = Required rate of return

g   = Dividend growth rate

It is worth noting that the model relies on two unknown assumptions: the dollar amount of future dividends and the growth rate of those dividends. As such, estimated values vary dramatically based on the assumptions used to measure value. Also, if the dividend growth rate exceeds the required rate of return a null value is obtained.

Planning Strategy 29: Calculate Key Financial Statement Ratios as a Stock Valuation Technique

The use of the following types of financial statement ratios can provide an important insight into the relative value of individual equities:

- **Profit margin:** net income/total sales

- **Return on equity:** net income/shareholder's equity

- **Debt-to-equity ratio:** long-term debt/shareholder's equity

- **Price-to-earnings ratio:** market capitalization/net income

- **Price-to-sales ratio:** market capitalization/total sales or total revenue

- **Price-to-book ratio:** market capitalization/shareholder's equity

Each of these ratios can also be determined on a per-share basis by dividing the formula outcome by the number of shares outstanding. Keep in mind that financial ratios provide a picture only of past performance. Should a firm's sales, net income, debt, or other calculation inputs change, estimated values will also change. Nonetheless, these ratios are widely used by financial planners to determine the relative value of a particular stock. Value investors tend to search for companies that exhibit low cost qualities. A price-to-sales ratio of, say, 1.0 or less would be considered a bargain. Growth investors generally are interested in return on equity, sales, and earnings growth rates.

Planning Strategy 30: Understand What Causes "Variance" of Returns

Default risk, or **credit risk**, is the risk that investors might not be paid what they are owed contractually. Because U.S. Treasury issues are backed by the full faith and credit of the U.S. government, these issues are said to be **default-risk free**. However other investments, such as money market mutual funds or bank accounts, are also virtually default-risk free and therefore offer similar rates of return.

The **Treasury bill** (T-bill) rate is often quoted as the **risk-free rate**, although even the risk-free rate of return is not totally free of risk. The T-bill rate is quoted as a **nominal rate of return**, and thus its return is influenced by inflation. However, because inflation affects all nominally priced investments, freedom from default risk earns the T-bill the risk-free designation. A premium on the risk-free rate is needed for clients to be willing to accept any additional risk. The **risk premium** depends on the type, severity, and probability of the risk, as well as the time horizon of the investment.

When a client is considering investing in other corporate or municipal issues, either equity or debt, it is always prudent to consider the default or credit risk of the entity. Financial planners typically rely on reviews made by credit rating agencies to assess default risk. Figure 10.16 shows the most common rate agencies and each firm's rating categories.

Figure 10.16. Bond Rating Agencies and Descriptions

Investment-grade Bonds			
Moody's	**S&P**	**Fitch**	**Rating Description**
Aaa	AAA	AAA	Highest investment bond rating
Aa	AA	AA	Very high investment grade rating
A	A	A	Medium investment grade rating
Baa	BBB	BBB	Lower investment grade rating
Speculative-Grade Bonds—High Yield			
Moody's	**S&P**	**Fitch**	**Rating Description**
Ba	BB	BB	Highest grade junk bond
B	B	B	Speculative grade junk bond
Caa	CCC	CCC	Low grade junk bond
Ca	CC	CC	Default grade junk bond
C	C	C	Issue that pays no interest
---	D	D	Issue in default

Possibly the costliest risk faced by investors is **inflation risk**.[7] Clients can spend either now or later. But to spend later in an inflationary environment means that a client will need to spend more money, in nominal terms, to purchase the same amount of goods and services. The purchasing power of money declines over time. If, for instance, inflation averages 4 percent and an account earns only 1 percent in interest, the real purchasing power of the savings declines by approximately 3 percent annually—before taxes are incorporated into the calculation.[7] Minimally, clients expect compensation that offsets this reduction.

Risk is at the root of most clients' concerns when they make investments. Beyond individual sources of risk, investors face two primary forms of risk: systematic and unsystematic. **Systematic risk,** also called **market risk,** is embedded in the system of financial markets. This type of risk generally cannot be eliminated through diversification. Assume, for example, that the markets experience a significant one-day drop in value, such as occurred in 1929 and 1987. Regardless of the amount of diversification within a portfolio, anyone invested in the stock market lost money on unhedged investments on those days.

Examples of systematic risks that investors face include **political risk** (regulatory or tax code) and **exchange rate risk.** Political changes can have a widespread impact on the markets. For U.S. investors, impacts can range from changes in the tax code to increased regulation of business. Political risks can be even more exaggerated if a portfolio contains overseas investments, particularly in emerging markets. Generally, the political systems in such countries are less developed and new leadership can signal dramatic change. U.S. investors who invest overseas must also account for changes in exchange rates. In general, a declining dollar makes U.S. exports and foreign investments more attractive. When the dollar strengthens against foreign currencies, U.S. investors can actually lose money on foreign investments, even if the investments make money nominally.

Another important type of systematic risk is the overall level of compensation investors require for taking risk. During the internet bubble of the late 1990s, investors were willing to accept little compensation for additional levels of risk. At any time, investors as a whole might demand more compensation for the risks they take, which can cause the value of securities either to stop increasing (stagnate) or to decline (deflate). This was the case immediately following September 11, 2001.

Unsystematic risk or **firm risk,** on the other hand, is a type of risk that can be managed and reduced through diversification. **Diversification** involves blending assets that are not highly correlated within a portfolio to reduce risk exposure. Business failure is perhaps the greatest unsystematic risk. Businesses can fail because of poor management **(business risk)** or for taking on too much debt **(financial risk).**

Quantitative/Analytical Mini-Case Problems

Tad and Tyler Mendoza

1. Use the information provided in the table below to calculate the weighted-average before-and-after tax rate of return of the portfolio held by Tad and Tyler Mendoza.

			Rate of Return	
Asset	Allocation	Amount	Before Tax	After Tax
Fund A	Large Cap Growth	$ 75,000.00	9.00%	6.75%
Fund B	Mid Cap value	$100,000.00	8.00%	6.00%
Fund C	Money market	$ 94,000.00	2.00%	1.50%
Fund D	Small Cap Growth	$ 14,000.00	12.00%	9.00%
Fund E	Small Cap Value	$ 35,000.00	4.00%	3.00%
Fund F	High Grade Bond	$ 45,000.00	3.00%	2.25%
Fund G	Low Grade Bond	$112,000.00	5.00%	3.75%

TJ Bartlett

2. TJ Bartlett would like to know how her portfolio is doing. Use the information shown in the following table to calculate the statistics below. (Refer to the Appendix, if necessary, for applicable formulas and purpose of each formula.)

Year	Portfolio Return	Market Return
1	12.00%	9.00%
2	9.00%	8.00%
3	22.00%	19.00%
4	–4.00%	–1.00%
5	2.00%	5.00%
6	25.00%	19.00%
7	15.00%	15.00%
8	–6.00%	–4.00%
9	11.00%	9.00%

a.   Geometric average of portfolio and market.

b.   Arithmetic average of portfolio and market.

c.   Standard deviation of portfolio and market.

Uma Johnson

3.   Uma Johnson has been tracking the performance of her portfolio benchmarked against a passive index. Here are her returns over the past few years, along with the return of the market index:

Year	Portfolio	Market Index
1	12%	9%
2	9%	8%
3	22%	19%
4	–4%	–1%
5	2%	5%
6	25%	19%
7	15%	15%
8	–6%	–4%
9	11%	9%

Based on Uma's data, answer the following questions:

a.   What is the standard deviation of Uma's portfolio and the market index?

b.   What is the geometric mean for her portfolio and the market index? How does this compare to the arithmetic mean?

c.   What is the correlation between Uma's portfolio and the market index?

d.   Based on the calculations from above, what is the beta of Uma's portfolio?

e.   Assuming a risk-free rate of 2 percent, and using the arithmetic mean, what is Uma's CAPM? Does the CAPM change if the geometric mean is used?

f.   Based on the geometric mean, has her portfolio done worse, the same, or better, on a risk-adjusted basis, compared to the market index? How do you know?

g.   Given your calculations, what should Uma do with her portfolio?

Nick Baker

4. Nick Baker is considering hiring a money manager to manage a portion of his sizable portfolio. He has narrowed his choices to the following money management firms. Each firm's historical mean return, portfolio standard deviation, and the risk-free rate is shown below:

	Benchmark	Manager 2	Manager 3	Manager 4	Manager 5
Mean	9.52%	16.00%	9.20%	18.00%	7.00%
Standard Deviation	10.65%	15.00%	5.60%	25.00%	6.00%
Risk-Free Rate	3.50%	3.50%	3.50%	3.50%	3.50%

Use this information to answer the following questions:

a. Which money manager took the most risk? Rank the money managers by the risk taken (highest to lowest).

b. Which money manager had the best risk-adjusted performance? Rank the money managers by the Sharpe ratio (highest to lowest).

c. Use the Modigliani measure to derive an estimate of what each money manager's return should have been given the amount of risk taken.

d. Which money manager should Nick hire? Why?

Chyna Snow

5. Chyna Snow considers herself to be a savvy value-oriented investor. She is always on the lookout for bargains in the market. Chyna is considering the purchase of one or more of the following stocks. Use the information provided below to estimate the value of each company's shares. Based on your analysis, using the dividend growth model, which stock or stocks should Chyna purchase?

	Stock A	Stock B	Stock C	Stock D	Stock E
Current Price	$60.00	$25.75	$145.00	$9.35	$89.50
Current Dividend	$ 2.00	$1.85	$3.56	$0.80	$3.68
Dividend Yield	3.33%	7.18%	2.46%	8.56%	4.11%
Dividend Growth Rate	4.00%	3.50%	5.20%	2.50%	3.75%
Chyna's Required Rate of Return	9.40%	9.40%	9.40%	9.40%	9.40%

Julie Cupples

6. Julie Cupples is in the process of evaluating her portfolio. Help her answer the following questions:

    a. She is considering two bonds for addition to her portfolio. Bond A has a modified duration of 8.0. Bond B has a modified duration of 3.0. Julie expects interest rates to fall over the next three years. Based solely on this information (assume the investments have equivalent bond ratings), which bond should she purchase?

    b. Julie is currently in the 22 percent marginal tax bracket. She can purchase a AAA corporate bond with a 4 percent yield to maturity. Alternatively, she can purchase a AAA municipal bond that yields 3.25 percent. Which is the better option for Julie?

    c. Julie is a gambler. She thinks the value of a stock she has been tracking is going to drop dramatically over the next three months. Julie does not have enough money in her brokerage account to short the stock. What strategy can she use to bet that the price of the shares will fall without having to hold shares directly?

    d. Julie is interested in buying a real estate investment trust for her portfolio. The REIT's price is currently $95 per share. Julie uses a value investing approach when managing her portfolio—she likes bargains. If the stock currently pays a $4 dividend should she make the purchase if her required rate of return is 9 percent and the dividend is growing at 5 percent annually?

Ron Carr

7. Ron Carr is an income investor who has a relatively low risk tolerance. He is considering the purchase of a $1,000 face value bond with the following characteristics:

    - Coupon: 4 percent

    - Coupon payments per year: one

    - Maturity: five years

    - Current market interest rate: 8 percent

    - Yield to maturity: 8 percent

        a. What is the bond's current price?

        b. What is the bond's modified duration?

        c. Based on your answer to the previous question, what will happen to the value of the bond if interest rates increase by 1 percent?

Kimberly Rabbani

8. Kimberly Rabbani would like help in estimating the convexity of a bond with the following characteristics:

- Face value: $1,000

- Coupon: 3 percent

- Coupon payments per year: two

- Maturity: five years

    a. Fill in the following table with the correct data.

Yield	Yield Change	Price	Change in Price	Change in Value
0.00%	−3.00%			
1.00%	−2.00%			
2.00%	−1.00%			
3.00%	0.00%			
4.00%	1.00%			
5.00%	2.00%			
6.00%	3.00%			

    b. Use the data from the table to graph the bond's convexity.

Chapter Resources

Benninga, S. *Financial Modeling*, 3rd Ed. Boston: MIT Press, 2008.

Boone, N., and L. Lubitz. *Creating an Investment Policy Statement*. Denver, CO: FPA Press, 2004.

California Debt and Investment Advisory Commission. *Issue Brief, Duration*, CDIAC# 06-10, 2007.

Ellis, C.D. Investment Policy: How to Win the Loser's Game. New York: McGraw-Hill, 1993.

FinaMetrica Risk Profiling System (www.riskprofiling.com/home).

FINRA Mutual Fund Expense Analyzer (apps.finra.org/fundanalyzer/1/fa.aspx).

Guy, J.W. *How to Invest Someone Else's Money*. Chicago: Irwin, 1994.

Haughey, B. *Bond Convexity:* What Is It, and Why Should You Care? *AAII Journal* 40 (5): 26-28, 2018.

Investment Risk Tolerance Quiz (http://pfp.missouri.edu/research_IRTA.html).

Leimberg, S., et al. *The Tools and Techniques of Investment Planning*, 4th Ed. Cincinnati, OH: National Underwriter Company, 2017.

Murray, N. *Behavioral Investment Counseling*. Mattituck, NY: The Nick Murray Company, Inc., 2008.

Shefrin, H., & Mario B. "Behavioral Finance: Biases, Mean-Variance Returns, and Risk Premiums." *CFA Institute Conference Proceedings Quarterly*. June (2007): 4–11. Available at: www.ifa.com/pdf/behavioralfinancecp.v24.n2.pdf.

Siegel, L.B. *Benchmarks and Investment Management*. Charlottesville, VA: CFA Institute, 2003.

Susan Bradley's Sudden Money Institute (www.suddenmoney.com).

Trone, D.B., Allbright, W.R., & Taylor, P.R. *The Management of Investment Decisions*. Chicago: Irwin, 1996.

Endnotes

1. A financial risk tolerance questionnaire can be found at: http://pfp.missouri.edu/research_IRTA.html

2. Most online financial data websites and publications, such as Morningstar, report R2 coefficients for individual stocks, mutual funds, and exchange traded funds.

3. These formulas assume a normal distribution.

4. Estimated cash flow calculated as follows: $80/(1.05)1; $80/(1.05)2; $1,080/(1.05)3

5. Data for the curve (the change in price shows the effect on a bond's price when interest rates change):

Yield	Yield Change	Price	Change in Price	Change in Value
0	–10	$ 2,000.00	$ 1,000.00	$ 145.57
1	–9	$ 1,854.43	$ 854.43	$ 132.61
2	–8	$ 1,721.82	$ 721.82	$ 120.92
3	–7	$ 1,600.90	$ 600.90	$ 110.36
4	–6	$ 1,490.54	$ 490.54	$ 100.81
5	–5	$ 1,389.73	$ 389.73	$ 92.18
6	–4	$ 1,297.55	$ 297.55	$ 84.36
7	–3	$ 1,213.19	$ 213.19	$ 77.28
8	–2	$ 1,135.90	$ 135.90	$ 70.86
9	–1	$ 1,065.04	$ 65.04	$ 65.04
10	0	$ 1,000.00	$ -	$ -
11	1	$ 940.25	$ (59.75)	$ (59.75)
12	2	$ 885.30	$ (114.70)	$ (54.95)
13	3	$ 834.72	$ (165.28)	$ (50.58)
14	4	$ 788.12	$ (211.88)	$ (46.60)
15	5	$ 745.14	$ (254.86)	$ (42.98)
16	6	$ 705.46	$ (294.54)	$ (39.68)
17	7	$ 668.78	$ (331.22)	$ (36.67)
18	8	$ 634.86	$ (365.14)	$ (33.93)
19	9	$ 603.44	$ (396.56)	$ (31.42)
20	10	$ 574.32	$ (425.68)	$ (29.12)

6. A lesser-known threat is liquidity risk. This is the risk that an investor will not be able to convert an asset into cash in a timely manner or without a loss in value.

7. The actual reduction in purchasing power is 2.97 percent [(1.04/1.01) -1].

Modern Portfolio Statistics— Mean-variance Analysis

ASSET MEAN "AVERAGE"

As discussed in Chapter 2, the most basic investment statistic is the **average return**, known as the arithmetic average, or **mean**. The mean is sometimes designated by the Greek letter μ. Typically, this is an easily understood investment statistic, the one most sought after by investors, and the most quoted by investment providers. This statistic is also the basis of all other modern portfolio theory related statistics, such as variance, standard deviation, the coefficient of variation, and the Sharpe ratio. The formula is:

$$\frac{r_1 + r_2 + r_3 + \cdots + r_n}{n}$$

Where:

r   = return for period

n   = number of periods

For longer forecasting periods, or for forecasting using a more highly varied return, a **geometric average** is most often used by financial planners. A geometric mean is computed using a geometric series. A geometric mean takes on more of the characteristics found in long-term averages and corrects for any upward bias. As discussed in Chapter 2, unless the variation of returns is zero, the geometric average will always be lower than the arithmetic return. The formula for calculating a geometric average is as follows:

$$\left[\left(1 + r_1\right) \times \left(1 + r_2\right) \times \left(1 + r_3\right) \times \ldots \times \left(1 + r_n\right)\right]^{1/n} - 1$$

Where:

r   = return for period

n   = number of periods

However, unless a client is investing in a fixed-return asset, such as a bank CD, it is important to remember that most periodic returns vary over time. An average return tells only half of the story. Although returns should average out in the end, returns during any given period likely will be either above or below the expected long-term average. When returns vary around an average, most predictions of future returns assume that the average will prevail.

Expected Return

The formulas described thus far have been calculated based on historical—or known—data. But as a common financial planning investment disclaimer states, "Past performance does not guarantee future results." For a financial planner to plan appropriately, some assumptions about the future must be made. These assumptions become the basis of expectations.

Clients expect a certain level of return to compensate for a variety of risks. This **expected return**, denoted $E(r)$, can be mathematically calculated by adding the appropriate risk premiums to the risk-free rate of return, as follows.

$$E(r) = r_f + IP + DP + BP + \dots$$

Where:

$E(r)$ = expected return

r_f = risk-free rate

IP = inflation risk premium

DP = default risk premium

BP = business risk premium

For simplicity, these **risk premia** are typically grouped together as one aggregated risk premium that accounts for both systematic and unsystematic risks. Once an expected rate of return is calculated, it is important for a financial planner to determine whether rates of return available in the marketplace are adequate for the level of risk that the client is willing to accept. Also, a financial planner must perform a **sensitivity analysis** to determine how likely the projected returns are.

Expected Return (Using Probabilities)

A typical financial planner task involves conducting a scenario analysis that considers possible outcomes under various market conditions. However, to facilitate client communication, these scenarios can be aggregated into the most likely outcome—or at least an average representation of the various scenarios.

Assigning and using probabilities is the easiest way to aggregate these outcomes. If a financial planner looks at three possible market conditions—boom, normal, and bust—and assigns each outcome a probability, then the financial planner can determine an "average" or most likely outcome.

Example: A financial planner determines that in any given year there is a 20 percent likelihood of above-normal returns (boom), a 65 percent chance of average returns (normal), and a 15 percent possibility of below-normal returns (bust). The financial planner also determines that the corresponding returns would be 21 percent, 9 percent, and –12 percent, respectively. With this information, and using the following formula, the planner can calculate the most likely—or average—outcome to be 8.25 percent.

$$E(r) = (p_1 \times r_1) + (p_2 \times r_2) + (p_{n-1} \times r_{n-1}) + ... + (p_n \times r_n)$$

Where:

E(r)   = expected return

p   = probability of outcome

r   = return (outcome)

n   = number of outcomes

In this example, E(r) = (20% × 21%) + (65% × 9%) + (15% × -12%) = 8.25 percent

Asset Variance

A fundamental measure of risk deals with the fluctuation of individual returns around an average return. The greater the dispersion of returns, the higher the return volatility; hence, the higher the risk. The difference between the average return and the range of possible outcomes is known as **variance**, denoted by σ^2. Variance is calculated by subtracting each individual outcome from the average outcome and then squaring the difference, as shown below:

$$\sigma^2 = X_t - \mu$$

Where:

σ^2 = variance

X_t = outcome

μ = average (mean)

Although individual security variance statistic is informative, average variance is the more important statistic. This calculation involves adding variances together and then dividing the sum by one less than the number of outcomes in the sample, as illustrated below:

$$\sigma_i^2 = \frac{(x_1 - \mu)^2 + (x_2 - \mu)^2 + (x_3 - \mu)^2 + \cdots + (x_4 - \mu)^2}{n - 1}$$

Where:

n   = number of observations or units

Example. Assets A and B have the following returns.

Nominal Rates of Return	Asset A	Asset B
2015	−12.0%	−2.9%
2016	4.2%	6.5%
2017	11.8%	9.0%
2018	6.1%	−3.7%
2019	9.3%	7.5%
Arithmetic mean	3.88%	3.28%

By applying the preceding formula, a financial planner can determine that Asset A has a variance of 0.00873, whereas Asset B has a variance of 0.00370.

Asset Standard Deviation

Standard deviation, denoted as a lower-case sigma (σ), is a risk measure related to and predicated on variance. Standard deviation is the square root of variance and is more often quoted and used in investment statistics than variance. Standard deviation can be very useful in determining the dispersion of possible—or past—outcomes in relation to an expected outcome. **Total risk**, which comprises systematic and unsystematic risk, is typically measured by standard deviation.

$$\sigma_i = \sqrt{\frac{(x_1 - \mu)^2 + (x_2 - \mu)^2 + (x_3 - \mu)^2 + \cdots + (x_4 - \mu)^2}{n - 1}}$$

Where:

σ = standard deviation

n   = number of observations or units

r_i = actual return

μ = average return

Using the table of data from the variance example, it is apparent that, because the annual outcomes are different, the standard deviation will be greater than zero. (In fact, the only time that standard deviation and variance are zero is when all outcomes over the analysis period are identical.) Using standard deviation formula, or applying the square root formula to the variance derived above, the standard deviations are as 9.34 percent and 6.08 percent, respectively, for Assets A and B.

Asset Coefficient of Variation

The **coefficient of variation** (CV) is another measure of dispersion (**range**), but in this case CV is a relative measure based on average returns. CV is the ratio of unit of risk per unit of return. It is easy to see that, for this ratio, smaller numbers are superior to larger ones. CV is useful when comparing the risks of various investments with different expected returns. The equation for CV is:

$$CV = \frac{\sigma}{\mu}$$

Where:

σ = standard deviation

μ = mean

Consider the same two possible investments, Asset A and Asset B, from above. To determine which asset offers the greatest return for a given level of risk, the risk of each asset (standard deviation) must be divided by the average return of each asset (arithmetic mean) as follows:

Nominal Rates of Return	Asset A	Asset B
2012	–12.0%	–2.9%
2013	4.2%	6.5%
2014	11.8%	9.0%
2015	6.1%	–3.7%
2016	9.3%	7.5%
Arithmetic mean	3.88%	3.28%
Variance	0.87%	0.37%
Standard deviation	9.34%	6.08%

CV Asset A = 9.34/3.88 = 2.41

CV Asset B = 6.08/3.28 = 1.85

By comparing the two assets without an adjustment for risk, a financial planner might choose Asset A, the riskier asset, because of its higher average return. However, after calculating the CV for both assets, the financial planner would rightly conclude that Asset A does not offer enough additional return for the increased level of risk.

Another use of CV involves determining the appropriate level of return for an increased level of risk. Returning to the preceding example, a financial planner sees that Asset B offers 1.85 points of risk for each point of return. Therefore, for the financial planner to choose Asset A, a similar or lower ratio is needed. It is possible to use the following formula to determine the level of return necessary for the level of risk associated with Asset A:

$$\text{Required return of Asset A to equalize the CV} = \frac{\sigma_A}{CV \text{ of Asset B}}$$

$$\text{Required return to select Asset A} = \frac{9.34\%}{1.85} = 5.05\%$$

Correlation and Covariance of Two Assets

As noted above, diversification is a method used to reduce the unsystematic risk in a portfolio. However, to maximize the benefit derived from diversification, it is important for a financial planner to select assets that do not react the same way to a given economic environment. **Covariance** and **correlation** are measures of the degree to which multiple assets move in tandem.

Covariance measures the linear relationship between two random variables. The formula for covariance is:

$$\sigma_{ij} = \sigma_i \sigma_j \rho_{ij}$$

Where:

σ_{ij} = covariance of assets i,j

σ = standard deviation

ρ_{ij} = correlation of assets i,j

Notice that the covariance formula and the formula for solving for correlation are identical. The variables have simply been rearranged to isolate the unknown. Unfortunately, if both correlation and covariance are unknown, then the equation is rendered useless. Therefore, an alternative equation must be used, one that is not predicated on the other, but on the periodic returns of each asset. The formula to solve for covariance if the correlation is unknown is:

$$\sigma_{ij} = \frac{1}{n-1} \sum_{t-1}^{n} (r_{i,t} - \mu_i)(r_{j,t} - \mu_j)$$

Where:

σ_{ij} = covariance of assets i,j

n = number of observations or units

r_i = actual return at each period "t"

μ = average return

The easier to interpret of these two statistics is the **correlation coefficient,** which scales covariance based on the product of the standard deviation of two measured assets. The correlation coefficient is often denoted by the Greek letter *rho* (ρ).

Correlation is measured on a scale of –1.0 to +1.0, with a value of zero indicating that there is no relationship between two variables. If assets are positively correlated, this means that as one asset rises in value (or falls) the other asset usually does the same. If the assets are negatively correlated, then as one asset rises in value the other asset falls, and as one asset falls in value the other asset rises. If assets are positively correlated to a degree of +1.0, meaning that the assets are perfectly correlated, then not only will both assets rise at the same time, they will rise at the same rate. The inverse of this is also true if the assets are perfectly inversely correlated (-1.0). The formula for correlation is:

$$\rho_{i,j} = \frac{\sigma_{i,j}}{\sigma_i \sigma_j}$$

Standard Deviation of a Two-Asset Portfolio

Now that all of the statistics about Assets A and B are known, the power of investment statistics can be applied to the combination of these two assets—a portfolio. Unfortunately, a financial planner cannot simply weight asset standard deviations to calculate the standard deviation of a portfolio as can be done with returns because this ignores the covariance of the assets when used in tandem. Instead, the following equation must be used to determine the standard deviation of a two-asset portfolio.

$$\sigma_p = \sqrt{w_i^2 \sigma_i^2 + w_j^2 \sigma_j^2 + 2 w_i w_j \sigma_{i,j}}$$

Where:

σ = standard deviation

w = weight "allocation" of each asset

α_{ij} = covariance

Standard Deviation and Confidence Levels

If returns are normally distributed, nearly 100 percent of all possible outcomes will fall within three standard deviations above or below the mean. As such, a financial planner can reasonably predict the minimum and maximum periodic return value for any period of time.

Risk can be quantified using measures of **volatility.** Standard deviation is a measure of historical returns as the returns are dispersed around an average. Although the standard deviation of a portfolio can change, financial planners usually assume that historical standard deviation is somewhat predictive of the future volatility of a portfolio. To use this measure of risk effectively, a financial planner needs to understand the following confidence levels.

1. Approximately 68 percent of all observations fall within one standard deviation of the mean.

2. Approximately 95 percent of all observations fall within two standard deviations of the mean.

3. Approximately 99 percent of all observations fall within three standard deviations of the mean.

Example. A portfolio returned an average of 12 percent while the standard deviation was 15 percent. Applying the three confidence levels, a financial planner can be 68 percent confident that a client's actual returns fell within a range of –3 percent and 27 percent (12% +/– 15%). A 95 percent confidence level suggests that returns ranged from –18 percent to 42 percent (12% +/– 30% (2 × 15%)) in any given year. A 99 percent confidence level suggests that returns ranged from –33 percent to 57 percent (12% +/– 45% (3 × 15%)) in any given year.

Standard deviation plays a central role in helping financial planners understand the dynamics of portfolio management. The measure of standard deviation, along with covariance and variance, makes up the core basis of modern portfolio theory.[1]

Log-Normal Distributions

The **log-normal probability** distribution arises from a continuous distribution of returns where the logarithm of those returns is normal, rather than the returns themselves being normal. This results is a distribution curve of returns that is skewed slightly to the left or right; it has been determined that, in developed markets, skewness is to the left. For a financial planner and client, this skewness means that the **geometric mean** (average) and the **geometric median** (50 percent level) are unequal. In other words, if a distribution is skewed to the left, then more than 50 percent of the outcomes are below the mean outcome.

Asset Semi-variance

Semi-variance generally can be defined as one-half of the original variance. If a financial planner is working with a normal distribution this assumption is correct. However, in the case of log-normal distributions, semi-variance is either greater than or less than one-half, depending on the direction of skewness and which side of the distribution is being measured.

Downside Risk (DR)

Because clients dislike losses even more than they like gains, it makes sense to target the side of the return distribution that fails to meet the standard rather than the side that exceeds it. In this case, the standard is the expected or mean outcome, and the side that fails is the left side where relative returns are negative (even if absolute returns can be either positive or negative). As a note, the target can be defined as any minimum return deemed acceptable. For example, the **internal rate of return** that satisfies an investment objective can be used as the target. The semi-variance should be calculated by squaring only the negative deviations from the mean (all outcomes above the target would be entered as the target, thereby resulting in a squared difference of zero). Taking the square root of the sum of these squared deviations results in **semi-deviation**, also known as **downside deviation**, a measure of **downside risk**.

The Sortino Ratio

The most popular method for ranking investment opportunities is by ratio. Typically, the ratio is of excess return (return greater than a target) over a measure of risk (e.g., total [σ], systemic [β], negative outcome [DR]). Whereas the **Sharpe ratio** measures excess return over total risk and the **Treynor index/ratio** measures excess return over systemic risk, the **Sortino ratio** measures excess return over only the risk of negative outcomes, or **downside risk**. This ratio is very useful when attempting to determine the likelihood of a particular investment or strategy not meeting the minimum acceptable return when the distribution of outcomes is non-normal, which has been previously determined. This utility arises from the fact that the minimum acceptable return target can be any number; it is not limited to a simple arithmetic or geometric mean.

CAPM as Expected Return

Once a financial planner knows the return of the market, the risk-free rate of return, and the beta of a portfolio, the financial planner can calculate an **expected risk-adjusted rate of return** for the portfolio. The formula used to calculate an expected rate of return is known as the **capital asset pricing model** (**CAPM**). The CAPM formula is shown below:

$$R_{Exp} = R_f + \beta(R_m - R_f)$$

Where:

R_{Exp} = expected risk-adjusted rate of return

R_f = risk-free rate

β = beta

R_m = return on the market

The risk-free rate of return is most often indexed to Treasury bill rates, or other risk-free, short-term rates. Some financial planners use the 10-year interest rate to approximate the long-term horizon assumed with holding equities or the one-year rate as a proxy for a one-year forecast horizon. The return on the market used most often for domestic portfolios is the S&P 500. However, other benchmarks can be used. For example, if a portfolio is composed of technology and internet stocks, the NASDAQ index cab be an appropriate benchmark. A portfolio comprised primarily non-U.S. stocks might be benchmarked against the **Europe, Australia, and Far East** (**EAFE**) index.

Example. Assume that Chris has a well-diversified retirement portfolio. Over the past three years, the beta of the portfolio was calculated to be 0.85. The risk-free rate at the time of the analysis was 3 percent, and the market returned 12 percent. What risk-adjusted return should Chris have received during the three-year period?

CAPM Return = 0.03 + [0.85 × (0.12 − 0.03)] = 10.65 percent

This means that Chris should have received 10.65 percent on a risk-adjusted basis over the three-year period. Anything below this expected rate of return indicates that Chris took unsystematic market risk that he was not compensated for.

Beta

The main weakness associated with measuring volatility using standard deviation is that standard deviation is security/portfolio specific. It is difficult to compare one portfolio against another using standard deviation. Many financial planners instead use **beta** as a measure of volatility to solve this problem. Beta is a relative measure of risk and is most often used as a measure of systematic risk in the stock market, but it can also measure the volatility of a portfolio compared to a market index. As noted above in the CAPM calculation, beta is used to determine an investor's expected rate of return.

Beta is generally estimated by using a linear regression for each asset, based on historical asset returns and the corresponding market returns. If standard deviation and correlation data are available, beta can also be measured as:

$$\beta = (\sigma_p / \sigma_m) \times \rho_{p,m}$$

Where:

σ_p = standard deviation of the portfolio

σ_m = standard deviation of the market

$\rho_{p,m}$ = correlation between portfolio and market

Example. Assume that the standard deviation of a portfolio of stocks is 14 percent and the standard deviation of a market index, such as the S&P 500, is 12 percent. If the correlation between the portfolio and market is 0.90, the beta of the stock portfolio will be 1.05 [(0.14 ÷ 0.12) × 0.90].

The **beta of the market** is, by definition, 1.0. Typically, the S&P 500 is used as the market index by U.S. investors. A portfolio with a beta of less than 1.0 is considered less volatile than the market. On the other hand, a beta of greater than 1.0 implies volatility in excess of the market. Beta is useful because the number can be used to tell a client approximately how much less or more volatile a portfolio is in comparison to the market. A beta of 1.10 indicates, for example, that a portfolio is approximately 10 percent more volatile than the index. Beta coefficients are theoretically continuous, meaning that scores can range from less than zero to a positive number. In practice, however, beta coefficients for diversified portfolios rarely exceed 4.0 on the high side or –2.0 on the low side.[2]

Endnotes

1. The two primary flaws of modern portfolio theory are that statistical analysis assumes that returns are normally (symmetrically) distributed around the mean, and that standard deviation is the appropriate measure of risk. Both of these assumptions tend to fail in practice. First, investment returns are not normally distributed; returns are closer to log-normal with slightly negative (left) skewness. This is important because the normal distribution erroneously assumes that one-half of the outcomes are below the average outcome and one-half are above. Second, clients dislike a negative surprise more than they like positive surprises. Put another way, the risk of the undesirable outweighs the risk of the unknown, and standard deviation simply measures the likelihood of the unanticipated happening—whether the outcome is positive or negative. To overcome these shortcomings, Markowitz (the Nobel Laurate who founded modern portfolio theory) suggested that models based on semi-variance (focusing on downside risk) are preferable.

2. One note of caution in relation to beta is in order. Financial planners who use beta should do so only with well-diversified portfolios. Beta becomes very unstable and unreliable when used with single securities or non-diversified portfolios. In such cases, it is often best to use standard deviation as the measure of portfolio risk.

Chapter 11

Education Planning

Learning Objectives

- Learning Objective 1: Estimate a client's education funding need.

- Learning Objective 2: Describe the features of different education saving plans.

- Learning Objective 3: Explain the tax associated with providing and obtaining financial assistance for higher education costs.

- Learning Objective 4: Provide strategies a client can use to meet an education funding goal.

CFP® Principal Knowledge Topics

- CFP Topic: C.17. Education Needs Analysis
- CFP Topic: C.18. Education Savings vehicles
- CFP Topic: C.19. Financial aid
- CFP Topic: C.20. Gift/income tax strategies
- CFP Topic: C.21. Education financing

Chapter Equations

Future Value of a Lump Sum:

$$FV = PV (1 + i)^n$$

Present Value of a Growing Annuity:

$$PV = \frac{PMT}{i - g} \left(1 - \frac{(1 + g)^n}{(1 + i)^n} \right)(1 + i)$$

Present Value of a Lump Sum:

$$PV = \frac{FV}{(1 + i)^n}$$

Present Value of an Annuity Payment:

$$PV = \frac{PMT}{i - g} \left(1 - \frac{(1 + g)^n}{(1 + i)^n} \right)$$

Payment Required to Achieve a Savings Goal:

$$PMT = \frac{PV(i - g)}{\left(1 - \frac{(1 + g)^n}{(1 + i)^n} \right)}$$

EDUCATION PLANNING STRATEGIES

While not all financial planning situations will entail the development of education funding recommendations, cases that do require education planning compel a financial planner to apply their knowledge of a broad array of educational planning tools and techniques. The following education planning strategies represent a sampling of approaches financial planners use when working with clients.

Planning Strategy 1: Estimate a Client's Education Funding Need Using a Consistent Methodology

Several interrelated steps are involved in the analysis of a client's education planning situation. To complete not only an education funding assessment but also a comprehensive financial plan, it is essential that a client's goals and objectives guide the process. It is possible—and likely—that a wide range of personal client beliefs and expectations will affect the education funding analysis and the type of recommendations ultimately made. In fact, client attitudes and beliefs, especially as they are converted into planning assumptions, may be more important and potentially more problematic in relation to education planning compared to other core content planning areas.

Two fundamental questions require answers when conducing an education funding analysis:

1. How much will the education cost?

2. How will these costs be paid?

Numerous underlying factors need to be considered when addressing these questions. Foremost among these is framing the goal of 'college' broadly to include education, higher education, or post-secondary education. These terms allow clients to acknowledge that their children might or might not be interested in a traditional college education, but that other options such as trade, technical, or arts programs may be a more appropriate choice. For some clients, the topic of paying for education can focus on the cost of private elementary or secondary school rather than public education. The following questions offer one way to explore some of the client-specific factors that underlie education planning:

*   Do you plan to save enough to pay for higher education before the child enters the educational program?

*   Do you plan to pay for the educational program after or while the child is enrolled in the educational program?

*   Do you expect others to pay for some or all the child's education?

*   Do you plan to use a combination of sources (e.g., personal, family, loans) to pay for the child's education?

Once a client has defined the direction of the education planning effort, focused planning with the client can begin. Thoroughly and openly discussing these questions can help a financial planner and client explore the range of client characteristics that impact education planning decisions. For example, some clients may firmly refuse to fully pay for college costs, although they may be financially capable of doing so. Based on their values and attitudes, some clients may want the child to contribute through earnings or loans. Other clients might insist on funding college costs to the exclusion of other planning needs. These examples illustrate how personality, values, attitudes, experience, and socioeconomic descriptors converge to influence education planning efforts.

For example, clients who plan to accumulate funding before a child enters college will likely initiate disciplined savings early and focus on the desired amount. Those who plan to pay during or after the student attends college may be doing so by necessity or choice—because of a failure to start early, competing financial goals, life events that prevented or interrupted savings, or any number of other reasons. These clients may have few reservations about incurring debt through public or private sources or postponing other goals to contribute to educational expenses. They, as well as clients who plan on someone else paying, may expect the child to contribute through borrowing or working while in school. Other clients may view student loan debt or employment during the academic year as an unnecessary burden on their child.

In addition to the child, others may be asked to help fund educational costs, including providers of **scholarships** and **grants** based on need, aptitude (e.g., scholastic, athletic, artistic), or interest (e.g., leadership, community service). Other family members (e.g., grandparents, siblings, etc.) might also be expected to contribute to a child's educational funding need before, during, or after college through direct or indirect gifts, trusts, or estate distributions. A combination of funding sources may sometimes result in an optimal funding solution.

In summary, the choice of which or how much of each goal to fund is complicated by the uncertainty of the assumptions used when determining education funding needs. Prior to quantifying this need, financial planners should first understand what priority a client places on education planning and which assumptions to include in the planning. For some clients, education funding will be the highest priority. For others, education funding will rank below other financial planning goals. Many of these issues can be revealed during the data-gathering discovery and the goal identification process, but if not, then a discussion focused on education planning should occur. Specific issues to address with a client include:

- Determining how much value a client or household places on attending institutions of higher education

- Prioritizing education planning within the comprehensive planning framework

- Establishing the primary reason education funding is desired, including feelings of obligation or benevolence, as well as tax considerations (e.g., preferences for tax-advantaged savings opportunities to defer or avoid income taxes, availability of income tax adjustments, or credits reductions in estate taxes)

- Establishing guidelines regarding what the client or household believes is a reasonable amount to pay for a college education for one or more dependents

- Identifying the level of control a client wants to retain in the management of assets devoted to education funding needs

- Assessing a child's probability of receiving a scholarship or grant based on unique skills, abilities, or interests

- Determining a child's expectation of receiving financial aid

Of these factors, some are wholly determined by the client, and as such, a financial planner must respect the client's opinion without judgment. Other fact-based considerations, such as preferences regarding taxes and control over accounts, can be used by financial planners to directly influence strategic recommendations. Once a financial planner has a solid understanding of a client's perceived roles, attitudes, and preferences underlying education planning, the financial planner can move on to determining the cost of the goal. Essentially, the analysis should help answer the following question: Is the client on track to meet the goal(s)? The analysis can be guided by the following questions:

1. When will the child(ren) begin college?

2. What type of college might the child(ren) want or be encouraged to attend?

3. How much are college costs increasing annually for this type of college?

4. What are the projected costs for the targeted college when the child(ren) begins college?

5. How much of the projected college cost does the client intend to provide?

6. How much of the projected cost does the client expect to be funded by scholarships, grants, and loans?

7. Does the client currently have assets earmarked for this goal?

8. How much is the client, or other family members, currently saving for this goal?

9. Does education planning include funding for graduate education? (If yes, the preceding questions must be reconsidered for this scenario.)

Assessing a client's educational funding need is a relatively straightforward procedure. Figure 11.1 illustrates the information needed to complete a basic education funding needs analysis, the likely source of data, and the calculations required.

Figure 11.1. Summary of Data and Calculations Required for a College Savings Need Analysis

Data Needed for Analysis	Source of Data
Rate of return	Client/planner assumption
Years to complete college	Client/planner assumption
Initial additional periodic savings amount	Client/planner assumption
Initial periodic increase in savings amount	Client/planner assumption
Annual cost of college today	Planner research
College expense inflation rate	Planner research
Current age of child	Client data
College age of child	Client data
Present value of assets currently saved	Client data

Calculations Required for Analysis	Completed by
College real interest rate	Financial planner
Future value cost of college	Financial planner
Future value of assets currently saved	Financial planner
Future value of additional periodic savings	Financial planner

In order to complete the analysis, a financial planner must determine the rate of return most likely to be generated on assets and savings dedicated to the goal. This return assumption should match the client's financial risk tolerance. The choice of a single rate-of-return figure may be overly simplistic because it is possible for clients to use a combination of before- and after-tax investments earmarked for education, and/ or use an age-based portfolio where the rate of return will decrease over time as risk is removed from the portfolio and goal realization nears. It is also likely that some investments (e.g., U.S. Savings Bonds and Section 529 plans) will generate tax-free returns. Once individual account returns have been determined, a financial planner can then calculate the weighted-average return on which to base future value calculations.

Other information needed to complete an analysis includes the assumed rate of inflation for tuition and other college expenses, the child's current age, expected age when entering college, and the number of years of college to be funded. The current cost of the college of choice is needed.[1] Finally, the amount of assets already saved, and a projected annual savings amount, must be determined. The following is a step-by-step process[2] that can be used to conduct an education funding analysis.

Step One

Determine the future value (FV) cost of education for a single year at the time the child begins college, using the future value equation below, where the present value (PV) is the current annual cost of college, the interest rate (i) is the projected annual increase (inflation rate) in college cost, and n is the number of years until college begins.

Future value of a lump sum

$$FV = PV(1 + i)^n$$

Step Two

Find the total cost of education (all years) at the time the child begins college using the present value of a growing annuity equation, where the payment (PMT) is the first-year cost of college as calculated in Step One. Because college tuition is normally paid as an annuity, the annual increase in college cost is the growth rate (g), the estimated rate of return becomes the interest rate (i), and n is the number of years in college. This estimate is an annuity due because college tuition is typically paid at the beginning of each semester.

Present value of a growing annuity

$$PV = \frac{PMT}{i-g}\left(1 - \frac{(1+g)^n}{(1+i)^n}\right)(1+i)$$

Step Three

To determine the cost of college today (as if the client were going to set aside the requisite amount immediately), calculate the present value (PV) of the total cost of education discounted from the first year of college back to today, using the present value of a lump sum equation, where the future value (FV) is the total cost in Step Two. The interest rate (i) is the estimated rate of return, and n is the number of years until college begins.

Present value of a lump sum

$$PV = \frac{FV}{(1+i)^n}$$

Step Four

If funding has already been dedicated to the goal, this amount should be subtracted from the total present cost of education in Step Three. The result is the **funding shortfall**, which is the lump sum amount needed immediately to meet the education goal.

Funding Shortfall = Total Need – Amount Already Dedicated to Goal Achievement

Step Five

If the client plans to fund the shortfall on a periodic basis, the financial planner needs to determine the monthly savings required until college begins.[3] This amount can be estimated using a present value of an annuity payment formula, where the present value (PV) is the lump sum amount in Step Four. The inputs for the formula include the expected rate of return (i) and the anticipated growth rate of the periodic payment (g), if applicable. Again, n is the number of years until college begins.

Present value of an annuity payment

$$PV = \frac{PMT}{i-g}\left(1 - \frac{(1+g)^n}{(1+i)^n}\right)$$

Rearranging the formula to isolate PMT yields the payment required to achieve the savings goal:

$$PMT = \frac{PV(i-g)}{\left(1 - \frac{(1+g)^n}{(1+i)^n}\right)}$$

The resulting payment is the required periodic payment, assuming that the client wants to save enough to achieve the goal without regard to other funding sources.

To illustrate this process, consider the following example used to determine a one-time lump sum payment (as well as monthly savings) to fully fund a child's educational need. Assume that the current annual cost of college is $12,000, and to ensure adequate funding, assume an annual cost increase of 5 percent per year both before and during college. Assume the child will begin college in exactly four years, will attend for four years, and has no money set aside for the goal. Finally, assume an effective annual rate of return of 8.30 percent.[4] What is the required savings amount if the client is going to set aside the entire amount today? What is the required monthly savings amount?

Step One. Determine the future value cost of education for the first year of school:

$$FV = PV\,(1 + i)^n$$

or

$$FV = \$12,000(1.05)^4 = \$14,586.08$$

Input	Keystroke	Result
0	[PMT]	PMT = 0.00
12000 [+/−]	[PV]	PV = −12,000.00
5	[I/Y]	I/Y = 5.00
4	[N]	N = 4.00
[CPT]	[FV]	FV = 14,586.08
Note: The PV is input as a negative figure because an investment is an assumed outflow. For this step, the inflation rate is treated as an interest rate to determine the "inflated" cost of the goal.		

Step Two. Find the total cost of education (for all years) needed at the time the child begins college:

$$PV = \frac{PMT}{i - g}\left(1 - \frac{(1 + g)^n}{(1 + i)^n}\right)$$

or

$$PV = \frac{\$14,586.08}{0.083 - 0.05}\left(1 - \frac{(1.05)^4}{(1.083)^4}\right)(1.083) = \$55,731.37$$

Input	Keystroke	Result
14586.08	[PMT]	PMT = 14,586.08
0	[FV]	FV = 0.00
3.1429*	[I/Y]	I/Y = 3.1429
4	[N]	N = 4.00
[CPT]	[PV]	PV = −55,731.37**
*The calculator needs a serial rate to handle growing annuities. See Chapter 2 for details. **Disregard the negative sign in the solution.		

Step Three. Determine the present value of the savings required as a lump sum:

$$PV = \frac{FV}{(1 + i)^n}$$

or

$$PV@t_0 = \frac{\$55,731.37}{(1.083)^4} = \$40,512.20$$

Input	Keystroke	Result
0	[PMT]	PMT = 0.00
55731.37	[FV]	FV = 55,731.37
8.30	[I/Y]	I/Y = 8.30
4	[N]	N = 4.00
[CPT]	[PV]	PV = –40,512.20*
*Disregard the negative sign in the solution.		

Step Four. Estimate the savings shortfall:

Since nothing has been saved to date, the lump sum amount needed immediately to meet the education goal equals $40,512.20 ($40,512.20 – $0).

Step Five. Determine the monthly savings needed to meet the education goal:

To solve for a monthly payment, the equivalent monthly rate for both the rate of return and the rate of payment growth, if applicable, must be used.

$$PMT = \frac{PV(i - g)}{\left(1 - \dfrac{(1 + g)^n}{(1 + i)^n}\right)}$$

or

$$PMT = \frac{\$40,512.20(0.00667)}{\left(1 - \dfrac{1}{1.00667^{48}}\right)} = \$989.02$$

Input	Keystroke	Result
40512.20	[PV]	PV = 40,512.20
0.667*	[I/Y]	I/Y = 0.667
48	[N]	N = 48.00
0	[FV]	FV = 0
[CPT]	[PMT]	PMT = –989.02**
*To calculate the monthly payment, either the interest rate must be in input as a monthly EPR or the number of payments per year must be reset to 12.		
**Disregard the negative sign in the solution.		

The last step in the analysis involves subtracting out any current monthly savings from the estimate. Because the client in this example was not saving towards the goal, the monthly savings needed to meet the education goal equals $989.02.

While the needs estimation approach described above can be used to estimate an education funding need for almost any client situation, nearly all financial planners prefer to use an automated spreadsheet to more quickly estimate a college funding need. Figure 11.2 illustrates the type of information typically included in a needs analysis model. This spreadsheet is available in the Financial Planning Analysis Excel package included with this book.

Figure 11.2. Education Planning Needs Analysis Spreadsheet

COLLEGE SAVINGS ANALYSIS			
ASSUMPTIONS			
Child/Scenario Name	Child 1	Child 2	Child 3
Combined Federal and State Marginal Tax Bracket			
Assumed After-Tax Rate of Return Before College			
Assumed Before-Tax Return of Tax-Advantaged Plans			
Assumed Rate of Return After College Begins			
Assumed College Expense Inflation Rate			
Age			
College Age			
Years In College			
Yearly Cost of College TODAY			
Value of After-Tax Assets Saved Today			
Value of Tax-Advantaged Assets Saved			
Annual After-Tax Savings			
Annual Tax-Advantaged Savings			
Annual Savings Growth Rate			
CALCULATIONS			
College Serial After-Tax Interest Rate Before College Starts			
College Serial Before-Tax Rate Before College Starts			
College Serial Interest Rate After College Starts			
FV of College			
FV of Assets			
FV of Savings			
Gross Assets Needed (1st Day of College) without Savings			
Assets Needed (1st Day of College)			

BEFORE-TAX ASSET CALCULATION			
Present Value of Assets Needed			
BEFORE-TAX SAVINGS REQUIREMENTS			
Annual Level Savings Needed			
Serial Adjusted Savings Needed*			
AFTER-TAX ASSET CALCULATION			
Present Value of Assets Needed			
AFTER-TAX SAVINGS REQUIREMENTS			
Annual Level Savings Needed			
Serial Adjusted Savings Needed*			
*Serial adjusted savings require that the amount saved for college increases each year by the savings growth rate.			

Planning Strategy 2: Recommend Saving for College Using a Section 529 Plan

Section 529 savings plans, named after Section 529 of the Internal Revenue Code (IRC), offer a number of advantages for clients who want a tax-advantaged education funding tool.

- First, a significant dollar amount can be contributed on an annual basis. This makes a Section 529 plan advantageous compared to a Coverdell Education Savings Account (CESA), which is described in more detail later in the chapter.

- Second, investments in the account grow tax-deferred, and if withdrawals are used for qualified college expenses, withdrawals are free from federal income tax.

- Third, some states offer state income tax advantages in addition to those offered by the federal government. States with an income tax often provide a state income tax exclusion for qualified withdrawals. Furthermore, most—but not all—states allow a deduction or credit for contributions to a Section 529 plan, and some offer direct grants or monetary incentives. Some states have "tax-parity" legislation that extends state tax deductions to residents investing in out-of-state Section 529 plans.

- The fourth benefit involves control over the account. The account owner maintains control over how funds are invested and distributed. A parent, grandparent, relative, or friend can establish an account for a designated beneficiary. The owner can even decide when withdrawals should be taken and for what purpose.

- Fifth, up to $10,000 may be used to pay down student loan debt on a tax free basis.

Another unique advantage associated with Section 529 plans involves the plan's usefulness in estate planning. A client may contribute up to $75,000 to a Section 529 plan in 2020 without triggering the federal gift tax. In effect, by implementing this strategy a client can use up to five years of gift tax annual exclusions in one year. Joint tax filers can contribute twice as much, and there are no limits to the number of beneficiaries for gift tax purposes. In addition, amounts in a Section 529 plan account are generally not included in the account owner's gross estate for federal tax purposes, though there could be a "clawback" of a portion of a five-year lump sum funding of a 529 plan should the donor pass away during the ensuing five-year period.

A beneficiary may use Section 529 plan college savings program funds at any accredited college, university, technical, vocational, or graduate school anywhere in the United States. This means that withdrawals can be used to pay for expenses in Kansas, for instance, even though the Section 529 plan was sponsored by Nebraska.

Furthermore, no income limitations or age restrictions are associated with Section 529 plans. Lifetime contribution limits for Section 529 plans are considerably higher than any other tax-advantaged college saving plan. The lifetime maximum contribution is based on each state's projected cost of college. In many states, the maximum lifetime contribution limit can exceed $250,000.

Financial planners need to be aware of some potential drawbacks associated with Section 529 plans. A beneficiary may decide not to attend college or to attend a less expensive school. Earnings withdrawn for *nonqualified* expenses are generally subject to federal and state income tax as well as a 10 percent federal penalty tax. Instead of taking a nonqualified distribution, an account owner is allowed to transfer an account to another family member, including siblings, first cousins, spouses, and even back to the client.

Another potential problem involves investment choices within Section 529 plans. Nearly all states have pre-established asset allocation models that are used to direct investments within a plan. Accounts for young beneficiaries typically are invested aggressively, and in some cases annual management and maintenance fees can be high. Asset allocation typically becomes more conservative as the beneficiary ages. The choice of mutual funds within an account is almost always restricted, and historically the number of times an account owner can make changes within a plan has been limited to once a year. Finally, investments held in the account are considered assets of the parent, and as such, asset values increase the expected family contribution (EFC) for financial aid, but not as much as if the child held the assets.

In some states, a **Section 529 prepaid tuition plan** may be available. This is a special form of Section 529 plan that provides an opportunity to prefund college expenses. Three important issues must be acknowledged before using a Section 529 prepaid tuition plan. First, the amount of contribution is based on the age of the beneficiary and anticipated college costs in the state offering the plan. Second, the account owner has no control over how the account is invested. The sponsoring state manages the account and guarantees that tuition will be paid, regardless of account value. Third, and maybe most important, Section 529 prepaid tuition plans typically guarantee benefits only for public institutions within the state sponsoring the plan, although some plans offer more flexibility.

In addition to the above, under the recently-enacted Tax Cuts and Jobs Act legislation, up to $10,000 of a 529 plan's assets may be used for public, private or religious school K-12 education expenses annually.

Planning Strategy 3: Know the Options Available with Unspent Section 529 Plan Assets

While contributing to a Section 529 plan can be a good way to save for a family member's college education, there are times when money saved in a Section 529 plan is not used. When this occurs, clients have several options.

- One alternative is to withdraw the account balance as cash; however, doing so will cause the account owner to owe tax on the earnings, plus a penalty equal to 10 percent on account earnings.

- Another option is to keep the money in the Section 529 plan. Doing so will allow a beneficiary to use the funds for graduate school expenses.

- An alternative is to change the recipient beneficiary. The only requirement is that the new beneficiary be a family member. Family member has been rather broadly defined under the regulations, and isn't limited to immediate family relations.

- Another alternative exists. Up to $10,000 may be used to pay down student loan debt on a tax free basis.

In situations where Section 529 plan assets remain unspent because a beneficiary received a scholarship, it is possible for the client to withdraw money up to the value of the scholarship. The portion of the withdrawal attributable to earnings will be taxable, but the distribution will not be penalized. The same holds true if the beneficiary becomes disabled or dies. Finally, a client should feel no rush to make any changes to a Section 529 plan as long as the named beneficiary is still alive. The assets will continue to grow on a tax-deferred basis until used or withdrawn. In rare cases when no future beneficiary is anticipated, the client may decide to donate the account to a charity and receive a tax deduction (assuming the client itemizes deductions).

Planning Strategy 4: Recommend Savings for College Using a Coverdell Education Savings Account

A **Coverdell Education Savings Account (CESA)** is a trust or custodial account set up for the purpose of paying qualified education expenses for a designated beneficiary. Principal and earnings from the account can be used to pay qualified higher education expenses, including tuition, fees, books, supplies, and equipment required for enrollment or attendance. Other expenses include amounts contributed to a qualified tuition program and room and board expenses. Distributions can be used to pay expenses at public, private, and religious elementary and secondary schools, as well as for postsecondary education expenses. This means that, unlike any other tax-advantaged program, a CESA can be used to pay for private day school expenses; though see the recently expanded K-12 distribution options for 529 plans above.

The designated beneficiary of a CESA must be under the age of eighteen when an account is established, unless the beneficiary has special needs. Any balance in a CESA must be distributed within thirty days after the date the beneficiary reaches age thirty, unless the beneficiary has special needs. There is no limit to the number of CESAs that can be established for one beneficiary. However, contributions can be made only in cash, and the total contributions made to all CESAs for any beneficiary in one tax year cannot be greater than $2,000. This means that a client cannot contribute $2,000 to an account while a grandparent contributes another $2,000. Also, contributions to CESAs are restricted by income phase-out rules.

The primary financial planning advantage associated with a CESA is that distributions are tax free to the extent the distribution does not exceed the beneficiary's qualified education expenses. If a distribution does exceed the beneficiary's qualified education expenses, a portion of the distribution may be taxable. A CESA can be rolled over into a Section 529 plan. Also, the Hope Credit or the Lifetime Learning Credit can be claimed for certain qualified higher education expenses in the same year in which a tax-free withdrawal from a CESA is made. However, the distribution cannot be used for the same educational expenses for which the credit was taken.

Two limitations are associated with this college savings approach.

- First, many financial planning clients find that their income exceeds threshold limits, making contributions out of the question.

- Second, and more importantly, the annual $2,000 contribution limit severely restricts the usefulness of this tool in accumulating assets for education.

Planning Tip

There is no hard-and-fast rule about the best time to convert a traditional IRA to a Roth IRA (**Roth conversion**); however, there is a worst possible time—while a client's child is in college. Qualified retirement accounts are excluded from assets when calculating the **expected family contribution** (EFC) for financial aid; however, income derived from those sources is not. So, although a distribution from IRAs to pay qualified educational expenses is allowable and will not trigger a tax penalty, a distribution will count as income and could affect the income component of the EFC the following year.

A lesser-known consideration is the impact of conversion. Converting a traditional IRA to a Roth IRA is a taxable event. In other words, the amount of the conversion is typically taxable as ordinary income in the year of conversion. So, a financial planner must consider long-term tax implications of IRA distributions and conversions to the account owner, as well as the near-term financial aid implications to the dependent student of the account owner.

To maximize this type of account, a client must start saving early in a child's life and save the maximum allowable each year. If, for instance, a client saved $2,000 each year for fifteen years earning 9 percent, on average, the account would be worth only $58,722 at the end of the period. Also, if assets are not used by the child's thirtieth birthday and are not assigned to a close family member, the client will incur income tax and a 10 percent penalty on earnings that accumulated on a tax-free basis within the account.

Planning Strategy 5: Recommend Saving for College Using a Roth IRA

For those eligible to do so, contributing to a **Roth IRA** is an excellent strategy for clients who want to save for a contingent educational funding need, but who have a primary goal of saving for retirement. If funds are needed for college or other education needs, distributions of contributions (not the earnings on contributions) can be received tax free (essentially, the distribution is a return of the account owner's original after-tax contribution). If earnings are withdrawn prior to the account owner being age 59½ and used to pay qualified educational expenses, taxes may be due on such distributions, but the early distribution penalty will not apply.

The primary disadvantage associated with this strategy is that it is unlikely that enough funding can be generated to cover 100 percent of college costs at a moderate- to high-expense college. Also, while using this retirement asset may benefit a client's child, the strategy can jeopardize the Roth IRA owner's retirement plan. Thus, this strategy may be more appropriate for a grandparent than a parent, depending on other situational factors. Additionally, distributions from Roth IRAs can adversely affect a subsequent financial aid application because of the increased income.

Planning Strategy 6: Utilize Variable Universal Life (VUL) Insurance to Save for College

This strategy, which is somewhat unorthodox outside the insurance industry, can be quite effective in meeting education funding goals. The principal advantages associated with this strategy include being able to maximize funding and investing in assets that can grow substantially over time. Ultimately, this strategy is beneficial if growth within the variable account is high enough to allow the client to take loans to pay for college expenses and have remaining assets generate returns to pay the interest and repayment charges. Also, if the insured dies, insurance proceeds can be used to pay for education.

The chief disadvantage associated with this strategy is that to fully fund a VUL at the level necessary to accumulate a significant account value, a large face value policy is needed. The premium cost of such a policy can be prohibitive. Furthermore, ongoing administrative and subaccount fees can reduce overall rates of return on assets. Unless managed and invested well, a VUL can terminate with a zero cash balance. Also, rates credited by the insurer are reduced when a loan is made.

Planning Strategy 7: Recommend Saving for College Using Series EE and Series I Bonds

Under current tax law, a parent's (or grandparent's) **EE savings bonds** can be cashed in tax free to pay for a child's (or grandchild's) college tuition. Clients must meet certain requirements for distributions from EE and **I savings bonds** to be tax free.

- First, a client must be at least twenty-four years old on the first day of the month in which the bond was purchased.

- Second, when using bonds for a child's education, the bonds must be registered in the *client's and/or spouse's name*. A child can be listed as a beneficiary on the bond but not as a co-owner.

- Third, if a client uses bonds for the client's own education, the bonds must be registered in the client's name.

- Finally, if a client is married and uses the bonds for educational purposes, the client must file a joint return to qualify for the exclusion.

When considering this strategy, it is important to remember that only payments made to **postsecondary institutions**, including colleges, universities, and vocational schools that meet the standards for federal assistance (such as guaranteed student loan programs) qualify for favorable tax treatment. **Qualified educational expenses** include tuition and fees such as lab fees and other required course expenses. Expenses paid for any course or other education involving sports, games, or hobbies qualify only if required as part of a degree- or certificate-granting program. The costs of books, room, and board are not considered qualified expenses. When determining the amount of qualified expenses, a client must reduce the amount of total expenses by the amount of scholarships, fellowships, employer-provided educational assistance, and other forms of tuition reduction received. Additionally, expenses must be incurred during the same tax year in which the bonds are redeemed.

Planning Tip

Another funding approach involves using savings bonds to fund a qualified state tuition plan, such as a Section 529 plan.

Up to $30,000 in Series EE and Series I savings bonds can be purchased by married clients ($15,000 for single clients) in any given year. To exclude the interest from gross income, a client must use both the principal and interest from bonds sold to pay qualified expenses. If the amount of eligible bonds cashed during the year exceeds the amount of qualified educational expenses paid during the year, the amount of excludable interest is reduced using a pro rata formula.

For example, assume that bond proceeds equal $20,000 ($16,000 principal and $4,000 interest) and the qualified educational expenses are $16,000. The amount of interest that can be excluded is $3,200 ([$16,000 expenses ÷ $20,000 proceeds] × $4,000 interest).

Like nearly all other tax benefits, certain household income limitations apply. The full interest exclusion is available only to clients with modified adjusted gross income (which includes the interest earned) under certain limits. Also, savings bonds are included as a parent asset, which can increase the EFC used in financial aid formulas. Furthermore, rates of return are relatively low, which limits a client's ability to fund expenses from interest earned. The early withdrawal penalty during the first five years and the relatively low rate of return require that this strategy be implemented well in advance of when the funds are needed.

Planning Strategy 8: Utilize Retirement Accounts Rather than Education Savings Products to Save for College Expenses

Although not universal, many **401(k)** and some **403(b)** plans allow an account owner to borrow the greater of $50,000 or 50 percent of account value at any given time. Typically, loans can be taken for up to five years with a minimal rate of interest. Student financial aid formulas generally do not take into account assets held in defined contribution plans or self-employed retirement plans, such as a **Keogh** plan.

By maximizing contributions to these plans, and then taking loans against account values if needed, it may be possible to reduce the EFC when applying for financial aid. In effect, this strategy allows a client to minimize the financial aid EFC by sheltering assets in a 401(k) or 403(b) plan, and then later use loan proceeds to pay for excess college expenses.

The primary disadvantage associated with this strategy is that if early withdrawals are needed, a 10 percent penalty may apply. Also, some private universities may require that retirement assets be listed for calculating the EFC for financial aid purposes. Additionally, access to plan loans may be limited for some clients. It is important to note that using retirement assets to fund a dependent child's college expenses can cause a client's retirement plan to become underfunded. Once a loan is taken, loan proceeds stop earning market rates of return. An opportunity cost exists where the amount of interest repaid will almost always be less than the amount of interest and capital gains that could have been earned. Additionally, loan repayments start immediately. If employment ends, the loan must be repaid in thirty days or less or taxes and penalties may apply.

Planning Strategy 9: Recommend Appropriate Student Financial Aid Alternatives to Meet Client Funding Needs

Financial aid comes in three basic forms: (1) **scholarships**, (2) **loans**, and (3) **grants**. Nearly all scholarships offered in the United States are university or program specific. However, a number of national scholarships are available. Scholarships can be either need or merit based. Students interested in scholarships should generally apply through their university, college, and academic unit.

Federal student loans are available as **Stafford loans** (Perkins loans were discontinued in 2015). Stafford loans are federally sponsored loans for educational expenses. Prior to July 2010, Stafford loans were offered under the Federal Family Education Loan Program, and funds were provided by private banks and credit unions. After passage of the Health Care and Education Reconciliation Act of 2010, the Federal Direct Loan Program began administering all Stafford loans, while the federal government provides funding directly through participating schools.

There are two types of Stafford loans: **subsidized** and **unsubsidized**. A subsidized Stafford loan is a **need-based loan** where the federal government pays the interest for the student on the loan as long as the student is enrolled at least half-time. Unsubsidized Stafford loans are available to all students (who are eligible for federal aid) regardless of need. An unsubsidized Stafford loan accrues interest from the date of disbursement. Both loans offer payment deferral, meaning the student is not required to make interest payments while attending college at least half-time, and both offer a six-month grace period after the deferment period ends before repayment is required.

Annual loan limits for undergraduate students are determined by their grade level and dependency status. Interest rates on Stafford Loans are quite reasonable—the rates are set periodically by Congressional Act. Loans disbursed prior to July 2006 carry a variable interest rate capped at 8.25 percent.[5] Some currently enrolled students may hold a **Perkins loan**, which is a need-based loan that charges a flat 5 percent interest rate, allows repayment to be deferred until nine months following graduation, and features a ten-year repayment period.[6] These loans were discontinued after 2015.

Parents rather than students apply for a **Parent Loan for Undergraduate Students (PLUS)**. A PLUS loan can be taken out for an amount equal to the difference between the college-defined cost of attendance and all other financial aid received. For loans disbursed prior to July 2006, the interest was variable based on market conditions and capped at 9 percent; however, loans disbursed since that time have rates ranging from less than 7 percent to more than 9 percent annually.[7] A primary difference between Stafford and PLUS loans is that PLUS loans require repayment beginning approximately sixty days after the loan is fully disbursed rather than being deferred until graduation.

All direct loan program loans offer a variety of **repayment plans**, as listed below:

- *Standard repayment*: up to ten years, with a minimum monthly payment of $50.[8]

- *Extended repayment*: up to twenty-five years, with the option of fixed or graduated payments (increasing every two years); must have more than $30,000 in qualifying debt to be eligible.[9]

- *Graduated repayment*: up to ten years (or twenty years if also qualified under the extended plan) with payment increasing every two years. Later payments are prohibited from being more than three times any other payment on the loan.[10]

- *Income contingent repayment*: an applicant income-based formula capped at 20 percent of discretionary income with a repayment period of twenty five years, after which any outstanding balance is forgiven but taxed as current income.[11] The annual payment calculation is based on adjusted gross income (AGI), plus spouse's income (if applicable), family size, and the total amount of Federal Direct Loans.

- *Income based repayment*: maximum repayment period can exceed ten years, but it is only available to those experiencing partial financial hardship. Under certain circumstances, loan cancellation may be available.[12] Payments may adjust annually matched to income. Partial financial hardship is determined by a calculation where, under a standard ten-year repayment plan for all eligible loans, the total annual payment due exceeds 15 percent of discretionary income.[13] The Health Care and Education Reconciliation Act, passed in 2010, reduced the maximum payment percentage from 15 to 10 percent and also reduced the forgiveness of any remaining loan balance from twenty-five years to twenty years.

Another repayment option exists. Beginning in 2015, any US citizen who has or had ever borrowed money using a federal government loan, either for college or graduate school, can enroll in the **pay-as-you-earn** debt repayment program. This program sets the maximum monthly debt repayment equal to 10 percent of a borrower's **discretionary income**, which is defined as adjusted gross income (AGI) less 150 percent of the poverty level. Under the rules, payments can be made for twenty years. For those with graduate student debt, the repayment period can be extended to twenty-five years. At the end of the period (i.e., either twenty or twenty-five years), any remaining balance is forgiven; however, all amounts forgiven are subject to regular income taxes. Two things are worth remembering. First, parents who took out loans to pay for a child's college costs are not eligible for pay-as-you-earn. Second, while this repayment plan will appeal to many people, it is important that clients be reminded that more interest will be paid over the life of the loan.

Planning Strategy 10: Evaluate the Use of Alternative Educational Loans and Grants

Supplemental loans can be obtained to fund unpaid educational costs. These private education loans, also known as **alternative education loans**, are available through private lenders. Private education loans tend to cost more than education loans offered by the federal government, but private loans tend to be less expensive than credit card debt. These loans are not subsidized and origination, guarantee, or repayment fees may apply. Repayment is typically deferred while a student is in school (interest payments may be paid or deferred), and the repayment periods can be as long as those of direct loans, although such features vary by lender.

An alternative is a **Pell grant**. A federal Pell grant is a tax-free gift to a student to offset college expenses. This type of grant is awarded based on family need as determined by the EFC. Universities and colleges can award **Federal Supplemental Educational Opportunity Grants** directly to needy students. Priority for these need-based federal grants is given to federal Pell grant recipients. Some states and universities also provide grants, but almost always such grants are based on need rather than merit.

Planning Strategy 11: Pre-Plan for FASFA Requirements

In some situations, a client's situational factors or beliefs may require a financial planner to determine alternatives to cover the projected cost of education. In other cases, the estimated cost of education may be so exorbitant that additional, cost mitigation methods are necessary. An important service a financial planner can provide is to help a client better understand the financial aid system and how planning choices can affect the likelihood of receiving aid. It is likely that nearly all clients (or their children) will apply for financial aid at some point in the educational planning process. In fact, this should be encouraged, regardless of family income.

It is important that parents and children start to discuss acceptable college costs early. Financial aid planning should begin in earnest no later than a child's junior year in high school. The longer planning is postponed, the more likely the chance to exercise certain strategies to increase financial aid offers will be lost. The following discussion highlights some of the most popular forms of financial aid available today and how a client, working with a financial planner, can assess the current situation to determine financial aid availability.

The first step involves understanding the basic financial aid application process. Information related to parent and student income and assets is input into a form called the **Free Application for Federal Student Aid (FAFSA)**, which can be opened, completed, and saved at the Department of Education Web site.[14] (Some private colleges and universities also require families to complete a **College Scholarship Service (CSS) Financial Aid Form**). Once the application has been completed online, a **Student Aid Report** is sent to the client. This report provides the client with an **expected family contribution (EFC)**, an indicator of a family's ability to pay for college. Schools use the EFC to determine a student's eligibility for various financial assistance programs.

Eligibility may vary among schools. If the cost of college is higher than the EFC, the student may be eligible for need-based student financial aid. Four financial factors influence the expected family contribution for a dependent student: (1) the parents' income; (2) the parents' assets; (3) the child's income; and (4) the child's assets. Parental income includes all sources of income, taxable and nontaxable, received by the parents in the previous year. Certain adjustments are made.

Because student status is significant in determining financial aid, it is important to understand the difference between a dependent and an independent student. Except for some exceptional circumstances, a student is considered a **dependent student** for financial aid purposes unless one of the criteria for independent student status is met. For financial aid purposes, students are not automatically independent if parents stop claiming the child on Form 1040 or refuse to provide support for college education. A common misconception is that not being claimed on a parent's income tax for two years establishes the child as an independent student. *Tax status and federal financial aid status are not the same.* To qualify as an **independent student** for financial aid purposes, a child must meet one or more of the following criteria:

- be twenty-four years of age or older during the year they apply for financial aid;

- be married;

- have legal dependents of their own (i.e., provide more than half of their support);

- be enrolled in graduate school;

- since turning age thirteen, be a ward of the court, be in foster care, or have both parents deceased;

- be a veteran of the U.S. armed forces or serving on active duty;

- be (or have been) an emancipated minor or in legal guardianship;

- be homeless or at risk of being homeless as defined (criteria apply); or

- be judged "independent" by a university administrator, even though the preceding criteria do not apply but documentation for the extenuating circumstance is provided.

Financial planners and clients must determine not only the amount of money that will be available for college expenses, but who will own that money. Ownership is important because the percentage of assets required to fund college costs depends on whether the assets are held in a child's, parent's, or guardian's name. Dependent students are expected to contribute 20 percent of assets and 50 percent of income to fund education expenses, whereas parents are expected to contribute 22 percent to 47 percent of income and 2.6 percent to 5.6 percent of assets.[15] These amounts differ for independent students. Figure 11.3 summarizes the impact asset ownership can have in terms of financial aid and the use of tax credits.

Figure 11.3. Potential Impact of Asset Ownership on Financial Aid and Tax Credits

Education Savings Plan	Change in Expected Family Contribution	Hope[1] and Lifetime Learning Tax Credit Impact
Assets Owned by the Dependent Student		
UGMA/UTMA	Increased (20% of balance)*	No impact
§ 529 savings plan (UGMA/UTMA)	Increased (2.6% – 5.6% of balance)*	Expenses paid with distribution cannot be claimed for tax credit**
Coverdell Education Savings Account (CESA)	Increased (2.6 %– 5.6% of balance)*	Expenses paid with distribution cannot be claimed for tax credit**
Crummey trust	Increased (20% of balance)*	No impact
Assets Owned by the Parent		
§ 529 savings plan	Increased (2.6% – 5.6% of balance)*	Expenses paid with distribution cannot be claimed for tax credit**
Series EE savings bonds (tax-free education withdrawals)	Increased (2.6% – 5.6% of balance)*	Expenses paid with distribution cannot be claimed for tax credit**
Retirement plans	None	No impact
Variable universal life insurance	None	No impact
Assets Owned by Others (e.g., Grandparent) but with Student as Beneficiary		
§ 529 savings plan	None***	Expenses paid with distributions cannot be claimed for tax credit**

*Hurley, Joseph F. (2011). *Family guide to college savings 2011–2012*, JFH Innovative, LLC, Pittsford, NY.

**Clients can take distributions from these plans. However, distributions must be spent on expenses not already claimed with the Hope or Lifetime Learning Credits.

***Distributions from plans owned by a third party will be added back as income on the FAFSA.

Armed with some knowledge of the financial aid system, a financial planner can advise parents regarding how to work more proactively with high school staff and targeted college financial aid programs to determine more accurately the likelihood of merit- or need-based financial assistance. The same strategy can be applied to identifying institutions, both public and private, that may offer the most assistance given a student's profile. Finally, this information, plus projected payment scenarios, can help clients feel more comfortable about taking on education loan debt for themselves or their children.

Planning Strategy 12: Utilize a 2503(c) Minor's Trust before a Client's Child Reaches Age Twenty-one

Funding a **2503(c) minor's trust** completes a gift to a minor under Internal Revenue Code section 2503(c), thereby removing the assets from the estate of the grantor while maintaining some level of control over the distribution and use of the assets. There are caveats to consider before implementing this strategy. Gifts made to the trust are irrevocable and must be made before the child turns age twenty-one. Additionally, all the proceeds from the trust should ideally be used for the benefit of the beneficiary prior to the age of twenty-one, unless a "window" is provided to the beneficiary immediately following the twenty-first birthday, which grants the beneficiary access to assets before the trust converts to an irrevocable trust for an additional time period. As with all trusts, set-up and administration fees can be high in comparison to the corpus of the trust. Additionally, trust assets are considered assets of the child, and income derived from the trust is income to the child; therefore, the account will have a significant impact on financial aid contribution calculations.

Planning Strategy 13: Utilize a Crummey Trust to Transfer Educational Funds to a Child

Funding a **Crummey trust** completes a gift to a minor by allowing temporary access to the gift, thereby removing the assets from the estate of the grantor while maintaining some level of control over the distribution and use of the assets. Another benefit is that Crummey trusts, unlike Section 2503(c) trusts, can name multiple beneficiaries. Gifts made to the trust are irrevocable. Similar to other trusts, set-up and administration fees can be quite high in comparison to the corpus of the trust. Finally, trust assets are considered assets of the child, and income derived from the trust is income to the child; therefore, it will have a significant impact on financial aid contribution calculations.

Planning Strategy 14: Recommend Shifting UGMA/UTMA Assets Two Years before the Child Turns Age Eighteen

Current financial aid formulas penalize families when a child holds sizable assets in **UGMA/UTMA** accounts. Although a parent cannot take back money held in a UGMA/UTMA account, it may be possible to use account assets to purchase goods and services for a child above and beyond items generally thought of as basic living expenses. For example, assets can be used to pay tuition to a pre-college camp. Doing so increases the likelihood of receiving a larger financial aid award because the UGMA/UTMA account will be reduced in value. Keep in mind that this strategy can cause increased IRS and college scrutiny. Gifts made to an UGMA/UTMA account are irrevocable. Assets should not be used for the benefit of a parent or guardian or for costs that are deemed to be basic expenses the parent or guardian may be obligated to pay under local law. Also, the effectiveness of this strategy disappears if account transfers are not made at least two years before filing for financial aid.

Planning Strategy 15: Recommend Using EE Savings Bonds to Fund a Section 529 plan

Although discussed previously, this strategy is worth reviewing again. Proceeds from the sale of *Series EE* and *Series I* savings bonds can be received tax free when used either to pay for a family member's educational expenses or when funding a Section 529 plan or a CESA. Several requirements must be met.

- The account beneficiary must be the client, the client's spouse, or a dependent of the client.

- To qualify for the interest exclusion, the bonds must be issued in the parent's name and purchased after 1989, must be used to pay for qualified higher education expenses or funding a Section 529 plan or CESA, and the parent must meet the modified AGI guidelines for the interest exclusion (income phase-outs apply).

Those filing "married filing separately" are ineligible for the exclusion. This allows savings bonds to be used on a tax-free basis to earn a potentially higher rate of return in a Section 529 plan. Furthermore, because many states provide an incentive to contribute to an in-state (and in some instances an out-of-state) Section 529 plan, doing so can yield a higher overall tax benefit. There are downsides associated with this strategy. By transferring savings bond assets to a Section 529 plan, a client limits the availability and use of these assets for other goals, especially if the client's child does not need to use account assets for education.

Planning Strategy 16: Recommend Increasing Annual Savings Dedicated to Goal Achievement in a Funding Analysis

An obvious education funding strategy involves having a client increase the amount of savings dedicated to the client's education funding goal. The more that can be saved on a monthly or yearly basis, the more likely that the goal will be met. It may be possible to involve grandparents or other family or friends in this effort. This strategy is based on the premise that the client or others have additional discretionary cash flow and unallocated savings to contribute to an educational goal. If this assumption is incorrect, this strategy will not work.

Planning Strategy 17: Recommend Decreasing the Cost of College Assumption in a Funding Analysis

Clients who attempt to achieve an education funding objective, but still find themselves coming short of their goal, may want to consider decreasing the cost-of-college assumption used in the analysis. Although it is nice to want to fund a child's full educational costs at an expensive university, it may be fiscally impossible. Therefore, reducing the cost to be covered and focusing on obtaining scholarships, grants, and loans may be a way to meet at least a portion of future educational costs. It is important to remember, however, that reducing the cost assumption and instead relying on a child to receive grants and scholarships can be a problematic approach to planning. The uncertainty associated with grants and scholarships makes these sources of funding difficult to predict. An unrealistic reliance on these forms of funding can leave a client significantly short of actual future assets to fund these expenses and limit alternative funding planning alternatives.

Planning Strategy 18: Recommend Increasing Risk/Return Trade-off Assumptions in a Funding Analysis

One way to force a funding analysis to balance saved assets and expected expenses involves increasing the rate of return assumption in a funding analysis. Often, this strategy is used, particularly when funding efforts are postponed (not initiated when a child is young) and the time horizon for goal attainment is shortened. If this is the case, this strategy calls for the client to reallocate assets to increase the rate of return assumption on savings. Increasing the rate of return on investment assets will amplify the compounding of returns, which helps make an education goal more achievable.

Of course, this strategy can have problematic outcomes, particularly when a client tolerance for financial risk is lower than the rate of return assumption. When this happens, a client may reallocate assets during a market downturn, which can negatively impact previously made plans. It is also worth noting that not all educational funding products allow a client to systematically change the asset allocation of savings to increase returns. For instance, many Section 529 savings plans use a fixed asset allocation based on the beneficiary's age. In other words, the risk exposure in the portfolio decreases as the beneficiary gets closer to college age. Also, if a Roth IRA or retirement plan is used to partially offset college costs, increasing the return may not match well with the return assumptions used in the retirement plan.

Planning Strategy 19: Recommend a Lower Assumed College Inflation Rate in a Funding Analysis

One factor that drives the future high cost of funding educational goals is the constant increase in the price of **tuition and fees**. One way to manipulate an educational funding analysis is to decrease the assumed rate of tuition inflation. Doing so will make the future cost of education appear more affordable; that is, the amount of savings necessary will be less. The **inflation rate** for college costs varies over time and by type of institution, but valid data on which to base assumptions are available. However, once a reasonable inflation rate has been determined, it is unwise to manipulate the numbers just to assuage a client's concerns. A better alternative is to explain the discrepancy in funding the education goal and to consider other alternatives.

It is worth noting that this is a complicated strategy that should be used only in extreme cases where the cost of college is significantly more than the projected future value of client educational assets. In effect, decreasing the tuition inflation rate assumption goes against twenty years of historical data, which suggest that tuition costs will continue to rise, with some projections indicating double-digit increases. But implementation of this strategy may give a client some solace that their efforts will pay off as long as the actual rate of inflation is less than originally projected.

Planning Strategy 20: Use Educational Tax Credits and Deductions Appropriately

The **American Opportunity Tax Credit (AOTC)** was originally introduced as an enhancement to the **Hope Scholarship Tax Credit**. Currently, the AOTC allows a tax credit up to 100 percent of qualified tuition and related expenses for each eligible student up to a maximum of $2,500. Additionally, up to 40 percent of the credit may be refundable. The tax credit can be used for four years of an eligible student's postsecondary education. Generally, the credit can be claimed if a client pays qualified tuition and related higher education expenses for an eligible student (including the client). The availability of the credit phases out when modified adjusted gross income (MAGI) reaches $90,000 for a single filer and $180,000 for joint filers. It is important to remember that those who file "married filing separately" may not claim the tax credit.[16]

The **Lifetime Learning Tax Credit (LLTC)** allows clients to claim a credit on 20 percent of the first $10,000 in college expenses. The maximum credit of $2,000 is per taxpayer. Expenses such as room and board, insurance, and transportation are not eligible. The LLTC is useful for clients who are funding a child's or their own education to acquire or enhance job skills. This can include part-time enrollment in college courses, trade school courses, and graduate courses. Income phaseouts apply.

It may also be possible to deduct interest paid on qualified student loans. If a client's modified adjusted gross income (MAGI) is less than $80,000 ($160,000 if filing a joint return), there is a special deduction allowed for paying interest on a student loan (also known as an education loan) used for higher education. This deduction can reduce the amount of income subject to tax by up to $2,500. Keep in mind that the student loan interest deduction is taken as an adjustment to income. This means a client may claim the deduction even if they do not itemize deductions. Figure 11.4 compares the AOTC, LLTC, and the tuition and fees deduction.

Figure 11.4. College Savings Analysis.

COLLEGE SAVINGS ANALYSIS			
ASSUMPTIONS			
Child/Scenario Name	Child 1	Child 2	Child 3
Combined Federal and State Marginal Tax Bracket			
Assumed After-Tax Rate of Return Before College			
Assumed Before-Tax Return of Tax-Advantaged Plans			
Assumed Rate of Return After College Begins			
Assumed College Expense Inflation Rate			
Age			
College Age			
Years In College			
Yearly Cost of College TODAY			
Value of After-Tax Assets Saved Today			
Value of Tax-Advantaged Assets Saved			
Annual After-Tax Savings			
Annual Tax-Advantaged Savings			
Annual Savings Growth Rate	0.00%	0.00%	0.00%
CALCULATIONS			
College Serial After-Tax Interest Rate Before College Starts	0.0000%	0.0000%	0.0000%
College Serial Before-Tax Rate Before College Starts	0.0000%	0.0000%	0.0000%
College Serial Interest Rate After College Starts	0.0000%	0.0000%	0.0000%
FV of College	$0.00	$0.00	$0.00
FV of Assets	$0.00	$0.00	$0.00
FV of Savings			
Gross Assets Needed (1st Day of College) without Savings	$0.00	$0.00	$0.00
Assets Needed (1st Day of College)			
BEFORE-TAX ASSET CALCULATION			
Present Value of Assets Needed			
BEFORE-TAX SAVINGS REQUIREMENTS			
Annual Level Savings Needed			
Serial Adjusted Savings Needed*			
AFTER-TAX ASSET CALCULATION			
Present Value of Assets Needed			
AFTER-TAX SAVINGS REQUIREMENTS			
Annual Level Savings Needed			
Serial Adjusted Savings Needed*			

*Serial adjusted savings require that the amount saved for college increases each year by the savings growth rate.

Planning Strategy 21: Prioritize Strategies to Help Clients Meet their Education Funding Goals

Developing education planning recommendations follows the same general process used in other areas of financial planning. Specifically, education planning recommendations flow directly from a client's primary education funding objective. Recommendations should evolve from both a quantitative analysis of a client's current situation and a review of household factors, such as the expectations of the child receiving financial aid, the client's willingness to fund certain expenses while not funding others, and the level of control a client wishes to maintain over assets and savings. These personal expectations and attitudes strongly influence the type of recommendations that are most suitable for a client.

The process of combining education funding strategies into one or more client-specific recommendations depends on a number of factors. At least initially, the choice of appropriate strategies should be driven by the education planning need. Figure 11.5 illustrates a hierarchical approach that can be used to select appropriate strategies for a client recommendation.

Figure 11.5. Ranking and Using Education Funding Techniques

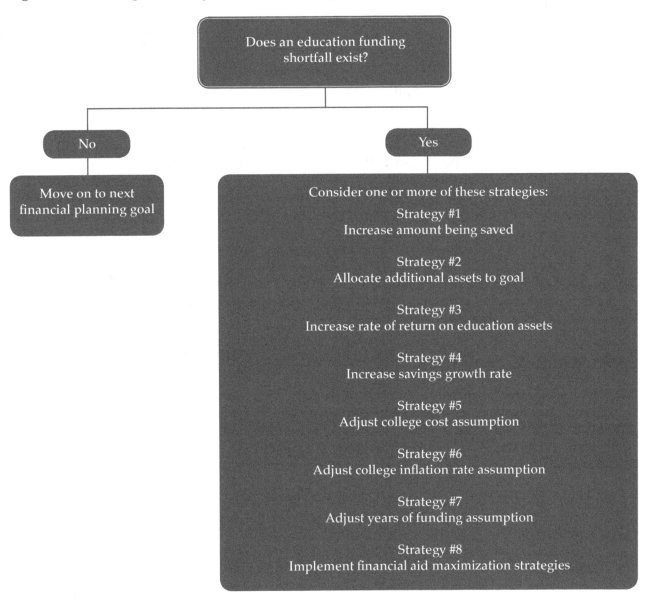

Does an education funding shortfall exist?

No

Move on to next financial planning goal

Yes

Consider one or more of these strategies:

Strategy #1
Increase amount being saved

Strategy #2
Allocate additional assets to goal

Strategy #3
Increase rate of return on education assets

Strategy #4
Increase savings growth rate

Strategy #5
Adjust college cost assumption

Strategy #6
Adjust college inflation rate assumption

Strategy #7
Adjust years of funding assumption

Strategy #8
Implement financial aid maximization strategies

Before a recommendation is presented to a client, steps should be taken to confirm that the recommendation meets both the education funding need and the client's stated expectations. For instance, recommending that a client reduce the college cost assumption to make funding feasible might run contrary to a client's strong desire to their or his child attend an elite (expensive) university. It may be better, in a situation similar to this, to determine whether the client may be willing to maintain the high cost assumption but realize that only a portion of the child's education costs can be funded. Such a candid approach helps a financial planner more effectively manage client expectations. It also enables the client to consider other options to maximize goal funding relative to any trade-offs in lifestyle that may be called for or the attainment of other goals. As with all aspects of financial planning, an overriding objective of education planning is to empower clients to make decisions more effectively.

Quantitative/Analytical Mini-Case Problems

Johanna and Ryan Younan

1. Johanna and Ryan Younan just put their two boys (grades 6 and 2) on their respective school buses for the first day of school and realized that they are growing up fast. As their financial planner, Johanna and Ryan called you and stated that they wanted to save, starting today, at the beginning of every month for the next six years (until the older child goes to college) to pay for one-half of school expenses for both children. You know that tuition, room, and board this year cost $18,000 at their selected school, and you expect 5 percent effective annual inflation for education expenses. Johanna and Ryan also said that they know the children's grandparents are going to make a gift of $48,000 toward this cause in exactly three years.

    Assume that both children attend the same college for four years each. Also assume that the annual tuition bill is due at the beginning of each academic year, and the first payment is exactly seventy two months away. How much money will Johanna and Ryan need to invest on a monthly basis to meet their education goal assuming a required effective annual rate of 10.471 percent (10 percent APR with monthly compounding)?

Balik Antone

2. Balik Atone, a new financial planning client, wants to begin a savings program for her eight-year-old son. She has been reading about the various accounts available for college savings programs, but she is confused about which type of account would be best. Her primary concerns are taxes, account ownership, and flexibility. She has developed a list of questions that she would like answered at the next meeting.

    a. Which account will allow for the greatest flexibility given that she is a single mother, is not expecting to have any additional children, and is not absolutely certain that her son will attend college?

    b. Given the following assumptions, which account requires the lowest monthly contribution to attain her goal of saving $50,000 in ten years? (The savings goal ends at the beginning of her son's first year of college.) Assume that she makes a fixed payment at the end of each month for the next 120 months. Also assume that any account set-up fees or annual fees are paid on a monthly basis in addition to the required savings deposit.

	Account Type		
	Nonqualified	Roth IRA	§ 529 plan
Projected market gross annual return	9.5%	9.5%	9.5%
Annual expense ratio (target date fund)	0.0%	1.1%	1.1%
Program fees*	0.0%	0.0%	0.6%
Annual account fee	$0	$12.00	$24.00
Annual applicable tax rate**	20.0%	0.0%	0.0%

*Program fees include management and state administration fees.

**Assume that all withdrawals from qualified accounts are used for a qualified purpose and therefore are not subject to income tax or early withdrawal penalties.

c. Depending on the account type chosen in part b, who should "own" the account, assuming her son has earned income? Consider both financial aid eligibility and flexibility of use.

Broderick Baatz

3. Broderick Baatz, an independent student, graduated from college in May 2018 with $37,000 (not including accrued interest charges) in unsubsidized Stafford Loan debt and realized that he is in over his head. He has come to you for answers. Answer the questions based on the following disbursement schedule:

Disbursement Date	Total Disbursement Amount	Interest Rate
Aug 2014	$8,000	6.8%
Aug 2015	$9,000	6.8%
Aug 2016	$10,000	6.8%
Aug 2017	$10,000	6.8%

a. What was the actual aggregated balance on his loans the August after he graduated?

b. What is the monthly payment if he chooses the standard ten-year repayment plan?

c. How much will he pay in total to pay off the aggregate loan? How much interest will he pay, assuming all payments are made as agreed?

d. What is the monthly payment if he chooses the extended twenty-year repayment plan?

e.   How much will he pay in total to pay off the aggregate loan? How much interest will he pay, assuming all payments are made as agreed?

f.   How much additional interest would Broderick pay if he chose the extended payment option?

Rahel Osei

4.   Rahel Osei, a dependent student, graduated from college in May 2018 with the maximum ($31,000) allowable amount in Stafford Loan debt; however, this was far less than the total cost of her schooling. Additionally, her parents had planned far enough in advance that Rahel demonstrated each year sufficient financial need to qualify for the maximum amount under the subsidized loan program. Her parents are wondering how much their planning paid off. Her parents have posed the following questions to you. Base your analysis on the disbursement schedule.

Disbursement Date	Total Disbursement Amount	Subsidized Amount	Unsubsidized Interest Rate	Subsidized Interest Rate
Aug 2015	$5,500	$3,500	6.8% (APR)	6.8% (APR)
Aug 2016	$6,500	$4,500	6.8%	6.0%
Aug 2017	$7,500	$5,500	6.8%	5.6%
Aug 2018	$7,500	$5,500	6.8%	4.5%

a.   What was the actual total balance on her loans the August after she graduated?

b.   How much total interest did Rahel avoid on her subsidized loans during college and since her graduation (the subsidy continues during the six-month grace period) as a result of the subsidy?

c.   What is the combined monthly payment, based on the standard ten-year repayment plan, for her subsidized loans?

d.   What would her combined monthly payment have been if her loans had not been subsidized? (Although not completely accurate, assume that the balance in August will still be the same.)

e.   How much additional interest would Rahel have paid if she had not qualified for any subsidized loans?

f.   How much was the subsidy worth?

Simon Garfield

5.   Simon Garfield has come to you with several questions related to creating an education plan for his daughter Whitney. Simon summarized his current situation as follows:

- Simon, who is single, has an AGI of approximately $265,000.

- Because of scholarships and grants, Simon anticipates that Whitney will need $35,000 in college funding.

- Whitney has several thousand dollars' worth of EE Savings bonds held in her name.

- Whitney has a brokerage account valued at $9,000 held as an UGMA.

- Whitney's grandfather has been saving into a 529 plan for Whitney. The account has a value of $49,000. The value of contributions is $45,000.

- Simon is willing to use one of his 401(k) plans, with a balance of $18,000, to help fund any excess college tuition expenses Whitney may incur.

Use this information to answer the following questions:

a. How much of Whitney's EE Savings bonds may she distribute tax free to help offset her college expenses?

b. What type of educational expenses may the 529 plan assets be used to cover?

c. What options does Whitney's grandfather have in relation to the 529 plan if, in fact, Whitney's college expenses are $35,000 and Whitney relies entirely on the 529 plan account balance?

d. If Simon needs to use his 401(k) assets to help fund college expenses for Whitney, how much may be borrowed from the account under current tax law?

e. What, if any, education tax credits may Simon claim on his federal tax return in relation to Whitney's college expenses?

f. Which of the assets listed will have the largest negative impact on the family's expected contribution calculation?

Jamal and Chyna Gwynn

6. Your clients, Jamal and Chyna Gwynn, would like you to determine if they are on track to meet the education funding objective of their son Jarius. Jarius is currently 13 years of age. Jamal and Chyna have high hopes for Jarius's future education. Use the following data to determine whether or not Jamal and Chyna need to save more to fund Jarius's educational need.

- Combined federal and state marginal tax bracket: 29 percent

- After-tax rate of return before college: 7.90 percent

- Before-tax rate of return of 529 plan: 9.75 percent

- Rate of return on educational assets after college begins: 5 percent

- College expense inflation rate: 4 percent

- Year Jarius begins college: Age eighteen

- Number of years in college: four years

- Yearly cost of college today: $60,000

- After-tax assets earmarked for Jarius's education: $25,000

- 529 plan assets earmarked for Jarius's education: $60,000

- After-tax educational annual savings: $0

- Annual tax-advantaged educational savings: $18,000

- Annual education savings growth rate: 3 percent

    a. Approximately how much will Jamal and Chyna need (gross need) on Jarius's first day of college?

    b. After accounting for the future value of assets and savings, how much additional (if any) do Jamal and Chyna need on Jarius's first day of college?

    c. Based on your answer to the question above, how much must Jamal and Chyna save annually in the 529 plan to meet the educational saving goal?

    d. If instead, Jamal and Chyna decide to save outside of a 529 plan or other tax-advantaged plan, how much must they save each year?

Chapter Resources

Department of Education, Student Loans Overview, *Fiscal Year 2012 Budget Request:* www2.ed.gov/about/overview/budget/budget12/justifications/s-loansoverview.pdf, p. S-12.

FinAid, The Smart Student™ Guide to Financial Aid. *Student Loans:* www.finaid.org/loans/studentloan.phtml.

"Interest Rates and Fees on PLUS Loans: www.edvisors.com/college-loans/federal/parent-plus/interest-rates/

Department of Education: https://studentaid.ed.gov/sa/repay-loans/understand/plans

Equal Justice Works. *Partial Financial Hardship.* Available at: www.equaljusticeworks.org/resources/student-debt-relief/income-based-repayment/partial-financial-hardship.

Joseph F. Hurley, *Family Guide to College Savings 2011–2012* (Pittsford, NY: JFH Innovative, 2011), 66.

Information about education tax credits: www.irs.gov/publications/p970/ch02.html#d0e1386.

Information about student financial aid: www.fafsa.ed.gov.

Endnotes

1. The U.S. government provides estimates of college costs at collegecost.ed.gov/catc/default.aspx.

2. This process assumes that periodic savings payments occur at the end of each period; that periodic savings payments for college will cease when the child begins college; and the annual college expense payment occurs at the beginning of each school year. Each of these assumptions can be changed to fit a client's individual situation, but corresponding changes in the calculations will be necessary.

3. This approach assumes that savings will end when the child enters college. Alternatively, an assumption can be made the savings will continue while the child is in college, thus reducing the annual saving need.

4. An effective annual rate (EAR) of 8.30 percent is equivalent to an 8 percent rate compounded monthly.

5. Department of Education, Student Loans Overview, *Fiscal Year 2012 Budget Request*. Available at: www2.ed.gov/about/overview/budget/budget12/justifications/s-loansoverview.pdf, p. S-12.

6. FinAid, The Smart Student™ Guide to Financial Aid. *Student Loans*. Available at: www.finaid.org/loans/studentloan.phtml.

7. Department of Education: https://studentaid.ed.gov/sa/repay-loans

8. *Ibid.*

9. *Ibid.*

10. *Ibid.*

11. *Ibid.*

12. *Ibid.*

13. Equal Justice Works. *Partial Financial Hardship*. Available at: www.equaljusticeworks.org/resources/student-debt-relief/income-based-repayment/partial-financial-hardship.

14. For more information see: www.fafsa.ed.gov.

15. Department of Education: https://fafsa.ed.gov/

16. Additional information is available online at IRS, *American Opportunity Credit*, at: www.irs.gov/publications/p970/ch02.html#d0e1386

Chapter 12

Retirement Planning

Learning Objectives

- Learning Objective 1: Describe the process involved in conducting a retirement capital needs analysis.

- Learning Objective 2: Describe the tax implications associated with different retirement saving plans.

- Learning Objective 3: Describe the role of Social Security in shaping a client's retirement alternatives.

- Learning Objective 4: Identify appropriate retirement planning recommendations that can be used to help a client reach their retirement objectives, accounting for client goals, resources, and household characteristics.

- Learning Objective 5: Describe optimal ways to withdraw accumulated assets to fund retirement income needs.

CFP® Principal Knowledge Topics

- CFP Topic: D.27. Annuities
- CFP Topic: G.52. Retirement Needs Analysis
- CFP Topic: G.53. Social Security and Medicare
- CFP Topic: G.55. Types of Retirement Plans
- CFP Topic: G.56. Qualified Plan Rules and Options
- CFP Topic: G.57. Other Tax-Advantaged Retirement Plans
- CFP Topic: G.58. Regulatory Considerations
- CFP Topic: G.59. Key Factors Affecting Plan Selection for Businesses
- CFP Topic: G.60. Distribution Rules and Taxation
- CFP Topic: G.61. Retirement Income and Distribution Strategies

Chapter Equations

Present value of a growing annuity (PVGA):

$$\frac{PMT_1}{(i-g)} \left[1 - \frac{(1+g)^n}{(1+i)^n} \right] (1+i)$$

Present Value (PV):

$$PV_n = \frac{FV}{(1+i)^n}$$

Serial Rate:

$$\frac{(1+i)}{(1+g)} - 1$$

RETIREMENT PLANNING STRATEGIES

The number and types of retirement planning strategies a financial planner can use when working with clients is quite large. As with other financial planning topics, the choice of one or more particular strategies should always be based on a client's unique goal(s), situation, needs, and desires, as well as the client's financial situation. It is important to remember, however, that often strategies are dictated, in part, by the products and services offered through a financial planner's firm. Even so, there are generally multiple ways to help a client reach their retirement goal(s). The following strategies provide an insight into some of the most widely used retirement planning tools and techniques used by financial planners on a day-to-day basis.

Planning Strategy 1: Estimate a Client's Retirement Capital Need Using a Consistent Methodology

Conducting a retirement capital needs analysis is a key aspect of any retirement planning exercise. The steps involved when estimating the level of assets needed to support retirement income needs requires the application of time value of money concepts. It is each financial planner's responsibility to develop assumptions related to rates of return, inflation, life expectancy, and timing of payments, and once developed, to balance these assumptions against each client's retirement aspirations and financial goals. The following discussion highlights one approach that can used to determine whether a client is on track to meet their retirement goal.

Prior to beginning a quantitative retirement analysis, either pre- or post-retirement, it is important to review lifestyle and client characteristics that may impact retirement planning assumptions. Client characteristics to consider—from the perspective of the client and spouse, partner, or significant other—include the following:

- attitude about retiring, or specifically about retiring early

- motivation for retiring or retiring early

- willingness to continue working in another firm or profession

- willingness to establish a consulting practice or other business venture

- types of personal, leisure, or volunteer activities that the individual(s) will engage in while retired

- health status

- willingness to relocate, either to a specific designation or to a lower-cost area

- willingness or need to provide support for other family members (e.g., children, grandchildren, parents, in-laws)

Although financial planners who work with pre-retirees should analyze the following quantitative financial factors to assess a client's retirement readiness, those considering early retirement must carefully consider these issues:

- ability of the accumulated asset base, plus other forms of income, to provide adequate retirement income

- impact of early retirement on Social Security benefits

- impact of early retirement on defined benefit plan distributions

- effect of retirement on health benefits

- impact of early retirement on the working status of a spouse or partner

- tax implications of lump-sum benefits (e.g., unused sick and vacation days) received from an employer

- relocation and retirement transition expenses.

Calculating a Retirement Need

Once a client and their financial planner have finalized a retirement goal, incorporating lifestyle and income desires, and considering both the active and inactive years associated with aging, attention must turn to quantifying the cost of the projected retirement need. Fundamentally, retirement planning involves:

1. documenting a client's specific retirement income funding goal;

2. determining the gross amount needed to pay for expenses over a client's life expectancy; and

3. determining whether the client is on track to meet her or his asset accumulation objective given all other assumptions about the funding situation.

Although the analytical approach may appear straightforward, these three elements of the projection must be accurately matched to each client's unique situation.

The retirement needs analysis process begins by calculating an income or living expense **replacement ratio**. This is a measure used to estimate a client's **retirement income funding goal**. An accepted generalization is that a client will need 70 percent to 80 percent of currently available income in retirement. That is, the target should be to replace at least 70 percent of current income on the client's first day of retirement. In general, low- and high-income earning households need the highest replacement ratios.

Assume, for example, that a client currently earns $169,000 annually. If it is determined that the client needs to replace 80 percent of this amount in retirement, the income funding goal becomes $135,200. This amount should be reduced by guaranteed sources of retirement income, such as expected defined benefit payments, Social Security benefits, and annuity payments. The result is the dollar amount needed in a capital needs analysis. Because the figure is in today's dollars, a future value estimate must occur using (1) an inflation rate assumption and (2) the number of periods between the retirement date and the current period as the period input.

Planning Tip

The Social Security Administration provides information on estimating a client's life expectancy. The following website can be used to obtain an estimate of a client's life expectancy: socialsecurity.gov/ planners/lifeexpectancy.html

Determining the gross pool of assets needed over a client's life expectancy involves conducting a traditional **retirement capital needs analysis**. This projection determines the capital needed from all sources to support a client's estimated retirement income requirement, while accounting for the effects of inflation over a client's life expectancy. Three types of **capital needs analyses** are typically used by financial planners:

1. Capital depletion

2. Capital preservation

3. Inflation-adjusted

Each approach is based on relatively simple time value of money equations. However, a financial planner must first make several assumptions, in consultation with the client, before estimating a client's retirement planning need:

*   The first assumption involves determining whether contributions toward the retirement goal will grow or remain fixed. That is to say, will each subsequent payment increase by a predetermined amount, such as the inflation rate? In effect, this assumption comes down to using a fixed annuity or a geometric varying annuity assumption.

*   A second assumption involves the length of the retirement period.

*   The third assumption involves determining the rate of return expected during retirement.

Once these calculation inputs have been determined, the financial planner—again working closely with their client—must calculate the amount of the first retirement payment. The amount of this payment should be based on the client's current (or projected) income. The projection can simply be an estimated target value, such as a dollar figure (e.g., $100,000), or a percentage of current living expenses using a replacement ratio. Once all variable inputs are known, the financial planner can calculate the amount required to fully fund the level of savings needed on an annual basis to meet the accumulated asset objective as of the retirement date.

To facilitate the presentation of these calculations, two loosely defined terms can be used. The first is a **retirement annuity**, which is the amount of money required to fund a client's retirement over a given period. The second is a **legacy pool**. This is the amount of money that a client wants or hopes to leave unspent at the end of the retirement period. Typically, this is the amount the client wants to bequeath to other people and/or organizations.

The most basic needs analysis approach is called the **capital depletion approach**. This approach assumes that at the end of the retirement planning period no additional client assets will remain available to the client or heirs. In other words, the legacy pool will be zero. Here is an example.

Example: Assume a client desires to fund a retirement account with enough money to last 30 years. The financial planner knows that the client wants the first payment to be $100,000, to be received at the beginning of the first year of retirement. [The $100,000 figure can either be an assumption or it can be based on taking a client's current household income multiplied by the income replacement ratio, less any guaranteed forms of retirement income, such as Social Security, and inflated to the date of retirement (i.e., a future value calculation).] A further assumption is the financial planner knows that subsequent payments are to increase 4 percent annually to keep pace with anticipated inflation. Assuming an effective annual rate of return of 10 percent, how much, in total assets, will the client need at retirement? Using the present value of a growing annuity formula, it can be determined that the client requires $1,492,564, as shown below:

Present value of a growing annuity

$$PVGA_n = \frac{PMT_1}{(i-g)}\left[1 - \frac{(1+g)^n}{(1+i)^n}\right](1+i)$$

Where,

$i = 10$ percent

$g = 4$ percent

$PMT_1 = \$100,000$

$n = 30$

$$PVGA_n = \frac{\$100,000}{(0.10-0.04)}\left[1 - \frac{(1.04)^{30}}{(1.10)^{30}}\right](1.10) = \$1,492,564$$

The capital depletion approach results in the lowest retirement annuity need because it is assumed that the client will deplete the account over the course of retirement. Many clients are uncomfortable with the fundamental assumption of depleting all assets over their life expectancy. First, there is the possibility of outliving the available assets. Second, the capital depletion approach leaves nothing as a legacy to heirs or charities. In cases where the minimum capital depletion scenario can be satisfied with asset projections, a financial planner should also calculate the retirement need using the **capital preservation approach.**

To determine the legacy pool needed to preserve a client's capital so that the client's asset base does not decline during retirement, a financial planner must conduct one additional time value of money calculation. As with the previous method, the retirement annuity figure must be estimated. The legacy pool should then be added to the present value of the retirement annuity to determine a new amount needed on the first day of retirement. In effect, the present value of the legacy pool grows while the present value of the retirement annuity is depleted. At the end of the planning period, the client should have exactly the same nominal amount available that they had on the first day of retirement. The following example illustrates the steps necessary to estimate a capital preservation retirement annuity.

Example: Return to the previous example where a client requires a growing annuity with a beginning payment of $100,000. However, in addition, the client desires to leave a legacy equal to the beginning value of the retirement annuity. Given these assumptions, the client needs to accumulate an additional $85,537 by the first day of retirement.[1] This is the amount that will result in a future value equal to $1,492,564 at the client's death. Using this approach, the client needs a total of $1,578,101 saved at retirement ($1,492,564 + $85,537). The present value of a lump sum is used to solve for the additional amount needed.

Present Value,

$$PV_n = \frac{FV}{(1+i)^n}$$

Where,

i = 10 percent

FV = $1,492,564 (the amount needed to fund the retirement annuity)

n = 30

$$PV_n = \frac{\$1,492,564}{(1.1)^{30}} = \$85,537$$

In cases where capital preservation can be achieved, a third retirement needs estimation can be used: the **inflation-adjusted capital preservation approach**. It may be possible not only to preserve a client's assets, but also to account for inflation such that at life expectancy the real value of the retirement assets is equal to the nominal value at retirement. The following illustration example extends the case from above.

Example: Again, the client requires a growing annuity with a beginning payment of $100,000. However, in addition, the client wishes to leave a legacy with an ending purchasing power equal to the beginning purchasing power of the retirement annuity. To maintain equivalent purchasing power, the client needs to a have an additional $277,429 saved at the time of retirement. Using this approach, the client needs a total of $1,769,993 saved on the first day of retirement ($1,492,564 + $277,429).

Serial Rate,

$$\text{Serial Rate} = \frac{(1+i)}{(1+g)} - 1$$

$$\text{Serial Rate} = \frac{(1.10)}{(1.04)} - 1 = 5.77\%$$

Using the serial rate, the following present value equation is used to calculate the required additional amount needed to preserve the purchasing power of the client's legacy.

$$PV_n = \frac{FV}{(1 + i)^n}$$

Where,

i = 5.77 percent

FV = $1,492,564 (the inflation-adjusted amount desired at the end of retirement)

n = 30

$$PV_n = \frac{\$1,492,564}{(1.0577)^{30}} = \$277,429$$

Once the retirement annuity figure has been determined, a financial planner must then estimate the future value of retirement assets and savings. These assets will be used, in most client situations, to generate income as an element of the retirement annuity. Making appropriate rate of return, inflation, and tax rate assumptions is important at this stage of the analysis.

Assume, for example, that a client currently has twenty-four years remaining until retirement, can earn an annualized rate of return equal to 7 percent, has 401(k) assets of $86,000, and is saving $9,000 per year (including employer matching contributions). Using these figures, a financial planner can estimate the future value as follows:

- 401(k) = $436,224

- savings = $523,590

These amounts should then be subtracted from the capital needs analysis estimate to determine a surplus or shortfall need. If a shortfall exists, a time value of money calculation can be used to pinpoint the amount of additional annual savings needed.

Figure 12.1 illustrates the type of information typically included in retirement capital needs analysis. This spreadsheet is available in the Financial Planning Analysis Excel package included with this book.

Figure 12.1. Capital Needs Analysis Spreadsheet

CAPITAL NEEDS ANALYSIS	
Assumes that income and savings grow at a constant rate prior to retirement	
ASSUMPTIONS	
Current Household Earned Income	
Other Retirement Income Excluding Social Security (today's dollars)	
Non-Tax Deferred Retirement Assets (Stocks & Bonds)	
Tax Deferred Retirement Assets (e.g., 401k)	
Tax-Free Retirement Assets (e.g., Roth)	
Tax Deferred Annual Savings (e.g., 401k) Including Employer Matching Contributions	
After Tax Annual Savings Specifically Allocated to Retirement Needs	
Tax-Free Savings Contributions (e.g., Roth)	
Other Annual Savings Specifically Allocated to Retirement Needs	
Retirement Income Replacement Ratio	
Age	
Retirement Age	
Age to Begin Social Security Benefits	
Life Expectancy	
Years Until Retirement	
Years in Retirement	
Inflation Prior to Retirement	0.00%
Inflation After Retirement	0.00%
Growth Rate of Savings	0.00%
Growth Rate of Salary	0.00%
Assumed Return While Retired	
Assumed Rate of Return Before Retirement	
Inflation Adjusted Retirement Return	0.00%
Inflation Adjusted Pre-Retirement Return	0.00%
CALCULATIONS	
Ratio Reduced Income Need (Today's Dollars)	$0.00
FV of Ratio Reduced Income Need @ Retirement Age	
FV of Non-Deferred Retirement Assets	
FV of Tax-Deferred Retirement Assets	
FV of Tax-Free Retirement Assets	
FV of Tax-Deferred Savings	
FV of After-Tax Savings	
FV of Tax-Free Savings	
FV of Other Savings	
FV of Social Security Benefits	
Total Retirement Assets/Savings Available on First Day of Retirement	
CAPITAL DEPLETION METHOD	
Amount Needed on FIRST DAY of RETIREMENT for CAPITAL DEPLETION	
Additional Net Assets Needed @ Retirement	
Additional Level Annual Savings Needed	
CAPITAL PRESERVATION METHOD	
Assets Needed on FIRST DAY of RETIREMENT for CAPITAL PRESERVATION	
Additional Net Assets Needed @ Retirement	
Additional Level Savings Needed (Capital Preservation)	

Retirement Distribution Calculations

Almost all retirement planning calculations are based on the assumption that a client is in the process of saving for retirement. It is, however, equally important to understand how to estimate appropriate retirement distribution amounts for those who are already retired. There are multiple ways to calculate the optimal withdrawal strategy for a client. Some financial planners use a simple heuristic, such as the **4 percent rule**, which states that a retiree can safely withdraw four percent of the value of savings each year during retirement. The academic literature offers a multitude of similar strategies, ranging from withdrawals based on increasing equity holdings over retirement to reducing the safe distribution to 4 percent or less, and in some cases, includes reverse mortgages and home equity in distribution estimates.

Two other approaches are widely used to determine the appropriate distribution from a **capital withdrawal process**. The first is based on a **deterministic model**. Deterministic models use a static, or constant, mean return throughout the modeling period. The output is a very elementary projection on which to base a safe withdrawal strategy. The second is called a **stochastic model**. Stochastic models add variability to distribution calculations. The following discussion highlights steps necessary to estimate withdrawals using a deterministic model.

1. Determine the value of the pool of available assets at the beginning of retirement. Although not all client assets will be used to fund retirement (home equity is often excluded), assets that can be used should be valued at the market value as of the projected date of retirement.

2. Choose a reasonable after-tax rate of return for retirement. A financial planner should always take into account a client's risk tolerance, expectations, time horizon, and preferences, including asset class limitations, when establishing a rate of return projection. The return should not subject a client's assets to risks beyond those necessary to achieve a desired standard of living.

3. Choose a realistic average rate of inflation during retirement (or determine the client's desired rate of increase for the retirement annuity). Although not always the case, using a conservative estimate is a best practice (i.e., slightly overstate projected inflation). Just as investment losses are more detrimental early in the withdrawal period, high inflation early during a withdrawal period can create a quicker depletion of assets, making it problematic that a client can maintain their standard of living.

4. Calculate the inflation-adjusted rate of return applicable to the client using the serial interest rate formula:

    $$\text{Serial Rate} = \frac{(1 + i)}{(1 + g)} - 1$$

5. Determine the client's life expectancy. A client's individual life expectancy can be estimated using the Period Life Expectancy Table shown in Figure 12.2.[2]

If a client is married, the client's and spouse's joint and survivor life expectancy (i.e., how long at least one of the two will live, or until both will be deceased) can be determined using a joint and survivor life expectancy table. These tables should be used as a starting point in an analysis. Other important information, including a client's ancestral life expectancy patterns, current health status, occupation, and hobbies, can be used to increase or decrease assumptions regarding a client's life expectancy. For financial planners who want a conservative estimate, using a table factor life expectancy and adding at least five years can be a practical approach.

Figure 12.2. Social Security Actuarial Life Expectancy Table

\multicolumn{15}{c}{**2015 Period Life Table[2]**}

Age	Male	Female	Age	Male	Female	Age	Male	Female	Age	Male	Female
56	24.63	27.88	70	14.30	16.44	84	6.30	7.41	98	2.34	2.73
57	23.83	27.02	71	13.63	15.69	85	5.87	6.91	99	2.22	2.57
58	23.05	26.17	72	12.97	14.96	86	5.45	6.43	100	2.11	2.42
59	22.27	25.32	73	12.33	14.24	87	5.06	5.98	101	2.00	2.27
60	21.51	24.48	74	11.70	13.54	88	4.69	5.54	102	1.89	2.14
61	20.75	23.64	75	11.08	12.85	89	4.35	5.14	103	1.79	2.00
62	20.00	22.81	76	10.48	12.17	90	4.03	4.76	104	1.69	1.88
63	19.27	21.99	77	9.89	11.51	91	3.73	4.41	105	1.59	1.76
64	18.53	21.17	78	9.33	10.86	92	3.46	4.09	106	1.50	1.64
65	17.81	20.36	79	8.77	10.24	93	3.21	3.80	107	1.41	1.53
66	17.09	19.55	80	8.24	9.63	94	2.99	3.54	108	1.33	1.43
67	16.38	18.76	81	7.72	9.04	95	2.80	3.30	109	1.25	1.33
68	15.68	17.98	82	7.23	8.48	96	2.63	3.09	110	1.17	1.24
69	14.98	17.20	83	6.75	7.93	97	2.48	2.90	111	1.10	1.15

Calculate the withdrawal amount. There are two basic methods that can be used at this step of the process. Both methods can be adjusted to account for inflation to preserve purchasing power. If inflation is accounted for, withdrawals will increase each year to reflect inflation. The first method assumes a depletion of all assets at the end of the client's life expectancy (i.e., at the end of retirement), which is referred to as the **capital depletion withdrawal method**. This approach is based on a growth-adjusted present value of an annuity due calculation.

Example: Assume a client has retirement assets equal to $500,000 at the time of retirement, that yearly distributions will increase by 4 percent, assets earn 8 percent annually, and retirement is planned to last for twenty years, at which time assets will be depleted. As shown below, the amount that can be withdrawn at the beginning of the first year equals $34,947. This amount must then be increased by 4 percent in each succeeding year.

$$\text{Serial Rate} = \frac{(1+i)}{(1+g)} - 1 = \frac{1.08}{1.04} - 1 = 3.846\%$$

$$\$500,000 = \frac{\text{PMT}}{0.03846}\left(1 - \frac{1}{1.03846^{20}}\right)(1.03846)$$

$$\text{PMT} = \frac{\$500,000 \times 0.03846}{(1 - 1.03846^{-20}) \times 1.03846} = \$34,947$$

Where,

i = 3.846 percent

FV = 0

PV = $500,000

n = 20

Solving for PMT also returns approximately $34,947, which is an annuity due estimate.

The second distribution approach is called the **capital preservation method**. This approach assumes that a client's assets at retirement will be preserved throughout the client's lifetime. The capital preservation method can also increase the yearly payment to reflect inflation. Payments can be determined using a present value of a growing perpetuity due calculation.

Example: Assume a client has retirement assets equal to $500,000 at the time of retirement, that yearly distributions will increase by 4 percent, assets earn 8 percent annually, and retirement is planned to last for twenty years, at which time assets will still be equal to the inflation-adjusted future value of $500,000. As shown below, the amount that can be withdrawn at the beginning of the first year equals $18,519. This amount, which is significantly less than the capital depletion withdrawal method, will then increase by 4 percent in each succeeding year. Using the same serial rate as before:

$$\$500,000 = \frac{\text{PMT}}{0.03846}\left(1 - \frac{1}{1.03846^{20}}\right)(1.03846) + \frac{\$500,000(1.04^{20})}{1.08^{20}}$$

$$\$500,000 = \frac{\text{PMT}}{0.03846}\left(1 - \frac{1}{1.03846^{20}}\right)(1.03846) + \$235,050.77$$

$$\$500,000 - \$235,050.77 = \frac{\text{PMT}}{0.03846}\left(1 - \frac{1}{1.03846^{20}}\right)(1.03846)$$

What is actually available to support retirement is the difference in the $500,000 saved and the $235,051 needed to ensure the inflation-adjusted future value of the account.

$$PMT = \frac{\$264{,}949.23 \times 0.03846}{(1 - 1.03846^{-20}) \times 1.03846} = \$18{,}519$$

Where,

$i = 3.846$ percent

$FV = 0$

$PV = \$264{,}949.23$

$n = 20$

Solving for PMT also returns approximately $18,519.

In other words, the present value of the account continues to increase in perpetuity by the rate of inflation. As a result, if the account is increasing in value at a rate equal to increases in the annual withdrawal, then it turns out to be a simple present value of a growing perpetuity.

$$\$500{,}000 = \frac{PMT}{0.08 - 0.04}(1.08)$$

$$PMT = \frac{\$500{,}000 \times (0.08 - 0.04)}{1.08} = \$18{,}519$$

A **non-random deterministic withdrawal model** can also be developed to help a client gain an idea of how long their retirement account balance(s) will exist into the future. Figure 12.3 illustrates how Excel™ can be used to project estimated withdrawal amounts for a client who enters retirement at age sixty-five with $100,000 in assets. The data in Figure 12.3 are based on the following assumptions:

- A 5 percent annualized before-tax rate of return,

- A 3 percent annualized inflation rate,

- A 4 percent annual distribution rate,

- A distribution rate that increases by the rate of inflation, and

- A required minimum distribution (RMD) based on the Uniform Lifetime Table.[3]

Planning Tip

Keep in mind that a calculator cannot easily handle a growing annuity problem using the TVM keys because there is a future value involved and serial rates typically cannot be used to directly solve for future values. Therefore, the present value of the remaining balance must be subtracted before beginning an analysis. As a reminder, a TVM calculator should be set to beginning-of-period payments.

Figure 12.3. Deterministic Withdrawal Illustration

Age of Client	Beginning Balance	Yearly Distribution	Distribution Rate (percent)
65	$500,000	$20,000	4.00
66	504,000	20,600	4.09
67	507,570	21,218	4.18
68	510,670	21,855	4.28
69	513,256	22,510	4.39
70	515,283	23,185	4.50
71	516,702	23,881	4.62
72	517,462	24,597	4.75
73	517,508	25,335	4.90
74	516,781	26,095	5.05
75	515,220	26,878	5.22
76	512,759	27,685	5.40
77	509,328	28,515	5.60
78	504,853	29,371	5.82
79	499,257	30,252	6.06
80	492,455	31,159	6.33
81	484,361	32,094	6.63
82	474,880	33,057	6.96
83	463,914	34,049	7.34
84	451,359	35,070	7.77
85	437,103	36,122	8.26
86	421,030	37,206	8.84
87	403,015	38,322	9.51
88	382,928	39,472	10.31
89	360,629	40,656	11.27
90	335,972	41,876	16.46
91	308,801	43,132	13.97
92	278,952	44,426	15.93
93	246,253	45,759	18.58
94	210,519	47,131	22.39
95	171,557	48,545	28.30
96	129,163	50,002	38.71
97	83,119	51,502	61.96
98	33,198	33,198	100.00
99	0	0	0.00

The first column in Figure 12.3 shows the client's age from sixty-five to an assumed death at age ninety-nine. The second column shows the client's account balance adjusted for each annual withdrawal and account earnings. The third column shows the annual 4 percent distribution, adjusted for inflation. The effective distribution rate shown in the last column can be estimated by dividing the yearly distribution amount by the beginning balance. Over time, the effective distribution rate will rise in response to inflation.

The use of a stochastic retirement withdrawal model is another way financial planners make retirement withdrawal estimates. Stochastic modeling, or what is known as Monte Carlo modeling, has gained favor as a projection tool for withdrawal analyses. A stochastic approach randomizes rate-of-return, inflation, and life expectancy assumptions using thousands of data point observations to estimate features of plan success or failure. The primary drawback to stochastic models is the need to use software or advanced data worksheet applications. While certainly not impossible, it would be very time intensive to use a calculator as a stochastic modeling tool.

Planning Strategy 2: Begin a Retirement Needs Analysis Using the Capital Depletion Method

Figure 12.4 outlines the hierarchical steps to follow when evaluating a client's current situation. The decision tree begins by asking whether a client needs additional savings to meet a capital depletion objective. If the answer is yes, a series of assumption changes and strategies is presented, beginning with allocating additional resources to the goal. If these adjustments do not allow a client to meet the retirement savings goal, a financial planner is prompted to determine the client's willingness to reduce the level of income needed in retirement. The process continues until the capital depletion projection is achieved, adjusted for the client's life expectancy. However, caution must be exercised when changing retirement planning assumptions to ensure that the assumptions are valid and defensible. Overly conservative estimates can compromise a client's current standard of living, whereas assumptions that are too generous can seriously threaten retirement funding by generating savings recommendations that will be insufficient if rate of return or inflation estimates deviate significantly from reality.

Once the capital depletion model is fully funded, the focus of potential funding strategies proceeds to Step Two at any point on the decision tree. Here, attention turns to projecting the funding needed for the capital preservation and inflation-adjusted models, depending on the client's preferences.

Figure 12.4. Decision Tree for Determining Appropriate Retirement Planning Strategy

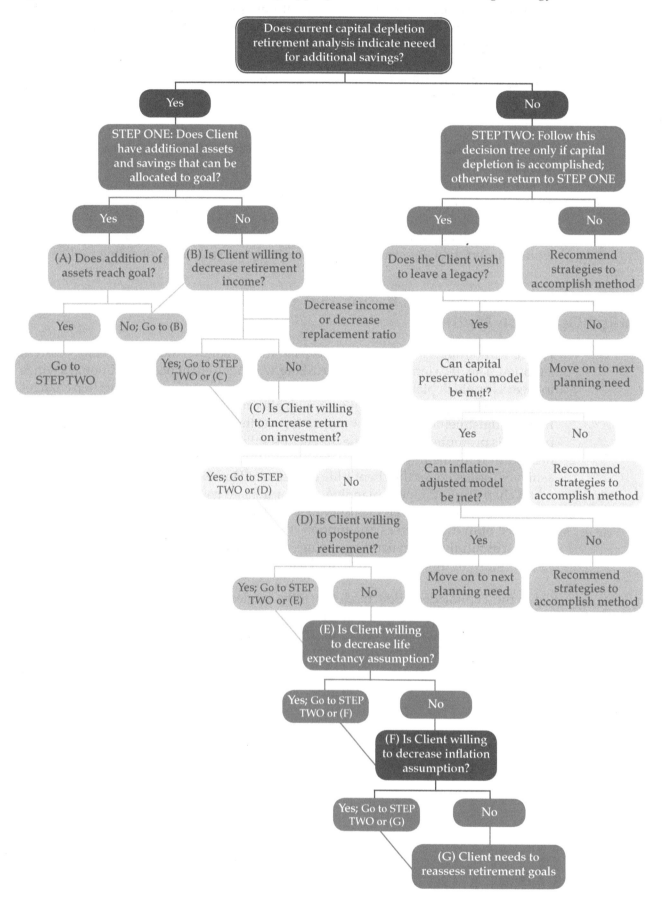

Planning Strategy 3: Identify Sources of Retirement Income

Financial planners often use the analogy of the **three-legged stool** as a framework for considering a client's retirement planning situation. The three commonly identified legs of the stool supporting retirement are:

1. resources from the government through Social Security benefits—a government-backed retirement system that provides monthly inflation-adjusted benefits;

2. resources from employer-provided retirement plans; and

3. resources from personal savings.

In light of the Baby Boom generation's recent and expanding efforts to redefine retirement, some professionals have suggested adding other legs to the stool: employment during retirement and the use of home equity. A Fidelity Research Institute Retirement Index report noted that, although 60 percent of pre-retirees plan on working to supplement their retirement income, 22 percent of retirees in that same survey were forced into early retirement because of poor health.[4] So, although employment, either in the same or a different professional pursuit, may be an alternative, like other retirement funding sources, the option of post-retirement employment is characterized by unique benefits and risks. The same also can be said of home equity, which prior to the global financial crisis, most assumed was stable or appreciating. The significant loss of value resulting from home losses between 2007 and 2010 eroded the retirement portfolios of many pre-retirees, forcing them to postpone retirement because of concerns over the value and liquidity of real estate.

Planning Strategy 4: Adjust Retirement Planning Assumptions to Help a Client Meet Their Retirement Planning Need

Sometimes meeting a client's retirement income need cannot be accomplished without adjusting key assumptions. A shortfall in retirement savings can exist even after committing unallocated assets and savings toward a client's retirement goal. When this happens, a financial planner, working with the client, will need to alter previously made assumptions and/or forecasts. The following discussion highlights areas within a retirement needs analysis that can most easily be adjusted.

- It is possible that the amount of income or living expenses being replaced is too high. This strategy calls for the client to reevaluate their retirement income need. By reducing the need, it might be possible to use existing resources to fully fund retirement. Emotionally, asking a client to reassess their income need can be quite difficult. Also, it is possible that a client's income need is realistic and that income cannot be cut without seriously decreasing a client's quality of life in retirement.

- Changing the years in retirement assumption (i.e., life expectancy) is one way to decrease a client's total asset need without decreasing the projected amount of annual income received. The obvious disadvantage associated with this strategy is that a client may outlive the accumulated asset base. The fiscal and emotional strain on a client and other family members, should this occur, can be devastating. Elderly clients who have planned well for retirement often worry about outliving their resources. Adjusting the life expectancy assumption, unless there is valid information on which to base this decision, can mislead a client and further limit alternative retirement saving options or available spending reductions.

- Increasing the rate-of-return assumption within retirement planning models is the easiest way to obtain the theoretical feasibility of retirement goals. Hypothetically, it is possible to meet retirement objectives, holding all other inputs static, by increasing portfolio returns. Rate-of-return assumptions must be based on a combination of a client's time horizon, risk tolerance, capacity for risk taking, asset class preference, and expectations about the future. Assuming a rate of return that is higher than is commensurate with a client's risk profile almost inevitably leads to plan failure. So, even though it is theoretically possible to make a retirement plan work by increasing portfolio return assumptions, in practical terms, it may not be possible to actually manage assets in a way that generates such returns without exposing the client to greater levels of risk. Further, overestimating expected returns in a portfolio might subject a financial planner to suitability challenges if returns are not realized.

Planning Tip

Deterministic retirement capital needs analysis models sometimes fail as a result of **sequence of returns risk**. This is the risk associated with receiving a below-average return during the first few years of distributions compared to earning higher returns later. Clients who begin distributions just before a market decline must earn higher rates of return in the future to reach an average return need. This means that the likelihood of having an asset shortfall is greater for such clients.

- It may be reasonable to recommend that a client postpone retirement one or more years. The advantage associated with this strategy is that it generally results in a higher Social Security benefit. The strategy also allows existing assets to grow for additional years. This strategy may not be feasible for clients who face forced retirement because of medical problems or loss of employment. Also, this strategy forces clients to work longer than hoped and expected, which can result in a reduced level of morale and willingness to maintain proactive financial planning strategies.

- In cases where adjusting other assumptions leaves a client short of their capital accumulation goal, another strategy is to reduce the assumed inflation rate for the retirement time period. This will result in a lower assumed gross asset need at retirement, which will make the value of assets and savings appear more likely to meet client needs. Implementing this strategy is fraught with risk. Inflation is often the greatest financial risk facing retirees on a fixed income. If actual inflation exceeds the assumed level, then it is likely that a client's assets will quickly be depleted over the course of the client's life.

- Another strategy calls for decreasing a client's income need while in retirement. The advantage associated with this strategy is that decreasing the percentage of income projected to be replaced will result in a lower total funding need at the date of retirement. Implementing this strategy can reduce a client's standard of living to a level that is less than optimal, and in an extreme situation, unrealistic. The ultimate consequence is less money to fund leisure activities, gifting strategies, travel, entertainment, or other expenses.

- Recommending that a client work in retirement has the dual advantage of providing additional cash flow in retirement while providing meaningful activity for the client while retired. For some executives and former business owners, this can mean periodic consulting. For others, it might mean working a permanent part-time job. The additional cash flow reduces the amount of retirement income to be replaced from assets, savings, and retirement plans. Working while retired is also an excellent way to keep both mind and body active. Some retirees find that their dreams of retirement are larger than the reality. When this happens, employment provides some with an opportunity to contribute to society in a meaningful way.

Planning Tip

It is worth remembering that working while retired can have a significantly negative impact on Social Security benefits. Clients who receive Social Security benefits before reaching full retirement age (FRA) are limited in the amount that can be earned without losing benefits.

Planning Strategy 5: Incorporate Social Security Claiming Strategies into the Retirement Planning Process

Virtually all working Americans are covered by Social Security, which is funded through employee and employer payroll deductions. A few categories of workers are not covered through the Social Security system. For instance, certain municipal or state employees whose employers have opted out of the system are exempt from Social Security taxes. Federal workers hired before 1984 are generally not covered by Social Security. Some religious ministers and Christian Science practitioners can also opt out of Social Security. The largest category of privately employed exempt workers includes railroad workers covered under the Railroad Retirement Act. Although most Social Security benefit calculations can be estimated online, customized to the client's earnings record online, or estimated by a Social Security representative, it is important that financial planners have a working knowledge of Social Security terms and benefit calculation methods.

The **Social Security Administration** uses an **average indexed monthly earnings** (AIME) calculation to determine a worker's Social Security benefit upon early, regular, or postponed retirement. According to the Social Security Administration, two primary calculations need to be made, consecutively, to arrive at AIME:[5]

- The first calculation is the adjustment for inflation of the retiree's top thirty five years of earnings, not to exceed the Social Security maximum taxable income in that specific year (fewer years may sometimes be used). The calculation begins by dividing the current national average wage index by the national average wage index in the year the individual incurred wages. This calculation is made for each year. This indexing adjustment is completed for all years with the exception of the most recent two years. The total indexed earnings amount is then divided by the total number of months in those years.

- The second calculation involves multiplying each year's earnings by the index calculated for that specific year. This effectively adjusts each year's earnings to the current year's wages, as indexed for inflation. Calculation outcomes are added together and then divided by the number of months to arrive at AIME. AIME is then used to calculate the Social Security **primary insurance amount (PIA)**, which is a term used to describe the monthly benefit.[6]

Social Security benefits are generally based on an average of the thirty five years of highest earnings, although the PIA is specifically used to determine retirement, disability, and survivor benefits that are paid *monthly* to a single individual. According to the Social Security Administration, PIA is calculated by first determining a worker's AIME, a factor the Social Security Administration provides. The PIA calculation is as follows:

PIA = 90% of the first $X of AIME

+ 32% of the AIME in excess of $X and less than $Y

+ 15% of the AIME in excess of $Y

In the preceding equation, $X and $Y are called **bend points**, which are adjusted annually according to the national average wage index. Although the figures change annually, the following examples are based on the value for $X as $767 and the value for $Y as $4,624. PIA is the amount the worker will receive for retirement at full retirement age.

> *Example*: Irina Dalakis, a forty-year-old account executive for a major pharmaceutical company, has begun to wonder how much she can expect to receive as a monthly benefit from Social Security to supplement her other retirement savings. Based on her AIME of $6,875, she would receive $2,262.00 per month in retirement benefit.[7]
>
> $PIA = (0.90 \times 767) + (0.32 \times (4,624 - 767)) + (0.15 \times (6,875 - 4,624))$
>
> $PIA = \$691.30 + \$1,234.24 + \$337.65$
>
> $PIA = \$2,262.19$

To be **fully insured** in the Social Security system, a client must generally have forty quarters of employment coverage. It is possible to be currently rather than *fully* insured. Individuals with at least six quarters of coverage credits in the last thirteen quarters are considered currently insured.

Planning Tip

It is important to note that PIA is reduced or increased for early or delayed retirement. When designing a retirement plan, it is worth remembering that those who are eligible for Social Security may receive retirement, disability, survivorship, and Medicare benefits concurrently. A small lump sum death benefit of $255 is also available to survivors of a fully insured person.

Planning Strategy 6: Differentiate Between Normal, Early, and Delayed Social Security Claiming Strategies

A client who is fully insured is entitled to Social Security benefits at retirement. **Full retirement age (FRA)** is sixty five for clients born before 1938. The FRA increases in two-month increments for every year an individual is born between 1938 and 1943. Anyone born from 1943 to 1954 has a full retirement age of sixty six years. For anyone born from 1955 to 1960, the FRA increases in two-month intervals until age sixty seven. Age sixty seven is currently the maximum Social Security full retirement age.

It is possible to retire prior to one's FRA. Age sixty two is the earliest age at which Social Security retirement benefits can be received. A retiree's monthly benefit is reduced:

- by 5/9 of 1 percent for every month of early retirement for the first thirty six months, and

- by 5/12 of 1 percent for every month in excess of thirty six.

Someone whose FRA is 66 and claims benefits at age sixty four, for example, will receive a 13.33 percent reduction in benefits (5/9 × 0.01 × 24). Someone whose FRA is age sixty seven, who claims benefits at age sixty two, will receive a 30 percent reduction in benefits, as shown below:

$$[(5/9 \times 0.01 \times 36) + (5/12 \times 0.01 \times 24)]$$

Clients also can *delay* the receipt of Social Security benefits. Doing so results in a permanent increase in benefits. The actual increase depends on the age of the client, but generally a worker can expect between a 6.5 percent and 8.0 percent increase in benefits for every year of deferment between FRA and age seventy.

Planning Strategy 7: Evaluate Social Security Spousal Rules

For retirement planning purposes, **spousal Social Security benefits** are available to the spouse of an insured individual. A spouse who has no work history or a limited work history can draw Social Security benefits based on their spouse's work history. The payment is typically 50 percent of the insured's benefit, but this can be reduced if the surviving spouse is younger than the insured. The Social Security Administration regularly sends statements to persons covered by Social Security that provide an estimate of future Social Security benefits in today's dollars, based on actual Social Security wages. Another easy way to estimate a client's approximate annual benefit in today's dollars is to use the Social Security Benefit Estimator.[8] This tool can be used to estimate how much a client and spouse can expect to receive at retirement.

Planning Strategy 8: Increase Contributions to Retirement Plans and IRAs to Maximize Asset Accumulation

Assuming that a client's retirement goal(s) and assumptions are realistic, one of the simplest strategies for meeting a retirement accumulation goal is to allocate additional assets and savings to an existing or new retirement plan. Certain defined contribution plans, and some IRA-based plans, allow clients fifty years of age or older to make catch-up contributions beyond the maximum annual allowable contribution. The contribution catch-up information shown in Figure 12.5 summarizes catch-up provisions as they apply to 401(k), 403(b), 457, and IRA plans.

Figure 12.5. Retirement Plan Catch-up Provisions

Plan	2020 and beyond
401(k)	$6,500Indexed to inflation in $500 increments
Roth 401(k)	$6,500
403(b)	$6,500 Indexed to inflation in $500 increments
457	$6,500 Indexed to inflation in $500 increments
SIMPLE IRAs and SIMPLE 401(k) plans	$3,000 Indexed to inflation in $500 increments
IRA	$1,000

It is important to note that reallocating assets and savings toward retirement plan goals can jeopardize other important financial planning goals, including building an emergency fund, funding insurance needs, and paying for a client's household educational expenses. However, depending on the type of account used, some retirement savings offer options for certain expenses. Using a Roth IRA, for example, can be a way to save for retirement while providing a secondary source of education funding if needed.

Planning Strategy 9: Fully Fund an Individual Retirement Agreement/ Arrangement to Maximize Asset Accumulation

Assuming a client has maxed out a defined contribution plan, at least up to the point of receiving the maximum employer match, investing in an **Individual Retirement Arrangement** (IRA) should be a high priority. The choice of traditional or Roth IRA generally depends on two factors: (1) the ability to deduct contributions to a traditional IRA and (2) the marginal tax rate at the time of contribution and withdrawal.

Clients who are eligible to make tax-deductible contributions generally find a traditional IRA attractive whenever the marginal tax rate will be lower when the client retires (when distributions begin). Clients who are eligible to make contributions to Roth IRAs will generally find a Roth IRA attractive if marginal tax rates will be higher after retirement (assuming Roth IRA distributions are qualified). A Roth IRA is generally a better choice when a contribution to a traditional IRA is not deductible, unless contributions cannot be made to a Roth IRA based on income limitations. Figure 12.6 illustrates how tax rates impact IRA funding decisions. It is worth noting that in some cases, it may be worth fully funding a client and spouse Roth IRA before contributing to a qualified plan, especially in cases where employer matching is unavailable.

Figure 12.6. Impact of Tax Rates on Traditional and Roth IRA Distributions

Type	Contribution	Contribution Tax Rate	Distribution Tax Rate	After-tax Distribution
Traditional IRA	$5,000	25%	25%	$13,659
Roth IRA	$3,750	25%	25%	$13,659
Traditional IRA	$5,000	25%	15%	$15,481
Roth IRA	$3,750	25%	15%	$13,659
Traditional IRA	$5,000	15%	25%	$13,659
Roth IRA	$4,250	15%	25%	$15,481

Data in this table are based on the following assumptions:
- Number of years until distribution = 15
- Rate of return = 9 percent
- Roth IRA contribution = traditional IRA contribution × (1 – pre-retirement tax rate)
- Roth distribution is a "qualifying distribution"

Choosing to contribute to either a traditional or Roth IRA before funding a qualified plan means that a client will lose an important tax reduction tool (i.e., the ability to fund qualified retirement savings with pretax dollars). Another disadvantage associated with this strategy is that contributions to and accumulations in IRAs are not always protected from creditors. **IRA asset protection** differs from state to state. Furthermore, deductible contributions to a traditional IRA or contributions to a Roth IRA may be unavailable because of income phase-outs based on modified AGI (many high-income clients may be phased-out of participation and unable to contribute).

Planning Strategy 10: Recommend a Pension Maximization Strategy to Maximize Retirement Income

According to the IRS, "a **qualified joint-and-survivor annuity (QJSA)** is used when retirement benefits from a pension plan or annuity are paid as a life annuity to the participant and a survivor annuity over the life of the participant's surviving spouse (or a former spouse, child or dependent who must be treated as a surviving spouse under a *QDRO*) following the participant's death. The amount paid to the surviving spouse must be:

- No less than 50 percent and no greater than 100 percent of the amount of the annuity paid during the participant's life.

- Alternatively, a participant who waives a QJSA may elect to have a qualified optional survivor annuity (QOSA). The amount paid to the surviving spouse under a QOSA is equal to the certain percentage (as chosen) of the amount of the annuity payable during the participant's life. Typical QOSAs are $66^{2/3}$ percent and 100 percent annuities.

Pension maximization generally starts by foregoing a QJSA or QOSA and instead taking a 100 percent single life payout from a defined benefit plan or annuity. Keep in mind that the person who is entitled to a QJSA must waive their right to the benefit. As a result of the single life payout, the monthly benefit will be significantly larger than a comparable joint and survivor annuity payout. Under a pension maximization arrangement, the extra amount is then used to purchase life insurance, which is used to fund a survivor's income need if the participant predeceases the spouse. If a permanent form of insurance is used, a portion of the cash value can be used in later years to supplement retirement income. Pension maximization will not work when a client is uninsurable. The strategy also might not work when a client's life expectancy is significantly longer than an affordable term of insurance, or when the amount of insurance that can be purchased is insufficient to fund the difference between the single life payout and the joint and survivor payout.

Planning Strategy 11: Use a Reverse Mortgage to Increase Retirement Income

A **reverse mortgage** is a type of loan that is generally provided to a client on either a monthly payout or a line of credit basis. Reverse mortgages offer several benefits:

- No interest or principal is due until the end of the mortgage term.

- Payments received by a client are not taxable.

- Payments received do not impact Social Security or Medicare benefits.

Although a reverse mortgage allows a client to convert a portion of home equity to current income while living in the home, it is possible that all equity will be used by the end of the loan term, leaving nothing for the client or heirs. Furthermore, if a client saves a portion of the payments received, this could negatively affect Medicaid and Supplemental Security Income eligibility. Additionally, interest paid is not deductible until the end of the loan term. Before recommending this strategy, a financial planner should ensure that the costs associated with a recommended product are reasonable.

Planning Strategy 12: Use Variable Universal Life as a Retirement Planning Tool

In some cases, a highly compensated client may need to shelter income and assets to such an extent that qualified plans are of modest help. For example, a highly paid executive might quickly exhaust their ability to shelter assets in an employer-sponsored retirement plan due to maximum annual contribution limits. It is also likely, given the executive's income level, that contributions to a Roth IRA will be phased-out. When this happens, what is a highly paid client to do? If the client is a business executive, one solution might be for the client's firm to implement a non-qualified retirement plan. This can be an expensive option. It could also be a risky alternative for the executive because assets held in a non-qualified plan may be subject to possession by firm creditors, as well as forfeiture due to resignation or termination for cause. One realistic solution for solving this issue involves the use of a variable universal life insurance policy.

A **variable universal life policy** (**VUL**) provides a method to save money on a tax-deferred basis with a great deal of premium flexibility (the policy owner may change the face value of a policy and yearly premiums paid). In effect, a VUL allows a client to purchase a term insurance policy while also investing in tax-deferred mutual funds. If invested appropriately, the cash account can grow in value over time. Unlike qualified plans that restrict annual contributions, a VUL can accept very large annual premiums. In fact, a VUL can easily be funded with multiples of the yearly limit applied to qualified defined contribution plans. Furthermore, the cash value in such accounts is sheltered from taxes and creditors. Once the cash value within a VUL generates enough annual income to cover policy expenses (called the **tax-free funding level**), all additional earnings and premiums work to increase cash values.

For example, assume an executive is ready to retire. Also assume that over the course of twenty or thirty years, the executive funded the VUL to the fullest extent. If the account has gone up in value, the executive can start to take policy loans out against the value of the account. The insurance company will charge interest on these loans, but the executive will generally owe no tax on the borrowed amounts unless they fail to make a loan payment. With a large enough account cash balance, the interest plus insurance expenses can continue to be covered by account earnings. Year after year, the executive can borrow money from the account on what is an essentially tax-free basis.

Obviously, multiple factors come into play when using this type of financial planning technique. First, the level of funding necessary to make the scenario realistic over time is quite large. Second, and most importantly, the client must invest aggressively over the VUL holding period. It is important to note that the account value must be of such size at the time of retirement to meet ongoing retirement income needs and also pay interest and insurance expenses. Another disadvantage is that this strategy is appropriate in only a limited number of cases, which limits the usefulness of the product in meeting the needs of many clients. Keep in mind that if a VUL policy is deemed to be a modified endowment contract, loan payments are treated as taxable distributions to the extent that cash value exceeds investment in the contract.

Planning Strategy 13: Use Glide Path Portfolios That Match a Client's Investment Time Horizon

A retirement **glide path portfolio** refers to the allocation of investments within a retirement account, most often mutual funds or exchange traded funds, which automatically adjust from risky to conservative as the client/investor ages. The glide path refers to the notion that the portfolio slowly adjusts to an increasingly conservative asset allocation the closer to retirement or the target-date maturity of the fund. At that time, the portfolio will be almost entirely in Treasury securities or other low risk/return assets. When this occurs, the client will have the choice of continuing to own the fund, purchasing an annuity, or reallocating the assets into a retirement income portfolio. These products provide two main advantages. First, the need to reallocate holdings is eliminated. Second, portfolio risk falls as the client's risk capacity declines.

It is worth noting that the term glide path portfolio is a marketing term used to describe what are generally known as **target-date maturity funds**. Although each company that provides a target-date product defines the glide path differently, all funds using this strategy reduce equity exposure over time. Depending on the reallocation from equity to low risk/return assets, this can run counter to academic studies showing that nearly everyone, regardless of age, should have some exposure to equities as an inflation and longevity hedge. By following a traditional glide path strategy, clients can find that their overall portfolio is too conservative based on the ratio of these retirement assets within the client's broader portfolio. For example, fixed-income assets (e.g., Social Security benefits, pensions, annuities, bond holdings, etc.) tend to make up a high percentage of income sources for the majority of retirees. Care must be taken that when glide path portfolios are included in a client's broader portfolio the allocation to fixed-income securities is not too great.

Planning Strategy 14: Incorporate Deferred Income Annuity Strategies into a Client's Retirement Plan

As the name implies, a **deferred income annuity (DIA)** provides an income stream to a retired client at some later point in retirement. A special subset of DIA is a **qualified longevity annuity**, which starts payments after age seventy five. The difference between a DIA and an immediate annuity payment can be quite large. Based on a $100,000 purchase, an immediate annuity might pay out $5,400 per year (assuming a return-of-premium feature). A similar DIA that starts payments at age seventy five will generate about $10,500 per year. A DIA will appeal to conservative clients who want a guaranteed source of lifetime income. It is worth noting that under IRS Regulations, a standard DIA (non-QLAC) owned within a qualified retirement plan (401(k), IRA) will typically exhaust by age 84 of the account owner. The IRS changed minimum distribution regulations regarding annuities in July 2014. The new regulations allow *qualifying longevity annuity contracts* (**QLAC**) to be excluded from minimum distribution rules that usually begin when a client turns age 72. This means that current required distributions can be reduced, which might allow for a greater legacy transfer at death (assuming a return-of-premium policy is purchased).

In order for a QLAC to be deemed qualifying, the amount used to fund the annuity is limited to the lesser of $135,000 (2020) or 25 percent of a client's total retirement holdings. Also, a QLAC must be specifically identified as such; distributions cannot be postponed beyond age eighty five. While a DIA carries a lower overall commission rate, few DIA products provide inflation protection. Additionally, some insurance experts have expressed concern that the internal rates of return are too low to make these products viable for most clients.

Planning Strategy 15: Recommend Early Retirement When Appropriate

A question commonly asked of financial planners is whether a client should take early Social Security retirement benefits. Before answering this question, a financial planner should perform a present value break-even calculation to determine the best time to begin drawing the benefit. Issues to consider when addressing this question include the client's life expectancy, current earnings projections, prospects for salary increases, and other employment opportunities. Some financial planners recommend that a single person should take early Social Security benefits only if the rate of return earned on the benefits exceeds the inflation rate by 5 percent.[9]

In effect, a client who postpones retirement benefits is wagering that they will live long enough to recoup the opportunity cost associated with delaying the benefit, and as such, the client must earn a sufficient real return to break even on the reduced benefit received. As long as the recipient's age and health profile match statistical averages, the 5 percent rule is usually appropriate. Someone who takes an early benefit may think that having additional cash flow now rather than later is worthwhile both financially and psychologically. As suggested by the 5 percent rule, this may be true if the early paid benefits can be saved and reinvested at a rate higher than inflation.

It is important to take into account possible tax issues when helping clients make decisions regarding the timing of benefits. Social Security payments can increase a client's income tax liability. The amount of benefits subject to tax depends on each client's combined income (not solely adjusted gross income [AGI]) and filing status). **Combined Social Security income** is the sum of AGI, tax-exempt interest, and one-half the Social Security benefit.

> *Example.* If the combined income of a single filer in 2020 is between $25,000 and $34,000, up to 50 percent of Social Security benefits could be taxed. If the combined income of a single filer is more than $34,000, up to 85 percent of the benefits can be taxed. For those filing joint returns, break points are $32,000 and $44,000, respectively. For married individuals filing separate returns, the break point is $0.

A client who retires before their FRA and receives Social Security retirement benefits can lose some or all of the benefits by working. Retirees who have not yet reached their FRA for all of 2020 can earn up to $18,240 without losing benefits. If earnings exceed this amount, part of the Social Security benefit is lost; the penalty in lost benefits is severe. For every $2 a client earns above this amount, $1 in benefits is lost. For those who will reach their FRA in 2020, the Social Security Administration will deduct $1 from benefits for each $3 earned above $48,600 until the month a client reaches full retirement age. After FRA has been reached, a retiree can earn an unlimited dollar amount without penalty.[10]

Planning Strategy 16: Use Qualified Employee Plans Appropriately

Employer-provided retirement plans can be broadly categorized as either qualified or non-qualified. **Qualified retirement plans** are recognized and described in the Internal Revenue Code (IRC). Qualified plans provide employees and employers certain tax advantages because they meet qualifications established by tax law. Contributions to an employee's qualified retirement plan are generally excluded from current taxable income. Employers enjoy an immediate tax deduction for contributions made to a qualified retirement plan for their employees. Although certain rules place limits on contributions, it is possible for some employers to offer more than one kind of plan.

Qualified retirement plans can be further differentiated into two categories: defined benefit plans and defined contribution plans. A **defined benefit plan**, or **pension plan**, provides a specific guaranteed benefit at retirement that is usually calculated using a **unit-benefit formula** typically based on a percentage of salary and years of service.

> *Example.* A benefit of 1.5 percent of final pay for each year of service up to twenty-five years is common. Using this formula, someone who has worked at a firm for

twenty years will be eligible to receive 30 percent of final pay as a yearly benefit in retirement for the remainder of the retiree's life.

A **defined contribution** plan provides an individual account for each participant and offers benefits to employees based on the value of that account upon retirement. The most common form of employer-provided retirement plan in the United States is a defined contribution plan.

The most common type of defined contribution plan today is a 401(k) plan. A **401(k) plan** offers employees the opportunity to contribute pre-tax dollars to their accounts. Many plans provide some form of matching contribution by the employer. A 401(k) plan can also include a **Roth 401(k)** feature, which allows the contribution of after-tax dollars. Two specialized types of 401(k) plan designs are available: the **SIMPLE 401(k) plan** and the **safe harbor 401(k) plan**.

Defined contribution plans include all profit-sharing plans, as well as stock bonus plans and employee stock ownership plans (ESOP). Money purchase plans and target benefit plans are also included. Certain types of retirement plans are not technically qualified plans, yet each operates in a similar manner and provides tax-deferred earnings growth. Examples include simplified employee pension accounts (SEP accounts) and Keogh plan accounts for small businesses, 403(b) tax-sheltered annuities for nonprofit employers, and 457 plans for state, local, and municipal government employers. Figure 12.7 provides summary data for each of these defined contribution plans.

Figure 12.7. A Comparison of the Funding Characteristics of Defined Contribution Plans for 2020

Plan Type	Maximum Contribution per Participant (Elective Deferral)	Maximum Annual Addition[1] per Participant (based on Max. Compensation of $285,000)[2]	Mandatory Yearly Employer Contributions?	CODA/ 401(k) Permitted?	Forfeitures Generally Required to Be Distributed?	In-Service Withdrawals Allowed?	Immediate, Mandatory Vesting for Employer Contributions?
Large-employer-sponsored Plans							
Money purchase	After-tax allowed	The lesser of 100% of income or $57,000	Yes	No	Yes	No, but loans are allowed	No
Target benefit	Not allowed	The lesser of 100% of income or $57,000	Yes	No	Yes	No	No
Profit-sharing	Not allowed	The lesser of 100% of income or $57,000	No[3]	Yes	Yes	Yes	No
Stock bonus	$57,000	The lesser of 100% of income or $57,000	No[3]	Yes	Yes	Yes	No
ESOP	$57,000	The lesser of 100% of income or $57,000	No[3]	Yes	Yes	Yes	No

401(k)[4]	$19,500 + $6,500 age 50+ catch-up	The lesser of 100% of income or $57,000	No	NA	No	Yes	No
Roth 401(k)	$19,500 + $6,500 age 50+ catch-up (after-tax)	The lesser of 100% of income or $57,000	No	NA	No	Yes; after five years of participation, or age 59½	No
Thrift and savings	Varies	The lesser of 100% of income or $57,000	Generally, yes	No	Yes	Yes	No
403(b)[4]	$19,500 + $6,500 age 50+ catch-up	The lesser of 100% of income or $57,000	No	No	No	Yes	Yes
457[4]	$19,500 + $6,500 age 50+ catch-up or 100% of compensation	$19,500 or 100% of compensation	Not allowed	No	NA	Yes; unforeseen emergency only	NA
Small-business-sponsored Plans							
SEP[5]	Not allowed	The lesser of 25% of net earnings or $57,000	No	No	NA	Yes; same as IRA	Yes
SARSEP/ 408(k)[6]	The lesser of 25% of compensation or $19,500	The lesser of 25% of net earnings or $57,000	No	No	NA	Yes; same as IRA	Yes
Keogh[5] money purchase	Employees may not contribute	Up to 25% of earned income	Yes	No	Yes	No	No
Keogh[5] profit-sharing	Employees may not contribute	Up to 25% of earned income	No[3]	No	Yes	Yes; after 5 years of participation, or age 59½	No
SIMPLE IRA	$13,500 + $3,000 age 50+ catch-up	See[7] below	Yes	No	NA	Yes; same as IRA	Yes
SIMPLE 401(k)[4, 8]	$13,500 + $3,000 age 50+ catch-up	$21,400 or $24,400 age 50+	Yes	Yes	NA	Yes; same as IRA	Yes

[1.] Annual additions are equal to the sum of employer contributions, employee contributions, both deductible and nondeductible, and unvested forfeitures. The maximum combined contribution to a defined contribution plan for a participant age 50 or higher in 2020 is $63,500, consisting of the sum of $57,000 plus a $6,500 "catch-up" contribution.

[2.] There is an additional limitation on the maximum amount of employer contribution that is tax-deductible to the employer.

[3.] No mandatory annual employer contributions required, but employers must make substantial and regular contributions.

[4.] A targeted, non-refundable tax credit for low- to moderate-income savers is available for 401(k), 403(b), 457(b), and IRA contributions.

[5.] SEP and KEOGH: the effective maximum contribution percentage considers net earnings instead of total compensation.

[6.] Salary Reduction (SAR) SEPs have not been eligible for new establishment since 1997.

[7.] For a SIMPLE IRA, employers must make either a dollar-for-dollar matching contribution up to 3 percent of an employee's compensation (can elect to lower the percentage to no less than 1 percent for no more than 2 out of 5 years ending in the current year), or 2 percent of compensation for all eligible employees earning at least $5,000 regardless of elected salary reductions.

[8.] The maximum total contribution to a SIMPLE 401(k) plan is $30,000 (salary deferral + 3 percent contribution of maximum salary of $285,000 + catch-up contributions). The maximum permitted contribution for a SIMPLE 401(k) plan is the maximum elective deferral plus the 3 percent matching contribution.

Planning Strategy 17: Use Non-Qualified Employer Provided Plans within the Funding Mix

Employers may find that non-discrimination rules and dollar limits placed on qualified plans restrict the usefulness of these retirement planning tools, especially as a means for providing benefits to executives and highly compensated employees. **Non-qualified plans** give employers more flexibility in offering benefits to those belonging to select groups, but non-qualified plans also generally offer fewer tax advantages.

An example of a non-qualified plan is a **non-qualified deferred compensation plan (NQDC)**, which is defined as an agreement between an employer and employee where the employee agrees to accept payments at some specified time in the future. Employees are sometimes allowed to contribute to an NQDC, in which case contributions are considered fully vested. However, employer contributions are not as secure compared to contributions to a similar qualified plan. In exchange for less security, an employee can be compensated with contributions far exceeding current limits on qualified plans.

Two non-qualified deferred compensation arrangements are commonly used by employers when benefit plans are negotiated with highly compensated employees: rabbi and secular trusts.

- A **rabbi trust** is an irrevocable arrangement between an employer and employee. (The name stems from the first trust assessed by the IRS in which a congregation established this type of arrangement for its rabbi.) Under this agreement, the trust is considered to be unfunded, meaning that the employee cannot access assets until all contractual obligations have been met (typically at retirement). Because the plan is unfunded, the employer cannot deduct contributions to the trust until distributions are made. The employee is not taxed until the employee receives a trust distribution (e.g., upon retirement, death, disability, or employment termination). Because of the non-qualified status of the plan, assets held in the trust must be subject to a "substantial risk of forfeiture" prior to distribution, such as loss due to incomplete vesting, termination for cause or voluntary resignation. In addition, assets may be subject to claims of the employer's creditors in case of bankruptcy.

- A **secular trust** provides employees additional security. Assets held in the trust are not subject to creditor claims against the employer. However, because the assets are more secure, all employer contributions to the plan are immediately income taxable to the employee.

Planning Strategy 18: Use Personal Savings within the Funding Mix

Nearly all Americans who hope to retire comfortably must rely on their own willingness and ability to save money on a regular basis. It is important for clients to generate a pool of assets, combined with those from qualified and non-qualified sources, that can be used to fund all or a portion of a retirement income needs.

A traditional or Roth IRA is typically one of the first personal retirement saving plans recommended outside of an employer-sponsored plan (assuming a client has earned income). IRAs provide an option to grow assets on a tax-deferred (traditional) or tax-free (Roth) distribution basis. Characteristics of traditional and Roth IRAs are summarized in Figure 12.8.

Figure 12.8. A Comparison of Traditional and Roth IRAs

Features	Traditional IRA	Roth IRA
Who may contribute?	Client may contribute if she/he (or spouse if filing jointly) has taxable compensation, regardless of age.	Client may contribute at any age if she/he (or spouse if filing jointly) has taxable compensation and modified adjusted gross income is below certain amounts: Single taxpayer for Roth IRA: $124,000 to $139,000. Married filing jointly taxpayer for Roth IRA: $196,000 to $206,000.
Are contributions deductible?	Client may be able to deduct contributions subject to the following phase-outs: Single taxpayer covered by workplace retirement plan: $65,000 to $75,000 Married filing jointly taxpayer covered by retirement plan: $104,000 to $124,000 Married filing jointly taxpayer who is not covered by retirement plan and is married to someone who is covered: $196,000 to $206,000.	Contributions are not deductible.
How much can be contributed?	The most a client may contribute to all traditional and Roth IRAs is the smaller of: • $6,000 (2020) or $7,000 if client is age 50 or older by the end of the year; or • the client's taxable compensation for the year.	
What is the deadline to make contributions?	Tax return filing deadline (including extensions).	
When can client withdraw money?	Client may withdraw contributions anytime.	
Does client need to take required minimum distributions?	Client must start taking distributions by age 72.	Not required if client is the original owner.

Are client withdrawals and distributions income taxable?	Any deductible contributions and earnings withdrawn or that are distributed from a traditional IRA are taxable. Also, if a client is under age 59 ½, the client may have to pay an additional 10 percent tax for early withdrawals unless she or he qualifies for an exception under IRC §72(t).	None if the withdrawal is a qualified distribution. Otherwise, part of the distribution or withdrawal may be taxable. If client is under age 59½, she or he may also have to pay an additional 10 percent tax for early withdrawals unless she or he qualifies for an exception.

Source: IRS (https://www.irs.gov/retirement-plans/traditional-and-roth-iras)

As illustrated in Figure 12.8, some features are common to both types of IRAs. First, almost any type of investment can be purchased, excluding life insurance and collectibles. Second, IRAs cannot be used as collateral for a loan. Third, under federal bankruptcy law, IRAs enjoy limited (up to $1 million) protection from creditors.

Beyond the taxation differences of traditional and Roth IRAs, there are four distinct types of IRAs typically used by clients. Each is determined by the funding source: contributory, rollover, inherited, and spousal.

- A **contributory IRA** is the most common, being funded with earned income. The other IRA types do not have an earned income requirement, whereas only the spousal IRA has an annual funding limit.

- **Rollover IRA** and **inherited IRA** accounts are distinctive for two reasons. First, the owner cannot contribute to these accounts after establishment, and second, these IRAs may not be commingled. This means that the owner cannot combine assets from one IRA with those of another, with one exception: if the rollover IRA is funded with assets that were originally contributed to another qualified retirement account (e.g. 401(k), 403(b), etc.) and distributed, typically as the result of a separation of service.

- An inherited IRA is an account originally funded by another person, with the original owner bequeathing the account to an heir. Multiple inherited IRAs from the same owner and of the same type (e.g., traditional or Roth), can be combined, or commingled, if all rules are followed.

Planning Strategy 19: Apply Inherited IRA Rules Correctly

It is important for financial planners to understand rules related to the inheritance of IRAs as a way to help clients avoid paying unnecessary taxes and penalties. The following points highlight important inherited IRA rules for non-spousal beneficiaries:[11]

1. When a **non-spouse beneficiary** inherits an IRA, they must either begin lifetime distributions by December 31st of the year after the year of the decedent's death or choose a five-year distribution alternative. The five-year distribution option is available only if the owner died before the required distribution beginning date for a traditional IRA. If the five-year distribution plan is chosen, the beneficiary can elect to revert to a lifetime distribution plan as long

as the first distribution is made by December 31st of the year following the decedent's death. Alternately, where the five-year distribution plan is chosen, the beneficiary can defer distributions until up to the fifth year following the year of the account owner's death, at which point 100 percent of the account balance must be withdrawn.

2. The 10 percent penalty for distributions prior to age 59½ does not apply to inherited IRAs; only taxes will be due upon distribution. The sixty-day rollover rule does not apply to inherited IRAs; however, any distribution is subject to tax.

3. Non-spouse beneficiaries cannot roll over inherited IRAs into an existing or new IRA, but beneficiaries are allowed to transfer funds to a new custodian or combine multiple inherited IRA accounts of the same type and from the same owner into one account. Care must be taken in titling the account according to IRS requirements, as follows:

   'IRA FBO Jane Smith as beneficiary of Dan Brown" or "IRA FBO Dan Brown (dec'd); Jane Smith (beneficiary).'

4. Non-spouse beneficiaries may not convert an inherited IRA into a Roth IRA or an inherited Roth IRA.

5. When calculating required minimum distributions (RMDs), inherited IRAs must remain separate from other IRAs owned by the beneficiary. For more information, see IRS Publication 590, *Individual Retirement Arrangements (IRAs)*. Non-spouse beneficiaries of Inherited IRAs are required to use Appendix B, Table I, Single Life Expectancy, to compute their first RMD following the death of the account owner. Subsequent annual distributions reduce the factor obtained for the first year's distribution by one.

Most rules are similar for a spouse who inherits an IRA, although a spouse can roll over an inherited IRA into an existing or new IRA of the same type. This tax provision allows for more discretion about RMDs from a traditional account. Figure 12.9 illustrates these general rules. However, extreme caution is warranted when working with a client inheriting spousal retirement assets or IRAs because the options are contingent on several different factors (e.g., age of spouse at death, age of surviving spouse, financial situation and the need for and timing of need for assets, potential estate tax situation of the surviving spouse), including the following:

- Transferring the inherited assets into an inherited IRA with rules fairly similar to that for a non-spousal inherited IRA, excepting the calculation method of RMDs in the second and subsequent year; or

- Rolling over the assets into an existing or new IRA with the RMD based on the age of the surviving spouse; or

- Rolling over or converting the assets into a new or existing Roth IRA; or

- **Disclaiming**, within nine months of the spouse's death, all or part of the inherited assets.

Finally, an important caveat is the reminder that clients complete necessary documentation to establish a beneficiary(ies) for an inherited IRA or a new spousal IRA funded with inherited assets. This is important to ensure that the client's wishes for bequeathing assets are satisfied and to protect the client's estate from potential additional estate taxation.

Figure 12.9. Decision Tree for Planning for an Inherited IRA

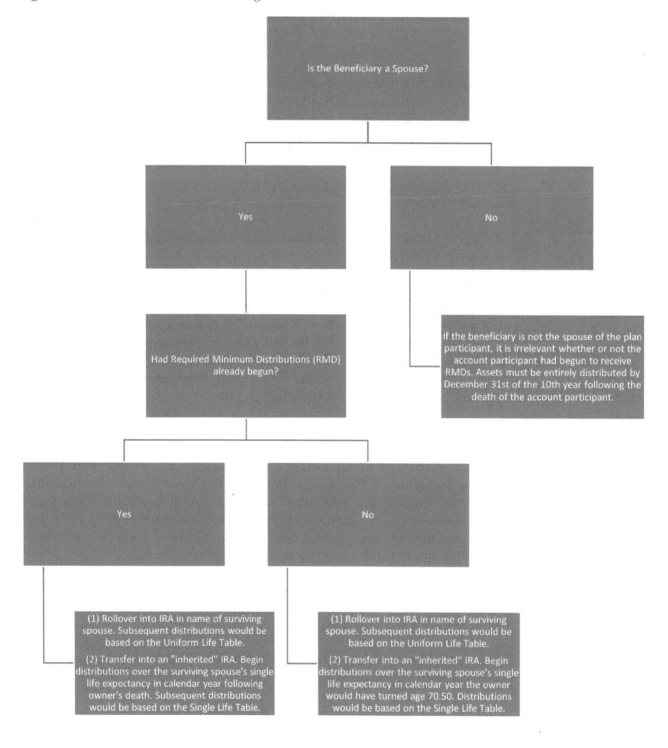

Planning Strategy 20: Apply IRA Transfer, Rollover, and Conversion Rules

The IRS currently allows assets to be transferred tax free from a qualified retirement plan or another IRA to an IRA. Three transfers are allowed.

- A **trustee-to-trustee transfer** occurs when one trustee directly moves a client's assets to another trustee. Because there is no distribution to the client, the transfer is tax free. According to the IRS, because this type of transfer is not a rollover, it is not affected by the one-year waiting period required between rollovers.

- The second transfer is called a **rollover**. An **IRA rollover** is a tax-free distribution of cash or other assets from a retirement plan made directly to a client. It is the client's responsibility to contribute assets to the IRA. Clients must generally roll over the entire contribution by the sixtieth day after receiving the distribution. There are two types of rollovers: indirect and direct. In the case of an **indirect rollover** the owner takes temporary (sixty days or fewer) ownership—called **constructive receipt**—of the funds. The original custodian sends the assets to the owner, who then sends the assets to a new custodian, thereby completing the rollover. The **direct rollover** method works the same as the transfer, where the owner never has constructive receipt of the funds. Generally, if a client makes a tax-free rollover of any part of a distribution from a traditional IRA, they cannot, within a one-year period, make a tax-free rollover of any later distribution from that same IRA. Clients are also prohibited from making a tax-free rollover of any amount distributed within the same one-year period from the IRA into which they made the tax-free rollover. The one-year period begins on the date that clients receive an IRA distribution, not the date they roll it into an IRA.

- The third transfer method is known as **transfers incident to divorce**. If assets in a traditional IRA are transferred from an ex-spouse to your client via a divorce or separate maintenance decree, the assets held in the IRA, starting from the date of the transfer, are treated as belonging to the client. The transfer is tax free.

Another method for moving funds—**conversion**—creates an income tax liability. Converting a traditional IRA to a Roth IRA is a strategy frequently used to gain the benefits of the Roth IRA. In its most basic form, a **Roth IRA conversion** occurs when a client converts assets held in a traditional IRA into a Roth IRA. Conversion triggers income tax in the year of the conversion on the value of the account (excluding any non-tax-deductible contributions that were previously taxed) on the day of the conversion. This allows the assets to continue to grow tax deferred with the option of making withdrawals on a tax-free basis. Because of the tax implications, and the potential to push some clients into a higher tax bracket, care must be taken when using this strategy. Prior to passage of the Tax Cuts and Jobs Act (2017), completed conversions were permitted to be reversed in a strategy known as "recharacterization." Some taxpayers found this to be desirable should the tax situation, the cash flow to pay the taxes, or the value of the converted assets declined significantly subsequent to conversion. This planning technique has now been legislated out of existence, effective January 1, 2018.

Beginning in 2010, income limits associated with Roth conversions were removed. This was the result of the Tax Increase Prevention and Reconciliation Act of 2005. The Act, however, did not eliminate the income restrictions associated with Roth contributions, thereby creating a significant tax loophole. High-income clients, who believe that their marginal tax rate will be higher in retirement, and those who wish to postpone RMDs are the most anxious to hold wealth in Roth IRAs. These clients are also the most likely to convert traditional IRA assets into Roth IRAs. This is where the loophole comes into play. High-earning households typically are excluded from contributing to a Roth IRA, but not to *non-deductible* traditional IRAs. Some financial planners recommend, therefore, that high-income clients contribute the maximum allowed to a *non-deductible* traditional IRA. Clients are then encouraged to convert assets in the *non-deductible, traditional*, IRA to a Roth IRA.

Planning Tip

If an eligible rollover distribution is paid directly to a client, the payer must withhold 20 percent for federal tax purposes. This rule applies even if the client plans to roll over the distribution to a traditional IRA. Clients must utilize assets from other personal sources to complete a 100 percent rollover (i.e., to "make-up" the 20 percent withheld for taxes) within the 60-day period and then seek a refund of the 20 percent withheld when filing their federal income tax return in the following year.

Although this strategy is being used, financial planners should be forewarned that the IRS requires IRA aggregating when calculating taxes due on conversions. If a client holds any pre-tax IRA assets, it is likely that this conversion strategy will trigger income taxation. Further, some have argued that the IRS could assert the **step transaction doctrine**, which states that a series of actions taken to complete a single comprehensive transaction will be taxed on the overall economic outcome of the transaction. That is, the IRS may conclude that clients who use this type of conversion strategy constructively made an improper Roth IRA contribution. As such, this loophole should be used with great caution.

Planning Strategy 21: Understand Social Security Eligibility for Divorced Clients

Increasingly, financial planners are called on to help clients prepare for retirement prior to, after, or during a divorce. It is important to understand how divorce can impact a client's eligibility for Social Security benefits. According to the Social Security Administration, if a client is divorced (even if the other person has since remarried), the client can qualify for benefits on the record of the ex-spouse. This is an important consideration for many women who were primarily homemakers, without an earnings record, prior to a divorce. To receive benefits, a client must:

- have been married to the ex-spouse for at least ten years;

- have been divorced at least two years;

- be at least sixty-two years old;

- be unmarried; and

- be ineligible for an equal or higher benefit on their own work or someone else's work.

These eligibility rules can place some clients in a financially awkward position. For example, if a client was married for less than ten years, they might not be eligible for benefits under an ex-spouse's record. The rules also prohibit a client from remarrying and receiving benefits based on a previous spouse's record; however, clients sometimes marry first only to discover that their benefits have been lost. The primary disadvantage for younger divorced clients under current rules is that to receive benefits and/or to be considered insured for Medicare, the client may have to reenter the workplace to establish an income record.

Planning Strategy 22: Understand Qualified Plan Coverage Rules

When designing or evaluating a qualified retirement plan for an organization (e.g., a small business owner) it is important to understand the following coverage eligibility rules:

- Defined benefit plans must benefit the lesser of 40 percent of eligible employees or fifty eligible employees.

- Defined contribution plans must provide a benefit to 70 percent or more of:

    o non-highly compensated employees, or

    o the ratio of non-highly compensated employees to highly compensated employees, or

    o the average benefit ratio for non-highly compensated employees to highly compensated employees must be at least 70 percent, and

    o the plan must not be nondiscriminatory.

Any plan that fails these coverage rules is considered non-qualified for tax purposes, resulting in lost tax deductions for the organization and potential loss of tax deferral for employees.

Planning Strategy 23: Understand Who May Be Excluded from a Qualified Retirement Plan

Providing a qualified retirement plan can often be an expensive benefit for a client who owns a business with employees. By understanding who can be excluded from plan participation, it is possible to save plan expenses for a business owner client. Employers who offer a qualified retirement plan (excluding collectively bargained plans) must allow participation to an employee who has (1) one year of service (defined as 1,000 hours) or (2) three consecutive years of service with at least 500 hours of work completed. The employer may exclude employees who qualify under the second rule from nondiscrimination testing, other coverage rules, top-heavy rules. Limiting participation, while financially feasible, may not be the best business recommendation. Excluding certain employees from a qualified plan can result in reduced productivity, resulting in higher employee turnover. Furthermore, business owners must weigh the potentially negative effects of excluding employees (e.g., low morale) against the actual dollar amount saved in benefit costs.

Planning Strategy 24: Understand how State of Residence Can Impact a Client's Retirement Saving and Spending Options

An important factor determining the feasibility of a retirement capital needs analysis involves a client's place of residence. Each state taxes pension benefits—and in some cases even Social Security benefits—differently. Various sources, such as Kiplinger, AARP, and the National Conference of State Legislatures, provide a state-by-state comparison of taxes—income, sales, and real estate, for example—levied on retirees. By understanding the income tax status of Social Security and private, state, and federal pensions at the state level, a financial planner can provide a more accurate income projection.

For example, some states like Nebraska, Rhode Island, North Dakota, Utah, and Vermont offer no income tax exemptions for Social Security or pension benefits.[12] Other states, such as Georgia, exempt Social Security benefits and up to $35,000 of retirement income from state taxation. Kentucky also exempts Social Security benefits from state income taxes plus more than $41,000 per person in retirement income, including public and private pensions and annuities.[13] It is important to remember that for some clients, it may be impossible to relocate to a state that provides a more competitive tax environment. There might also be situations when a client would rather pay higher taxes than move. Under such circumstances, tax information should be used to help clients plan for avoiding or paying taxes rather than as a comparison of tax havens.

Planning Strategy 25: Understand the Role Played by the Pension Benefit Guaranty Corporation in Retirement Planning

The **Pension Benefit Guaranty Corporation (PBGC)** was created when President Ford signed the **Employee Retirement Income Security Act (ERISA)** into law in 1974. The primary role of the PBGC is to protect participants in qualified defined benefit plans from losing benefits when a plan is terminated because of underfunding. PBGC is a government corporation that serves the role of insuring pension plan account balances. PBGC insurance covers only a fraction of the benefit level of a terminated pension plan. PBGC benefits are based on an employee's age, the previous promised defined benefit plan payout, and the amount of plan benefits that remain after plan termination. PBGC insurance is funded by premiums collected from pension plan sponsors (based on a premium per participant), earnings from assets held by PBGC, and recoveries from the sponsors of terminated defined benefit plans.

Planning Strategy 26: Determine Which Assets to Tap First for Retirement Income Needs

Upon retirement, retirees face an important question regarding the distribution of income from accumulated savings. Financial planners typically recommend that clients withdraw funds from taxable accounts before taking distributions from qualified retirement plans (e.g., a 401(k), 403(b), 457 plan). This approach maximizes the tax deferral of the other accounts.[14] Assets held in tax-free accounts (e.g., a Roth IRA) are generally distributed last. Two exceptions to this general rule exist:

- First, clients who will not take meaningful distributions prior to death may want to withdraw from tax-deferred accounts first to obtain the maximum step-up in basis on other assets at the time of death.

- Second, whenever the after-tax return on taxable accounts exceeds the return on qualified tax-deferred account assets, distributions from the tax-deferred accounts should occur first.[15] The one caveat to this point is the risk aspect because higher returns normally mean higher risk.

Planning Strategy 27: Understand Retirement Plan Alternatives Available to Clients Who Separate Service

Clients who have assets held in employer-sponsored qualified retirement plans often encounter complex distribution rules upon separation of service. Employers often require employees who separate from service to take a distribution. Distributions from qualified plans (401(k), 403(b), 457 plan, etc.) can generally be made in a couple of ways. Accumulated assets can, depending on plan policy, be left in the plan itself, which may allow the client to take distributions as needed—on a regular periodic or irregular basis, or the employer may require the former employee to take a lump sum distribution of all plan assets.

A client who takes a **lump sum distribution** from a qualified defined contribution plan must be given the opportunity to roll over the proceeds of the distribution into an IRA or other eligible qualified plan. Once the plan assets have been rolled over to an IRA, the client has the same distribution options as the law applies to any other IRA account. The following discussion examines two forms of distribution and associated income tax considerations:

1. Non-annuitized payments (e.g., lump sum "one-time" distributions, discretionary installment payments, irregular distributions)

2. Annuitized payments

Nearly all qualified retirement plans offer lump sum distributions. Clients who take a lump sum distribution will trigger a 20 percent federal income tax withholding requirement. The IRS requires plan sponsors who issue lump sum payments to withhold taxes as a way to ensure that the recipient can pay any tax liability. The benefit of a lump sum payment is that the total account value (minus tax withholdings) is available to make a subsequent investment or purchase. The drawback is that a client will lose tax-deferred compounding of the earnings. This disadvantage is another reason why financial planners often suggest that a client roll over an account balance into an IRA or other qualified retirement plan. Rollovers allow retirement assets to be managed in a way that preserves the tax-deferral of the retirement account proceeds.

Additionally, a plan participant can opt, if available, to receive discretionary periodic withdrawals, which can be received on a planned or an ad hoc basis. This is the most common method for handling distributions because the strategy maintains the greatest flexibility and can be matched most closely to the deterministic withdrawal streams estimated in a retirement capital needs analysis.

If an annuity or other periodic taxable distribution option is taken, all or a portion of the payments received will most likely be taxable. If the annuity is imbedded in an IRA, the entire payment will be taxable as ordinary income, but if the annuity is held outside an IRA, any return of principal will avoid taxation. In other words, the extent to which distributions are taxed is based on the adjusted taxable basis of plan assets. In a case where all contributions to a plan are made with "pretax" dollars, meaning that the IRS has not collected tax revenue on the money invested, as is the case with most employer-sponsored retirement plans, all distributions from the plan will be fully taxable. At the other extreme are Roth accounts, either IRA or 401(k)/403(b). Assets held in these accounts are based on money contributed to the plan that is taxed prior to deposit. Thus, distributions from such a plan will be exempt from federal taxation in most cases.

Planning Strategy 28: Understand How Annuity Payouts are Taxed

Retirement distribution planning becomes more difficult when some client assets have been contributed on a pre-tax basis, while other assets have been saved on an after-tax basis, or when there is some other reason why the adjusted tax basis of one or more assets is not zero. In these situations, annuity distributions from a traditional IRA (or any tax-qualified annuity) are taxed using an **inclusion ratio** (or the inverse **exclusion ratio**). The taxable portion of a periodic distribution can generally be estimated using the following formula.

$$\text{Inclusion Ratio} = \frac{(\text{Annual Dist.} \times \text{Expected Dist. Time}) - \text{Aftertax Cont.}}{\text{Annual Dist.} \times \text{Expected Dist. Time}}$$

Example: Assume a client retires and receives a $2,000 monthly annuity payout. Also assume the client's life expectancy is twenty years. If the client contributed $150,000 to the annuity, 68.75 percent of each distribution will be subject to income taxes, based on the formula.

$$\text{Inclusion Ratio} = \frac{(\$2,000 \times 240) - \$150,000}{(\$2,000 \times 240)} = 68.75\%$$

Planning Strategy 29: Estimate Required Minimum Distributions Correctly

A **required minimum distribution** (RMD), also referred to by some sources as minimum required distributions, or MRDs, is a mandatory distribution from a qualified retirement plan, traditional IRA, or other similar plan. An RMD generally must begin by April 1st of the year following the year in which a client turns age seventy-two if born on or after July 1, 1949. Individuals born prior to July 1, 1949 must begin distributions by April 1 of the year following the year in which a client turns age 70½. (Different rules may apply to pre-1987 contributions to 403(b) plans.) Certain retirement plans might permit employees (other than 5 percent owners) to wait until April 1 of the year following retirement, if not later, to take distributions from their employer's qualified plan. This delayed option is not available for IRAs. A penalty of 50 percent applies to the extent that RMDs are not made. Generally, RMDs are computed by dividing the account balance at the end of the preceding year by the client's life expectancy factor, based on one of three tables: (a) the Uniform Lifetime Table (Table III), (b) the Single Life Expectancy Table (Table I) (for use by certain eligible beneficiaries), or (c) the Joint and Last Survivor Life Expectancy Table (Table II) (for use by clients whose spouses are more than ten years younger and are the sole beneficiaries of the client's IRA(s)). The appropriate table to use depends on the type of account, beneficiaries, and ages of the account owner and beneficiary, although lifetime distributions are generally based on the Uniform Lifetime Table factors shown in Figure 12.10. The above notwithstanding, any beneficiary who is not an "eligible beneficiary" as defined in the Internal Revenue Code must withdraw 100 percent of the account by December 31st of the 10th year following the year of death of the account owner.

Planning Tip

Learn more about required minimum distributions by visiting the IRS website: www.irs.gov/Retirement-Plans/Required-Minimum-Distributions-for-IRA-Beneficiaries.

Figure 12.10. Uniform Lifetime Table Factors

Uniform Lifetime Table				
Age	Divisor		Age	Divisor
70	27.4		94	9.1
71	26.5		95	8.6
72	25.6		96	8.1
73	24.7		97	7.6
74	23.8		98	7.1
75	22.9		99	6.7
76	22.0		100	6.3
77	21.2		101	5.9
78	20.3		102	5.5
79	19.5		103	5.2
80	18.7		104	4.9
81	17.9		105	4.5
82	17.1		106	4.2
83	16.3		107	3.9
84	15.5		108	3.7
85	14.8		109	3.4
86	14.1		110	3.1
87	13.4		111	2.9
88	12.7		112	2.6
89	12.0		113	2.4
90	11.4		114	2.1
91	10.8		115 +	1.9
92	10.2			
93	9.6			

Source: IRS. *Individual Retirement Arrangements (IRAs)*, Publication 590, p. 102.[16]

Note: These factors are scheduled to change for distributions beginning January 1, 2021.

The Uniform Lifetime Table can be used by all IRA owners (i.e., unmarried owners; owners whose spouses are fewer than ten years younger; owners for whom the spouse is not the sole beneficiary), except under the following circumstances:

- IRA owners for whom the sole beneficiary of the account is a spouse who is more than ten years younger than the owner. In this situation, the Joint Life Expectancy Table (Publication 590, Appendix B, Table II) must be used. The **younger spouse exception** provides a longer payout for IRA owners whose sole beneficiary is a spouse who is younger by more than ten years and the only beneficiary of an account. These owners can calculate their lifetime RMD based on the ages of both owner and spouse, using a Joint and Last Survivor

Life Expectancy Table. This effectively reduces the amount of the required distribution, thereby preserving the tax-deferred status of the account balance.[17]

- Inherited IRA owners (non-spousal or spousal if titled as an inherited IRA). In this situation, the Single Life Expectancy Table should be used.

Example: Assume an individual turned age eighty two this year and had a traditional IRA valued at $100,000 at the end of the previous year. A financial planner would simply divide $100,000 by 17.1 to determine the current year RMD of $5,848.

Planning Strategy 30: Calculate Early Distribution Penalties Correctly

Nearly all distributions from qualified plans before age 59½ are subject to federal and state income taxation, as well as a 10 percent early distribution penalty.[18] The following exceptions from the **early distribution penalty** are available for certain distributions:

- Distributions made at the death of the owner/participant;

- Distributions attributable to the disability of the owner/participant;

- Certain distributions made in the form of substantially equal periodic payments over the life of the person (or lives of the person and a beneficiary);

- Distributions to the extent of medical expenses that exceed 7.5 percent of a person's adjusted gross income;

- Distributions made to someone age fifty five or older who has separated from service (this exception does not apply to IRAs);

- Certain distributions ordered by a court, such as a qualified domestic relations order (QDRO) (not applicable to IRAs);

- Distributions to the extent of health insurance premiums paid during unemployment (IRAs only, not applicable to qualified plans);

- Distributions to the extent of certain college costs (not applicable to qualified plans); and

- Certain distributions for the first-time purchase of a home, up to $10,000 (not applicable to qualified plans).

Planning Strategy 31: Understand How the Bi-Partisan Budget Act of 2015 Changed Social Security Claiming Strategies

The 2016 U.S. budget led to significant changes in Social Security rules related to restricted application and voluntary suspension claiming strategies. **Restricted application** refers to a strategy that allowed someone who was eligible for either their own or one-half of their spouse's Social Security benefit to claim the spousal benefit, allow their own benefit to grow at 8 percent per year, and at age seventy switch to their own benefit, which would be higher at that time. While there are a few exceptions, restricted application no longer exists. Once a client chooses either their own or a spousal benefit, the client is locked into the choice.

One exception exists for those who are not eligible for a spouse benefit because their spouse has not yet filed for Social Security. Assuming a client claims their own benefit, when the client's spouse does claim benefits, and if one-half of the spouse's benefit is larger than the current benefit, an election to change may be made.

Strategies related to **voluntary suspension** have also been eliminated. Voluntary suspension occurred when a married client, age sixty two or older, filed for Social Security benefits so that their spouse could claim a spousal benefit. Once established, the client suspended their benefit. This allowed the higher benefit to grow at 8 percent per year until age seventy, when the client would refile for benefits. Today, once a benefit is suspended, Social Security benefits stop for both spouses. Additionally, the law now disallows requests for retroactive lump sum distributions of benefits between the time of the request and the date of suspension. Taken together, these changes will require additional creative thinking for financial planners working with clients nearing retirement.

Planning Strategy 32: Understand How 2019 SECURE Act Impacts Retirement Planning

In 2019, Congress made sweeping changes to the tax code. Many of these changes have a direct impact on retirement plans, IRAs, and general retirement planning. The following discussion highlights some of the most important changes that will likely impact financial planning recommendations in the future:

- Beginning in 2020, the age to begin required minimum distributions from qualified retirement plans and IRAs changes from $70^{1}/_{2}$ to age 72.

- Beginning in 2024, 401(k) plans must allow any employee who has worked 500 or more hours for three consecutive years to contribute to the employer's 401(k) plan; in these cases, the employer will not be required to make matching contributions.

- Parents who have a child or adopt a child may withdraw up to $5,000 from a retirement account within one year of birth or adoption without paying a distribution penalty (regular income tax is still required).

- If someone is investing in an annuity within a 401(k) plan, and the employer stops offering the annuity, the person may transfer the annuity to an IRA without penalty or taxation; the person may also continue to contribute up to current year IRA limits into the annuity even if otherwise prohibited.

- Individuals who inherit an IRA must withdraw the assets held in the IRA within ten years rather than being based on their own life expectancy. The law does not require annual distributions; it is possible to postpone distributions and take one lump-sum distribution at the end of the ninth year. There are four exceptions to the rule:

  ○ Heirs of IRAs who received an inheritance prior to 2020;

- o Surviving spouses (the surviving spouse may use her or his life expectancy);

- o Disabled or chronically ill heirs; and

- o Minor children up to the age of majority or age twenty-six if the child is still enrolled in college (after which point the IRA must be depleted within ten years).

Quantitative/Analytical Mini-Case Problems

Marybeth and Anneal Yao

1. Marybeth and Anneal Yao are beginning to contemplate retirement. They are each forty-five years of age and have saved a total of $500,000 for retirement. Marybeth and Anneal realize that they have not saved sufficiently to be able to retire early, fully retire without some part-time employment, or replace 100 percent of current pre-retirement income. As such, they are willing to explore different approaches to reach retirement.

    Marybeth and Anneal have a combined annual income of $125,000. They believe their salaries will keep pace with inflation at 4 percent per year. They are also comfortable assuming that the effective annual rate of return on their retirement assets will be 9.0 percent before retirement and 6.5 percent after retirement. For now, Marybeth wants to keep the planning simple, projecting that they will both die in exactly forty years and that their retirement assets will be depleted with the exception of $100,000 to cover funeral and burial costs. Lastly, they do not want to continue saving after they retire (either partly or fully).

    As their financial planner, provide some assistance in calculating the amount of retirement assets needed on the first day of retirement, based on the two options listed below. Considering the information presented in the case, which outcome requires the lowest monthly (end-of-month) contribution if they also require that their retirement annuity grow by 4.0 percent per year to keep pace with inflation? (Ignore the effects of income taxes and Social Security on the answer.)

    a. To retire at age fifty-five with an income replacement ratio of 60 percent.

    b. To retire at age fifty-five with an income replacement ratio of 100 percent but work part-time for an additional ten years to offset half the projected annual need for those ten years. (In other words, Marybeth and Anneal will have a 50 percent replacement ratio for ten years and a 100 percent replacement ratio thereafter.)

    c. To retire at age sixty-five with an income replacement ratio of 100 percent.

Tara Woodyard

2. Tara Woodyard, age forty-four, plans to retire at age sixty-seven. Her life expectancy, accounting for family medical history, is age ninety-seven. Tara is single and currently earns $56,000 per year as a university librarian. At her normal retirement age, she expects to receive $28,700 in Social Security benefits (today's dollars). She will also receive a small defined benefit pension in the amount of $13,500 from a local municipality. She has come to you to determine whether she is on

track to meet her retirement goal. Use the following assumptions and information to answer the questions that follow:

- She would like to use a 90 percent income replacement ratio, based on current earnings.

- She is currently contributing $2,400 per year into a 403(b) plan [no employer match].

- Inflation is assumed to be 3.50 percent.

- She can earn a 6.50 percent after-tax rate of return on assets before retirement.

- She can earn a 4.50 percent after-tax rate of return on assets after retirement.

  a. How much does Tara need, on her first day of retirement, to fund a capital depletion model of retirement?

  b. Given her current level of savings, is Tara on target to reach her retirement goal?

  c. If she has a capital needs shortfall, how much more must she save per year to reach her goal?

  d. If she would like to obtain a capital preservation goal for retirement, how much will she need to have saved on her first day of retirement?

  e. Given a capital preservation goal, is she saving enough on a yearly basis currently?

  f. How much, in total, must she save yearly to reach a capital preservation model of retirement?

Annette Robinson

3. Annette Robinson is a sixty-three-year-old recent widow. Annette is attempting to do some tax and investment planning pertaining to her late husband's traditional IRA account. She is seeking your advice as to the best course of action. She has informed you that her husband was sixty-nine at the time of his death and had not started taking a RMD.

  a. What are the three distribution methods available to Annette?

  b. Which method should she choose to maximize tax deferral? Based on the appropriate life expectancy table, how much will her first required distribution be? When will this distribution happen?

  c. Which method should she choose to maximize the distribution? Based on the appropriate life expectancy table, how much will her first required distribution be? When would this distribution happen?

  d. Which alternative would not have been available had her husband begun his required distributions?

  e. If Annette had been younger than age fifty-nine, which alternative would have allowed her to take distributions without incurring a tax penalty?

Lyle and Melissa Murray

4. Lyle and Melissa Murray plan to retire when Lyle turns age sixty-five, even though his normal retirement age is age sixty-seven. Lyle has worked at the same firm for over thirty years. Melissa has worked only occasional temporary jobs over her lifetime. The Murrays have a few questions about Lyle's defined benefit pension benefit and expected Social Security benefits. Use the following information to answer their questions:

    *   Lyle must choose from the following four defined benefit plan distribution options:

        o $3,000 for life with no survivor benefit

        o $2,700 for life with a 50 percent survivor benefit

        o $2,350 for life with a 67 percent survivor benefit

        o $2,000 for life with a 100 percent survivor benefit

    a. Assuming (a) Lyle lives ten years after retiring, (b) Melissa lives an additional ten years beyond Lyle's passing, and (c) the pension has no cost of living adjustment, which of the four alternatives should they choose in order to maximize their combined lifetime benefit?

    b. What benefit alternative should they choose if Lyle lives another twenty years beyond retirement and Melissa lives an additional ten years beyond that?

    c. If Lyle's Social Security retirement benefit at age sixty-seven is $2,300 per month, how much will they receive in yearly benefits if they both claim benefits when Lyle turns age sixty-five?

Juwan and Timi Clarke

5. Juwan and Timi Clarke are planning for retirement. Juwan has a number of retirement related questions he needs help answering. Use your retirement planning knowledge to address the following questions.

    a. Juwan would like to withdraw $365,000 from retirement savings when he retires. Assuming he can earn a 6.0 percent annualized rate of return on retirement assets, and that inflation will average 2.0 percent during retirement, how much will he need on his first day of retirement to fund twenty-four yearly payments?

    b. What will be the inflation-adjusted rate of return (serial rate) if Juwan changes the rate of return and inflation assumptions to be 12.0 percent and 3.0 percent, respectively?

    c. Timi will turn age fifty seven this year. She currently contributes to a 401(k) plan and wants to make an IRA contribution. Is she eligible to use the catch-up provision?

    d. Juwan is eligible for a modest defined benefit pension when he retires at age sixty-seven. If Juwan elects a 100 percent joint and survivor annuity will he and Timi receive more or less than a 50 percent joint and survivor annuity? If Juwan elects an annuity payment without a survivor benefit, will he receive more or less than a 50 percent joint and survivor annuity? What must occur to obtain a no survivor annuity?

e. Juwan's employer uses the following unit benefit formula to determine benefits in the defined benefit plan: 2 percent of final pay for each year of service. If Juwan works for twenty years and has a final year income of $160,000 how much will he receive from the pension on a yearly basis?

f. If Timi is age fifty-five and earns $46,000 per year, what is the maximum in annual additions that can be contributed to her qualified 401(k) account this year?

Jamal and Chyna Gwynn

6. Your clients, Jamal and Chyna Gwynn, would like you to determine if they are on track to meet their retirement goal. Use the following assumptions to answer the Gwynns' retirement planning questions:

- Jamal: Age forty eight

- Chyna: Age fifty

- Desired Retirement Age: When Jamal turns Age sixty two

- Age to Begin Receiving Social Security Benefits: Age sixty two

- Full Retirement Age: Age sixty seven

- Earned Income: Jamal $145,000

- Earned Income: Chyna $210,000

- Bonus: Jamal $25,000

- Retirement Income Replacement Ratio: 90 Percent

- Investment Rate of Return Before Retirement: 7.90 Percent

- Investment Rate of Return After Retirement: 5.50 Percent

- Inflation Rate Assumption (Presently and Going Forward): 3.00 Percent

- Growth Rate of Retirement Savings and Social Security Benefits: 3.00 Percent

- Marginal Federal and State Marginal Tax Rate Before Retirement: 29 Percent

- Marginal Federal and State Marginal Tax Rate After Retirement: 29 Percent

- Annual Social Security Benefit at Full Retirement: Jamal $42,000

- Annual Social Security Benefit at Full Retirement: Chyna $39,000

- Other Income in Retirement: $80,000

- Combined Retirement Assets Held in Tax-Deferred Assets: $1,500,000

- Combined Retirement Savings Using Tax-Deferred Accounts: $42,000

- Other Retirement Assets: $0

    a. What is the retirement asset value needed on the first day of retirement, plus any additional annual savings needed per year, to fully meet a capital depletion retirement goal?

    b. What is the value of assets needed to fund the capital preservation model of retirement? Can the Gwynns' currently meet this need?

Chapter Resources

Baldwin, B., *The New Retirement Investment Advisor* (New York: McGraw Hill, 2002).

Belth, J. M., *Retirement: A Consumer's Handbook*, 2nd ed. (Bloomington, IN: Indiana University Press, 1985).

General retirement and tax source: *Tax Facts on Retirement & Employee Benefits* (Cincinnati, OH: National Underwriter Company, published annually).

Leimberg, S. R.; Buck, K.; and Doyle, R.J. *The Tools & Techniques of Retirement Planning*, 6th ed. (Cincinnati, OH: National Underwriter Company, 2015).

Life and Health Insurance Foundation for Education, general retirement information (www.naifa. org/consumer/life.cfm).

Endnotes

1. In practical terms, this extra amount is segregated from a client's other retirement assets and left to grow at the post-retirement rate of return. At the end of the client's retirement period, the original dollar amount should be worth approximately $1,492,564. Any yearly tax liability is assumed to be paid from regular cash flows.

2. For ages 0 to 55 and 112 to 119, see Social Security Actuarial Life Table, 2015 Period Life Table. https://www.ssa.gov/oact/STATS/table4c6.html.

3. See Figure 12.10. Source: IRS Publication 590, Appendix B, Table III, Uniform Lifetime Table

4. Fidelity Research Institute. (2007, March). "The Fidelity Research Institute Index." Research Insights Brief. Summary report available at: nsresearch.com/media/Mar.12.07_Retirement.pdf.

5. Social Security Administration. *Social Security Benefit Amounts*. Available at: www.ssa.gov/OACT/COLA/Benefits.html.

6. A complete calculation example can be found at: www.ssa.gov/oact/ProgData/retirebenefit1.html.

7. Social Security benefits are always rounded down to the next lower dollar. For more information, see www.ssa.gov/oact/ProgData/retirebenefit2.html.

8. Available online at: www.socialsecurity.gov/OACT/quickcalc/index.html.

9. Lemons, D., "When to start collecting Social Security Benefits: A Break-even Analysis," Journal of Financial Planning 25, no. 1 (2012): 52–60.

10. Social Security Administration (https://www.ssa.gov/pubs/EN-05-10003.pdf).

11. Caudill, A., "Inherited IRA myths." *Journal of Financial Services Professionals,* 65 no. 5 (2011): 38–41.

12. National Conference of State Legislatures, *State Personal Income Taxes on Pensions & Retirement Income: Tax Year 2010.* Available at: www.ncsl.org/documents/fiscal/TaxonPensions2011.pdf , pp. 9, 10, and 11.

13. Kiplinger's, *Retiree Tax Heavens (and Hells).* Available at: www.kiplinger.com/tools/retiree_map/.

14. W. Reichenstein, "Tax-efficient sequencing of accounts to tap in retirement." Trends and Issues, TIAA-CREF Institute, (2006, October). Available at: www.tiaa-crefinstitute.org/ucm/groups/content/@ap_ucm_p_tcp_docs/documents/document/tiaa02029501.pdf.

15. J. J. Spitzer and S. Singh, "Extending Retirement Payouts by Optimizing the Sequence of Withdrawals," *Journal of Financial Planning,* 19 *no.* 4 (2006): 52–61.

16. Full table available at: Available at: www.irs.gov/pub/irs-pdf/p590.pdf.

17. See IRS Publication 590 at: www.irs.gov/publications/p590/ar02.html.

18. See Internal Revenue Code §72(t).

Chapter 13

Estate Planning

Learning Objectives

- Learning Objective 1: Describe the importance of estate planning within a comprehensive financial planning plan.

- Learning Objective 2: Explain the three purposes of estate planning.

- Learning Objective 3: Identify influential client characteristics and questions that help determine a client's estate planning needs.

- Learning Objective 4: Estimate a client's potential gift and estate tax liability.

- Learning Objective 5: Identify estate planning strategies that can be used to help a client reach their estate planning goals.

CFP® Principal Knowledge Topics

- CFP Topic: H.63. Characteristics and Consequences of Property Titling
- CFP Topic: H.64. Strategies to Transfer Property
- CFP Topic: H.65. Estate Planning Documents
- CFP Topic: H.66. Gift and Estate Tax Compliance and Tax Calculation
- CFP Topic: H.67. Sources of Estate Liquidity
- CFP Topic: H.68. Types, Features, and Taxation of Trusts
- CFP Topic: H.69. Marital Deduction
- CFP Topic: H.70. Intra-Family and Other Business Transfer Techniques
- CFP Topic: H.71. Postmortem Estate Planning Techniques
- CFP Topic: H.72. Estate Planning for Non-Traditional Relationships

Chapter Equations

There are no equations in this chapter.

ESTATE PLANNING STRATEGIES

Estate planning is the process of determining:[1]

- how and by whom a client's assets will be managed for the client's benefit during their life in event the client becomes incapacitated;

- when and under what circumstances it makes sense to distribute a client's assets during the client's lifetime;

- how and to whom a client's assets will be distributed after death; and

- how and by whom a client's personal care will be managed and how health care decisions will be made during a client's lifetime if the client becomes unable to care for himself or herself.

Imbedded within this definition is the notion that a financial planner will take steps to review a client's estate planning wishes, concerns, and current estate planning documents to ensure that the estate planning process is completed thoroughly. Before reviewing specific strategies, it is worth remembering that while it is appropriate for a financial planner to make estate planning recommendations, unless a financial planner is a licensed attorney, a financial planner may not draft legal documents. Instead, financial planners typically use referral networks to facilitate implementation of estate planning recommendations within a comprehensive financial plan. The following estate planning strategies represent some of the most common tools and techniques used by financial planners during an estate planning analysis.

Planning Strategy 1: Estimate a Client's Estate Tax Situation Using a Consistent Methodology

Estate planning tends to be focused on two aspects of a client's situation. The first is a review of estate planning documents and procedures. The second is a review of the future potential tax liability facing a client due to death and/or previously made gifts. Estimating gift and estate taxes can become quite complicated. This is one reason it is important to utilize a consistent methodology when making asset value and tax calculations. In this regard, the following four-step process can be used to describe and calculate a client's gift and estate tax situation.

1. Estimate the value of the client's gross estate.

2. Calculate the taxable estate by subtracting from the gross estate funeral and administrative expenses, debts, taxes, charitable donations, and any marital transfers.

3. Add the value of taxable lifetime gifts back into the taxable estate figure. This results in what is known as the adjusted taxable estate.

4. Determine the tax payable. To arrive at this figure, any remaining exclusion amount is subtracted from the adjusted taxable estate. What remains is subject to taxation. Alternatively, the tax can be calculated first with the applicable credit amount then subtracted to determine the remaining liability.

The Estate Tax Calculation

It is worth remembering that although a client's values, social position, or culture are influential factors in determining and quantifying planning needs across all core financial planning content areas, these types of personal characteristics are particularly relevant in estate planning. Sensitivity to a client's family, cultural, and religious beliefs and attitudes is an important financial planner skill. Estate planning needs can run the gamut from providing care to a family member or even a pet to determining the optimal donation to a charity. The primary estate planning calculation centers on estimating a client's potential federal estate tax liability. The calculation hinges on the value of a client's **taxable estate** (i.e., the taxable value of assets owned by a decedent at their death) relative to the federal estate tax threshold—a figure currently over $11 million per person (over $22 million for a married couple).

The **estate tax** is a levy on a client's right to transfer property at death. The tax is based on the value of a client's taxable estate at the time of death. A client's taxable estate is the gross estate less allowable deductions.

The gross estate includes the fair market value of all property that a client owned or had an interest in at the time of death, or in some cases within three years of death. IRS Form 706 is used to account for these assets. The **fair market value of assets** at a client's death (or as of an alternative valuation date) is used to determine the gross estate. Assets included in the gross estate consist of cash and securities, real estate, revocable trusts, business interests, as well as:

- life insurance proceeds payable to the estate or, if the client held incidents of ownership in the policy, to the client's heirs;

- the value of certain annuities payable to the estate or heirs;

- the value of certain property transferred within three years before death; and

- trusts or other interests established by the client or others in which the client had certain interests or powers.

A client's **taxable estate** is determined by subtracting certain deductions from the gross estate. Allowable deductions include outstanding mortgages and other debts, as well as the following deductions:

- expenses associated with estate administration, including funeral expenses paid out of the estate, debts owed at the time of death, taxes, and certain estate losses;

- marital deductions, including all property passing to a surviving spouse;

- charitable deductions; and

- a state death tax deduction, if any.

It is important to deduct only the portion of a liability attributable to the client. Specifically, only the part of a client's debt attributable to a listed asset is deductible.

For example, married couples holding a principal residence as **joint tenants with right of survivorship (JTWROS)** can list only half of the fair market value of the property as an asset. As such, the deceased client can deduct only one-half of the outstanding mortgage balance.

A **marital deduction** is available for the value of all property that passes from one spouse to another. Under current law, the marital deduction is unlimited, meaning that one spouse can leave all their assets to a spouse free of estate and gift taxes. A **charitable deduction** is available for the value of the property that passes to a charity or qualified non-profit organization.

After the net amount is computed, **adjusted taxable gifts** or the value of lifetime taxable gifts made after 1976 are added to this figure, resulting in the taxable estate. The tax is then computed on the new balance or taxable estate. Tax is also calculated on the adjusted taxable gifts and subtracted from the tax on the taxable estate. The tax is then reduced by the available **applicable credit amount** and other available credits, such as the credit for prior taxes paid or a foreign death tax credit. A **credit**, in this case, is similar to an income tax credit (i.e., a dollar amount that reduces or eliminates a tax).

Planning Tip

Keep up to date on estate tax rates, the marital deduction, the applicable credit amount, and other important data by visiting the IRS website yearly: www.irs.gov/Businesses/Small-Businesses-&-Self-Employed/Estate-Tax.

An additional tax, beyond the standard estate tax calculation, may be necessary for estate assets classified as **income in respect of a decedent (IRD)**. This tax is based on any income that the deceased client was entitled to receive prior to death but was not actually received until after death. Examples of IRD include salary earned but not paid until after a client's death, retirement account distributions, royalties, rents, dividends, interest, and other similar forms of income. IRD items must be included in a decedent's gross estate. The beneficiary of the income is then taxed at the beneficiary's marginal income tax rate. However, the beneficiary might be able to deduct a portion of any estate taxes generated by the inclusion of the IRD.

The gift and estate tax process can be formalized as shown in Figure 13.1 or as an Excel™ spreadsheet, as shown in Figure 13.2. (The spreadsheet is available in the Financial Planning Analysis Excel package included with this book.)

Figure 13.1. Estate Planning Calculation Process

STEP	CALCULATION	NOTES				
1.	Calculate Gross Estate	Calculation is based on the fair market value at date of death or alternate date value of the decedent's ownership interest.				
2.	Calculate the Taxable Estate	Subtract Funeral/Burial Expenses, Estate Administration and Legal Expenses, Outstanding Liabilities, Income Taxes, Executor Fees, Charitable Contributions, and other reductions, including the Qualified Marital Transfer, directly attributable to the decedent.				
3.	Add back Adjusted Taxable Gifts					
4.	Estimate Tax liability based on Estate and Gift Tax Rates	**For Taxable Estates Between ...**	**And ...**	**You'll Pay This Amount of Tax ...**	**Plus, You'll Pay This Percentage on the Amount in Excess of the Lower Limit**	
		$0	$9,999	$0	18%	
		$10,000	$19,999	$1,800	20%	
		$20,000	$39,999	$3,800	22%	
		$40,000	$59,999	$8,200	24%	
		$60,000	$79,999	$13,000	26%	
		$80,000	$99,999	$18,200	28%	
		$100,000	$149,999	$23,800	30%	
		$150,000	$249,999	$38,800	32%	
		$250,000	$499,999	$70,800	34%	
		$510,3010	$749,999	$155,800	37%	
		$750,000	$999,999	$248,300	39%	
		$1,000,000	----------	$345,800	40%	
5.	Subtract Tax on Adjusted Taxable Gifts					
6.	Equals Tentative Estate Tax					
7.	Subtract Credits	In 2020, the **applicable exclusion amount** was $11,580,000, which was equivalent to an **applicable credit amount** of $4,577,800.				
8.	Equals Estate Tax Liability					

Figure 13.2. Estate Planning Calculation Process Using an Excel™ Spreadsheet

ESTATE TAX PLANNING ANALYSIS	
Assumed Asset & Expense Growth Per Year	0%
Checking Account	
Savings Account	
Money Market Account	
Other Monetary Assets	
EE/I Bonds	
Mutual Funds	
Other Investment Assets	
Primary Residence	
Other Housing Assets	
Vehicles	
Personal Property	
Retirement Assets	
Other Assets	
Life Insurance	
GROSS ESTATE	**$ -**
Deductions from Gross Estate	
Less Funeral & Burial Expenses	
Less Estate Fees, Legal Fees & Executor Fees	
Less Mortgage, Debts & Losses	
ADJUSTED GROSS ESTATE	**$ -**
Taxable Estate (Exclude Marital Deduction)	
Charitable Donation Deduction	
TAXABLE ESTATE BEFORE MARITAL DEDUCTION	**$ -**
Tax Assuming No Marital Deduction	
Gross Tax	$
Less Unified Credit	$
TAX DUE WITHOUT MARITAL DEDUCTION	**$**
Assets Available For Marital Deduction	$
Spouse's/Co-Client's Gross Estate After Marital Deduction Transfer	
Assumed Asset & Expense Growth Per Year	0%
Checking Account	
Savings Account	
Money Market Account	
Other Monetary Assets	
EE/I Bonds	
Mutual Funds	
Other Investment Assets	
Primary Residence	
Other Housing Assets	
Vehicles	
Personal Property	
Retirement Assets	

Other Assets		
Life Insurance		
Marital Transfer	$	-
GROSS ESTATE	**$**	**-**

Deductions from Gross Estate		
Less Funeral & Burial Expenses		
Less Estate Fees, Legal Fees & Executor Fees		
Less Mortgage, Debts & Losses		
ADJUSTED GROSS ESTATE	**$**	**-**

Taxable Estate (Exclude Marital Deduction)		
Charitable Donation Deduction		
TAXABLE ESTATE	**$**	**-**

Tax Calculation		
Gross Tax	$	-
Less Unified Credit	$	
TAX DUE	**$**	

Planning Strategy 2: Recommend that a Client Prepare or Amend a Will

While not all clients need a will, generally, this estate planning strategy should be the first advice given to a client who does not currently have a will and for those clients whose will is out of date. A **will** ensures that a client's wishes are followed appropriately rather than relying on the intestate laws of the client's state of residence. Dying without a valid will and having state law dictate the distribution of assets is called intestate succession. This should be avoided.

When reviewing a client's current will, financial planners should look for signs that a change or **codicil** might be needed. The following list includes a number of indicators that a client's will or estate plan should be reviewed by an attorney.

- The will was drafted more than five years ago.

- The client has additional beneficiaries who are not listed in the will.

- The client now has fewer beneficiaries than are listed in the will.

- There has been a major change in the beneficiaries' family or financial circumstances.

- The client has indicated verbally that the client wishes to distribute assets differently from what is listed.

- The client's health has diminished since drafting the will.

- The client's marital status has changed since drafting the will (marriage, remarriage, divorce, or death of a spouse).

- The birth or adoption of one or more grandchildren has occurred.

- A significant estate planning law was passed since the date of the will or the date of the last review, if any.

- There has been a significant increase or decrease in the client's wealth or income since the will was drafted.

- The client has purchased additional life insurance.

- The client has started a business.

- A change in the named guardian is needed.

- A change in the executor or contingent executor is needed.

- Property has been purchased in a different state.

- The client has moved, thereby changing the state of residence.

It is important for clients to recognize that having a valid will does not avoid **probate** and the associated advantages and disadvantages associated with probate. It is worth reminding clients that, upon the death of a decedent, a will becomes a public document through the probate system. The value of the assets conveyed through a will is subject to probate fees, and in some states the probate process can be lengthy and expensive. The cost of a will might also be a deterrent. Clients can expect to pay between $200 and $1,000 for a basic attorney drafted will, with the cost increasing with the complexity of the situation. Given the urgency of recommendation implementation, a financial planner may need to patiently encourage their clients to act rather sooner rather than later.

Planning Strategy 3: Encourage Clients to Draft a Letter of Last Instruction

A general estate planning recommendation calls for clients to draft a letter of last instructions. This letter can include special wishes that might not otherwise be included in a will or trust document.

Example. A client can specify where they would like to be buried, the name of the caterer that the client would like to use at the funeral, and other requests.

Clients who write a letter of last instructions should take care to update the letter whenever they rewrite a will or other legal documents. Great confusion can result if more than one letter is found at the date of death.

Planning Strategy 4: Recommend that a Client Utilize a Living Will, Power of Attorney, and Advanced Medical Directive

A **living will** is a legal document that establishes the medical situations in which a client no longer desires life-sustaining or life-prolonging treatment. A living will is most often drafted as a partnership between a client and the client's physician. Typically, a living will includes a client's wishes regarding the use of cardiopulmonary resuscitation, intravenous therapy for nutrition or medication, feeding tubes, and ventilators for artificial breathing. It is very important that a client's family be informed of the content within a living will. A living will is relevant only in situations of terminal illness or injury when an individual is incapable of making care decisions.

Planning Tip

A living will is sometimes known as a **declaration** or **directive to physicians** or in some states as an advanced medical directive.

An alternative to a living will is a durable power of attorney for health care, also called a medical power of attorney. This legal document appoints another person, called an agent, attorney-in-fact, or proxy, to make health care decisions for the client when the client is unable to do so as a result of physical or mental incapacitation. The addition of the term durable makes this, or another power of attorney, remain in effect or take effect in the event of mental incompetence. The agent can make decisions for non-terminal situations or, if a living will is available, help ensure compliance with a client's wishes.

Generally, a **medical directive** or **advanced medical directive (AMD)** combines the protection of a living will in terminal situations with the broader powers of a durable power of attorney for health care into one document. A proxy or attorney-in-fact is appointed, as well as a contingent individual, or successor agent, should the primary person be unavailable to serve. Neither the medical power of attorney nor the medical directive obligates the agent or proxy with financial responsibility for the costs of medical care.

A power of attorney appoints a person or organization to handle a client's affairs. As noted above, a **durable power of attorney** remains in effect or takes effect in the event of subsequent disability or incapacity. A power of attorney can be general, giving broad powers for most—if not all—financial affairs, or be limited to a specific list of responsibilities. With an extremely broad general power of attorney, a client might, in effect, give a third party "all legal powers that I have myself." A **powerholder** with an unlimited power of attorney may or may not be able to make gifts to himself or herself or family members. This right depends on state law and the prior history of the client. Powers of attorney are relatively inexpensive to establish, simple, private, and flexible. Courts also universally recognize powers of attorney.

The greatest disadvantage associated with this strategy is psychological, not financial. A financial planner may face resistance among some clients when this strategy is presented. Occasionally, clients find the thought of planning for their own incapacity and the sharing of decision-making authority difficult and uncomfortable. As a result, some clients might resist implementing this strategy. The use of a **springing power of attorney** (i.e., powers available only after a specific event, such as an illness or disability, and perhaps after validation by a physician) is one way to alleviate client fears. Clients should also be assured that a power of attorney can be revoked at any time. Depending on individual state law, an attorney or witnesses may or may not be required, so minimal costs are generally involved. It is worth noting that clients who own property or live for periods of time in different states each year should exercise particular caution with these documents, because state reciprocity may not apply.

Planning Tip

When planning for incapacitation and overall health care issues, clients should be encouraged to have a living will and a medical power of attorney, as well as a power of attorney for financial affairs. In this way, the client's care and death decisions can be made confidentially using state-specific documents, and the client's financial affairs can be managed with a power of attorney.

Planning Strategy 5: Recommend the Use of Trusts for Incapacity Planning

Because a trust transfers the rights of ownership to a third-party trustee, a trust is a useful strategy to financially provide for a person or persons unable to care for themselves because of legal or medical incapacity. **Incapacity** can be defined in several ways, including lack of ability, lack of legal standing, lack of legal power, or the inability to plan, delegate, provide for, or manage one's legal and financial affairs. Medical incapacity is usually the result of illness or accident, whereas legal incapacity is most common in situations where minor children or developmentally disabled adults are involved. Less acknowledged are situations where an adult has maladaptive behaviors such as a drug or gambling addiction, legal issues, behavioral problems, or a history of poor financial decision making. Trusts are often established in response to the need to provide care for incapacity. However, in some situations, clients should be proactive in planning for their own incapacity. Individuals who fail to plan for the possibility of incapacity face potential risks and costs, including:

- placing the management of assets and health decisions under the control of a third party

- the loss of standing to direct the distribution of assets to heirs and charities before and after death

- the inability to legally execute or delegate their own financial affairs

- the possibility of depleting family assets because of legal battles associated with conservatorship issues

Planning Strategy 6: Understand How Trusts are Taxed

Financial planners most often provide advice to clients regarding revocable and irrevocable trusts. The taxation of these trusts differ. For instance, all income and deductions associated with a **revocable trust** are treated as part of the grantor's individual tax return, although grantors are required to complete the entity part of **IRS Form 1041**. At the death of the grantor, the executor of a grantor's estate is also required to file IRS Form 1041 for the revocable trust.

Planning Tip

The IRS classifies all trusts as simple or complex for the purposes of annual income taxes; complex trusts, whether living or testamentary, are subject to their own tax rates as reported on IRS Form 1041. The Internal Revenue Code (IRC) defines a simple trust as one that:

- distributes its income, instead of allowing discretionary distributions;

- makes no mandatory or discretionary distributions of principal; and

- makes no distributions to or has any principal set aside for charity.

Should a trust not meet the preceding criteria, it is classified as a complex trust and is subject to trust income tax rates for that tax year.

An **irrevocable trust**, on the other hand, is considered a separate entity from the grantor, and as such, IRS Form 1041 must be completed each year that the trust has non-distributed income. With an irrevocable trust, income that is distributed is taxed first to beneficiaries. If income remains in the trust (more than $100 in gross income), the trust itself is subject to the following trust tax rates and must file IRS Form 1041 and pay applicable income taxes.

- 10 percent on income up to $2,600

- 24 percent on income up to $9,450

- 35 percent on income up to $12,950

- 37 percent on income greater than $12,950

Planning Strategy 7: Use Appropriate Property Titling Techniques

Titling assets properly is one tool that can be used to help a client manage their estate plan. Generally, whenever a person is added to the title of a property, the IRS considers the addition a **taxable gift** to the new owner equal to the fair market value of the new ownership position. Understanding when a taxable gift might be incurred can save a client significant gift and estate taxes. If the original owner can make a withdrawal from the asset account without the permission of the new owner, no gift tax will be due until the new owner takes a distribution.

For example, no gift tax is due when a joint owner is added to a bank account until the new owner makes a withdrawal.

The following titling methods can be used for property owned by more than one person:

- **Tenancy in common**: Used by two or more individuals; ownership interests need not be equal; each owner can sell, exchange, or otherwise dispose of their interest without the consent of the other owners; there are no survivorship rights.

- **Joint tenancy with right of survivorship (JTWROS)**: Used by two or more individuals; ownership is equal among owners; ownership passes automatically to survivors upon the death of an owner; ownership can be terminated by death, mutual agreement, and divorce.

- **Tenancy by the entirety**: Used only by married couples; survivorship interests pass automatically to the surviving spouse.

- **Community property**: Used only by married couples living and acquiring property in community property states; survivorship interest does not automatically pass to the surviving spouse.

In the case of JTWROS and tenancy in common, creditors can access the value of the co-owner's interest. Only tenancy by the entirety protects a couple's home from creditors or liability claims against one member of the couple. Some states, such as Virginia, also allow married couples to title investment assets as tenants by the entirety.

Planning Tip

Separate property is:

- Property a client owned before marriage;

- Property client and spouse agreed to convert to community property under state law;

- Property purchased with separate funds;

- Money a client earns while living in a non-community property state;

- Property received as a gift or inheritance.

- Community property is any property acquired during marriage while living in a community property state if the property was commingled with spouse or purchased with community assets.

Ten states provide married couples with an alternative to tenancy by the entirety. **Community property** refers to all assets obtained while a couple is married. Each spouse legally owns one-half of each asset purchased as community property. Community property is available to residents of Alaska, Arizona, California, Idaho, Louisiana, Nevada, New Mexico, Texas, Washington, and Wisconsin.

Community property is unique in that any property owned by a spouse prior to marriage remains the sole property of that spouse unless it is commingled with community property assets. Furthermore, if a spouse receives a gift or inheritance while married, those assets remain the separate property of the spouse unless comingled. Upon the death of one spouse, all assets receive a 100 percent **step-up in basis**. This compares favorably to the 50 percent step-up in basis for assets held by spouses as **JTWROS** (i.e., titling procedure in which ownership of an asset transfers automatically at death to the surviving owners) or as tenancy by the entirety. Few banks, title companies, or other financial service firms automatically title marital assets as community property. A financial planner who fails to guide their community property clientele in the appropriate use of this titling option could cause clients to pay higher taxes in the future because of the lost step-up in basis associated with JTWROS titling.

Planning Strategy 8: Recommend the Use of a Qualified Disclaimer to Transfer Property

One way to transfer ownership of an asset is through the use of a **qualified disclaimer**. According to Internal Revenue Code (IRC) 2518, a qualified disclaimer refers to "an irrevocable and unqualified refusal by a person to accept an interest in property."[2] For the disclaimer to be qualified, the disclaimer must meet the following guidelines:

- It must be in writing.

- It must be received no later than nine months after the bequest is made, or if the beneficiary is a minor at the time of the bequest, no later than nine months after the child reaches the age of twenty-one.

- The beneficiary must not accept any interest or benefit from the bequest.

- The beneficiary must not maintain any control or interest concerning who is to receive (inherit) the asset after filing the disclaimer.

A disclaimed asset is treated as though the asset was never transferred, which allows the asset to be transferred to another person or entity. This strategy can be useful in situations where a beneficiary already has a sizable estate and additional assets are not needed or desired. For a disclaimer to be qualified for federal and state tax purposes, the written disclaimer must be in compliance with IRC 2518, as well as any state disclaimer statues that might apply.

Planning Strategy 9: Use a Living Trust to Help a Client Avoid Probate

Two reasons to consider establishing a **living trust** (i.e., a trust created during a client's life) are minimization of probate court involvement and a reduction in publicity surrounding public documentation of a client's financial situation at death. Other advantages include continuation of income and distributions to heirs from assets held in the trust after the death of a client, the ability of a trustee to manage assets, and the likely appropriate distribution of assets to heirs at a client's death. Other advantages include reducing the possibility of someone claiming that asset transfers are or were against the decedent's wishes, as well as a reduction in legal costs for those who own property in more than one state.

Client confusion is sometimes associated with this strategy. Clients occasionally confuse avoiding probate with avoiding estate taxation. Assets held in a revocable living trust are included in a client's (grantor's) gross estate for estate tax purposes. Also, income that is taxable to the trust, rather than to the grantor or other trust beneficiaries, is generally taxed at a higher rate (e.g., tax rates on trusts are based on compressed income tax brackets). It is worth noting that although living trusts are effective in helping a client avoid probate, unless all titled assets are retitled or originally titled in the name of the trust, the ability to avoid the probate process will be nullified.

Planning Strategy 10: Recommend an A-B Trust Arrangement for Clients with a High Net Worth

An **A-B trust** arrangement is another name for a strategy that uses a **credit shelter bypass trust** in conjunction with a marital deduction trust (also known as a standard **family trust**). This technique can save a high net worth household substantial amounts in estate tax if properly implemented. As shown in Figure 13.3, this strategy guarantees that both spouses will maximize the use of their estate tax applicable exclusion amount. This strategy can also be an effective way to guarantee that a surviving spouse receives annual income but avoids some of the pitfalls associated with asset ownership, with the remaining assets going to ultimate beneficiaries upon the death of the surviving spouse.

Figure 13.3. A-B Trust Arrangement

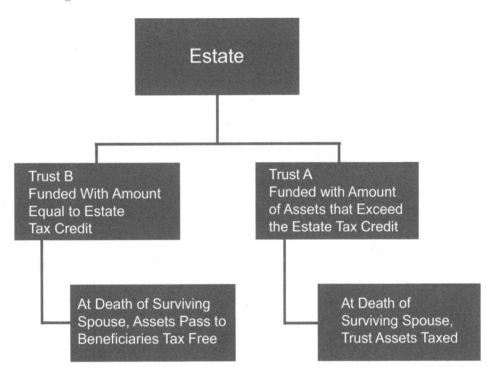

In this arrangement, the **marital trust**—the **A Trust**—is established at the same time as the **bypass trust**—the B Trust. The marital trust is typically funded with assets in excess of the estate tax unified credit applicable exclusion amount using the **unlimited marital deduction**. The marital trust is usually either a **POA trust** or a **QTIP trust**. With either of these types of trust arrangements, the surviving spouse must be given an income interest in the trust. In a POA trust, the surviving spouse must also be given a general power of appointment over trust assets. As a result, marital trust assets are generally included in the surviving spouse's gross estate. For this reason, a bypass trust is also established, which is funded with assets protected by the applicable credit amount remaining of the first spouse to die. At the death of the surviving spouse, the trust assets bypass the surviving spouse's estate.

When the Tax Relief Act of 2010 created the portable estate exemption, the law effectively eliminated the need for most A-B trust arrangements. The law allows a surviving spouse to utilize any unused exclusion amount from the first-to-die spouse. As long as the couple was married at the date of the first death, and the surviving spouse elects the exemption on IRS Form 706, the full value of a joint estate, more than $23 million, can be sheltered from federal estate taxes in 2020. A-B trust arrangements will continue to be used regardless of the federal exclusion amount. These trust arrangements allow for asset protection, particularly for those with estates exceeding $23 million. Another advantage associated with this strategy is that assets held in a B trust are generally inaccessible to creditors. A-B trusts also provide asset protection in cases where a surviving spouse remarries. If the portable estate exemption is elected, and the surviving spouse remarries, the exemption amount can be reduced.

Potential problems are associated with this strategy. First, establishing the trust agreements requires that all other estate planning documents be revised, including the "evening out" of assets through retitling. Retitling can result in a sizable upfront cost in both time and money for clients who implement the strategy. This makes the strategy less attractive for clients whose combined assets are not, or will not be, greater than the estate tax unified credit applicable exclusion amount in the future. Second, the irrevocable nature of the bypass trust means that the surviving spouse generally can routinely access only income generated from assets, with trust principal being limited to an "ascertainable standard" limited to health, education, maintenance and support. In some situations, an ascertainable standard can limit the surviving spouse's standard of living if the assets fail to generate adequate income in the future.

Planning Strategy 11: Decrease Estate Tax Liability and Generate Income Using a CRAT, CRUT, or Pooled Income Fund

This estate planning strategy is designed to benefit a charity while enhancing a client's financial situation. If proper gift planning is conducted and implemented, it may be possible to accomplish several distinct goals simultaneously. First, income tax liabilities can be reduced, although the amount of the income tax charitable deduction is affected by the type and use of the asset given. Second, gift and estate taxes can be reduced. Third, benefits can be provided to charitable organizations. Fourth, engaging in charitable giving can provide the donor with a feeling of goodwill.

Charitable giving involves providing gifts of money, income, and assets to charitable organizations. To qualify for a charitable donation, a client must give assets to a recognized charity in the United States, a United States territory, or a political subdivision. **Nonprofit organizations** include most religious, scientific, and charitable organizations, some fraternal societies and associations, and certain veteran's associations and organizations. To receive a tax deduction and exclude assets from an estate, a client should consider outright gifts, as well as the use of one or more of the following trust arrangements: a charitable remainder annuity trust, a charitable remainder unitrust, a pooled income fund, or a charitable lead trust.

Planning Tip

Charitable lead trusts *annually* pay *charitable* beneficiaries a percent of the value of assets in the trust; the charity *receives distributions annually* for the term of the trust; at the end of the term, the assets are transferred to the donor's heirs without federal income or estate tax.

When a client contributes to a **charitable remainder annuity trust (CRAT)**, the non-charitable beneficiary generally receives, on an annual basis, a fixed annuity payment equal to or greater than 5 percent, but not more than 50 percent, of the initial net fair market value of the trust. The benefit may be structured as an annuity for life or a term certain. Once established, no additional contributions can be made to the CRAT. At the end of the term, the remainder goes to charity.

A **charitable remainder unitrust trust (CRUT)** is similar to a CRAT, but fundamentally different in the way in which payments are made to the beneficiary. The non-charitable beneficiary generally receives, annually, a payment equal to a fixed percentage between 5 percent and 50 percent of the assets held in the trust as revalued on an annual basis. The benefit can be structured as a unitrust for life or a term certain. In some instances, payments are set at the lower of the unitrust amount or trust income, with or without a make-up provision. This means that distributions can be limited to earnings, and there is no requirement to use principal to pay beneficiaries. Further, additional donations to a CRUT are allowed. At the end of the term, the remainder goes to charity.

A **pooled income fund** is a charitable device created and maintained by a charity. The donor makes an irrevocable gift that is pooled with similar gifts from other donors. The charity manages the commingled assets, and payments based on the income earned by the account are made to beneficiaries on a pro-rata basis for life. At the end of the term, the remainder goes to charity.

It is important to remember that gifts made to charitable organizations are irrevocable. It is also possible that payments from charitable trusts will not keep pace with inflation over time. Because a unitrust is a variable annuity, a CRUT can provide a hedge against this possibility. In general, clients must be committed to the charity and acknowledge that the use of donated assets might not represent the client's values or aspirations in the future. The irrevocable nature of charitable gifts is something each client must weigh against the qualitative and quantitative benefits received.

A **charitable lead trust (CLT)** (see Strategy 19) reverses the role of the charity, which takes the lead interest, and family members, which take the remainder interest, after the lead interest expires. Similar to a CRAT or CRUT, a charitable beneficiary receives, at least annually, a percentage equal to 5 percent or greater, of the assets placed in trust. A **CLAT** payment is based on the initial fair market value of assets placed in trust, while a **CLUT** payment is based on the value of assets as revalued on an annual basis. The term of a CLT generally cannot exceed twenty years. At the expiration of the term of the charitable lead interest, assets remaining in the CLT pass to lower generation family members.

Planning Strategy 12: Recommend that a Client Establish a Donor-advised Charitable Fund

A **donor-advised charitable fund** is an irrevocable account established by a custodian to accept, manage, and distribute donations to a client's selected charities. The donor, while losing access to the assets for personal use, controls which charity receives a donation, when the donation will be made, how often the donation will be granted, and how much will be distributed. Although distributions cannot be used for pledges, private benefit, or political contributions, any legitimate charitable activity can receive benefits from a donor-advised fund.

The primary advantage associated with establishing a donor-advised charitable fund is that, although contributions are irrevocable, the client retains control over the timing and amount of annual distributions to a charity. Furthermore, a client can generally determine which charity will receive distributions. This choice can change yearly, so if a charitable organization veers from the client's objectives for giving, a different charity can be chosen in subsequent years.

There are tax advantages as well. Just like a regular charitable contribution, assets transferred to a donor-advised fund reduce a client's gross estate. Gifts of appreciated stock offer the added benefit to the donor of avoiding capital gains taxes on the appreciation. A portion of contributions can also be used to reduce federal income tax liabilities through itemized deductions.

Several disadvantages are associated with this strategy. First, the number of donor-advised charitable fund providers is relatively limited, although financial services providers like Charles Schwab, Fidelity, and Vanguard offer trust services. Second, the costs associated with donor-advised funds can be quite high. Annual fees of 2 percent to 5 percent are common, but even these high fees are reasonable in comparison to establishing a private foundation. Third, unlike CRATs and CRUTs, a donor cannot retain the right to receive payments from the fund.

Planning Strategy 13: Recommend that a Client Establish a Foundation

Private and public foundations are tax-advantaged entities that allow individuals to donate goods, services, and assets while receiving an income tax deduction (assuming the donor itemizes deductions).

- **Private foundations** generally receive their asset contributions from one or a few sources. Assets are then used to fund the ongoing operations of a charity or nonprofit organization.

- **Public foundations** typically receive funding from a wider public audience. Assets are then used to support a variety of community charities.

Caps on the deductibility of contributions to foundations exist. The maximum deductibility for cash donations to private foundations is capped at 30 percent of adjusted gross income. Cash donations to public foundations are capped at 60 percent of adjusted gross income. Private foundations have very strict reporting requirements that require disclosure of asset values and donation sources. Private foundations must, by law, also distribute the equivalent of 5 percent of the fair market value of all investable assets per year.

Planning Strategy 14: Use a Section 529 Plan to Help Decrease a Client's Gross Estate

This strategy works well when a client's objective is to help save for a child or grandchild's education while reducing their own estate tax liability. A single client may contribute up to five years of annual exclusion gifts to a **529 plan** for a beneficiary in any given year (once every five years). The gift will avoid the gift tax. A married couple may double the amount contributed on a tax-free basis. Clients who use this strategy will be required to file a gift tax return at the time of the contribution to account for the gift. If a client should pass away prior to the expiration of the five-year period, the "unexpired" portion of the used annual exclusion will be included in the client's gross estate at death.

Planning Strategy 15: Recommend Establishing a Qualified Personal Residence Trust (QPRT) or Grantor Retained Annuity Trust (GRAT) to Reduce Estate Liabilities

A **qualified personal residence trust (QPRT)** is designed to hold a client's home for later transfer to an heir(s). QPRTs are used by clients who would like to reduce the value of their gross estate in the future but still retain the right to live in their home, which may be the client's single largest asset. If a client outlives the term of the trust, the property is transferred to the beneficiary. At that point, the client may continue to live in the property by agreeing to pay rent (based on an independent appraiser's fair market value rental) to the new property owner. If the client should die before the trust terminates, the full value of the home will be included in the client's gross estate. Figure 13.4 illustrates the QPRT process.

Figure 13.4. The Qualified Personal Residence Trust (QPRT) Process

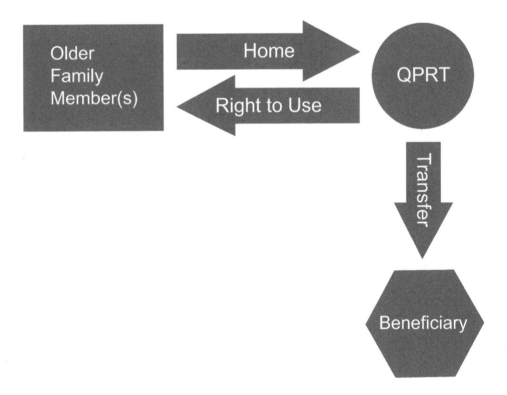

A **grantor retained annuity trust (GRAT)** is similar to a QPRT, but instead of holding a personal residence, the trust holds other assets, such as stocks, bonds, mutual funds, and income producing real estate. The trust makes annuity payments to the grantor for

a pre-determined number of years. At the trust's termination, the assets are transferred to the trust's beneficiaries. A GRAT is shown in Figure 13.5.

Figure 13.5. The Grantor Retained Annuity Trust (GRAT) Process

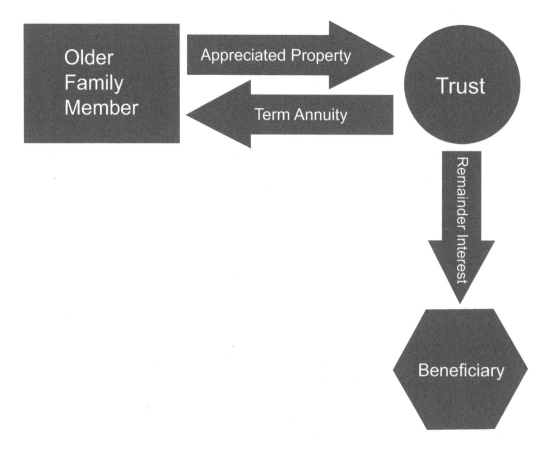

QPRTs and GRATs can be effective tools for use in reducing a client's gross estate while providing a client with immediate access to housing or an annuity stream. Implementing this strategy allows a client to remove a potentially rapidly appreciating personal residence or other asset from the client's estate (assuming the client outlives the term of the trust).

Several issues are associated with this strategy. For example, the trust asset(s) will generally be includable in a client's (grantor's) gross estate if the client (grantor) dies during the trust term. Although the value of the property can be excluded from the gross estate if the client (grantor) survives the trust term, the client (grantor) may owe a gift tax on the present value of the remainder held in a QPRT or GRAT. The shorter the term of the trust, the higher the potential gift tax will be. However, the longer the term, the more likely that the client will not outlive the trust term, which can defeat the purpose of the strategy. To simultaneously mitigate the payment of gift tax and hedge against the mortality concern, a client with substantive assets may opt to create a series of "rolling GRATs." For example, a client desiring to transfer $10 million to lower generation family members may create a series of five equal-sized GRATs, with terms of two, four, six, eight and ten years. As each term period expires, an increasing amount of property is removed from the client's gross estate.

Planning Tip

Even though a QPRT owns a client's personal residence, it is the client's responsibility to pay all expenses related to upkeep, insurance, and taxes on the property. Also, if a client should outlive the duration of a QPRT, the client will need to negotiate with the owners of the property to continue living in the house.

Planning Strategy 16: Recommend that a Client Establish a Family Limited Partnership

A **family limited partnership (FLP)** is a tool that can be used by high net worth business owner clients to reduce estate tax liabilities, decrease income tax liabilities, and transfer ownership of a business to relatives over time. In its simplest form, client establishes a **limited partnership**, keeping a general partnership interest in the partnership, as well as some limited partnership interests. This enables the client to retain control over the day-to-day activities of the business. Initially, some limited partnership interests can be given or sold to family members. Over time, the client can give interests in the limited partnership to children, grandchildren, and other family members. Figure 13.6 illustrates how a FLP works.

Figure 13.6. A Family Limited Partnership

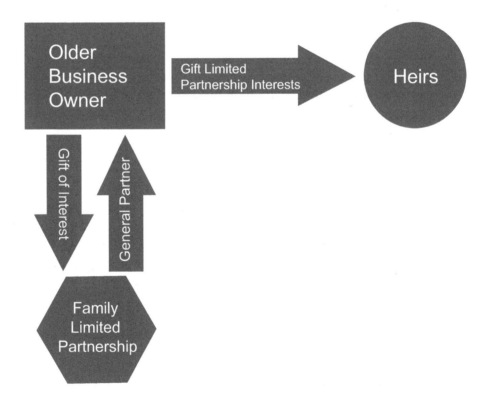

As income is generated in the business, the limited partners will need to report their share of earnings. This can help a client reduce current income tax liabilities. Keep in mind, however, unearned income of a child under age nineteen (twenty-four if a full-time student) is generally taxable to the child at the custodial parent's highest marginal federal income tax rate.

The real advantage associated with this estate planning technique is that it is possible to transfer ownership of a privately held firm from one generation to another on a tax-free basis, using a combination of the gift tax annual exclusion and the unified credit. Furthermore, valuation discounts are often available for transfers of minority interests, as well as discounts resulting from lack of marketability.

Planning Tip

Family Limited Partnerships:

- Allow parents to transfer wealth to their children at a discount to FMV;

- Allow parents to transfer income tax liabilities to others in a lower bracket;

- Allow parents to retain some control over the transferred property; and

- Offer limited liability to the partners, although the parents continue to have unlimited liability as general partners.

Some key issues are associated with this strategy. First, even though a partnership can be established with relatively few upfront costs, the actual partnership document must be thorough and the parties need to continually observe partnership formalities to obtain tax benefits. Second, ongoing costs can become high because of accounting issues. Third, by establishing a partnership, the client may be taking on general liability risk for family members that the client might not otherwise want. Fourth, a gift tax might apply if future partnership gifts exceed the annual gift tax exclusion. Finally, implementing this strategy can result in a higher probability of being audited. An alternative strategy involves the establishment of a **limited liability company (LLC)**.

Planning Strategy 17: Recommend the Use an Irrevocable Life Insurance Trust to Reduce a Client's Gross Estate

An **irrevocable life insurance trust (ILIT)** strategy can be one of the best ways to remove a high value asset from a client's gross estate. Using this strategy, a client transfers an existing life insurance policy to a trust. Premiums are then funded using the gift tax annual exclusion (i.e., the client gifts the premium amount to the trust, which then pays the insurance premium). Assuming the grantor-insured lives for more than three years after the original life insurance gift is made, the face value of the life insurance policy will be removed from the client's gross estate. A further estate reduction occurs whenever annual gifts are used to fund premium payments.

A significant disadvantage associated with this strategy is that the transfer of ownership in a life insurance policy is considered a gift. If the value of the gift exceeds, or for some reason does not qualify for the gift tax annual exclusion, a client may need to use up some or all of their unified credit and perhaps owe a gift tax. Another disadvantage is that the cost of establishing and maintaining an ILIT to some extent offsets the tax benefits gained. It is worth remembering that this strategic technique is generally appropriate for transfers of cash value insurance policies.

Planning Strategy 18: Recommend that a Client Establish a QTIP Trust When Applicable

A **QTIP trust** is often used to obtain a marital deduction for **qualified terminable interest property (QTIP)**. A QTIP trust can be a useful tool for divorced individuals entering a remarriage with children, or when a wealthy spouse wishes to ensure adequate income for a surviving spouse but has a strong desire to ensure that, at the surviving spouse's death, assets remaining in the trust will pass to the wealthy spouse's children. Two important rules apply to the use of QTIP trusts:

1. The surviving spouse must be given the right to all income from the trust (paid at least annually).

2. No one can be given the right to direct that the property held in the trust will go to anyone else as long as the surviving spouse is alive.

If these rules are met, assets passing to the trust become eligible for the marital deduction. Property that remains in the trust after the surviving spouse's death then pass to the beneficiary(ies) originally named by the donor or decedent. Like any marital deduction trust, a QTIP trust is subject to estate tax at the surviving spouse's death. That is, QTIP trusts are ineffective tools for those wishing to reduce or eliminate estate tax liabilities.

Planning Strategy 19: Help Clients Reduce Taxes by Recommending the Use of a Charitable Lead Trust

A **charitable lead trust (CLT)** allows a client to gift assets to a charity, receive a tax deduction for the gift, and potentially reduce estate tax liabilities. Unlike other charitable gifting strategies, a CLT provides a charity with an annuity income rather than assets. At the end of the annuity period (e.g., in twenty years), any assets remaining in the trust are distributed to the client's remainder beneficiaries. The longer the term of the annuity payment, the larger the tax deduction and reduction in estate value.

For estate tax purposes, the return of the asset to the remainder beneficiary is considered a gift; however, the gift value will be based on current market interest rates and the present value of the assets when donated, not the appreciated value. Internal Revenue Service (IRS) rules make the use of a CLT strategy complicated. Gifts to CLTs do not qualify for the annual gift exclusion. Also, a CLT is treated as either a "grantor" trust or a "complex" trust for income tax purposes, meaning that capital gains incurred on the trust's assets, plus ordinary income, will either be income taxable to the grantor, or to the trust itself. This determination depends upon the provisions as drafted and incorporated in the trust agreement. Finally, a CLT may be disallowed if the IRS suspects self-dealing.

Planning Strategy 20: Suggest the Use of Intra-Family and Other Business Transfer Techniques When Appropriate

Planning Tip

Clients who own one or more businesses, and those who have substantial real estate holdings, need to preplan ways to transfer these assets to co-owners, heirs, and other beneficiaries. Buy-sell agreements are used to facilitate the transfer of a business ownership to other owners. The simplest type of agreement outlines the manner in which the ownership interest of one owner will be transferred to other owners, usually through the use of company assets.

A simple way to remember how many policies are needed in a buy-sell agreement involves the use of the following formula: N x (N – 1), where N is the number of owners.

An **entity purchase agreement** can be used to transfer business interests. With this agreement, the company owns life insurance with each business owner as the insured and the company as the beneficiary. Figure 13.7 shows how an entity purchase agreement can be established.

Figure 13.7. Entity Purchase Agreement

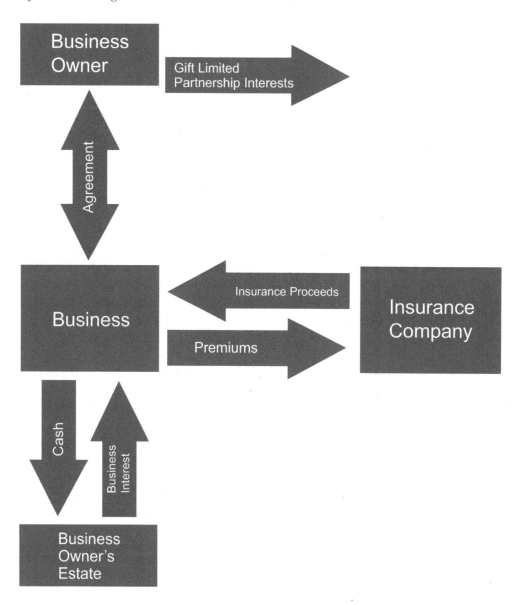

An alternative is a **cross-purchase agreement** where each business owner purchases a life insurance policy naming themselves as the beneficiary and the other owners as the insureds. Figure 13.8 illustrates how a cross-purchase agreement works.

Figure 13.8. Cross-Purchase Agreement

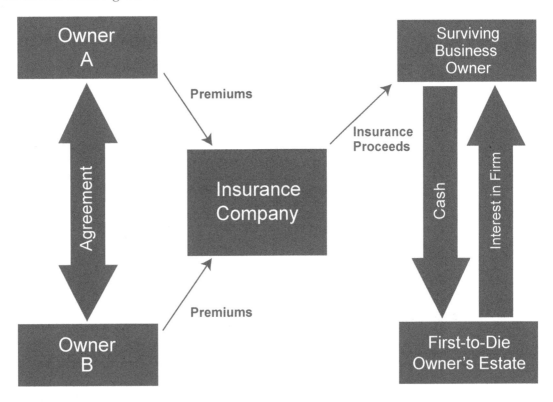

A third option is a **wait-and-see buy-sell agreement**. Within this strategy, the business is given the first right to purchase a deceased owner's interest in the firm, after which the remaining owners are given an opportunity to purchase the decedent's shares.

Financial planners should ensure that a client has incorporated the following elements into any buy-sell agreement: wording that clarifies who is and is not covered by the agreement, what events beyond death might trigger the agreement, the buyout price, and how often the agreement should be reviewed and revised.

When considering family transfers, clients are often faced with the dual goals of reducing gift tax liabilities and ensuring family unity. Providing gifts while retaining an interest in an asset is one way to remove the value of an asset from a client's estate over time. A grantor retained annuity trust can be used to facilitate this process. With this type of trust, a donor gifts property to a trust and receives an annual payout from the trust for a pre-determined number of years. At the end of the period, the remaining value is passed to one or more beneficiaries, thereby reducing both gift and estate taxes.

A **qualified personal residence trust** is a special form of **grantor retained annuity trust** that helps transfer a home to beneficiaries. Some financial planners also use **defective grantor trusts**. These types of trust, as shown in Figure 13.9, are designed so that the grantor is liable for income taxes, which reduces distributions from the trust to pay income taxes and ensures a larger transfer later in time. GRATs, GRUTs, QPRTs, and some charitable lead trusts are all examples of intentionally defective grantor trusts.

Figure 13.9. Defective Grantor Trust

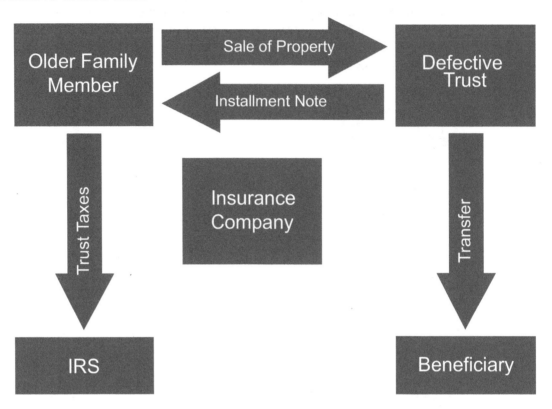

Several additional strategies can be used to facilitate intra-family transfers.

- The first involves an **intra-family loan** where one family member loans money to another for the purchase of the lender's property. No gift tax consequences are involved if the loan is an arms-length transaction; however, if the loan's rate of interest is zero or below the market, the foregone interest may be considered imputed income.

- The second approach involves the establishment of a **private annuity**. With this strategy, an older family member purchases a lifetime income from an obligor—a younger family member—using assets from the elder's estate. The annuity becomes an uninsured promise to pay, but sometimes a life insurance policy is purchased on the obligor's life to ensure income payments to the annuitant. When the annuitant (the elder family member) dies, the property's basis is adjusted for the annuity payments already made, which may generate a tax liability for the obligor. As long as the present value of the payments is equal to or more than the fair market value of the property used to purchase the annuity, the property will be excluded from the gross estate.

Sometimes a **self-cancelling installment note (SCIN)** is used to facilitate intra-family transfers. An **installment sale** occurs when an older family member sells property to someone younger in the family using a loan. The transaction is a SCIN if the loan automatically cancels after the death of the seller. The principal amount of the note needs to be based on the fair market value of the property and include a "risk premium" based either on the seller's life expectancy or carry an above market rate of interest on the note. If the buyer and seller are not related, any cancelled payments are excluded from the seller's gross estate but are taxed as income in respect of a decedent; however, if the parties are related, this strategy can get complex, which explains why this strategy is rarely used.

Planning Tip

Advantages of an installment sale include:

- deferral of capital gains;

- removing an asset from the gross estate; and

- helping family members acquire property.

If the transferred property is a business, vacation home, or primary residence, the borrower may deduct the interest paid.

Occasionally, a business owning family will use a **gift leaseback** strategy. As illustrated in Figure 13.10, using this technique, a parent will gift a depreciated asset to a child but continue to use the asset in the business. The parent and child then enter into a lease agreement where the parent makes tax-deductible payments to the child for use of the asset. The income is taxable to the child. As long as the value of the gift is below the annual gift exclusion amount, the gift tax can be avoided.

Figure 13.10. Gift Leaseback Process

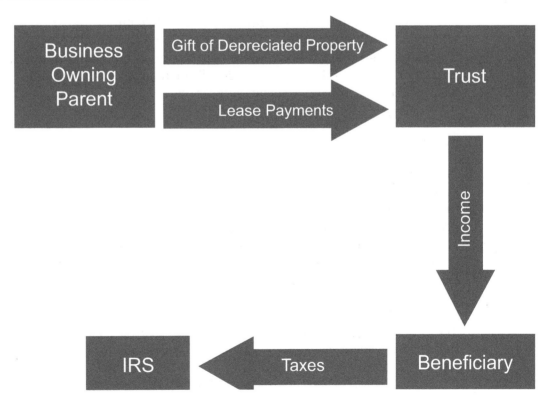

A **sale leaseback arrangement** is similar to a gift leaseback. The primary difference, as shown in Figure 13.11, is that the depreciated property used in the transaction is sold to a trust. As long at the sales price is based on a true fair market value, the gift tax can be eliminated.

Figure 13.11. Sale Leaseback Process

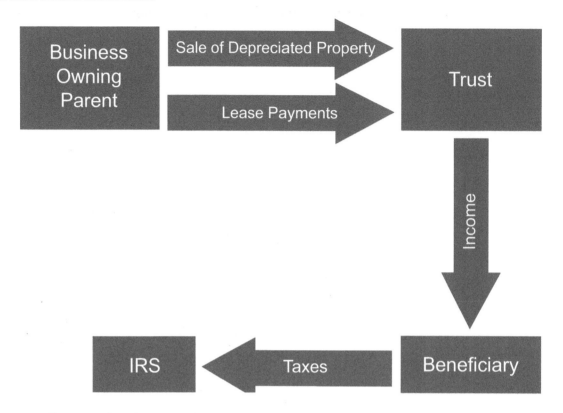

Finally, some families use a **bargain sale** to facilitate intra-family transfers. This occurs when the sales price of an item is less than the fair market value. The difference is considered a taxable gift from the seller to the buyer if the amount exceeds the annual gift exclusion amount. The purchaser will then adopt either the seller's carried over basis or the amount paid, whichever is larger.

Planning Strategy 21: Minimize Taxes Associated with Gifting

The federal **gift tax** is linked to the estate tax. Planning for gifting does require additional strategizing. Under current law, gifts are taxable to the giver (**donor**) rather than the receiver (**donee**). The gift tax applies to transfers of property by **gift** and occurs whenever property (including money) or the use of or income from property is given without expectation of receiving something of at least equal value in return. Additionally, if a client sells something at less than the asset's full value, or if an interest-free or reduced-interest loan is made, the IRS will consider the foregone interest to be a taxable gift.

The general rule is that any gift is a taxable gift. However, there are certain exceptions to this rule. Generally, the following gifts are not subject to gift tax:

- Annual gifts that do not exceed the exclusion per donee for the calendar year;

- Gifts to a client's US citizen spouse (limits apply for a non-US citizen spouse);

- Tuition expenses a client pays directly to the educational institution for the benefit of someone else;

- Medical expenses a client pays directly to the institution or person providing care for the benefit of someone else;

- Gifts to a political organization for its use; and

- Gifts to qualified charities (a deduction is available for these contributions).

One of the most effective ways to decrease a client's gross estate involves taking full advantage of the $15,000 (in 2020) **gift tax annual exclusion** per donee. Using this strategy, a client may give up to $15,000 per year, gift tax free, to as many individuals (related or not) as the client desires. Married couples may double gifts through gift-splitting techniques and provide up to $30,000 per year to each donee gift tax free. It is possible to reduce an estate substantially over time by systematically making gifts to one or more persons. The primary disadvantage associated with this strategy is that, once a gift has been made, the transfer is irrevocable. Further, gifts to others cannot be used to generate income for the donor. Gifts made of more than the annual exclusion amount per recipient in a calendar year effectively decrease a client's unified credit and subject the donor to gift taxation.

Planning Tip

- Present interest gifts greater than the annual exclusion are currently taxable.

- Future interest gifts are currently taxable.

- No gift tax is due as long as the current gift plus all lifetime gifts do not exceed the applicable exclusion amount.

Generally, clients need not file a **gift tax return**, IRS Form 709, unless the value of a gift exceeds the annual exclusion amount. Although a tax return may be required, no actual gift tax will be payable until cumulative lifetime taxable giving exceeds the applicable exclusion amount. Clients who give money or assets to others are primarily responsible for the payment of the gift tax. When discussing gift tax issues with clients, it is important to remind clients that the person who receives the gift generally will not have to pay any federal gift tax.

Example. Assume that a client gifts $25,000 to her son, $25,000 to her daughter, $8,000 to her niece, and $2,500 each to the seven other members of her bridge group. Further assume all gifts are made within the same calendar year—in this example, 2020. Although the client made gifts totaling $75,500, each gift is treated separately. After applying the $15,000 annual exclusion, none of the individual gifts under $15,000 are taxable; only the individual gift amounts in excess of $15,000 to each child are taxable. The gift tax will be calculated on the $20,000 [($25,000 − $15,000) × 2] in non-excludable gifts. Because the gift to each child is taxable, the client must file IRS Form 709 to report the gifts, although the client can opt to subtract the tax from her unified credit rather than pay the tax.

Tax basis must also be considered when gifting property, in that the donee's basis will be different depending on whether the property was received as a gift or an **inheritance**. When property is inherited, the donee's tax basis becomes the value of the property as of the donor's date of death (or alternate valuation date if chosen by the executor of the estate); however, if the property is transferred as a gift, the donee does not receive a step-up in basis. This means the donee's original tax basis still applies.

> *Example.* A client's parent left her the family farm, which has an original tax basis of $145,000. The market value is $500,000. If the farm was received as a gift and then sold for the market value, the client would owe capital gains tax on the $355,000 difference between the basis and sales price. Additionally, the client's parent might be responsible for gift tax on the $485,000 difference between the annual exclusion and the market value. However, if the client instead inherited the property upon her parent's death, the client would not owe any capital gains tax on the sale, and so long as the total value of lifetime taxable gifts did not exceed the exclusion, the client's parent's estate would not owe any estate tax on the transfer.

Some financial transactions are difficult to classify as a gift. Adding a joint tenant to a bank account is not considered a gift until the new owner withdraws the funds. But adding a joint tenant to real estate is a gift if the new owner has the right to sell their interest in the property, even if the owner does not exercise this right. Finally, it is important to realize that although many other taxes can be filed jointly, gift tax returns are filed on an individual basis. So, if a married couple gives a single person a gift in excess of twice the annual exclusion, the gift will be evenly split and each spouse will need to file Form 709 for one-half of the amount in excess of twice the exclusion amount.

Planning Strategy 22: Account for a Possible Generation-Skipping Transfer Tax

A **generation-skipping transfer tax (GSTT)** is a levy on the portion of an estate that skips over one generation. Each U. S. Citizen is allowed a **GST Exemption** equal to the Applicable Exemption Amount ($11,580,000 in 2020) that may be used during life or at death on any Generation Skipping Transfers. Any gift or property assignment to a direct descendant two or more generations below the person making the transfer (or 37½ years younger than the donor, if unrelated), known as a **skip person**, is generally considered a **generation-skipping transfer**. Typically, a generation skip occurs when a distribution is made from a grandparent to a grandchild, thereby skipping a generation. This is known as a **direct skip**. Direct skips can occur whether the donor/decedent is living or deceased, but in cases where the death of the middle generation occurs before the gift is made, the GSTT tax is avoided. The tax can also be avoided whenever a donor/decedent and beneficiary are unrelated and the beneficiary is no more than 37½ years younger than the donor.[3] Transfers to a trust today that may benefit a skip person in the future—as well as certain transfers within or from a trust to a skip person—are subject to the GSTT tax. All GST transfers are taxed at the highest marginal estate tax rate in effect at the time of transfer, on the portion that exceeds any allocated GST Exemption that may have been applied to the transfer.

Planning Strategy 23: Help a Client Elect the Correct Estate Valuation Date

The **personal representative** of a decedent's estate may choose to value assets for tax purposes at the fair market value on the date of death or, under certain circumstances, the value six months after death. The use of the **alternate valuation date** is permitted whenever estate assets have decreased in value during the six-month period after death and the federal estate tax payable is reduced. A few caveats are worth noting. First, if a decedent's property is sold, exchanged or distributed within the six-month period, the alternate valuation of those assets becomes the value on date of sale, exchange or distribution. Second, if the alternate date is used, all assets must be valued using the technique, including those that may have increased in value. Third, certain depreciating assets and those whose value is subject to decline due to mere lapse of time (i.e., automobiles, patents, life estates, remainder interests) must be valued at date of death value, not the depreciated or amortized value six months following death. Additionally, if an estate owes generation-skipping transfer taxes, the sum of estate taxes and generation skipping transfer taxes payable must be lower on the alternate valuation date than on date of death. The personal representative must elect the alternate valuation date within one year of the estate tax return filing date, including granted extensions.

Planning Tip

When valuing an estate, the following must be added back to arrive at an appropriate gross estate figure:

- Certain transfers made within 3 years of death;

- Gift taxes paid on gifts made within 3 years of death;

- Transfer of a life insurance policy within 3 years of death; and

- Transfers where the decedent retained an interest in the transferred property.

Planning Strategy 24: Identify Sources of Estate Liquidity

At death of a client, the surviving family or estate is typically faced with immediate expenses; however, in some cases a decedent's assets may be frozen, making access to cash and other liquid assets difficult. Immediate expenses include funeral costs, medical bills, debts, probate costs, and possibly state and federal taxes. Identifying sources of **estate liquidity** prior to death is an important financial planning function.

In addition to cash and cash equivalents held by a decedent, the three primary sources of estate liquidity include life insurance, loans, and asset sales. Life insurance is widely used to meet a liquidity need. It is important to note, however, that if the beneficiary of a decedent's life insurance policy is the estate, the proceeds will be included in the decedent's gross estate. Additionally, if the Internal Revenue Service deems life insurance proceeds as essential to the payment of taxes, claims, and other estate expenses, the death benefit will be included in the gross estate. This is true even if the beneficiary is an ILIT or another person who is legally obliged to pay the decedent's final expenses. Careful drafting of an ILIT by a skilled estate planning attorney is essential so that ILIT assets may be available, but are not obligated, to meet estate expenses, including death taxes.

Planning Tip

Thirty states have filial responsibility laws that require children to provide financial support to parents who are indigent.

The second liquidity strategy involves pledging unencumbered property held by the estate as security for a short-term loan. It may also be possible to borrow from a decedent's ILIT. A third option involves selling assets. Assets that are included in the gross estate typically receive a step-up in basis. (Note that this strategy does not work for **ordinary income property**, such as 401(k), 403(b), annuity, and savings bond assets.) Shortly after the decedent's death, assets can be sold with little, if any, income tax liability. It may also be possible to sell assets to a decedent's ILIT. Another liquidity source for some clients includes assets from a closely held business.

Planning Strategy 25: Recommend that a Client Make Gifts to Custodial Accounts (UGMA/UTMA)

State laws for custodian accounts are titled either **Uniform Gifts to Minors Act (UGMA)** or **Uniform Transfers to Minors Act (UTMA)**. If a UGMA/UTMA is used, an adult must be named **custodian** of the account. When a child reaches the **age of majority**, which is typically age eighteen or twenty one depending on the state of the child's residence, the assets become the full property of the non-custodian owner.

Certain tax advantages are associated with using UGMA/UTMA accounts. First, a donor's gross estate can generally be reduced through the use of the annual gift tax exclusion. Second, income-producing assets can be shifted to children and grandchildren in a way that possibly reduces the total amount of income tax paid by the donor. Third, gifts to custodial accounts qualify for the annual exclusion for both gift tax and generation-skipping transfer tax purposes.

It is important to keep in mind several disadvantages associated with this strategy. To begin with, all gifts to custodial accounts are irrevocable, and upon the child's age of majority—typically eighteen or twenty-one—the assets become the sole property of the child. Additionally, unearned income of a child under age nineteen (twenty-four if a full-time student) is generally taxable to the child at the trust and estate marginal tax rate. The loss of property use and the inability to guarantee that assets will be used for a specific purpose make this strategy problematic for some clients.

Planning Strategy 26: Make Gifts to § 2503(b) or 2503(c) Trusts for a Minor Child

Certain trusts can be used to transfer assets to minor children and grandchildren using the gift tax annual exclusion. A Section **2503(b) trust** generally requires income from assets held in the trust to be distributed for a child beneficiary's benefit at least annually. Typically, this income will be taxable at the trust and estate marginal income tax rate. However, the principal need not be distributed at the age of majority.

A Section **2503(c) trust** allows all income to grow within the trust, but distribution of trust assets must generally occur at the child beneficiary's age of majority. A Section

2503(c) trust is similar to a UGMA/UTMA in this respect, but different in that a clause can be inserted into a Section 2503 trust document that gives the child a right to demand distribution from the trust for a limited period of time upon reaching the age of majority. If the distribution is not requested within this time period, the trust can continue into later years. As such, unlike a gift to a UGMA/UTMA, property can remain within the trust beyond the child's age of majority.

It is worth reminding clients who are interested in this strategy that, with either trust, the asset and the income from the asset will no longer be available to the donor. Furthermore, if a Section 2503(b) trust is used, income generated within the trust must be distributed at least annually to the child beneficiary. Last, separate trusts must be established for each child with either strategy, possibly increasing expenses associated with drafting and administering these trust arrangements.

Planning Strategy 27: Provide Advice about Adding Co-owners to Accounts

Many times, clients feel an emotional obligation to add family members to bank and brokerage accounts. Sometimes clients are tempted to add co-owners in an attempt to avoid probate. If a client wants an account to pass automatically at death, clients should instead consider using a **payable on death (POD)** or **transfer on death (TOD)** account.

- A POD is used for bank accounts.

- A TOD is used for security titling.

Although adding a spouse, child, or other person as a co-owner to property may sound like a viable strategy, the long-term ramifications of this strategy can be quite negative. For example, co-owning all assets with a spouse almost guarantees that the co-owned assets will transfer directly to the surviving spouse through the unlimited marital deduction. This can result in **over-qualifying the spouse's estate** for the marital deduction, resulting in more federal estate tax due at the surviving spouse's death than might otherwise have been the case. Adding a co-owner other than a spouse to property can also result in gift tax. Additionally, co-owners can lose the ability to receive a full step-up in basis on co-owned property, and in blended family situations, children from previous marriages may be inadvertently omitted as a beneficiary at the death of a parent. Finally, care is needed to avoid a conflict with POD or TOD arrangements that take precedence over intentions stated in a client's will.

Planning Strategy 28: Make Complete and Appropriate Use of Property Transfer Law by Using Appropriate Beneficiary Designations

One of the simplest ways to reduce **probate fees** and retain client privacy is to ensure that all financial assets owned by a client have designated beneficiaries and contingent beneficiaries, and that these designations are kept up to date. Changes precipitated by a death, divorce, or other personal situation should not be overlooked. Like many other estate planning topics, beneficiary designations require clients to face their mortality and make choices. Too often, no designation is made or "payable to the estate" is chosen by default. A financial planner can add value to the financial planner-client relationship by ensuring the appropriate beneficiary designations have been made.

Planning Strategy 29: Take Care to Accurately Account for Life Insurance in the Gross Estate

It is important to know when and how much life insurance should be included in a client's gross estate. The face value of a policy is always included if a decedent owns the insurance and is the insured. The face value amount should be reduced by any outstanding policy loans and accrued dividends. If a decedent owned a policy but was not the insured, the **interpolated terminal reserve** value of the policy, plus any unearned premium, will likely be included in the gross estate. Often, this value is close to the cash value of a non-term policy. Failing to account for the appropriate value of life insurance in a client's gross estate can produce significant estate miscalculations.

Planning Strategy 30: Valuing Art and Collectibles

The valuation of art, collectibles, and other keepsakes owned by a deceased relative often causes heirs confusion. Two values exist: the catalog value, available for most items; and the market value. Catalog values are used primarily for insurance purposes; however, heirs sometimes assume that an inventory based on catalog values is equivalent to market value. This is rarely true. In the case of collectibles, such as stamps and books, market value may be as little as 20 percent of the unadjusted (for condition of the item[s]) catalog value.[4] That is, a collection will almost always generate less in cash value than the cost it would take to replace the collection. In some situations, catalog and market values tend to be close. The valuation of precious metals, for example, usually falls much closer to catalog valuation. When reporting the worth of a valuable collection for estate planning purposes, it is important to work with an experienced appraiser who can translate catalog values into market values.

Planning Strategy 31: Ensure That Each Client Has Appropriate Estate Planning Documents in Place

According to an ABC News poll, only 50 percent of adults living in the United States have a will—a document written to direct the distribution of one's property at death, and even fewer—only 42 percent—have a living will, health care proxy, or advance medical directive (AMD) for directing end-of-life or health care decisions.[5] A financial planner should continually evaluate the strategies, products, and legal techniques a client is currently using to accumulate, preserve, and distribute assets over time. Although no one but an attorney should ever draft a legal document, every financial planner who performs comprehensive financial planning should help clients think through the complex issues associated with planning an estate. As part of this review, it is imperative that a financial planner determine whether a client (and spouse or partner) possesses any of the following documents and evaluate when documents were drafted and whether existing documents are still applicable.

- Client will(s): A legal document outlining how property will be transferred at death.

- Letter(s) of last instruction: A document written to a significant other (usually a spouse) to provide directions regarding the execution of a client's will.

- Codicil: An attachment or amendment to an existing will.

- Power of attorney (medical or financial): A legal document appointing another person to act for the client if the client becomes incapacitated.

- Living will or advance medical directive (AMD): A directive written for the use of a physician or hospital that outlines a client's wishes regarding medical and end-of-life treatment in the event of the client's incapacitation.

In addition to these legal documents, any prepaid, contracted, or informal final arrangements should also be discussed and the location of any contracts determined, if applicable. Finally, it is important to verify and review the following documents to develop a comprehensive profile of the client situation and confirm locations for future use:

- Birth certificate(s) for all household members;

- Marriage certificate(s) and/or divorce decree(s);

- All in-force insurance policies with beneficiary designations;

- Life, health, long-term care, and annuity policies and beneficiary designation form(s) for individual and group policies;

- Title(s) to personal property and deed(s) to real property in the state of residence or other states;

- Inventory of any special property such as jewelry, fine art, or a collection (e.g., stamps, coins, wine, firearms) including a schedule of beneficiaries;

- Brokerage account statements or other evidence of security ownership (e.g., stock certificates);

- Business agreements and documentation for any outstanding unpaid debts or unsettled legal claims;

- Income tax returns for the previous three years; and

- The location of a safety deposit box, an inventory of contents, the location of key(s), and a determination of whether state law requires that the box be sealed until inventoried by a representative of the court.

Planning Strategy 32: Use a Legal Document Checklist to Ensure Proper Estate Planning

After reviewing a client's current estate plan, a variety of issues may need to be addressed. Relevant issues and concerns should drive the estate planning recommendation development process. The checklist shown in Figure 13.12 can be used to guide a review of a client's current estate planning situation.

Figure 13.12. Estate Planning Documentation Checklist

Estate Planning Documentation Checklist		
Question	Yes	No
1. Is the client's name correct on all documents?		
2. Is the spouse's or partner's name correct on all documents?		
3. Are the children's names and ages (if applicable) correct on all documents?		
4. Is the executor properly named?		
5. Is a guardian for dependent children named?		
6. If named, is the guardian still the appropriate choice?		
7. Are special bequests adequately identified?		
8. Are charitable bequests up to date and adequately identified?		
9. Is the simultaneous death clause appropriate for the state of residence?		
10. Are trust documents referred to in the will?		
11. Does the will refer to a particular trust if a trust exists?		
12. Have trusts, other than testamentary trusts, been funded?		
13. Have special considerations been made for parents?		
14. Have special considerations been made for siblings?		
15. Have special considerations been made for grandchildren?		
16. Are codicils up to date and accurate?		
17. Does the client have a power of attorney in place? If so, what kind and what powers are included?		
18. Has the client written a letter of last instructions?		
19. Depending on the state of residence and need, has the client drafted: • a living will? • an advance medical directive? • a medical power of attorney? • a HIPAA authorization?		
20. Does the client share time in different states? If so, are all documents appropriate and in place?		
21. Is there a current list of all financial professionals, including the estate attorney, available for the survivors or the executor?		

Quantitative/Analytical Mini-Case Problems

Sandomir and Rasia Kolbe

1. Sandomir and Rasia Kolbe, ages fifty eight and fifty seven respectively, and their three grown children, recently attended Sandomir's father's funeral in Poland. They realized that they did not know the effect of federal estate tax on their own estate, nor did they have any legal documentation supporting end-of-life medical or financial decisions. So, upon returning home, Rasia called her mother for a recommendation regarding estate planning help. Rasia's mother suggested an attorney for the legal documents and her own financial planner for other estate planning needs. For the purposes of this problem, assume all family members are citizens of the United States. Financial information for the Kolbe family follows:

Current Division of Assets				
Assets	Total	Sandomir	Rasia	Joint
Cash and savings	$83,500	$4,500	$7,000	$72,000
Securities and annuities (nonqualified)	$625,000	0	0	$625,000
Securities and annuities (qualified)	$55,000	0	$55,000	0
Retirement plans	$605,000	$425,000	$180,000	0
Automobiles	$105,000	0	0	$105,000
Personal property	$150,000	0	0	$150,000
Residence	$500,000	0	0	$500,000
Other real estate	$350,000	0	0	$350,000
Business interests	$225,000	0	$225,000	0
Life insurance (see table below)	$164,000	$84,000	$80,000	0
Total assets	$2,862,500	$513,500	$547,000	$1,802,000

Current Life Insurance Information					
	Face Value	Cash Value	Owner	Insured	Beneficiary
Life Policy # 1 (Term)	$220,000	$0	Employer	Sandomir	Sandomir
Life Policy # 2 (Whole)	$250,000	$45,000	Sandomir	Sandomir	Rasia
Life Policy # 3 (Whole)	$150,000	$30,000	Rasia	Sandomir	Children
Life Policy # 4 (Term)	$20,000	0	Rasia	Rasia	Sandomir
Life Policy # 5 (VUL)	$300,000	$50,000	Rasia	Rasia	Sandomir
Life Policy # 6 (Whole)	$50,000	$9,000	Sandomir	Rasia	Sandomir
Life Policy # 7 (Whole)	$150,000	$30,000	Sandomir	Rasia	Children
Total life insurance	$1,140,000	$164,000			

Based on the Kolbes' financial information, the lawyer and the financial planner jointly made the following recommendations:

Recommendation 1: Establish testamentary trusts for both Sandomir and Rasia.

Recommendation 2: Retitle assets in preparation of funding trusts.

Recommendation 3: Transfer life insurance ownership to the three children.

To assist the Kolbes with their estate planning, answer the following questions.

a. What type of trust(s) might be recommended in keeping with the clients' desires of minimizing estate taxes, maximizing privacy, and easing asset ownership transfers?

b. How might the assets be retitled to ensure that all trusts can be adequately funded?

c. What are some of the challenges associated with transferring ownership of the insurance policies to the children? Describe some of the problems with the current life insurance designations. What other strategies can also be considered to alleviate any potential estate, gift, or income tax issues?

d. Besides completing wills and trust documents, what other legal documents should the Kolbes consider?

Jane and John Williams

2. Assume the following estate planning information for Jane and her spouse John.

	Client (Jane)	Spouse (John)	Joint*
Assets	$16,300,000	$9,200,000	$4,500,000
Debts			1,000,000
Funeral	120,000	120,000	
Estate administration	200,000	200,000	
Charitable contribution	400,000	400,000	
Marital plan	A/B	A/B	

*Jointly owned with right of survivorship between client and spouse. Assume an exclusion amount of $11,580,000 and a unified credit of $4,577,800

a. If Jane were to pass away first, what is her tax liability before the marital deduction?

b. If John were to pass away first, what is his tax liability before the marital deduction?

c. Using the portable estate exemption, how much of their combined estate is taxable today?

d. If Jane and John fail to take advantage of the portable estate exemption by forgetting to file IRS Form 706 at the death of the first spouse, will there be a tax liability this year, assuming the second spouse also passes shortly thereafter? Describe an estate planning strategy that can be used to minimize any estate tax liability in this situation.

Brenda Chatterjee

3. Brenda Chatterjee is wealthy, single, and generous. During the previous year she made the following gifts:

*   Gift of stock to the local art museum (a 501(c)(3) nonprofit organization): $245,000

*   College tuition payment for niece: $29,000 made directly to the institution

*   Medical bills for elderly neighbor: $18,000 paid directly to the hospital

*   Home down payment gift to daughter: $30,000 paid directly to the mortgage lender

*   Cash gift to son: $17,000

*   Use the gift tax rates shown below as a guide to answer the following questions:

For Taxable Estates Between ...	And ...	You'll Pay This Amount of Tax ...	Plus, You'll Pay This Percentage on the Amount in Excess of the Lower Limit
$0	$9,999	$0	18%
$10,000	$19,999	$1,800	20%
$20,000	$39,999	$3,800	22%
$40,000	$59,999	$8,200	24%
$60,000	$79,999	$13,000	26%
$80,000	$99,999	$18,200	28%
$100,000	$149,999	$23,800	30%
$150,000	$249,999	$38,800	32%
$250,000	$499,999	$70,800	34%
$500,000	$749,999	$155,800	37%
$750,000	$999,999	$248,300	39%
$1,000,000	-----------	$345,800	40%

a.   What is the total amount of taxable gifts this year?

b.   What is Brenda's gift tax liability this year?

c.   Assume that Brenda has not used any portion of her unified credit. What alternative does Brenda have in terms of paying the gift tax liability?

Malek and Nelda Goetz

4.   Malek and Nelda Goetz live in Nevada. They are working with you to deal with several estate planning questions and concerns. Use your estate planning skills to answer the following questions:

a.   Nelda read that it is a good idea to have a power of attorney in place to help deal with incapacitation issues. She is worried, however, that providing someone power over the family's financial situation now could lead to unnecessary problems and confusion. What type of POA can Malek and Nelda establish that will address her worries? What needs to occur to trigger this type of POA?

b.   Malek and Nelda were married in Nevada. In fact, they have lived their entire life in Nevada. If Malek were to pass away, with the family home valued at $500,000 at Malek's death, what will be Nelda's new basis in the property? Assume the basis in the home is $100,000.

c.   Avoiding probate is a primary concern for Malek. Which of the following assets will be subject to probate?

- A personal residence owned JTWROS with a child.

- Life insurance proceeds paid to a non-insured beneficiary.

- Property titled as tenants in common.

- Brokerage account.

d.   Malek would like to reduce the value of the family gross estate by transferring ownership of the family's second home to his daughter; however, he is worried that he and Nelda may need to live in the house in the event they sell their primary residence (the primary residence is under contract for sale). Malek and Nelda should consider establishing what type of trust to deal with this potentiality?

e.   Nelda owns a small business with three other individuals. The business is growing and profitable. Nelda would like to establish a buy-sell agreement to ensure business continuity. What type of agreement should she establish, with her business partners, if she hope that each business owner will purchase life insurance on the life of each other business owner?

f.   At what age can Malek's son elect to access assets held in a Section 2503(b) trust (the son is named as the beneficiary)?

Mary Eddy and Mack Baker

5.   Your clients, Mary Eddy and Mack Baker, have come to you for help addressing their combined estate plan. Mary, age sixty eight, is contemplating marriage to Mack, age thirty eight. Mack is a handsome man with many attributes that women find appealing. Mary, although an older lady, has maintained her fine figure, but occasionally she finds other younger women glancing at Mack. She finds this disconcerting and worries that someday, maybe soon, Mack will leave her for a younger woman.

It is unlikely that Mack would ever do such a thing. Besides having professed great love for Mary in his marriage proposal, it is also an established fact that Mack has potentially much to gain from this marriage. Four years ago, he was divorced from his wife after a lengthy bankruptcy filing. Although the bankruptcy filing stopped creditors from harassing him, he has recently received calls from creditors about bills that he is either late on currently or has just failed to pay. He has no children of his own. He currently works as a lawn and supply stocker at a home supply store, where he earns $9.50 per hour. He has no assets other than a 2001 Ford F-150 with 125,000 current miles.

Mary is a self-made woman. Five years ago, she sold her cosmetics company that she started in the 1960s with her now deceased husband. The proceeds of the sale include approximately $24,500,000 in cash and stock in a new cosmetic company worth $3,000,000. She has four grown children and two grandchildren by her first son. Although not a close family, Mary would like for her children to share equally in her estate when she passes. She would also like to leave a legacy for her grandchildren, both living and yet unborn, to pay for college expenses at a private east coast university. If she marries Mack, as she thinks she will, she would like for his needs to be met during his lifetime, unless he has an affair while she is living, regardless of her health or incapacitation, or if he remarries within three years of her death.

Mack recently read a book on probate and investing. He has concluded that avoiding probate is a good thing to do. He has suggested that he and Mary place the bulk of their assets in joint tenancy with the right of survivorship. He also wants to have a general power of attorney for Mary beginning at the lesser time of her incapacitation or five years. He has suggested to Mary that she need not have a living will but rather a health care proxy with Mack as the proxy. Mary agrees with Mack that her house should be retitled as joint tenants with right of survivorship shortly after they are married. She is unsure how this will affect Mack's relationship with his creditors. This question, along with others, has prompted Mary to seek your advice about what steps she should take next. Please use the following asset and liability data to answer Mary's questions.

Property	Owner	Value
Checking and Savings Accounts	Mary/Mack	$16,000/$250
Money Market Account	Mary	$24,530,000
Mutual Fund	Mary	$60,000
Cosmetic Company Stock	Mary	$3,000,000
Vacation Home	Mary	$655,000
Paintings	Mary	$300,000
Vested Profit Sharing	Mary	$95,000
Furniture and Household Goods	Mary	$55,000
Jewelry and Gems	Mary	$75,000
Automobiles	Mary	$45,000
Automobile (Ford F-150)	Mack	$2,200
Life Insurance Owner, Insured, and Beneficiary	Mary	$800,000
Primary Residence	Mary	$550,000
Mortgage on Residence	Mary	$95,000
Charitable Donation	Mary	$1,000,000
Debts	Mary	$240,000
Car Loan	Mary	$15,000

Unpaid Medical Bills	Mary	$20,000
Unpaid Bills	Mack	$8,000
Expected Funeral Expenses Estate Expenses and Fees	Mary/Mack Mary/Mack	$40,000 $85,000 (assuming Mary and Mack marry)

a. Assume Mary and Mack get married. If Mary dies first shortly after marriage, what is the non-inflation adjusted value of her gross estate?

b. Assume Mary dies first and leaves all her assets to Mack. What will be her federal estate tax liability without the marital deduction?

c. Assume Mary dies first and leaves all her assets to Mack. What will be the non-inflation adjusted value of Mack's gross estate if he dies shortly thereafter?

d. How much will Mack owe in federal estate taxes should Mary dies first, leave all her assets to Mack, with Mack dying shortly thereafter?

e. How does retitling assets as JTWROS conflict with Mary's family legacy goal?

f. Should Mary add Mack to the title of her home as JTWROS? What would be an alternative recommendation?

g. Why should Mary still have a living will, even though Mack disagrees?

Chapter Resources

Legal Information Institute, Cornell University Law School, 26 USC § 2518 – Disclaimers. Available at: www.law.cornell.edu/uscode/text/26/2518.

Gary Langer, *Poll: Americans Not Planning for the Future*. Available at http://abcnews.go.com/Business/story?id=86992&page=1#.TvpMeZg5tFI.

Napoleon, Philatelic Estate Disposition for the Novice, *American Philatelist*. Available at: stamps.org/userfiles/file/Estate/PhilatelicEstateDispositionfortheNovice.pdf, p. 159.

IRS Form 706 Instructions: Generation Assignment. Available at http://www.irs.gov/instructions/i706gst/ch01.html.

Endnotes

1. http://www.calbar.ca.gov/Public/Free-Legal-Information/Legal-Guides/Estate-Planning#1

2. Legal Information Institute, Cornell University Law School, 26 USC § 2518 – Disclaimers. Available at: www.law.cornell.edu/uscode/text/26/2518.

3. *IRS Form 706 Instructions: Generation Assignment.* Available at http://www.irs.gov/instructions/i706gst/ch01.html.

4. Napoleon, Philatelic Estate Disposition for the Novice, American Philatelist. Available at: stamps.org/userfiles/file/Estate/PhilatelicEstateDispositionfortheNovice.pdf, p. 159.

5. Gary Langer, *Poll: Americans Not Planning for the Future.* Available at http://abcnews.go.com/Business/story?id=86992&page=1#.TvpMeZg5tFI.

Chapter 14

Financial Planning Cases

Learning Objectives

- Learning Objective 1: Utilize the seven step financial planning process when solving financial planning cases.

- Learning Objective 2: Apply financial planning strategies and skills when solving financial planning cases.

- Learning Objective 3: Use professional judgment when selecting appropriate financial planning recommendations to meet a client's unique needs.

Chapter Equations

There are no equations in this chapter.

CASE STUDIES: AN INTRODUCTION

This section of the book includes seventeen mini-cases: (a) ten ten-question mini-cases, (b) five twenty-question cases, (c) an ethics case, and (d) a comprehensive open-ended case. Each case has been written to test both definitional and basic applied financial planning concepts. The longer twenty-question cases provide more detail in terms of background, assumptions, and complicating factors. Those interested in solving the ethics case will find material published in *Fundamentals of Writing a Financial Plan: A Seven Step Process* helpful when answering questions. The Ruiz open-ended, comprehensive case was written to test complex analytical and strategic management skills. Each of the other longer cases, although comprehensive in context, focuses on one central theme, as follows:

1.   Graham case: general financial planning

2.   Cantrell case: investment planning

3.   Mayfield case: retirement planning

4.   Butterfield Case: insurance planning

5.   Tun Case: education planning

Instructors and students interested in additional writing applications will find the Graham, Cantrell, Mayfield, Butterfield, Tun, and Ruiz cases appropriate for use as either modular/targeted or comprehensive financial planning narratives. That is, each case contains enough information, when supplemented with appropriate assumptions, to be used as the foundation for a written financial plan.

The ethics case is intended to be used as an interactive in-class exercise. The ethics case was designed to be lighthearted and obvious in the main character's violation of multiple professional standards. The case was written to help students assess competencies related to key Certified Financial Planner Board of Standards, Inc., (CFP Board) practice standards, terms, rules, and ethical requirements.

Before beginning work on any of the cases, it is important to consider each case in relation to the following assumptions:

- Case data, information, and associated assumptions can be linked to the Financial Planning Analysis Excel™ package provided with the book. Using the assumptions provided, financial planning students should be able to use the spreadsheets to arrive at mathematical solutions to all core financial planning problems (e.g., cash flow, net worth, retirement, etc.). This does not mean, however, that the cases can be solved only by using the spreadsheet package. To the contrary; it is possible to solve each case using traditional calculators, formulas, and commercially available software.

- Assumptions within a particular case are divided into sections. For example, each case has unique assumptions related to insurance planning, retirement planning, estate planning, and other relevant financial planning topics. *Students should use only the assumptions provided in each section to solve math and strategic planning questions related to that section.* In other words, it is possible—and likely—that rate-of-return assumptions, for instance, will be different for insurance and retirement planning purposes. It is also likely that current market data will be different from what is shown in each case. As such, when solving any question, students should use the assumptions related to the specific section in the case narrative. Bringing in additional assumptions, rate-of-return data, or other information from the "real world" will result in widely divergent solutions, and in cases where multiple choice questions are asked, results may lead to incorrect answers and student frustration.

- Instructors and students who would like to add realism to each case may want to consider changing the Anystate and Anycity location assumption to a specific state. Income tax information was originally developed for each case based on a model state, as shown below:

  - Graham case: Arizona

  - Cantrell case: South Dakota

  - Mayfield case: Ohio

  - Butterfield case: Virginia

  - Tun case: Georgia

It is hoped that the cases that follow will be challenging, yet rewarding in helping to identify student competencies related to the financial planning process.

The Bonita Zimmer Case

A FINANCIAL SITUATION MINI-CASE

Today's date is December 31, 20XX. Bonita Zimmer has stopped by your office for her year-end annual financial planning review. The following narrative provides important details about Bonita.

Bonita just turned thirty years of age. She lives in a house that she purchased three years ago for $110,000, right before housing prices began to skyrocket in her area. She was fortunate to purchase the home with $18,000 in down payment money received from her father (who is married) and a loan for the remainder of the home price. She was able to obtain a 6.5 percent thirty-year mortgage.

Bonita is a hard worker and good saver. Over the past eight years—since graduating from college—she has accumulated a nice-sized nest egg. Table I.1 summarizes her asset and liability situation.

Table I.1. Bonita Zimmer's Assets and Liabilities

Assets	Value	Liabilities	Value
Savings account	$9,000	Mortgage balance	$88,704
Checking account	$2,000	Credit card balances	$3,200
6-month CD	$2,500	Car loan	$9,500
Principal residence	$367,000		
Car	$12,000	**Total assets**	$403,500
Personal property	$11,000	**Total liabilities**	$101,404
		Net worth	$302,096

Bonita has been saving for an emergency fund. Her goal is to maintain a liquid account balance equal to six months of total expenses. Table I.2 summarizes Bonita's income and expense situation. Note that Bonita lives in an income tax-free state.

Table I.2. Bonita Zimmer's Income and Expenses

Income or Expense	Amount (Yearly)
Income	
Annual income	$55,000
Reinvested interest income	$400
Expenses	
Mortgage payment	$6,978
Real estate taxes and insurance	$2,200
Utilities	$2,400
Groceries	$3,000
Dining out	$2,400
Credit card payments	$960
Car payments	$4,400
Gas	$900
Auto insurance	$1,200
Auto and household maintenance	$1,800
Entertainment	$3,200
Federal taxes	$6,540
FICA	$4,320
Personal care	$1,500
Clothing	$3,000
Charitable donations	$2,200
Gifts to others	$3,000
Miscellaneous expenses	$2,400
Reinvested interest	$400

Please use the information provided in the case narrative to answer the following case questions.[1]

Case Questions

1. If Bonita sells her current residence for full fair market value (excluding commissions and closing costs), and then purchases a new residence for $180,000 in the same calendar year, the amount of proceeds subject to capital gains tax will be:

    a. $7,000

    b. $28,296

    c. $187,000

    d. $257,000

2. Which of the following statements is true assuming that the money Bonita received for the down payment for her house from her father was a gift rather than a loan?

    I. Bonita must pay a gift tax on the amount that exceeds the gift tax annual exclusion.

    II. Her father should have filed a gift-splitting election with the IRS to avoid incurring a gift tax liability.

    III. Bonita should have filed a gift-splitting declaration with the IRS to avoid incurring a gift tax liability.

    IV. The basis in the house is increased by the amount of any taxes paid on the down payment gift.

    a. II only

    b. I and III only

    c. II and IV only

    d. III and IV only

    e. I, III, and IV only

3. Bonita is concerned that she could be overextended on her monthly mortgage payment. Do you agree with her?

    a. Yes, because her total debt-to-income ratio exceeds the accepted benchmark of 36 percent of gross income.

    b. No, because her monthly housing cost-to-income ratio is less than the accepted benchmark of 28 percent of gross income.

   c.   Yes, because her monthly housing cost-to-income ratio is greater than the accepted benchmark of 28 percent of gross income.

   d.   No, because her monetary assets are greater than six months of total expenses, which allows her to overextend her monthly mortgage obligation.

4.   Which of the following statements is correct regarding Bonita's cash flow situation?

   a.   Her level of discretionary cash flow, if used for savings, is below the recommended benchmark average of 10 percent of gross income.

   b.   Her level of expenditures for principal, interest, tax, insurance (PITI), and other debt payments exceeds the recommended maximum of 36 percent of gross income.

   c.   She needs to save additional money in liquid assets to achieve her six-month emergency fund goal.

   d.   Both (a) and (c) are correct.

   e.   Answers (a), (b), and (c) are correct.

5.   Bonita has been dating Jason for nine months. He has proposed marriage. If Bonita accepts the proposal and Bonita and Jason purchase a home together after they get married, which method can Bonita and Jason use to title the property that will provide automatic survivorship rights, assuming they live in a non-community property state?

      I.   Joint tenants with right of survivorship (JTWROS).

      II.   Tenants by the entirety.

      III. Tenants in common.

   a.   I only

   b.   II only

   c.   I and II only

   d.   I and III only

   e.   II and III only

6.   Bonita is considering changing jobs and plans to roll over the vested portion of her qualified retirement plan into either an IRA or the qualified retirement plan of her new employer. Reasons why a direct rollover into the new plan, rather than an IRA, would be more appropriate include which of the following?

      I.   The new employer's plan is the only way Bonita can obtain a distribution at retirement in the form of a life annuity.

      II.   The new employer's plan contains a provision for loans.

III. There will be no tax penalty if a lump sum benefit is withdrawn from the new plan at early retirement after attaining age fifty.

IV. Lump sum withdrawals from the new employer's plan after age 59½ will be eligible for five- or ten-year forward-averaging.

a. II only

b. I and III only

c. II and III only

d. II and IV only

7. Bonita received a bequest of 100 shares of XYZ stock from a relative who died on March 1 of this year. The relative bought the stock at a total cost of $5,500. The value of the one-hundred shares of XYZ stock was $5,750 on March 1. On July 1 of this year, Bonita sold the stock for $6,250, incurring expenses from the sale of $250. The taxable gain on the sale will be a:

a. $250 long-term capital gain.

b. $250 short-term capital gain.

c. $500 long-term capital gain.

d. $500 short-term capital gain.

8. Bonita is considering establishing a trust for her mother that will pay out $1,000 each month. The trust department at a local bank will act as trustee. Bonita will retain the right to revoke the trust and be the remainder beneficiary of the trust. If the trust earns $15,000 for the year, who must pay income tax on earnings?

a. Bonita will pay on $15,000.

b. Bonita's mother will pay on $12,000, whereas the trust will pay on $3,000.

c. Bonita's mother pays will pay on $12,000, whereas Bonita will pay on $3,000.

d. The trust will pay on $15,000.

9. If Bonita and Jason do get married and buy a house together, they have identified two mortgage alternatives when taking out a loan. The first alternative is a thirty-year, 7 percent mortgage with five discount points to be paid at closing. The second alternative is an 8 percent mortgage with two discount points to be paid at closing. Assuming Bonita and Jason can qualify for either loan, which of the following aspects should Bonita and Jason consider when choosing between these two alternatives?

I. Monthly PMI expenses.

II. Estimated length of ownership.

    III. Monthly utility expenses.

    IV. Cash currently available.

    a. I and II only

    b. II only

    c. II and IV only

    d. IV only

    e. I, III, and IV

10. Bonita is considering purchasing an expensive piece of jewelry next month. The local jeweler is offering a three-year financing plan to help her pay for the jewels. For the purposes of preparing Bonita's financial statements for next year, you should:

    I.   List the jewels as an investment asset.

    II. List the loan amount as a current or short-term liability.

    III. List the jewels as a use or general household asset.

    IV. List the loan payment as a fixed expense on the household cash flow statement.

    a. I and II only

    b. II and III only

    c. III and IV only

    d. I and IV only

    e. II and IV only

The Larry and Lolita Ande Case

A TAX PLANNING MINI-CASE

Today's date is July 1st. Larry and Lolita Ande, both age forty-four, are reviewing their household tax situation for the current year. Larry and Lolita have been married for a number of years and have one adult child. Larry and Lolita file their own tax returns. This is the first year the Andes have run into filing questions. Table II.1 summarizes their financial position for tax purposes. Use this information to answer the Andes' tax questions.

Table II.1. The Andes' Annual Tax Position

Tax Item	Amount
Larry's earnings	$79,000
Lolita's earnings	$43,000
Federal tax withholdings	$12,300
State income tax withholdings	$4,100
State and local sales taxes paid	$2,300
FICA withholdings	$6,273
Bank account interest*	$1,600
State tax refund from previous year	$900
Home mortgage interest paid	$5,300
Real estate taxes paid	$1,800
Charitable contributions	$4,000
Unreimbursed medical expenses	$800
Stock ownership: United Motor Company**	Current value: $4,000 Basis: $8,000
Whole-life insurance policy	Face value: $100,000 Cash value: $7,800 Owner: Larry Beneficiary: Lolita Insured: Larry Policy dividend: $300
*Larry and Lolita earn 4.0 percent on the bank account balance. In comparison, short-duration municipal bond funds are currently yielding 3.4 percent.	
**Larry and Lolita purchased the stock three months ago and still own the stock today.	

The Andes itemized deductions for their federal return last year. Currently, neither Larry nor Lolita have access to a qualified retirement plan through their work. Neither Larry nor Lolita have taken steps to fund an IRA up to this point. Lolita has access to a Section 125 flexible spending account through her employer. To date, the Andes have not funded the account. Open enrollment for the Section 125 account lasts for the next thirty days.

Case Questions

1. Which of the following statements is true?

    I.   If Larry were to pass away this year, Lolita would be required to claim the face value of the life insurance received for federal income tax purposes.

    II. If Larry uses a transit pass valued at $100 per month given to him by his employer to commute to and from work, he will be required to add the value of the pass to his income for tax purposes.

    III. If the Andes want to reduce gross income for tax purposes, Larry and Lolita could contribute to a flexible spending plan to cover the cost of unreimbursed medical expenses.

    IV. Although the face value of the life insurance policy can be received tax free by Lolita if Larry were to pass away, the cash value will be fully taxable as income at the federal level.

    a. II only

    b. III only

    c. I and III only

    d. II and IV only

    e. II, III, and IV only

2. Larry and Lolita are considering moving their bank account balance to a safe municipal bond mutual fund. Before making the switch, they should be aware of which of the following?

    I.   Given their federal marginal tax bracket, the bank account provides a higher after-tax yield.

    II. Interest and capital appreciation from the municipal bond fund is federally income tax exempt.

    III. Interest from the bonds will be state income tax free if the bonds held in the fund are from the state where the Andes live.

    IV. Municipal bond interest that is used to reinvest in the fund will grow on a tax-free basis.

a. I only

b. III only

c. II and III only

d. II, III, and IV only

e. I, II, III, and IV

3. Which of the following tax items will be included when calculating the Andes' gross income this year?

    I.   Lolita's salary.

    II.   The state tax refund from the previous year.

    III.   The capital loss in United Motor Company.

    IV.   Dividends earned, but not received, on the insurance policy.

a. I and II only

b. I and IV only

c. II and III only

d. I, II, and IV only

e. I, III, and IV only

4. The Andes do not know whether they should take the standard deduction or itemize deductions this year. Which of the following statements is true in relation to this issue?

a. It does not matter which deduction amount Larry and Lolita choose because they are equal.

b. Larry and Lolita should claim itemized deductions because this amount is greater than the standard deduction.

c. Larry and Lolita should claim the standard deduction because this amount is greater than itemizing deductions.

d. If Larry and Lolita sell the United Motor Company stock, the loss will reduce their itemized deductions, making the standard deduction more attractive.

e. Both c and d are correct.

5. Lolita and Larry are thinking about adding to their family next year. If Larry and Lolita do have a child, Lolita plans to be a stay-at-home mom. Larry is concerned about what will happen to their tax situation when Lolita stops working. One issue, in particular, that Larry and Lolita would like to discuss with their financial planner is whether they should sell the United Motor

Company stock this year or wait until next year. What is the best recommendation given their current and projected income tax situation?

a.   Larry and Lolita should sell the stock this year because this will result in a larger deduction than waiting and selling when they are in a lower bracket.

b.   Larry and Lolita should sell the stock next year, making the deduction more valuable as an offset to Lolita's lost income.

c.   Larry and Lolita should sell the stock this year because the full value of the loss can be used this year to reduce their gross income level.

d.   Larry and Lolita should sell the stock next year because they currently do not need a tax loss to reduce their reportable income.

6.   The Andes are considering the possibility of moving to another state across the country so that Larry can work with his brother. Larry and his brother are employed in a similar line of work. If the Andes do move, which of the following expenses will be an allowable moving expense deduction?

   I.   Payment of real estate expenses on the sale of their current home.

   II.   Any loss that Larry and Lolita incur when selling their personal residence.

   III. Cost of travel expenses, such as lodging, while in transit from one town to another.

   IV.   Cost of meals while in transit from one town to another.

a.   III only

b.   I and III only

c.   II and III only

d.   III and IV only

e.   None of these expenses is deductible

7.   Which of the following tax planning strategies provides the greatest immediate tax benefit for the Andes?

a.   Contributing the maximum allowable to a Roth IRA.

b.   Making the maximum allowable deductible contribution to a traditional IRA.

c.   Establishing and contributing to an immediate fixed annuity.

d.   Purchasing additional whole life insurance.

8. Larry is considering changing jobs. A potential employer has offered him several employee benefits that make the job offer very attractive. Which of the following employee benefit alternatives will help reduce the Andes' reportable gross income for federal income tax purposes if Larry takes the job and signs up for the benefit?

    I.   The immediate right to contribute to a 401(k) plan.

    II. Employer-provided parking.

    III. Group term life insurance equal to three times salary.

    IV. The right to contribute to a Section 125 plan.

    a. I only

    b. I and II only

    c. I and IV only

    d. II, III, and IV only

    e. I, II, III, and IV

9. One month ago, Lolita's uncle gave Larry and Lolita a check for $25,000. Lolita's uncle lives in California, and on a recent trip to Reno, he hit a big jackpot. Lolita's uncle gave the gift as a way to share his good fortune with the family. Larry is concerned about the tax ramifications of the gift. Which statement(s) below is (are) true in this situation?

    I.   Larry and Lolita are responsible for paying any applicable state and federal income tax on the full $25,000.

    II. Larry, Lolita, and Lolita's uncle are jointly responsible for paying any applicable any tax liability.

    III. Lolita's uncle is responsible for paying pay any applicable state and federal income taxes on the winnings.

    IV. Lolita and Larry need not pay any applicable income tax because the $25,000 is a gift.

    a. I only

    b. II only

    c. III only

    d. II and III only

    e. III and IV only

10. If Larry and Lolita finalize a divorce this year and the court orders Larry to pay alimony in the amount of $700 per month for six months (through December), and then $700 per month for fifteen years or until Lolita dies, which of the following statements will be true?

   a. Larry and Lolita may not file married filing jointly when completing this year's tax return.

   b. Lolita must file as head of household when completing this year's tax return.

   c. Larry may take a $4,200 deduction from gross income related to the alimony payments.

   d. Lolita must report the alimony she receives as taxable income in future years.

   e. Both c and d are correct.

The Ira and Flora Roth Case

A TAX PLANNING MINI-CASE

Your clients, Ira and Flora Roth, have come to you for some basic tax planning advice and guidance. Here are the facts you need to help them.

- Ira's earned income: $65,000

- Flora's earned income: $52,000

- Ira and Flora live in Kansas and own a municipal bond issued by the city of Wichita (not a private activity bond). The bond's face value is $100,000; the bond has a 3.5 percent coupon.

- Ira paid $12,000 in alimony for the year to a former spouse.

- During the year, Ira and Flora had the following transactions:

  ○ Sold XXP stock for $11,000; originally purchased many years ago for $5,000.

  ○ Purchased 100 shares of HHP stock for $3,000 in April of the year.

  ○ Sold a KSU corporate bond originally purchased on February 6 of the year for $15,000 (basis); Ira and Flora received $11,000 for the bond on November 12.

  ○ Redeemed $4,300 worth of EE savings bonds in July that Ira and Flora had held for twelve years; the bonds earned 6 percent interest and had doubled in value.

  ○ Sold 1,000 shares of UNR stock at $7 per share that Ira and Flora had purchased earlier in the year for $13 per share.

- Flora (age sixty-one) received annuity distributions of $22,000 from a nonqualified annuity (with payments made over Flora's life). At the beginning of the year, the annuity had a value of $300,000 and an after-tax basis of $100,000.

- Ira (age fifty-seven) terminated employment and took a distribution of $100,000 from his 401(k) plan with the intent of rolling the money over to a Fidelity IRA in thirty to forty-five days.

- Ira and Flora paid $3,000 in housing expenses for their grandchild Chuck as a way to help offset some of his college expenses. They paid the $3,000 directly to Chuck.

- During the year, Ira and Flora paid the following items:

  - $12,600 in unreimbursed medical expenses,

  - $7,000 in mortgage interest,

  - $3,500 in property taxes,

  - $500 in legal fees,

  - $750 donation to alma mater,

  - $100 in safe deposit box fees,

  - $3,000 in state income taxes,

  - $2,800 in state and local sales taxes,

  - $1,000 to the Salvation Army, and

  - $2,400 to their church.

- Ira and Flora also contributed $3,200 to a Section 529 plan to help pay for their grandson's college expenses.

Life expectancy table:

Single-life Expectancy Table							
Age	Divisor	Age	Divisor	Age	Divisor	Age	Divisor
56	28.7	70	17.0	84	8.1	98	3.4
57	27.9	71	16.3	85	7.6	99	3.1
58	27.0	72	15.5	86	7.1	100	2.9
59	26.1	73	14.8	87	6.7	101	2.7
60	25.2	74	14.1	88	6.3	102	2.5
61	24.4	75	13.4	89	5.9	103	2.3
62	23.5	76	16.7	90	5.5	104	2.1
63	22.7	77	16.1	91	5.2	105	1.9
64	21.8	78	11.4	92	4.9	106	1.7
65	21.0	79	10.8	93	4.6	107	1.5
66	20.2	80	10.2	94	4.3	108	1.4
67	19.4	81	9.7	95	4.1	109	1.2
68	18.6	82	9.1	96	3.8	110	1.1
69	17.8	83	8.6	97	3.6	111+	1.0

Case Questions

1. How much in long-term capital gains did the Roths incur for the year?

   a. –$3,000

   b. $0

   c. $1,000

   d. $6,000

2. What is the net gain or loss position of the Roths' capital transactions for the year?

   a. The Roths suffered $1,000 in net short-term losses for the year.

   b. The Roths suffered $4,000 in net short-term losses for the year.

   c. The Roths suffered $10,000 in net short-term losses for the year.

   d. The Roths suffered $15,000 in net short-term losses for the year.

3. How much (rounded) of Flora's annuity distribution will be taxable this year?

   a. 19 percent

   b. 67 percent

   c. 81 percent

   d. 100 percent

4. Which of the following statements is true?

   a. Ira's employer will withhold $20,000 in federal taxes from the 401(k) distribution.

   b. Ira will owe an immediate 10 percent penalty on the 401(k) distribution.

   c. Ira will need to contribute only $80,000 to the IRA rollover to avoid penalties.

   d. Ira needs to roll over the 401(k) distribution to the IRA within thirty days to avoid taxes and penalties.

5. Had Ira and Flora decided to give the XXP stock to a charity, they should have:

   I. sold the stock first and then made the donation for a deduction.

   II. donated the stock first and then taken the deduction.

   III. donated cash to the charity then sold the stock.

    a.   I only

    b.   II only

    c.   III only

    d.   I, II, or III, because each strategy results in the same tax outcome

6.   Rather than donate cash to a charity, assume Ira and Flora decide to donate the KSU bond to a charity. In this situation, Ira and Flora should:

    I.   sell the bond first and then make a donation for a tax deduction.

    II.   donate the bond first and then take a tax deduction.

    III.   donate the bond first and then deduct the loss.

    a.   I only

    b.   II only

    c.   III only

    d.   I, II, or III, because each strategy results in the same tax outcome

7.   How much can the Roths deduct from their federal income taxes for the Section 529 plan contribution?

    a. $0

    b. $1,000

    c. $2,000

    d. $1,600

    e. $3,200

8.   In addition to the information already known about the Roths, you learn that Flora owns a vacant lot in Topeka that she purchased as an investment. She would like to exchange the lot so that she does not incur a tax liability. Which of the following properties can she take in trade to receive like-kind tax treatment?

    a.   A duplex in Wichita.

    b.   Collector coins owned by a coin dealer.

    c.   A mortgage on a rental house in Topeka.

    d.   Either a or c.

9. Instead of doing a straight exchange with someone, assume Flora finds a person who is willing to provide her a combination of property and cash for her vacant lot. Flora will receive $5,000 cash and a similar vacant lot across town valued at $10,000 (basis of $8,000). If her original lot has a fair market value of $20,000 and a basis of $5,000, how much will Flora *realize* on this transaction?

    a. $0

    b. $5,000

    c. $8,000

    d. $10,000

    e. $15,000

10. Using the information presented in the previous question, how much gain must Flora *recognize* on the exchange for income tax purposes?

    a. $0

    b. $5,000

    c. $10,000

    d. $15,000

    e. $20,000

The Kevin and Sonya Shim Case

AN INSURANCE PLANNING MINI-CASE

Kevin and Sonya Shim are conducting an insurance review with their financial planner. Kevin and Sonya consider themselves middle-class Americans—with a small but positive cash flow and a modest net worth. Kevin (age sixty-three) is just a few years away from retirement, whereas Sonya (age sixty-one) plans to work a few more years once Kevin officially retires. The following discussion provides a summary of the Shims' insurance planning situation.

Life Insurance

Kevin owns a $250,000 universal life insurance policy. Sonya is the insured and their son Wilbur (age thirty-seven) is the beneficiary. The policy has a cash value of $23,450 and a living benefits provision; all account earnings are used to offset premium expenses. Sonya owns a twenty-year $100,000 level-term life policy that she purchased five years ago. She pays approximately $450 per year in premium costs.

Property and Casualty Insurance

Kevin and Sonya own a home as JTWROS that has a market and replacement value of $245,000. The house is insured with a Standard HO-3 policy for $210,700. The policy requires that the Shims pay a $500 deductible per claim occurrence. Other provisions include the following:

- 10 percent coverage on detached structures,

- coverage up to $250 for cash,

- coverage up to $1,500 for collectibles, artwork, and similar assets,

- personal property contents coverage equal to 20 percent of the insured dwelling,

- living expense coverage for six months,

- coverage up to $100,000 for personal liability, and

- a replacement cost coverage endorsement is in place.

The Shims' two cars are insured under a personal automobile policy with split-limit coverage of $250,000/$500,000/$50,000. Kevin and Sonya also have a $1 million dollar excess liability policy.

Health Insurance

The Shims are covered under Sonya's group health insurance plan. The traditional plan has a no lifetime maximum benefit, a $500-per-person deductible, and a 20 percent coinsurance clause, with a family stop-loss limit of $2,500.

Use the preceding case information to answer the questions that follow.

Case Questions

1. In preparation for retirement, Kevin is exploring his Social Security and Medicare insurance coverage options. Which of the following is a benefit provided by Medicare?

   a. Hospice benefits for terminally ill persons.

   b. A stop-loss limit for annual medical expenses in excess of $2,500.

   c. Coverage for custodial care.

   d. Coverage for non-prescription drugs.

2. Kevin is considering purchasing a twelve-year-old pickup truck for use when he goes hunting. The truck that he has his eye on has 90,000 miles but is in generally good condition. If Kevin's insurance goal is to decrease the annual premium while retaining appropriate coverage, which of the following insurance coverage(s) should Kevin exclude when purchasing an insurance policy for this truck?

   I. Part A—liability coverage.

   II. Part B—medical payments coverage.

   III. Part C—uninsured motorist coverage.

   IV. Part D—damage to insured's auto coverage.

   a. IV only

   b. II and IV only

   c. I, II, and III

   d. I, III, and IV

   e. II, III, and IV

3. If Sonya were to die today, which of the following is true in relation to the $250,000 universal life insurance policy owned by Kevin?

   a. Kevin will continue to own the policy for the benefit of Wilbur.

   b. Kevin will be deemed to have made a taxable gift of the life insurance proceeds to Wilbur.

c.   Kevin will receive an amount equal to the cash value, while Wilbur will receive the remainder of the life insurance value as a tax-free gift.

d.   Kevin will receive the proceeds of the policy.

e.   Kevin must include the $250,000 face value of the policy as an asset when he calculates Sonya's gross estate.

4.   What will be the result if Sonya decides to cancel her term life insurance policy?

a.   She will incur a $2,250 tax liability based on the level of premium paid over the past five years.

b.   She will receive $450 in premium paid for last year's coverage as a refund from the insurance company, and this amount will be fully taxable at the Federal level.

c.   She will not have a tax liability associated with the cancellation.

d.   She will incur a tax liability on the face amount received if she were to die after canceling the policy but before receiving refunded premiums.

5.   If the Shims sustain an $80,000 loss to their dwelling from a fire, how much will the insurance company pay (after the deductible) toward the dwelling loss claim?

a. $64,000

b. $68,000

c. $79,500

d. $80,000

6.   If a shed valued at $13,000 in the backyard is also destroyed in the fire, what is the maximum amount that the insurance company will pay, prior to the deductible, to replace the shed and any other detached dwellings?

a. $225,000

b. $25,000

c. $21,070

d. $13,000

e. $1,300

7.   Sonya believes that her husband is a reckless driver, and she worries about what will happen if he is ever in a serious car accident. If Kevin is involved in a car accident that causes physical harm to another motorist in the amount of $300,000, how much will be paid from the personal automobile policy (PAP) and how much will be paid from the excess liability policy?

a. $300,000 PAP and $0 excess liability.

b. $0 PAP and $300,000 excess liability.

    c. $150,000 PAP and $150,000 excess liability.

    d. $50,000 PAP and $250,000 excess liability.

    e. $250,000 PAP and $50,000 excess liability.

8.   How much will the Shims' health insurance company pay if Sonya files a claim for a broken foot that cost $2,000 for emergency room treatment, $700 for bone setting, and $300 in rehabilitation services?

    a. $0

    b. $500

    c. $2,000

    d. $2,500

    e. $3,000

9.   The Shims are curious about the alternatives available when planning for possible nursing home care costs in the future. Which of the long-term care insurance strategies listed below is an appropriate financial planning alternative for the Shims?

    I.   Use the living benefits provision within an accelerated death benefit rider available in the universal life insurance policy.

    II.   Purchase a life insurance policy that has a long-term care insurance endorsement.

    III.   Systematically save for future health care costs and use Medicare as the primary insurance coverage for long-term care expenses.

    IV.   Use Medicaid coverage for long-term care expenses after age sixty-five.

    a.   II only

    b.   I and II only

    c.   II and III only

    d.   III and IV only

    e.   I, II, and III only

10.   Currently, neither Kevin nor Sonya has disability insurance coverage. Kevin and Sonya would like more information about disability insurance. Which of the following statements is (are) true in relation to disability insurance?

    I.   Shorter elimination periods result in lower premium costs.

    II.   Benefits paid from employer-provided group disability plans are received income tax free.

III. If a guaranteed renewable contract is used, the insurance company cannot increase premiums on individual policies but can raise premiums for all individuals covered by the policy.

IV. Disability policies are nearly always designed to provide lifetime benefits.

a.   I only

b.   I and II only

c.   II and III only

d.   III only

e.   II, III, and IV only

The John and Haley Butterfield Case

AN INSURANCE PLANNING CASE

John Butterfield, age forty-nine, and his wife Haley Butterfield, age forty-four, live in a relatively new home on the outskirts of Anycity, Anystate. John and Haley have been married for twenty-three years and have three children. Both John and Haley are in excellent health. Their son Troy, age twenty, is a baseball player on scholarship at the University of Anystate. Daughter Holly, age seventeen, hopes to attend State University next fall as a cadet to begin pursuing a career in the Marine Corps.

The choices of their first two children have allowed the Butterfields to concentrate their college saving goals on Naomi, the youngest, at age thirteen. John and Haley have come to you for help in addressing several insurance planning questions and concerns. Use the following information to conduct a review of their financial situation and use your analyses to answer the questions that follow the case narrative.

Global Assumptions (Valid unless otherwise Specified in Certain Instances)

- Inflation: 3.5 percent

- All income and expense figures are given in today's dollars.

- Federal marginal tax bracket: 22 percent

- State marginal tax bracket: 5.75 percent

- Any qualified plan or IRA contribution growth rates are assumed to stop at the federally mandated limit unless otherwise restricted.

- All nominal rates of return are pretax returns.

Income Issues

- John has worked for the last fourteen years as an engineer for CNS Design. He has an $81,000 salary. He would like to retire at age sixty-seven.

- Haley has worked as a CPA for seventeen years, the last fourteen of which have been out of their home. She also does consulting work from home. Though her earnings vary from month to month, she estimates that she will earn $65,000 this year. She wants to retire at the same time as John.

- John and Haley also assume that their salaries will increase, on average, by 3.5 percent per year over their working lives. This year John and Haley anticipate earning $600 in interest and non-qualified mutual fund dividend distributions, which will be reinvested.

Expense Issues

Table V.1 provides a summary of the Butterfields' fixed (non-discretionary) and variable (discretionary) expenses.

Table V.1. Summary of Income and Expenses

Expense	Amount	Frequency
Pretax health care premiums	$200	Monthly
401(k) contributions	$540	Monthly
Keogh contributions	$7,800	Annually
Mortgage	$1,600	Monthly
Home equity loan	$625	Monthly
Auto loan #1	$310	Monthly
Auto loan #2	$500	Monthly
Credit cards and installment debt	$2,100	Annual
Auto insurance	$1,100	Semiannual
Homeowner's insurance	$825	Annual
Disability insurance (pretax)	$200	Monthly
Life insurance	$400	Annual
IRA contributions (Haley)	$750	Quarterly
IRA contributions (John)	$750	Quarterly
Subscriptions	$650	Annual
Telephone	$1,560	Annual
Digital cable television	$125	Monthly
Hobbies	$750	Annual
Entertainment	$1,500	Annual
Education payments (spending money Troy)	$5,000	Annual
Travel costs for first child while in college	$1,200	Annual
Groceries	$75	Weekly
Food away from home	$3,400	Annual
Real estate taxes	$1,300	Annual

Household maintenance	$2,700	Annual
Utilities	$175	Month
Clothing	$1,500	Annual
Dry cleaning	$50	Month
Personal care	$500	Annual
Furnishing	$1,000	Annual
Allowances	$2,000	Annual
Medical copayments	$700	Annual
Prescriptions	$250	Annual
Gas	$2,500	Annual
Personal property tax	$400	Semiannual
Banking fees	$75	Annual
IRA fees	$80	Annual
Travel	$100	Monthly
Contributions to church	$125	Monthly
Vacations	$3,000	Annual
Christmas gifts	$2,400	Annual

Home mortgage. John and Haley are eight years into a thirty-year 7.5 percent mortgage that had an original balance of $228,850. The loan has a current outstanding balance of $206,602.

Home equity loan. The loan balance was used to make an addition to their home. The monthly payment is approximately 2 percent of the outstanding balance. The credit line expires and will be due and payable in seven years. John and Haley have paid $3,000 in interest over the past year.

Auto Payments.

- Auto 1: Balance is $8,500 with thirty months remaining.

- Auto 2: Balance is $25,000 with fifty-seven months remaining.

Tax Issues

After reviewing their pay stubs, John and Haley calculated that their total annual federal withholdings and/or estimated tax payments total $20,250. State withholdings amount to $8,000. Social Security withheld is $10,985. The Butterfields file taxes as "married filing jointly" and have $30,241 in itemized deductions for the year.

The Butterfields are eligible for a $5,000 state income tax deduction, and five $1,000 state-level personal exemptions. The marginal state tax bracket is 5.75 percent.

Information about the Butterfields' assets and liabilities is shown in Table V.2.

Table V.2. The Butterfields' Asset and Liability Situation

Asset	Amount	Ownership
Checking account	$950	Client
Large-cap mutual fund	$9,000	Client
Checking account	$1,200	Co-client
Small-cap mutual fund	$17,250	Co-client
Life insurance cash value	$3,800	Co-client
Checking account	$2,800	Joint
Savings account	$7,500	Joint
Money market account	$10,050	Joint
Mid-cap mutual fund	$40,000	Joint
Artwork	$25,000	Joint
401(k)	$62,000	Client
Keogh retirement plan	$125,000	Co-client
Individual retirement account (IRA)	$38,000	Client
Individual retirement account (IRA)	$41,500	Co-client
Home	$315,000	Joint
Honda	$17,500	Joint
Toyota	$38,000	Joint
Collectibles	$13,000	Co-client
Furniture	$17,500	Client
Other assets	$69,000	Joint
Misc. assets	$39,000	Joint
Liabilities	**Amount**	**Ownership**
Visa credit card	$2,500	Co-client
MasterCard	$4,900	Joint
Mortgage	$206,602	Joint
Home equity loan	$32,000	Joint
Honda	$8,500	Joint
Toyota	$25,000	Joint
Short-term installment debt	$21,000	Client

Current Insurance Data

Property and Casualty

Auto. All vehicles

- Liability: $300,000 single limit (including uninsured motorist)

- Medical payments coverage: $1,000 limit per person

- Deductible: $250 collision; $100 comprehensive

- Premium: $1,100 every six months

Auto 1: 20XX Honda Accord LX Sedan

Mileage: 30,000

Color: light blue

Engine: 6-cylinder

Transmission: manual

Payment: $310/month

Balance: $8,500 with 2.5 years remaining

Worth: $17,500

Auto 2: 20XX Toyota Sequoia Limited (4×4)

Mileage: 5,500

Color: silver

Engine: 8-cylinder

Transmission: automatic

Payment: $500/month

Balance: $25,000 with fifty-seven months remaining

Worth: $38,000

Home. Single-family dwelling

- Insured value: $245,000

- Replacement value: $315,000

- Deductible: $500

- Personal property: 50 percent of dwelling

- Bodily injury: $100,000

- Personal injury: $0

- Other endorsements: None

Umbrella: None

Professional liability: None

Business: None

Life and Health Insurance

Life. Haley owns a $50,000 universal life policy with XYZ Insurance Co. She pays the annual premium of $400. The policy has a current cash value of $3,800 (the cash value at the beginning of the period was $3,600). John is the primary beneficiary and Haley is the owner. At the time of purchase, policy projections were based on after-tax U.S. Treasury rates of 6 percent.

John has an employer-provided term policy that pays one times his annual salary. The face amount of the policy is reduced by 50 percent, regardless of his salary, at age sixty-five and terminates at age seventy.

Other life assumptions:

- For planning purposes, the Butterfields would like to use 80 percent of their combined incomes, before taxes, to represent their total household expenses in the event of a death.

- Final illness and burial expenses are estimated to be $15,000 each.

- Estate administration expenses are expected to be approximately $5,200 each.

- Child care expenses will be $10,000.

- Full retirement age, for insurance purposes, is assumed to be age sixty-seven.

- The Butterfields need $100,000 in annual income per year, before taxes, while retired. They would like to use this assumption for both insurance and retirement planning purposes.

- Social Security benefit while children are still at home is $32,000 if John dies, and $29,000 if Haley dies, in today's dollars.

- At age sixty, Haley is eligible for a $13,000 annual Social Security survivor benefit, while John is entitled to a $10,000 annual survivor benefit (in today's dollars).

- In the event of either spouse's death, the other spouse plans to stop working at age sixty and begin taking early retirement survivor benefits (if available).

- For conservative planning purposes, the Butterfields do not plan on using interest and/or dividends as an income source when planning insurance needs.

- At full retirement (i.e., at age sixty-seven) John will receive $18,000 per year in Social Security benefits; Haley will receive $16,500 in benefits (in today's dollars).

- Assumed ages at death for John and Haley are ninety and ninety-two, respectively.

- The assumed gross rate of return on insurance assets, in the event of death, is 9 percent.

Health. The Butterfields' health insurance is provided by Blue Cross/Blue Shield. Coverage currently includes everyone in the immediate family. The monthly premium of $600 is paid 66 percent by John's employer, with the remainder paid out of pocket by John. The plan has a deductible of $250 per person and a family co-insurance provision of 20 percent. The out-of-pocket per family cap on co-payments is $1,000 per year.

Long-term care. None.

Disability. John's disability coverage is a group disability contract provided by his employer. The policy pays a $5,000 monthly benefit until age sixty-five. The contract has a liberal "own occupation" definition. The elimination period is 120 days. Haley does not have a disability policy. In the event of a disability, the Butterfields would like to continue saving for other goals; however, John and Haley do not want to rely on Social Security disability benefits when estimating disability income needs.

Vacation/medical leave. John has accumulated thirty sick days, which is the maximum he is allowed to carry. He is eligible to accrue one week per year if he falls below the maximum. He also is eligible for three weeks of vacation per year. He can carry over one week, but this has not previously been done.

Education Funding Goals

The Butterfields would like to assume that education expenses will increase 6.50 percent per year. John and Haley are comfortable assuming a growth rate of 9.00 percent per year for educational assets and savings in a tax-advantaged account before and after college begins (6.75 percent if assets are held in a taxable account). Each of the children is talented academically (GPA > 3.5) and each participates actively in extracurricular activities.

Troy is currently enrolled at University of Anystate. Current cost: $14,700/year (waiver).

- He is on a 3/4 baseball scholarship. His parents budget $5,000 per year in extra support. John and Haley pay tuition not covered in the scholarship and give Troy what is left from their $5,000 budget as a spending allowance.

- The Butterfields have also allocated $1,200 per year to help pay for Troy's travel expenses.

- Troy has completed one year of college.

- Troy's health insurance is provided under John's group health insurance plan.

- Holly wants to attend State University; current cost: $10,500/year (possible tuition waiver).

- Holly would like to go to school on an ROTC scholarship and fund any additional expenses out of pocket from money earned during summer vacations.

- Naomi's college funding goals have not yet been formalized; however, John and Haley want to plan for college costs of $16,500 per year (in today's dollars).

- John and Haley prefer to use tax-advantaged savings plans to fund current and future college expenses.

Retirement Information

John and Haley would like to retire when John turns age sixty-seven. Based on today's dollars, John and Haley are willing to reduce their income by 80 percent of current income while retired.

- At full retirement, John will receive $18,000 per year in Social Security benefits (in today's dollars);

- Haley will receive $16,500 in Social Security benefits (in today's dollars) at age sixty-seven.

- When planning for retirement, John and Haley are comfortable assuming a 9.00 percent rate of return before retirement, and a 5.75 percent return after retirement.

- Contributions to defined contribution plans are anticipated to increase 3 percent annually.

- John and Haley anticipate being in a combined federal and state tax bracket of 25 percent in retirement.

- Inflation before and after retirement will be 3.50 percent; their incomes should keep pace with inflation.

- John's employer matches 401(k) contributions $0.50 cents on the dollar.

- IRA assets are held in Roth accounts. Assumed age at death for John is age ninety and age ninety-two for Haley.

Estate Information

John and Haley have simple wills. John's will leaves his estate to Haley, whereas Haley's will leaves her estate to John. They believe that, on average, the surviving spouse's estate will grow by 4 percent after the first spouse's death. Other assumptions include:

- Funeral expenses are expected to be approximately $12,000 each.

- Estate administrative expenses will be $5,200 each.

- The Butterfield do not expect to pay any executor fees.

Specific Client Goals

- Under any circumstance, John and Haley want to provide 50 percent of the cost of Holly's and Naomi's college education costs, and all of Troy's education costs that are not covered by scholarships.

- John and Haley want to maintain their current standard of living in retirement or in the event of either spouse's premature death.

- John and Haley want to protect their income and assets in the event of a catastrophic accident or illness, so that they can pass on their assets to their children.

- John and Haley want to continue funding IRAs to the current maximum limit.

Case Questions

1. Which of the following strategies can the Butterfields use to improve their cash flow situation?

   a. Pay off credit card balances with monetary assets.

   b. Decrease insurance deductibles.

   c. Reduce IRA contributions and use the proceeds to purchase a variable universal life insurance policy.

   d. All of the above.

2. The Butterfields' current ratio is (rounded):

   a. 0.62

   b. 0.79

   c. 1.68

   d. 3.00

3. The Butterfields' savings ratio, using gross earned income and including employer 401(k) matching but excluding reinvested interest and dividends, is (rounded):

    a.   4 percent

    b.   10 percent

    c.   16 percent

    d.   22 percent

4. John and Haley have retirement account balances. John and Haley would like to know what their options will be in relation to these balances when John and Haley reach retirement. Which of the following statements describes their IRA retirement situation?

    I.   John can roll over his 401(k) account balance into an IRA.

    II.   Haley cannot roll over her account balance because her assets are held in a Keogh.

    III. Both John and Haley can roll over their account balances into an IRA and take a special five-year averaging tax technique on amounts withdrawn at that time.

    IV. Haley can roll over her Keogh account balance into an IRA.

    a.   III only

    b.   I and II only

    c.   I and III only

    d.   I and IV only

5. Which of the following is true if Haley closes her CPA practice to join a large consulting company this year?

    a.   Because she will be changing jobs, she will no longer be covered under her current health insurance plan; instead, she will need to continue coverage using COBRA provisions until she become eligible for coverage with the consulting company.

    b.   She can remain on John's health insurance policy until she is eligible for benefits under her new employer's insurance plan.

    c.   Because of her good health status, if she were to drop off of John's health insurance plan and move to a policy offered by the consulting company, John's health insurance premiums will increase.

    d.   She must enroll in a marketplace health insurance plan in the state where she resides.

6. If John, Haley, and Naomi are involved in an accident that requires medical care, how much will John's health insurance pay, including deductibles and copayments, given the following expenses? Assume no annual limits have been met. John $1,800; Haley $3,700; Naomi $4,200.

   a. $1,750

   b. $7,160

   c. $7,950

   d. $8,950

7.   An HO-3 policy (Special Form) with no endorsements excludes which of the following perils?

   a.   Flood

   b.   Fire

   c.   Collapse caused by a covered peril

   d.   Weight of ice

   e.   Volcanic eruption

8.   If the Butterfields suffer a $47,000 homeowner's loss due to fire, how much will the insurance company pay on the claim, accounting for any deductible and co-pay provisions?

   a. $45,193

   b. $45,693

   c. $46,500

   d. $47,000

9.   The Butterfields recently lived through a major wind storm. The experts said the storm was not a tornado, but John and Haley would argue otherwise. Their home was terribly damaged. It has been estimated that it will cost $250,000 to make repairs to the house. Excluding listed deductibles and copayments, how much must the Butterfields pay out of pocket toward the repairs?

   a. $0

   b. $500

   c. $5,000

   d. $7,500

10.   The Butterfields might be able to reduce their personal automobile policy insurance premiums by taking which of the following discounts?

   a.   A good student discount.

   b.   A multicar discount.

c. A farm use discount.

d. Both a and b.

11. Which of the following statements is (are) true about the Butterfields' PAP?

    I.   They are covered if injured while driving someone else's car.

    II. They are covered while driving either the Honda or Toyota.

    III. They are covered if John and Haley rent off-road motorcycles to tour the desert while on vacation.

a. I only

b. II only

c. I and II only

d. I, II, and III

12. During a recent thunderstorm, the Butterfields' Honda Accord received $2,300 in damage from hail. How much will the PAP pay for this claim?

a. $0

b. $2,050

c. $2,200

d. $2,300

13. Haley is worried that Troy will be without health insurance after he graduates from college with his B.S./B.A. degree in a few years. Haley's primary worry is that Troy may not immediately find employment or be eligible for employer-provided coverage for an extended period of time, such as ninety days. Given these concerns, which of the following is optimizes Troy's insurance coverage once he graduates?

a. Purchase no coverage; Haley's concerns are not valid as the Affordable Care Act (ACA) of 2010 extends coverage under a parental policy until young adults reach the age of twenty-six.

b. Purchase no coverage; Haley's concerns are not valid as the Affordable Care Act (ACA) of 2010 extends coverage under a parental policy until the age of twenty-six as long as the young adult does not have coverage available through an employer plan. When available, he will have coverage.

c. Extend Troy's current coverage through a COBRA extension.

d. Purchase insurance through an Affordable Care Act (ACA) of 2010 high-risk pool.

14. Which of the following risk management recommendations is(are) most appropriate to help the Butterfields manage their risk exposures?

      I.   Purchase an excess liability insurance policy.

      II.   Decrease their homeowner's coverage to 80 percent of the home's value.

      III. Eliminate collision coverage on the Toyota.

      IV. Purchase an endorsement to cover the family's art collection.

    a.   I and III only

    b.   II and IV only

    c.   II and III only

    d.   I and IV only

15. Which of the following strategies can the Butterfields use to increase their current discretionary cash flow situation?

    a.   Increase the deductible in their PAP policy.

    b.   Purchase an umbrella liability insurance policy.

    c.   Decrease the deductible in their HO policy.

    d.   All of the above.

16. John and Haley are not sure whether they are paying an appropriate premium for Haley's universal life insurance policy. Which statement below is true in relation to this concern?

    a.   The universal life policy is fairly priced according to the yearly-price-per -thousand formula.

    b.   Even though the yearly-price-per-thousand formula states that the policy is overpriced, given Haley's health status, she should hold the policy because she probably will not qualify for another policy.

    c.   Even though the universal policy is expensive, Haley should not replace the policy because the cost is less than two times the yearly-price-per-thousand formula benchmark price.

    d.   Haley should replace the universal policy because, according to the yearly-price-per-thousand formula, the cost is more than two times the benchmark price.

17. Haley would like to know the difference between variable life insurance and universal life insurance. Which of the following statements most accurately describes the difference?

    a.   Variable life insurance uses subcontracts that are invested to generate a guaranteed rate of return.

    b.   Universal life insurance uses a fixed mortality charge, whereas variable life insurance does not.

c.   Variable life insurance has a death benefit that varies, whereas universal life insurance provides only a fixed death benefit.

d.   Universal life insurance provides a crediting rate based on the insurance company's general account subject to a minimum guarantee, whereas variable life insurance uses subaccounts that can fluctuate based on market returns.

18.   Which of the following is an advantage for John and Haley if they decide to fund their children's college expenses using a Section 529 plan?

a.   The contribution will allow John and Haley to take a federal and state income-tax deduction, which will reduce their overall tax liability.

b.   If a beneficiary of the Section 529 plan does not use the assets, John and Haley may name a new beneficiary of the account.

c.   Because of the special tax structure of Section 529 plans, the assets held in the plan will not increase the expected family contribution for financial aid.

d.   All of these answers are advantages.

19.   Which of the following is an advantage associated with the Butterfields' current health insurance coverage?

a.   John's employer pays two-thirds of the total premium, which makes the cost of the group health policy reasonably low.

b.   The annual per person deductible and family maximum co-insurance amount associated with the policy is very reasonable, as compared to the maximum allowable family out-of-pocket limits set by the ACA of 2010 for a Health Insurance Marketplace plan.

c.   Once Troy and Naomi graduate from college and obtain health insurance coverage through an employer, John and Haley should drop John's employer-provided health insurance coverage and purchase a plan through an Affordable Care Act of 2010 exchange because the costs will be lower and the benefits higher.

d.   All of the above statement are true.

e.   Only statements a and b are correct.

20.   Which of the following is true for John if he purchases additional life insurance through his employer?

a.   Few exclusions are associated with these types of policies.

b.   Because most group term policies have a conversion feature, he can be assured that upon termination of employment he can continue his coverage.

c.   He can tailor the coverage to his own needs.

d.   All of the above are true.

Supplemental Questions

Assume the following, given the facts of the case:

21. The Butterfields paid their 96th mortgage payment in March 20XX (they were "eight years in"). Based on your suggestion, John and Haley have decided to refinance their mortgage. John and Haley will make the April payment on April 15 and close on April 20.

    a. What is the outstanding balance after the April payment? How much interest will be due on the mortgage at closing on April 20? In other words, what is the total payoff for the mortgage at the closing?

    b. Assuming a high credit score and a low new mortgage rate of 4.0 percent for a twenty-year mortgage, can John and Haley qualify to (1) refinance and (2) payoff the balance on the home equity loan? For simplicity, use the outstanding balance shown in the case for the home equity loan and ignore any reduction in the April balance.

    c. If the answer to the question above is yes, what issues should you, as their financial planner, discuss with the John and Haley as a precaution?

    d. If the answer is yes to the question above, is it possible to also pay off the short-term installment debt?

22. Given the increase in cash flow resulting from a mortgage refinance strategy, what are the top three (no priority) goals or identified needs toward which the excess discretionary cash flow should be redirected?

Discussion Points and Questions

1. Briefly summarize the relevant facts of the case relating to insurance planning.

2. If John and Haley were going to purchase additional life insurance, what type of policy, what face value, and what riders would be most appropriate given their ages and needs?

3. Explain the advantages and disadvantages of having John purchase additional life insurance through his employer.

4. Describe the 80 percent homeowner's co-insurance rule and report to the Butterfields how this rule affects their homeowner's coverage.

5. What actions can the Butterfields take to reduce their insurance premiums while maintaining adequate coverage in terms of liability and property coverage?

6. Explain why the Butterfields should consider purchasing an excess liability insurance policy.

7. Describe the purpose of long-term care insurance and indicate whether and when John and Haley should consider purchasing this type of insurance.

8. Report on the advantages and disadvantages associated with the Butterfields' current health insurance policy.

The Lucas Little Case

AN INVESTMENT PLANNING MINI-CASE

Lucas Little, a financial planning professional, has been asked by his client to review the financial statements of Stuff Stores Company. Mr. Little's client is considering making a substantial purchase of Stuff Stores stock. Before doing so, the client would like to know a bit more about the financial stability of the company. The information in Table VI.1 should be used to conduct a fundamental analysis of Stuff Stores' financial situation.

Table VI.1. Annual Financial Data for Stuff Stores Company ($ millions)

Financial Attribute	Year 1	Year 2	Current
Market capitalization	200,000.5	212,234.0	249,926.5
Total sales	139,208.0	166,809.0	193,295.0
Net income (earnings)	4,430.0	5,377.0	6,295.0
Dividends per share	.16	.20	.24
Shares outstanding	4,474.8	4,443.8	4,464.5
Total assets	64,654.0	70,349.0	78,130.0
Debt	16,891.0	18,712.0	18,824.0
Shareholder's equity	19,136.0	24,216.0	31,343.0
Cash flow	7,580.0	8,194.0	9,604.0

Other relevant data include:

- Beta for Stuff Stores stock: .85

- Standard deviation for Stuff Stores stock: 14.5 percent

- Average return for Stuff Stores stock: 10.5 percent

- Risk-free rate of return: 4.0 percent

- Return on the market: 9.0 percent

Information on similar stocks is shown in Table VI.2:

Table VI.2. Data for Similar Stocks

Company	Stock Beta	Stock Standard Deviation	Average Stock Return
Wigwam Stores, Inc.	.90	15.5%	8.0%
Maryland Markets	.80	12.0%	9.0%
Pacific Mercantile, Inc.	.89	15.0%	11.0%

Please use this information to answer the following questions:

Case Questions

1. Based on the current information available, what is the net profit margin for Stuff Stores?

    a.   1.98 percent

    b.   2.97 percent

    c.   3.26 percent

    d.   3.56 percent

    e.   3.88 percent

2. Based on the current information available, the price to earnings ratio (P/E) for one share of Stuff Stores stock is:

    a.   1.29

    b.   7.97

    c.   20.08

    d.   26.02

    e.   39.70

3. When comparing Stuff Stores stock to similar stocks in the market, which has the highest required rate of return?

    a.   Stuff Stores Company.

    b.   Wigwam Stores, Inc.

    c.   Maryland Markets.

    d.   Pacific Mercantile, Inc.

    e.   Stuff Stores Company and Pacific Mercantile, Inc. are the same.

4. Based solely on past performance compared to the required rate of return, which stock should Mr. Little's client avoid?

    a. Stuff Stores Company.

    b. Wigwam Stores, Inc.

    c. Maryland Markets.

    d. Pacific Mercantile, Inc.

    e. Both Maryland Markets and Pacific Mercantile, Inc.

5. Mr. Little would like to rank the four stocks in a standardized way before making a recommendation to his client. Using the average stock return data provided, rank the four stocks from highest to lowest using the Sharpe ratio.

    I.   Stuff Stores Company.

    II.   Wigwam Stores, Inc.

    III. Maryland Markets.

    IV. Pacific Mercantile, Inc.

    a. II, III, I, and IV

    b. IV, III , II, and I

    c. III, I, IV, and II

    d. IV, I, III, and II

    e. I, IV, III, and II

6. Mr. Little's client pointed out during a recent meeting that the price of Stuff Stores Company stock has remained steady during the past six months. The client is convinced that the stock will continue to trade in a narrow range. The client, however, would like to make money on the stock. Which of the following strategies will cause Mr. Little's client to experience the greatest potential loss if Stuff Stores' stock price begins to fluctuate more widely?

    a. Selling a naked put option.

    b. Selling a naked call option.

    c. Selling a covered call option.

    d. Buying a call option.

    e. Buying shares in Stuff Stores Company directly.

7. Assume that Mr. Little's client decides to purchase shares in Stuff Stores stock to add to his sizable portfolio. The client tells Mr. Little that although he is worried about price declines in his portfolio, he does not want to incur the cost of selling the stock or the entire portfolio. The client also does not want to risk mistiming the market should stock prices start to fall. One strategy for the client to protect against a possible decline in both Stuff Stores stock price and the value of the portfolio would be to:

    a. buy an index call option.

    b. sell an index call option.

    c. buy an index put option.

    d. sell an index put option.

    e. avoid all options strategies because the client cannot protect against the decline with these options.

8. If the market risk premium were to increase, the value of common stocks, including Stuff Stores Company stock, (holding all other factors constant) would:

    a. not change because the market risk premium does not affect stock values.

    b. increase to compensate an investor for increased risk.

    c. increase because of higher risk-free rates.

    d. decrease to compensate an investor for increased risk.

    e. decrease because of lower risk-free rates.

9. Mr. Little thinks that he has found an interesting bond investment for his client's portfolio. Mr. Little, when searching for investment ideas, focused on his client's goal of return maximization. The bond has a face value of $1,000 with a maturity date in seven years. The bond's coupon rate is 6.25 percent compounded annually. Today, the bond sells for $1,185.00. The indenture agreement states that the bond can be called for $1,100 after five years. Which of the following statements is true?

    a. The current yield is greater than both the yield to maturity and yield to call.

    b. Given the client's investment objective, this bond should do particularly well if interest rates start to increase.

    c. Mr. Little can lock in a yield to maturity that is higher than the current yield by purchasing the bond today.

    d. The value of the bond today, in comparison to the spread in the yield to maturity and the current yield, indicates that this bond will not be called early.

10. According to the discounted dividend valuation model of stock valuation, which of the following statements is true, assuming that Mr. Little's client has a required rate of return of 16 percent and that the dividend has grown from 16 cents to 24 cents in three years?

    I.   The current Stuff Stores stock price exceeds the calculated value.

    II.   The current Stuff Stores stock price is less than the calculated value.

    III.   Using the discounted dividend valuation model as the only measure, the Stuff Stores stock is undervalued.

    IV.   The market price and the calculated value for Stuff Stores match closely, as expected given the high degree of efficiency in the markets.

    a.   I only

    b.   III only

    c.   II and III only

    d.   III and IV only

The Gabriel and Sarah Cantrell Case

AN INVESTMENT PLANNING CASE

Gabriel and Sarah Cantrell, both age twenty-six, were married four years ago. Gabe and Sarah have one daughter, Joyce, who is now age three. They also have a young son, Lee, who is age one. Gabe and Sarah live at 1315 Devonshire Drive in Anytown, Anystate, 88901.

Gabe works for TG Ag Services as a sales representative. He has been working since he turned age sixteen and has spent the last five years with TG Ag Services. Gabe earns $45,000 per year.

Sarah started working when she was fifteen years old. Four years ago, she took a clerk position at Dave's Discount Store in downtown Anytown. She makes $27,500 per year.

Use the following information to conduct a review of the Cantrells' financial situation.

Global Assumptions (Valid unless otherwise Specified in Certain Instances)

- Inflation: 3.5 percent

- Anystate has no state-imposed income tax.

- All income and expense figures are given in today's dollars.

- Planned retirement age: sixty-seven for both

- Federal marginal tax bracket: 15 percent

- State marginal tax bracket: No state income tax

- All nominal rates of return are pretax returns.

Income Issues

Currently, Gabe earns $45,000 per year. Sarah earns $27,500. Both Gabe and Sarah assume that their salaries will increase at the rate of inflation. Combined, Gabe and Sarah make approximately $60 (all of which is reinvested) in interest annually. Gabe and Sarah have no other sources of income.

Expense Summary

Before meeting with you, Gabe and Sarah summarized their income and expense situation. Household expenses are shown in Table VII.1. Household assets are listed in Table VII.2, whereas household liabilities and debts are shown in Table VII.3.

Table VII.1. The Cantrells' Fixed and Variable Expenses

Expenses	Amount	Frequency
Health care expenses (Gabe)*	$300.00	Monthly
Health care expenses (Sarah)*	$50.00	Monthly
401(k) contribution (Gabe)**	$1,800.00	Annually
401(k) contribution (Sarah)**	$1,375.00	Annually
SS/Medicare (FICA) withholdings	$5,225.00	Annually
Federal tax withholdings	$4,500.00	Annually
Mortgage payments	$714.25	Monthly
Credit card payments	$20.00	Monthly
Auto insurance	$800.00	Semiannually
Homeowner's insurance	$600.00	Annually
Subscriptions	$480.00	Annually
Telephone expense	$1,800.00	Annually
Home Internet	$90.00	Monthly
Hobbies (Sarah)	$1,450.00	Annually
Recreation/entertainment	$200.00	Monthly
Groceries	$400.00	Monthly
Food away from home	$3,000.00	Annually
Real estate taxes	$1,482.00	Annually
Private mortgage insurance	$50.00	Monthly
Household maintenance	$750.00	Monthly
Other Home Expenses	$750.00	Annually
Utilities	$3,300.00	Annually
Clothing	$2,200.00	Annually
Laundry services	$300.00	Annually
Personal care	$50.00	Monthly
Furnishing	$750.00	Annually

Child care***	$600.00	Monthly
Eye glasses	$300.00	Annually
Medical deductibles	$50.00	Monthly
Unreimbursed medical expenses	$100.00	Annually
Gasoline	$1,100.00	Annually
Car registrations	$575.00	Annually
Personal property tax	$450.00	Annually
Safe deposit box fee	$1.00	Monthly
Accounting fees	$150.00	Annually
Charitable contributions	$100.00	Monthly
Vacations	$2,800.00	Annually
Gifts to family members	$1,000.00	Annually
*Pretax Section 125 plan expenses		
**Pretax expenses		
***The child care provider is licensed in Anystate.		
Note: Last year, the Cantrells paid $711 in Anystate sales taxes.		

Asset Summary

Table VII. 2. A Summary of the Cantrell's Assets

Asset	Amount	Ownership
Financial Assets		
Checking account	$350.00	Joint
Savings account	$500.00	Joint
EE savings bonds	$1,000.00	Joint
Retirement 401(k) Assets		
Large-cap funds	$5,000.00	Gabe
Mid-cap funds	$2,500.00	Gabe
Small-cap funds	$2,500.00	Gabe
Government bond funds	$1,000.00	Sarah
Mid-cap funds	$2,500.00	Sarah
Small-cap funds	$1,000.00	Sarah

Other Assets		
Primary residence	$124,000.00	Joint
Buick Regal	$12,000.00	Joint
GMC pickup	$9,800.00	Joint
Collectibles	$1,200.00	Joint
Golf clubs and equipment	$3,800.00	Joint
16-foot sailboat w/2-HP motor	$9,600.00	Joint
Furniture	$13,000.00	Joint
Other assets	$4,700.00	Joint

Liability Summary

Table VII.3. A Summary of the Cantrells' Liabilities

Liability	Amount	Ownership
Visa credit card*	$2,400.00	Joint
MasterCard**	$500.00	Joint
Mortgage	Unknown	Joint
*17.95 percent APR		
** 14.25 percent APR		

Gabe and Sarah purchased a new home in town exactly two years ago today. The original mortgage was in the amount of $116,000 for thirty years at a 6.25 percent interest rate. Gabe and Sarah have made precisely twenty-four payments on the mortgage.

Life Insurance and Planning Issues

Gabe and Sarah would like you to analyze their life insurance situation using the following assumptions and facts:

- Upon the first death, household expenses will decrease to $55,000 per year.

- Final expenses are expected to be $9,500 each.

- Estate administration costs are anticipated to be $3,500 each.

- All outstanding liabilities will be paid at the first death.

- Gabe and Sarah would like to prefund $10,000 in child care expenses at the death of the first spouse.

- Gabe and Sarah would like to prefund college costs in the event of a spouse's death. They plan to invest any insurance proceeds for this goal in a tax-advantaged educational savings plan.

- Gabe and Sarah can earn 7 percent before taxes on any life insurance proceeds both pre- and postretirement.

- Gabe and Sarah anticipate that their marginal federal tax rate will increase to 25 percent in retirement.

- Gabe and Sarah would like to replace $58,000 in retirement income for the surviving spouse.

- Gabe and Sarah are willing to use all of their retirement savings to offset life insurance needs.

- In the event of either spouse's death, the other spouse plans to stop working at age sixty and begin taking early retirement survivor benefits (if available).

- For conservative planning purposes, the Cantrells do not plan to use interest and/or dividends as an income source when determining insurance needs.

- Gabe's employer provides a term policy for two times his salary at no cost, which continues during periods of disability but terminates at retirement. Sarah is the beneficiary of the life insurance policy.

- Sarah's employer also provides two times her salary in term coverage at no cost, which continues during periods of disability but terminates at retirement. Gabe is the beneficiary of the life insurance policy.

- The surviving spouse's income is not expected to change after the death of the first spouse.

Table VII.4 provides information about the Cantrells' Social Security expected benefits.

Table VII.4. Social Security Survivor Benefit Information

Beneficiary	Amount (Monthly)*
Sarah and children (until last child turns age 18)	$2,582.50
Gabe and children (until last child turns age 18)	$1,843.10
Sarah (ages 60–67)	$1,048.00
Gabe (ages 60–67)	$1,118.00
Sarah (at age 67)	$1,466.00
Gabe (at age 67)	$1,563.00
* Income test limits could apply. See www.ssa.gov for more information.	

Additional Insurance Information and Financial Planning Issues

Both TG Ag Services and Dave's Discount Store are large employers in the area; each employs more than twenty people at any given time. The Cantrells do not currently have disability or long-term care insurance policies. Both are healthy, with both sets of parents still alive and well. Their home is currently covered by an HO-3 policy with an inflation rider and a $1,000 deductible. Both automobiles are insured with split-limit coverage of $25/$50/$10 and a $500 deductible.

Retirement Information and Planning Issues

The following information should be used when evaluating the Cantrells' current retirement planning situation:

- Gabe and Sarah anticipate being in a combined federal and state 25 percent marginal tax bracket after retirement (Gabe and Sarah are considering moving to another state at retirement).

- Gabe and Sarah are comfortable assuming that working with you, their financial planner, they can generate a 10.00 percent annualized rate of return before retirement.

- When retired, Gabe and Sarah would prefer to maintain a conservative growth asset allocation that will generate an 8.25 percent annualized rate of return.

- If retired today, Gabe and Sarah would like to replace 80 percent of their combined income.

- At retirement, Gabe will be eligible to receive $1,563 in monthly Social Security benefits.

- At retirement, Sarah will be eligible to receive $1,096 in monthly Social Security benefits (this figure is different from the amount shown in Table VII.4).

- Gabe and Sarah are comfortable assuming a life expectancy of one-hundred years.

- Gabe currently contributes 4 percent of his salary to his company's 401(k) plan; his employer matches 50 percent on the first 6 percent contributed; his plan has a maximum deferral limit of 12 percent of salary.

- Sarah currently contributes 5 percent of her salary to her company's 401(k) plan; her employer matches 50 percent on the first 5 percent contributed, up to the maximum annual limit.

- Inflation before and after retirement is assumed to be 3.50 percent.

- Contributions to 401(k) plans will increase by 3 percent even though salaries are expected to increase by the rate of inflation.

Estate Information and Planning Issues

Both Gabe and Sarah have professionally prepared wills; Gabe's will leaves all his assets to Sarah, whereas Sarah's will leaves all her assets to Gabe. Each will names their attorney as the estate executor, and in the event of a simultaneous death it is assumed that Gabe will predecease Sarah. Other estate planning assumptions include:

- Funeral and burial expenses will be $7,500 each.

- Estate and legal costs will be $2,000 each.

- Executor fees will be approximately 2 percent of the gross estate before the marital transfer.

- The net growth rate of the survivor's estate is estimated to be 4 percent annually.

- Both wills name Sarah's sister Lindsey as the guardian of their children.

- All individually owned assets that pass via property law or contract (e.g., IRAs, qualified plans, bank accounts, life insurance) name the surviving spouse as the primary beneficiary; no contingent beneficiaries have been named.

- No other estate planning documents are known to exist.

Table VII.5 provides a summary of the current yield and rate of return information applicable to this case.

Table VII.5. Yield and Rate of Return Information

Investment Class	Yield
Checking account	0.00%
Savings account	3.00%
Taxable money market fund	3.50%
EE and I bonds	3.50%
Loan Rates	
thirty-year mortgage*	6.50%
1five-year mortgage*	6.00%
Home equity line of credit*	7.25%
Home equity loan*	7.35%
five-year auto loan	7.90%
Personal loan	8.50%
*APR includes closing costs over life of loan.	

Goals and Objectives

The Cantrells' primary financial planning objective at this point is to fully fund four years of college for their two children. Gabe and Sarah have already been in contact with the universities they hope their children will attend. Gabe and Sarah learned that the annual cost of college (including tuition, room, and board), in today's dollars, is $18,000 at each school. College costs are estimated to increase by approximately 6 percent annually.

Gabe and Sarah would like to have the total amount needed to pay for each child's college costs available on the first day of college. Given their combined moderate level of risk tolerance, Gabe and Sarah are comfortable planning for college expenses using a 7.00 percent annualized rate of return assumptions. Gable and Sarah would also like to use a tax-advantaged investment to save for college.

Their second goal is to retire at age sixty-seven, using the assumptions already listed.

In preparation for a meeting with the Cantrells, you have been given a monitored list of mutual funds used by your firm. Your firm's investment committee will allow you to use any of the funds listed in Table VII.6 when developing investment recommendations.

Table VII.6. Mutual Funds Approved for Cantrell Recommendations

Market Indexes					
		RoR*	SD	Corr (r) with Index	Yield
T-bills		4.00%	2.00%	1.00	4.00%
Equity market		12.00%	17.00%	1.00	2.00%
Bond market		8.00%	9.00%	1.00	4.70%
Approved Mutual Funds					
Fund	Fund Objective	RoR*	SD	Market Correlation (r)	Yield
Super Big Fund	Large-cap fund	13.00%	18.00%	0.95	2.00%
Maxi Fund	Large-cap fund	12.20%	17.40%	0.92	2.00%
Multivariate Fund	Mid-cap fund	14.00%	18.30%	0.90	1.00%
Germain Fund	Mid-cap fund	13.30%	16.90%	0.89	1.25%
Efficacy Fund	Small-cap fund	11.00%	19.00%	0.85	0.25%
Software Fund	Small-cap fund	12.00%	21.00%	0.70	0.00%
Clinical Fund	International fund	10.00%	13.00%	0.68	2.00%
Image Fund	International fund	9.80%	11.00%	0.63	1.00%
Measures Fund	Precious metals fund	6.00%	13.00%	0.40	0.50%
Thumb Fund	Real estate fund	11.00%	11.00%	0.99	4.00%
Factors Fund	Real estate fund	9.90%	12.00%	0.89	5.30%
Column Averages		**11.11%**	**15.51%**	**0.80**	**1.75%**

Fund	Fund Objective	RoR*	SD	Market Correlation (r)	Yield
Alumni Fund	Gov't bond fund	7.80%	8.00%	0.95	4.50%
Bush Fund	Gov't bond fund	8.20%	8.50%	0.90	5.00%
National Fund	Corporate bond fund	8.40%	9.00%	0.98	5.10%
CDR Fund	Corporate bond fund	7.56%	9.20%	0.85	5.40%
Fast Fund	High-yield bond fund	9.90%	13.00%	0.75	7.00%
Mobile Fund	High-yield bond fund	10.30%	12.80%	0.60	8.20%
Column Averages		**8.69%**	**10.08%**	**0.84**	**5.87%**
*Rates of return include yields.					

Use the information provided in the case narrative to answer the questions that follow.

Case Questions

1. How much total Section 79 income (rounded) for the year must the Cantrells report for tax purposes?

    a. $0

    b. $6

    c. $29

    d. $32

    e. $35

2. Which of the following is true?

    a.   Interest earned by the Cantrells adds to their level of discretionary cash flow.

    b.   Section 79 income earned by the Cantrells adds to their level of discretionary cash flow.

    c.   Contributions to Gabe's 401(k) plan reduce discretionary cash flow.

    d.   All of the above are true.

    e.   Only statements a and b are true.

3. The Cantrells are eligible for which of the following tax credits?

    I.   Income tax credit.

    II. Child and dependent care tax credit.

      III. Child tax credit.

      IV. Low-income housing tax credit.

  a.   I and II only

  b.   II and III only

  c.   III and IV only

  d.   II, III, and IV only

4.   The Cantrells' current net worth situation can best be described as:

  a.   A positive $78,356

  b.   A negative $2,900

  c.   A positive $116,094

  d.   A negative $113,194

  e.   A positive $194,950

5.   When completing their federal tax return, the Cantrells should:

  a.   file married filing separately.

  b.   claim a deduction from AGI for retirement plan contributions.

  c.   use the sales tax deduction when calculating the amount claimed (if any) for itemized deductions.

  d.   claim Anystate income taxes as a tax credit.

6.   Which of the following strategies can the Cantrells use to improve their discretionary cash flow situation?

      I.   Refinance their first mortgage using a fifteen-year loan.

      II. Pay off some or all credit card debt with financial assets.

      III. Reduce the amount being withheld for federal taxes.

      IV. Increase the amount of reinvested interest earned on investments.

  a.   I and III only

  b.   II and III only

  c.   II and IV only

  d.   II, III, and IV only

7. The Cantrells' current level of discretionary cash flow is enough to:

    a. fund this year's savings need for one child's college education.

    b. fund both children's savings need for college education this year.

    c. pay off credit card debts within one year.

    d. fund both a and c.

8. Which of the following statements is true?

    a. The Cantrells need to save an additional $3,700 per year to meet their retirement goal.

    b. The Cantrells will fall short of their retirement goal by more than $1.5 million using their current retirement planning strategy.

    c. The Cantrells must reduce their life expectancy in retirement to retire at age sixty-seven.

    d. Statements a and c are correct.

    e. None of the statements are correct.

9. Which of the following statements is true regarding the Cantrells' estate situation?

    I. The value of Gabe's group life insurance policy will be excluded from his gross estate.

    II. The full value of jointly held liabilities can be deducted as an expense from the gross estate at the passing of the first spouse.

    III. If Gabe and Sarah establish Section 529 plans for their children by contributing $5,000 to Section 529 plans, the assets held in the accounts will be excluded from Gabe's and Sarah's gross estate.

    IV. The Cantrells should begin a gifting strategy to reduce their taxable estate.

    a. I only

    b. III only

    c. I and II only

    d. II and III only

    e. I, III, and IV only

10. All of the following are examples of tax-advantaged education savings alternatives appropriate for use by the Cantrells except:

    a. A Section 529 plan.

    b. A Coverdell savings plan.

c. EE savings bonds.

d. An immediate annuity.

11. Sarah's grandmother has decided to gift Gabe and Sarah $150,000. Which of the following strategies can the Cantrells fund with this gift?

I. Fully prefund each child's college education costs.

II. Earmark the gift as a source of emergency funds.

III. Use the gift to fully offset Gabe's need for additional life insurance.

a. I only

b. III only

c. I and II only

d. II and III only

12. Rank the following mutual funds in terms of total portfolio risk (volatility), highest to lowest:

I. Maxi Fund

II. Software Fund

III. Image Fund

IV. Clinical Fund

a. I, II, IV, and III

b. I, II, III, and IV

c. II, I, IV, and III

d. II, I, III, and IV

13. Which mutual fund's expected rate of return, as measured by CAPM, is the lowest?

a. Super Big Fund

b. Efficacy Fund

c. Image Fund

d. Measures Fund

14. Rank the following mutual funds based on the Sharpe ratio (highest to lowest):

I. Thumb Fund

II. Germain Fund

III. Multivariate Fund

IV. Super Big Fund

a. I, II, IV, and III

b. I, II, III, and IV

c. II, I, IV, and III

d. II, I, III, and IV

15. Rank the following mutual funds based on the Treynor index (highest to lowest):

    I. Clinical Fund

    II. Image Fund

    III. Measures Fund

    IV. Thumb Fund

a. I, II, IV, and III

b. I, II, III, and IV

c. II, I, IV, and III

d. II, I, III, and IV

16. Rank the following mutual funds based on the Sharpe ratio (highest to lowest):

    I. Germain Fund

    II. Image Fund

    III. Multivariate Fund

    IV. Thumb Fund

a. I, II, IV, and III

b. I, II, III, and IV

c. II, I, IV, and III

d. IV, I, III, and II

17. Rank the following mutual funds based on the Treynor index (highest to lowest):

    I. Germain Fund

    II. Image Fund

    III. Multivariate Fund

    IV. Thumb Fund

  a. I, II, IV, and III

  b. I, II, III, and IV

  c. II, IV, I, and III

  d. IV, I, III, and II

18. Which of the following mutual funds has the highest alpha?

  a. Super Big Fund

  b. Thumb Fund

  c. Germain Fund

  d. Factors Fund

19. Assume that the correlation and standard deviation data for the bond mutual funds are linked to the bond market index. Which bond mutual fund has the highest alpha?

  a. Mobile Fund

  b. Fast Fund

  c. National Fund

  d. CDR Fund

20. Which of the following statements is correct?

    I. High-yield mutual bond funds are affected by both interest rate changes and changes in the economic performance of the company issuing the bonds.

    II. Risk-adjusted performance can best be measured by beta.

    III. An investor who wants to rank a list of diversified mutual funds can feel comfortable using the Treynor index.

    IV. If an investor wants to rank a list of sector funds, the Treynor index is more appropriate than the Sharpe ratio.

  a. II only

  b. I and IV only

  c. I and III only

  d. II and IV only

The Alpha Corporation Case

A RETIREMENT PLANNING MINI-CASE

Alpha Corporation is considering its alternatives in relation to establishing a retirement plan for its employees. Please help the CFO of Alpha Corporation answer the following questions:

Case Questions

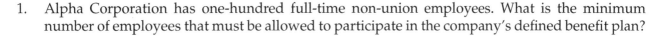

1. Alpha Corporation has one-hundred full-time non-union employees. What is the minimum number of employees that must be allowed to participate in the company's defined benefit plan?

    a. 40

    b. 50

    c. 75

    d. 100

2. The CFO would like to implement a 401(k)/profit sharing plan. If 75 percent of the firm's employees stay with the company for only two years (i.e., the firm has high turnover), and the remainder stay for an average of at least ten years, which vesting schedule should the CFO choose if she wants to minimize plan administration costs?

    a. 2–6 year graduated

    b. 3-year cliff

    c. 3–7 year graduated

    d. five-year cliff

3. Jana, age twenty-five, has worked for Alpha Corporation on a part-time basis (i.e., 900 hours per year) for four years. Is she eligible to participate in the firm's 401(k) plan?

    a. Yes, because she meets IRS service and hours requirements.

    b. No, because she has not accumulated enough hours for the year.

    c. Yes, because all employees, regardless of years of service, must be allowed to participate in the plan.

    d. No, because she has not worked for at least five years.

4. The CFO's husband, Bud (age forty-three), also works at Alpha Corporation. He earns $28,000. Bud just contributed $3,000 to a Roth IRA. When must he begin taking distributions from the Roth IRA?

    a.   Never

    b.   At age 59½

    c.   At age 72

    d.   At age 75

5. The CFO would like to establish a deferred compensation plan for the firm's management (including herself). She wants any money contributed to the plan to be protected from the firm's creditors. Which non-qualified deferred compensation plan should she choose?

    a.   A rabbi trust

    b.   A secular trust

    c.   A 457 plan

    d.   An unfunded promise-to-pay plan

6. The CFO feels bad about having a plan for the exclusive benefit of key employees. She would like you to recommend a qualified plan that will allow her to restrict employee contributions but will permit the firm to make contributions as a tool to increase employee productivity. Which of the following three plans should she use?

    I.   A defined benefit plan

    II. A stock bonus plan

    III. An ESOP

    a.   I only

    b.   II only

    c.   II or III only

    d.   I, II, or III

7. Which type of plan should the CFO choose if she wants Alpha Corporation to absolutely guarantee benefits to eligible employees (i.e., employees will know exactly how much they will receive when they retire)?

    a.   A 401(k) plan

    b.   A profit-sharing plan

c. A target benefit plan

d. A defined benefit plan

8. Micala, an employee of Alpha Corporation, is fifty-three years old. She is considering divorcing her husband Jack. Micala and Jack have been married for nine years. If Micala obtains a divorce, is she eligible to receive a spousal benefit from Jack's Social Security benefit?

a. No, because Micala and Jack have not been married for ten years.

b. Yes, because Micala and Jack have been married for at least five years.

c. No, because as someone with a job she can claim only her own Social Security benefit.

d. Yes, because she is younger than age sixty at the time of divorce.

9. Assume Christina (age forty-one) terminates employment with Alpha Corporation. Further assume that she rolls over her 401(k) account balance to an IRA. Which of the following statements is true, assuming that she takes the distribution directly before rolling it over to the IRA?

I. She must roll over the full amount of the distribution within sixty days to avoid taxation and penalties.

II. If she distributes $200,000 from the 401(k) plan, she must roll over $160,000 to avoid a penalty.

III. If she fails to roll over the full distribution, she will incur a 10 percent penalty.

a. I only

b. III only

c. I and II only

d. I and III only

10. Which of the following health insurance options does Christina have as a result of quitting her job with Alpha Corporation?

a. She is ineligible for COBRA coverage because Alpha Corporation employs fewer than one-hundred employees.

b. She is eligible for COBRA coverage because Alpha Corporation employs more than twenty employees.

c. A COBRA extension will cover expenses associated only with pre-existing conditions.

d. Statements b and c are correct.

The Nick Edwards Case

A RETIREMENT AND EMPLOYEE BENEFITS MINI-CASE

Nick Edwards owns a used car dealership. He is age sixty, has worked in the business for thirty years, and earns $210,000 per year. He has several employees with varying years of experience and tenure at the dealership. As the owner of the company, Nick has come to you for advice regarding the establishment of a retirement plan. He is also interested in learning more about employee benefits as a tool to help him recruit and retain good salespersons.

Over the course of several weeks of meetings with Nick you have compiled a list of attributes he would like to see in a retirement plan:

- He wants his employees to contribute to the plan.

- He is willing to match employee contributions if necessary.

- He wants the plan to be an incentive to increase productivity.

- He is willing to pay all the plan's administrative costs.

- He would prefer not to assume any investment risk on the part of employees.

- He would be happy with a payroll deduction for his firm of 10 percent to 15 percent per year.

- Although he is willing to match contributions, he would prefer to maintain flexibility so that in low-profit years he can skip matching if needed.

- He does not want 100 percent immediate vesting for employees.

- He has no opinion regarding the ability of employees to make in-service withdrawals.

- He would like to maximize his own benefits, but not at the expense of running afoul of IRS highly compensated employee rules.

You have learned that, in addition to retirement benefits, Nick offers a mix of employee benefits, including life, health, and disability insurance for his employees. Information about these plans is summarized below:

- Group term life insurance equal to two times annual earnings.

    o Table IX.1 shows the cost per $1,000 of life insurance protection offered through the Nick's firm on a monthly basis for tax purposes.

- Group health insurance benefits:

    o   Traditional plan with a $500 annual deductible and 80/20 coinsurance provision.

    o   Out-of-pocket maximum equal to $5,000 annually.

    o   Benefit coverage includes employee and spouse only.

    o   Financed 100 percent through the dealership.

- Group short-term disability insurance:

    o   Benefit equal to 50 percent of salary for six months.

    o   Thirty-day waiting period.

Table IX.1. Cost per $1,000 of Employer-provided Life Insurance Protection

Attained Age on Last Day of Employee's Tax Year	Cost Per $1,000 of Protection for One-month Period
Under 25	$.05
25–29	.06
30–34	.08
35–39	.09
40–44	.10
45–49	.15
50–54	.23
55 – 59	.43
6 –64	.66
65–69	1.27
70 and above	2.06

Nick's best employee is Emily James. Emily has worked at the dealership full-time for seven years. She is fifty-six years old and makes $74,000 per year. Other employees' relevant data are shown in Table IX.2.

Table IX.2. Relevant Employee Data

Name	Salary	Years w/Firm	Age	Status
Kate	$36,000	6	28	Full-time employee
Mark	$32,000	4	47	Full-time employee
Joyce	$32,000	4	34	Full-time employee
Bill	$30,000	2	36	Full-time employee
Jack	$15,000	3	20	Part-time employee (< 1,000 hours/year)
Andy	$12,000	2	17	Part-time employee (< 1,000 hours/year)
Mary	$6,000	1	19	Part-time employee (< 1,000 hours/year)

Use this information to answer the following questions.

Case Questions

1. How much must Emily James report in yearly Section 79 income (rounded) for tax purposes, assuming she stays employed for the year?

   a. $42

   b. $98

   c. $506

   d. $6,000

2. Nick purchased a $100,000 participating whole-life insurance policy on his life. To date, he has paid $50,000 in total premiums and received $10,000 in dividends. The policy currently has a net cash value of $15,000 and is subject to a $30,000 outstanding loan. If Nick decides to surrender the policy, he would realize a gain of:

   a. $0

   b. $5,000

   c. $10,000

   d. $15,000

3. Currently, Nick's brother Tommy owns an auto repair shop across town. Tommy owns the shop as a sole proprietorship. Nick has suggested that Tommy think about converting the shop to a

corporation. Advantages for incorporating the repair shop into a C corporation include which of the following?

> I.   Allowing the flow-through of corporate profits to shareholders that can then be taxed at each owner's marginal tax bracket.
>
> II. Withdrawing accumulated profits at capital gain rates.
>
> III. Providing tax-favored fringe benefits to employee shareholders.
>
> IV. Changing the form of business with ease once a corporation has been formed.

a.   II only

b.   III only

c.   I and III only

d.   I and IV only

4. Assuming that Nick is most interested in implementing a retirement plan that offers flexibility, low costs, and limited paperwork and regulation, he should consider establishing a:

a.   Cash balance plan

b.   401(k) plan

c.   Roth 401(k) plan

d.   SIMPLE plan

e.   Stock bonus plan

5. Based on Nick's desires, as outlined in the case narrative, which of the following plans will meet his needs?

> I.   A 403(b) plan
>
> II. A profit sharing plan
>
> III. A stock bonus plan
>
> IV. A defined benefit plan

a.   I and IV only

b.   II and IV only

c.   II and III only

d.   I, II, and III only

e.   II, III, and IV only

6. Using the most restrictive vesting schedule and participation rules available, Nick can exclude which of the following employees from participating in a qualified defined contribution plan?

    I.   Bill

    II.   Jack

    III. Andy

    IV. Mary

  a.   I and II only

  b.   II and III only

  c.   I and IV only

  d.   I, II, and III only

  e.   II, III, and IV only

7. Nick is concerned about how he will fund contributions to a defined contribution plan. You recommend that he use a unit formula based on employee compensation and years of service. The formula is calculated using one unit of credit for each year of service and one unit of credit for each $10,000 in earnings. If Nick is willing to allocate $30,000 in total contributions in any given year, using a total allocation of eighty units (and disregarding any key employee or top-heavy restrictions), what is the maximum amount that will be contributed to Nick's account?

  a. $9,675

  b. $13,225

  c. $19,125

  d. $22,750

8. Nick's daughter, who is hoping one day to take over ownership of the car dealership, is interested in your discussion with her father. She would like her father to receive the maximum plan benefit available before and after retirement. She would also like to establish a plan that guarantees her father a steady source of income during retirement. If you follow the daughter's desires, which of the following plans would be most appropriate?

  a.   A SIMPLE plan

  b.   A money purchase plan

  c.   A stock bonus plan

  d.   A defined benefit plan

  e.   A target benefit plan

9. Nick is intrigued by his daughter's questions. However, he is still adamant about providing the best possible benefits to his employees, in addition to himself. The thought of maximizing tax deductions for contributions is something he would like to consider. Assuming that the car dealership has steady to increasing levels of cash flow, which of the following plan(s) would be most appropriate?

    I.   A defined benefit plan

    II.   A target benefit plan

    III. A 401(k) plan

    IV. A stock bonus plan

    V.   A Roth 401(k) plan

  a.   I and V only

  b.   I and II only

  c.   IV and V only

  d.   II, III, and IV only

  e.   I, II, III, and V only

10. Joyce, one of Nick's employees, has come to you for advice. She would like guidance on choosing between contributing to a defined contribution plan and a Roth IRA. Assuming that Nick establishes a 401(k) plan, which of the following statements is true for Joyce?

  a.   If Nick's firm matches contributions to the 401(k) plan, she should contribute to the plan at least to the point of obtaining the match.

  b.   Under no circumstances will the 401(k) plan provide a better after-tax return than the Roth IRA.

  c.   If Joyce believes that tax rates in retirement will be higher than rates today, she should contribute to the 401(k) plan rather than the Roth IRA.

  d.   Regardless of employer matching, Joyce should maximize her contribution to the Roth IRA before contributing to the defined contribution plan.

The Peter and Ann Mayfield Case

A RETIREMENT PLANNING MINI-CASE

Peter and Ann Mayfield, both age fifty-two, have reached out for your help in planning their financial future. Peter is the Anytown, Anystate, city manager. Ann is active in many civic organizations but not employed outside of the home. They live at 123 Maple Street, in Anytown. Peter and Ann have been married for nearly twenty-five years.

Their two children, Nick and Nedra, have both moved away from home. Nick and Nedra have their own families. In fact, Nick and his wife have two children, Lisa and Timmy, ages three and two, respectively. Table X.1 presents additional information about the Peter and Ann.

Table X.1. Additional Personal Information

Occupation—Peter	City Manager
	123 Elm Street
	Anytown, Anystate 01010
	26 years of employment
Occupation—Ann	Homemaker
	26 years of employment

Global Assumptions (valid unless otherwise specified in certain instances):

- Inflation: 3.0 percent.

- All income and expense figures are given in today's dollars.

- Federal marginal tax bracket: 22.0 percent.

- State marginal tax bracket: 4.5 percent.

- Any qualified plan or IRA contribution growth rates are assumed to stop at the federally mandated limit unless otherwise restricted.

- All nominal rates of return are presented as pretax returns.

- Peter and Ann are currently qualified for Social Security benefits.

Income Issues

Peter currently earns $90,000 per year and expects his salary to increase at 3.0 percent per year until retirement. As shown in Table X.2, Peter contributes 10 percent of his salary to his employer-sponsored 403(b) plan. He receives a 33 percent match from the city. Ann and Peter are covered by an employer-sponsored health care plan, which has a premium of only $50 per month and is paid for directly out of Peter's paycheck on a pre-tax basis. The Mayfields currently use interest earned from their municipal bond holdings to supplement their income. Table X.2 summarizes the variable and fixed household expense situation. Table X.3 presents asset and liability information for Peter and Ann.

Table X.2. Fixed and Variable Household Expenses

Source of Expense	Amount	Frequency
Pretax medical premiums	$600	Annually
403(b) contributions	$750	Monthly
Social Security withholdings	$6,839	Annually
Federal tax withholdings	$10,000	Annually
State tax withholdings	$3,400	Annually
Mortgage payment (P&I)	$511.63	Monthly
Credit card payments	$450	Annually
Auto insurance	$550	Semi-Annually
Homeowner's insurance	$50	Monthly
Life insurance (private policy)	$780	Annually
Other insurance	Not calculated by client	
Umbrella policy	$150	Annually
Peter's traditional IRA contribution	$2,000	Annually
Ann's traditional IRA contribution	$2,000	Annually
Unallocated savings	$1,000	Quarterly
Subscriptions	$50	Monthly
Telephone charges	$1,560	Annually
Alarm system	$40	Monthly
Internet and cable	$90	Monthly
Hobbies	$100	Monthly
Recreation	$400	Monthly
Health club dues	$90	Monthly
Groceries	$3,900	Annually

Eating-out expenses	$4,900	Annually
Real estate taxes	$1,600	Annually
Household maintenance	$90	Monthly
Utilities	$2,160	Annually
Clothing	$1,700	Annually
Dry cleaning	$60	Monthly
Personal care	$100	Monthly
Stereo equipment	$800	Annually
Yard maintenance service	$900	Annually
Eye glasses	$725	Annually
Health insurance co-pays	$500	Annually
Prescriptions	$400	Annually
Other medical expenses	$350	Annually
Gas and car maintenance	$800	Semiannually
Car licenses (not tax deductible)	$250	Annually
Parking in city	$100	Annually
Trains and taxis in city	$300	Annually
Personal property tax	$750	Annually
Safe deposit fees	$40	Monthly
Bank fees	$4	Monthly
IRA fees	$45	Annually
Tax preparation fees	$450	Annually
Charitable contributions	$300	Monthly
Business travel*	$1,500	Annually
Vacations	$1,000	Quarterly
Business expenses*	$250	Annually
Alcohol expenses	$250	Semiannually
Postage stamps	$125	Annually
Gifts to children/grandchildren	$1,300	Semiannually
Other misc. expenses	$500	Annually

*Peter's employer does not reimburse these expenses.

Table X.3. Asset and Liability Information

Asset/Liability	Value	Notes
Checking account	$13,000	No interest earned on asset
Municipal money market fund (general obligations)	$240,000	2.50% federal annual tax-free yield
I-bonds*	$42,000	Market value
Peter's 401(k)	$975,000	Invested in equities
Peter's traditional IRA	$52,000	Invested in equities
Ann's traditional IRA	$35,000	Invested in equities
Primary residence	$375,000	
Mazda	$6,700	5 years old
Honda	$5,200	6 years old
Household furnishings	$30,000	
Yard equipment	$7,500	
Other misc. assets	$14,000	
Visa credit card	$2,500	14.90% interest rate
MasterCard	$4,000	9.90% interest rate
Discover card	$1,000	18.90% interest rate
Macy's credit card	$500	21.00% interest rate
First mortgage	$25,685	Home purchased 25 years ago; $75,000 financed at 7.25% for 30 years; 300 payments made to date
Note: All nonretirement assets are jointly owned.		
*The I bonds have been owned for 4 years.		

Tax Information

The Mayfields' marginal state tax rate is 4.5 percent. The state income tax is tied to the federal AGI figure. The Mayfields are eligible for two state exemptions in the amount of $1,300 each and a state standard deduction of $10,000. Peter and Ann are also eligible for $6,000 in state income tax adjustments. The municipal money market mutual fund is made up of general Anystate state obligations.

Insurance Information and Planning Issues

Life Insurance

Peter purchased a $250,000 ten-year term policy when he turned age fifty. Peter is the owner and insured. Ann is the beneficiary. In addition, Peter's employer provides him with a group term policy in the amount of one times his salary. When estimating life insurance needs, the Mayfields would like to make the following assumptions:

- Life expectancy: age ninety-five each.

- Final expense needs: $12,000 each.

- Estate administration needs: Peter: $36,500; Ann: $9,500.

- Other immediate needs: $12,000 each.

- Peter and Ann would like to pay off all debts at the first death.

- Anticipated expense needs at first death: $85,000 per year before and after retirement (in today's dollars).

- Peter and Ann believe they can earn 6 percent on any proceeds from insurance prior to retirement.

- Peter and Ann believe they can earn 5 percent on insurance proceeds after retirement.

- Peter and Ann anticipate being in a combined 25 percent federal and state marginal tax bracket after retirement.

- Projected inflation rate: 3.0 percent.

- In the event of a spouse's death, Peter and Ann plan to stop working and collect early Social Security benefits at age sixty. They will receive $16,500 in annual benefits at that time.

- For conservative planning purposes, the Mayfields do not plan to use interest and/or dividends as an income source when planning for life insurance needs.

- Full retirement benefits, at age sixty, are $23,580.

- In addition to Peter's life insurance, Peter and Ann are willing to use all their retirement, investments, and monetary assets to meet life insurance needs.

Disability Insurance

Peter's employer provides both short- and long-term disability coverage. Peter's short-term coverage pays 100 percent of his earned income for the first six months of disability. There is no wait period for this coverage. Peter's long-term coverage has a six-month wait period and pays a benefit equal to 60 percent of earned income until age sixty-five. All premiums, for both policies, are employer paid. If Peter were to become disabled, Peter and Ann will not continue to save for other goals. In case of disability:

- Total household expenses in the event of death or disability are $85,000.

- When calculating disability insurance needs, the Peter and Ann are willing to use all their combined retirement savings to offset insurance needs.

- Peter and Ann prefer to assume that in the event of a possible disability neither will be eligible for Social Security disability benefits.

- For disability insurance planning purposes only, Peter and Ann would like to replace $85,000 per year, in today's dollars, for retirement.

Long-term Care Insurance

The Mayfields do not currently have long-term care insurance.

Retirement Information and Planning Issues

The following information should be used when evaluating the Mayfields' current retirement planning situation:

- Peter does not have access to a defined benefit plan at this time.

- Retirement age for reduced Social Security benefits is age sixty-two; Peter and Ann plan to retire and take benefits at the earliest possible date.

- Retirement age for full Social Security benefits is age sixty-six.

- Their individual life expectancies are ninety-five years of age.

- In the event of the death of one spouse, the surviving spouse is eligible to receive $16,500 per year starting at age sixty from Social Security.

- At age sixty-two, Peter's annual Social Security benefit will be $17,950 in today's dollars; Ann is eligible to receive a survivor benefit equal to $8,367.

- At age sixty-six, Peter's annual Social Security benefit will be $24,420 in today's dollars; Ann is eligible to receive one-half of this amount.

- At age seventy, Peter's annual Social Security benefit will be $32,900 in today's dollars; Ann is eligible to receive a survivor benefit.

- Peter and Ann would like to replace $90,000 in yearly income, in today's pretax dollars, on their first day of retirement. (Note that this figure is different from the assumption used for insurance planning purposes.)

- Ann is the beneficiary of Peter's qualified retirement plan assets.

- For retirement planning purposes only, Peter and Ann believe they can earn a 7.6 percent rate of return prior to retirement and a 5.0 percent rate of return after retirement.

- Inflation before and after retirement is expected to be 3.0 percent.

- Peter's salary will increase at the rate of inflation.

- All annual retirement savings will increase by the rate of inflation (3.0 percent) prior to retirement.

- Peter and Ann are willing to assume that they will remain in the same marginal tax bracket after they retire.

- All nonretirement assets are owned as JTWROS at this time.

Estate Information and Planning Issues

- Final funeral, burial, and medical expenses for life insurance and estate planning purposes will be $12,000 each.

- Estate administration costs are anticipated to be $1,500, whereas executor fees will be approximately $35,000 for Peter and $8,000 for Ann.

- In the event of death, the Mayfields will need approximately $12,000 to cover immediate needs.

- Peter and Ann would like to leave a legacy for their grandchildren by fully funding both children's college education costs should Peter or Ann die.

- Assumed investment return on assets in the event that one spouse dies is 6.0 percent annually.

- The value of the surviving spouse's net estate is expected to grow by 4.0 percent annually.

Additional Planning Assumptions

Peter and Ann would like to maintain their monetary assets as an emergency fund if possible and use interest earned as a "slush fund" while in retirement.

Goals and Objectives

Peter and Ann are very much looking forward to retirement. They hope to spend more time with their growing grandchildren. Given this goal, Peter and Ann plan to retire when Peter turns age sixty-two. Peter and Ann would like to know if they are currently on track to meet this goal.

Their second goal involves establishing an education funding plan to help their grandchildren pay for college expenses. Peter and Ann would like to fund one year of college tuition and room and board for each grandchild. Tuition plus expenses for colleges Peter and Ann have looked at average $18,000 per year. Peter and Ann believe that college costs will continue to rise at a 6.0 percent rate, but to offset some of this increase Peter and Ann are comfortable assuming an 8.0 percent rate of return in a tax-advantaged education savings account, which is roughly equivalent to a 5.5 percent after-tax rate of return.

Use the information provided in this narrative to answer the following case questions.

Case Questions

1. How much money market fund income did the Mayfields earn during the year?

    a. $0

    b. $6,000

    c. $6,325

    d. $7,200

2. Which of the following statements is true?

    I.   Peter must report $110 in Section 79 income for tax purposes.

    II. Because Peter is over age fifty, he does not need to report Section 79 income.

    III. Section 79 income helps reduce a client's taxable income.

    IV. Section 79 income should be accounted for as a taxable expense on the income and expense statement.

    a. II only

    b. I and II only

    c. I and IV only

    d. II and III only

    e. II, III, and IV only

3. How much of the Mayfields' gross income is considered total income for tax purposes on IRS Form 1040?

    a. $96,110

    b. $90,000

   c. $86,510

   d. $80,510

4.   All of the following statements about the Mayfields' level of discretionary cash flow are *incorrect* except:

   a.   After paying all dedicated and discretionary expenses, Peter and Ann have a negative cash flow.

   b.   Total dedicated expenses are greater than discretionary expenses.

   c.   Savings expenses make up the largest dedicated/fixed expense item for Peter and Ann.

   d.   The Mayfields' savings ratio, including employer matching contributions, exceeds 10 percent.

5.   Which of the following is a strength(s) related to the Mayfields' financial situation?

   a.   The savings rate, as measured by the savings ratio, is acceptable at this time.

   b.   Debt, as a percentage of net worth, is low as measured by industry ratios.

   c.   Peter and Ann can easily pay off all of their debt using monetary assets.

   d.   All of the above statements represents strengths.

6.   Which of the following is true?

   a.   Peter and Ann should choose to itemize deductions on IRS Form Schedule A.

   b.   Given their age, Peter and Ann will receive enhanced personal exemptions for this year's taxes.

   c.   Peter and Ann may claim a tax credit for gifts made to their grandchild this year.

   d.   The Mayfields' standard deduction is greater than the itemized deduction amount.

   e.   Statements a and b are correct.

7.   During a benefits presentation for all city employees, the presenter talked about the need for those in attendance to think about long-term care needs. Peter was shocked to learn how much one year of nursing home care might cost. He is worried about depleting assets if he or Ann should need this type of care. Peter wants to know whether he and Ann should purchase long-term care insurance. Which of the following statements best represents a strategy that the Mayfields should consider?

   a.   Purchase long-term care insurance because their net worth, exclusive of home value, is less than $1.5 million.

   b.   Peter and Ann do not need long-term care insurance because they can afford to self-insure the costs of care.

c. Peter and Ann should expect to spend down assets to a point where they will become eligible for Medicaid, and as such, they do not need long-term care insurance.

d. Peter and Ann do not need long-term care insurance because they can use a combination of assets, Medicare funding, and Medicaid reimbursement to fund care needs.

8. Peter was recently approached by a financial advisor who wanted Peter to consider investing in a variable annuity for retirement. A few days later the advisor called Peter again and said that a variable universal life (VUL) insurance policy can also be used to fund retirement needs. Which of the following statement(s) is (are) true in relation to annuities and VULs?

   I.   Given their favorable tax treatment, variable annuities and VUL policies allow earnings to grow tax deferred until withdrawn.

   II. Distributions from an annuity, after age 59½, will be taxed at the long-term capital gain rate if the annuity has been in existence for at least one year.

   III. Distributions from a VUL policy, if made in the form of a loan, will be taxed at a policy owner's marginal tax rate.

   IV. Distributions in the form of a VUL loan need not be reported on IRS Form 1040 for tax purposes.

   a. I and II only

   b. III and IV only

   c. I and IV only

   d. II, III, and IV only

9. When estimating a life insurance need, reducing a client's life expectancy assumption will have which of the following effects?

   a. Increase the amount of life insurance needed.

   b. Decrease the amount of retirement assets needed.

   c. Increase the amount of retirement assets needed.

   d. Statements a and c are correct.

10. Which of the following disability insurance statements is true?

   a. All the benefits received by Peter from his disability coverage will be taxable because his employer paid the premium.

   b. None of the benefits received by Peter from his disability coverage will be taxable because his employer paid the premium.

   c. If Ann becomes disabled, she will be eligible for coverage under her state's workers' compensation program.

    d.   Statements a and c are correct.

    e.   Statements b and c are correct.

11. Peter and Ann have been discussing the possibility of retiring as early as age sixty. What do the Mayfields need to consider as factors that will impact the costs, risks, and benefits of this objective when conducting their retirement planning?

    a.   Distributions from the qualified retirement plans at that time will be subject to a 10 percent early withdrawal penalty.

    b.   Peter and Ann can deal with the loss of health insurance by extending their current health insurance coverage using both COBRA and HIPAA benefits until age sixty-five, at which time they will be eligible to enroll in Medicare.

    c.   The cost of Medicare will increase dramatically for each year that Peter and Ann postpone enrolling after age sixty.

    d.   None of these statements are correct.

12. Which of the following strategies should the Mayfields consider as a way to increase their level of discretionary cash flow?

    a.   Pay off credit card debt with monetary assets.

    b.   Opening and using a home equity line of credit.

    c.   Increase contributions to Peter's 403(b).

    d.   Increase IRS W-4 withholdings on an annual basis.

    e.   Answers a and b only.

13. If Peter and Ann want to pay off their credit card debt, which of the following assets should they use first?

    a.   Money market fund

    b.   Proceeds from a 403(b) loan

    c.   I-bonds

    d.   Home equity

14. Suppose the Mayfields decide to retire at age sixty. How much do Peter and Ann need in assets at that time to fund income needs from ages sixty to sixty-two, assuming that they still want $90,000 (in today's dollars) in annual income starting on their first day of retirement?

    a. $114,009

    b. $225,847

    c. $228,018

    d. $231,438

15. Peter and Ann are concerned about estate planning issues. They have heard about income in respect of a decedent (IRD). Peter and Ann realize that their retirement plans could be subject to IRD taxation. Which of the following statements is true in relation to IRD property?

    I.   IRD property will be included in the estates of Peter and Ann at fair market value.

    II.   IRD property does not receive a step-up in basis.

    III.   IRD property is subject to income taxation when the heir or estate collects income from the property.

    IV.   IRD property will be included in the estates of Peter and Ann at a step-up in basis value.

    a.   I and III only

    b.   II and IV only

    c.   I, II, and III only

    d.   II, III, and IV only

16. Which of the following factors should help drive the Mayfields' decision to fund a capital preservation approach of retirement planning compared to a capital depletion method?

    a.   Their desire to leave a legacy at the death of the second spouse.

    b.   Their willingness to dedicate additional cash flow today to fund the higher retirement asset need in the future.

    c.   Their willingness to decrease their income replacement ratio assumption.

    d.   Each of the factors listed should drive the decision.

17. Calculating the future value of regular savings using a geometrically varying annuity assumption will tend to:

    a.   reduce the future value of the asset.

    b.   reduce the tax liability of the asset.

    c.   increase the future value of the asset.

    d.   increase the interest rate used to calculate future value.

18. Peter and Ann would like to establish a gifting program for their grandchildren. Peter and Ann have two desires. First, they want to implement a strategy that does not allow the grandchildren to access principal prior to age twenty-one, except to pay expenses for the welfare of the child.

484   Case Approach to Financial Planning

Second, they want to maintain the maximum flexibility in terms of the types of assets that can be gifted. Which of the following alternatives meet(s) their desires?

a.   A Uniform Gifts to Minors Act account

b.   A Section 2503(b) trust

c.   A Section 2503(c) trust

d.   All of the above

e.   Only b or c

19. What is(are) the advantage(s) associated with suggesting that Peter and Ann prepay their mortgage at this time?

a.   The loss of the interest deduction will require them to claim the standard deduction.

b.   Their annual level of discretionary cash flow will increase, which can be used to fund other financial goals and objectives.

c.   Peter and Ann will have the satisfaction of knowing that they own their home outright.

d.   Each of these statement is true.

e.   Statements b and c are true.

20. Peter and Ann should consider which of the following estate planning strategies to reduce the likelihood of owing federal estate taxes in the future?

a.   Maximizing the use of the marital deduction.

b.   Gifting strategies to reduce the value of Peter's gross estate.

c.   Using a credit equivalency or bypass trust arrangement.

d.   Both a and b will reduce the possibility of owing federal estate taxes in the future.

e.   Both b and c will reduce the possibility of owing federal estate taxes in the future.

The Marcel and Clio Dion Case

AN ESTATE PLANNING MINI-CASE

Marcel and Clio Dion are taking steps to begin evaluating their estate planning situation. Marcel is sixty years old. Clio is fifty-three years old. They have two children, ages thirteen and eighteen. Marcel is a successful executive with a Fortune 500 company, while Clio has achieved success as a cosmetics home sales trainer.

Currently, Marcel's and Clio's wills state that if either Marcel or Clio were to pass away, the surviving spouse will inherit everything. Both Marcel and Clio value their privacy, but they have not established a trust at this time. Marcel and Clio have an interest in providing charitable support to their church, but they have not made any sizable contributions. Table XI.1 summarizes the asset, liability, and estate expense situation for Marcel and Clio.

Table **XI.1.** Asset, Liability, and Expense Situation for the Dion Household

Assets	Value	Ownership
Checking account	$26,000	JTWROS
Savings account	$20,000	JTWROS
Money market account	$90,000	JTWROS
Other monetary assets	$0	JTWROS
EE/I bonds	$100,000	JTWROS
Mutual funds (basis less than fair market value)	$11,720,000	JTWROS
Other investment assets	$250,000	JTWROS
Primary residence	$700,000	JTWROS
Other housing assets (vacation home)	$240,000	JTWROS
Vehicles	$86,000	JTWROS
Personal property	$134,000	JTWROS
Retirement assets (e.g., 401(k) and IRA)	$2,768,000	Marcel
Retirement assets (e.g., 401(k) and IRA)	$2,345,000	Clio
Other assets	$48,000	Jointly held but not titled
Life insurance (variable universal life)*	$1,500,000	Marcel
Life insurance (universal life)	$250,000	Clio

Liabilities	Value	Ownership
Mortgage on vacation home	$112,000	Joint
Debts	$86,000	Joint
Expenses	**Costs**	
Funeral and final expenses assumed the same for both	$25,000	

*Clio is the beneficiary of Marcel's policy, and Marcel is the beneficiary of Clio's policy.

Use this information to answer the questions that follow:[2]

Case Questions

1.   Identify the statement(s) below that correctly characterize(s) property interests held by Marcel that, at death, pass by operation of law.

   I.   If the property passes according to the operation of law, the property avoids probate.

   II.   If the property passes according to the operation of law, it will not be included in the decedent's gross estate.

   III. Property that passes by operation of law cannot qualify for the marital deduction.

   IV.   The titling on the instrument determines who shall receive the property.

   a.   I only

   b.   I, II, and III only

   c.   I and IV only

   d.   I, II, and IV only

   e.   II and III only

2.   As Marcel and Clio think about the value of their adjusted gross estate, they are unsure which assets and expenses might be deductible. Which of the following is a deduction from the gross estate used to calculate the adjusted gross estate?

   a.   Costs associated with maintaining estate assets.

   b.   Nontaxable gifts made within three years.

   c.   Federal estate tax marital deduction.

   d.   Property inherited from others.

3. Currently, the Dions own their personal residence as JTWROS. If instead they owned the property as tenancy by the entirety, how can this form of ownership be terminated?

> I.   Death, whereby the survivor takes the property.
>
> II. Mutual agreement.
>
> III. Divorce, which converts the estate into a tenancy in common or a joint tenancy.
>
> IV. Severance, whereby one spouse transfers their interest to a third party without the consent of the other spouse.

a. IV only

b. I and III only

c. II and IV only

d. I, II, and III only

e. I, II, III, and IV

4. One of Marcel's primary financial planning goals includes making lifetime gifts to his children. He would like to do this to help his children and to reduce the family's potential future estate tax liability. If he moves forward with his plan to maximize the value of the strategy, he should make gifts of property that:

> I.   are expected to depreciate in the future.
>
> II. are expected to appreciate in the future.
>
> III. have already depreciated significantly.

a. I only

b. II only

c. III only

d. I and III only

e. I, II, and III

5. What is the value of Marcel's adjusted gross estate if he were to pass away today and before Clio?

a. $2,475,000

b. $3,975,000

c. $9,591,000

d. $10,851,000

6.   There are several weaknesses associated with the Dions' current estate plan. Which of the following are the significant weaknesses within their plan?

   I.   Failure to utilize the marital deduction.

   II.   Failure to maximize the unified credit.

   III.   Failure to utilize charitable gift strategies to reduce the taxable estate.

   IV.   Failure to avoid probate.

   a.   I and III only

   b.   II and IV only

   c.   I, II, and III only

   d.   II, III, and IV only

   e.   I, II, III, and IV

7.   In view of the combined estate values for Marcel and Clio, and knowing that one of their planning objectives is the reduction of estate taxes, which of the following estate planning techniques is appropriate?

   I.   Placing the life insurance policies in an irrevocable trust.

   II.   Establishing a revocable living trust and funding it by using the unlimited marital deduction and the full unified credit.

   III.   Making use of the gift tax annual exclusion.

   IV.   Establishing a qualified terminable interest property (QTIP) trust to pass property to their children.

   a.   II and III only

   b.   I and III only

   c.   II and IV only

   d.   II, III, and IV only

   e.   I, II, III, and IV

8.   Calculate Clio's taxable estate assuming that Marcel passes away first, followed closely the death of Clio.

   a. $6,029,000

   b. $10,851,000

c. $20,153,000

d. $20,029,000

e. $22,894,500

9. Marcel and Clio are considering making a sizable charitable gift to a local university using assets held in their joint mutual fund accounts. The primary purpose of their gifting strategy is to reduce the taxable estate while providing a benefit for the university. Which of the following strategies will maximize the effectiveness of this estate planning strategy?

a.   Give the mutual funds first to their oldest child, who can then sell them with a stepped-up basis and use the proceeds as a donation to the university.

b.   Donate the mutual funds directly to the university and allow the university to sell the mutual funds.

c.   Sell the mutual funds first and then donate the cash proceeds to the university.

d.   Transfer the mutual funds to a non-charitable irrevocable trust and then donate the trust income to the university.

10. A local university has approached the Dions about making a charitable contribution. After discussing the possibility of making a donation, Marcel and Clio have decided that they are willing to make the donation if they can receive an immediate tax deduction and an income stream for life based on a fixed percentage of the amount donated (valued annually). Marcel and Clio would also like to have the ability to increase their donation amount in future years. Which of the following charitable giving alternatives best serves the Dions' desires?

a.   A charitable remainder unitrust.

b.   A charitable remainder annuity trust.

c.   A pooled income fund.

d.   A grantor retained annuity trust.

The Onslo and Daisy Graham Case

A GENERAL FINANCIAL PLANNING CASE

Onslo Graham is fifty-nine years of age. His wife, Daisy, is age fifty-eight. Onslo and Daisy have been married for nearly thirty years. The Grahams currently live at 3456 Speedway, Anycity, Anystate 01010. They have an adult child, Rose, who recently turned age twenty-eight. Rose also lives in Anycity.

Because of their strong relationship, Onslo and Daisy have titled all property jointly, even though Daisy has been a homemaker and not directly contributed to the purchase price of household assets. Onslo does have one real estate asset that is not jointly owned.

Onslo is the general manager of Tarantula Industries, a closely held corporation, which owns a hockey team in an expanding southwestern minor league. The team is headquartered at 555 West Verity Road, Anycity, Anystate 71010. Onslo has been involved in professional sports management for approximately twenty-five years. He currently earns $137,500 per year in income. Rose is also actively involved with the team. She works in the front office and manages day-to-day operations. Onslo and Daisy hope that Rose will eventually take over management of the team once Onslo retires.

Use the following information to conduct a review of the Grahams' financial situation.

Global Assumptions (Valid unless otherwise specified in certain instances):

- Inflation: 4.0 percent.

- All income and expense numbers are presented in today's dollars.

- Planned retirement age: When Onslo turns age sixty-six.

- Combined federal and state marginal tax bracket: 29.72 percent.

- All qualified plan or IRA contribution growth rates are assumed to stop at the federally mandated limit unless otherwise restricted.

- All nominal rates of return represent pre-tax returns.

- As of the date of the case, Onslo and Daisy are not subject to the alternative minimum tax (AMT).

- Onslo and Daisy are currently qualified for Social Security benefits.

Income Issues

Onslo currently earns $137,500 per year and expects his salary to increase at 5.0 percent per year until retirement. As a household, Onslo and Daisy also receive $15,403 in non-qualified dividends and interest from miscellaneous other investments, all of which are reinvested. Onslo and Daisy are covered by employer-sponsored health care. The premium, which is paid by Onslo directly, is $2,400 per year. Onslo also contributes $9,600 annually into a 401(k) plan. The plan provides matching at 33 cents on the dollar with no maximum beyond IRC statutory limitations. These expenses are paid for with pre-tax dollars.

Expense Summary

Based on his salary, Onslo had $27,000 withheld for federal, Social Security, and Medicare taxes. He also had $6,565 withheld for state taxes. Table XII.1 summarizes other household expenditures.

Table XII.1. Other Household Expenses

Expense	Amount	Frequency
Mortgage payments	$1,829.50	Monthly
Home equity loan payments	$286.67	Monthly
Auto payments	$483.33	Monthly
Credit card payments	$3,500.00	Annually
Auto insurance	$1,300.00	Semiannually
Homeowners insurance	$450.00	Semiannually
Life insurance	$3,200.00	Annually
Umbrella liability insurance	$125.00	Annually
Disability insurance	$2,250.00	Annually
IRA contributions (Daisy)	$2,000.00	Annually
IRA contributions (Onslo)	$2,000.00	Annually
Subscriptions	$500.00	Annually
Telephone expense	$91.67	Monthly
Home Internet	$50.00	Monthly
Hobbies (Daisy)	$500.00	Yearly
Hobbies (Onslo)	$100.00	Yearly

Recreation/entertainment	$100.00	Monthly
Club dues	$500.00	Yearly
Groceries	$500.00	Monthly
Food away from home	$400.00	Monthly
Real estate taxes	$600.00	Semiannually
Household maintenance	$200.00	Monthly
Utilities	$300.00	Monthly
Clothing (Daisy)	$300.00	Monthly
Clothing (Onslo)	$600.00	Semiannually
Laundry services	$100.00	Monthly
Personal care	$100.00	Monthly
Furnishing	$1,000.00	Yearly
Yard maintenance	$100.00	Monthly
Medical copayments (Daisy)	$10.00	Monthly
Medical copayments (Onslo)	$10.00	Monthly
Prescriptions (Daisy)	$300.00	Yearly
Unreimbursed medical expenses	$10.00	Monthly
Gasoline	$100.00	Monthly
Car registrations	$320.00	Yearly
Parking and tolls	$400.00	Yearly
Personal property tax*	$450.00	Yearly
Safe deposit box fee	$100.00	Yearly
Monthly bank fees	$2.00	Monthly
IRA fees	$40.00	Yearly
Accounting fees	$400.00	Yearly
Charitable contributions	$400.00	Monthly
Travel expenses	$2,500.00	Yearly
Vacations	$2,500.00	Semiannually
Alcohol expenses	$350.00	Annually
Gifts to family members (Daisy)	$500.00	Quarterly
Gifts to family members (Onslo)	$500.00	Annually
Other miscellaneous expenses	$500.00	Semiannually
*Amount includes applicable car registration property tax.		

Tax Issues

Onslo and Daisy complete their own tax returns using a nationally known tax preparation software package. Onslo pays his company's accountant to double-check his calculations. Onslo and Daisy file married filing jointly. Onslo and Daisy are eligible for a $1,250 state standard deduction and a $275 state exemption per person. Onslo is considered an employee of his firm and does not pay self-employment income taxes. Household held assets are summarized in Table XII.2. Household debts and liabilities are shown in Table XII.3.

Table XII.2. Asset Summary

Asset	Amount	Ownership
Financial Assets		
Checking account	$6,500	Joint
Savings account	$10,000	Joint
Taxable money market mutual fund	$230,000	Joint
I-bonds	$15,000	Joint
Government bond funds	$41,000	Joint
Corporate bond funds	$45,000	Joint
High-yield bond funds	$15,000	Joint
Large-cap funds	$151,600	Joint
Mid-cap funds	$70,600	Joint
Small-cap funds	$37,000	Joint
Rental real estate portfolio*	$2,100,000	Onslo
Retirement Assets		
Large-cap funds (401k)	$40,000	Onslo
Mid-cap funds (401k)	$35,000	Onslo
Small-cap funds (401k)	$15,000	Onslo
Corporate bond funds (401k)	$27,000	Onslo
International funds (IRA)	$19,000	Onslo
High-yield bond funds (IRA)	$17,500	Daisy

Other Assets		
Primary residence	$375,000	Joint
Mazda MPV	$25,000	Joint
Ford Taurus	$7,800	Joint
Artwork	$2,500	Joint
Hockey collectibles	$1,500	Joint
Sporting/hobbies supplies	$3,500	Joint
14-foot aluminum boat	$7,000	Joint
Furniture	$28,000	Joint
Other assets	$6,500	Joint
*The rental real estate is income and tax neutral; the property does not generate income or losses for cash flow or tax purposes.		

Table XII.3. Debt and Liability Summary

Liability	Amount	Ownership
Visa credit card	$12,000	Joint
MasterCard	$8,000	Joint
Discover card	$7,500	Joint
Garts sporting goods card	$5,000	Joint
Loan due in 45 days	$2,500	Onslo
Mortgage	$235,984	Joint
Home equity loan*	$29,471	Joint
Mazda loan	$9,177	Joint
*Loan used to pay for a vacation and to pay off debts owed by Rose.		

Loan Factors	Home Mortgage	Home Equity Loan	Mazda Loan
Original loan amount	$275,000	$30,000	$25,000
Interest rate	7.00%	8.00%	6.00%
Length of loan	30 Years	15 Years	5 Years
Number of payments made	120	6	40

Life Insurance Information and Planning Issues

Onslo and Daisy would like you to analyze their life insurance situation using the following assumptions and facts:

- In the event of a death, household expenses will drop to $105,000 per year.

- Final expenses (funeral and burial costs) will be $25,000 for each person.

- Estate and legal costs will be $69,930 for Onslo and $16,135 for Daisy.

- All outstanding liabilities will be paid at the first death.

- Other immediate needs should be funded with $10,000 each.

- Onslo and Daisy would like to plan conservatively in the event of a death by assuming a 6.0 percent before-tax rate of return on any insurance proceeds both pre- and post-retirement.

- For planning purposes, assume Onslo and Daisy will be in a combined state and federal tax bracket of 30.0 percent before retirement.

- Full retirement age is sixty-six for both Onslo and Daisy.

- Onslo and Daisy would like to replace $90,000, before taxes, while in retirement for the surviving spouse.

- Daisy is eligible to receive $1,958 per month (in today's dollars) as a Social Security survivor benefit at age sixty-six (assumes that Onslo dies today).

- Onslo will receive $2,024 Social Security benefits per month (in today's dollars) in retirement at age sixty-six.

- Onslo and Daisy are eligible to receive survivor benefits equal to a 71.5 percent reduction in full benefits from age sixty to sixty-six.

- In the event of either spouse's death, the other spouse plans to stop working at age sixty and begin taking early retirement survivor benefits.

- For conservative planning purposes, the Grahams do not plan on using interest and/or dividends as an income source when determining insurance needs.

- Onslo and Daisy are willing to use all their retirement savings and $350,000 in other assets to offset life insurance needs.

- Onslo expects his salary to remain the same following Daisy's death.

- Daisy does not expect to work after Onslo's death.

Table XII.4 summarizes life insurance policy information for Onslo and Daisy.

Table XII.4. Life Insurance Policies Owned by Onslo and Daisy

Policy Type	Face Value	Cash Value	Owner	Insured	Beneficiary	Premium
twenty-year term (12 years remaining)*	$250,000	NA	Onslo	Onslo	Daisy	Paid by Onslo and Daisy; $1,000 yearly
twenty-year term (20 years remaining)*	$150,000	NA	Onslo	Onslo	Daisy	Paid by Onslo and Daisy; $1,200 yearly
Group term	$50,000	NA	Onslo	Onslo	Daisy	Employer paid
Whole-life**	$100,000	$21,250	Onslo	Daisy	Rose	Paid by Onslo and Daisy; $1,000 yearly

*Both insurance companies are rated A by A.M. Best.

**Cash value at beginning of year was $21,250; current dividend is $100; an equivalent after-tax yield is 6 percent.

Disability Insurance Information and Planning Issues

Onslo and Daisy have not focused too heavily on disability planning issues. Onslo and Daisy do know that they do not want to account for Social Security benefits in the event of a disability. A few years ago, Onslo purchased a long-term disability insurance policy in the private market (not through a cafeteria plan at work). Information about the policy is summarized below:

- The policy is defined as own-occupation and is issued by an A.M. Best A- rated company.

- The policy has a six-month elimination period.

- The policy pays 50 percent of Onslo's current salary until age sixty-five.

- All premiums are paid with after-tax dollars.

- If disabled, Onslo and Daisy would like to continue to save for other financial objectives.

Other Insurance Information and Planning Issues

The Grahams do not currently have a long-term care insurance policy. In the case of a long-term care need, Onslo and Daisy are comfortable assuming nursing home costs of $65,000 per year in today's dollars, with a four year funding need. Both are healthy with both sets of parents still alive and well. In fact, Onslo and Daisy skate twice a week at the team's local indoor practice arena.

Onslo and Daisy have worked with the same property and casualty insurance agent for twenty-five years. Their agent encouraged them to purchase a $1 million umbrella policy four years ago. This required that the Grahams increase the split-limit coverage on their personal automobile policies to $100/$300/$100. Their current HO-3 homeowner's policy provides 100 percent inflation protection coverage.

Current yield information for use when solving case questions is provided in Table XII.5.

Table XII.5. Current Yield Information

Investment Class	Yield
Checking account	0.00%
Savings account	2.00%
Taxable money market fund	3.00%
Anystate municipal money market fund	2.40%
EE savings bonds	3.50%
I bonds	4.50%
Government bonds	4.50%
Corporate bonds	5.00%
High-yield bonds	6.50%
Real estate	3.75%
Gold	0.00%
Large-cap stocks	2.00%
Mid-cap stocks	1.00%
Small-cap stocks	0.00%
Loan Rates	
thirty-year mortgage*	5.95%
1five-year mortgage*	5.75%
Home equity line of credit*	5.85%
Home equity loan*	7.35%
five-year auto loan	6.10%
Personal loan	8.25%
*APR includes closing costs	

Retirement Information and Planning Issues

The following information should be used when evaluating the Grahams' current retirement planning situation:

- Onslo and Daisy would like to retire when Onslo reaches age sixty-six.

- Although the actual tax rate will likely be less, Onslo and Daisy would like to assume that they will be in a 25 percent combined federal and state marginal tax bracket while in retirement.

- Prior to retirement, Onslo and Daisy are comfortable assuming that future rates of return will be 10.72 percent, before taxes, on retirement assets and savings.

- If retired today, they would like to replace 90 percent of Onslo's salary.

- At retirement, Onslo will be eligible to receive $2,024 (in today's dollars) in Social Security benefits per month.

- Daisy has not yet earned forty quarters for Social Security benefits, but she does qualify for spousal benefits.

- Onslo and Daisy are comfortable assuming a life expectancy of ninety-five years.

- Contributions to Onslo's 401(k) will increase by 3 percent each year.

- Daisy is the primary beneficiary of Onslo's retirement assets.

- All qualified assets held outside of the 401(k) are in traditional IRAs.

- After retirement, Onslo and Daisy plan to allocate retirement assets to generate a before-tax return of 8.70 percent.

Estate Information and Planning Issues

Onslo and Daisy have separate wills. Onslo's will leaves all his assets to Daisy. Daisy's will leaves all her assets to Onslo. Each person's will names their attorney as the estate executor, and in the event of a simultaneous death, it is assumed that Onslo predeceases Daisy. Other estate planning assumptions include:

- Funeral and burial expenses will be $25,000 each.

- Estate and legal costs will be $5,000 each.

- Executor fees will be approximately 2.0 percent of the gross estate before the marital transfer.

- The net growth rate of the survivor's estate is estimated to be, on average, 4.0 percent annually.

- Daisy is the sole beneficiary of Onslo's IRA and retirement plan assets.

- Onslo is the sole beneficiary of Daisy's IRA assets.

- Daisy has a strong allegiance to the University of Anystate. She would like to leave a legacy gift to the university, if possible.

- No other estate planning documents are known to exist.

Goals and Objectives

Onslo and Daisy have two primary goals. First, they would like to know whether they are on or off track to meet an age sixty-six retirement goal. Second, they feel that a thorough review of their current estate situation is in order. Specifically, Onslo and Daisy would like to minimize any estate and/or gift taxes paid in the event of death. Other planning objectives include reviewing the discretionary cash flow, net worth, and life insurance situation. Onslo and Daisy are looking for guidance on ways to improve their general financial well-being.

Case Questions

1. Which of the following statements most accurately reflects the Grahams' current discretionary cash flow position?

    a. Their discretionary cash flow is greater than $0 but less than $1,000.

    b. Their discretionary cash flow is less than $0 but greater than –$1,000.

    c. Their discretionary cash flow is greater than $1,000 but less than $8,000.

    d. Their discretionary cash flow is less than $–1,000 but greater than –$8,000.

2. Which of the following statements is (are) true?

    I.   Retirement plan assets make up approximately 5 percent of the Grahams' total assets.

    II. Given their age and income profile, one would expect Onslo and Daisy to have a substantially higher level of net worth.

    III. The Grahams' savings ratio, including reinvested dividends and interest, is below financial planning benchmark levels.

    IV. The Grahams' emergency fund ratio is adequate at this time.

    a. I and II only

    b. II and III only

    c.   I and IV only

    d.   I, III, and IV only

3.   Which of the following strategies can the Grahams use to increase their discretionary cash flow situation?

    I.   Refinance the first mortgage using a fifteen-year fixed-rate loan.

    II.   Pay off outstanding credit card debt using money market mutual fund assets.

    III.   Use a six-year home equity loan to refinance the Mazda car debt.

    a.   II only

    b.   I and II only

    c.   II and III only

    d.   I and III only

4.   According to your tax calculations, which of the following statements is(are) true?

    a.   Onslo and Daisy should use the standard deduction rather than itemize expenses.

    b.   Given their AGI, the Grahams can deduct Daisy's IRA contribution because she is not an active participant in a qualified retirement plan.

    c.   Even though Onslo is an active participant in a qualified plan, the Grahams can deduct his IRA contribution because he is over age fifty this year.

    d.   Statements a and b are correct.

5.   Which of the following tax planning statements is true?

    I.   Onslo and Daisy should, based on tax-equivalent investment calculations, transfer the money market mutual fund assets to an Anystate municipal money market fund.

    II.   By paying off the home equity loan early, Onslo and Daisy will increase discretionary cash flow but lose a tax deduction.

    III.   Using municipal bond investments will increase both the Grahams' level of discretionary cash flow and their taxable income.

    IV.   Increasing 401(k) contributions will decrease the amount of taxes the Grahams will pay at the federal level.

    a.   I and II only

    b.   I and IV only

c. I, II, and IV only

d. II, III, and IV only

6. All of the following life insurance observations are true except?

a. Based solely on the relative cost of the policy, Onslo should consider using a Section 1035 exchange procedure to replace the $100,000 whole-life insurance policy.

b. The death benefit from Onslo's current life insurance policies is less than his calculated life insurance need.

c. Term life insurance will provide the Grahams with the maximum amount of coverage for the lowest premium but leave them uninsured at some point in the future.

d. Using the nonforfeiture provision in the whole-life insurance policy will result in a decrease in discretionary cash flow.

7. Which of the following statements is true?

a. The Grahams can afford to self-insure short-term disability needs by using a combination of cash flow and non-retirement assets.

b. Because Onslo purchased his disability policy in the private market, if he receives benefits, then 100 percent of the benefit received will be subject to federal income taxation.

c. If the Grahams use all of their financial assets, excluding insurance cash values and Onslo's rental real estate interests, they will be able to self-insure Onslo's net long-term disability need.

d. Statements a and c are correct.

8. Assume that long-term care (LTC) costs in Anycity are currently $45,000 per year. Also assume that LTC costs are increasing by 5.0 percent annually. If the Grahams anticipate that Daisy will enter a nursing home when she turns age seventy-one and will need care for five years, and they can earn a 7 percent rate of return on investments, which of the following statements is true if Onslo and Daisy are willing to reduce retirement income expectations in the event of a LTC need?

a. The Grahams currently have enough financial assets to self-insure nursing home costs for Daisy.

b. The Grahams do not need to worry because Daisy will qualify for Medicaid benefits at that time.

c. The cost of coverage for five years will exceed the Grahams' ability to self-insure the loss.

d. Even if Onslo and Daisy wanted to purchase long-term care insurance, the cost to purchase this insurance today is prohibitively high.

9. To retire at age sixty-six—based on the value of their current retirement assets—Onslo and Daisy need to consider which of the following?

    a. Be willing to reduce their income need in retirement.

    b. Increase the rate of return earned on retirement savings and assets.

    c. Increase the age-of-death assumption.

    d. All of the above.

    e. Only statements a and b are correct.

10. Given what Onslo and Daisy currently have saved, which of the following statements is(are) true in relation to Onslo's and Daisy's current retirement planning situation?

    a. Onslo and Daisy currently have adequate cash flow to fund their retirement goal.

    b. If Onslo can convert his rental real estate holdings to cash prior to age sixty-six, the Grahams can meet their retirement goal.

    c. Postponing retirement by one year will allow them to reach their retirement goal without using any additional assets.

    d. None of these statement is correct.

    e. Only statements b and c are correct.

11. Which of the following assets will pass directly to Daisy (thus avoid probate) if Onslo were to die today?

    a. His 401(k) assets.

    b. Proceeds from his group term life insurance policy.

    c. His ownership interest in their house.

    d. Each of the assets listed will pass directly to Daisy.

12. What is the approximate value of Onslo's gross estate today?

    a. $1,000,000

    b. $2,000,000

    c. $3,000,000

    d. $4,000,000

13. At Onslo's death, assuming Daisy is still alive:

    a. if Anystate is a community property state, Daisy will receive a step-up in basis equal to 50 percent on all jointly owned taxable property.

    b. if Anystate is a community property state, Daisy will receive a step-up in basis equal to 100 percent of all community property.

    c. Daisy will retain the original basis in all property held jointly.

    d. Daisy will be required to pay estate and gift taxes on all property received from Onslo.

14. What action(s) can Onslo take today to ensure a smooth transfer of his rental real estate holdings to either Daisy or Rose at his death?

    I.   Change the title from individual to trust ownership.

    II. Consider a buy-sell agreement provision by funding the agreement with a life insurance provision so that the daughter can then buy the rental company from Daisy (assume Daisy will be the owner because she is the beneficiary of the property).

    III. Use a grantor retained annuity or unitrust to pass these assets to Rose.

    a. I only

    b. III only

    c. I and II only

    d. I, II, and III

15. Which of the following estate planning tools can be used to allow Onslo to maintain full control of his assets today while minimizing estate taxes at his death in the future?

    I.   An A-B trust arrangement funded at his death.

    II. A QTIP trust arrangement.

    III. An irrevocable living trust arrangement.

    IV. A funded revocable living trust arrangement.

    a. I only

    b. I and II only

    c. I and III only

    d. III and IV only

16. Onslo and Daisy have indicated to you that they are considering adding Rose as a co-owner on their checking and savings accounts. Onslo and Daisy heard that gift and/or income taxes might apply if they decide to move forward with the idea. Which of the following statements best describes the tax consequences of adding Rose to the account?

    a.   Rose will owe a gift tax on one-third of the account balance when she is added to the account.

    b.   Onslo and Daisy might owe a gift tax when Rose makes a withdrawal from the account.

    c.   Rose will owe only federal income tax on her share of the account when either Onslo or Daisy dies.

    d.   Onslo and Daisy will owe a gift tax when Rose is added to the account.

    e.   Statements a and d are correct.

17. Daisy has been talking with a planned giving officer from the University of Anystate about funding a charitable trust that will also provide income to Onslo and Daisy during retirement. She and Onslo would like to begin funding the trust immediately and retain the right to add to the fund in future years. Which of the following gift alternatives will meet the Grahams' objective?

    a.   A charitable remainder unitrust.

    b.   A charitable reminder annuity trust.

    c.   A pooled-income fund.

    d.   All of the above will meet Daisy's objectives.

    e.   The alternatives listed in a and c will meet Daisy's objectives.

18. Recently, Onslo indicated being concerned about the general strength of the stock market. As he and Daisy get closer to retirement, he is worried that the market will drop at just the moment they need to be drawing money from their equity fund holdings. Even so, he is reluctant to sell his stock funds at this time. Which of the following investing strategies provides Onslo with a solution to his dilemma?

    a.   Periodically sell an index option put.

    b.   Periodically buy an index option put.

    c.   Periodically write a covered put.

    d.   Periodically buy an index option call.

19. Onslo has occasionally thought about buying municipal bond securities, but he never has because he does not have great faith that his local elected officials will make good on the bonds (i.e., pay back the full-face value upon maturity). Which of the following municipal bond alternatives would be most appropriate for Onslo, assuming that he wants to know that bond interest and principal will be paid from earnings on a project rather than tax revenues?

a. Debenture bonds.

b. General obligation bonds.

c. Revenue bonds.

d. Income bonds.

20. Before selling their taxable bond securities and purchasing municipal bond securities to reduce tax liabilities, Onslo and Daisy ought to consider which of the following factors as true in their situation?

a. Given their level and sources of income and deductions, there is the possibility that owning certain municipal bond securities that generate preference item interest will subject them to the AMT.

b. Anystate will tax all interest earned on bonds issued by another city in their state but not by Anycity, where Onslo and Daisy file taxes.

c. Although state income tax free, any municipal bond interest that Onslo and Daisy earn will still be taxable at the federal level.

d. Statements a and c are correct.

Discussion Points and Questions

1. Briefly summarize the relevant facts of the case.

2. Are there any areas in the Grahams' expense summary that can be reduced to improve their cash flow situation?

3. If the Grahams were going to purchase additional life insurance, what type of policy would be most appropriate given their age and needs?

4. What factors do the Grahams need to take into account regarding health insurance as they begin to think about retirement?

- The Grahams' current retirement plan assumes the depletion of assets at the death of the surviving spouse. How much more do the Grahams need in assets on their first day of retirement to fully fund a capital preservation model of retirement if the following assumptions are used?

- Onslo and Daisy want to replace 90 percent of Onslo's salary in retirement.

- Onslo's salary is increasing by 5 percent annually.

- Social Security benefits are increasing by 4 percent annually.

- Inflation will remain at 4 percent throughout retirement.

- Onslo and Daisy can earn an 8.7 percent rate of return on investments in retirement.

- At retirement, Onslo and Daisy have a twenty-nine-year life expectancy.

5. Discuss property ownership and titling characteristics for Onslo and Daisy, assuming that Onslo and Daisy live in a community property state.

6. What can Onslo and Daisy do to avoid probate?

7. What action(s) can Onslo take today to ensure a smooth transfer of his rental real estate holdings to either Daisy or Rose at his death?

8. What type of gifting strategies can be used by the Grahams to reduce their estate tax situation (assuming the value of their assets grows to a taxable level)?

9. What other creative estate planning techniques can be used in this case?

The Adora and Jorge Tun Case

A CASH FLOW AND EDUCATION PLANNING CASE

Adora and Jorge were married seven years ago when Jorge was thirty-five years old. He met Adora, who was also thirty-five years of age at the time, at a Caribbean resort. Jorge had flown down for the week with his golfing buddies. Adora was on the island taking a well-earned break from her hectic life. When they met, Adora was recently divorced, and although she had sworn off ever getting married again, when she got to know Jorge she knew that they were destined to be married.

Before meeting Jorge, Adora's life was chaotic. She married her high school sweetheart one week after graduation. Adora reasoned that it was better to get married, pool resources, and grow old with a man she loved. It wasn't long before she and her husband had their first baby. Adora was nineteen years old. She felt blessed to hold her newborn son, whom they named Amado.

The realities of married life with a child soon hit Adora and her husband with full force. He was working as a construction worker, while Adora held a job as a cashier at a local card shop. As a couple, they were making a bit more than minimum wage, which was just enough to pay rent, cover car loan payments, pay for food, and cover baby expenses. There was nothing left at the end of the month. Adora knew that her family was in trouble. They were on a dead-end financial road.

At age twenty-one, Adora made a life-changing decision. She quit her job and enrolled in a business program at a local community college. Her husband was skeptical, but he reluctantly agreed that Adora should go to college, if for no other reason than to get a better paying job after graduation. In two years Adora completed an Associate's degree in Business Administration. Her instructors encouraged her to apply for a scholarship that would allow her to complete her Bachelor's degree from the local state university. Adora did not know if she would qualify, but with prompting by the community college faculty, she filled out the scholarship application. Adora was thrilled when she learned that the final two years of her college education would be paid for from a special fund that was available to assist first generation mothers complete college. At age twenty-five, Adora completed her Bachelors of Science degree in Business Administration. Her graduation was a day of celebration.

Shortly after graduation, Adora took a job as a teller at a local bank. Amado started Kindergarten, while her husband continued to work as a tradesman. Maybe it was good fortune or just hard work, but it wasn't long before Adora was promoted to Head Teller. From there she moved into the loan department doing both personal and commercial loans. Time flew by while Adora remained at the bank. Today, she is a loan manager and a highly valued employee of the bank.

During Adora's rise through the ranks at the bank, her husband's career remained basically unchanged. He was still working construction jobs with local contractors. During the summer months he made good money but was rarely home. During the winter months, when construction subsided, he stayed at home more often and tended to spend his days drinking. By her late twenties, Adora had a feeling that her marriage was in trouble, but she continued to work at making the relationship function. Her primary thought was of Amado—making sure that Amado had a stable home environment. When Adora was thirty-four years she could no longer take her husband's drinking. She decided to end the marriage. It was not too long afterward that the divorce proceedings were finalized. The week after the divorce was final, she sent Amado to stay with his grandparents. She caught a plane for the Caribbean and it was there that she met Jorge.

Jorge grew up in a small Midwestern town. After graduation from high school he worked at the local Co-Op. He started as a day worker in the grain elevator, but soon was promoted to work inside selling all sorts of farm and ranch supplies. Because he is an outgoing person, easily likeable, and a generally sincere person, people immediately gravitate to him for advice and friendship. The problem, for both Adora and Jorge, was that life soon intruded on their budding relationship. Adora's life—her house, job, and son—were in one state. Jorge was living in another state. The romance would only work if Jorge was willing to move, which is exactly what he did. Jorge quit his job, loaded up his pick-up truck, sold what he could not take, and headed east to be with Adora. After a whirlwind time together, Adora and Jorge were married in a small church. That was seven years ago.

The Tuns' Current Situation

Before marrying Jorge, Adora made it quite clear that they should work as a couple to achieve their financial goals. Adora and Jorge agreed to pool their income to pay household expenses and to save for future goals. However, they were of the same opinion that some expenses should not be jointly paid. For example, Jorge agreed to fund his own health insurance premiums. This strategy helped reduce Adora's monthly expense by allowing her to provide coverage for herself and Amado.

Since their marriage, Adora's position at the bank has become even more secure. Last week, her manager pulled her aside and told her how valuable she was to the success of the branch. The manager also indicated that should she ever get a competing job offer, the bank would do everything possible to allow her to stay. This not only made her feel good, but it also helped her think about Jorge's situation.

Because of Jorge's good nature and skills, he was hired immediately by a regional hardware store when he arrived in Adora's hometown. He has been working at the store for seven years. He, like Adora, is considered a valuable employee. It is because of this that Jorge faces a life changing decision in relation to his job. Last week he learned that the store's owners are in the process of expanding. The owners hope to open five new branches over the next three years. The owners want to hire store managers from within the firm. There is just one problem. The firm has a policy of hiring only managers with a college degree. The preference has been to hire individuals with a marketing and accounting background. Of course, the owners know that hardware skills are critically important too, but in the final analysis, the owners are looking to hire managers who have an understanding of the financial operations of each store.

Yesterday, Jorge met with the firm's regional manager. The regional manager made the following offer. If Jorge can complete a Bachelor's degree in Marketing within the next three years the firm will guarantee him a manager position at one of the new stores. If he chooses to not pursue a college degree or does not finish in time, the firm will have no choice but to hire someone else for the position. The regional manager also made it quite clear that while Jorge is a valued employee, opportunities for management are restricted to those with a college degree.

The Tuns' Questions, Dreams, and Goals

That night, Jorge went home in a rather excited, yet confused state. After dinner, he sat down with Adora and explained the opportunity. Adora was excited for Jorge but was concerned as well. Questions such as, "How will we pay for this?" and "Is it worth the expense?" came immediately to mind. Adora looked at Jorge and asked, "What would you like to do?" He knew his answer immediately. "I would love to be a store manager. I know that I can do the job. I love the company, and I can see great potential with the firm."

Adora replied, "Is this your dream job?"

Jorge was quick to reply, "I really think that this is my dream." He was quick to add, "If it makes financial sense to do it. Otherwise, I am happy being your husband and working at the store. I would only go to school if it was financially the smart thing to do."

Unfortunately, neither Adora nor Jorge knows if going back to college makes financial sense. This is the reason Adora and Jorge have come to you as a financial planner. During your initial meeting with them meeting you learn the following:

- Jorge's primary goal is to find a way to improve the family's financial situation. Together, the family income is just barely enough to make ends meet. Becoming a manager might help the Tuns' overall financial situation, but Jorge wants to know if the investment, both time and money, will be worth the effort.

- The bottom line question for Jorge is this: Should he should stay in his current job and make do with what he and Adora live on, or should he return to school and work towards a marketing degree. While in your meeting you also noted the following:

  ○ Jorge loves his job and would not be crushed if you recommend that he does not go back to school. In fact, he is a bit nervous about going to college, but he knows that without a college degree his current job might be the best he can hope for, not only with the firm but in town as well.

○ Neither Adora nor Jorge is willing or able to move so that Jorge can find a better job. Adora has deep ties in the community that make moving unacceptable.

○ Jorge does not want to earn a degree online; he performs better in a classroom situation.

○ Given Jorge's work hours and variable work schedule, there is no way he can hold down a second job as a way to increase his income.

The Tuns' Financial Position

When Adora and Jorge arrived at your office they had several folders containing financial records, tax returns, and other information they thought might be helpful in the financial planning process. Because Adora works at a bank, she had a good idea that you would need information about their incomes, expenses, assets, and liabilities. She and Jorge also brought information about their financial goals and objectives, time horizon for meeting objectives, expectations about their employment future, and their risk tolerance. The following discussion summarizes what you learned during your interview with Adora and Jorge.

Income and Expenses

When reviewing their financial documents, you made a note of one thing immediately. The Tuns are very good at cutting costs and watching where they spend their money. Their annual cash flow statement is an example of frugality. When asked, Adora is quick to note her philosophy: it is important to live within one's means. While she is not opposed to debt, both she and Jorge are reluctant to go into more debt unless it makes financial sense to do so.

During your meeting, Adora disclosed that given their income and expense situation, she and Jorge have been unable to save anything over the past several years. In fact, neither Adora nor Jorge have contributed to their 401(k) plans.[3] There are several reasons for their lack of savings. First, the household income is just not sufficient to meet daily needs, let alone fund retirement objectives. Second, expenses associated with raising Amado have been higher than expected. Since her divorce, Adora has received nothing in terms of alimony or child support. Third, Amado is about to begin college,[4] and Adora wants to help her son with some of those expenses (if possible), so she feels saving for retirement would only work against that goal. Finally, when Adora and Jorge were married neither had much in terms of assets. Adora's wealth was depleted during the divorce, while Jorge basically had very little in terms of financial assets to begin with. While Adora and Jorge are happily married, the one area of their life that has been somewhat stressed is their financial situation. The following table summarizes the Tuns' income and expense situation:

Table XIII.1. Yearly Income and Expense Figures ($ rounded)

Income	Amount	Variable Expenses	Amount
Jorge's Wages	$27,900	Electricity	$2,400
Adora's Salary	$55,000	Other Utilities	$900
Interest	$2,000[5]	Telephone/Cell phone	$2,700
Other Income	???	Cable TV	$1,100
TOTAL	???	Home Repairs	$750
Fixed Expenses	Amount	Home Improvements	$1,500
Mortgage Principal and Interest[6]	$15,932	Food at Home and Eating Out	$5,800
Automobile Payments[7]	$5,366	Clothing	$2,750
Credit Card Payments[8]	????	Auto Gas and Oil	$3,000
Medical Insurance (Jorge)[9]	$1,170	Personal Care	$2,500
Medical Insurance (Adora)[6]	$1,950	Entertainment	$2,300
Other Insurance	???	Travel	$1,700
Homeowner's Insurance	$1,200	Donations and Gifts	$4,800
Automobile Insurance	$1,500	Unreimbursed Medical Expenses	$700
Federal Income Taxes	$9,122[10]	Amado's Education	$1,000
State Income Taxes	$1,050	Other	$0
FICA	$6,108		
Real Estate Taxes	$2,450		
Personal Property Taxes	$600		
TOTAL FIXED	???	**TOTAL VARIABLE**	???
TOTAL INCOME			???
TOTAL EXPENSES			???
ANNUAL DISCRETIONARY CASH FLOW			???
Note: ??? indicates the need for a calculation by the financial planner.			

Assets and Liabilities

Adora and Jorge are concerned that they will not be able to retire given the rate at which they are accumulating debt and saving money. Currently, every dollar in earnings that Adora and Jorge make is spent on fixed (non-discretionary) and variable (discretionary) expenses. During the interview, Adora pointed out that she and Jorge are not able to save money from the family's budget at the current time. The only savings the family has is shown on the balance sheet below. The Tuns have taken every step that they can think of to protect their assets. Adora is adamant about not wanting to spend down their assets to pay current bills if at all possible—after all, she reasons, this is their nest-egg. Also, Adora and Jorge feel it would be difficult (you sense high reluctance when talking with Adora and Jorge) about efforts to slash their cash flow budget, especially in the areas of food, personal care, entertainment, and travel.

Table XIII.2. Assets and Liabilities ($ rounded)

Assets	Amount	Liabilities	Amount
Cash	$250	Visa Credit Card[11]	$9,250
Checking Account	$500	MasterCard Credit Card[12]	$15,250
Savings Account[13]	$100,000	Mortgage	???
EE Savings Bonds[14]	$600	Automobile Loan[15]	$22,000
Primary Residence	$199,000	Other	$0
Automobile #1 (new car)	$22,000		
Automobile #2[16]	$9,000		
Furniture and Household Goods	$11,000		
Personal Property[17]	$5,000		
401(k) Plan Assets (Adora)	$160,000		
401(k) Plan Assets (Jorge)	$19,000		
TOTAL ASSETS	???	TOTAL LIABILITIES	???
NET WORTH			???
Note: ??? indicates the need for a calculation by the financial planner.			

Other Information

During the course of the interview, Adora and Jorge were able to provide information about other areas of their family financial situation. The key information is summarized below:

- All titled assets are jointly owned unless otherwise indicated.

- Tax information is based on their most recent 20XX tax return.

- Adora and Jorge pay a 3 percent marginal state tax[18] with the following adjustments:

    - one state deduction worth $14,750

    - three state exemptions worth $4,700 each

    - medical insurance of $3,120 can be used as a state adjustment

- Adora and Jorge make a $400 monthly contribution to their church, which is the *minimum* that they want to provide as a charitable contribution.

- Adora and Jorge currently use all of the interest earned on the savings account to help cover household expenses—i.e., interest is not reinvested.

- Their checking account is free of monthly charges but does not pay interest.

- Their homeowner's policy is an HO-3 policy with replacement coverage; the policy does not have an inflation-adjustment rider.

  - The house is insured for $141,000.

  - The replacement value of the home equals the current market value.

  - Liability coverage is equal to $100,000.

  - Deductible information: 1 percent deductible.

- No personal property insurance endorsements are currently in place.

- Adora and Jorge carry a $50/$150/$100 split limit PAP coverage on their automobiles (comprehensive coverage is included on both vehicles).[19]

  - Deductible information: $250 deductible.

- Adora's health situation is excellent,[20] and because she works at the bank, she is covered by an excellent PPO plan.[21]

  - Deductible information: $25 per visit with a $250 stop-loss limit.

- Jorge's health is also excellent. His insurance policy has a $2,500 annual deductible, with an 80/20 co-insurance provision, and $3,500 stop-loss provision.

- Adora's employer provides her with $100,000 group term life insurance coverage.

- Jorge's employer provides him with $35,000 in group term life insurance coverage.

- Adora's will is very basic; she has decided to leave all of her assets to Jorge with Amado as the secondary beneficiary. Jorge does not have a will.

- Neither Adora nor Jorge are worried about probate; in fact, Adora would like a full public disclosure of her final asset and liability position. Jorge has no opinion about probate issues.

- Besides Adora's will, Adora and Jorge have no other estate planning documents.

- In the event of death, final administrative estate expenses are estimated to be 1 percent of each person's gross estate.

- Jorge has a relatively low level of financial risk tolerance, whereas Adora's risk tolerance is in the moderate range.

- Adora is willing to use her inheritance and the family's savings to help pay for Jorge's educational needs, but she is not comfortable investing the money outside of federally insured bank accounts or short-term certificates of deposit, if the money is to be used for college or as an emergency fund. This is not really an issue related to risk tolerance but rather a need to know that the money is safe and accessible if needed. It is reasonable to assume a 2.25 percent rate of return on these funds.

Research Findings[22]

The research process that was started as part of the data gathering phase of the client engagement revealed several areas where the Tuns could immediately improve their financial position. You plan on making recommendations in the areas of cash flow, net worth, insurance planning, and estate planning immediately. Addressing their second goal (question), within the context of education and retirement planning, has taken more research on the part of your planning staff. Here is what your paraplanner uncovered during the additional background analyses:

- Inflation has been averaging 3.40 percent annually; you feel this rate of inflation will continue into the future.

- Adora's salary is expected to increase at the rate of inflation.

- Jorge's current wage is tied to the inflation rate and should increase over time. If he obtains a management position, the salary associated with the job will increase at the rate of inflation.

- Money market mutual funds and short-term certificates of deposit currently yield 2.25 percent.

- The thirty-year fixed rate mortgage interest rate is 7.00 percent.

- The twenty-year fixed rate mortgage interest rate is 6.25 percent.

- Closing costs for a refinanced mortgage are 2 percent of the amount borrowed.

- The current interest rate on home equity lines of credit is 7.25 percent. The typical draw period is ten years.

- The bank's 401(k) plan will match employee contributions $1 for $1 up to 3 percent of salary contributed to the plan.

    ○ The 401(k) plan does not currently allow for plan loans.

    ○ The hardware store's 401(k) plan does not provide matching contributions.

- A private college located forty-five miles away offers an accredited marketing degree program that can be completed in three years. The college's annual tuition fee is $14,000. This cost includes tuition, books, and all other college and program costs.

- The degree is a full-time intensive academic program.

- In order to complete the program in three years, Jorge must take a full load of classes fall, spring, and summer semesters. He plans to work ten hours per week at the hardware store (on weekends) while in school.

  - Jorge can earn $13 per hour while working part-time.

- The cost of tuition is increasing at a 4.00 percent annual rate.

- Adora is willing to use their $100,000 savings to help fund Jorge's education goal, if you feel it is appropriate. Assume that these assets remain in the savings account until needed for education purposes.

- Student loans (a combination of federal subsidized and institutional sources) can be obtained up to a maximum of $35,000 per year at a fixed 6.80 percent APR for ten years.

  - Loans may exceed the cost of college up to the maximum of $35,000 per year.

  - Payments can be postponed until after graduation.

  - Loans do not accrue interest during the payment deferral period.

  - If Jorge returns to school, Adora and Jorge will need approximately $20,000 in additional income to offset his full-time income.[23] Adora and Jorge expect this income need while in school to increase at the inflation rate of 3.4 percent.

- Household expenses will increase at the rate of inflation.

• If Jorge leaves employment he will lose his health and life insurance benefits; however, he will be eligible for low-cost health benefits through the private college (or through a federal exchange). The monthly cost of the coverage is $45. The policy provides reasonable coverage for those in college.[24]

• After talking with the Jorge, you believe that Jorge can earn $43,500 (in three years) during his first year as a store manager, assuming he begins working after graduation from college.

• Life insurance planning assumptions:

- Burial expenses: $15,000.

- Adora and Jorge will pay-off all outstanding debts at death.

- Total (anticipated) household expenses are defined as all expenses less savings.

- o   In order to help the family manage the transitional period, Adora and Jorge would like to have $10,000 in cash available at death.

- o   *For life insurance planning purposes only*, assume a combined federal, state, and local marginal tax bracket of 18 percent.

- o   Before retirement, assume a 7.00 percent before-tax rate of return; after retirement, assume a 5.00 percent rate of return [these assumptions only apply for insurance planning purposes].

- o   Inflation is assumed to be 3.40 percent.

- o   In the event Adora or Jorge passes prior to retirement, the survivor plans to work until age sixty-seven.

- o   For life insurance planning purposes only, assume a survivor's annual retirement income need of $59,000.

- o   Adora and Jorge are willing to allocate Adora's $100,000 nest egg towards life insurance needs.

- o   The income replacement ratio for the capital retention method is 90 percent.

- o   Adora and Jorge will make no charitable donations at death.

- o   Adora and Jorge do not wish to fund any additional educational expenses for Amado in the event of Adora or Jorge's death.

- •   Disability insurance planning assumptions:

  - o   Given their current income, assume a 100 percent income replacement in the event of disability.

  - o   If disabled, Adora and Jorge plan to retire with full Social Security benefits at age sixty-seven but claim Medicare benefits at age sixty-five.

  - o   Adora and Jorge are willing to allocate Adora's $100,000 in savings to help offset short- and long-term disability needs.

  - o   In the event of disability, Adora and Jorge are be willing to reallocate assets to earn a slightly higher return (4.50 percent).

  - o   The bank provides a 180-day waiting period disability policy. If approved for long-term disability, employees receive 50 percent of their annual salary, payable in equal monthly installments, until age sixty-five. This income may be reduced by monies received from Workers' Compensation and/or the Social Security Administration.

  - o   Adora and Jorge do not wish to plan for Social Security benefits in the event of disability.

- The hardware store does not provide disability insurance for non-managers; however, managers receive a core disability benefit similar to the one offered to Adora.

- The regular retirement age for Adora and Jorge, for Social Security, is age sixty-seven.[25]

  - They would like to stop working at full retirement age, which is the end of the year of Adora's sixty-seventh birthday (December 31st).

  - Adora and Jorge would like to be debt free upon entering retirement.

  - At Adora's current salary, she will earn $1,800 per month in Social Security benefits at age sixty-seven.

  - At Jorge's current salary, he will earn $1,113 per month in Social Security benefits at age sixty-seven.

    - His Social Security benefit is expected to be larger than 50 percent of Adora's benefit.

  - If Jorge were to earn $43,500 per year and take Social Security benefits at age sixty-seven he would receive $1,471 per month.

- Even though Adora and Jorge are earning 2.0 percent on their savings and 3.5 percent on the EE Savings Bonds, when calculating retirement savings needs, use the following assumptions:

  - Adora and Jorge are willing to allocate their savings bonds towards the retirement goal.

    - The savings bonds have a fixed 3.50 percent yield

  - Inflation pre- and post-retirement is/will be 3.40 percent.

  - It is possible to receive a 5.90 percent annualized tax-adjusted rate of return using a diversified portfolio of mutual funds prior to retirement. This rate of return matches Adora's risk tolerance and their joint risk capacity. In other words, Adora and Jorge are willing to have you invest the $100,000 (if available) and their 401(k) assets in a portfolio of mutual funds earning 5.90 percent for retirement purposes.[26]

  - Adora and Jorge can invest *after* retirement and earn 4.35 percent per year annualized (tax-adjusted).

  - Adora and Jorge will continue to be in the 15 percent federal marginal income tax bracket pre- and post-retirement.

  - Adora believes that she and Jorge can live comfortably on approximately 75 percent of *current* earned income, in today's dollars, when retired, regardless if Jorge takes a manager's position or not. (Note: the income replacement ratio is significantly less if Jorge goes back to school and earns a higher income as a store manager.)

- Adora is comfortable using her $100,000 inheritance for retirement (if available) or for education funding; if used for retirement, assume a 5.90 percent annualized tax-adjusted rate of return.

  ○ If at all possible, she would like to leave a financial legacy for her son Amado and future grandchildren.

- Their joint life expectancy is age ninety-five.

Please use only the assumptions and data shown in the case when addressing the client's questions.

Case Questions

1. How much are the Tuns spending on PITI each month?

   a. $1,328

   b. $1,425

   c. $1,632

   d. $15,932

2. How much should Adora and Jorge list as the outstanding balance on their mortgage today?

   a. $165,000

   b. $147,338

   c. $147,559

   d. $150,286

3. Assume you recommend that Adora and Jorge create a three-month emergency savings fund with the fund based on total fixed and variable expenses. Which of the following statements is true?

   a. Adora and Jorge have just enough in monetary assets to meet this need.

   b. Not only can Adora and Jorge meet the need, they also have enough for a six-month funding emergency fund.

   c. Monetary assets are insufficient to meet the three month need.

   d. Adora's and Jorge's financial situation today will allow them to fund only a two-month emergency fund.

4. How are Adora and Jorge doing in relation to their current housing costs? Use the front- and back-end mortgage ratios to answer this question.

    a. Adora and Jorge meet the 36 percent ratio but not the 28 percent ratio guidelines.

    b. Adora and Jorge meet the 28 percent ratio but not the 36 percent ratio guidelines.

    c. Adora and Jorge meet both the 28 percent and the 36 percent ratio guidelines.

    d. There is not enough information to answer this question.

5. Which of the following recommendations should be implemented by Adora and Jorge in an effort to improve their current cash flow situation?

    a. Payoff the credit card debt using monetary assets.

    b. Refinance the mortgage.

    c. Begin contributions to a Roth IRA.

    d. All of the above strategies will improve their cash flow situation.

    e. Solutions a and b will improve their cash flow situation.

6. Based on tuition and living expense estimates, what is the total cost of college over the three-year time period, assuming Jorge begins college this year (rounded)?

    a. $95,671

    b. $102,000

    c. $105,766

    d. $109,000

7. Assume that Adora is willing to allocate $50,000 of her savings to help fund Jorge's educational goal. How much in student loans will Jorge need to obtain in order to fund tuition and expenses (rounded)?

    a. $43,702

    b. $61,383

    c. $67,415

    d. $74,744

8. Which of the following strategies can be used to (a) reduce the Tuns' federal income tax liability this year, (b) increase saving for retirement, and (c) help increase the likelihood that Jorge might qualify for a need-based scholarship?

    a. Contribute the maximum yearly amount to a Roth IRA.

    b. Implement an income shifting strategy by having Adora max out her 401(k) contributions while using her $100,000 in savings to offset living expenses.

c. Contribute fully to a qualified section 529 plan.

d. Purchase a variable annuity using Adora's $100,000 in savings in order to defer taxes on distributions into the future, thereby decreasing assets available to fund Jorge's college costs.

9. How much do the Tuns need in retirement, on their first day of retirement, assuming no other recommendations have been implemented. In other words, taking into account current assets, liabilities, and assumptions, how much do Adora and Jorge need as a lump sum when they retire (rounded)?

   a. $675,451

   b. $984,294

   c. $1,543,958

   d. $1,558,143

10. Assume the Tuns' house catches on fire and Adora and Jorge experience a $150,000 loss. How much will the insurance company reimburse Adora and Jorge for the loss?

    a. $139,500

    b. $141,000

    c. $148,500

    d. $150,000

11. Based on the human life value approach to estimating a life insurance need, what is the total amount of life insurance Adora needs today assuming that income from the insurance policy begins immediately for the beneficiary (rounded to the nearest thousand)?

    a. $557,000

    b. $686,000

    c. $757,000

    d. $915,000

12. Which of the following are *client* characteristics and factors that need to be evaluated prior to making a financial planning recommendation?

    I. The current level of interest rates in the marketplace.

    II. Both Adora's and Jorge's financial risk tolerance.

    III. Jorge's inter-personal communication preference.

a. I only

b. II and III only

c. I and II only

d. I, II, and III

13. After evaluating the Tuns' financial situation, your paraplanner noticed that interest rates have come down since Adora first purchased her home. Based on this observation and their current cash flow situation, which of the following recommendations is most appropriate in terms of increasing their current cash flow situation?

a. Suggest that Adora maintain with the original mortgage in order to obtain a higher mortgage interest deduction.

b. Suggest that Adora refinance the mortgage using a fifteen-year loan because this will reduce the amount of interest paid over time.

c. Suggest that Adora refinance to a thirty-year fixed rate mortgage as a way to lower the monthly payment.

d. Refer the analysis and recommendation to a mortgage broker.

14. During the course of the initial financial planner-client meeting, the topic of retirement planning came up. Adora made a comment that she and Jorge are probably not on track to meet their retirement objective. As their comprehensive financial planner, you agree. How should you direct the discussion regarding retirement planning at this stage of the systematic financial planning process?

a. Tell Adora and Jorge that they must increase their monthly retirement savings immediately.

b. Recommend no changes because you anticipate an improvement in market conditions, which should get the Tuns back on track towards their retirement goal.

c. Discuss alternatives currently available to increase the likelihood of success in the future.

d. Suggest that Adora and Jorge postpone retirement by at least three years.

15. Adora is interested in helping Amado fund some of his college costs. Assuming that Adora and Jorge can improve their cash flow situation, which of the following strategies will ensure that the Tuns do not trigger the gift tax?

a. Contribute funds to a UTMA account for Amado.

b. Pay tuition and other expenses directly to the college or university.

c. Contribute to a Section 529 qualified tuition plan.

d. Each of the strategies listed will ensure that the gift tax is not triggered.

16. Adora and Jorge are feeling overwhelmed with all the different financial planning strategies that are available to them. For example, Adora was recently informed that she is eligible to receive stock options and restricted stock that is tied to her company's performance. Because of the tentative nature of the options and stock, Adora has requested that you do not include these assets in your planning calculations. The stock options did prompt additional questions about what she and Jorge should do next in terms of implementing recommendations. Given the information in the case narrative, which of the following strategies would you recommend Adora and Jorge implement first?

    a. Exercise the stock options.

    b. Diversify their investment holdings.

    c. Draft new wills.

    d. Create and fund an irrevocable life insurance trust.

17. Your paraplanner is concerned that the Tuns are living beyond their financial means. The paraplanner wants to recommend that Adora and Jorge reign in their spending immediately and stop using credit cards. The paraplanner is concerned that you will waste a lot of time and effort working with these clients. As their financial planner, which of the following is a reasonable financial planning strategy?

    a. Terminate the client-planner relationship based on the insights of your paraplanner.

    b. Ask the paraplanner to talk with Adora and Jorge about their poor spending habits and stress that unless Adora and Jorge change their behavior the client-planner relationship will be terminated.

    c. Review the Tuns' current and potential income streams to identify ways to solve their immediate cash flow problem.

    d. Recommend a reallocation of assets in Adora's 401(k) plan as a way to increase portfolio income that can be used to offset household expenditures.

18. Jorge has been approached by two friends who are interested in opening a new landscaping business. Jorge's friends are sure the economy is about to make a turn for the better, which should create demand for their services. Jorge's friends would like Jorge to invest $25,000 into the new venture. Which of the following is the most suitable recommendation for Jorge as he considers this possible business opportunity?

    a. Borrow the $25,000 using a home equity line of credit (HELOC).

    b. Cash out Adora's 401(k) plan.

    c. Statements a and b are both suitable recommendations.

    d. Given his financial risk tolerance and low risk capacity, walk away from the business opportunity.

19. Which of the following strategies provides a way for Adora and Jorge to save for retirement while keeping the option open to fund college expenses for Amado or Jorge on a tax- and penalty-free basis?

   a. Fund a 529 plan for Jorge and transfer funds to Jorge if necessary.

   b. Contribute the maximum amount to a Roth IRA and use distributed contributions to fund college expenses if necessary.

   c. Contribute the maximum amount to a tax-deductible IRA and use distributions from the account to fund college expenses if necessary.

   d. None of the strategies match the criteria.

20. Given an analysis of the Tuns' financial situation and goals, which of the following conclusions is correct?

   a. Jorge should go back to school because he will earn more income over the course of his working life.

   b. Jorge should not go back to school because the standard student loan payment will exceed the extra income he can earn as a store manager.

   c. Jorge should only go back to school if he can get a scholarship that will pay 100 percent of tuition expenses.

   d. Jorge should postpone college for at least five years until the Tuns' financial situation stabilizes and Amado is out of school.

The Abed Menjivar Case

A PROPERTY OWNERSHIP CASE

Your client Abed Menjivar is curious about the process of buying property—both autos and homes—as well as property insurance. Imagine that he comes to you with the following questions. Help him work out the math and details of his questions so that he obtains a better understanding of the purchase process and insurance aspects of financial planning.

Case Questions

1. Abed has determined that he needs a new car. By new he means either brand new or a relatively new "used" car. He has been going through his budget and he thinks he can afford $295 per month as an auto payment. He saw an advertisement on television stating that he can get a three-year loan at a 3.9 percent annualized APR. Given this information, what is the maximum loan that he can afford?

    a. $8,202.08

    b. $10,006.95

    c. $11,246.87

    d. $22,421.80

2. Help Abed calculate his monthly PITI, based on the following facts:

    - He currently earns $66,000 per year.

    - The loan has a 4.5 percent annualized APR.

    - The loan is a thirty-year mortgage (fixed rate).

    - $200,000 loan amount.

    - $150 monthly HO insurance premium.

    - $300 monthly HO tax.

    a. $1,013

    b. $1,463

    c. $1,540

    d. $3,278

3.   Based on your answer to the previous question, does Abed meet the front-end mortgage qualification rule?

    a.   Yes, because his monthly PITI is less than 36 percent.

    b.   No, because his monthly PITI is greater than 28 percent.

    c.   Yes, because his monthly PITI is less than 28 percent.

    d.   No, because his monthly PITI is greater than 36 percent.

4.   If Abed tells you that he also has a $100 furniture loan payment and that he pays $200 monthly on an outstanding credit card balance, do you think a bank will loan him money to buy a house with a $200,000 mortgage?

    a.   Yes, because the combination of all his loan payments will be less than $1,980 monthly.

    b.   No, because the passes neither the front-end or back-end mortgage qualification rules.

    c.   Yes, because his monthly income is more than 2.5 times the actual loan amount.

    d.   No, because while he passes the front-end mortgage qualification rule, he does not have enough income to meet the loan rule that states, "A borrower must not borrow more than 2.5 times their annual income."

5.   Based on the front-end mortgage qualification rule, and assuming the Abed goes to the maximum PITI level based on the rule, how much can he afford to borrow? Assume the following:

    •   He currently earns $66,000 per year.

    •   The loan has a 4.5 percent annualized APR.

    •   The loan is a thirty-year mortgage (fixed rate).

    • $200,000 loan amount.

    • $150 monthly HO insurance premium.

    • $300 monthly HO tax.

    a.   215,124

    b. $283,540

    c. $303,936

    d. $390,775

6. Abed has obtained several loan offers from banks, credit unions, and mortgage brokers. Assuming he does not qualify for a VA or FHA loan at this time, which of the following borrowing strategies will enable him to pay the least amount of interest over the course of the loan? Assume the purchase price of the home is $200,000?

    a. Obtain a thirty-year fixed rate 4.5 percent APR mortgage with a loan to value ratio of 80 percent.

    b. Obtain a thirty-year fixed rate 4.5 percent APR mortgage with a loan to value ratio of 50 percent.

    c. Obtain a fifteen-year fixed rate 3.9 percent APR mortgage with a loan to value ratio of 100 percent.

    d. Obtain a twenty-year fixed rate 4.0 percent APR mortgage with a loan to value ratio of 90 percent.

7. Help Abed do some worst-case planning. Assume Abed purchases an HO policy with a maximum limit of $150,000 (assume that his house has a replacement value of $200,000). If he has a $40,000 loss, how much will he receive as a reimbursement (exclude the deductible for this problem)?

    a. $0

    b. $37,500

    c. $40,000

    d. $150,000

8. In order for Abed to qualify for an excess liability insurance policy, which of the following statements is true?

    a. He must not have received a speeding ticket within the last year.

    b. He must own a house and car and bundle the insurance together.

    c. He must increase his liability coverage on his auto and home above the state required minimums.

    d. Each of the statements listed is correct.

9. Abed is a collector. Last week he estimated the following values on his collections:

    1) Postage Stamps: $3,000

    2) Jewelry: $1,000

    3) Signed 1st Edition Books: $3,500

    4) Silver Coins: $800

Which of these collections needs a personal articles floater?

a.   Only #3

b.   #1 and #2 only

c.   #2 and #4 only

d.   #1 and #3 only

e.   All of the items

10. Abed has a PAP with the following split limit coverage: 100/300/50. If he is involved in an accident, which of the following statement is true?

a.   The maximum amount his insurance will pay to fix or repair damage to his car is $50,000.

b.   The maximum his insurance will pay in medical expenses, per person, for himself, his family, and those in the other car is $100,000.

c.   The maximum his insurance will pay, if he is liable in the accident, for medical expenses of one other person in the other car is $100,000.

d.   Statement a and b are correct.

The Case of the Good Gone Bad

A PLAY IN THREE SCENES[27]

To solve this case, you must have access to Certified Financial Planner Board of Standards, Inc. (CFP Board) *Code of Ethics and Standards of Conduct, Disciplinary Rules and Procedures,* and *Candidate Fitness Standards,* which can be found at http://www.cfp.net. Information from *The Fundamentals of Writing a Financial Plan,* the companion text to this book, can also be used to help answer questions.

Characters:

Ashley: A CFP® professional

Bill Jackson: Ashley's client and friend

Jane Jackson: Bill's wife and Ashley's friend

Phil Rheem: A prominent attorney in the area

Ben Pyles: Ashley's broker/dealer representative

Background

Ashley has been a Certified Financial Planner (CFP®) professional and registered representative for more than ten years. She prides herself on her excellent work and ethical standards. Ashley was recently ranked by her local newspaper as one of the top fifty planners in her region, and she was recently recognized at an awards banquet.

At 9:30 on a bright Thursday morning, Ashley received a phone call from a long-time client, Bill Jackson. Although Bill is married, Ashley manages only Bill's sizable investment portfolio. Bill is one of the wealthiest men in the area. He and Ashley have had a long client-planner relationship, and he considers her to be worthy of his full trust. Ashley and Bill have long been good friends and dealing with Bill has always been a pleasure for her. When Ashley answers the phone, she is aware of Bill's altered mood and she immediately becomes concerned.

Bill: *(In a hushed tone.)* Ashley, I need to talk with you about asset protection.

> **Narrator:** Ashley could sense that Bill was quite disturbed, and she wondered why this type of question might cause such panic in a person.

Ashley: Bill, your assets are fully protected. Your trust is fully secure, and your brokerage account has comprehensive SIPC coverage. Why the concern about asset protection all of a sudden?

Bill: *(More persistent.)* Listen Ashley, I just need to know how not to let anyone touch my investments or my property without my permission.

> **Narrator:** Ashley was now getting annoyed; she could not figure out for the life of her what brought on this sudden panic about asset protection.

Ashley: Bill, are you in some sort of trouble? What is going on?

> **Narrator:** There was silence on the other end of the line, and Ashley could sense the tension as she held the receiver. Finally, a long sigh came from Bill, and Ashley was temporarily relieved.

Bill: *(Pauses.)* Ashley, you and I have been friends for a long time. Our kids played with each other. For heaven's sake, I couldn't even count the number of barbecues our two families have had in my backyard .... Those were the easy times, Ashley—everything was so simple back then. Ashley, I don't know how to tell you this, *(long pause)* but I am leaving Jane. Another thing, she doesn't know yet.

> **Narrator:** Ashley was shocked. She and Jane had been good friends for years—better friends than she was with Bill.

Ashley: Bill, what are you talking about? Why would you and Jane split up?

> **Narrator:** Again, there was a long sigh on the other end of the line; then Ashley heard a voice—a female voice—but it wasn't Jane's. Ashley now knew why Bill wanted a divorce. He had met someone new. It wasn't a unique scenario for Ashley; she had seen it happen to a few of her other "fifty-something" friends. "After Jane had supported Bill for so long, he is going to trade her in for a newer model. What a creep!" Jane thought to herself. Well, there was no way she was going to let Bill leave Jane with nothing. In fact, Ashley thought to herself, "I'll fix it so that Jane is better off than she has ever been, and I'll make that slimeball pay!"

Ashley: Bill, you know I will do anything to help you out. I mean, after all, you have been so good to me over the years. Let me look into the situation, and I will call you back on Monday morning. Can you wait that long?

> **Narrator:** Ashley smiled on the other end of the line as she waited for Bill's response. She leaned back in her chair and began planning out her strategy. Bill's voice came back over the line a lot calmer than it had been at the beginning of their conversation.

Bill: Thanks Ashley, Monday will be fine.... I really didn't think you would understand, I mean … you know … since you and Jane have been such good friends.

Ashley: Well, Bill, you are my client, and what you do with your personal life is not a professional concern of mine. I'll call you on Monday. Have a good weekend.

Ashley: *(Talking to herself.)* Yeah, have a *great* weekend, you weasel—because it is the last good one you'll have after I get through with you.

> **Narrator:** As soon as she hung up the phone, Ashley immediately called Jane at the club. Ashley knew Jane always played tennis on Thursday mornings with a group of other "housies," as Jane and her friends liked to refer to themselves. When Jane finally got to the phone she sounded winded from the run up to the clubhouse.

Jane: *(In a cheerful voice.)* Hello Ashley, what in the world has given me the pleasure of hearing from you this morning?

Ashley: Jane, listen, I think there are some things we need to discuss; is there any way you can meet me for lunch this afternoon?

Jane: *(Suddenly serious.)* Well, normally I have lunch with my tennis group, but I'm sure they won't mind if I cancel. What is this about?

Ashley: Jane, I'll talk to you about it at lunch. Does *Le Marie* sound good to you … say 1:00?

Jane: Yes, that will be fine. I'll see you there at 1:00.

> **Narrator:** Later that afternoon when Ashley and Jane were at Le Marie for lunch, Ashley finally looked Jane in the eye and began to tell her the whole story.

Ashley: Listen, Jane, this is really hard for me to say. I don't even know where to begin. But, this morning I got a phone call from your husband. Can I just ask you one question?

Jane: *(Concerned.)* Ashley you know you can talk to me about anything. What is it?

Ashley: Jane, how is your marriage?

Jane: Ashley, what is this about? What do you mean how is my marriage?

Ashley: Bill is having an affair.

Jane: (*Suddenly angry.*) What are you talking about? Bill has always been faithful and for your information our marriage is fine. Now, if you have nothing else to say I will be leaving.

> **Narrator:** As Jane is getting up to leave, Ashley's voice softens and she touches Jane's arm.

Ashley: (*More softly.*) Jane, I know Bill is having an affair. Today when he called me I heard "her" voice in the background. And Bill was calling to figure out how he could protect his assets from someone—(*long pause*)—and that someone is you.

> **Narrator:** Jane sat down quietly and leaned her head in her hands. She was clearly shaken but didn't seem to be too surprised.

Jane: Oh, Ashley ... if you only knew how hard it's been these last few years. Bill has been so distant. But, I never expected him to be unfaithful. I mean after all of this time. After everything I have given him. I mean I gave up my life and my career to be his perfect "trophy wife."

> **Narrator:** Jane was suddenly struck with anger. She didn't know what she could do, but there was no way she was going to let Bill leave her with nothing. After all she had sacrificed; she was not going to let him make her a poor little old lady without a penny to her name!

Jane: So, what can you do to help me? Would you act as my financial advisor?

Ashley: I thought you would never ask. First, I need some information. Who is your lawyer? You know you are going to need to hire a good divorce attorney—do you have someone in mind?

Jane: I have always worked with Phil Rheem. He was a dear friend of my father, and he was the one who handled my father's estate when he passed away; normally all he handles are divorce cases. I will stop by his office after I leave here.

Ashley: Also, I will be setting up a trust for your assets.

Jane: Are you qualified to do that sort of thing?

Ashley: Oh, don't worry, I can take care of it—I've got a lot of experience with trusts and it will save us some time instead of having to worry about jumping through all the legal hoops.

> **Narrator:** On the way back from lunch, Ashley was thinking about where to begin. She knew she wanted to leave Bill with nothing, but she also needed to make sure Jane was able to continue living the life she had become accustomed to.

Scene II

Narrator: Later that afternoon Ashley returned to her office. She knew that the day ahead was going to be a long one.

After she left her office she stopped by Phil Rheem's law practice. Even though Ashley only knew Phil on a casual basis, she had worked with him on a number of different occasions when she had clients with complicated estate matters. Ashley told Phil's secretary that the matter was urgent and she needed to see him immediately. When she entered Phil's office he was reviewing a case file that he placed to the side as he stood up to greet her.

Phil: Well ... Good afternoon, Ashley. What is it that gives me the good fortune to see your pretty face in my office today?

Narrator: Ashley had never really cared for Phil's charming style—she found it to be condescending and irritating. Nevertheless, he was the perfect type of attorney who had the power and connections to do what she needed him to do for her.

Ashley: (*Sounding charming herself.*) Good afternoon to you too, Phil. You know it is always *my* pleasure when I have a chance to work with you.

Narrator: Phil motioned for Ashley to sit down in one of the overstuffed leather chairs in front of his giant mahogany desk. As Ashley took a seat, she noticed the open file on Phil's desk. She glanced at it only briefly, but she noticed the name typed at the top of the papers. Ashley then realized that the file contained all of the legal documents for Bill Jackson's trusts. Of course, she also had a copy of them, but these were the originals, and the man who had signed and prepared them was sitting right in front of her. She silently crossed her fingers that Mr. Rheem would be as helpful as she was hoping.

Ashley: Phil, (*Pausing, then speaking in a direct tone.*) I am going to get right down to business here. (*Pausing again.*) I am here about Jane Jackson. Her husband has been a client of mine for more than 10 years. I am sure you are acquainted with Bill?

Phil: Yes, I have worked with Bill on a few previous business matters.

Ashley: Well, this morning Bill contacted me. He was interested in protecting his assets. When I talked to him he seemed so frantic that I was concerned, of course. I could not understand where this sudden panic had come from, and it wasn't until I found out that he was going to leave his wife that it all made sense to me. Bill wants to make sure that his wife, Jane, will not be able to lay a finger on any of his wealth, which—if I may say say—Jane helped him to build. So, as you can see, this little situation has put me in quite a bind.

Phil: Yes, I can see where it would. Well, (pause) as Jane may have told you, I have been acquainted with her family for a long time. Her father and I used to play golf together out at the club. He was a great man. He helped me get my start in this profession. It saddened me greatly to see him pass away. (*Leaning back in his chair and sighing.*) I must tell you that I would have done anything for that man—I would be willing to do whatever it takes to protect Mrs. Jackson; she deserves at least that much.

Ashley: (*Leaning back in her chair.*) Thank you, Phil. I knew you would understand. Jane and I have talked, and she is willing to do whatever it takes also. I know she will be getting in touch with you soon about filing for divorce, but I felt like I needed to see you myself—I am sure you understand.

Phil: Of course, I understand. (*Pause.*) Now don't you worry your pretty little head about a thing; I will make sure Jane is completely taken care of. Now, if you'll excuse me I'll make a few calls and see what I can do for you.

Ashley: Thank you, Phil. And you know that if you ever need anything, just give me a call. I will always be glad to return the favor.

Scene III

Narrator: Later that night, Ashley sat down in her still, dark office and pulled a file out of her briefcase. She switched on the desk lamp and opened the file containing Bill Jackson's original trust documents. Yesterday, when she was in Phil's office, she had secretly slipped them into her briefcase when he momentarily stepped out to talk with his secretary. She knew that she was treading in deep waters here, but it seemed so simple to her. Slowly, Ashley stood up and walked over to the shredding machine in the corner of the room, and one by one, she fed each sheet into the metal teeth that ground up the original documentation that Bill Jackson had ever established a trust.

The following morning, she returned to her office. She picked up the phone and hit the speed dial. She was directly connected with Ben Pyles, her broker/dealer representative.

Ashley: Ben, yes, hello? And how are you this morning? Yes, it is early. Well, you know I wanted to get a jump on a few things before heading off for the weekend. Listen, I need to make a few trades for a client—his name is Bill Jackson. His account number is 9008765. (*Pausing, waiting for him to answer.*) Yes, that's right. I want to go ahead and liquidate the account. (*Pause.*) No, I do not want to reinvest the proceeds into a money market account. Just make a check out to Bill and Jane Jackson and send it to their home address. Secondly, I would like for you to liquidate Bill's second account and invest the proceeds in the following penny stocks.

Narrator: Ashley listed several penny stocks, directing Ben to split the assets evenly among the stocks she had given him. Ashley was fully aware that by moving the assets from the second account into penny stocks that Bill would almost certainly incur a loss. She also knew that this could hurt Jane by reducing the amount of assets available in the divorce, but she suspected that the account was nothing more than a place where Bill stashed money to pay for his own personal expenses. She felt justified in taking the action.

Ashley: *(Pausing and softly giggling.)* Now, Ben, you know I wouldn't do anything that wasn't in the best interest of my client. I tried to talk him out of these trades, but he was insistent. I guess he read some article in a personal investing magazine. It is all a bunch of bologna if you ask me, but I work for him so I have to do what he wants. You know…that's just the way the business goes. *(Pausing again.)* Well, I guess that will be all for me. You have a nice weekend. Tell your wife hello for me. Take care now. Goodbye to you, too.

> **Narrator:** When the receiver finally clicked down, Ashley leaned back in her chair. She sighed to herself. She hated to see Bill and Jane's marriage end; it seemed like Bill and Jane were always so happy. But she wasn't going to allow Bill to make a mockery of all of Jane's sacrifice and devotion. No, Bill Jackson was going to be the sorry one in the end. By Monday morning, he wouldn't know what had hit him.

Case Questions

1. When asked later about her actions, Ashley affirmed that she did what she thought was right at the time because it served the interest of her friend. She argued that even though her actions might be wrong, the consequences for Jane were positive. Her view of the ethical situation was driven by which ethical outlook?

    a. Normative ethics

    b. Teleological ethics

    c. Deontological ethics

    d. Disclosure ethics

2. When conceptualized broadly, which of the following statements is true?

    I.   Ashley is in violation of CFP Board's *Code of Ethics and Standards of Conduct*.

    II. Ashley is in violation of SEC financial adviser rules.

    III. Although some of Ashley's actions are questionable, nothing she did would fall under the rule making of FINRA.

    a. I only

    b. III only

    c. I and II only

    d. I, II, and III

3. Which of the following will provide liability protection for Ashley in this case?

    a. Errors and Omission (E&O) insurance.

    b. The arbitration clause in an investment management contract.

    c.   Disclaiming fiduciary status as a registered representative.

    d.   None of the above.

4.   According to the definition of what constitutes a client, found in the terminology of financial planning practice standards section of CFP Board's *Code of Ethics and Standards of Conduct*, who among the following is not considered Ashley's client?

    a.   Bill

    b.   Jane

    c.   Phil

    d.   Both Bill and Jane

    e.   Both Jane and Phil

5.   Did Ashley break CFP Board's *Code of Ethics and Standards of Conduct* confidentiality rules when she contacted Phil Rheem without the consent of Jane—even though Jane was most likely not going to be upset with Ashley?

    a.   Yes, because personal information was given without Jane's consent, a violation occurred.

    b.   No, because Jane could not be harmed by the use of her personal information.

    c.   No, because Ashley is allowed to share client information with other professional advisors.

    d.   Because Jane is only a friend of Ashley's, the CFP Board's Code of Ethics and Standards of Conduct do not apply.

6.   Does Jane's attorney, Phil Rheem, need to follow the CFP Board's *Code of Ethics and Standards of Conduct*?

    a.   Yes, because any professional who deals with a CFP® professional must also follow the standards.

    b.   No, because Phil is not a CFP® professional.

    c.   Yes, because as an attorney, he must abide by all applicable and published ethical standards.

    d.   Attorneys have no ethical standards, so he does not have to follow CFP Board rules—or any other rules, for that matter.

7.   The Principle of Integrity states that "A CFP® professional must perform professional services with integrity." Which of the following statements is true in relation to this principle?

    I.   This principle allows for honest mistakes and innocent errors.

    II.   This principle allows a client who is dissatisfied with their financial planner to sue for lack of disclosure.

    III.   This principle requires CFP® professionals to provide fee-only services whenever a client requests an initial planning review.

a. I only

b. II only

c. III only

d. I and II only

e. II and III only

8. Prior to her trouble with the Jacksons, Ashley prospected for clients using seminars. She advertised herself as Ashley Smith, CFP®, RIA. Is this permissible?

a. Yes, so long as she describes what the certifications mean during her seminar.

b. No, because the SEC does not allow the use of RIA in marketing materials.

c. Yes, as long as she tells the audience that she is not also a registered representative.

d. It depends on the size of the seminar and whether or not she is promoting the sale of securities.

9. CFP Board's *Code of Ethics and Standards of Conduct* indicates that a CFP® professional may not solicit clients using false or misleading advertisements. Which of the following statements is not an example of a misleading statement/advertisement?

a. "Our mutual fund portfolios have averaged over 18 percent returns during the last three years."

b. "We guarantee a 100 percent improvement on your portfolio's annual return."

c. "Our firm offers fee-based services, but also receives commissions from the investment products sold."

d. "I practice as a fee-only planner, but I receive a commission on the insurance products I sell."

10. About a year ago Ashley was dealing with a client, Bob Hernandez, who was trying to minimize estate taxes. Ashley was not clear on all of the estate laws relevant to Mr. Hernandez's situation, so she called an attorney friend who deals primarily with criminal cases to help resolve a few of Bob's questions. Did Ashley violate rules related to planning competence within CFP Board's *Code of Ethics and Standards of Conduct*?

a. No; she called a qualified person for help.

b. Yes; she should not be dealing with estate planning issues at all as a CFP® professional.

c. Yes; she should have contacted a qualified estate attorney.

d. No; she acted in the best interest of her client.

11. Which of the following statements is true?

    I.   If a CFP® professional must earn continuing education credits from a licensing board other than CFP Board, he/she does not have to meet CFP Board continuing education credits.

    II.   A CFP® professional shall not engage in any conduct that reflects adversely on their integrity or fitness as a CFP® professional.

    III. All CFP® professionals are prohibited from actively practicing other professions and offering services in related fields, regardless of license and practice standards.

    a.   I only

    b.   II only

    c.   III only

    d.   II and III only

    e.   I, II, and III

12. A CFP® professional must disclose which of the following to a client?

    a.   A statement of philosophy the professional adopts when working with clients.

    b.   A statement identifying conflicts of interest..

    c.   A statement disclosing how the professional receives compensation.

    d.   Each of these must be disclosed.

    e.   Only b and c need to be disclosed.

13. CFP Board's *Code of Ethics and Standards of Conduct* states that a CFP® professional must always make timely disclosures of all material information to clients. Which of the following forms will meet this requirement when a client engagement has been signed?

    a.   SEC Form ADV, Part II.

    b.   A customized form that provides CFP Board required disclosure information.

    c.   A statement of the financial planner's life and business philosophy.

    d.   Each of these documents/statements can be used to meet the rule.

    e.   The SEC Form ADV, Part II and a customized disclosure form that includes all CFP Board required information can be used to meet the rule.

14. In which of the following situations is it impermissible to reveal personal information about a client?

    a.   To establish a brokerage account for a client.

    b.   While the planner is being audited for their own tax return.

    c.   To defend the CFP® professional against charges of wrongdoing.

    d.   In a civil dispute between the CFP® professional and the client.

15. After finding out what Ashley had done, Bill terminated his working relationship with Ashley and requested that she return all documents about his account immediately. Bill went on to bring a civil suit against Ashley. If one year goes by before she notifies CFP Board, is Ashley in violation of CFP Board's *Code of Ethics and Standards of Conduct*?

    a.   Yes, because she must allow the CFP Board thirty days to provide legal counsel to Ashley in defense of the allegation.

    b.   No, CFP Board gives planners at least two years to inform Board officials of the outcome(s) associated with a civil suit.

    c.   Yes, because she has thirty days from the date she learned of the law suit to inform CFP Board.

    d.   No, a CFP® professional is under no legal, moral, or ethical responsibility to inform CFP Board of a civil suit brought by a former client.

16. Which of the following statements is true?

    I.   According to the CFP Board's *Code of Ethics and Standards of Conduct*, a CFP® professional is not allowed to practice any profession unless a license is required by law to practice the profession.

    II.   CFP Board's *Code of Ethics and Standards of Conduct* requires a CFP® professional to always act in the best interest of clients, even when such an action may harm a CFP® professional financially.

    III.   When conducting a comprehensive financial planning engagement, CFP Board's *Code of Ethics and Standards of Conduct* requires a CFP® professional to make only recommendations that are suitable for each client.

    a.   I only

    b.   II only

    c.   II and III only

    d.   I, II, and III

17. Ashley, as a CFP® professional, is required to properly supervise subordinates when dealing with the subordinate's delivery of financial planning services. Which of the following would be considered properly supervised?

    a.   An intern makes recommendations that have not been reviewed by Ashley to a client.

    b.   Ashley's office manager, Marge, who is not licensed, is asked to research and suggest stocks to be included in a client's portfolio.

c. A licensed intern, before making a client recommendation, reviews the recommendation with Ashley.

d. An intern, who is not licensed, makes a trade, with Ashley's permission, in a client's account while Ashley is at lunch.

18. Which of the following statements is true?

a. When Ashley contacted Jane about Bill's divorce plans, she was also required by CFP Board's *Code of Ethics and Standards of Conduct* to disclose conflicts of interest in writing.

b. Instructing the broker to purchase penny stocks for Bill's account was a violation of the CFP Board's *Code of Ethics and Standards of Conduct*, which requires that recommended strategies and products be made in the best interest of a client.

c. Sharing information about Bill and Jane with Phil Rheem is a direct violation of CFP Board *Practice Standards and Code of Ethics*.

d. Each of these statements is true.

e. Only statements a and c are true.

19. Which of the following statements is true in relation to Ashley's reallocation of Bill Jackson's investment assets?

a. FINRA would find that these investments were unsuitable for Bill.

b. Ashley would be held harmless against a claim of unsuitability because she, in fact, conducted some research on the stocks before instructing the broker to place the buy orders.

c. Her actions are a prime example of churning.

d. If Ashley had discretion over Bill's account, she was entirely within her rights to make the penny stock purchases.

20. CFP Board's *Code of Ethics and Standards of Conduct* states that a CFP® professional must offer advice only in the areas in which they are is competent to do so. Ashley has obviously broken rules related to this standard. Why? Choose the best possible answer.

a. Ashley did not gain enough information from Bill before entering into the relationship with Jane.

b. Jane should have recognized Ashley's conflict of interest.

c. Ashley was unable to meet Bill's needs and objectives adequately.

d. Ashley was unable to provide competent services because of the conflict of interest concerning her friendship with Jane.

The Maria and Sancho Ruiz Case

A COMPREHENSIVE FINANCIAL PLANNING CASE

Maria Ruiz recently turned age fifty. She heard about your firm from a neighbor who recommended your services as a comprehensive financial planner. The neighbor, who you helped with retirement and education funding questions, was particularly pleased with the manner in which you incorporated cognitive, emotional, behavioral, relational, and economic concepts into your recommendations. She told Maria that you do an excellent job of getting to the root of the quantitative aspects of financial details as well as delving into each client's emotional relationship with money and financial issues.

Based on this recommendation, Maria called your office for an appointment. Your receptionist indicated that you would be delighted to meet with her if both she and her husband (Sancho) would come in for a meeting. This caught Maria off guard because she was not sure if she could convince her husband to come to the meeting. However, you heard back from Maria a few weeks later. She had persuaded her husband to meet with you.

Prior to the meeting, you sent Maria and Sancho a data gathering form and asked them to bring important financial documentation to the first meeting. You met for the first time in your conference room. You and your paraplanner (Emily) were able to determine the following from these data and the meeting:

- Maria has a relatively low level of risk tolerance.

- Sancho is a real risk taker.

- Their shared primary goal is to retire when Maria turns age sixty-five, assuming the following:

  ○ Maria and Sancho need to earn the equivalent of $495,000 before taxes per year—today's dollars—at that time.

  ○ Maria and Sancho anticipate living until Sancho is ninety-five years of age.

  ○ Maria and Sancho except inflation to average 3.0 percent annually into the future, which is also the anticipated growth rate of savings and salaries.

- Maria and Sancho have simple wills leaving assets to the surviving spouse. Neither Maria nor Sancho have any other estate planning documents or trusts in place.

Additionally, Maria has several questions she would like answered:

- First, is she adequately protected in case Sancho were to pass away?

  - This is a concern for Maria because she has split her time between being a stay-at-home mom and working in the family's rental real estate business and in Sancho's consulting firm for most of her adult life.[28]

- Second, she would like for you to investigate the family's financial situation because she cannot figure out why she and Sancho have been having a challenging time balancing their budget month-to-month.

  - Maria thinks that she and Sancho make a reasonably good income, but she is not able to see where all the money is going, particularly the family's investment earnings.

- Third, she is interested in other advice and counsel that can be used to benefit her and the family's financial situation.

Information about Sancho

During the meeting, you learned a few things about Sancho. He is a very busy person. He currently works for a high-tech firm. He is the senior vice president of cyber security. As a senior executive with the firm, his position is very secure. In addition, Sancho runs a business consulting firm. His firm provides executive leadership consulting to Fortune 500 company clients. Sancho's consulting firm has been very successful—even though it is run primarily as a small business. You did learn that Sancho runs the consulting practice as an LLC, but he has no full-time employees, although he does pay Maria a nominal wage so that she can fund her individual retirement account (IRA) and maintain a wage base for Social Security purposes.[29]

An interesting element of Sancho's business is that he needs to travel quite a bit. This is the reason he has established offices in Las Vegas, Nevada and St. Petersburg, Florida. He leases a car in each location so that one is available when he uses the office. Sancho chose these locations for two reasons:

- The first is that he and Maria already own a personal condominium in each city. Being familiar with each location made the decision easier.

- Second, Sancho thought having a base of operations on the east and west coasts would be an innovative idea in terms of client contact and entertaining.

Maria also liked the idea of establishing offices in each location because her family lives in Tampa and vacations in Las Vegas frequently.

Given the dynamic real estate markets in Las Vega and St. Petersburg, and economic signs of price appreciation, Sancho and Maria purchased condominiums as rental investments in each city.[30] Maria was involved in the purchase decisions but did not choose the initial (or current) tenants. Once the properties were rented, Sancho and Maria created an LLC to hold the condominiums. Sancho and Maria are each 50 percent managers. In order to avoid passive activity rules associated with owning rental real estate, Maria took the role of property manager. She devotes between fifteen and twenty hours per week working in the business managing the day-to-day real estate operations. Maria is responsible for screening potential new tenants,[31] scheduling repairs, paying expenses and homeowner's association bills, and ensuring that rent is collected on a timely basis. Given that Sancho frequently travels to Las Vegas and St. Petersburg, he has also asserted that he allocates approximately 500 hours per year to the real estate business. Essentially, he is the one that checks on each property's state of repair and condition.

As the initial meeting with Maria and Sancho ended, Sancho made the following comments:

- He noted that he was not interested in working with you. There was nothing personal in the comment. He stated that he already has an attorney and accountant on retainer, and as such, he did not think it was necessary to get involved with another financial adviser at this time.

- However, he made it quite clear that he felt it would be useful for Maria to have her own financial planner, and that if she wanted to move forward working with you he would support the idea.

  ○ He did note that Maria would need to fund the service fees charged by your firm.

  ○ In an effort to jumpstart your professional relationship with Maria, Sancho agreed to provide as much information as needed to get a financial plan in place that will (1) show if Maria and Sancho are on track, as a couple, to reach their retirement goal, and if not, how they can achieve the goal; (2) address Maria's concerns about premature death issues; and (3) provide Maria peace of mind related to the household's financial situation.

- Sancho noted that he would be pleased to receive any information about ways to increase the household's combined overall level of financial well-being.

Financial Notes

Personal Background

- Sancho is fifty-two years old.

- Maria is fifty years old.

- Manuel (son) is twenty-seven years old.

- All family members are in good health.

Business Notes

- Approximately two years ago, Sancho purchased a plane timeshare for $417,500. Monthly expenses are $5,035, plus $1,275 per hour of use. The timeshare includes fifty hours of guaranteed airtime (he must pay for the time used).

- As noted above, Maria works part-time for Sancho's consulting company, in addition to running the rental real estate LLC.

- Because the consulting practice is based on Sancho's expertise, he feels the company will have no value once he retires or dies.

Asset Summary[32]

- Principal Residence.

  - Purchased for $875,000 (loan amount) with a thirty-year 4.5 percent mortgage

  - Last payment: 81st.

- St. Petersburg Condo.

  - Purchased for $385,000 (loan amount) with a twenty-year 5.8 percent mortgage

  - Last payment: 24th.

- Las Vegas Condo.

  - Purchased for $280,000 (loan amount) with a thirty-year 5.0 percent mortgage

  - Last payment: 60th.

- Las Vegas Condo (rental).[33]

  - Purchased for $380,000 (loan amount) with a twenty-year 6.0 percent mortgage

  - Last payment: 36th.

- Florida Condo (rental).[34]

  - Purchased for $495,000 (loan amount) with a twenty-year 6.9 percent mortgage

  - Last payment: 36th

- 201X Lexus two years old; five-year loan with 0.0 percent loan.

- 201X Land Rover one year old; five-year loan with 1.0 percent loan.

- 201X BMW three years old; five-year loan with 2.5 percent loan.

- Universal Life Insurance Policy (Owner/Insured: Sancho; Beneficiary: Maria).

    ○ $1 million face value issued seven years ago.

- Term Life Insurance Policy (Owner/Insured: Sancho; Beneficiary: Maria).

    ○ $1 million thirty-year face value policy issued five years ago.

- Group Term Life Insurance Policy (Owner/Insured: Sancho; Beneficiary: Maria).[35]

    ○ $3 million face value policy.

Liability Summary

- Credit Cards.

    ○ Visa: several cards with an average APR of 14.50 percent.

    ○ MasterCard: several cards with an average APR of 13.90 percent.

    ○ Discover: one card with an APR of 18.00 percent.

    ○ Store Cards: several cards with an average APR of 23.90 percent.

    ○ Furniture Loan: APR 19.00 percent; five year installment loan.

- Student Loan.

- Parent Plus and bank loans to pay for son's college expenses.

    ○ Amount borrowed: $240,000.

    ○ Average interest rate: 6.9 percent.

    ○ Original loan term: ten years.

    ○ Last payment: 24th.

- Home Equity Loan.[36]

    ○ Amount borrowed: $145,000.

    ○ APY: 7.35 percent.

    ○ Last payment: 24th (original ten-year loan).

Expense Summary and Notes

- Gifts and donations are primarily charitable in nature (e.g., church, civic organizations, museums, etc.).

- Unreimbursed medical expenses include occasional chiropractic care, elective surgery, and insurance deductibles.

Information about Sancho's Consulting Business

- Sancho runs his consulting business as an LLC. He regularly transfers $100,000 from net earnings to his ABC brokerage account. The account is in Sancho's name only.

- All remaining net earnings from the business are transferred to the household budget.

The following balance sheet represents Maria's best attempt to summarize the household asset and liability situation. Emily—your paraplanner—needs your advice on completing the form:[37]

Figure XVI.1. Balance Sheet[38]

Assets	Value (Ownership)
Monetary Assets	
Checking Account	$ 6,700.00 (J)
Checking Account	$ 14,000.00 (H)
Savings Account	$ 37,000.00 (J)
Total Monetary Assets	*$ 57,700.00*
Investment Assets	
MNO Brokerage Account	$ 350,000.00 (J)
401(k) Account	$ 1,400,000.00 (H)
IRA Account	$ 169,000.00 (W)
ABC Brokerage Account	$ 905,628.81 (H)
XYZ Brokerage Account	$ 720,000.00 (H)
Life Insurance Cash Value	$ 82,500.00 (H)
Total Investment Assets	*$ 3,627,128.81*
Assets Associated with Sancho's Business	
Golf Club Membership	$ 75,000.00 (H)
Plane Timeshare	$ 400,000.00 (H)
Savings, Cash, & Checking Accounts	$ 11,000.00 (H)
Total Business Assets	*$ 486,000.00*
Real Estate LLC Assets	
Las Vegas Condo	$295,000 (LLC)
Florida Condo	$ 500,000.00 (LLC)
Total LLC Assets	*$ 795,000.00*

Housing Assets	
Primary Residence	$ 1,300,000.00 (J)
St. Petersburg Condo	$ 385,000.00 (J)
Las Vegas Condo	$ 300,000.00 (J)
Total Housing Assets	*$ 1,985,000.00*
Vehicles	
201X Lexus	$ 45,000.00 (J)
201X Land Rover	$ 60,000.00 (J)
201X BMW	$ 43,000.00 (H)
201X Harley Davidson Motorcycle	$ 16,500.00 (H)
Total Vehicle Assets	*$ 164,500.00*
Personal Assets	
Artwork	$ 79,000.00 (J)
Jewelry	$ 135,000.00 (W)
Coins and Stamps	$ 19,000.00 (H)
Furniture and Household Goods	$ 200,000.00 (J)
Jet Skis	$ 30,000.00 (J)
37 Foot Sailboat	$ 83,000.00 (H)
Golf Equipment	$ 15,000.00 (H)
Other	$ 250,000.00 (J)
Total Personal Assets	*$ 811,000.00*
TOTAL ASSETS	**$ 7,426,328.81**

Liabilities	Debt (Ownership)
Personal Liabilities	
Current Bills	$ - (J)
Short-Term Debt	$ - (J)
Total Short Term Debt	*???*
Credit Cards	
Visa	$ 40,000.00 (J)
MasterCard	$ 30,000.00 (J)
Discover	$ 20,000.00 (H)
Store Cards	$ 30,000.00 (J)
Total Personal Liabilities	*$ 120,000.00*

Mortgages	
Primary Residence	??? (J)
St. Petersburg Condo	??? (J)
Las Vegas Condo	??? (J)
Home Equity Loan	??? (J)
Total Mortgage Liabilities	*???*
Vehicle Debt	
201X Lexus	$ 35,540.00 (J)
201X Land Rover	$ 65,899.00 (J)
201X BMW	$ 23,110.00 (H)
201X Harley Davidson Motorcycle	$ - (H)
Total Vehicle Liabilities	*$ 124,549.00*
Other Liabilities	
Furniture Loan	$ 60,000.00 (J)
College Loans	$ 213,000.00 (J)
Bank Loan	$ -
Total Other Liabilities	*$ 273,000.00*
Liabilities Associated with Sancho's Business	
Leases	
Las Vegas Offices Lease	$ 192,000.00 (J)
Florida Offices Lease	$ 190,800.00 (J)
Las Vegas Car (Mercedes, lease)	$ 21,600.00 (J)
Florida Car (Acura, lease)	$ 19,800.00 (J)
Total Business Liabilities	*???*
Real Estate LLC[39]	
Las Vegas Condo (mortgage)	???
Florida Condo (mortgage)	???
Total LLC Liabilities	*???*
TOTAL LIABILITIES	$ 3,256,517.14
ASSETS	???
LIABILITIES	???
NET WORTH	???

Sancho is the primary household earner. The following is a summary of his W-2 income from his cyber security position. Please note that Sancho was unable to obtain an exact figure for other compensation. He hopes that you can calculate that.

Figure XVI.2. Sancho's Non-Business Income Situation[40]

Wages	$ 871,416
Other Taxable Compensation	$???
Taxable Income	$???
Federal Income Tax Withheld	$ 193,503
Social Security Wages	$ 128,400
Social Security Tax Withheld	$ 7,961
Medicare Wage and Tips	$ 894,308
Medicare Tax Withheld	$ 19,216
Qualified Plan Contributions*	$ 8,034
Medical Insurance Contributions*	$ 7,800
Disability Insurance Contributions*	$ 2,750
State and Local Taxes Withheld	$ 42,150
*Pre-tax contributions/payments	

The following income and expense statements represent the cash flow situation for the real estate LLC and Sancho's consulting business:

Figure XVI.3. Real Estate LLC

Income	
Las Vegas Rental Income	$24,000
Florida Rental Income	$19,200
Expenses	
Las Vegas	
Mortgage	$32,669
Insurance	$450
Tax	$6,300
Condo Fees	$6,000
Florida	
Mortgage	$45,697
Insurance	$700
Tax	$6,700
Condo Fees	$3,600

Figure XVI.4. Sancho's Consulting Business Income

Business Income and Expenses	
Yearly Income	**Dollars**
Business Income	$ 702,000
Other Income	$ 0
Total Income	**$ 702,000**
Expenses & Payments	
Travel	$ 24,000
Meals with Clients[41]	$ 19,100
Professional Services	$ 28,000
Office Expenses	$ 15,000
Employee Expenses	$ 10,765
Las Vegas Office Lease[42]	$ 48,000
Florida Office Lease	$ 63,600
Las Vegas Car Lease	$ 7,200
Florida Car Lease	$ 6,600
Insurance Expenses	$ 4,350
Plane Timeshare	$ 124,170
Misc. Tax-Deductible Business Expenses	$ 33,000
Total Expenses	**$ 374,235**
Income	**$ 327,765**
FICA	$ 13,413
Employer Element of FICA	$ 12,732
Federal Tax Withholdings	$ 108,000
Income After Expenses	$ 193,638
State Income Tax Withholdings	$ 25,000
Earnings Contributed to Business Brokerage Account	$ 00,000
Transfer to Household Account	$ 68,638
Note: Expenses are paid using American Express	

The following represents the Ruizs' cash flow position. Please note that Maria and Sancho were unable to complete the form.

Figure XVI.5 Household Cash Flow Statement

Cash Flow Worksheet	
Yearly Income	**Current Year**
H Income	$ 871,416
W Income	$ 10,765
H Business Income	$???
H Business Interest & Dividends	$??? See portfolio data
H Interest & Dividends	$??? See portfolio data
W Interest & Dividends	$??? See portfolio data
Group Benefit Income	$???
Total Income	**$???**
Expenses & Payments	
Principal Residence P&I	$???
St. Petersburg Condo P&I	$ 32,568
Las Vegas Condo P&I	$ 18,037
Home Equity Loan	$???
201X Lexus	$ 12,730
201X Land Rover	$ 17,101
201X BMW	$ 14,630
Mortgages and Vehicle Total	**$???**
Universal Life Premiums	$ 22,000
Term Life Premiums	$ 3,500
Homeowner's Insurance	
Principal Residence	$ 1,300
St. Petersburg Condo	$ 600
Las Vegas Condo	$ 750
Automobile Insurance	$ 5,500
Group Benefit Insurance	$???
Other Misc. Ins. Premiums	$ 0
Insurance Total	**$ 42,942**

Federal Income Taxes Paid	$ 301,503
State Income Taxes Paid	$ 67,150
FICA Paid	$ 54,127
Payroll Tax Total	**$???**
Homeowner's Tax	
Principal Residence	$ 8,000
St. Petersburg Condo	$ 4,100
Las Vegas Condo	$ 7,000
Personal Property Taxes	$ 2,300
Quarterly Federal Tax Withholdings	$ 0
Tax Total	**$ 34,400**
Brokerage Account (J)	$ 3,493
401(k) Account (H)[43]	$ 8,034
IRA Account (W)	$ 6,500
Brokerage Account (H)	$ 36,000
Regular/Allocated Savings	$ 0
Reinvested Interest & Dividends	$ 47,998
Reinvested Interest & Dividends	$ 26,036
Other Tax Advantaged Retirement Savings	$ 0
Savings Total	**$ 128,062**
Utilities	$ 7,200.00
Telephone	$ 3,600.00
Utility Total	**$ 10,800**
Condo Fees	$ 9,000
Home Maintenance & Repair	$ 4,800
Home Expense Total	**$ 23,400**
Food at Home	$ 10,800
Food Eating Out	$ 19,000
Clothing	$ 20,000
Automobile Repairs	$ 3,200
Daily Living Expense Total	**$ 53,000**

Entertainment & Vacation	$ 48,000
Gifts & Donations	$ 95,000
Personal Liabilities	
Short-Term Debt	$ 0
Student Loan Debt	$ 34,013
Credit Cards	
Visa	$ 6,000
MasterCard	$ 6,000
Discover	$ 6,000
Store Cards	$ 6,000
Ongoing Expenses	**$ 201,013**
Unreimbursed Medical Expenses	$ 6,000
Miscellaneous Expenses	$ 7,200
Miscellaneous Expense Total	**$ 13,200**
Discretionary Cash Flow	
Total Income	$???
Total Fixed Expenses	$???
Total Variable Expenses	$???
Discretionary Cash Flow	**$???**

Figure XVI.6. Portfolio Data[44]

Account	Account 1	Account 2	Account 3	Account 4	Account 5
Name	MNO Brokerage	Sancho 401k	Maria IRA	ABC Brokerage	XYZ Brokerage
Title	Joint	H	W	H	H
Value	$350,000	$1,400,000	$169,000	$905,629	$720,000
Years Invested	26	22	15	10	15
Annual Contribution	$3,493	$8,034	$6,500	$100,000	$ 36,000
Allocation					
Stocks	75%	80%	25%	20%	50%
Bonds	15%	0%	50%	60%	30%
T-Bills	5%	0%	25%	20%	10%
Hard Assets	5%	20%	0%	0%	10%
Taxable Yield/Return	0.260%	n.a.	n.a.	1.040%	0.5200
Qualified Dividend Yld	1.065%	0.000%	3.550%	4.260%	2.130%

Notes: Joint = joint ownership; H = owned by husband (Sancho); W = owned by wife (Maria)

Historical Portfolio Rate of Return Assumptions (past and forward looking)

- Stocks: 10.32 percent (Standard Deviation: 19.70 percent).

- Municipal Bonds: 7.10 percent (Standard Deviation: 9.75 percent).

- T-Bills: 5.20 percent (Standard Deviation: 5.00 percent).

- Hard Assets and Real Estate: 7.78 percent (Standard Deviation: 21.00 percent).

- Thirty-Year Mortgage APR: 6.00 percent.

- Twenty-Year Mortgage APR: 5.00 percent.

- Fifteen-Year Mortgage APR: 4.80 percent.

- Home Equity APR: 6.25 percent (Based on ten-Year Loan).

Financial Planning Assumptions

The following assumptions and data should be used in addition to the information already provided in the case narrative:

Taxes

- Emily, your paraplanner, estimates Social Security and Medicare taxes to be *approximately* $47,310; however, this number is based on the case assumptions and the case marginal tax rates. She recommends that you confirm this figure using your own calculation.

- All dividends and capital gains are reinvested.

- Maria and Sancho are in the 35.0 percent federal marginal tax bracket.

- Maria and Sancho pay a 6.0 percent state marginal tax.

  o The state deduction amount is $8,000.

  o The state exemption amount is $2,500 per person.

  o The family is not eligible for a state tax credit.

Retirement

- Sancho's monthly Social Security retirement benefit (PIA) in today's dollars: $3,400 (Maria is eligible to receive 50 percent of Sancho's benefit).[45]

- Sancho and Maria hope to replace the equivalent of $495,000 before taxes per year in today's dollars in retirement, which is a replacement ratio of approximately 56.1 percent of earned household income.

- For insurance planning purposes, assume that the Ruiz family is in the 35.0 percent federal marginal tax bracket and the 6.0 percent state tax bracket pre- and post-retirement.

- Maria and Sancho plan to retire when Sancho turns age sixty-seven (his full normal Social Security retirement age).

- Sancho would like to invest aggressively prior to retirement. Maria would prefer to take less risk. Sancho and Maria are willing to compromise by assuming a simple return calculated as: (Sancho's 401k RoR + Maria's IRA RoR)/2.

- Sancho and Maria plan to invest in a diversified portfolio of stocks, municipal bonds, T-Bills, and hard assets/real estate during retirement. For initial planning purposes, assume an equal weighting in each of these asset classes to determine the expected RoR.

- Retirement savings contributions (pre- or post-tax) are assumed to grow at the rate of salary inflation (3.0 percent).

- Sancho and Maria are willing to allocate $500,000 from Sancho's personal investment account for retirement if needed.

- Maria and Sancho plan to sell the rental properties at retirement to help offset retirement needs. Sancho stated that he believes these assets will increase in value, on average, by a 7.60 percent rate of return until retirement.[46]

Insurance

In the case of death:

- Expenses at death:

  - Final expenses: $40,000 each.

  - Estate administration: $12,000 each.

  - Miscellaneous final needs: $20,000 each.

  - Transitional funding need: $10,000 each.

- For life insurance planning purposes only, Maria and Sancho would like to ensure that the surviving spouse will receive $625,000 in income per year until retirement.

- Sancho and Maria hope to replace the equivalent of $495,000 before taxes per year in today's dollars in retirement.

- Maria will earn $10,765 per year until retirement; Sancho is expected to earn $871,416 until retirement.[47]

- Maria and Sancho feel a 80 percent capital retention replacement ratio is appropriate when planning for life insurance needs.

- For insurance planning purposes, assume that the Ruiz family is in the 35.0 percent federal marginal tax bracket and the 6.0 percent state tax bracket pre- and post-retirement.

- Sancho and Maria plan to invest any life insurance proceeds and other assets in the case of death in a diversified portfolio of stocks, municipal bonds, T-Bills, and hard assets/real estate. For initial planning purposes, assume an equal weighting in each of these asset classes to determine the expected RoR.

- Inflation pre- and post-retirement is assumed to be 3.0 percent.

- Maria and Sancho are agreed that they would like to pay off all short-term, mortgage, vehicle, business, and other debts at the death of the first spouse.

- Maria's Social Security retirement benefit, should Sancho die, is $20,400 per year in today's dollars; she will receive the benefit starting at age sixty. No survivor Social Security benefit is expected if Maria dies first.

- Sancho's monthly Social Security retirement benefit in today's dollars: $3,400 (Maria is eligible to receive 50 percent of Sancho's benefit).

- Maria and Sancho are willing to sell the rental properties and second homes at the death of the first spouse to offset life insurance needs.

- Other assets to be used in the event of death: All brokerage accounts and retirement plan assets.

In the case of disability:

- Sancho has a long-term disability policy with a $60,000 annual benefit.

  - The plan is employer provided at no cost to Sancho.

  - Benefits last until age sixty-seven.

  - The plan has a 180-day elimination period.

- Maria has no disability coverage.

- Maria and Sancho would like to replace 60 percent of household current income.

- The couple is willing to self-insure the risk that Maria may become disabled.

- Assume a life expectancy of life expectancy of age ninety-five for Sancho and age ninety-three for Maria.

- Sancho has earmarked $974,000 of investment and monetary assets to cover short-term and elimination period disability needs.

- Maria and Sancho are willing to allocate $1,255,628 to help fund other disability needs.

- For insurance planning purposes, assume the Ruiz family is in the 35.0 percent marginal tax bracket and the 6.0 percent state tax bracket.

- Sancho and Maria plan to reallocate investment assets, in the event of disability, into a diversified portfolio of stocks, municipal bonds, T-Bills, and hard assets/real estate. For initial planning purposes, assume an equal weighting in each of these asset classes to determine the expected RoR.

- Maria and Sancho will use earnings from the MNO and XYZ brokerage accounts to help offset yearly long-term disability income needs.

- Neither Maria nor Sancho expect Social Security benefits if either becomes disabled.

In the case of a long-term care need:

- Maria and Sancho are comfortable using all brokerage account assets to fund any LTC needs.

- Assume an LTC inflation rate of 4.0 percent.

- Assume $12,000 annual prescription costs per person if long-term care services are needed (in addition to long-term care costs).

- The average long-term care cost in their area is $85,000 per year.

- Assume age seventy-five for LTC needs for Maria and age seventy-seven for Sancho.

- Maria and Sancho are comfortable assuming a four-year long-term care need.

- Sancho and Maria plan to reallocate investment assets, in the event of a LTC need, into a diversified portfolio of stocks, municipal bonds, T-Bills, and hard assets/real estate. For initial planning purposes, assume an equal weighting in each of these asset classes to determine the expected RoR.

Property Insurance

- The couple's principal residence is currently insured based on a replacement value of $1 million.

- The St. Petersburg condominium is insured for a replacement value of $347,000.

- The Las Vegas condominium is insured for a replacement value of $285,000.

- The Las Vegas rental is insured for a replacement value of $295,000.

- The Florida rental is insured for a replacement value of $500,000.

- Each vehicle is covered by a 100/300/100 split-limit coverage policy.

- A $1 million excess liability policy is in place; the premium is $150 per year.

Use these data and assumptions to craft a comprehensive financial plan for your client. Be sure to address Maria's questions through cash flow/net worth, tax, insurance, investment, retirement, estate, and 'special needs' analyses.

Discussion Points and Questions

1. Briefly summarize the relevant facts of the case.

2. Estimate the amount of income earned from non-business source. Be sure to account for federal, state, and FICA taxes withheld at the household level.

3. Estimate the net taxable income from Sancho's consulting business. Be sure to account for FICA taxes, federal tax withholdings, and state tax withholdings. Also determine how much of the net income from the business flows to Sancho's brokerage account versus the household budget.

4. Estimate net income from the rental real estate LLC.

5. Estimate the Ruizs' current discretionary cash flow position.

   a. Identify strengths and weakness associated with their cash flow situation.

   b. Use financial ratios to evaluate areas for improvement.

   c. Draft a list of potential recommendations that can be used to improve or enhance the situation.

6. Estimate the Ruizs' current net worth situation.

   a. Identify strengths and weakness associated with their net worth situation.

   b. Use financial ratios to evaluate areas for improvement.

   c. Draft a list of potential recommendations that can be used to improve or enhance the situation.

7. Determine the weighted average rate of return for each portfolio, based on the current asset allocation.

   a. Estimate the amount of qualified dividends from the MNO, ABC, and XYZ portfolios.

   b. Estimate the amount of interest earned from the MNO, ABC, and XYZ portfolios.

   c. Determine whether the current value of each portfolio account matches an estimate of the account value based on contributions, time invested, and rate of return assumptions.

8. Develop an estimate of this year's tax situation for the Ruiz family? Can Maria and Sancho expect a federal income tax refund?

   a. Identify strengths and weakness associated with their federal tax situation.

   b. Draft a list of potential recommendations that can be used to improve or enhance the situation.

9. Do Maria and Sancho need long-term insurance coverage at this time? If yes, how much?

10. Does Sancho need additional short-term disability coverage? Does Sancho need additional long-term disability coverage? If the answer is yes to either question, how much? Provide an estimate of the cost of coverage?

11. Do Maria and Sancho need additional life insurance coverage? Answer the question based on:

   I.   A full needs analysis.

   II. The human life value approach.

   III. The capital retention approach.

   IV. The income retention approach.

   a. How much additional life insurance, if any, does Maria need?

   b. How much additional life insurance, if any, does Sancho need?

   c. If either has a need, what type of insurance policy would be most appropriate? How much might such a policy cost?

   d. Draft a list of other potential recommendations that can be used to improve or enhance the situation.

12. Are Maria and Sancho on track to meet their retirement goal(s) based on the current case assumptions?

   a. Identify strengths and weakness associated with their retirement situation.

   b. Draft a list of potential recommendations that can be used to improve or enhance the situation.

13. Do Maria and Sancho need to worry about paying federal estate taxes should either die prematurely this year?

   a. Identify strengths and weakness associated with their estate planning situation.

   b. Draft a list of potential recommendations that can be used to improve or enhance the situation.

14. Identify other issues Maria should be aware of as she evaluates the information provided in the context of a comprehensive financial plan.

The Case of Betty and Bob Shultz

A RETIREMENT AND TAX PLANNING MINI CASE

Betty and Bob Schultz are sixty-nine and seventy-one years of age, respectively. They reside in Anytown, USA, which does not impose any state or local income taxes. Bob will retire on September 1 of this year from the architectural firm where he has been employed for the past twenty-five years; Bob does not have any ownership in the firm. Betty has been an elementary school teacher for forty-five years, and she plans to retire at the end of the current academic year on July 1, which will be her seventy-first birthday.

Betty earns an annual salary of $65,000, contributing the full allowable amount annually to 403(b) and 457(b) Plans. Bob earns a salary of $85,000 and typically receives a year-end bonus, payable in the first quarter of the subsequent calendar year equal to 15% of his salary. Bob contributes fully to his firm's 401(k) Plan; the firm matches 50% on the first 6% of deferred salary contributions. Since Bob is over age seventy, he receives Social Security monthly benefits of $3,050. Betty has opted to defer receipt of her Social Security benefits until her seventieth birthday. Her Social Security statement estimates her PIA benefit at age seventy to be $2,635 per month. The Schultzes claim the standard deduction for federal income tax purposes.

The Schultzes have three adult children, ages forty-two, forty, and thirty-seven, and six grandchildren ranging in age from three to sixteen. Betty and Bob own the following assets:

Assets	Value
Checking Account (joint)	$ 15,000
Savings Account (joint)	30,000
Automobiles (2 - joint)	47,000
Furniture & jewelry	25,000
Primary Residence (joint)	195,000
Anytown School District 403(b) Plan (Bob primary beneficiary)	462,000
Anytown School District 457(b) Plan (Bob primary beneficiary)	184,000
XYZ Architectural Design 401(k) Plan (Betty primary beneficiary)	725,000
Twenty-year Term Life Insurance Policy on Bob's Life, Betty primary beneficiary, policy fifteen years ago; annual premium $175	75,000
Total Assets	$ 1,758,000

Liabilities	
Credit cards (balances paid in full monthly)	$ 2,500
First Mortgage Loan @ 4.5% fixed; $125K mortgage (original term 25 years; 3 years remaining)	22,348
Total Liabilities	$ 24,848

Case Questions

1. Based on the case information, Bob:

    a. was required to take his first RMD from his employer's 401(k) plan by December 31st of the previous year.

    b. must take his first RMD from his employer's 401(k) plan by the end of December this year.

    c. must take his first RMD from his employer's 401(k) plan by April 1st of next year.

    d. must take his first RMD from his employer's 401(k) plan by December 31st of next year.

2. Based on the case information:

    a. both Bob and Betty may contribute the full amount to either a Regular IRA or Roth IRA for this calendar year.

    b. Betty, but not Bob, may contribute the full amount to either a Regular IRA or Roth IRA for this calendar year.

    c. Bob, but not Betty, may contribute the full amount to either a Regular IRA or Roth IRA for this calendar year.

    d. Neither Bob nor Betty may contribute to a Regular IRA or Roth IRA for this calendar year.

3. Betty is eligible to contribute to her employer's 403(b) plan and 457(b) plan. What is the maximum dollar amount she may defer in this calendar year?

    a. The annual contribution limit amount, including catch-up, to each plan.

    b. The annual contribution limit amount, excluding catch-up, to each plan.

    c. One annual contribution limit amount, including catch-up, to be allocated between the two plans

    d. One annual contribution limit amount, excluding catch-up, to be allocated between the two plans.

4. When must Betty begin to take RMDs from her 403(b) plan?

    a. December 31st of the year she turns age 70½.

    b. April 1st of the year she turns age 70½.

    c. December 31st of the year she turns age 72.

    d. April 1st of the year she turns age 72.

5. Given their age and household situation, the current tax code, and current market conditions, which of the following is an appropriate recommendation for Bob and Betty in relation to their residential mortgage debt?

    a. Keep the mortgage in force for the balance of its term.

    b. Refinance the mortgage to obtain a lower interest rate.

    c. Pay off the mortgage balance as soon as possible.

    d. Maintain the existing mortgage and apply for a home equity line of credit not to exceed $100,000.

6. Given the Schultzes taxable income for the current calendar year, what would their long-term capital gains tax rate be if they recognized a hypothetical long-term capital gain of $10,000?

    a. 0%

    b. 15%

    c. 20%

    d. 23.8%

7. Assuming the Schultzes are eligible to contribute to either a Roth IRA or Regular IRA, which should they choose to fund during the current year to minimize future tax obligations while optimizing their long-term financial planning situation?

    a. Both should contribute to a Roth IRA.

    b. Betty should contribute to a Regular IRA and Bob should contribute to a Roth IRA.

    c. Bob should contribute to a Regular IRA and Betty should contribute to a Roth IRA.

    d. Both should contribute to a Regular IRA.

8. Which of the following statements below is correct?

    a. If Betty should die today, the value of her 457(b) account will pass income tax free to Bob.

    b. If Betty should die today, Bob may elect to roll Betty's 457(b) account into an IRA Account in his name.

c. If Betty should die today, Bob will be required to take an RMD from Betty's 403(b) account by December 31st of the current year.

d. If Betty should die today, Bob will be entitled to collect Betty's full Social Security Benefit as a widower's benefit.

9. Assume Betty dies today and Bob inherits her 403(b) and 457(b) plan accounts. How will Bob determine his RMD for next year and annually thereafter assuming he elects to roll both accounts into an IRA Account in his name?

a. Bob will have to calculate RMDs using his single life expectancy as of Betty's year of death and recompute his life expectancy annually thereafter.

b. Bob will have to calculate RMDs using his single life expectancy for next year and reduce the factor by 1 in each successive year.

c. Bob will have to withdraw the entire account balance no later than 10 years following the year of Betty's death; annual RMDs are not required in the interim.

d. Bob will calculate his RMD annually using the Uniform Lifetime Table.

10. Assume Betty and Bob die this year and their retirement accounts designate their three children as contingent beneficiaries equally. How will the children determine their RMD amounts following their parents' death?

a. The children will have to calculate RMDs using their individual single life expectancies as of their parent's year of death and recompute their life expectancy annually thereafter.

b. The children will have to calculate RMDs using the eldest sibling's single life expectancy as of next year and reduce the factor by 1 in each successive year.

c. The children will have to withdraw their entire 1/3rd share of the account balances no later than 10 years following the year of their parent's death; annual RMDs are not required in the interim.

d. The children will calculate their respective RMDs annually using the Uniform Lifetime Table based on their respective ages.

Endnotes

1. Questions 6, 7, and 8 were adapted from "Released CFP® Certification Examination Questions," "2004 Case Scenario and Questions," and "1994 & 1996 Certification Exam Questions." Copyright © 2008, Certified Financial Planner Board of Standards, Inc. All rights reserved. Used with permission.

2. Questions 1, 2, and 3 are from "Released CFP® Certification Examination Questions," "1994 & 1996 Certification Exam Questions," and "1999 Case Scenario and Questions." Copyright © 2008, Certified Financial Planner Board of Standards, Inc. All rights reserved. Used with permission.

3. Adora began contributing to her company's 401(k) plan when she started as a teller, but she stopped contributing a few years ago.

4. Adora estimates that it will take five years for Amado to finish college. Amado is now age twenty-three but he is considered a full-time student.

5. Interest earned is based on receiving 2 percent interest on $100,000. The $100,000 was an inheritance received by Adora from her Aunt Haley.

6. Adora and Jorge live in Adora's home from her first marriage. Adora originally took out a $165,000 mortgage at 9.00 percent for thirty years. She and Jorge recently made the 120th payment on the mortgage.

7. Adora purchased a new car two weeks ago with a $22,000 zero down five year 7 percent APR loan.

8. The Tuns pay the minimum *monthly* payment, which is approximately 3 percent of the outstanding credit card balance. The balance has remained steady for several years.

9. Pre-tax contributions within the employer-sponsored health care plans.

10. Tax figures are based on 20XX actual liabilities.

11. 18.50 percent annual interest rate.

12. 19.10 percent annual interest rate.

13. The savings account currently pays 2 percent on deposits greater than $5,000.

14. Purchased by Adora during the first few months of employment; Adora has not purchased savings bonds in over a year. The average annualized interest rate is 3.50 percent. She is willing to allocate these assets towards retirement.

15. They purchased a new car two weeks ago using a zero down five year 7 percent loan.

16. Second car is a four-year old Honda.

17. Family heirlooms primarily, including a silver bracelet with an estimated value of $3,000.

18. For planning purposes, assume that their state income tax liability is approximately 11.50 percent of their federal tax liability.

19. Both Adora and Jorge are good drivers—no accidents in the past five years.

20. Adora and Jorge are non-smokers.

21. When Amado graduates from college Adora's health insurance premium will drop by 33 percent.

22. The assumptions shown should be used to solve the case. Note that the assumptions used are case specific. Data, rates, and other information may be different in your location; however, use the information provided in the case when conducting calculations. *Do not use any assumption or input other that what has been provided.*

23. The figure is less than Jorge's current income because he will continue to work part-time on weekends, while reducing other work-related expenses. The $20,000 need is above what he can earn on the weekends.

24. Adding Jorge to Adora's health insurance policy will cost $1,800 yearly.

25. Assume that Adora and Jorge will retire sometime after Adora turns age sixty-seven but before age sixty-eight; that is, twenty-five years in the future.

26. Their current 401(k) assets are earning an after-tax return of 5.90 percent annualized.

27. This fictional (and lighthearted) play is intended to be acted out in class. The case takes approximately fifteen minutes to complete. A minimum of thirty minutes should be allocated to answer case questions.

28. She is also interested to know if she is adequately insured.

29. Sancho's LLC is considered a personal service firm.

30. The properties are owned by an LLC controlled by Maria and Sancho.

31. The properties have been rented by the same tenants the entire time, resulting in no tenant search activity.

32. All real estate was purchased prior to December 2017.

33. Assume that the property has been fully depreciated for tax purposes.

34. Assume that the property has been fully depreciated for tax purposes.

35. Premium paid by employer.

36. The home equity loan was used to fund personal and household expenses, including a family vacation.

37. Your firm uses ??? to indicate that additional information/calculations are needed from you.

38. H = Husband (Sancho); W = Wife (Maria); J = Joint; LLC = Limited Liability Company.

39. Maria and Sancho are jointly responsible for the leases and the mortgages for the properties held in the LLC.

40. A "???" indicates that Emily, your paraplanner, was not able to obtain this number for you. You will need to calculate these figures.

41. Subject to limitations.

42.   Maria and Sancho are jointly liable for the property leases.

43.   Sancho's employer does not provide a 401(k) match.

44.   Assume a cost basis in each taxable portfolio equal to 50 percent of the current fair market value. Also assume investments within each portfolio have been held for more than one year.

45.   Social Security benefits are expected to increase at the inflation rate.

46.   The rental real estate growth factor is different than the assumed rate of return on other pre-retirement assets.

47.   Income data have not been adjusted for inflation.

Index